DCPL0000393426

22

Items should be returned on or before the last date
shown below. Items not already requested by other
borrowers may be renewed in person, in writing or by
telephone. To renew, please quote the number on the
barcode label. To renew online a PIN is required.
This can be requested at your local library.
Renew online @ www.dublincitypubliclibraries.ie
Fines charged for overdue items will include postage
incurred in recovery. Damage to or loss of items will
be charged to the borrower.

Leabharlanna Poiblí Chathair Bhaile Átha Cliath
Dublin City Public Libraries

Dublin City
Baile Átha Cliath

DOLPHINS BARN LIBRARY
TEL

Date Due	Date Due	Date Due
16 FEB 2011		16 JUL 2012
15 APR 2011		26 JUL 2012
		2 JUL 2012
		27 JUL 2012
		13 JUN 2017

D1422494

THE RELUCTANT TAOISEACH

John A. Costello

THE RELUCTANT TAOISEACH

John A. Costello

DAVID McCULLAGH ∾

Gill & Macmillan

Gill & Macmillan Ltd
Hume Avenue, Park West, Dublin 12
with associated companies throughout the world
www.gillmacmillan.ie

© David McCullagh 2010
978 07171 4646 8

Index compiled by Helen Litton
Typography design by Make Communication
Print origination by Carole Lynch
Printed and bound in Great Britain by MPG Books Ltd,
Bodmin, Cornwall

This book is typeset in Linotype Minion 11/13.5pt
and Neue Helvetica.

The paper used in this book comes from the wood pulp
of managed forests. For every tree felled, at least one
tree is planted, thereby renewing natural resources.

All rights reserved. No part of this publication may be
copied, reproduced or transmitted in any form or by
any means, without permission of the publishers.

A CIP catalogue record for this book is available
from the British Library.

5 4 3 2

CONTENTS

PREFACE

Most days that the Dáil is sitting, on my way to the Press Gallery, I walk past the portrait of John A. Costello which is on the jacket of this book. For the last couple of years, I have been silently promising the painting that I was nearly finished this biography. At last, I will be able to look Jack Costello's likeness in the eye again.

John A. Costello's interests were (not necessarily in this order) golf, the law, religion, politics, and his family. Whatever about the others, the last mentioned enthusiasm is easy to understand for anyone who has met the extended Costello family. Doubtless there is much in this book with which they will disagree, but I hope they will feel that it is fair.

The idea of writing this book has been at the back of my mind for at least ten years, but it wouldn't have happened if it hadn't been for Declan Costello, who encouraged me to undertake it, facilitated access to his father's papers in UCD, and smoothed my way with various contacts. Unfortunately, a recent illness means that he hasn't been able to see it finished, a fact I will always regret.

Declan's brother, John, kindly put some memories on paper for me. I have also been helped by a number of the Costello grandchildren, who have shared memories of the private side of the public man: Jacqueline Armstrong and her husband Fergus, Kyran FitzGerald, Joan Gleeson, Georgina Sutton and Isabelle Sutton (who supplied a treasure trove of photographs).

Many others gave me information about John A. Costello, in interviews or through correspondence, including Jack Christal, Liam Cosgrave, Ronan Fanning, Tom Finlay, Alexis FitzGerald, Ronan Keane, Harvey Kenny, Mick Kilkenny, the late Patrick Lynch, Muiris Mac Conghail, Risteárd Mulcahy, the late Louie O'Brien, Niall O'Carroll, Michael V. O'Mahony, Pat Russell, Richie Ryan and T.K. Whitaker.

Much of the research for this book was carried out in the UCD Archives—many thanks to Seamus Helferty and his colleagues, particularly Orna Somerville who catalogued the Costello Papers. Stephen MacWhite (acting on behalf of Mrs Kathleen MacWhite) kindly granted access to the papers of his grandfather, Michael MacWhite; as did Mella Crowley to her father, Freddie Boland's memoir. The UCD-OFM partnership facilitated access to the de Valera and MacEoin papers. Thanks also to the staff of the National Archives of Ireland, the British National Archives, the Public Records Office of Northern Ireland, and the National Library of Ireland (especially Mary Broderick).

I am also grateful to: Jonathan Armstrong, King's Inns Library; Patricia Boyd, Registry of Deeds; Damien Burke, Irish Jesuit Archive; Mary Clark, Dublin City Archives; Joe Curry, Dominican College, Eccles Street; Noelle Dowling, Dublin Diocesan Archivist; Peter Durnin, Papal Knights Association of Ireland; Estelle Gittins, Trinity College Manuscripts Department; Greg Harkin, All Hallows archives; Elizabeth Keane, biographer of Seán MacBride, who pointed me in a useful Canadian direction; Fran Leahy, Property Registration Authority; Martin Long, Catholic Communications Office; Seán MacCárthaigh and Pascal Letellier at the Arts Council; and Darragh O'Donoghue, Allen Library.

Across the Atlantic, I thank Richie Allen, Library and Archives Canada; Erica Flanagan of the Truman Library; Herb Pankratz at the Eisenhower Library; and John Vernon and Matthew Olsen, United States National Archives, College Park, Maryland.

Friends and colleagues with specialist knowledge have been bothered for information: Eamon Kennedy clarified some legal aspects, Alan Finan interpreted some medical terms, Joe Mac Raollaigh did some translation, and Senator Cecilia Keaveney explained the latest legal developments concerning Lough Foyle. Michael Webb kindly gave me a copy of the Memoirs of his father-in-law (William Bedell Stanford). My father, Robin McCullagh, supplied some information on the stamp marking the centenary of John A. Costello's birth, and more importantly he and my mother, June, performed child minding duties above and beyond the call of duty.

At Gill & Macmillan, I'd like to thank Fergal Tobin for taking on the book in the first place (a decision I hope he won't regret!); D Rennison Kunz who oversaw the editorial process; Nicki Howard who commissioned the jacket and looked after marketing; Teresa Daly who dealt with publicity; and photo researcher Jen Patton. Thanks also to editor Esther Kallen, and to Helen Litton for compiling the index. My gratitude to them all.

Elaine Byrne and Maurice Manning made helpful suggestions on the manuscript, as did John Fanagan, who kindly proof-read the entire draft, despite the fact that we had never met. Any errors that remain are, of course, entirely my fault. I really should have listened to them.

Finally, to my family, who have had to put up with my absences, physical and mental, as this was written. My wife, Anne-Marie Smyth, encouraged me to start the project, to find a publisher, and to keep going. Our daughter, Rosie, also urged me towards the finishing line, with the encouraging words: "Are you not finished that book *yet*?" My love, and my thanks, to them both.

David McCullagh
May 2010

Introduction ∼

THE RELUCTANT TAOISEACH

"I agree that I was a reluctant Taoiseach, but I was never a reluctant politician."[1]

JOHN A. COSTELLO, 1969

"It was because John A. Costello happened to be available at that time, in those circumstances, that ... the First Inter-party Government was born."[2]

TOM O'HIGGINS, 1969

John A. Costello was unique among Irish heads of government for two reasons. Firstly, he wasn't the leader of his party—he was chosen as Taoiseach in 1948 as a compromise among the five parties who wished to form a government. The second difference between him and other holders of the office was even more fundamental: his genuine reluctance to take the job. Not only did he not seek the top job in Irish politics, he actively fought against taking it.

Other holders of the office have struggled to attain it; Jack Costello had it thrust upon him. The only other politician to hesitate before accepting a chance to take the job was Jack Lynch of Fianna Fáil in 1966. Lynch has sometimes been described as a reluctant Taoiseach. But his reluctance was entirely due to consideration for his wife[3]—there was no doubt that he, unlike Costello, actually wanted the job.

Apart from being essentially a part-time politician, other factors seemed to militate against Costello. For the first 44 years of the State's existence, the other three men who headed Irish governments had played prominent parts in the 1916 Rising. Costello, by contrast, had been playing golf when the Rising broke out, and many years later still seemed aggrieved at having had his journey home interrupted by a roadblock.[4] He played no role either in the War of Independence, apart from representing prisoners in a couple of court cases.

In fact, like the vast majority of his contemporaries, he had been a Home Ruler rather than a Republican during most of this period, one of the rising

Catholic middle class who saw the introduction of Home Rule as their ticket to greater political, economic and social status. One of the ironies of Irish history is the ultimate triumph of such people, who seemed to have been cast to the margins by the War of Independence.

In office, Costello was to provide surprises, too, not least his success in holding together two disparate coalition governments for considerable lengths of time—comparable, indeed, to the tenure of the single-party government which came between them. Despite his earlier key role in the development of the Commonwealth, he declared the Republic, a development not without its controversies, but nonetheless significant. And while he was seen as a temporary or stop-gap Taoiseach, he served longer in the office than any of his Fine Gael successors to date.

It has been widely known that his reluctance to take the job was, at least in part, due to his desire not to leave the law—for both professional and financial reasons. His love of the practice of law was obvious to all who knew him, and he could even say in an interview while Taoiseach that "his biggest moment was not when he became Prime Minister, but when 'winning a big case'".[5]

But there was another reason, as he revealed in an extraordinary letter to his son Declan, then in Switzerland, written just days after he became Taoiseach: "I think I can honestly say that it was not the financial loss or even the parting from my life's work as an advocate ... that made me fight so hard against acceptance, but a fear amounting almost to terror that I would be a flop as Taoiseach and bring discredit on the new administration if it was formed. I felt that such a new departure would be looked upon with distrust and be subjected to severe criticism. If I proved unfit it would be disastrous for them all."[6]

This engaging self-doubt was also, to say the least, untypical in holders of the office of Taoiseach. However, Costello's reluctance, while real enough, should not be exaggerated. Once he agreed to take on the job, he did so with his characteristic determination, energy and application. Indeed, in the same letter to his son, he concluded by saying that despite his initial doubts, "I can now assure you that I am perfectly and supremely happy and contented, and face the future and what it holds with resignation, and with confidence and hope."[7]

Anyone watching, or listening to, John A. Costello would have been surprised at his admission of a lack of confidence. As an *Irish Times* editorial at the time of his death noted, he was a man who "breathed belligerence".[8] This public image was reinforced by his tendency to scowl in photographs— apparently he didn't smile for the camera because he didn't like having his photograph taken.[9] In later life, with his hat, his cigar and his scowl, he reminded one of his granddaughters of "a Mafioso boss, particularly as he dived into his big black State car at the end of a working day".[10]

His belligerence was evident on the political platform, in interviews, and most particularly in the courts. One of those on the receiving end of his forensic brilliance was Dr Harry Parker, an acquaintance who was appearing as an opposing witness. "I remember one occasion when you attacked me most savagely in the witness box and for, as far as I could see, no good reason. Feeling hurt, I asked Cecil Lavery what was the reason. This most gifted counsel, like little Audrey, laughed, and laughed, and laughed. He intimated that you simply wanted to win your case ..."[11]

But this belligerence was only part of the story. As the same *Irish Times* editorial observed, his manner was misleading, his belligerence "the armour he put on against his sensitive and compassionate disposition".[12] Those who worked with and for him praised his kindness—even Noël Browne, the Minister for Health who never forgave Costello for his handling of the Mother and Child crisis. There are many examples in his personal papers of his charitable instincts,[13] and he maintained his interest in the Society of Saint Vincent de Paul throughout his life.

The law was, arguably, his first love. Political opponents like Seán Lemass accused him of being prepared to argue any brief, in politics as in the law. "He was still at the Bar as it were: he was not really concerned about the soundness of the brief. He argued to the brief given to him by his Party or his officials."[14] This was unfair, but then Lemass had a famous aversion to lawyers in general, and Fine Gael lawyers in particular. Interestingly, Ronan Keane, a future Chief Justice who saw both Lemass and Costello speak at a debate at UCD's Literary and Historical Society in 1951, felt that Costello was by far the more effective speaker, because of his ability to appeal to ordinary people. It was this which made him such a "great jury operator"—he knew how to come across as one of them.[15]

His secretary, Patrick Lynch, who knew him well, said his background in the law was not always an advantage. "Acceptance of the law's delays did not foster an overnight conversion to consistent punctuality. The vehement rhetoric of the courts did not necessarily match the changing moods of the Dáil, and he sometimes found it hard to avoid flowery diction and the purple patch."[16] His forceful speaking style could be both a blessing and a curse in political terms—his speeches were generally quite entertaining, and his aide-de-camp and political assistant Mick Byrne always urged him to throw away his script and speak off the cuff during election meetings in the constituency.[17] But what pleased a crowd could also cause trouble.

As his son-in-law Alexis FitzGerald tactfully pointed out to him, "it is impossible to speak frequently *ex tempore* without the eloquence of some moment reaching further than the facts warrant ... whenever Mick Byrne tells you to do without a script, please remember that if I were present I would howl for one. As many of the words that you have as Taoiseach to utter should be thought out carefully before they are uttered, I am certain that you should suffer the glory of the moment to pass by. The cheers cease but *litera scripta manet* [the written word remains]. The local enthusiasm will be less, the national greater."[18] FitzGerald also warned his father-in-law that Fianna Fáil planned to play on another characteristic—his notoriously short fuse—by provoking him into a rage. "As I believe they think this the chink in your armour, you should watch always for this line of attack."[19]

Though he was not a particularly intellectual Catholic, his deep religious commitment cannot be doubted—as was made more than clear during the Mother and Child controversy. For much of his life he went to Mass every day, either at his local church in Donnybrook in south Dublin or in the Church of Adam and Eve on the quays on his way to the Four Courts.[20] He was, according to a former parish priest, "an example in every way", both as a parishioner and a sodality member.[21] His son Declan recalled that while he would say the Rosary every night, he never suggested the entire family should join in, as would have been reasonably common at the time. Instead, once the children had gone to bed, he would kneel down beside the fire in his study to perform his devotions alone, rather than insisting on conformity.[22]

His pugnacity could frequently extend to religious matters—famously in an address to the Trinity College Philosophical Society in October 1948, when he referred several times to the "so-called Reformation"[23]—a reference which caused considerable offence to Protestants. It was also, according to Patrick Lynch, quite deliberate. Lynch had drafted a speech for him, but the Taoiseach had rewritten parts of it, adding in the "so-called Reformation" reference as an expression of his dislike and suspicion of Trinity.[24]

Apart from religion, John A. Costello's other great comfort in life was his family. Evenings were spent in the study, the children listening to the radio while their father read briefs by the fire—he claimed to have learned to ignore noise and concentrate on his work in the Law Library, where he worked with conversations going on around him.[25] A profile in the (British) *News Review* in 1949 noted that "most of the family fun is found at home", referring to the then Taoiseach's liking for listening to music, playing bridge, taking his dachshund Slem for a morning walk, and reading thrillers.[26] What he referred to as his "pernicious habit" of reading detective stories did prove politically useful on one occasion, giving him the background knowledge to make an informed Dáil contribution about the training of police in detection techniques.[27]

He had a ritual of going every spring to the Dublin Mountains to pick primroses with the family. The journey, given his famously fast driving, must have been a bit rough—his daughter Eavan later said looking at a painting of primroses which had belonged to her father made her feel carsick because it reminded her of those trips.[28]

And then there was golf, to which he cheerfully admitted he was "addicted", even in old age.[29] At the time of his election as Taoiseach, he was Captain of Portmarnock Golf Club, and an editorial in *Irish Golf* magazine remarked that his choice for both posts was wise, as "John Costello despite his very retiring manner makes one respect him and feel confidence in him."[30]

However, it would appear that despite his "addiction", he wasn't a particularly strong golfer—his son recalled that, even being generous, he was no more than "average".[31] The *Irish Golf* editorial noted that "he never played golf except for the fun and exercise of it", and went on to pay a rather back-handed compliment: "When one has seen a golfer take the rough with the smooth in the most equable of manners, when he could miss a shortish putt without thinking the world was collapsing, then one can have confidence in the new Taoiseach. A broad fairway to him, though if he does find the rough he will get out of it calmly and well."[32] Every Sunday for years, Costello played in the same four-ball in Portmarnock, with Dick Browne of the ESB, an old school friend; Dick Rice, chairman of the Revenue Commissioners; and Seamus O'Connor, the Dublin City Sheriff.[33] It was on one such occasion in 1948 that he wrestled with the dilemma of whether he should accept the position of Taoiseach.

A less benign addiction was to smoking—he was an inveterate smoker of Churchman cigarettes, although according to his son he didn't actually inhale.[34] In conversation, an observer noted, he had two habits—"twiddling a pencil, and keeping his cigarette tucked in the corner of his mouth while talking".[35] One of his more impassioned contributions to the Dáil was on the question of tobacco, which he argued was a necessity rather than a luxury, and should be taxed accordingly. "It enables everyone, whether rich or poor, to carry on his work ... In addition to giving a certain amount of comfort, and soothing the nerves ... it gives him a certain amount of relaxation, and enables him to do his work better."[36]

He was a famously dapper dresser.[37] In 1948, the British Lord Chancellor, William Jowitt, paid him a compliment by suggesting he might visit a tailor in Dublin while on holidays in Ireland "to see if I can approach nearer your standard" of sartorial elegance.[38]

Another factor much remarked upon was Jack Costello's modesty. Tom Finlay, later to be Chief Justice, recalled his "absolute humility" as one of the most remarkable things about him. He would have been taken aback if Finlay, as a young barrister appearing in court with him, let him through a door first.[39] Again, the *News Review* noted in 1949 that as Taoiseach, "the idea of anyone wanting to write an article about him still amuses him".[40] The young Fine Gael activist Richie Ryan had the job of announcing Costello's arrival into the Drawing Room of the Mansion House during the 1949 Fine Gael Ard Fheis. As he called out, "Ladies and Gentlemen—the Taoiseach!" he got an "almighty thump" in the back and heard Costello growl, "Cut that out, Richie, I don't want any of that nonsense."[41]

This modesty, as well as his personal kindness, had major political implications, as it played a role in his selection as the inter-party group's candidate for Taoiseach. Noel Hartnett was a leading figure in Clann na Poblachta who fell out with Seán MacBride—and, by extension, with Costello—over the Mother and Child Scheme and the Battle of Baltinglass (a controversy over political influence in the filling of a post office appointment). In 1959 he wrote that Costello's faults as a politician sprang "almost exclusively from excessive loyalty to his colleagues". This loyalty, Hartnett said, "led him occasionally to defend actions and policies which would better have been condemned". Hartnett pointed to another of Costello's characteristics—his avoidance of bitterness—as the reason for his choice as Taoiseach, and pointed out that the members of all the parties in the Inter-party Governments "trusted and respected him".[42]

This judgment had been borne out at the time of his election by others, including High Court judge T.C. Kingsmill Moore, a former Independent senator who told Costello, "you were almost unique in the Dáil in that all parties liked and trusted you, no matter how bitterly opposed to you".[43] Similarly, The O'Mahony, a former Fine Gael TD (who was also to fall out with Costello over the Baltinglass issue), wrote to him in 1948, "If you are able to keep that varied coalition of parties together I think you will have brought about a miracle, but from what I saw of you during the eleven years I was in the Dáil I don't believe anyone else would ever have a chance."[44]

Reluctant he may have been. But John A. Costello, thanks to his background, his career, and most importantly his personality, was in 1948 in a pivotal position to make history.

Chapter 1 ～

THE VALUE OF PRACTICE

" ... fluency of speech in public is as much an acquired talent as a natural gift."[1]

JOHN A. COSTELLO, JULY 1911

"Mr Jack Costello is an example of the value of practice. He improves every meeting and is now really worth listening to ..."[2]

UCD MAGAZINE *THE NATIONAL STUDENT*, MARCH 1912

A fter John A. Costello's election as Taoiseach, one of his former schoolmates, John Keane, produced a photograph of a group of pupils at O'Connell School, and asked his children to guess which one grew up to be the leader of the Government. The clue, it turned out, was that Costello was the only boy in the photograph wearing a watch chain[3]—a suitable symbol of the future wealth and upper middle class status of one of the leading barristers of his day. The watch chain also fits neatly into the widespread perception that Costello, like some of his colleagues in Cumann na nGaedheal and later Fine Gael, was the product of a privileged background.

But in fact, unlike other members of the pro-Treaty leadership such as Kevin O'Higgins, Patrick Hogan and Patrick McGilligan, the future Taoiseach was not a past pupil of the elite private school Clongowes. He was a Christian Brothers boy, his father a mid-ranking civil servant, and his upbringing modest, though comfortable.[4] If the watch chain was symbolic, it was symbolic of an aspiration rather than a status achieved. And the story of Jack Costello's early years is the story of how hard work and natural ability allowed him to make good on that aspiration.

John Aloysius Costello was born on 20 June 1891, at the home of his parents at 13 Charleville Road[5] on the northside of Dublin, not far from the city centre. The house is a pleasant mid-terrace redbrick with a bay window. Charleville Road, quiet and tree-lined, runs from Cabra Road down to the North Circular

Leabharlanna Poiblí Chathair Bhaile Átha Cliath
Dublin City Public Libraries

Road. Although Costello's birth certificate describes it as being in Cabra, it's actually closer to Phibsborough, just down from the massive gothic St Peter's Church (begun in 1862, but only finished in 1911).

Costello was part of the last generation to grow to adulthood in an Ireland that was part of the British Empire. His birth came in the middle of political crisis—the Home Rule Party had split in December 1890 over the continued leadership of Charles Stuart Parnell, who was to die the following October. Costello's year of birth also put him, in terms of age, almost exactly halfway between two of his great political rivals—Eamon de Valera, born in 1882, and Seán Lemass, born in 1899.

His father, John Costello senior, was born in Barefield in Clare on 25 May 1862,[6] while his mother, Rose Callaghan, was three years younger and a native of Westmeath. The couple married in 1888.[7] When he became Taoiseach, Jack Costello was asked if he was related to various branches of the Costello clan, but had to reply that he had "made only very little study of his genealogical tree".[8] However, he apparently spent boyhood summers in Barefield, playing with the local children and eating apples from the local orchard—whether with permission or not is not clear.[9] In later years, he enjoyed telling his family stories about Clare, particularly the West Clare Railway immortalised by Percy French in the song "Are You Right There Michael". Costello claimed a printed notice in one station outlined a revised timetable and ended with the warning that "there will be no last train".[10]

Just four miles from Ennis, Barefield was less a village than a "small cluster of houses", although it was significant enough to have an RIC hut under the command of a sergeant. It was described in the mid-1940s as "a very undulating parish, and its good and bad land is just as much mixed as its contour". At that time, it had two pubs, a Catholic church, a post office, a dispensary, and a national school.[11] The latter, described in 1943 as a "fairly new, substantial four teacher school" was built on Costello family land.[12]

John Costello senior began working in the Registry of Deeds in Dublin in 1881, shortly before his nineteenth birthday.[13] His progress through the ranks of the organisation was steady if unspectacular—by 1898 he was a Second Division Clerk,[14] in 1903 he became one of three Higher Grade clerks,[15] and a decade later he became a Staff Officer—a senior position but still quite a bit down the pecking order, behind the Registrar, First and Second Assistant Registrars and the Chief Clerk.[16] He was in the same position when he retired.[17] His brother Jim also went into the Civil Service, in his case the post office, but appears to have had a more successful career, as in later life he had a house on the fashionable Alma Road in Monkstown.[18]

Outside work, John Costello was a prominent temperance activist in Father Mathew Hall in Church Street for over 40 years.[19] He gave lectures in the Hall on diverse subjects, ranging from "Some Incidents in the Land War of the Last Century"[20] to "The Rise of the Peasant in Ireland"[21] and even "A holiday by the Cliffs of Moher", which was to be "illustrated by limelight view".[22] Of more significance, he served as chairman of the Father Matthew Health Insurance Society, which among other things campaigned for the extension of medical benefits to Ireland.[23] He was also active in trade unionism, being involved in the formation of the Civil Service Guild[24] and serving on its Executive.[25] As an active politician, his son was to champion the cause of civil servants, helping to bring about an arbitration system to resolve disputes over pay.[26]

Jack Costello recalled in later years that his father was "a great Parnellite".[27] This was a common position in the capital, as Tom Garvin has pointed out: "bourgeois and working-class Dublin became Parnellite in contrast to the mainly anti-Parnellite countryside."[28] Of course, the son was also a supporter of Home Rule, and of John Redmond, in the years leading up to the First World War—as he said later, "everyone in Ireland was a Home Ruler with the exception of a very small minority who were in the IRB ..."[29] As we shall see in Chapter 5, Costello senior was to become a Fine Gael Councillor on Dublin Corporation after his retirement.

John and Rose Costello had three children. Mary, known as May in the family, was born the year after their marriage. She was to live on in the family home, caring for her parents, and never married. Thomas Joseph, who was a year younger, became a doctor and emigrated to England—as we shall see, he was a larger-than-life character, and in their university days overshadowed Jack, who was two years younger than him. Their father was keen on walks— perhaps in the nearby Phoenix Park—so keen, in fact, that Jack was put off organised walks for life.[30]

By the time of the 1911 Census, the Costello family was living at 32 Rathdown Road, in the parish of Grangegorman. Rathdown Road is just across the North Circular from Charleville Road, and runs down towards what was then Grangegorman mental hospital. Number 32 is part of a long terrace of red brick houses, and is similar in appearance to Costello's birthplace on Charleville Road, with a bay window on the ground floor and two windows upstairs.

Rose Costello's family may have helped with the purchase of both these houses, which could have been slightly beyond John Costello's salary as a relatively junior civil servant. Just three months after buying the house at Charleville Road, he signed an indenture of assignment with his brother-in-law, James Callaghan, a grocer in North King Street, and with John McKeever, a draper from Navan married to one of the Callaghan sisters.[31] This suggests they had some financial interest in the house, perhaps after lending their brother-in-law some money. Another of the Callaghan sisters, Bridget, had an interest in the house in Rathdown Road, and in her will, made in November 1921, she left that interest to Rose, stipulating that after Rose's death it should pass to May. In a codicil to the will made in 1930, after Rose's death, the interest in 32 Rathdown Road was left to John senior and May.[32]

John Aloysius became a pupil at St Joseph's, Marino, in the autumn of 1903, when he was 12. The school (later better known as "Joey's") was run by the Christian Brothers. One of its three rooms was devoted to the 43 pupils in the intermediate (secondary) class. The 300 primary pupils were divided between the other two rooms.[33] Among his classmates was Dick Browne,[34] later Chairman of the Electricity Supply Board, who was Costello's greatest friend, godfather to his son Declan, and one of his golfing partners on Sunday mornings in Portmarnock for many years.[35]

As Marino had no senior classes at the time, the two friends transferred to the O'Connell School in North Richmond Street,[36] also run by the Christian Brothers. The school was named after Daniel O'Connell, who laid the foundation stone in 1828.[37] It prided itself on its success in the Intermediate Examinations, frequently boasting the highest number of passes and distinctions in the country.[38] The school's centenary book in 1928 noted the number of senior Government officials it had produced, including Costello, who was then Attorney General, Dick Browne, who was a Senior Inspector of Taxes, and the Secretary of the Department of Local Government, E.P. McCarron. With some self-satisfaction, R.C. Geary (later Director of the Central Statistics Office) wrote, "Your 'Richmond Street' boy makes a good official. In the first place he possesses the necessary academic qualifications to place him high on the examination lists. He has, in addition, certain qualities which make him a good colleague. This is an essential point. However clever an official he may be, he has to pull with the team ..."[39]

As well as civil servants, the school produced a great many rebels, with more than 120 pupils or former students believed to have taken part in the 1916 Rising, including three of the 16 leaders who were executed—Eamonn Ceannt, Con Colbert, and Seán Heuston.[40] The latter, in fact, was among John A. Costello's classmates.[41] Other past pupils included President Seán T. O'Kelly, Taoiseach Seán Lemass, and Judge Cahir Davitt, a son of Land League founder Michael Davitt, who became President of the High Court in 1951.[42] Other notable legal figures who attended the school were Ireland's last Lord Chief Justice, Sir Thomas Molony, and Aindrias Ó Caoimh and Charles Casey, both of whom became High Court judges after serving as Attorney General (Casey having been appointed to that position by Costello).[43]

At O'Connell School, in a pattern that would be repeated throughout his education, the young Costello performed well academically, winning prizes and distinctions. He also improved as he went along—another pattern that would be repeated in college, at the Bar and in politics.

At the time, the State examination, the Intermediate, was divided into Junior, Middle and Senior Grades, the latter corresponding to the Leaving Certificate, which was introduced in 1924 (along with, confusingly, another examination known as the Intermediate Certificate, the equivalent of the old Junior Grade).[44] In the Middle Grade, in 1907, Costello received Honours results in English, French, Irish, Algebra, Trigonometry and Science, with passing grades in Arithmetic, Shorthand, Geometry and Latin. The results were good enough to win him a £3 book prize.[45] In his final year, 1908, he took honours in English, French, Irish, Arithmetic and Algebra, Trigonometry and Physics, and passed Geometry, winning £3 prizes for modern literature and experimental science, as well as a £1 prize in mathematics. It was a fairly broad education. Costello appears to have been keen on Science—he had the joint highest (in 1907) or highest (1908) hours spent at Science according to the school records.[46] More importantly, he won the Fanning Scholarship, worth a substantial £50 a year for three years,[47] which was to pay his college fees.

It had been a successful school career, and while Costello didn't speak much of his time at the school in later life, he didn't complain about it either.[48] The link with the school was played on by an enterprising 11-year-old when Costello was elected Taoiseach. Tom Fahy of Vernon Park in Clontarf wrote to congratulate him on his election—which he felt could best be marked by a free day. Unfortunately, there is no record of whether the new Taoiseach did, as suggested by Master Fahy, contact the school authorities to let his successors off for the day.[49]

When Costello won the Fanning Scholarship in 1908, he was one of its first recipients. The scholarship, set up two years previously, aimed to pay the college fees of the son of a civil servant receiving the highest marks in the Senior Grade of the Intermediate. It stipulated that the person holding the scholarship should carry out his studies at UCD. According to Costello, who paid a visit to the founder of the Trust after receiving the scholarship, Francis A. Fanning was "a very strong Catholic" who wanted to encourage Irish students to go to the new National University rather than Trinity College, which "in those days was regarded as the bastion of the then Protestant Ascendancy".[50]

The institution which he joined was in a state of flux, to put it at its mildest. He was in the last group of students who attended 86 Stephen's Green under the old Royal University—the next year the new National University was established under the 1908 Irish Universities Act (introduced by Irish Secretary Augustine Birrell to placate Catholic opinion). The Act joined UCD with the former Queen's Colleges in Cork and Galway to form the NUI. In a foretaste of partition, the other Queen's College, in Belfast, became a separate university.

Costello claimed in later life that the authorities dithered so much about faculty positions that they ended up appointing a number of professors to the wrong chairs. "There was general confusion and we had not merely ... no Professors to lecture us, we had not even a chair to sit on, we were walking around Stephen's Green wasting our time until the National University authorities made up their minds to give us some Professors to lecture us."[51] The complaint was an echo of that made at the time, in an editorial in the first edition of a student newspaper, the *National Student:* " ... there has been little academic work done this year. The Professors have been occupied busily in securing their positions, in making boards and committees on which to sit, and then in sitting on them ... There is a vague but general feeling that no attention is being paid to the students, that they are regarded as necessary evils, whose sole duty is to pay fees and keep quiet ..."[52]

The new college was small, with only 530 students in its first academic year, 1909–10, although numbers grew quickly, almost doubling (reaching 1,017) by 1916.[53] As George O'Brien, a future senator and professor of economics, noted, "We were few enough to get to know each other very well, even if some of us did not like each other very much. Indeed, some of the developments in the political history of Ireland in the years since the Treaty grew out of the affinities and dislikes of my contemporaries. Old alliances and old quarrels reappeared in the wider field of public life."[54] Among Costello's contemporaries in UCD were future ministers Kevin O'Higgins, Patrick McGilligan and Patrick Hogan; his successor as Attorney General after the change of government in 1932, Conor Maguire; and the leading solicitor Arthur Cox.

These young men and their fellow NUI graduates were to provide much of the leadership of the new Irish Free State, in politics, the Civil Service and the professions. Of course, they could not have foreseen that the then dominant Irish Parliamentary Party would be destroyed within a decade by Sinn Féin. According to O'Brien, "we took it for granted that, if Home Rule was achieved, we would be among the politicians of the new Ireland ... So certain were we of the approach of Home Rule that some of our students neglected to prepare for a profession, believing that they would get a good job when self-government came ..."[55] While Arthur Cox could not be accused of neglecting his studies, his enthusiasm for imminent Home Rule is clear from his diary for 1913, in which he counted down the days to the Bill coming into force.[56]

Academically, Costello progressed in much the same way he had in school, starting off with mediocre results but quickly improving. He received a pass mark in his First Arts exam in 1909;[57] first class honours in Irish and French, as well as a pass in Biology, in 1910;[58] and graduated with a First in Irish and

French in 1911.[59] His interest in Irish was later demonstrated in government when he established the Department of the Gaeltacht. He had travelled to the Aran Islands to learn Irish while still at school,[60] although the experiment was not an unqualified success. He later complained that the islanders were "much more concerned with picking up little scraps of English and getting me to talk English to them than they were about speaking Irish to me".[61] This perhaps explains why, despite his exam results, there was some doubt about his fluency. At a meeting of the Literary and Historical Society in March 1912 a motion was proposed criticising the Records and Correspondence Secretaries, Tom and Jack Costello, for "incompetence ... in not being able to answer questions in Irish". The motion was only defeated by 20 votes to 18.[62]

Among the lecturers Costello got to know were James Murnaghan, later a judge of the Supreme Court, Swift MacNeill, then an Irish Party MP, and Arthur Clery, whose favourite pupil he was.[63] George O'Brien described the latter lecturer: "Clery was a bachelor who liked the society of young men. He used to invite us to very pleasant dinner parties where we met some of his own generation. He was kind to us and I appreciated his friendship at the time. I learned later that he was very bigoted against the British and against Protestants and a great extremist in politics, although he took no active part in revolutionary movements. I am afraid he influenced some young men in the direction of his own views and that he sowed the seeds of a good deal of bitterness."[64] As O'Brien's biographer makes clear, this somewhat jaundiced account may have been influenced by O'Brien's dislike of John A. Costello.[65]

As a later interviewer put it, "in college his interests were intellectual rather than athletic",[66] but the young Costello did have some sporting interests—he was a member of a football club based at Goldsmith Street.[67] However, he was to have a more enduring interest in golf. He joined a golf club in Finglas,[68] a forerunner of his membership of clubs at Portmarnock, Milltown and Rossapenna, Co. Donegal. He also, at least occasionally, was prevailed upon to sing at musical evenings.[69] According to his children Declan and Eavan, he spoke in later years about singing at parties as a young man, sometimes accompanied by his wife, Ida, on the piano.[70] Costello also regaled his children with reminiscences of the 1907 Great Exhibition in Ballsbridge, with its giant water slide and a Zulu tent featuring "real live Africans", obviously an exotic sight at the time.[71]

In July 1911, just turned 20, Costello wrote a lengthy and mildly amusing article for the *National Student,* the college magazine, contrasting the old Royal with the new National University, suggesting that he saw some improvement in the situation of students. He claimed that the Royal "was little better than a glorified Boarding and Day School ... The residents ... rose in the morning by rule, lived mechanically, and even voted in the Societies mechanically and as they were told. The outdoor students of the College came to lectures, met casually, chatted desultorily outside the lecture room, and dispersed." The new structure had a higher purpose than the old, which had served merely as an exam factory. "The National has been created to send forth students better equipped mentally and bodily than heretofore; to produce students with broader views and wider knowledge ... Its aim should be culture rather than erudition; learning rather than pedantry." Exams, he suggested, were "a necessary evil, and must be tolerated ... The importance attached to them should, however, be reduced to a minimum: the true end of a real University should be culture, not examination."

Of his fellow students, he observed mordantly that "students always take themselves and their opinions seriously", before going on to criticise certain "types" of student, which could be divided into sots and swots. Of the first, he wrote, "These gentlemen often accost some meek and unoffending student whom they wish to impress; buttonhole him and tell him of the number of times they were on the bend; how hard it is to study when in such a state; what head-aches they had after it; what daring tricks they had played on their professors; and what damage they had done to other people's property. These gentlemen in their first year wish to make it believed that they are real wits and veritable roués!" (It is impossible to know who Costello had in mind when he was writing this, but it sounds rather like the "dissipated" student Kevin O'Higgins, as described by his biographer, a regular at Mooney's pub in Harry Street.)[72]

Costello had this to say about the swots: "They walk rapidly, at the sound of the bell, from the Library to the lecture hall and install themselves in a place convenient to the professor and without losing an instant. They are fearful of being late. They are fearful of losing some of the words of wisdom which fall from the learned professor's lips. They are fearful of incurring his ire. They take copious and meticulous notes and accept his opinions as final without demur. The lecture finished, they hasten back to their interrupted studies. No loitering, no conversation, no stories—all study concentrated and unlimited. No Society ever sees them. At social functions they are conspicuous by their absence—nor are they missed. Their one desire is success in examinations, and their one aim is to stuff their brains with a store of book learning, thereby taking the shortest path to pedantry."

This leads him on to extol the virtues of the College societies, which are beneficial and, in fact, indispensable. "By means of books we may come under the influence of dead genius; by means of social intercourse we may be influenced by living talent. For the formation of student character there must be frequent conversation between the students, they must live and work together, and must get to know each other. What a blank student life would be if it merely consisted of daily attendance at lectures!"

Given his experience in the Literary and Historical Society (the L&H), his assessment of the quality of debate there is interesting: "The ideas of the members of these societies may not, and seldom are, either strikingly original or alarmingly learned, but at all events by speaking in public they are taught self-confidence and self-mastery, and even from listening to commonplace and mediocre ideas there is something to be gained ... The real *raison d'être* of College Societies is to be found in the fact they are conducive to culture and refinement, and that fluency of speech in public is as much an acquired talent as a natural gift."[73] He was an example of the truth of this observation—his future success in politics and the law was built on his ability as a public speaker, an ability honed in college debates.

It is possible that involvement in college societies conferred culture and refinement on students, but a more immediate reward was status—especially in the L&H, success in which "was firmly established as a significant benchmark against which any ambitious student's career in university was measured".[74] As Costello later observed, the lack of resources under both the old Royal and the new National Universities denied students the university life known in older academic institutions, but "they made it for themselves by congregating around the steps of the National Library, and by their activities in the famous Literary and Historical Society".[75]

The Library steps, according to George O'Brien, "were the scenes of much conversation. The conversations on the Library steps in Joyce's *Portrait of the Artist* bring back vivid memories of the hours that we used to spend on the same spot ..."[76] The L&H, meanwhile, was the place where "many of the young men who helped to establish the new Irish State from 1922 onwards received their first lessons in politics and public speeches".[77] If UCD was where the future elite of the Irish Free State met, the L&H was where they cut their teeth, learned the arts of public speaking and of politics, and made friendships and enmities that were to last a lifetime. Those young men included John A. Costello. He later claimed that his first appearance in print was as a "Voice" during an address by Chief Secretary Augustine Birrell to the L&H in the Aula Maxima in 86 St Stephen's Green. He "was at the back of the hall, a very young student in my first year, and very tentatively I am afraid shouted out 'What about the new University?'"[78]

A contemporary, slightly tongue in cheek, description of the L&H sets the scene: "About a hundred and twenty people, some eighty men and forty women, sit from 8 p.m. till 11 p.m. in a room decorated with grisly pictures of skeletons [meetings were held in the same room as medical lectures], and in an atmosphere almost solid with tobacco-smoke. The first hour is occupied with a 'discussion of rules'. The majority of the meeting have not the least idea what the rules are, but a handful of men spend an hour heckling the officers of the Society with regard to them ... The debate begins ... It was perfectly obvious to me after listening to a very few of the speeches that the real object of a speaker was not to say something new or weighty ... but to talk good nonsense ..."[79]

Chief among the hecklers was Costello's brother, Tom, a flamboyant figure who had preceded him to UCD in 1907 and was studying medicine.[80] The elder Costello quickly made a name for himself as a tormentor of the Society's officials: "There are some who expend, in inventing posers for the Record Secretary, a wealth of time and ability that, otherwise applied, would make them medallists of the society. But ... [Mr] Costello ... and others of that ilk prefer asking questions to making speeches. And the society would be much duller if they did not."[81] Arthur Cox, a friend and rival of Jack Costello's, described Tom as "dominant in private business. Caring little for more formal debate, he seemed to be for ever in opposition, thundering from the topmost bench down on the committee at their table below, moving votes of censure and perpetually taking the officers to task for some breach of Palgrave's *Parliamentary Procedure* which ruled all our proceedings. Had he remained in Ireland ... he would have been a leader."[82] Another contemporary, Michael McGilligan, said, "Tom was at that time the more dynamic of the two. Tom laid about him in the Society ... Jack ... was not then the Costello of the Courts ..."[83]

The younger Costello was very much overshadowed in his first few years in college by his brother, as is shown in the pages of the *National Student*, where Tom was frequently a target for good-natured banter. When Jack was mentioned, it was usually in relation to his more flamboyant brother.[84] The younger Costello made his maiden speech to the L&H in November 1908, shortly after starting in UCD. The then auditor, Tom Bodkin, later a good friend, remembered the speech as being "on the trite subject: 'That the pen is mightier than the sword'",[85] while Costello described it as "most undistinguished".[86] It appears he was right—his effort received the lowest score of any speaker that evening, at just 3.92 out of 10.

In February 1911, Tom Costello's badgering of the committee finally produced results, and led to advancement for him and his brother. Tom's motion of censure on the committee was passed by the necessary two-thirds majority.[87] Elections were held for a new committee. Arthur Cox topped the poll, with 46 votes. Jack Costello was second, with 39, one more than Tom.[88] As a speaker, Jack Costello had not yet hit his stride. The *National Student* observed, "One cannot get over the idea that he does not believe in what he is saying ... that he makes no distinction between his strong and his weak points—that he is not impressive."[89] He was, for instance, ranked twentieth out of 23 speakers in the impromptu debate in May (which was won by Arthur

Cox, with Patrick McGilligan second),[90] despite a fairly easy topic—"That the worst of things must come to an end". His brother, the *National Student* noted, "denied stoutly, for several reasons, mainly personal, 'That a large mind is impossible in a small family' ..."[91]

Drama was provided by the 1911 auditorial election between Patrick McGilligan, the previous year's runner-up, and John Ronayne. A contemporary account read, "Who that has been through it either as active partisan or harried voter will ever forget it? ... It was the final incident in the fierce struggle that has been going on between the two parties in the Society ... the parties may well ask themselves what they were fighting for, and what is their exact point of difference ... we do wish to deprecate the excessive bitterness which marred, grievously marred, the late election ..."[92] Michael McGilligan described the campaign as having "bitterness of a kind and degree that I had not seen in any previous election. I do not remember why: I am not sure that I ever knew why ..."[93]

Ronayne was declared the victor, by 83 votes to 80, but a petition was immediately lodged challenging the validity of a number of the votes. The row was so bitter that the President of UCD, Dr Denis Coffey, asked for legal advice from the Solicitor General, Ignatius O'Brien, himself a former auditor (and later Lord Chancellor). O'Brien ruled that a number of the votes for Ronayne were indeed invalid, and recommended a new election. Dr Coffey wisely decided to avoid a further divisive contest, and instead proposed a compromise, with Ronayne to continue as auditor until (perhaps appropriately) St Valentine's Day, when McGilligan was to take over. This compromise was ratified by the Society on the proposal of Jack Costello,[94] though Ronayne later attempted to repudiate it.

The split in the Society appears to have left the Costello brothers on different sides—when it came to the division of offices within the committee, Tom first proposed Alec Maguire, who declined the nomination, and then Arthur Cox as Correspondence Secretary, in opposition to Jack. The younger Costello, however, was elected to the post by five votes to three. Tom was Records Secretary and Michael J. Ryan was Treasurer. Cox had been nominated for all three posts, and lost all three.[95] One of Jack's more novel suggestions on the committee was for the society to hold a dance—a proposal later vetoed by Dr Coffey.[96] This was perhaps an attempt to appeal to members in advance of the next auditorial election.

In debate, meanwhile, Jack Costello was now a very regular contributor, with improved though still not spectacular marks—although by now he was occasionally beating Arthur Cox in debate as well as in elections.[97] As the *National Student* put it, "Mr Cox has, we think, the best style of speaking in the Society. While he is speaking he is very impressive, it is only when he has sat down that one is tempted sometimes to think that he has said nothing and said it very well. Mr Jack Costello is an example of the value of practice. He improves every meeting and is now really worth listening to ..."[98] In May, he read a paper on "Ireland's Literary Position" to the Society, receiving the very high mark of 9.16 out of 10.[99] According to the account in the *National Student*, he "enhanced his reputation by the excellence of his paper. It was so good ... that his brother sat beaming with a look on his face which said quite plainly, 'See what I could have done if I had only bothered'."[100]

This paper was delivered in the midst of an auditorial election campaign, which pitted Costello against Arthur Cox. Cox, who was to become Ireland's leading solicitor in mid-century, was a Belvedere boy from a well-off family—his father, Dr Michael Cox, was the closest friend of John Dillon, at this point deputy leader of the Irish Parliamentary Party.[101] He and Costello were to be friendly rivals for many years, although at this time the rivalry rather than the friendship was dominant, certainly as far as Cox was concerned. In later years, Cox remembered the campaign as intense, because "electioneering tactics had been brought to a high perfection ... no device was omitted by the supporters of either".[102] Costello's recollection was probably more accurate: "I was the complete amateur. He knew every trick in the bag and always defeated me."[103] In February 1961, a half century after the contest, Costello presided over a meeting of the L&H "and spoke of how he had been deprived of that office ... by the ruthless methods of that most respectable Dublin solicitor Mr Arthur Cox. It was clear that the result still rankled after all the years."[104]

On nomination night, Cox was proposed by George O'Brien, who, in the lively account of the *National Student*, "gave us a list of Mr Cox's successes from his earliest childhood up to the time he became a nut and went to dances. Nobody blames Mr Cox for winning a lot of medals—everyone must have his little hobby—but everyone blames Mr O'Brien for reminding us of them. Mr Davoren seconded, and in polished tones talked about the magnificent speeches which Mr Cox had made at every meeting of the society. As Mr Davoren had been present at not more than three meetings this year his opinion on the subject was of undoubted value. Mr C.A. Maguire proposed and Mr Dwyer seconded Mr J. Costello. They told us, of course, that Mr Costello had had 'the interests of the Society at heart', and had read a magnificent paper, and so on ... All the voters on the authorised list—to the number of 200—listened breathlessly to the speeches ... There were also many present whose subscriptions had been paid, but who did not know Mr Ryan, the treasurer, who were so unbiased that they did not know which was Mr Costello and which was Mr Cox, and who went out as they came in—with their minds made up for them. That insignificant minority, the lay, stay-at-home members who had attended regularly during the year and had paid their own subscriptions, sat there unnoticed and unaddressed. What did their votes matter?"[105]

The final touch of brilliance on the part of the Cox campaign was to appeal to female members. Admission of women had been a controversial subject in the Society until 1909, when they had outmanoeuvred their opponents by the simple expedient of paying their subscriptions to the Treasurer. Auditor Michael Davitt then ruled that as paid up members they could themselves vote on whether or not they should be admitted.[106] Both Costello and Cox had spoken against the admission of women, but the latter appears to have been more committed to the anti-suffragette cause, even telling a debate at the King's Inns that women cause wars, as was proved by Helen of Troy.[107] But an election is an election. A number of female members informed Cox that they would not vote for him unless they were invited to the traditional auditor's victory tea in the Café Cairo, which, equally traditionally, was male-only. As the National Student reported, "Mr Cox gave in, and 'bought their votes with penny buns'. That was the way some brutes of men put it."[108]

But Cox had more going for him than such tactical shrewdness. He was the best speaker in the Society that year, winning the Gold Medal, and his opponent clearly recognised that this was an electoral advantage. Cahir Davitt, also a former O'Connell School boy, recalled being canvassed by Costello, and replying evasively that he hadn't been to enough meetings to judge which of the candidates was the better speaker. Costello replied "that of course if that were the only matter that was to be considered I should vote for Cox".[109] As it happened, Davitt voted for Costello, presumably because the school tie trumped eloquence; but the exchange is indicative of the future Taoiseach's diffidence, modesty, and lack of a killer instinct—it is difficult to imagine Cox giving a similar reply.

On election night, Cox won 112 votes to Costello's 63, a crushing defeat. George O'Brien, ever unsympathetic to Costello, wrote in his unpublished recollections in 1950, "If anybody had ventured to predict that one of the parties to this contest would have become prime minister of an Irish Republic his prophecy would have been received with some scepticism. If a hearer had chosen to believe that the prophecy would come true and had been asked to say which of the candidates was destined for this distinction, he would have unhesitatingly chosen Cox. I do not think that anybody would have chosen Costello, who matured late and whose elevation was the result of unforeseen political circumstances."[110] In his contribution to the L&H centenary history, published when Costello was in his second term as Taoiseach, O'Brien diplomatically left out the final two sentences of the quote above.[111]

Costello had a respectable showing in the committee elections, coming in second with 95 votes, which kept alive his hopes for another run the following year. Ominously for his prospects, though, first place was taken by M.J. Ryan, an ally of Cox, who received 122 votes.[112] During the 1912/13 academic year, Costello was again a frequent and effective speaker—he was to end the year placed fourth overall,[113] but, crucially, Ryan was first, winning the Society's Gold Medal and cementing his claim to the auditorship. Among the topics Costello addressed were the future of the Intermediate System of Education (the *National Student* judged him "thoughtful and effective ... his speech was, perhaps, the most interesting of the evening"), and, appropriately, International Arbitration ("Mr J.A. Costello cleverly sketched out the history of the growth of arbitration, and if Locke be correct when he asserts that a young man who is versed in the Jus Civile is assured of success, Mr Costello's knowledge of international law should ensure his future").[114] He also successfully led the opposition to a motion calling for women to be given the vote,[115] and to a motion by Ryan that the three Irish Universities should be federated.[116]

In a further sign of his stature within the L&H, he was one of the three members (the others were George O'Brien and Conor Maguire) elected to join the auditor, Cox, in an Inter-debate with the King's Inns on the question of whether modern taste in literature was 'decadent'. Their opponents were led by Tom Bodkin, and included Charles Bewley, later Irish Minister to Berlin.[117] According to the following day's *Freeman's Journal*, Costello argued "that modern literature was a question of supply and demand. The commercialism of the day had gripped it, and the result was that it was not the finest taste that succeeded, but what was best from the point of view of the business man."[118]

By the beginning of March, two months before the vote, Cox noted in his diary that "the Auditorial fight has begun in earnest. Three Hotspurs are already in the field—Ryan, Maguire and Costello."[119] Three days later he recorded that "Costello seems downcast. I think Maguire has the ball at his feet."[120] The last prediction was spectacularly wrong, but Costello had every reason to be downcast. He had asked Cahir Davitt to propose him, which, the future President of the High Court later confessed, "I did very ineptly. I think he pulled me down before my peroration."[121] Ryan had the support of his fellow Engineering students. He also managed to project an image of being an outsider trying to overcome the "Establishment"—he was described by Michael Tierney, later the President of UCD, as "the candidate of the proletariat".[122]

In a four-way race, Ryan won with a majority of the votes cast—113. Costello had the consolation of coming second, with 44, two votes ahead of Conor Maguire, while J.B. Magennis, a medical student, got just 10 votes.[123] Costello later claimed that Ryan had pinpricked the ballot papers so he could see exactly who had voted for him. Addressing a meeting of the L&H in 1951, he turned to one of the other speakers, Seán Lemass, and assured him that "tactics were adopted here in connection with elections that have not even yet been thought up by the Opposition". He added that what he had learned in the Society about politics and electioneering had been "of inestimable value" in his later career.[124]

John A. Costello was in good company—James Joyce was an unsuccessful candidate for the auditorship (against Costello's future mentor, Hugh Kennedy), as were many other future legal and political stars.[125] As an unsuccessful 1980s candidate for the post wrote, "Losing an election is a horrible feeling, even if there is the consolation that some of the best talents in the L&H, such as James Joyce and John A. Costello, also lost the Auditorial contest."[126] In a sense, the L&H also lost out, as its most recent historian has suggested, "twice profligately dismissing what is perhaps at this stage likely to prove to have been its sole prospect of having an auditor who became Taoiseach."[127] Ryan, incidentally, became Reid Professor of Law at Trinity College,[128] and later still applied to be made a Senior Counsel—to the then Attorney General, John A. Costello.[129]

While their own internal politics naturally consumed a large amount of their attention, students at this period could not be unaffected by the dramatic events engulfing Ireland. It was the time of the crisis over Home Rule, of the Ulster Covenant, the formation of the Volunteers, and the 1913 Lockout. The L&H played its part at a huge Home Rule rally in the centre of Dublin on 31 March 1912. Professors and students of the National University occupied one of the four speakers' platforms—John Redmond was on the main platform, while John Dillon was on the second, and Belfast's Joe Devlin was the main speaker on the third. The speakers on the NUI platform, which backed onto the O'Connell monument facing College Green, included the President of UCD, Dr Denis Coffey, and its MP Professor Swift MacNeill. There were student speakers too, most notably Arthur Cox, Michael Davitt and John Ronayne. The latter stole the show with a vigorous denunciation of the Union Jack, "which for some extraordinary reason had been hoisted over the offices of a newspaper at Carlisle buildings".[130] Costello was there, and may have been on the platform, but there is no record of him speaking. Almost six decades later, he recalled the "tremendous demonstration", and in particular the speech by Patrick Pearse, in which he agreed to give the British a chance to introduce a "proper" Home Rule bill. "That was Pearse ... giving the British their chance and they didn't take it ... and they paid very dearly for that ..."[131]

There could be no doubt about young Jack Costello's political sym-pathies—he was a staunch Home Ruler. Many years later, he recalled listening to John Dillon address the L&H on the Home Rule Bill. "I was there as a very humble student indeed with no possible hope of ever attaining political significance in this country, but with a secret desire that if there was ever an

Irish parliament set up in this country, that it would be vouchsafed to me by an Almighty Providence the privilege of being a member of that body ..."[132] He also attended an early meeting of the Proportional Representation Society of Ireland in the Antient Concert Rooms in 1911, where he heard Arthur Griffith extol the virtues of PR.[133] But he doesn't seem to have been stirred by the more martial spirit that was demonstrated in November 1913 with the formation of the Irish Volunteers. While it was reported that "practically every male student of University College ... attended"[134] the public meeting in the Rotunda which established the movement, there is no evidence that Costello was one of them. By then he was deeply immersed in his legal studies.

The exams for the LL.B, a one-year law degree, in the summer of 1913 reignited the competition between Costello and Arthur Cox. As his biographer notes, Cox "had no interest in coming second. His academic brilliance was matched by a very competitive instinct."[135] This comes through clearly in his diary for 1913, which demonstrates his increasing concern about the exam (in fairness it should be pointed out that he was writing an M.A. thesis in English literature at the same time). On 1 May he judged that while he was assured of getting through, he couldn't depend on coming first. "O'Brien and Costello are formidable propositions."[136] Five days later, a rash of exclamation marks suggests mounting hysteria: "God help the 2nd Law! No work done! And George O'B and Costello working like blazes!"[137] A fortnight later Cox was sunk in despondency: "George O'Brien ... will probably beat me in the Law exam ... I am in despair ..."[138] He had a brief moment of exhilaration two days later: "George O'Brien is not going up for the Law exam!"[139] But this was quickly followed by a reminder that he wasn't out of the woods: "Davoren, Meagher and Costello all serious propositions."[140] The exams lasted three days, with five papers: Jurisprudence; Real Property I; Real Property II; Constitutional Law and Legal History; and Law of Public and Private Wrongs. By coincidence, the two rivals met on the train some days after the exam as both went to supervise exams, Costello to Fermoy and Cox to Killarney.[141]

It was there that Cox received a telegram from Arthur Clery telling him he had come first. Two days later, he had a letter from Costello congratulating him, a characteristic gesture much appreciated by Cox, who wrote in his diary, "Decent of him to write."[142] Costello had come second, and both received £20 as First Class Exhibitioners in the LL.B. degree,[143] which suggests there was not a great deal of difference in their marks. But for the ever-competitive Cox, winning was important, and remained important for the rest of his life. In the 1950s, Terence de Vere White wrote an article in the *Irish Times*, in which he said (wrongly) that Costello, the then Taoiseach, had been beaten only once in a law exam. He received an immediate complaint from Cox: "You did not say who it was beat Costello."[144]

Fortunately for their future friendship, the rivals opted for different branches of the law, Cox becoming a solicitor, while Costello went to the Bar, possibly under the influence of Arthur Clery, who was a barrister as well as a lecturer and who was to sign the certificate seeking his admission to the Bar when he finished his studies.[145] Costello was admitted as a student of King's Inns at the beginning of Michaelmas Term 1911 (his studies there continued at the same time as those in UCD).

The King's Inns date back to the time of Henry VIII, and like the Inns of Court in London, began as accommodation for the judges and lawyers working in the courts nearby. Later, the Inns developed a role in the education, administration and regulation of lawyers.[146] But it wasn't until 1850 that formal law lectures were introduced, after a select committee of the House of Commons revealed the inadequacies of legal education. Fourteen years later, examinations began, and students could opt either to attend lectures or sit exams—in 1872, both became compulsory.[147] As one product of the system, Rex Mackey, wryly remarked, "the course of legal education pursued at the King's Inns, or for that matter at the university, is nicely calculated to unfit the student for the practice of any profession whatsoever, and more especially for that of the Law". The graduate might be an authority on Roman or medieval law, but would have never seen a counsel's brief or been taught how to cross-examine a witness.[148] Tom O'Higgins, later Chief Justice, wrote that "interesting as our lectures were, the main purpose of attendance at the Inns was the eating of the required number of dinners".[149]

Students had to eat between four and six dinners in each of the four legal terms. The dinners were each of five courses, and included a bottle of wine and as much beer as one could drink—in 1939, the cost for all six was £1.[150] The original idea of Commons was that students would learn from listening to the conversation of more experienced barristers—it evolved at a time when there was no formal legal education. It may be, as one participant observed, that the conversation was "more likely to relate to next Saturday's prospects at the Curragh" than to complex legal problems, but the dinners had two advantages for the aspiring barrister: "they will, theoretically at any rate, teach him to hold his wine like a gentleman, and ... bring him into an easy and friendly intimacy with the Bench and Bar among whom he will spend his professional life".[151]

Despite such diversions, for an ambitious student, it was a place for hard work. Costello did well, although not quite as well as later writers claimed. He came third in his two law exams in his final year. In the final examinations for the Bar in June 1914, Costello won a £10 prize, compared to £25 for the winner, B. Fox, and £15 for James Francis Meagher of Trinity, who came second.[152] In the Honour Examinations in October, Costello again placed third—this time Meagher was first, winning the John Brooke Scholarship of £50 per year for three years. Arthur Black was second, taking the Society's Exhibition of £21 for three years. Costello won the Society's prize of £21 for one year.[153]

During his time at the King's Inns, he also won a prize at the Law Students' Debating Society for Legal Composition.[154] This was for an essay on "The Leading Principles of the Brehon Laws", which was subsequently published in the December 1913 issue of *Studies*. The 25-page essay demonstrated a firm grasp on the subject matter and a clear writing style. Costello's primary degree in Languages came to the fore, as he used a number of phrases in French (without translation) as well as many words in Irish (all of which are translated, presumably a recognition that his readers were more likely to know French than Irish). He concluded by comparing the Brehon Laws— imposing, but primitive—to "a certain wonderful fort which stands perched in lonely grandeur on the top of a high cliff on the Big Island of Aran ... This fort is Dun Aonghus." Even if his attempts to learn Irish there were not successful, his visit to the Aran Islands had left an impression.[155] Publication in a prestigious journal like *Studies* must have done his reputation no harm, and was noticed by his contemporaries—Arthur Cox mentioned reading the piece, without commenting on its merits, in his diary.[156]

On Monday 2 November 1914, John A. Costello was one of eight new barristers called to the Bar, second in the order of precedence behind Meagher, the winner of the Brooke.[157] The new barrister, having been admitted to the degree of barrister at law in the Benchers' Room in the Four Courts,[158] is formally called to his profession (nowadays by the Chief Justice, in Costello's time by the Lord Chancellor). The new barrister is asked if he wishes to move the court. "The person thus addressed merely bows, without saying anything. He has now been recognised and addressed as a barrister for the first time, but he is not to be obliged to declare that he is still without a brief. For this reason he bows and says nothing."[159] On the sixtieth anniversary of his call, Costello suggested the day hadn't had much impact on him. "To be honest I cannot remember much about it. It didn't impress me, I think."[160] Impressive or not, the call meant that he was now a fully fledged barrister—although, as one member of the profession observed, "tomorrow he will find that he is very small fry indeed in a very big pond".[161]

Chapter 2 ∽

| AN ARDUOUS ROAD

" ... the majority of successful barristers have an arduous road to travel before they can even make a bare living."[1]

JOHN A. COSTELLO

" ... were it not for the many occasions in our early days in which we had no money to employ a senior and you had to do all the work, you might have never come to the front as quickly as you did."[2]

JOHN L. BURKE, SOLICITOR

With no connections in the legal profession, Costello was warned he was mad to try to make a career in law. His first year as a barrister seemed to bear out those warnings, as he made a grand total of 5 guineas.[3] As he put it himself many years later, with some understatement, he "had very considerable trouble" making his way at the Bar.[4] And yet, within five years, he was successful enough to get married, and in another couple of years was able to purchase a very fine house in an upmarket part of Dublin. His success was partly due to natural ability, partly to luck, and very largely to sheer hard work.

One crucial element of luck was that he devilled with barrister Hugh Kennedy, and became "very great friends" with him.[5] Kennedy was to become Law Officer to the Provisional Government, first Attorney General of the Irish Free State, and then the first Chief Justice. He brought his young protégé into Government service, which provided him in turn with his route into politics. They remained close—when he died, the then Chief Justice left Costello an old English snuff box "in token of their friendship".[6] Devilling was a system of apprenticeship, during which the young barrister would carry out various mundane jobs for his "master", such as representing him in court on uncon-tested applications for adjournments and helping to draft pleadings. More importantly for the student, "by accompanying his master to court he would learn how to examine a witness and how to present evidence".[7] One practical benefit for Jack Costello was that Kennedy showed him how to do conveyancing—in later years he told colleagues this was how he got over the difficulty of breaking into a Bar still dominated by Protestants and Unionists.[8]

The profession which Jack Costello joined in 1914 was, on the surface at least, one governed by tradition—the wigs, the gowns, the formalities in court. The upper reaches were still overwhelmingly Protestant. In 1907, according to the Catholic Defence Society, only 7 of 22 County Court Judges, 19 of 66 Resident Magistrates, and 9 out of 44 Benchers of King's Inns were Catholic.[9] But the Bar was changing, as it became more open to Catholics of the rising middle class. Nationalist MP and barrister Tim Healy, writing just a couple of years before Costello's call, looked forward to "the swamping of the Ascendancy Party, and to the probability that clever youngsters on our side will have better prospects at the Bar in the coming generation than could have been hoped for previously".[10] Until 1885, Irish law students had had to keep several terms at an Inn of Court in London, as well as at King's Inns in Dublin—the removal of this expensive requirement "opened the Bar to a broader spectrum of society".[11] The change, which was to accelerate after independence and partition, was already well under way when Costello was called. In 1871, Protestants outnumbered Catholics at the Bar by more than two to one. Forty years later, the proportion of Catholics had risen to 44.5 per cent—still not a majority, but the trend was clear.[12]

The centre of the profession was the Bar Library, which, in the words of a near contemporary of Costello's, Maurice Healy, gave "the Irish Bar its corporate personality ... the Bar in Ireland was open to very poor men, who could carry out their profession without any of the expenses which the English system of chambers necessarily imposes".[13] Once the annual subscription was paid, the member had access to all the legal texts and reference books he would require. It was also, as Judge Matthias Bodkin pointed out, "the fair or market where barristers are hired ... Business or no business, he daily robes himself in full legal toggery, climbs a flight of stairs to the law library, and takes his place very literally like a cabman on his hazard, waiting for a fare."[14]

Costello's UCD rival, George O'Brien, "found the Library a very congenial place. In spite of a good many personal animosities and jealousies, the atmosphere was friendly. Professional esprit de corps was very high. Political and religious differences did not prevent amicable relations in the Library. In the smoking-room and the dressing-room much good conversation and many amusing stories were to be heard. To mix on terms of equality with my elders taught me a great deal about the way of the world."[15] It also taught young barristers a great deal about the law. One of the traditions of the Law Library was the "inflexible code of etiquette [which] prescribes that even the most junior barrister can invoke the assistance of even the most senior. The latter will immediately lay aside his work and give his advice. Accordingly, a solicitor can send a brief for an opinion to a newly called junior, in the comfortable assurance that even if his nominee does not know the answer, the opinion he will get back will have emanated from someone who does."[16] In later life, when he was an extremely successful barrister, Jack Costello was himself renowned for being helpful to more junior barristers—Patrick Lindsay recalled that despite being "the busiest man in the Library", he was "never too busy to offer a helping hand to even the most junior member".[17]

Costello's call to the Bar came three months after the outbreak of the First World War—and the war was to be a good time for those lawyers who stayed at home. Out of a practising Bar of around 300, almost 130 joined up, and 25 died in action.[18] The tone of the main legal publication, the *Irish Law Times and Solicitors' Journal*, was distinctly bellicose. It published, in February 1916, "a War Supplement which contains a full record of the members and sons of members of the legal profession in Ireland who are serving in His Majesty's Forces in the present war or have been killed in action ... The Supplement shows that the Bench, the Bar and the Solicitors' Profession in Ireland have promptly given of their best to the services of the country."[19] Even many of those involved in the law who remained at home tried to "do their bit", for instance forming a Four Courts Auxiliary Munitions Association to "keep the [munitions] factory going over the weekends while the ordinary workers are obtaining their well-earned rest".[20]

Of course, while Unionists naturally supported the war effort, so too did Redmondite Nationalists, as was demonstrated by Jack Costello's brother, Tom. Having qualified as a doctor and served for a time as house surgeon in the Mater Hospital and as a temporary doctor in Mountjoy Prison,[21] he joined the Royal Army Medical Corps, becoming a lieutenant in the Wessex Field Ambulance.[22] He was promoted to Captain in June 1916[23]—some eight months before his arrival at the front in France[24]—and was awarded the Military Cross at the end of 1917 in the New Year's Honours List.[25] After the war Tom married and settled in Darwen in Lancashire, where he had seven children,[26] was elected to the Town Council for the Liberal Party in 1927,[27] and served as Mayor for two terms from 1941 to 1943.[28] He died in March 1945.[29]

Jack Costello, though, was not moved by what he later referred to as Redmond's "generous gesture" in encouraging nationalists to enlist in the British Army. He said this led to the "sacrifice in vain of many thousands of Irish lives", but had "taught us the unforgettable lesson not to pay for the goods until they are actually and decisively delivered".[30] In any event, war held no attractions for Jack, then or later—he was far more interested in furthering his career. A week after his call, the Bar Council agreed to follow the example of the Inns of Court in London by adopting resolutions "as to the holding of briefs by counsel on behalf of brethren who have joined Lord Kitchener's army".[31] The idea was to preserve the practices of those who had volunteered for military service, with barristers urged "to make it a point of honour to ensure that an absent barrister should get back his practice intact when he resumed work at the Bar".[32] But these good intentions did not survive four years of war—as the *Irish Law Times* recognised in 1919: "Beyond doubt the position of lawyers who surrendered their positions in 1914 is unenviable. Juniors who stayed at home stepped forward, gained ground and held it tenaciously."[33]

Costello later recalled the advice of his mentor, law lecturer and barrister Arthur Clery, who said there were three ways for a young junior counsel in those days to make his way at the Bar—write a book, marry a solicitor's daughter, or go to Quarter Sessions, on circuit in the provinces. He chose the third option, and not surprisingly, given his connections through his father and his childhood visits to the county, he opted for Quarter Sessions in Clare, going for seven years to Ennis and the surrounding towns several times a year.[34] Clare had the further advantage that the presiding judge was Matthias Bodkin, the father of Tom, his friend from UCD. Judge Bodkin had been a journalist as well as a barrister and in the former guise wrote editorials for the nationalist *Freeman's Journal*, in which his opponents admitted he displayed "admirable political malice". He was appointed a County Court judge after the Liberals returned to Government. "At first he was not a conspicuous success; but his good nature and common sense took charge of his Court, and when he retired he was universally regretted."[35]

According to Maurice Healy's account of the Munster Circuit, which covered the jurisdictions of five County Court judges, in Clare, Limerick, Kerry, and the East and West Ridings of Cork, it was difficult to follow more than one judge as he went on his rounds four times a year. So "each judge usually was followed by a bar of some half-dozen members", each likely to end up with a few appeals to take to the half-yearly Assizes, which would rehear the whole case. Both civil and criminal cases were heard.[36]

In Clare, the young Jack Costello built up a steady stream of work, the foundation of his subsequent practice in the capital.[37] His time there also opened his eyes to the ways of the world—he later recalled asking a man he was defending in a slander case if he had used the words the plaintiff complained of. His client replied, "I have, but I have two witnesses here to swear I did not." Experiences like this led Costello to conclude that the Irish courts saw "rather wholesale perjury".[38]

In Dublin, he worked closely with the solicitor John Burke, who briefed him for his first jury action, a case involving payment for grazing horses, which earned him five guineas.[39] Burke later pointed to his inability to afford a more senior barrister in such cases as a stroke of luck for Costello's future career. "I think you will agree with me that were it not for the many occasions in our early days in which we had no money to employ a senior and you had to do all the work, you might have never come to the front as quickly as you did. For people who saw you then perform would ask round the Court who you were. I remember so well the day you appeared on a motion sent me by J. O'Connell Tralee whose agent I was. Those present were spellbound."[40]

This could, of course, have been flattery of a man who was by then Taoiseach—but flattery does not appear to have been in John Burke's line. He was not a political supporter of Costello's, despite their lengthy professional and personal relationship, and far from flattering the Taoiseach, he wrote to him some two months before the comments quoted above to say, "strange as it may seem I have never been able to summon any enthusiasm for your election to Taoiseach, not because we differed in politics, but just because the qualities we as friends admire in you made you seem unfit for such a task".[41]

There can be no doubt that Costello was very much fit for the task of being a barrister. But his performances, spellbinding or otherwise, did not happen by accident—the key to his lifelong success at the bar was hard work. Tom Finlay, a colleague in later years, recalled that he was "always very well prepared for a brief", and that, allied to his very effective cross-examination, made him perhaps the top barrister of his day.[42] As Finlay said of him at his retirement from politics, he led the Irish Bar "not only in brilliance ... not only in success [but also] ... in matters of standards, matters of integrity and matters of ethics. His talents never became the preserve of the great corporations, or of the vested bodies, much as they would have liked. Rather have they been untiringly, brilliantly, and, may I be permitted to say, belligerently at the disposal of the oppressed and the under-privileged."[43]

Even the son of his greatest political rival found that Costello showed him "nothing but kindness and consideration". As a solicitor, Terry de Valera often briefed Jack Costello in later years, "and a more learned, loyal and con-scientious leader one could not have". He recalled winning one case against Costello, after which the latter successfully argued that his client should be spared some of the costs. Outside court, the younger de Valera, somewhat woebegone, was called over by Costello, who said, "I'm sorry about the costs, Terry, but you know that I had to do my duty"—an extremely gracious com-ment in the circumstances.[44] Another testament to Costello's ability came from fellow barrister Kevin Liston, at a King's Inns tribute evening: "He passed the supreme test of a good advocate—he could win a poor case before a good judge."[45]

Ability, kindness, hard work—all were in evidence from the earliest days of his legal career. He was not, however, much interested in the revolutionary ferment which was about to sweep away his former schoolmate Seán Heuston. Costello candidly admitted he "hadn't the remotest idea what was going on ... I was engaged in laying the foundations for my practice at the Bar and it was difficult enough without my going into the Troubles at that time."[46]

In fact, on the day the Easter Rising broke out, Costello was—characteristically—playing golf. As he put it more than half a century later, with some evident lingering resentment, he had "very considerable difficulty in getting home. The IRA ... had a barricade across ... the North Circular Road and I lived down in Rathdown Road at the time. I was coming home on a bicycle from Finglas Golf Club and I had the greatest difficulty in getting through that barricade and it was only when the gentlemen who were armed keeping the barricade were not looking that I slipped behind them and got home where I remained for a solid week incarcerated, not able to go anywhere."[47] The *Irish Law Times* was equally put out, condemning the "deplorable rising in Dublin", during which the rebels "took possession of the Law Library and other buildings [in the Four Courts], piling textbooks, law reports, and books of record in the windows as barriers behind which to shoot".[48]

For the ambitious young barrister, career came before politics—but it would be a mistake to think he was unaffected by the events going on around him. Many years later, as Taoiseach, he remembered his first sight, in early 1922, "of men in the green uniform walking through College Green. He had felt then a thrill of pride at the concrete evidence of what had been achieved by the sacrifices of people over the centuries."[49] He was to make a contribution, in his own modest way, to the developments of the War of Independence. In the meantime, his career was progressing. During 1916, he became one of two barristers reporting cases for the *Irish Law Times* from the King's Bench Division of the High Court.[50] While paying very little, this was a way for a young barrister to gain some profile, while at the same time keeping up to date with case law.[51]

He was also fighting his own cases—appearing before the Master of the Rolls in July 1916, for instance, for a defendant, Hynes, who was trying to stop a mortgage company selling his land after he failed to meet repayments. Costello argued that under wartime regulations the plaintiff should have obtained leave from the court before instituting proceedings. He lost the case, but the fact that it merited mention in the *Irish Law Times Reports* suggests it was of some significance—and therefore that the young barrister was starting to make his mark.[52]

The legal establishment at this time was still rather splendid—and extraordinarily overstaffed. The Supreme Court of Ireland had no fewer than fifteen judges: the Chancellor, the Master of the Rolls and two others in the Chancery Division; the Lord Chief Justice and seven others in the King's Bench Division; two Lords Justice of Appeal; and the Judicial Commissioner of the Irish Land Commission.[53] This judicial hierarchy had its last moment of glory at the start of the Easter sittings of 1919, when for the first time since the war the Lord Chancellor, Sir James Campbell (later Lord Glenavy), held a levée in the Benchers' Chambers in the Four Courts. This was "largely attended by King's Counsel, Junior Barristers and officials. Subsequent to the levée there was the usual procession of the Judges to the Hall of the Four Courts. The Lord Chancellor and the other Judges in their official robes made a goodly show which attracted a large crowd of interested spectators ... The procession of judges went to the main entrance, and then turned and walked to the steps underneath the clock, where the Lord Chancellor took up his position for the reception of the judges. His Lordship was attended by his private secretary and purse bearer ... his permanent secretary; and by his train bearer, mace bearer, and other officials ..."[54] For the arduous task of holding the Lord Chancellor's train on the five occasions a year when he wore his full robes, his train bearer was paid £100 per annum.[55]

By the following year, the opening of the Easter Term was much more low-key—not least because several Judges missed it as a general strike had stopped the trains. "The Lord Chancellor's levée and the procession of the judges, which in former years formed a picturesque feature of the inauguration of the legal year, were abandoned ..."[56] By this stage, the War of Independence was in full spate, a war in which the legal system was becoming a hotly contested, if secondary, battleground.

The Dáil or Republican courts—with a full structure of parish, district, circuit and supreme courts—were established by a Dáil decree of 29 June 1920, functioning most openly in the summer and autumn of that year, and again after the truce in July 1921.[57] In the intervening period, they were driven under-ground by the British authorities. One of the judges, Kevin O'Shiel, recalled of this period, "To carry on, we had to assume fictitious names and disguises, and make ourselves and our courts as inconspicuous as possible. Accordingly, I ... assumed the calling of a commercial traveller."[58] The Republican Courts were a considerable challenge to the British, with Assistant Under-Secretary Andy Cope warning a Cabinet conference in London that they were "doing more harm to the prestige of the government than the assassinations".[59]

O'Shiel remembered that "local solicitors of every religious and political complexion pleaded in my courts, but it was somewhat different with the Bar whose superiors took a much more rigid view as to the propriety of their members countenancing our courts, which resulted in my having the assist-ance of comparatively few of them".[60] The Dáil Minister for Home Affairs,

Austin Stack, put it more bluntly, complaining that he found "the Irish Bar worthy of the bad traditions it always had; there were scarcely half a dozen patriotic men among them".[61] In fact, more than a dozen barristers were involved in the Dáil courts, including Arthur Clery, Hugh Kennedy, John O'Byrne, Cecil Lavery and Cahir Davitt.[62] The latter was approached about taking a judicial position by Arthur Clery, one of the two members of the Dáil Supreme Court, in July 1920. Davitt said the reason he, a relatively inexperienced barrister, was approached was that "men of more standing" had refused[63]—which raises the intriguing question of whether Clery approached another favourite former pupil, John A. Costello, who had a couple of years' more experience at the Bar than Davitt.

In fact, there is no reference to Costello being involved in the Dáil courts at this stage, although he did appear in them after the truce. He clearly confused his role in a newspaper interview half a century later, when he claimed to have "a happy memory" of the Republican Courts: "I'm delighted to say that as a result of them I was found guilty of 'professional misconduct'. You see, the Bar Council at the time passed a resolution saying that it was professional misconduct to appear in Sinn Féin courts. I appeared in them and I had many good men in company with me, some very eminent men."[64]

This presumably refers to a "very largely attended" meeting of the Bar Council in June 1920, which debated the question of the Dáil courts and whether it was professional misconduct, or simply a breach of professional etiquette, for members to appear as advocates before such courts. The Council resolved "that it is professional misconduct on the part of any member of the Bar to appear before such tribunals ..."[65] Despite Costello's later claim this decision did not affect him, as he doesn't seem to have appeared in the Republican courts.

The question arose again five months later, when another meeting of members of the Bar discussed a motion in the name of Tim Healy declaring the earlier resolution *ultra vires*. When Healy was called on to speak, he revealed that he had not drafted the resolution, or agreed to let his name be attached to it. But he believed the Bar Council "had no right to pass judgement upon the conduct of any member of the Bar ... the only body who had that right was the Benchers, who admitted men to the Bar. He had been 39 years at the Bar, and nothing like this had arisen in his time. He did not know what was to be done, but he felt that the senior members should do what they could to protect the junior members of the Bar." The only other speaker was S.L. Brown, K.C., who claimed "they had all been a happy family in the Library, and it would be a pity to introduce anything that would cause friction or disagreement". On his suggestion, it was agreed to adjourn the meeting indefinitely, without coming to a decision on the issue.[66]

The Bar Council found it easier to reach agreement when it was acting as a trade association—agreeing a new scale of minimum fees early in 1920.[67] It also complained to the Attorney General at the use of English barristers as prosecutors at courts martial at the end of the year, at a time when "there is no lack of Irish counsel who are willing to undertake this work ..."[68]—a comment Austin Stack might have taken as confirmation of his view of the Bar.

As well as setting up their own courts, Republicans were intent on ensuring that the established legal system didn't work. This they did through a mixture of intimidation of witnesses and jurors and the destruction of the physical infrastructure of the courts. In July 1920, only nine grand jurors and nine common jurors, out of a list of 78, answered the call at Waterford City Assizes, a situation the presiding judge described as "without parallel in the history of Ireland, England or Scotland", and which he blamed on "threatening notices in Dublin newspapers".[69] The judges attending the summer Assizes in Limerick had to be accommodated in the county courthouse, guarded by soldiers and police.[70] Westmeath County Council ordered the closure of all courthouses in the county and the eviction of Government officials from them, and refused to pay the salary of the Under Sheriff "on the grounds that that official was engaged in carrying out decrees and legal processes of courts not recognised by Dáil Éireann".[71] When the local Resident Magistrate and his clerk arrived at Newbridge Town Hall, venue for petty sessions courts for forty years, they found the doors locked on the orders of the Town Commissioners.[72]

Not surprisingly, given this level of hostility, 315 magistrates resigned between May and August 1920.[73] The pathetic state to which British law in Ireland had been reduced was illustrated at Borrisokane, Co. Tipperary, in the latter month. "The local courthouses having been recently destroyed by fire, the ... monthly petty sessions was held in the ruins of the burned building. Major Dease, R.M., who was the only magistrate that attended, occupied a seat inside the entrance gate, and the rain, which fell at intervals, made it very unpleasant for those present."[74]

By far the most prominent case with which Jack Costello was involved in the initial stages of the War of Independence was that of Father Thomas O'Donnell, a Tasmanian chaplain in the British army during the First World War, who was charged with making seditious remarks about the King during a visit to Killarney in October 1919. He was arrested and taken to the Tower of London, and faced a court martial in London's Guildhall.[75] The two senior barristers in the case were Paddy Lynch and the legendary Tim Healy,[76] previously a leading, if disruptive, figure in the Irish Parliamentary Party, and later first Governor General of the Irish Free State. As the junior counsel, Costello doesn't appear to have spoken at the court martial, which found the priest not guilty.[77]

More typical was Costello's continuing work in Clare. In March 1920, for instance, he was again junior to Paddy Lynch when they represented Clare County Council in a compensation case brought against it by the brother of an RIC sergeant killed in the War of Independence. The Council was liable for compensation under the Criminal Injuries (Ireland) Act, 1919, but successfully argued that the claimant had no prospect of benefit from the continuance of his brother's life.[78] The council at this time was controlled by Sinn Féin; the chairman was a local IRA commander, and almost all its members were on the run.[79]

Early in 1918, Clare had been declared a special military area after Volunteer activity. Permission was needed to enter and leave the county, mail was censored, and a curfew was imposed in some areas.[80] The legal profession was affected by these developments. With train services interrupted, barristers on the Munster Circuit were not guaranteed that their luggage would arrive, and so had to obtain "permission to appear in court without wig and gown".[81] A more serious problem was the partial or complete destruction of the court-houses of Ennistymon, Killaloe, Kilrush and Tulla, which meant the Quarter Sessions for those towns had to be held in Ennis.[82]

In these disturbed conditions, the local judge, Matthias Bodkin, lived up to his nationalist credentials by criticising the activities of the Black and Tans. As Costello later recalled, Bodkin "displayed great judicial courage when ... he read in open Court on the 5 February 1921 a report on the reprisals of the Black and Tans in Clare. He sent a second report to the British Authorities which was described by the late Lord Asquith in the House of Commons as 'one of the gravest indictments ever presented by a Judicial officer against the Executive Government in a free country' ..."[83] According to Maurice Healy, Bodkin "refused to be silenced, and at the imminent risk of his life continued to denounce the infamies that were being perpetrated by these notorious servants of the Crown. It was in a large part due to his efforts that black-guardism was at last checked; and many a Clare household can thank Judge Bodkin for having been spared from arson and loot."[84] He was later "blackbeaned" from membership of the RDS for his troubles.[85]

The legal aspects of the War of Independence were a constant problem for the British. While the legal system had largely broken down at a local level, the higher courts were still functioning—and were frequently prepared to hear appeals against decisions of the military courts. Dublin Castle officials had little regard for the legal establishment, one of them, Mark Sturgis, dismissing the Lord Chancellor, Sir James Campbell, as "a poltroon of the most con-temptible dye—does nothing and apparently thinks of nothing but the best way to show SF that he is neutral and passive. A coward and a shirker, and by God a thief too since he continues to draw his salary."[86] In order to minimise the chance of trouble with the civil courts over Habeas Corpus applications, the Judge Advocate General advised the military to carry out death sentences as soon as possible after they were handed down. As Sturgis mordantly put it, "Macready [the Army commander] must wait for the Act of Indemnity to be cleared of a murder charge."[87]

In order to protect military courts from judicial interference, the British had to demonstrate that a state of active hostility existed in the area concerned—which rather upset their repeated claim that there wasn't a war going on.[88] The law appeared to have been settled in the case of John Allen in February 1921. He had been arrested for possession of arms in January and sentenced to death. On 24 February, the King's Bench Division rejected an appeal for Habeas Corpus because a state of war existed, during which the Government was bound to repel force with force. It also ruled that military courts could act even though the ordinary courts were sitting, and that civil courts had no authority to control the military authorities during the period of war.[89] Allen was executed four days later.[90] Despite this ruling, further appeals were made, to the evident frustration of the authorities. Mark Sturgis wrote, "I *can't* understand why one High Court case doesn't settle this but it seems it doesn't."[91] In total, out of 37 death sentences in 23 cases, there were five appeals to the courts, all of which followed the Allen ruling, until the cases of Egan and Higgins,[92] in which John A. Costello was centrally involved.

John Joseph Egan, a motor engineer with Clare County Council, had been arrested on 26 May 1921. Some soldiers claimed they had seen him throw a parcel over a wall, at a place where they subsequently found a quantity of ammunition. He appeared before a military court on 11 June represented by Clare-based barrister Paddy Lynch. Egan was found guilty and sentenced to death.[93] Costello first became aware of the case when the condemned man's solicitor, Jack Lynch, "came up to Dublin and asked me if anything could be done as this man was to be shot the next morning". Costello arranged for Hugh Kennedy to come in as Senior, and together they decided to make their application for Habeas Corpus before the Master of the Rolls, Charles O'Connor.[94]

They chose their judge well. By his own admission, O'Connor's "practice at the Bar and ... life as a Judge of the Chancery Division have left me unqualified for criminal cases". But he recognised the right of anyone under arrest "to apply to any Judge of the High Court for the writ of Habeas Corpus, and if the writ is refused to proceed from Judge to Judge ... it is the duty of each Judge to form his independent opinion and to act upon it".[95] He had also been involved in unsuccessful attempts to broker a peace deal, accompanying leading Sinn Féiner Fr Michael O'Flanagan to Downing Street in early January to meet Lloyd George.[96]

The application was made on 14 June 1921.[97] As Costello recalled, "There was always the tradition at the Bar that an application for Habeas Corpus took precedence over all other business and when Hugh Kennedy and I went in to make this application and told him what it was about he immediately stopped the case which was at hearing before him, heard the application, granted the conditional order, [and] fixed a particular date for the hearing of the application."[98]

Costello's account of subsequent developments left out two important points. The first was the involvement of Lynch, who was to conduct practically all the legal argument in the main hearing of the case. Lynch was to have an interesting political career. A moderate nationalist, he represented the Parliamentary Party in the by-election arising from the death on the Western Front of Willie Redmond. His opponent, of course, was Eamon de Valera, and Lynch was defeated. However, he was later to serve as de Valera's Attorney General, a mark of the respect in which his by-election opponent held him. His courtroom style was described by Maurice Healy: "He loved to lull his audience into comfort with a succession of softly-spoken sentences, and then suddenly to thunder out some impassioned phrase in tones that caused everyone in court to jump. To hear Paddy lead a witness along the flowery path until every suspicion had been allayed, and then shout a fierce and fatal question, with a vicious 'Answer me that!!!' was an experience of the dramatic not to be equalled in any theatre."[99]

The second important point was that the legal team represented a second condemned man, Patrick Higgins, whose case ran in tandem with Egan's, but who is left out of nearly all accounts. Higgins had been arrested following an engagement at Clonmult, Co. Cork, on 20 February 1921. An informer had alerted the British forces to a house full of IRA men, which was duly surrounded. A gun battle erupted during which 12 IRA men were killed, four wounded, and four others captured.[100]

According to his statement, Higgins had until 1918 been a member of the Volunteers, "which at that time was more or less a hobby with young fellows and consisted of no more than marching". Hobby or not, it had resulted in a recurrence of an old illness—improper treatment of appendicitis some years before left him with an incision which did not heal permanently—and at the request of his mother he resigned. However, his name had come to the attention of the authorities, and he claimed he became a target for harassment and threats from the military. At the suggestion of a friend he went to the house at Clonmult, which he "knew ... was a hiding place ... He was hardly there ten minutes when the military arrived, surrounded the house and started firing ..." After he surrendered, Higgins said he was shot in the mouth by a stray bullet, but his statement insisted he "had no gun and there is no evidence connecting him with one".[101]

This was pure invention. In fact, Higgins was a captain in the IRA and Battalion Quartermaster, and had a central role in the Battle of Clonmult.[102] Although he was the most senior officer left in the house after the flying column's commander and deputy commander went on a reconnaissance, he was not left in charge because one of his superiors felt he "didn't show any great aptitude for the work" during an earlier engagement.[103] The historian of Clonmult, Tom O'Neill, believes Higgins' resentment at this slight impaired the flying column's effectiveness in the battle.[104] And far from being hit by a stray bullet, he was shot in the mouth after surrendering by Auxiliaries who executed six of the other IRA men and were only stopped from killing the rest by the arrival of an officer in the regular British Army.[105]

Higgins was detained in Victoria Barracks in Cork, but due to his injuries and a recurrence of appendicitis, his trial was delayed until June. A military court then sentenced him to death—two of the other prisoners captured at Clonmult had already been executed, on 28 April, after their own application for Habeas Corpus had been rejected. As Macready's affidavit in the Higgins case pointed out, he "was arrested at the same time and place and by the same persons and in the same circumstances [as the executed men] ... there is no distinction in law or in fact between the cases ...".[106]

O'Connor granted conditional orders of Habeas Corpus for both men.[107] In preparation for the main hearing of the case, their legal team gathered affidavits claiming that there was no state of war in either Cork or Clare, that the civil courts were still operating, and therefore there was no justification for resorting to military courts.[108] In response, affidavits on behalf of Macready detailed the activities of the IRA, the deaths of policemen and soldiers, and the difficulties of running the law courts.[109] By the time he came to deliver his judgment on 26 July, O'Connor's ruling was probably academic, as the truce had come into operation on 11 July. But it was a rather ingenious judgment all the same. He accepted that under the Prerogative of the Crown, the civil courts had no right to interfere with the military during a state of war—but then went on to argue that the Royal Prerogative had been limited by the Restoration of Order in Ireland Act of 1920. This Act gave the military special powers, but also imposed conditions, including the requirement that in a trial for an offence punishable by death, the court martial must include one member nominated by the Lord Lieutenant and certified to be a person of legal knowledge and experience. He rejected the proposition put forward by the military that there could be no limitation on the Prerogative of the Crown in a state of war, even by Act of Parliament, and found that "on the ground that the Restoration of Order Act has limited the powers of the Military Authority in the present state of war in Ireland, I must hold that the writ of Habeas Corpus must be issued".[110]

According to Macready, this ruling "caused a terrific stir in Sinn Féin circles, being described as 'a staggering blow' against military rule. So far as I was concerned I considered that the position of the military was unassailable, and had no intention of paying attention to the writ ...".[111] On the day the prisoners were due to be produced in court, Macready's counsel, Serjeant Hanna, said he was not going to do so, pending an appeal, although the authorities did undertake not to execute the two men.[112] Jack Costello later remembered that "the Master of the Rolls was very cross at this, he got as white as a sheet, he denounced the action of the military and said that if they persisted in their refusal to carry out the order, there would be nothing but red ruin and the break up of all law ...".[113] The Master issued a writ of attachment against Macready and the other senior officers named in the case, as well as the governor of Limerick Prison, for failing to produce the prisoners.[114] As Macready ruefully observed, O'Connor's outburst "was a perfect godsend for the press, and the next day the headlines were a joy to read", although he took some solace in the reported unhappiness of the High Sheriff, who, probably wisely, "had ... come to the conclusion that it was for the police rather than for him to carry out the order of the court".[115]

In his memoirs, the general tried to make light of the affair, referring to the "amusement it caused", and calling it a "breeze between the Master of the Rolls and myself [which] made no difference in our personal relations, which remained cordial up to the day on which I left Ireland ...".[116] But it is clear that Macready took it very seriously indeed at the time. Travelling from London, he decided "to go to Cork on my return [rather than travelling through Dublin] ... In the martial law area I should not have hesitated to arrest anyone, including the Master of the Rolls himself, who attempted to carry out the service of the writs." And he was most put out when Lloyd George, on the advice of the Irish law officers, agreed to release the two men. He was so annoyed that he wrote to the Army Council saying that "unless my authority as Chief Governor of the martial law area was not speedily restored I must ask to be relieved of a position I could no longer hold without loss of self-respect".[117]

On 1 August, a Cabinet sub-committee—including Irish Secretary Hamar Greenwood, Lord Privy Seal Austen Chamberlain, Secretary of State for War Worthington Evans and Lord Chancellor Birkenhead ("looking very holidayish in a light suit and soft white hat") met to consider the situation.[118] A week later, Chamberlain announced that the decision to release Egan and Higgins was due to the importance of avoiding conflict between the civil and military authorities in Ireland, and had nothing to do with the decision by the civil courts, which had no power to overrule the military courts in the martial law area in Ireland. According to Macready, "the pronouncement of the

Government ... was so unequivocal as to safeguard the position of officers charged in the future with the burden of administering martial law, and on that account alone was an ample compensation for the absurd position in which I and my officers had been placed".[119] Clearly, not a laughing matter.

In November 1921, the two cases came before the Court of Appeal, but counsel for Macready asked for them to be taken out of the list (with liberty to re-enter) because of the truce, and expressed the hope that "the Court might hear no more of the cases".[120]

Ironically, many of the arguments—and many of the same people—were to be involved in the case of Erskine Childers, the anti-Treaty Director of Publicity who had been arrested in possession of a revolver—given to him as a souvenir by Michael Collins—and sentenced to death by a military court during the Civil War. On the evening of 23 November 1923, just hours before he was due to be executed, his legal team applied for a writ of Habeas Corpus to none other than the Master of the Rolls, Charles O'Connor. The courts were then sitting in the King's Inns following the destruction of the Four Courts, and the emergency hearing was conducted by candlelight in the dining hall of the Inns.[121]

Childers' legal team—Patrick Lynch, Michael Comyn and Conor Maguire—based their appeal on O'Connor's ruling in Egan v. Macready, arguing that the Provisional Government was precluded from establishing military tribunals unless it did so by statute, because the Restoration of Order (Ireland) Act was still in force. This time, though, O'Connor was having none of it, declaring that the Provisional Government was *de jure* as well as *de facto* the ruling authority, with the right to organise an army to protect the people; accepting the government's case that war was raging; and arguing that the Restoration of Order Act only applied to British forces, so courts could not rule on the Irish Army's acts while suppressing the rebellion. He then referred to a number of cases, most notably that of Allen, neatly reversing the argument he had followed in Egan v. Macready, and rejected the application.[122] Childers was executed the following day.

In later life, Egan made the best of his moment of notoriety, and the contacts it had given him with lawyers who went on to greater things. In May 1924, by which time he was a lieutenant in the National Army attached to the staff of the GOC, he wrote to Hugh Kennedy, then still Attorney General, seeking an interview so he could "have the pleasure of thanking you, personally, for all you did for me during my trial in 1921".[123] A quarter of a century later, he was writing to the junior counsel in his case, by then Taoiseach, seeking help in being made permanent on the staff of Clare County Council. He had left his job with the Council in 1922 to join the Army, on the understanding that he would be reinstated when he was discharged. By the time he left the Army the Council was under Fianna Fáil control and refused to honour the understanding. At Costello's request, the Minister for Local Government, T.J. Murphy, successfully intervened on Egan's behalf.[124] Egan died in 1954.[125]

The Egan and Higgins cases were important for Costello's subsequent political career because they allowed him to answer the awkward question of what exactly he had "done during the war". When he was Taoiseach, the US magazine *Ave Maria* bluntly stated that "John Costello took little or no part in the revolution which won Irish freedom except occasionally to defend a patriot in the Court of Law."[126] His supporters, by contrast, were inclined to wildly overestimate the importance of these cases and the extent of Costello's role. Michael Hayes, for instance, described him as having "fearlessly, and I am sure without pay, devoted his legal talents to the defence of Irish Volunteers. With Hugh Kennedy he had achieved a resounding legal victory in a famous law case."[127] (In fact, Costello was paid for both cases—according to his copy of the Higgins brief he received £15.5.0 for his work on part of that case,[128] while for the Egan case, for which he was finally paid in 1927, he received £43.[129])

In February 1956, the *Fine Gael Digest* took a similar line, suggesting that Costello "had put his talents at the disposal of the Volunteers and the Sinn Féin movement", which was stretching it quite a bit. The magazine described the decision in the Egan case as "a resounding blow against the British Military and the British Government's methods of conducting the war in Ireland" which "undoubtedly helped in the making of a Truce"[130]—another very considerable imaginative leap. Costello himself was to make the same leap, telling David Thornley during their "Seven Days" interview that the case "had some considerable effect in bringing about the Truce some weeks afterwards".[131] As we have seen, the Master of the Rolls had only granted a conditional order of Habeas Corpus before the truce, only delivering his final judgment a fortnight after the cessation of hostilities. It is highly unlikely that such a conditional order had any bearing at all on the agreement of the truce. On the other hand, the lives of two men were saved; had it not been for the successful legal challenge, both Egan and Higgins would have been executed before the end of hostilities.

The outbreak of the Civil War was a disaster for the fledgling State—and it had ramifications for the legal profession too. The *Irish Law Times* thundered that the occupation of the Four Courts by anti-Treaty forces in April 1922 was "the event of the week—and indeed, it is no exaggeration to say, of the century, in legal circles". Legal business was at a standstill as a result, and the courts and the Law Library moved, temporarily, to the King's Inns.[132] But things were to get much, much worse in July, when Provisional Government forces shelled the Irregular garrison in the Four Courts, turning the historic buildings into "piles of gaunt ruins ... The magnificent Courts, with the adjoining Judges' Chambers, the Round Hall with its fine statues, the Law Library with three or four sets of the reports and of text-books, the Probate office, with records of all modern wills, and perhaps more especially the Records Office, with its priceless treasures of the past, which are absolutely irreplaceable, are all gone ... The legal profession has suffered a blow from which it will not recover for many years to come."[133] The courts remained at King's Inns for a year while Dublin Castle was being prepared, in premises that were "very restricted and most inconvenient ... King's Inns is too small, too much out of the way, and continuance there is bad for the health of Bench and Bar, and is also detrimental to business."[134]

The Castle proved to be a happier home, with "large and airy" court rooms and "very suitable" accommodation for the Law Library in St Patrick's Hall, all in "large and convenient premises in an accessible position".[135] The courts moved to Dublin Castle in April 1923, and were to remain there until October 1931, as the Four Courts were slowly rebuilt.[136] At this point, of course, the courts and the judiciary were still those inherited from the British. The Irish courts established under the Courts of Justice Act, 1924, did not come into being until 11 June 1924.[137] The new system was considerably less bloated, with a Supreme Court of three and a High Court of only six. Only two of the eight remaining judges appointed under the *ancien régime* opted to stay on in the service of the new State—Charles O'Connor, who stayed for one more year, and W.E. Wylie, who was to serve for a further 12 years. The others retired.[138]

And so it was that one of Costello's most colourful cases—involving ill-gotten gains from Tammany Hall and a putative Indian princess—was played out in June 1923 in Dublin Castle, before Lord Chief Justice Thomas Molony, the last British-appointed holder of that post. At issue was the will of Richard E. 'Boss' Croker, former head of New York City's Tammany Hall, the political machine which controlled the government of that city, and which was a byword for the corruption on which Croker's fortune was based. In comparison with his famous predecessor, Boss Tweed, he "spilt less blood and was less blatant"[139], but there was no doubt about the nature of his power. Born in Mallow, Co. Cork, in November 1841, he emigrated to the United States eight years later, becoming a mechanic and later joining the New York Fire Brigade.[140] At the age of 22, he demonstrated his enthusiasm for the political process by voting 17 times in one day for a Democratic candidate.[141] After he lost control of Tammany in 1902, he moved to England before finally settling in Glencairn in south county Dublin (later the residence of British Ambassadors to Ireland), where he bred and trained horses, most famously the 1907 Epsom Derby winner Orby. As a result of his Derby victory, he was granted the Freedom of the City of Dublin.[142]

He had formally separated from his wife in 1897, and following her death in 1914, when he was 73, he married Bula Edmonson, who was 43 years his junior.[143] The new Mrs Croker was somewhat exotic—she was one-sixteenth American Indian (on her mother's side) and claimed to be a direct descendant of Sequoyah, the deviser of the Cherokee alphabet, and entitled to the name "Keetaw Kaiantuckt Sequoyah".[144] Although she said in court that she had never claimed to be royalty, "she had come to be identified in the newspaper mind and in the public mind as an Indian princess". No doubt this was due to her appearance in full Indian costume, riding a black horse, at the head of a procession of Native Americans in President Woodrow Wilson's inauguration parade in March 1913.[145]

In any event, her stepchildren did not take kindly to her arrival, especially after their father altered his will to leave most of his wealth to his new wife, and removed his son Richard junior from the running of his affairs in the United States. The children took a court case in Palm Beach in 1920, alleging that their father was entirely under the domination of Mrs Croker, and that he was incompetent to mange his affairs. The court dismissed their claim.[146]

However, after the Boss died in April 1922—Arthur Griffith, Oliver St John Gogarty and the Lord Mayor of Dublin were among his pall bearers[147]—his children decided to try their luck in the Irish courts. Richard junior sought to have the will condemned, while his sister, Mrs Edith White, accused the widow of fraud, on the grounds that she was already married to an Italian tailor by the name of Guy Marone at the time of her supposed marriage to Boss Croker.[148]

Although he apparently "went on his knees, begging her to accept" an offer of settlement of the claim,[149] Mrs Croker's solicitor, Henry O'Hanlon, put together the best legal team he could find when she refused. It included Jack Costello as junior counsel, Paddy Lynch K.C. and Serjeant Hanna. The Attorney General, Hugh Kennedy, was put under pressure by Mrs Croker's friends to accept a brief in the case, which he was reluctant to do because of the pressure of his work as Attorney General.[150] He finally agreed to take the brief under certain conditions, to O'Hanlon's obvious delight:[151] he believed Kennedy was the man most competent to protect Mrs Croker's interests.[152] But within a week, Kennedy wrote asking to be relieved, after "one of the Counsel with whom I was to collaborate, unable to throw a veil of decency over his personal hostility to me, or perhaps to the government with which I am associated, has so acted in breach of the traditions of our profession and in violation of the recognised canons of that profession as to make it impossible for me to make any useful contribution to the case".[153] O'Hanlon was shocked at this "gross abuse of your rights" and observed, "one would imagine that the passing away of the old order in this Country and the coming of the new would make any man sufficiently liberal of thought to feel a pride in finding himself associated with another who, in a time of danger and contention, has handled with success the destinies of a nation".[154] The guilty party was either Lynch or Hanna, although Kennedy appears to have had cordial relations with the latter up to the start of the year, when he asked him to gather information on other legal systems in preparation for the new court system.[155]

The case was heard in Court Number 4—formerly the Throne Room of the Castle—and was the subject of intense public interest, every seat in the public gallery being taken.[156] Mrs Croker was taken through her evidence by Paddy Lynch, and was reported to have "replied to the questions calmly and clearly". She pointed out that the name of her alleged husband, Guy Marone, was never mentioned in the 26 days of the Florida trial.[157] Under cross-examination by Serjeant Sullivan, who had come over from London to lead Richard Croker junior's legal team,[158] she agreed that she had inherited around a million dollars' worth of property, bonds and shares.[159] The case against the will was that Croker "at the end of his days had become fascinated by a young, attractive and ... clever ... woman ... The result was that he lost control of his affairs, and although the hand that wrote was the hand of Richard Croker, the real hand and voice were those of Bula Edmondson ..."[160]

Richard junior's case was damaged by us newspaper reports that the witnesses he was producing to allege his stepmother had been married to Marone had been paid lavishly for their trouble. The *Boston Post* reported one of them as saying, "It will be a wonderful trip for us, and they, the Crokers' representatives, have taken care of every item of expense, even to engaging the taxi which called to our door to take us to the station ... If things come out right we shall never have to worry about money again; that will be made certain."[161] The case was further damaged by a bumbling performance by Richard's brother, Howard, who was given a rough time in the witness box by Serjeant Hanna.[162] Another major problem for the claimants was their failure to trace, and produce, the mysterious Guy Marone, supposedly Mrs Croker's real husband.

It would seem Mrs Croker's case was also helped by the attitude of Lord Chief Justice Molony, who in summing up, remarked that "the jury would probably have some difficulty, as he himself had" in accepting the description of her by her stepson's counsel as "cunning, calculating and clever ... a person lacking refinement, culture and reputation".[163] Counsel for the claimants objected to his summing up, but the Lord Chief Justice declined to recall the jury, and after an hour and a quarter, they returned, finding for Mrs Croker on all points at issue. "Immediately after the reading of the findings of the jury there was a loud outburst of cheering and hand-clapping in court ... When Mrs Croker left the court she was again warmly cheered outside. The demonstration of sympathy with her and approval of the verdict was renewed as she descended the staircase, several people approaching and cordially shaking hands with her. She was again cheered as she entered her motor car in the Castle Courtyard, and drove away waving her hand in acknowledgement."[164]

After a 12-day hearing, the case still had a surprise to offer—Mrs Croker claimed that the day after her victory that she had received a telegram from the real wife of Guy Marone, now living in Missouri.[165] The claimants sought and received an extension of the time allowed to consider an appeal,[166] but in the end opted not to lodge one.[167] According to Law Library legend, Mrs Croker thanked her legal team, including Costello, at a dinner in Glencairn, where the waiters removed the silver covers from the dinner plates to reveal a handsome bonus of 1,000 guineas for each lawyer. Whether or not this bonus was in fact paid, Costello made enough from his work on the case to put down a deposit on his first house.

Later, as Attorney General, Costello successfully lobbied for Henry O'Hanlon to be appointed Taxing Master of the superior courts, a position he assumed in 1930.[168] Mrs Croker was not done with the law, although her further brushes with litigation were back in the United States. In August 1929 she lost a case in which she was trying to break a nine-year-old agreement to sell a parcel of Palm Beach property at a fraction of its value—the difference was around $5 million, plus costs. And Richard Croker junior was not finished with his stepmother, continuing his legal actions against her.[169] As a result she had to file for bankruptcy in 1937. However, she was considered "a spirited addition to the Palm Beach social circuit", being nominated to the Town Council in 1930, running for Congress, and operating "a Caribbean pirate treasure salvaging company" as well. She died in 1957.[170]

Most of Jack Costello's cases were far less exotic—but some were legally significant. At this time, for instance, he represented a Ministry of Labour insurance officer, Major Fuge, whose decision to refuse unemployment benefit to striking rail workers was challenged (unsuccessfully) in the High Court.[171] This case was later to be appealed to the Privy Council, a development that will be considered in the next chapter. He also had an indirect connection with the Dáil courts, when he represented 24 people who had taken a case in the Land Court. The defendants in that case went to the High Court seeking a writ of prohibition against Conor Maguire and Kevin O'Shiel, the judges in the Dáil Land Court, to prevent them hearing the case. Lord Chief Justice Molony argued that because the Dáil Courts were not properly established, there was nothing he could do about it. " ... This Court, while it prohibits and quashes the orders of inferior tribunals which exceed their jurisdiction, does not take notice of bodies which act openly and avowedly in defiance of the law."[172] The plaintiffs didn't even get their costs for challenging what the court found was an illegal tribunal.[173]

As well as building a legal career, Costello was also building a family. According to family tradition, he met his future wife, Ida O'Malley, at a dance in the Gresham Hotel in 1912,[174] when he was still a law student. They "kept company" from then until their marriage in 1919. Ida had been educated at the Dominican School in Eccles Street in Dublin, and had spent the academic year 1907/8 in school in Amiens in France on an early exchange programme. This had been organised by Sophie Raffalovitch, the French wife of Irish Party MP William O'Brien.[175] After her husband's death, Madame O'Brien moved back to France, living in rather reduced circumstances. Ida visited her from time to time. When he was Taoiseach, Jack Costello tried to sort out her will, which was causing her some distress in her ninetieth year.[176] Jack and Ida shared an interest in the French language, even writing to each other in French at times.[177]

After taking a degree at UCD, Ida taught in Eccles Street until her marriage.[178] She was the eldest of 13 children, seven boys and six girls. Her father, Dr David O'Malley, was the "popular medical officer of Glenamaddy"[179] in County Galway. The family later lived at 11 Tudor Road in Ranelagh.[180] Like the Costello family, the O'Malleys were Redmondite Nationalists, and at least four of the boys joined the British Army during the First World War, two of them being killed.[181] The only other O'Malley sibling to stay in Ireland was Leilagh, the youngest of the family, who married and settled down in Cork. The rest emigrated to England, although one of Ida's nieces, Patricia, was to have a very close connection to the Costello family in later years.

John A. and Ida were married at the Catholic University Church in St Stephen's Green on 31 July 1919. The groom had just turned 28, while the bride was a few months older. The ceremony was performed by Costello's cousin, Fr John McKeever, to whom he was very close, the pair having swum together at the Forty Foot as students. In later life, a Costello family tradition was to visit the priest at Christmas, in whichever parish he happened to be based, for dinner. The best man was John Herlihy, a childhood friend of Costello's, who was to be godfather to his daughter Grace.[182] The other witness was Mary O'Meara from Waterford, a school friend of Ida's. She later taught English in Manchester, and came regularly at Christmas time to stay with the Costello family.[183]

The newlyweds spent the first four years of their married life in a flat at 22 Ely Place,[184] just off St Stephen's Green. They were living there when the first of their five children were born—Wilfrid ('Wilfie') in 1921 and Grace in 1922. They were to be followed by Declan in 1926, Eavan in 1927, and finally John in 1931.

Wilfie's birth was apparently difficult. He suffered a cerebral haemorrhage which left him with a mild mental disability.[185] His medical problems were compounded by the development of epilepsy when he was a teenager. Physically, he was rather clumsy, which marked him off from other children as he was growing up. He was able to go to school in Belvedere like his brothers, and later completed a History degree at UCD. But he wasn't capable of independent living, and was supported by his parents for the rest of his life. It appears that Wilfie could be quite difficult at times—a friend of his father's reported in 1952 that in a letter Wilfrid "admitted his unreasonableness to the family".[186]

At one point John A. Costello bought a tobacconist business for him in Fairview, which he went to every day, but it was largely run for him by a manager employed by his father. Eventually the shop had to be given up. On medical recommendation he lived in a psychiatric hospital in Scotland for a year, and later in St Patrick's Hospital in James Street, visiting home at week-ends.[187] His care was obviously of concern to his parents throughout their lives. It also led to a family interest in disability. When St Michael's House was established in 1955 to provide community-based services for people with intellectual disabilities, Ida Costello was offered, and accepted, the position of President. After her death, Declan Costello became President of the organisation, and worked for many years to improve what were, at that time, "absolutely inadequate" services.[188]

Two of the children, Grace and Declan, followed their father into the law, his eldest daughter being called to the Bar in 1943, and Declan in 1948.[189] Grace, who was to be close to her father throughout her life, and particularly after the death of her mother in 1956, married Alexis FitzGerald, a solicitor and economist who was to have a very great influence on Costello, particularly during his time as Taoiseach.[190]

As well as becoming a barrister, Declan also followed in his father's political footsteps, achieving lasting fame as the author of Fine Gael's "Just Society" policy, and finishing his legal career as President of the High Court. Eavan completed a history degree in UCD, later working in the library there before marrying barrister Ralph Sutton. The first 15 years of their married life was spent in Cork, where her home became a welcome refuge for her father when he was on circuit in the southern capital. The youngest of the family, John, who was to become an architect, was artistically inclined. When he was just 11, one of his watercolours, described by a visiting journalist as having "a strong Paul Henry influence", hung in his father's study.[191]

The growing Costello family clearly needed more space, and the answer was found in August 1923 at 20 Herbert Park, " ... a semi-detached red brick house with dark green drainpipes and window frames and an arched porch door. There is a wallflower border to a small lawn, and a laurel hedge. The garage is at the back and pear and apple trees grown in the garden ..."[192] The new house was clearly a step up in the world for Costello—it had a rateable value in 1924 of £60, compared to the £27 his father's house in Rathdown Road attracted. Costello also employed domestic staff, which at the time of his first term as Taoiseach consisted of a cook, two maids and a gardener.[193] The deposit on the house came from the Croker case, while Costello also took out a mortgage, on the advice of his solicitor Tommy Robinson. According to his son, he was very reluctant to do so as he didn't want to be indebted.[194]

His new address would provide useful contacts for his legal career, as well as increased social standing—among the neighbours were solicitor G.A. Overend and barrister Frederick Price K.C.[195] But contacts and status were also being provided by his almost simultaneous first steps into public service.

Chapter 3 ∿

HE HAS DONE WONDERFUL WORK

*"The Evening Mail ... stated that I had become
Attorney General by a strange concatenation of
fortuitous circumstances."* [1]

JOHN A. COSTELLO, 1969

*"John A. Costello came to see me and tell me of
developments. He has done wonderful work. I know
no one else who could have even tackled the job."* [2]

HUGH KENNEDY, 1929

When W.T. Cosgrave retired from politics in 1944, he wrote to John A. Costello thanking him for his service as Attorney General, saying that he had never been wrong in the advice he gave.[3] This tribute echoes the glowing comments of Hugh Kennedy quoted above, and contrasts with the rather lukewarm reaction of the *Evening Mail* to his appointment. But as with other phases of his life—at school, UCD and the Bar—Costello showed critics that by dint of hard work and a certain element of luck, he could succeed in a new role. The luck was once again to be in the right place at the right time and with the right contacts, in this case Hugh Kennedy.

In May 1922, Kennedy, Law Officer of the Provisional Government, was under pressure. He was faced with an "immense volume of work ... files from all Ministries and Departments ... not only with questions of Law and procedure, but also requiring the drafting of documents, letters, etc. I have been attempting to deal with all these single handed but it is quite impossible that I should do so efficiently." The solution, he suggested to the Minister for Home Affairs, Kevin O'Higgins, was the appointment of a junior counsel who could do some of the time-consuming tasks for him. Kennedy thought the appointment should be for a period of six months "to carry us over the enormous work of the initial stages".[4] This was to be John A. Costello's route into Government service, and he acknowledged it was due to his friendship with Kennedy.[5]

Costello later expressed pride at being appointed by a Government made up of prominent figures from the War of Independence, especially as he was "without what was then known as a National Record. I never died for Ireland, and don't intend dying for Ireland!"[6] Given his admitted lack of a "National Record", his promotion was open to criticism. Half a century later, interviewer David Thornley suggested that "people like yourself, typical of the Law Library, the professions, the bureaucracy, from 1922 on took over the fruits of what had been won violently without their having helped". Costello replied, "That is so, that's a fair comment ..."[7]

He was not alone. John M. Regan has argued that Kevin O'Higgins deliberately worked to bring into Government members of the Catholic nationalist elite who had been swept aside by the War of Independence. The appointment of John Marcus O'Sullivan as Minister for Education in 1926 marked a watershed as "there were now more non-combative Clongownians in the Cabinet than veterans of the 1916 Rising".[8] While not a Clongownian, Costello was certainly a non-combatant, and his rise can be seen as part of a wider process.

Costello described Kennedy's job as Law Officer as very difficult, "because at that time nobody knew what the law was ... when the transfer of functions from the British to the Irish was started ...".[9] So enormous was the task, in fact, that Costello was initially only the Second Assistant to Kennedy—Kevin O'Shiel, former Land Court judge, was the First.[10] Kennedy had sketched out the tasks he wanted performed by his new assistants in his letter to O'Higgins. "Many legal questions involve the hunting up and collation of Statutes and decisions, which often take a considerable amount of time. The drafting of documents in itself is a tedious process, and I think that you will agree that the only satisfactory way to do this class of work is to have the collection of materials and the rough drafting done by someone competent to do it, and then submit it for revision and final settlement by me."[11]

Costello later described himself as "working in a very unobtrusive and humble fashion",[12] but the range of issues he dealt with was wide. In October 1922 he provided opinions on exhumation and on Commissions of Inquiry, while in February 1923 he wrote about extradition, theatre patents, and illegal trawling.[13] A typical example of the sort of tedious work Kennedy wanted done related to the appointment of a stockbroker to the courts. The Lord Chief Justice, Thomas Molony, was claiming the right to make the appointment, and Kennedy asked Costello to find out whether such a post existed, who should make the appointment, and whether it should be made or at least approved by the Minister for Home Affairs.[14] A lengthy opinion from Costello informed Kennedy that the Lord Chief Justice did appear to have the right to make the appointment, and there was no basis on which the Minister for Home Affairs could establish a claim to make it—although, as he pointed out, the position had no salary or pension attached, and simply amounted to an indication that the appointee might receive "a certain proportion" of the stock exchange business connected with the courts.[15]

More substantial issues were raised by a Public Meetings Bill proposed by Kevin O'Higgins. According to the Department of Home Affairs, "very considerable inconvenience and loss have been caused to business people in Dublin by reason of the continued dislocation of traffic on account of meetings".[16] The Bill proposed a ban on public meetings unless permission had previously been given by the authorities.[17] Kennedy, however, expressed concern about the proposed Bill to O'Higgins, pointing out that it aimed to regulate an existing right of public meeting, but that no such right existed, while it was silent on the right of assembly in procession, and seemed to assume the right of meeting in private buildings for any purpose whatever.[18] The Executive Council agreed to the circulation of a 23-page memorandum on the Bill by Costello.[19]

The Legal Assistant argued that while people had a right to free expression of opinion and to free assembly under Article 9 of the Free State Constitution, there was no right to meet where and when they wanted, to meet on highways, or to enter private property. "The right must be exercised with due regard to the rights both of private individuals and those of the general public."[20] Kennedy noted that the memorandum "has confirmed the principles and views expressed by me ... I am satisfied that the first Section of the draft Public Meetings Bill is unconstitutional and bad ..."[21] O'Higgins agreed to modify the Bill to avoid the constitutional difficulties raised,[22] although the legislation was eventually abandoned because it proved impossible to avoid breaching Article 9 of the Constitution.[23] In this case Kennedy's—and Costello's—concern for the rule of law proved stronger than the authoritarian impulses of O'Higgins.

As well as his work for Kennedy, and his continuing private practice at the Bar described in the previous chapter, Jack Costello also represented the State at various inquests—a tricky assignment at a time when elements of the security forces were assassinating Republicans. In August 1923, for instance, he represented the authorities at the inquest into the death of Henry McEntee, a staff captain in the (anti-Treaty) IRA, who had disappeared from his home on 31 July, and whose body was discovered three days later in a field near Finglas with several bullet wounds. The next of kin were represented by Costello's friend from UCD days, Conor Maguire, who said the case was one of a series of murders in which there was such an air of mystery that it had been impossible to track down the parties responsible. He added that the Coroner and the jury stood between the public and a system of tyranny. Costello rather weakly replied that he was there to assist the Coroner and the jury in every way and that every possible step would be taken to trace the murderers.[24]

An even more notorious case was that of Noel Lemass, who was abducted from a Dublin street on 3 July 1923, and whose decomposed body was found in the Dublin Mountains in October. A friend of the family, Jimmy O'Dea— later a famous comedian, but who had trained as an optician—helped identify the corpse by recognising a pair of Noel's glasses.[25] When the inquest opened in Rathmines Town Hall, Coroner Dr J.P. Brennan (later a Clann na Poblachta TD) said he had received reports that "the teeth were torn from the jaws" which "suggested a barbarism of which the most pitiless savage would be ashamed". Costello sought an adjournment in order to seek medical evidence, but this was opposed by A. Lynn, counsel for the murdered man's brother, Seán Lemass. Lynn claimed some of his witnesses were afraid of being killed. Costello said that the forces of the State were available for their protection— which was not very reassuring given that the forces of the State were responsible for the murder of Noel Lemass. Lynn was allowed to call his witnesses, who disclosed death threats from the Free State forces warning them not to give evidence.[26]

Despite the extra assistance, Kennedy still appeared to be swamped by his work, receiving a blistering complaint from W.T. Cosgrave in April 1924 about delays in dealing with Colonial Office Despatches. "Many of these appear to have lain in your Office for over a year without attention ... I cannot but think that there is something seriously wrong in the administration of a Department where Despatches on important matters are allowed to remain undealt with for so long."[27] Kennedy sent a spirited response, expressing surprise that Cosgrave had accepted "apparently without question, the far from fair indictment which has been put up to you, I suppose by the Secretariat". He was able to give a reasonable excuse for the delay in dealing with each of the Despatches in question, and then addressed the wider issue of the running of his office. "I am afraid you lose sight of the fact that in a Department like mine ... every matter dealt with is a matter of a personal ruling by me, and not the mere initialling of a Civil Service file ... I must confess to having been overmuch accessible and agreeable to all and sundry who made demands upon my help regardless of time or my own convenience. The 'statement' you ask 'as to what steps I propose to take in the matter' need not go beyond the first step, namely, to cut out for the future accessibility and general agreeableness."[28]

Kennedy's period of inaccessibility and disagreeableness didn't have to last long—a month later he was appointed the first Chief Justice of the Irish Free State. He was replaced as Attorney General by John O'Byrne.[29] On the day of his appointment, O'Byrne wrote to W.T. Cosgrave reminding him to raise with the Executive Council his own appointment as a King's Counsel.[30] This was duly approved, and O'Byrne became the last barrister in the Free State appointed a K.C.[31] As we have seen, the new courts system came into operation a few days later, on 11 June, and in July the Executive Council agreed that from then on, barristers called within the Bar would be termed Senior Counsel rather than King's Counsel.[32]

Costello continued as Legal Assistant to the new Attorney General, who asked him to study the legal changes that would be necessary if, as expected, substantial portions of the territory of Northern Ireland were transferred to the Free State by the Boundary Commission.[33] In April 1925, Costello took silk, writing to Diarmuid O'Hegarty, Secretary to the Executive Council, that he was "anxious to be called to the Inner Bar at an early date ... I am authorised by the Chief Justice and by the Attorney General to say that they approve of and support my application."[34] Kennedy wrote in support of the application,[35] and on 5 May 1925 Governor General Tim Healy issued the patents for Costello, along with James Geoghegan and Martin Cyril Maguire.[36] The following day at the Supreme Court in Dublin Castle the three (wearing full-bottomed wigs) were duly called within the Bar by the Chief Justice, "whose formal inquiry, 'Have you anything to move?' they acknowledged with a bow".[37]

More preferment was to come to John A. Costello soon after. On Friday 8 January 1926, the Executive Council nominated O'Byrne to a vacancy in the High Court, and Costello as his replacement as Attorney General. The appointments were made by the Governor General the following day, a Saturday. On Tuesday 12 January, Chief Justice Hugh Kennedy admitted Costello to the "precedence at the Bar to which he is entitled by virtue of such appointment".[38] The golfing correspondent of the *Irish Times* noted that this meant that devotees of the game held the post of Attorney General on both sides of the Border. The North's Attorney, Anthony Babington, was "very closely identified in the game in Ireland" and "a regular competitor at our championship meetings". Jack Costello was said to be "very popular" at his Milltown Club, but in a case of damning with faint praise, it was noted that "he plays a good game, but figures but rarely in competitive golf".[39] Following his appointment as Attorney-General, Costello was also elevated to membership of the benchers of King's Inns,[40] a position he was proudly to hold for the rest of his life.

While reports of his appointment referred to his popularity at the Bar, he was undoubtedly young for the post at 35 and with just 12 years' practice behind him—of the first 17 Attorneys none was younger and only Cearbhall Ó Dálaigh was the same age.[41] He later said that any danger of his developing a swollen head as a result of his early promotion was dashed by the *Evening Mail*, which said he had become Attorney General by "a strange concatenation of fortuitous circumstances". Another deflation came from British M.P. Lady

Nancy Astor, who, on being introduced by W.T. Cosgrave to his new AG at the Imperial Conference of November 1926, responded, "That thing? Attorney General?"[42] While this incident was doubtless apocryphal, the fact that Costello repeated the alleged comment may indicate his nervousness at taking up such an important post at a relatively young age.

His new job carried the very respectable salary of £2,500 per year, the same as the President of the Executive Council (by comparison, Cabinet ministers received just £1,700).[43] The salary made up for the loss of his burgeoning practice at the Bar, and he was by the standards of the 1920s very well off. It appears he took some responsibility for the financial affairs of the wider family, paying for his mother's funeral in July 1929, for instance.[44] He also continued to make charitable donations, being included on the list of solid Catholic citizens subscribing to the St Vincent de Paul Night Shelter in January 1926. He gave £3.3.0, the same amount as Hugh Kennedy.[45]

Costello owed his handsome salary to Kennedy. It had been set at this level in 1922, possibly because of Kennedy's complaint that he had been unable to continue his private practice at the Bar (one of his conditions for taking the job) because of the volume of Government work he faced.[46] The question of private practice by the Attorney General continued to generate debate for many years to come. Kennedy himself, speaking in the Dáil during the debate on the Ministers and Secretaries Bill in 1923, rejected the notion that the office should be a full-time one. He pointed out that the "exceedingly exacting character of the position" which had prevented him from taking any private practice would probably not continue once the new State was firmly established. He added that no barrister could accept the job as a full-time office, as he would lose his position in the profession.[47]

Seven years later, Cosgrave sought Costello's views on the subject, enclosing a newspaper clipping reporting a case in Belfast in which Babington appeared.[48] Costello replied that while he had "kept the point open that in theory at least the Attorney General is entitled to take on private work, in practice I have never done so nor has either of my predecessors". He then went further, stating that "in principle I think it is wrong that the Attorney General should be entitled to take private work. Abuses might very easily result. It is, of course, essential that the Attorney General should be above suspicion and his remuneration has to be fixed with that object in view." He added that when the Attorney appeared in Court for the Government, the practice had been that he did not take any fee over and above his salary.[49] (Costello had represented the State in Court in a number of important cases, such as Leen v. President of the Executive Council in the High Court in 1926, and Fogarty v. O'Donoghue in the High and Supreme Courts in 1928.[50]) Cosgrave directed that the exchange should be filed to give a permanent record of the practice regarding fees.[51]

A further memorandum on the subject, dated 1 February 1932, is unsigned, but a note in the file suggests it should be attributed to Costello (an attribution accepted by J.P. Casey, the author of the standard work on the office of the Attorney General).[52] However, as the memorandum argues that the prevailing practice should be changed to allow the Attorney to carry out private practice, and as the incoming Fianna Fáil administration adopted this approach, it seems far more likely that it was written by Conor Maguire, who succeeded Costello as Attorney General, and added to the file after the change of government. Further support for this view comes in a letter from Costello to G.P.S. Hogan, secretary to the Committee of Inquiry into Ministerial and Other Salaries in 1937, in which he repeats his view that "in principle the Attorney General ought not to engage in private practice".[53]

When the new Fianna Fáil government took office in March 1932, it announced, with a great show of Republican virtue, that it was cutting the salaries of the President and the Attorney General from £2,500 to £1,500, and of ministers from £1,700 to £1,000 per annum. However, the virtue was somewhat more apparent than real—the old figures were before tax, while the new ones referred to after-tax income.[54] In addition, the new Attorney General had other compensations—the new Government allowed him to take private cases, and to keep fees earned in the course of his duties.[55] However, this position was later reversed—in December 1936 it was decided that such fees should be retained by the Exchequer, and in January 1946 it was formally decided that the Attorney should not take private work.[56]

Ironically, it was John A. Costello, back in government as Taoiseach in 1948, who reversed these decisions, agreeing to allow his Attorney General, Cecil Lavery, to "engage in such private practice as, in his discretion, he might deem not to be incompatible with the duties of his office",[57] and also to retain fees paid to him for the discharge of his duties.[58] He also insisted on the revival of the tradition that the Chief Justice should formally welcome Lavery and "summon him to his place as leader of the Bar", a practice which had died out after 1936.[59] Given his own attitude when Attorney General, it appears strange that Costello should revert to the practice established by his rival Conor Maguire. But in his 1937 letter about the role of the Attorney General, in which he stated that in principle the Attorney should not engage in private practice, Costello went on to point out that anyone taking on the job "would be called upon to make a very great personal and professional sacrifice. I may say that I personally would not accept the position unless I were assured that I could devote myself to a very considerable extent to private practice."[60] In 1948 he made a similar point to the Secretary to the Government, Maurice Moynihan, in relation to Lavery. Costello stated that it was in the public interest to appoint a leading member of the Bar, and it would be unreasonable to expect them to make the considerable sacrifice of income involved in accepting the office without the right to engage in private practice.[61]

Of course, Cecil Lavery in 1948 was a well established senior counsel, and would have been able to earn a much higher income than would Costello at the time of his own appointment in 1926, when he was an s.c. of just six months' standing. By the time he wrote in 1937 that he would not take the job without the right to practice privately, Costello would have been a consider-able earner himself, which probably explains the change in his own attitude to the job—although his view of the principle involved did not change: he recognised the potential for conflict of interest. In conversation with J.P. Casey in March 1975 about his appointment of Lavery, Costello once again stressed his opposition in principle to private practice by the Attorney because of the danger of abuse, but said "he believed that no such danger could arise in this instance." As Casey points out, in 1950 Lavery's successor as Attorney, Charles F. Casey, appeared for the respondent in the controversial Tilson case, which involved religion and adoption. "It is surprising that Costello did not inter-vene to prevent this. The case gave rise to considerable controversy about the implications of Article 44 of the Constitution, and it was hardly desirable for the AG to have been—unnecessarily—involved in this."[62]

The other potentially controversial aspect of the Attorney General's role concerned his involvement in politics. Hugh Kennedy, of course, had been elected to the Dáil in a by-election after his appointment—apparently at Cosgrave's suggestion.[63] But subsequently Cosgrave, and particularly Kevin O'Higgins, took the view that the Attorney should not be a TD. As Costello later recalled, "Mr Cosgrave, many a time, put it to me that his view was that the Attorney General occupied a quasi judicial position and he should be apart from politics and that the government should be ... enabled ... to get an opinion from the Attorney General that was unbiased and untinged with their political outlook and that it therefore could be relied upon as completely impartial and not being motivated or activated by politics."[64] Kevin O'Higgins, according to his biographer, "disliked the conventional legal careerist who takes up politics as a means of advancing himself in his profession ... O'Higgins wished to establish the practice of appointing, as law officer to the Government, a barrister who had no seat in the Dáil to think about and who could give a detached opinion, as though he were advising a private client."[65] Costello did not follow this principle himself—his first Attorney General, Cecil Lavery, was a senator, and a TD, Patrick McGilligan, was Attorney during his second administration.

However, not being a TD does not imply a lack of political commitment— in the case of an Attorney General, support of the party in power is a necessary qualification for the job. In a 1974 newspaper interview, Costello was reported as saying that Cosgrave and O'Higgins believed the Attorney "should not be a member of, or attached to, any political party".[66] This notion was described as J.P. Casey as "surprising",[67] which indeed it is; it is also completely inaccurate. Costello was 83 when he gave the interview, and it appears that he was simply a little confused. In the same interview he criticised modern-day barristers for getting married after just five years at the Bar, claiming that "in my day it was an accepted rule that no young barrister got married until he was 10 years at the Bar".[68] Evidently neither Costello, nor the interviewer, recalled that he was married in 1919, just five years after his call.

In any event, Costello as Attorney General was far from politically un-attached, describing himself in later times as "a convinced supporter" of Cumann na nGaedheal,[69] although as we shall see in Chapter 5 his first foray onto the hustings did not come about until the 1932 election. As J.P. Casey pointed out, the only way to have depoliticised the office of Attorney General would have been to make it a Civil Service post,[70] which doesn't appear to have been seriously contemplated by anyone. Indeed, by the 1970s, Costello had come to the view that Ireland should follow the British pattern, with the Attorney Generalship working as a full ministerial office[71]—a view which may well have been strengthened by his son Declan's then position as Attorney General and TD.

While the "immense volume of work" involved in setting up the State referred to by Hugh Kennedy had eased somewhat, the job of Attorney General was still extremely busy, as the Cosgrave government continued to face enormous challenges, many of them with a legal aspect. The range of Commonwealth and international relations, in which the government of the Irish Free State sought to widen and extend its status as an independent state, will be dealt with in the next chapter. But in domestic politics too, there were many thorny legal challenges—including relations with the Stormont government across the Border; the problem of emergency legislation to deal with the threat of Republican violence; the Fianna Fáil challenge on the Oath and Annuities issues; and the problem of appeals to the Privy Council. In each of these, Costello was to play a prominent part.

One of the first matters to be dealt with by the new Attorney General was the question of appeals to the Privy Council, a matter of considerable legal and political delicacy, but one with which Costello was well familiar. While the Treaty of December 1921 did not specifically mention the Privy Council, it was agreed that the Irish Free State was to have "the same constitutional status in the Community of Nations known as the British Empire" as Canada, Australia, New Zealand and South Africa, and specifically that the position of the Free State "in relation to the Imperial Parliament and Government and otherwise shall be that of the Dominion of Canada, and the law, practice and constitutional usage" governing relations between Canada and the Crown and Westminster would also govern those with the Irish Free State. One of those practices was the right of appeal to the Judicial Committee of the Privy Council (a group of Law Lords, sitting in London). In fact, the British deliberately chose Canada because the appeal was provided for in the British North America Act but was modified in the Australian and South African Constitutions.[72]

But the actual terms of the Irish Free State Constitution appeared to the British to renege on the Treaty. Article 66 stated that the decision of the Supreme Court "shall in all cases be final and conclusive, and shall not be reviewed or capable of being reviewed by any other Court, Tribunal or Authority whatsoever". However, it then continued, "Provided that nothing in this Constitution shall impair the right of any person to petition His Majesty for special leave to appeal from the Supreme Court to His Majesty in Council or the right of His Majesty to grant such leave." So, were decisions of the Supreme Court final, or were they not?

When Lloyd George saw the terms of the draft Constitution, he complained that it was "wholly inconsistent with the Treaty". He demanded answers on a range of issues which he felt were unclear in the Constitution—the oath, the declaration to be signed by members of the Provisional Government, common citizenship, the position of the Crown, treaty-making powers, and the Privy Council. "Are the courts of the Irish Free State to stand in the same relation to the King in Council (the Judicial Committee of the Privy Council) as do the courts of the Dominion of Canada?"[73]

In his response the following day, Arthur Griffith pointed out that the Privy Council question was "a matter of no small delicacy in Ireland", adding that the appeal procedure was being challenged in the Dominions and could well be abolished in the near future. He said objection would be taken to some of those likely to be members of the Judicial Committee, adding, "we must ask what guarantees can be given that the impartiality of the Court in question can be secured". And he objected to the appeal on grounds of expense. "It is a rich man's appeal which may well be used to the destruction of a man not well off." In conclusion, he said the Irish side "did not think that this appeal was a necessary incident of the Treaty position".[74]

Despite the British complaints, the Constitution became law with the relevant article intact. Hugh Kennedy believed "there is to be no appeal from the Irish Courts to the Privy Council in London, only some old supposed right of anyone personally to petition the King being reserved".[75] In a letter to Labour Party leader Thomas Johnson, Kevin O'Higgins explicitly stated that the proviso at the end of Article 66 was intended "to preserve only the prerogative right of appeal ... and not the wider appeal existing in Canada. It is intended to give us the South African position ... that is to say, no appeals from ordinary litigations, but only appeals in such matters as upon petition to the Crown it may be decided should be allowed for some special reason. The special reasons contemplated are such as arise from the litigation in question affecting the other members of the Commonwealth."[76] Two points should be made here. In trying to achieve the South African position, the Irish were explicitly trying to wriggle out of the Treaty stipulation that the Free State should have the same "law, practice and constitutional usage" as Canada. Secondly, it was largely up to the Privy Council itself to decide if they got away with it.

The first time this was tested was in July 1923, when two petitions for a hearing came before the Privy Council. The first was Bowman v. Healy and Others—the case in which Costello had represented insurance officer Major Fuge in the Free State Courts (see Chapter 2). He again appeared in the Privy Council hearing for the respondents, along with Hugh Kennedy. The petition was withdrawn, and Kennedy sought his costs, which were awarded by Lord Haldane.[77] The other petition came from the *Freeman's Journal*, which had been sued for breach of contract by Swedish paper company Follum Traeslileri. The Swedes claimed the *Journal* had agreed to buy 5,000 tons of paper for £365,000, but had then reneged when the market price dropped, offering only £200,000. The Swedes won damages of £165,000 in the High Court in March 1922,[78] a decision upheld in the Court of Appeal a year later, at which point counsel for the *Freeman's Journal* sought a stay of execution pending an appeal to the Privy Council. Counsel for the newspaper claimed they were entitled to do so as there was the same right of appeal in the Free State as in Canada. Lord Justice O'Connor pointed out that the right only existed "where large questions of law were involved", while Lord Chief Justice Molony asserted "there was no appeal in the ordinary sense now".[79] The irony of the last remnants of the British legal establishment refusing a nationalist newspaper the right to appeal to the King appears to have been lost on all concerned.

When the *Freeman* case came before the Privy Council in July 1923, the Free State was represented by its current and future Attorneys General—Hugh Kennedy and John A. Costello. The ruling, by Viscount Haldane, was all the Free State could have wished for. "Ireland is now by virtue of the Treaty ... a Dominion ... She has got immense control over her own internal affairs ... and it follows that she must in a large measure dispose of her own justice ... I was anxious not to rule out all the exceptional cases, but as the general principle is the first thing to start with, the general principles are principles of Dominion justice."[80] As Hugh Kennedy wrote to Cosgrave, the ruling allowed the Irish "to establish our position in this matter rigidly, and I need hardly say that this is a matter where, if they had been so dishonestly minded, the British side could have eaten into our rights very substantially".[81]

But the position in fact was not as rigid as Kennedy believed, and there were inevitably further appeals. Two of these were heard in December 1925, with Costello on the Free State's legal team. The first, Lynham v. Butler, arose out of the interpretation of the 1923 Land Act, while the second, the Wigg and Cochrane case, concerned compensation for civil servants who retired under the terms of the Treaty. In Lynham v. Butler, the Lord Chancellor, Viscount Cave, ruled that "it does appear to be a point of importance which may arise in other cases, and their Lordships will advise that leave to appeal shall be granted on the usual terms".[82] This decision caused particular annoyance to the Irish, as "this was a matter of purely internal law", and because questions asked by members of the Privy Council "revealed a complete misconception ... of an aspect of Irish Land Law which had been established for decades".[83]

The decision to grant leave to Wigg and Cochrane would appear to have had more justification, as the civil servants in question, who had won their case in the High Court but had it overturned on appeal to the Supreme Court, were trying to establish whether a claim to compensation under the Treaty was justiciable in the courts. According to Charles Bewley, who appeared before the Privy Council along with Costello, the Law Lords "obviously knew very little of the Pensions Act and nothing whatever of the various laws and orders governing the relations between Great Britain and Ireland". After the hearing, as the two Irishmen walked down Whitehall, Costello asked Bewley if he knew the average age of the judges. He didn't, but Costello had discovered from Who's Who that the youngest was 71 and the oldest 87, the average age being 75. "Now that I know what the Privy Council is like, I've made up my mind that it must go. It's a scandal that such a court should have the final decision in Irish cases."[84] Bewley's memoirs are generally unreliable (as well as betraying his unpleasantly pro-Nazi outlook) but his record of this exchange has the ring of accuracy. It would be typical of Costello to prepare thoroughly for such a case, including checking up on the judges; and his trenchant response to seeing the Council in action is also characteristic.

When Costello took office as Attorney General he was faced with the fall-out from these two cases. The Privy Council's decision in Lynham v. Butler was dealt with easily enough through the 1926 Land Act, passed into law on 11 March, which clarified the anomaly at issue and backdated it.[85] Costello explained to Justice Minister Kevin O'Higgins that such Declaratory Acts were not uncommon, and were used "to set aside what Parliament deems to have been a judicial error, whether in the statement of the Common Law or in the interpretation of a Statute".[86] The British Conservative Lord Cave, no supporter of the Free State, described the procedure as an "effective and ingenious" way of getting round the Privy Council.[87] Costello kept an eye on developments in the case through "cautious enquiries", which indicated that the Privy Council appeal would not now be proceeded with.[88] (A third case in which leave to appeal was granted, the Performing Rights Society v. Bray UDC, was also circumvented by introducing legislation, in this case, the Copyright Preservation Act, 1929.[89])

The Wigg and Cochrane case, however, was not so easily disposed of. It proceeded to hearing before the Privy Council, and the Free State lost the case, leading to a position where the civil servants were awarded benefits which the British Government did not grant to its own civil servants. Ernest Blythe, the Minister for Finance, estimated that the extra benefits granted by the Privy Council would cost £55,000 immediately as well as an unquantifiable continuing annual charge. He refused to make any payment to the individuals involved, and he and Costello agreed the form of a despatch to the British Government on the issue.[90] Complex negotiations ensued between the Irish and British Governments, and between the Irish Government and the Civil Service unions, led by the General Secretary of the Post Office Workers' Union, Bill Norton. Working closely together on this issue built up a significant level of trust between Costello and Norton, which would be important in later years. In 1929, agreement was reached on a new tribunal to assess compensation to civil servants. The Irish conceded the better terms, while the British agreed to repay the extra money involved. The settlement, which was embodied in legislation in both jurisdictions, was in effect "the first revision of the hitherto sacrosanct Treaty".[91]

Whatever practical measures might be taken to resolve problems thrown up by particular decisions of the Privy Council, it was clearly impossible to continue in a situation where litigants in seemingly innocuous cases might be granted leave to appeal. There was also the Constitutional principle at stake. British attempts to reform the operation of the Privy Council were opposed by the Free State, on the grounds that such efforts were "likely to make its eventual abolition more difficult".[92] In January 1931, the Executive Council asked Costello to examine the possibility of declaring that decisions of the Supreme Court were final.[93] His draft legislation was considered by the Executive Council in March. Costello offered his colleagues two drafts of the Constitution (Amendment No. 17) Bill, 1931, which differed only in their long title. The first described the act as one "making absolute the finality of decisions of the Supreme Court", while the second was more to the point, saying it would make "the decision of the Supreme Court incapable of review by His Majesty in Council".[94]

Ministers chose the first, more diplomatic, option, but decided to hold the legislation in reserve, as it was "possible that the question with which they are intended to deal may be solved by other means".[95] It appears Patrick McGilligan, the Minister for External Affairs, was hoping to reach agreement with the

British on the issue in the context of the Statute of Westminster, which will be discussed in the next chapter. In October it was agreed to defer consideration of the matter for another two months, while in December McGilligan indicated that he *didn't* want the subject put back on the agenda of the Executive Council.[96] The effect of this, of course, was to leave the matter for the incoming Fianna Fáil government to deal with.

The second major issue facing Costello as Attorney General was emergency legislation to combat IRA activities. Such measures were introduced three times during his term of office, in 1926, in 1927 (after the assassination of Kevin O'Higgins), and again in 1931. Costello was a most reluctant participant. Many years later, he was to describe himself as being "very tired and sick at heart at all the rows that were going on between Irishmen", and describing himself as having "the misfortune to have to prepare and ... put into practice" these measures.[97] Indeed, he claimed this distaste encouraged him to repeal the External Relations Act as a way of "taking the gun out of Irish politics".[98] Ironically, in a tribute after his death, then Taoiseach Liam Cosgrave stated that Costello's greatest contribution "was in the Constitutional sphere", citing his work in drafting "many of the original public order acts"[99]—which perhaps says more about Cosgrave's order of priorities than it does about Costello's. Curiously, his role in drawing up emergency legislation was later praised by one of the targets of such laws, Seán MacBride, who believed Costello insisted on their passage "in order to avoid the rule of law from being disregarded completely".[100] In other words, if the Government and the Gardaí were going to break the ordinary law anyway, it was better to suspend the operation of that law rather than ignore it.

Costello's first brush with emergency law came in November 1926, following a series of raids on Garda stations which led to the deaths of two Gardaí.[101] On 15 November, the Government approved "the immediate introduction" of a Public Safety (Emergency Powers) Bill, 1926, the text of which was approved the following day. The Bill was signed into law just three days later.[102] The legislation allowed for the declaration of a state of emergency, which would last for a renewable period of three months, during which persons suspected of committing a scheduled offence could be interned by ministerial order.[103] However, the legislation had to be suspended less than a month later, following reports of Garda violence towards detainees in Co. Waterford.[104]

Emergency legislation again became necessary following the murder of Kevin O'Higgins, the Minister for Justice and External Affairs, and Vice-President of the Executive Council, on Sunday 10 July 1927. The Government's response was twofold. It introduced public safety legislation suspending Habeas Corpus, establishing special non-jury courts and reintroducing internment—"essentially a return to the emergency measures of the Civil

War".[105] Secondly, it brought in a new law forcing Fianna Fáil TDs to take their seats in the Dáil. Following the election of June 1927, Fianna Fáil TDs had turned up in Leinster House to take their seats, but after telling the Clerk of the Dáil that they would not take the Oath prior to doing so, were removed from the premises by the Captain of the Guard. Two of their number, Seán T. O'Kelly and Seán Lemass, subsequently challenged this action in the High Court, naming as defendants Costello as Attorney General, Ceann Comhairle Michael Hayes, the Clerk of the Dáil and the Captain of the Guard. Costello armed himself with the legal opinion of four eminent counsel—A.K. Overend, W.G. Shannon, Charles Bewley and Cecil Lavery—who were "clearly of opinion that the Plaintiffs were not entitled to attend the meeting of Dáil Éireann so summoned without having first taken ... the prescribed oath ..."[106] Equally eminent counsel—Arthur Meredith, Albert Wood, and George Gavan Duffy—advised Fianna Fáil that "there is no authority in anyone under the Treaty or the Constitution or the Standing Orders of Dáil Éireann to exclude any member of that House (whether he has taken the oath or not) from any part of the House before the House has been duly constituted and the Ceann Comhairle thereof duly elected".[107]

O'Higgins was murdered while this legal action was still pending, so the Executive Council considered ways of forcing the issue. It initially proposed declaring the seats of existing deputies vacant if they failed to take the oath, but following discussion with Labour leader Thomas Johnson it was decided "not to vacate the Irregular Seats, but to make a sworn declaration of intention to comply with Article 17 ... a condition precedent to valid nomination for all future elections".[108] This was duly included in the draft legislation forwarded by Costello the following day, which required candidates to declare their intention of taking the Oath, set down a two-month time limit for them to do so, and provided for the seats to be declared vacant if they didn't.[109] In any event, the outcome was the same—de Valera led his deputies into the Dáil on 12 August, having taken what was now described as an "empty formula".

But while the legislation was passed by both Houses of the Oireachtas on 10 August, it wasn't actually signed into law for another three months. On the sixteenth, Cosgrave was handed a petition, signed by 64 Labour and Fianna Fáil TDs, asking that the Bill be suspended for 90 days under Article 47 of the Constitution. (This could have been avoided if both Houses of the Oireachtas had declared the Bill necessary for the immediate preservation of the public peace, as they had done for the Public Safety Bill.[110]) The signatures were sent to the Ceann Comhairle to confirm they were accurate,[111] while the Attorney General was asked for his opinion as to whether the Governor General should be advised to sign the legislation despite the petition.[112]

The Ceann Comhairle confirmed the accuracy of the signatures within two days.[113] Extraordinarily, as late as mid-October, the Assistant Secretary to the Government was writing to Costello to enquire if he had come to a conclusion on whether the Bill should be signed.[114] Speed may not have appeared that important as Fianna Fáil had already entered the Dáil, but until the legislation was actually signed by the Governor General, there was always the danger that the Opposition would be able to secure enough support to demand a referendum on the issue,[115] which makes Costello's apparent inertia inexplicable. Although the Executive Council had considered removing the Constitutional provision for referendum and initiative after O'Higgins' assassination,[116] they did not do so until the following year.[117]

This, along with the decision to apply the requirement to take the oath only on future election candidates rather than unseating those already elected, is another example of a paradox at the heart of the government's reaction to the assassination of its Vice-President. While portrayed as draconian, the response was in fact far more measured than might have been expected, or than was initially considered. For instance, five days after the murder, the Executive Council decided that rather than immediately suspending trial by jury, legislation should only give it the power to do so by proclamation.[118] A further decision three days later referred to "if and when extraordinary tribunals were set up".[119] Clearly, the Government was a lot less hard-line than is usually believed—in fact the power to set up courts martial was not used.[120] In November, Cosgrave indicated "in view of the altered circumstances which have arisen since that Act was passed that its duration might reasonably be limited to the 31st December, 1928".[121] The following May, the Minister for Justice, James FitzGerald-Kenny, told Eamon de Valera that while four people had been arrested under its terms, nobody was then detained under the Act, and nobody had ever been convicted under the Act of any offence.[122] It was, then, no great surprise when the Act was repealed at the end of 1928— although the repeal caused considerable annoyance to Garda Commissioner Eoin O'Duffy.[123]

While de Valera's decision to take the Oath contributed immeasurably to the long-term stability of the political system, it left Cumann na nGaedheal in a minority in the Dáil. Fianna Fáil agreed to support a Labour minority government in order to get Cosgrave out, in return for a Labour commitment to remove the Oath. This arrangement was later described by Costello as "a conspiracy by the Labour Party"[124]—a rather strange interpretation of democratic politics, but indicative of the intense suspicion of Fianna Fáil held by the government of the day. The Dáil debated a confidence motion put down by Labour leader Thomas Johnson on 16 August. Another party, the National League, agreed to support the motion, and Cosgrave and his colleagues were suddenly staring defeat in the face.

But good luck, a malleable Opposition TD and a large amount of alcohol intervened to save the day. The National League's Alderman John Jinks was waylaid by Bertie Smyllie of the *Irish Times*, plied with drink, and put on the train home to Sligo. A piece of evidence in Blythe's papers suggests Costello was aware of, if not involved in, these events. On the back of a card on which is typed "Attorney-General" is a hand-written note (presumably by Costello): "Jinks is gone away. It will be a tie with casting vote."[125] The vote was duly tied at 71 each and the Ceann Comhairle cast his vote for the status quo. Cosgrave then proposed a three-month adjournment, which after some haggling with the Opposition was reduced to two months, and the Dáil adjourned.[126]

Which was all well and good until the House resumed in October, and Cosgrave and his ministers would face the same arithmetic, with no guarantee that the disappearance of Jinks or some other deputy would work the next time. And once they lost a vote in the Dáil, they wouldn't even be able to call an election. Article 53 of the Constitution was very clear: " ... the Oireachtas shall not be dissolved on the advice of an Executive Council which has ceased to retain the support of a majority in Dáil Éireann." But at this point Jack Costello proved worth his legal weight in gold.

In both August 1923 and May 1927 the Dáil had voted on a dissolution motion before an election took place. The Executive Council believed that it had no right to dissolve the Dáil without the Dáil's own consent. But, according to Ernest Blythe, Costello pointed out that the wording of the Constitution did in fact allow for a dissolution by the Executive without a vote in the House, and while it *wasn't* in session.[127] Eleven days after the adjournment, Governor General Tim Healy proclaimed the dissolution of the Dáil, and in the subsequent election Cumann na nGaedheal and Fianna Fáil gained at the expense of the smaller parties (Jinks was among the casualties). With 62 seats and the support of the Farmers, Cosgrave was able to form a stable government.

When the new Dáil met on 11 October, the decision to call an election without consulting the Dáil was heavily criticised by Labour's T.J. O'Connell (whose vote could have unseated Cosgrave in August, had he not been absent at a conference in Canada[128]). O'Connell complained that the government had "used the powers which were given them in the most arbitrary fashion; they have trampled on the Constitution, and they have flouted the wishes, even the decisions, of the Parliament that elected them to power ... Why did not the President ... get a decision from that authority to have a dissolution and a general election? The President knows well, as everybody knows who sat in the Fifth Dáil, that if such a motion as that was put before the Fifth Dáil it would not have been carried. That is the reason he ignored the authority of the Dáil ..."[129]

O'Connell was undoubtedly right, and Costello's advice had proved invaluable to the Government—and was to prove equally valuable to de Valera in 1933, 1938 and 1944. In fact, de Valera widened the power of the Government to call an election at the time of its own choosing in the 1937 Constitution. The 1922 Constitution said a dissolution "shall not" be granted to a government which had lost its Dáil majority; the 1937 version merely gave the President *discretion* to refuse it. This is one of the few discretionary powers of the Presidency, and one that has never been used, despite the best efforts of Fianna Fáil to persuade President Patrick Hillery to refuse a dissolution to Garret FitzGerald in 1982. There are other options for a government after losing an important vote in the Dáil. For instance, when the Opposition parties defeated Cosgrave on a pensions bill in March 1930, he promptly resigned and successfully asked the Dáil to re-elect him;[130] when the First Inter-party Government lost a vote on the Estimates for the Department of Posts and Telegraphs, it simply resubmitted the unchanged Estimate the following day and won a vote. The defeat in the latter case was due to accident rather than an important policy issue—one Government TD had apparently locked himself into the toilet and therefore missed the vote.[131]

But to return to 1927, Cosgrave was now back in power, with a secure majority; Fianna Fáil were inside the political system; and the Government, as we have seen above, felt confident enough about the security situation to repeal the Public Safety Act in December 1928. That confidence was not to last long.

In January 1929, the foreman of a jury which had convicted an IRA member was shot, though not fatally; the following month Albert Armstrong, who had given evidence against a number of Republicans who tore down a Union Jack, was shot dead.[132] Armstrong had been worried about possible repercussions after he gave evidence, and approached Fianna Fáil TD Bob Briscoe, a friend. Briscoe later told Gardaí that Armstrong thought he might be kidnapped, not shot. After making enquiries, the TD told Armstrong that as far as he could judge he was not in any danger.[133] The Gardaí shared this assessment, reporting that an earlier assassination attempt had failed "owing to the faintheartedness" of one of the potential assassins.[134]

Worse was to follow at the beginning of 1931, with an IRA informer shot dead in January, Garda Superintendent John Curtin murdered in Tipperary in March, and a man who had given evidence against the IRA for Curtin killed three months later.[135] These murders were a direct challenge to the justice system, and could not be ignored by the Government. The Curtin assassination has been described by Eunan O'Halpin as "a monumental miscalculation" by the IRA, which was, "as usual ... taken aback by the cumulative consequences of its own operations when the government finally acted".[136]

In June 1931, Garda Commissioner Eoin O'Duffy claimed in a report to the Government that the IRA was on the verge of open insurrection—a claim given credence when thousands of Republicans defied the Government's ban on the annual march to Wolfe Tone's grave at Bodenstown that month.[137] The Executive Council requested a report on the extent of illegal drilling through-out the country.[138] The report claimed the IRA consisted of around 1,300 officers and 3,500 rank and file, that the organisation had successfully terrified jurors, and that in areas like Kerry and Tipperary "men are afraid to be seen speaking to the police".[139] O'Duffy added a personal complaint to the Department of Justice, claiming that the IRA and their followers "treat the Gardaí with absolute contempt". He complained that since the Courts had declared "harassing tactics" illegal, "the Irregulars have the field to them-selves". O'Duffy urged the Government to put those trying to overthrow the Constitution outside the protection of that document. "There is no good reason why an Organisation making war on the State should be afforded the protection which the State affords its loyal citizens ..."[140]

Proposals for new legislation were drawn up by Stephen Roche, the acting Secretary of the Department of Justice. In August 1931 he advised the Government that existing draft legislation, the Police (Powers) Bill, would be "entirely inadequate". He was directed to submit proposals which he believed would be sufficient, "regardless of the political or Parliamentary difficulties".[141] Cosgrave began seeking Church support, warning Cardinal McRory of "a situation which threatens the whole fabric of both Church and State".[142] The Justice memorandum was sent to the Catholic hierarchy, with a request from Cosgrave for "joint Episcopal action in the form of a concise statement of the law of the Church in relation to the present issues ... Doctrines are being taught and practised which were never before countenanced amongst us and I feel that the influence of the Church alone will be able to prevail in the struggle against them."[143] The bishops issued a hard-hitting joint pastoral on 18 October, the day after the new emergency powers became law.

From Geneva, Patrick McGilligan wrote to the Secretary of the Department of External Affairs, Joe Walshe, expressing a preference for a "simple" Bill, giving the Government powers to deal with the security situation by decree, rather than "a Bill of a repressive type with many clauses ... [which would] if it is to be put through the Dáil, give rise to interminable debates the propaganda effect of which will be very bad for us". McGilligan also mused that the Government might be better to go for an early election rather than trying to carry on, not only because of "the irregular and Bolshie situation", but also because of the economy. "I feel it would be sheer madness to think of trying to operate repressively throughout a miserable and poverty-stricken twelve-month. I wonder if a February election would be at all possible."[144]

McGilligan's analysis of the likely election date was spot on. And while the legislation was more detailed than he wished, it didn't spend too long going through the Dáil. Introduced on 14 October, it was law by the seventeenth. The Constitution (Amendment No. 17) Act set up a Special Powers Tribunal made up of military officers, gave special powers to the Gardaí, outlawed associations aiming to overthrow the Government by force, as well as prohibiting their publications, and gave the Executive Council the power to ban public meetings, among other things.[145] These new powers were inserted as a Schedule into the Constitution immediately after Article 2, and therefore called Article 2A. As soon as the Act was signed into law, the Government made the necessary order to bring it into force. In a statement, President Cosgrave noted that the powers in the Act were wide and the penalties drastic, but hoped they would only have to be used "to the minimum necessary". He added, "The State must protect the people from everything which involves the decay and downfall of the Irish nation."[146] Ironically, one of General O'Duffy's suggestions which was not taken up was a ban on "the wearing of uniforms or badges indicating membership of an unlawful association"[147]—a decision O'Duffy was to have cause to be grateful for a couple of years later.

Although the Government had given O'Duffy many of the powers he sought, there was evidently still nervousness about how they would be used. On the nineteenth, ministers approved a note on policy, prepared for Justice Minister James FitzGerald-Kenny by his civil servants. Mindful of previous abuses, it stressed that "any unnecessary act of violence by the police or any unnecessary discourtesy will be visited with most severe punishment". It also noted that the police now had "ample powers within the law to deal with political crime". Those powers were not to be exercised without political supervision—Republicans prepared to keep quiet were not to be harassed, while an executive minister was to approve the process of bringing a suspect before the Tribunal.[148] In fact, it was generally Costello and his successors as Attorney General who made the decision (this was long before the introduction of an independent Director of Public Prosecutions—a reform introduced by Declan Costello when he was Attorney General). The Gardaí sent copies of the relevant papers to the Attorney and to the Minister for Justice, but in practice the Attorney gave the direction without consulting the Minister.[149] The point was that the Gardaí did not make the decision about using special powers.

O'Duffy had different ideas. He informed the Minister for Justice that each Division had been asked to supply a list of unsolved "outrages", together with a list of suspects for each one. He anticipated that the provisions of the new law for "accounting for movements and actions at time of the crime should be very helpful in this respect". He also planned to arrest around a hundred leading Republicans and interrogate them, although he added, "I do not recommend internment. I believe the Act gives sufficient scope to frame some charge against any person worth arresting. There will always be a popular demand for the release of any person against whom no charge is preferred." He assured the Minister that his men had been "warned very definitely that anything in the nature of so-called third degree methods, flourishing of guns, or bullying tactics, will be severely punished".

The Commissioner also sought an increase in Garda numbers to cope with the extra work, asking for permission to admit two hundred retired officers into the Special Branch immediately.[150] A special meeting of ministers considered O'Duffy's memo on 22 October, ruling out an increase in recruiting, rejecting his suggestion that agrarian crime and mail-car robberies should come under the Act (unless firearms were used), and limiting the interrogation powers to outrages committed since the start of the year. "It would not be in accordance with Government policy to be presented with a large number of prisoners against whom there was no heavier charge than refusing to answer questions."[151]

The effect of the legislation, according to Eunan O'Halpin, was threefold: it removed the problem of jury intimidation; it increased the stakes for Republican opponents of the Government, who knew that internment and executions were real possibilities; and it succeeded in curbing political violence, allowing the February 1932 election to proceed in relative peace.[152] But again, as after the assassination of O'Higgins, the actual implementation of the draconian powers concerned was far less severe than is generally thought. Costello later outlined his view that "every person that went to prison under that Article was a monument to the failure of that Article. Its operation was effective merely because it was *in terrorem* ..."[153] In other words, it was a deterrent; and a deterrent that has to be used has failed. Costello made many references in later years to his unhappiness at being involved with Article 2A—viewing it as a deterrent that would not have to be used was one way of dealing with his doubts.

As soon as Fianna Fáil took office, the tribunals were suspended and the 17 men imprisoned by them pardoned. Gardaí trying to bring prosecutions against the IRA under other legislation found it almost impossible to get directions from the new Attorney General, Conor Maguire. "The message as far as the Guards was concerned ... was clear. It was 'Hands off the IRA'."[154] The suspension was to prove temporary—the tribunals were reappointed in August 1933 to deal with the Blueshirts, although the IRA was soon receiving attention as well. And following the introduction of the new Constitution in 1937, Article 2A provided the template for successive Offences Against the State Acts.

O'Duffy had managed to alienate his political superiors with his extremism, as well as by refusing to accept a pay cut for Gardaí. He was clearly becoming more erratic, and the Cosgrave Government had decided to dismiss him if returned to office—one suggestion was to appoint him consul to the United States.[155] He was also apparently considering a possible coup, as were some elements in the Army. As his biographer puts it, O'Duffy "had little faith in the government, indeed numerous reasons to resent it, and he regarded the opposition as unfit for power. His reports revealed his lack of respect for the constitution, and an underlying belief that the public lacked the civic virtues necessary for democratic rule."[156] The ministers planning to sack him knew all this, which makes their later decision to make him leader of Fine Gael all the more extraordinary.

As the election approached, the question of payments of the Land Annuities became a live political issue into which Costello was drawn. The Annuities were payments due for the purchase of land from landlords under the 1891 and 1909 Land Acts, amounting to £3 million per year. The Free State Government had committed itself in a number of agreements with Britain to continue collecting the annuities and paying them to Britain.[157] However, a vigorous campaign against paying the annuities was waged by the editor of *An Phoblacht*, Peadar O'Donnell. In December 1926, Costello as Attorney General advised the Department of Justice on the type of charges which might be brought against O'Donnell, suggesting that a charge of conspiracy to commit a wrongful act would be more likely to succeed than one of sedition.[158] Of more concern, though, was the attempted hijacking of the campaign by Fianna Fáil, which challenged the payments on technical legal grounds. The Government won a vote on the matter in the Dáil in May 1929, but the agitation continued, and Costello was instructed to draw up a comprehensive memorandum on the subject.

Despite the convention that the legal advice of the Attorney General is privileged and confidential to the Government, the 49-page memorandum was published as a Government White Paper.[159] It concluded that "the action of the Government of the Irish Free State in reference to the Land Purchase annuities is and has been strictly in accordance with the law and with the necessity of maintaining the credit and honour of the State".[160] Fianna Fáil, naturally, were not impressed, complaining that "it seemed hardly fair tactics to present such a document to the public on the eve of an election", and producing its own legal opinions which argued the opposite case.[161] When Fianna Fáil in power withheld the Annuities, sparking the Economic War, the British Treasury brief challenging their right to do so quoted Costello's memorandum in support of the British position.[162]

Throughout Costello's time as Attorney General, there was a continuing dispute involving Dublin, Belfast and London over fishing rights in Lough Foyle. The rights were claimed by the Irish Society, the body set up by Royal Charter in 1613 to govern the plantation of the Derry area by the City of London. The Society had leased the fishing rights to the Foyle and Bann Fisheries Company. Which was all well and good, except that Donegal fishermen in the Inishowen peninsula didn't recognise the Society's right to control fishing in the lough. Their fishing—or poaching, depending on the point of view—threatened to lead to violent confrontation. In 1923, Donegal District Court threw out a trespass case against the Donegal fishermen because jurisdiction over the lough was unresolved—and it was to remain unresolved despite intensive negotiations involving Costello and his counterpart in Belfast, Anthony Babington.

In July 1925 the Secretary to the Executive Council, Diarmuid O'Hegarty, wrote to the Boundary Commission pointing out that the Government of Ireland Act defined Northern Ireland as consisting of parliamentary counties, rather than counties. And in maps drawn up to show the parliamentary counties, the lough was not included in either Londonderry or Donegal. Therefore, the argument went, the lough by definition was not part of Northern Ireland and so belonged to the Free State.[163] Craig and Cosgrave met in London in December 1925 to agree, with the British, a settlement which shelved the report of the Boundary Commission in return for the removal of financial liabilities incurred by the Free State under the Treaty.[164] Craig came away with the impression that Cosgrave had "practically concurred" in the view that the lough was included in the parliamentary county of Londonderry. According to Craig's recollection, Cosgrave asked that this not be included in the Agreement, "as he would experience sufficient difficulty in dealing with the actual question of the Boundary Agreement in the Dáil".[165]

Given this recollection, Craig was confident that the Lough Foyle issue could be sorted out in talks with Dublin, even though "we were still in some doubt as regards our legal position".[166] Attorney General Babington was also "strongly of opinion that outstanding questions should be settled by an amicable arrangement with the Free State rather than having the matter contested in any Court".[167] At the end of July 1926, the Cabinet authorised Babington to go to Dublin to have an informal chat with his opposite number, Jack Costello, "to see whether some arrangement could be arrived at which would overcome the immediate difficulty".[168] The two men duly met in August, but their discussions don't seem to have made progress.[169]

The following March, the Northern Prime Minister, now elevated to the peerage as Lord Craigavon, wrote to Cosgrave saying that with the fishing season starting on 15 April "serious trouble may occur unless this question of jurisdiction is definitely settled before then". He said his government intended introducing legislation in the Northern Parliament to deal with the matter, and went on to outline his recollection of their discussion in London.[170]

This letter immediately set off alarm bells in Dublin. Cosgrave sent a copy to Costello, seeking material for a reply,[171] later telling him that the question raised by Craigavon in London was to do with shipping rights in the lough, not fishing.[172] In his reply to Craigavon, Cosgrave insisted that his recollection of their discussion in London was quite different, and that neither he nor any of his colleagues changed the position they had adopted since the Treaty, that all of Lough Foyle was within the Free State's jurisdiction. The proposed Northern Bill was based on an assumption of jurisdiction which Dublin "very strongly controverts", and would create "a very serious situation" if it proceeded.[173] He also wrote to British Prime Minister Stanley Baldwin advising him of the situation.[174]

Craigavon appeared somewhat taken aback by Cosgrave's response, agreeing that the question was now more serious than one of disputed fishery rights, and suggesting that his government should introduce its Bill, and if it was *ultra vires* the British Cabinet could then refer it to the Privy Council under the terms of the Government of Ireland Act[175]—a suggestion that was immediately and predictably rejected by Cosgrave, who proposed direct negotiations instead.[176] Craigavon, clearly wary of too much contact with Dublin, suggested that as it was a legal question, it might be better to have the respective Attorneys General discuss it, a suggestion Cosgrave accepted.[177]

J.M. Andrews, the North's Minister for Labour, had earlier expressed the fear that if news of the discussion with Dublin got out it would be misunderstood, with many people thinking it was "the thin end of the wedge towards a United Ireland".[178] It was not surprising then that the Northern side treated the issue with considerable circumspection, agreeing that discussions about Lough Foyle at Cabinet would not be circulated in the normal way,[179] while Babington suggested discretion to Costello, writing that "one may possibly be able to talk more freely if we met privately in the first instance".[180] When the two men met, they each put forward well established positions— Babington arguing that the starting point must be an admission by Dublin that the Irish Society owned the fishing rights, Costello countering that the Society should prove this by taking a case in the Free State courts. They came up with a suggested *modus vivendi*—each Government should pass legislation banning fishing with drift or other nets (other than those used by the Society for centuries). This would protect the Society's fishery without affirming or denying its ownership.[181] Shortly afterwards, Costello prepared a lengthy memorandum for his Government colleagues, stressing the strength of the Free State claim to the entire lough, but concluding that "a working arrangement ought to be effected between the two Governments".[182]

Desultory talks between the two Attorneys continued over the winter,[183] and in mid-February they met when Babington travelled to Dublin for the Ireland–England rugby match. There was a poor result in the rugby (Ireland lost by one point, 6–7, the team's only defeat in that year's Five Nations)[184] and deadlock on Lough Foyle. In some frustration, Babington wrote to Costello telling him that if Dublin couldn't accept the Northern proposals, they should come up with their own suggestions.[185] This led to the formation of a Cabinet sub-committee of Ernest Blythe (Minister for Finance), Desmond FitzGerald (Defence), Patrick McGilligan (Industry and Commerce) and James FitzGerald-Kenny (Justice).[186] Costello again gave his opinion to the Committee that the Lough belonged absolutely to the Free State, but that under international law they couldn't deny the Northern Government innocent passage for shipping through it. He added that the dispute had arisen from excessive and illegal drift-net fishing, which would have to be stopped even if the Free State exercised complete ownership of the Lough.[187] Babington's barrage of letters to Costello continued, with some effect, as he sought further meetings of the sub-committee because of the "insistent pressure" from the Northern Attorney.[188] The result was rather less dynamic than Costello or Babington might have wished. Fisheries Minister Fionán Lynch undertook "to have the whole question of fisheries in the Lough and in the river exhaustively examined", and then to bring forward proposals for how the two governments might agree to purchase and control the Foyle fisheries.[189]

At this stage, Baldwin reactivated proposals for a conference in London,[190] presumably as a result of pressure from the Irish Society.[191] The meeting took place in May 1928 in the offices of Dominions Secretary Leo Amery. Costello joined Blythe and McGilligan on the Free State delegation, while Babington was joined by John Milne Barbour, Parliamentary Secretary for Finance, and Northern Cabinet Secretary Charles Blackmore. Babington referred to his talks with Costello, and to the draft bill he had prepared to be passed by both parliaments, banning drift-net fishing on the Lough while ignoring the question of jurisdiction. But this solution was overruled by Costello's political superiors. Blythe said it was "politically impossible", and again called for the Irish Society to take a case in the Free State courts to sort the matter out once and for all. This was rejected by the Northern delegation, and finally Amery offered to contact the Irish Society to see if a solution could be found.[192] He put to them a suggestion made by the Free State delegation, who claimed it would be politically difficult to pass legislation protecting the fishery unless there was some benefit to Donegal. Amery suggested charitable donations of two or three hundred pounds a year, a suggestion the Society agreed to consider.[193] However, when the Society met representatives of the Free State Government, they found Costello in best barrister mode, claiming the sum was "absurdly low", and again insisting that they take a court case. "Establish your right and we will protect it."[194] With no legislation in prospect in Dublin, Babington wrote to Costello at the end of July putting an end to their discussions. "As we cannot get any further, things will have to remain as they are ... If at any future time your Government are both willing and able to deal with the matters we have discussed I shall be only too glad to take them up again ..."[195]

The long-threatened violence broke out the following year, when a patrol boat operated by the Fisheries Company was destroyed.[196] In response, the Company sought an injunction in the High Court in Belfast against Free State fishermen. When it was granted, Cosgrave claimed that the Court was acting beyond its powers, and warned London and Belfast that an attempt to enforce the injunction could lead to "breaches of the peace and possibly loss of life".[197] Craigavon replied that the only solution was to ban drift-net fishing, adding that legislation "jointly prepared" by Costello and Babington "admirably meets the case ... as it carefully avoids any reference to the boundary issue". He said he intended to include it in his legislative programme for the following year.[198] But Dublin stuck to the line that the only solution was for the Irish Society to take legal action in the Free State courts, a suggestion the British Government once again agreed to press on the Society. The British also agreed that the Belfast court action had been "very provocative".[199]

Violence continued with suspected involvement by the IRA, who were reported to be "anxious to make trouble" and "on the look out for Thompson machine gun ammunition".[200] But the Irish Society ignored the advice of the British and Irish Governments for quite some time, finally taking a case in the Irish courts in the mid-1940s which was still dragging on when Costello returned to government as Taoiseach. The fisheries issue was finally resolved by the purchase of the fishery by the two governments and the appointment of the Foyle Fisheries Commission to manage it—the first example, incidentally, of a North–South body with executive powers, an example much quoted at the time of the Good Friday Agreement.

Another legal issue involving Dublin, Belfast and London concerned the Order of Saint Patrick—and it too was to re-emerge when Costello was Taoiseach. The Order was created by George III in 1783, and was conferred only on peers connected to Ireland. The establishment of the Free State obviously created some question over the future of the Order, and in 1924, Craig made efforts to have it transferred to the North. He also wanted the Order conferred on the King's sons, the Prince of Wales and the Duke of York.[201] British Prime Minister Ramsay MacDonald ruled out any changes or new appointments.[202] However, the deaths of a number of knights in the next couple of years prompted the British Government to approach Cosgrave on the matter. Their emissary was Lord Granard, who was a member of the Free State Senate as well as the King's Master of the Horse.[203]

The Executive Council requested Costello to prepare a memorandum on the legal position of the Order,[204] which characteristically took 14 months to complete.[205] Costello concluded that the King was bound to act solely on the advice of Irish ministers in relation to the Order; that Northern Ireland had no role, as it had opted out of the Free State and had no jurisdiction over dignities or titles of honour; and that it was open to the Executive Council to decide that the Order should be allowed to lapse.[206] Ministers duly decided that this was the best course of action.[207] The British sent a further message, through Granard, that they did not share the Irish view, but Cosgrave ignored it.[208] Stumped by the Irish response, the British decided to keep the Order in being, but to restrict it to members of the Royal Family, and two more appointments were made, the last in 1936.[209]

However, the British managed to pull off something of a coup during the war, when the British Press Attaché (and spy) John Betjeman persuaded the Office of Arms in Dublin Castle to hand over the seal of the Order.[210] Costello was encouraged by officials to seek the return of the seal during the Anglo-Irish trade talks in 1948, but "found no opportunity of raising this matter".[211] However, his Northern counterpart, Sir Basil Brooke, did find an opportunity of raising it—the revival of the Order of Saint Patrick was one of the responses he suggested to Costello's declaration of the Republic in September 1948.[212] British Prime Minister Clement Attlee declined to act on the suggestion, and while the Order was never actually abolished, its last member died in 1974. Suggestions by Blythe for the creation of an independent State decoration, the Cross of the Legion of Saint Patrick, also came to nothing[213]—the question has resurfaced from time to time over the years but without much vigour.

Costello's position as Attorney General had involved him in several legal questions with important constitutional implications—it was also to give him a ringside seat as the Free State sought to establish its international position, and to change the British Commonwealth in ways that could hardly have been imagined in 1921.

Chapter 4 ∽

A LONG GAME

"It is not the pace that matters, but the direction. It's a long game, and I would like to see it played out."[1]

KEVIN O'HIGGINS, 1926

" ... there have been advances made that I did not believe would be made at the time."[2]

EAMON DE VALERA, 1932

"What was achieved was the final justification of the founders of this State."[3]

JOHN A. COSTELLO, 1946

The Commonwealth which the Irish Free State joined by virtue of the Treaty was in a process of evolution. In fact, the Treaty was the first official document to use the new title invented by General Smuts— "The British Commonwealth of Nations". But "the relationship of that Commonwealth remained obscure and the status of Dominion ... was not clearly defined".[4] As historian Nicholas Mansergh pointed out, Irish governments after the Treaty had two possible policies towards the Commonwealth. "The first was to refashion the Commonwealth in closer accord with Irish interests and outlook; the second to seek the first opportunity to unravel ... Irish ties with the Commonwealth." He goes on to argue that, broadly speaking, Cosgrave pursued the first policy while de Valera pursued the second.[5] However, it should be noted that the unravelling would have been impossible, or at the very least much more difficult, without the refashioning which had preceded it.

The Irish effort to establish and enhance the new state's status was fought on two fronts—at the League of Nations, and at a succession of Imperial Conferences. As the Government's chief legal adviser, Costello was part of the team which pursued the diplomatic struggle. In the words of Garret FitzGerald he was "the legal genius" of that team, whose "immense legal skill, his brilliance in any aspect of Constitutional Law, gave to our delegation of Ministers and civil servants such a basis of knowledge, experience and skill, that they were able to outmanoeuvre not just the delegations of the other countries of the Commonwealth, but the British themselves".[6] This, while perhaps an overstatement, captured the importance of his role. Costello's involvement in these events also gave him a grounding in diplomacy at the highest level—whether he used that experience to best advantage as Taoiseach will be examined in a later chapter.

The new Attorney General's first appearance on the international stage was very much a walk-on role, at the 1926 Imperial Conference in London. The official delegates to the Conference were W.T. Cosgrave, Kevin O'Higgins, Desmond FitzGerald and Patrick McGilligan.[7] Costello was to attend as an adviser, along with the Secretary of the Department of External Affairs, Joe Walshe, Secretary to the Executive Council Diarmuid O'Hegarty, and John Hearne, legal adviser to the Department of External Affairs, who had drawn up most of the memoranda for the delegation on the issues they could expect to face.[8] However, Cosgrave had no intention of staying in London for the duration of the Conference—O'Hegarty explained that he had had no holiday, and his wife had been ill. "He fears, and we all fear, that unless he gets some rest before the Dáil resumes, he will feel the strain very severely."[9] In his absence, it was clear that O'Higgins, Minister for Justice and Vice-President, would be in charge, rather than the Minister for External Affairs, FitzGerald. Cosgrave was asked which of his ministers should join him as the second Irish guest at a dinner in Buckingham Palace, being told that the chosen minister "will be regarded as the head of the delegation in your absence". He chose O'Higgins.[10] This may have been just as well—O'Higgins told his wife that the British "will stand more from me than from Desmond, whom they dislike".[11]

In advance of the Conference, Walshe summarised the difficulties in relations with Britain. They included the "usurpation by the British Government of the right to advise His Majesty" on matters affecting a particular Dominion; the use of the Foreign Office as the channel of communications between the Dominions and foreign governments; the failure to change the Royal Title to take account of the creation of the Irish Free State and its separation from the United Kingdom; the ban on Dominion legislation having extra-territorial effect; the British view that relations between members of the Commonwealth were not "international"; and the existence of the appeal to the Privy Council (see previous chapter). He concluded that the Conference was "incomparably more important for the Dominions than any one that has preceded it".[12]

In his own preparatory memorandum, Costello dealt with merchant shipping legislation, a fairly complex legal area which seemed unrelated to fundamental constitutional issues. But as the Attorney General pointed out, the existing 1894 Merchant Shipping Act gave the British Board of Trade the right to administer shipping throughout the Commonwealth. This, he argued, "appears to be inconsistent with the exercise of complete legislative and administrative control of their public services by the various members of the Commonwealth". Giving member states the right to control every class of shipping within their jurisdiction would be desirable "on grounds of con-stitutional propriety and ... on grounds of practical convenience in ... administration".[13]

If the British hoped discussion on the Constitutional question could be kept low-key, they were to be sorely disappointed. This was largely thanks to the actions of the Governor General of Canada, Lord Julian Byng, who was accused of acting in an "unconstitutional and autocratic" manner. He had refused a dissolution of Parliament to Liberal leader W.L. Mackenzie King after his minority government lost a vote of censure in the House of Commons on 26 June. Byng summoned the Conservative leader, Arthur Meighen, to form a government, but when he in turn was defeated in Parliament on 2 July he reversed course and granted the defeated Prime Minister a dissolution. Mackenzie King declared that the issue before the people was "whether or not the Government of Canada is to be carried out in accordance with the expressed will of the people's representatives in Parliament under a system of self-government".

Joe Walshe noted with some satisfaction that "the British would hardly regard a violent electoral contest on a big constitutional issue as a propitious preparation for calm discussion at an Imperial Conference".[14] The issue was discussed in London at a meeting between Dominion High Commissioners and the Dominions Secretary, Leo Amery, who insisted Byng had not sought or received any advice from London. The Irish High Commissioner, James MacNeill, shortly to become a Governor General himself, expressed some sympathy for Byng, but predicted that "hereafter the rubber stamp view will prevail".[15]

The idea of the Governor General as a "rubber stamp" acting on the wishes of the Dominion Government would have given considerable satisfaction to Dublin. The Irish Attorney General was developing his own, very firm, ideas on the role of the Governor General. In his notes, Costello wrote that his con-stitutional position should be the same as that of the King. "He should have no power to question or attempt to control executive action ... the possibility of the Governor General's refusal to act on advice weakens the sense of ministerial responsibility. It is not compatible with the ideal of equality of status that a Ministry which represents the choice of Parliament and the constituencies should be subject to control in their action by a nominee of the Imperial Government, even though his action is taken on his own initiative."[16]

Unlike other delegations to the Conference, the Irish rejected the British offer to provide accommodation, on the grounds that they did not have to pay heavy travel expenses. But it was clear that the Irish were really concerned with asserting their independence—Kevin O'Higgins stated his desire for "the Parliament and people of the Irish Free State to regard the Delegation as carrying on important business on their behalf as partners in the British Empire".[17] This decision signalled the attitude the Free State delegation would be taking during the conference. But it also led to constant rows with the Department of Finance over expenses. O'Hegarty complained bitterly to Finance official H.P. Boland: "The volume of work here is so enormous that we cannot reach half of it—and needless to say the financial end is the most annoying."[18]

The round of socialising took its toll of the main delegates. O'Higgins complained that "every day there is a lunch or dinner to be faced—generally both and it's all rather a strain on the 'innards'".[19] On the plus side, he found King George V "very gracious and affable" during a 15-minute conversation at the dinner in Buckingham Palace,[20] and even found time to experience his first flight at Croydon one Saturday, "which I enjoyed very much ... except for the noise there was nothing unpleasant".[21] O'Higgins, of course, was also engaged in other social activities at the time with his mistress Lady Lavery.[22] But mainly the Conference was hard work—especially for Costello and the rest of the backroom team, who found themselves stuck in the Hotel Cecil for days and nights on end because of the constant need for consultation. And while the official dinners were hard on the "innards", eating at the hotel was very hard on the finances. As Attorney General, Costello had a subsistence allowance of 30 shillings per night, but still found himself "very considerably out of pocket" after a six-week stay in London.[23]

In advance of the Conference, the Department of External Affairs had hoped to combat "subtle proposals" from the British by co-operating with the Canadians.[24] However, their hard line appeared to worry Mackenzie King. After meeting FitzGerald and Costello, the Canadian Prime Minister noted in his diary that the Irish were "inclined to the extreme view of having five countries, each with a separate King, operating in all particulars as distinct nations". He contrasted this with the British "desire for the single government of all", implying that he would seek a middle way.[25] The Irish weren't too impressed with Mackenzie King, with O'Higgins observing that he had "dis-improved since '23—gone fat and American and self-complacent".[26] According to Desmond FitzGerald, the Canadian Prime Minister annoyed O'Higgins at a dinner party with Lord Simon by referring to "the way he and we worked together when as a matter of fact we did the fighting and got damned little support".[27]

O'Higgins was also unimpressed with the South African Prime Minister, General Hertzog, "a very decent and likeable kind of man [who] has not been a success—he talks a lot and none too clearly ... The onus of the 'status' push ... has fallen very largely on ourselves and while we have made some headway, it would be greater if Hertzog were more effective and King a stone or two lighter."[28] After the conference, when the South African Prime Minister returned to Pretoria, he told the welcoming crowd, "We have brought home the bacon." To which O'Higgins retorted, "Irish bacon".[29] The South Africans were trying to gain a British declaration that they had a right to secede from the Commonwealth. Costello later claimed that he had advised General Hertzog "that the British would give any number of phrases recognising the right, but if it was ever being translated into practice the utmost pressure would be brought to bear to prevent it".[30] This assessment may have been in his mind during the debate on repealing the External Relations Act (see Chapter 8).

While Costello was not one of the main delegates, he was more than an advisor, representing the Free State on the Committee on Workmen's Compensation,[31] a subject he would have been very familiar with from his work in the courts. He also represented Ireland on a sub-committee of the Committee on Inter-Imperial Relations. The sub-committee dealt with Treaty Procedure. Costello forcefully put forward the Irish position, objecting to the use of "British Empire" to cover the entire Commonwealth when signing treaties. He suggested referring to the King instead, which "would preserve the unity of the Empire, and at the same time make it clear that each of the contracting States was a separate entity acting on the advice of separate sets of Ministers". Those parts of the Empire which were separate members of the League of Nations should not, he argued, be covered by Britain's signature on treaties.[32]

At the Committee on Nationality, O'Higgins rejected the British Home Office proposal to allow female British subjects a legal right to declare their nationality when they married aliens. The measure was proposed to deal with situations which had arisen during the First World War, when women who had lost their British nationality on marriage found themselves trapped when hostilities broke out. O'Higgins told the Home Secretary, Sir William Joynson Hicks, that he couldn't get such a proposal through the Dáil. "We are a conservative people despite superficial evidence to the contrary ... there is not in the Irish Free State the same pressure from Feminist movements which ... exists in Great Britain."[33] He observed mordantly that he and the South African representative, who also opposed change, "would be delivered into the hands of the feminist organisations of the Commonwealth of Nations as a whole burnt offering. They would be made the scapegoats and would be represented as the enemies of womankind." He pointed out that the British Government was itself divided on the issue, with the Foreign Office opposing the change proposed by the Home Office.[34] Costello, meanwhile, told the Conference that they were members of the British Commonwealth of Nations, not the Commonwealth of British Nations, but this important distinction did not find enough support[35]—yet.

In the privacy of his letters home to his wife, O'Higgins rejoiced that the Irish "are by far the best team in the Conference ..."[36] He also floated to his wife the idea of "a dual monarchy—two quite independent Kingdoms with a common King and perhaps a Defence Treaty ... It presupposes, of course, a united Ireland ..."[37] As the Conference drew to a close, he felt they had done well and made "quite definite and important progress" on Constitutional questions. " ... [I]f only people at home had a true sense of their interests they would seize the opportunity of next year's election to steam-roll the Irregular elements and go full steam ahead for a United Ireland and a Dual Monarchy ... all this lopping off of old forms and abandonment of old claims which has gone on for the last month has left a clear open avenue to that solution if only—if only we had a smaller percentage of bloody fools in our population ..."[38] O'Higgins, accompanied by Costello, went to a function at one of the Inns of Court specifically to meet Edward Carson in order to sound him out on the idea. Costello later claimed to believe that had O'Higgins lived, "Partition would have ended before 1932."[39]

There was plenty in the final report of the Conference for the Irish to be happy about. One recommended change was a simple comma. The King's Title referred to him being ruler "of the United Kingdom of Great Britain and Ireland and of the British Dominions beyond the seas" and so on. The Conference recommended the removal of an 'and' and addition of a comma, so the title would read "Great Britain, Ireland and the British Dominions beyond the Seas".[40] Dominions Secretary Leo Amery later recalled "O'Higgins's persuasive advocacy of the comma and I agreed with his general outlook. I was entirely prepared to accept the wording which indicated the historical difference between Ireland and the younger members of the Commonwealth and at the same time left the door open to eventual Irish unity."[41] The Conference also accepted the Irish view of the role of the Governor General, who was no longer to be the representative of the British Government but only of the King. In consequence, he would no longer be the channel of communication between the British and Dominion Governments.[42]

On the Privy Council, the Irish summary of proceedings recorded the British agreement that judicial appeals should be dealt with as the Dominion concerned wished. It also noted that the Irish Free State did not press for an immediate change, "though it was made clear that the right was reserved to bring up the matter again at the next Imperial Conference"—a conclusion that would be challenged by the British, as we shall see below.

But by far the most important conclusion related to Dominion status. The Balfour formula (named after the chairman of the Committee on Inter-Imperial Relations, Arthur Balfour) defined their position and mutual relations as follows: "They are autonomous Communities within the British Empire, equal in status, in no way subordinate one to another in any aspect of their domestic or external affairs, though united by a common allegiance to the Crown, and freely associated as members of the British Commonwealth of Nations."[43] Historian David Harkness wrote that the Declaration was, to the Irish, "of no importance: worse still, it was a distraction from the real issues".[44] This may have been the Irish attitude at the time—but the number of times the Declaration was cited in later years in various tussles with the British suggests that it turned out to be extremely useful.

As Costello later wrote, "The legal bonds which formerly bound together the fabric of the old Colonial Empire were to be entirely removed. The doctrine of the supremacy of the Parliament at Westminster and the para-mount power of its Statute Law was placed under sentence of elimination".[45] He quoted O'Higgins's words to members of the Delegation who felt more could have been achieved: "It is not the pace that matters, but the direction. It's a long game, and I would like to see it played out."[46] O'Higgins, of course, would not live to see the end of his long game—but Jack Costello would, playing a key part along the way. The first task was to ensure that the British lived up to the agreement.

Attention now switched to the wider international arena. The first test of the supposed equality of Dominions came with a conference in Geneva on the limitation of naval armaments. Clearly the Free State had no interest in the subject matter of the conference—but it had every interest in asserting its international status. Dublin advised London in March 1927 that if the Commonwealth states could not be represented individually, it would be better for the Dominions to abstain from the Conference altogether.[47] Dominions Secretary Leo Amery agreed that each Government would be able to appoint "a separate delegate who would hold a separate full power from His Majesty the King ... to negotiate ..."[48] However, it was only after further Irish pressure that he agreed that the British delegation's Full Power would be limited to the territory of the United Kingdom and the Colonies, rather than covering the Dominions as well. As Joe Walshe pointed out, "for the first time—if they are held to their agreement—the British will sign an international instrument of a purely political character on a basis of complete equality with the Dominions".[49] Given the important constitutional issues involved, Costello was named as a delegate, along with FitzGerald as Minister for External Affairs.[50]

In the event, FitzGerald was replaced as Minister for External Affairs by Kevin O'Higgins on 23 June, just four days before the Irish delegation arrived at the conference. They went, in Costello's words, "to represent at a Naval Conference a country without a Navy".[51] O'Higgins's first call in Geneva was to the head of the British delegation, First Lord of the Admiralty William Bridgeman. He explained that Irish interest in the conference "was mainly, if not entirely, based on Constitutional considerations", and that so long as its constitutional position was "rigidly respected and safeguarded" the Free State would back British technical proposals. Bridgeman agreed with O'Higgins's conclusion that "nothing should be done during the Conference to obscure in any way the exclusive right of the representatives of each State of the Commonwealth to accept responsibilities ... for ... their own Government".[52]

O'Higgins expressed frustration with the Canadians and South Africans, who "will only fight in support of us. They have not yet learned to take a stand on their own and in any case they only see things when they are pointed out to them." However, he grudgingly admitted that "they played up well enough yesterday—under tuition".[53] One Irish success related to the naval quotas to be agreed at the Conference. The British wanted a single quota, rather than one for each Commonwealth member, presumably so they could use any spare capacity. O'Higgins was happy enough with this proposal, but persuaded the Canadians to back his suggestion that instead of a quota for the "British Empire", it should be for the sum total of "all the States Members of the British Commonwealth", in order to stress their status as individual states. The Irish also forced the British to have a reference to the British Empire removed from the minutes of the Executive Committee. As Joe Walshe noted, "All this shows the necessity for careful watching of all subsequent proceedings ..."[54]

Having explained the Free State's constitutional position "to a roomful of British Admirals, Commanders of Submarines, Gunners and other experts", O'Higgins felt his work was done, and "relaxed and freely discussed his hopes and future plans" with Costello and the rest of the delegation.[55] He wrote to his wife that he was "feeling much less the leavings of an election campaign than I was four days ago. I rout out Walshe and Costello at 6.45 every morning and we swim in the lake before breakfast." They also enjoyed a day trip to the nearby ski resort of Chamonix, where they took a cable car up to the Alps. "Literally our heads were in the clouds—all round about us snow clad peaks glittering in the sun and Chamonix like a toy village down below."[56] But, despite the attractions of a short holiday, O'Higgins decided to return home early to get back to his work in Dublin.[57]

In his absence, Costello and Walshe went to a meeting of the Credentials Committee, taking advantage of its informality to sneak a look at the British Full Power "without appearing to have any definite object in view. The Power is in proper form and is restricted territorially according to their agreement with us."[58] Clearly the Irish were not taking any chances. But having made their point, and checked up on British bona fides, the work in Geneva was done. Costello went to a couple of meetings, but didn't speak, before leaving for home.[59] O'Higgins, meanwhile, had paid a high price for his early return. He left Geneva on 5 July,[60] apparently spending two days with Hazel Lavery in London on his way home.[61] After he returned to Dublin he was gunned down on his way to Mass, with political and legal consequences examined in the previous chapter.

Costello was to return to Geneva in the autumn, as Primary Irish Delegate to the Assembly of the League of Nations. McGilligan, the new Minister for External Affairs, was originally named as the leader of the delegation,[62] but the September election made it impossible for him to go. With Costello were the Irish Representative to the League, Michael MacWhite, Diarmuid O'Hegarty and Joe Walshe. The Irish had already been quite active in the League of Nations, registering the Treaty there in 1924 against British opposition— Dublin held it was obliged to register the Treaty as it was an international agreement, while the British took the view that it was an internal matter between two members of the Commonwealth. The Irish had also sought a seat on the Council of the League in 1926, again against British wishes. The point of this was not simply to prove that Britain did not speak for all the Commonwealth members, but also to vindicate the right of small League members to representation. As Desmond FitzGerald put it, "We not only defended Dominion rights but also countries like Austria, Hungary, Bulgaria, Abyssinia, etc. We got the ten votes with British against us ... I am quite satisfied that we could have been elected with a proper canvass in good time."[63]

In advance of the 1927 Assembly, Walshe suggested another run for the Council. "Only the actual election of another Commonwealth State [i.e. apart from Britain] to the Council will make our independent status in the League apparent at home and abroad."[64] It was agreed that the Free State should go forward unless the Canadians decided to do so.[65] Costello was a member of the Assembly's First Committee, which dealt with constitutional and legal questions. But apart from being appointed to a sub-committee looking into the question of international arbitration,[66] Costello made little impact, and the Irish candidacy for the Council was withdrawn in favour of the Canadians.

Costello was back for the following year's Assembly, as part of a much higher-powered delegation, led by Vice-President Ernest Blythe, and including FitzGerald, now Minister for Defence, and Education Minister John

Marcus O'Sullivan.[67] The First Committee again focused on the question of international arbitration, with Costello strongly backing a proposal for a General Act of the League, claiming that "a great step would have been taken in the development of arbitration throughout the world if that draft should be adopted".[68] The British delegate argued that a General Act, rather than a less binding Convention, would be "a source of danger to the League", but the draft supported by Costello was passed by the Assembly with no substantial modification.[69] The contrasting Irish and British attitudes to international arbitration were a forerunner of a more serious dispute the following year.

In letters home to his wife, Desmond FitzGerald grumbled that his committee sat in the afternoons, while Costello and the other delegates were free from lunchtime, having sat in the mornings.[70] It is unlikely, however, that FitzGerald was short of social diversion. He had written home in 1926 that "shyness is not a feature of diplomatic women—on the first meeting one may easily learn how often their husbands perform with them or how they like it done".[71] Such considerations seem unlikely to have occurred to the other members of the delegation. Michael MacWhite, the permanent representative to the League, was more concerned with the image of Ireland at Geneva. He complained that "the voice of the Saorstát has been scarcely heard in the Reformation Hall". A similar reticence was evident in the various committees, although he charitably gave the Irish members credit for exercising influence "in conversations with other delegates, in supporting proposals corresponding to our ideas and by a discriminating use of the vote ... In the long run, however, it is only those States whose representatives participate actively and openly in the general work of the Assembly who count ..." He advised another run for a Council seat when Canada's term expired in 1930, arguing that Irish chances would be boosted if it were to sign the Optional Clause of the Permanent Court of International Justice[72]—a question that was to dominate the 1929 Assembly.

The Optional Clause committed signatories to submit international disputes to the compulsory jurisdiction of the Permanent Court of International Justice. The Court, which sat at The Hague, had been provided for in the Covenant of the League. It was inaugurated in 1922, and dissolved in 1946, when it was succeeded by the International Court of Justice.[73] In 1924, Ramsay MacDonald's first Labour Government made moves towards accepting the Court's compulsory jurisdiction, although there were concerns about the British Empire's position in time of war.[74] The matter was shelved when the Tories came back to power, and at the 1926 Imperial Conference it was agreed that none of the Governments represented there would accept compulsory jurisdiction "without bringing up the matter for further discussion".[75]

However, shortly after resuming office in June 1929, MacDonald informed the Dominions that he felt it was time to accept the Court's jurisdiction, although he made it clear that Britain would sign with reservations.[76] These included the exclusion of disputes either submitted to or under consideration by the Council of the League. The British felt this would allow them to avoid making a specific reservation about disputes between belligerents at sea, as such disputes would inevitably come before the League Council. They also rejected as unnecessary an Australian suggestion that disputes between members of the Commonwealth should be excluded. The British held that "the declaration only accepts the jurisdiction in international disputes".[77] In other words, the British still did not accept the full sovereignty of the Dominions. McGilligan said the Free State wished to sign with as few reservations as possible. He also pointed out that the conclusions of the 1926 conference did not imply that a general agreement was needed before a member of the Commonwealth could sign.[78]

The Irish believed the British were intent on reviving what was called the *inter se* doctrine. This phrase, literally meaning "between or among themselves", held that disputes between members of the Commonwealth were internal, rather than international. They also objected to the British proposal to restrict jurisdiction to matters arising after ratification—which would obviously exclude disputes relating to interpretation of the Treaty.[79]

A lengthy memorandum by Costello outlined the sequence of events in Geneva. MacDonald managed to offend many of the Dominions at a meeting of the British Commonwealth delegations on 1 September, using language which "generally assumed paternal responsibility for all the Commonwealth Delegations. This attitude caused obvious resentment on the part of Canada, South Africa and ourselves and even on the part of Australia." The British subsequently blamed MacDonald's faux pas on his unfamiliarity with the Dominion position, but it was a bad start. The Prime Minister wanted to make an announcement at the League Assembly that Britain and all the Dominions had decided to sign the Optional Clause, believing this would "have a tremendous moral and psychological effect ... He appeared to be tremendously anxious to create somewhat of a stir by his announcement ..." McGilligan quickly put a stop to this suggestion. He also objected to the proposed British wording for acceding to the Optional Clause, claiming it had been designed to exclude intra-Commonwealth disputes from the jurisdiction of the Court. This was stoutly denied by MacDonald, who called in the Foreign Office legal adviser, Sir Cecil Hurst, to explain. To the Prime Minister's evident discomfort, Hurst confirmed that the Irish suspicions had been absolutely correct.[80] While Hurst's attitude came as a surprise to MacDonald, the Irish were well aware of his views. The previous March, he had argued at the League of Nations Committee of Jurists that disputes between two Dominions could not be brought before the court as they "were not international".[81]

A major disagreement ensued on whether Dominion disputes should or could be referred to the Court. The Irish delegates outlined their political problems—it would be portrayed as a surrender of sovereignty if they gave away even a theoretical right to bring a dispute with Britain to the Permanent Court. At McGilligan's suggestion, a sub-committee of Costello, Hurst, the South African Eric Louw, and the Australian Sir William Harrison Moore was set up to look at what sort of acceptable alternative to the Permanent Court could be established to deal with Commonwealth disputes. Having first cleared his suggestion with Costello, Louw proposed that the members of the Commonwealth should agree not to refer any disputes to the Permanent Court pending the next Imperial Conference.[82]

The matter was then referred to a full meeting of the Commonwealth delegations. The British suggested they should make a statement indicating that the reservations they attached to their signing of the Optional Clause had no effect on the international standing of the Dominions established at the 1926 Imperial Conference. Costello pointed out that nobody had suggested the British were trying to repudiate the 1926 Conference, and that their pro-posed statement was "in essence an insult to the British Government under their own hands". The Foreign Secretary, Arthur Henderson, "at this stage got greatly annoyed and stated that the British Government were entitled to insult themselves if they liked".[83] It wasn't the last time Costello would get under the skin of a British Labour politician.

Faced with this impasse, the Irish decided to go ahead and sign the Optional Clause without reservations. Costello advised that the British should be given as little notice as possible, "so that they would not be in a position to make an effort to obtain a group signature". McGilligan signed at 3.30 p.m. on Saturday 14 September 1929.[84] Having concluded their work in Geneva, Costello and McGilligan now turned their attention back to London, where an attempt was to be made to tease out some of the technical issues left over from the Imperial Conference of 1926.

Chaired by the Dominions Secretary, Lord Passfield (formerly Sidney Webb), the official title of the meeting was the Conference on the Operation of Dominion Legislation and Merchant Shipping Legislation. It opened on 8 October and finished on 4 December—a long time, but valuable from the Irish perspective because it set the ground for the 1930 Conference and the 1931 Statute of Westminster. McGilligan led the Irish delegation, with Costello in a very prominent role, along with O'Hegarty, Walshe and Hearne.[85] The Irish once again refused the British offer of hospitality during the conference.[86]

As John Hearne observed in advance of the conference, the merchant shipping legislation and the Colonial Laws Validity Act "illustrate the system which is now obsolescent better than any other statutes that we know". The

1894 Merchant Shipping Act limited the power of a Dominion to alter the Act, requiring the King's permission before changes were made.[87] The practical effect was that the Free State had been unable to legislate in this area, and while the tricolour was flown on Irish ships, it was not legally recognised.[88]

On the eve of the conference, Costello wrote to Education Minister John Marcus O'Sullivan reporting on meetings with the South African and Canadian delegations. The former were "quite sound on all points" and "were entirely *ad idem* with us". They agreed that everything contrary to the declaration of equality agreed in 1926 must go: reservation (under which Dominion legislation couldn't come into force until the British had approved it); the Colonial Laws Validity Act; restrictions on extraterritorial and shipping legislation. He was agreeably surprised by the Canadians: "Their attitude is more satisfactory than we ever dared to hope for. If they stick to their present intentions we ought to have a clean sweep." There was one potential fly in the ointment, though, which Costello explained with typical hyperbole. The British wanted special arrangements under which all Dominion Parliaments would agree on certain matters, such as the succession to the Crown. As Costello explained, the Irish had a difficulty with the provision relating to the religion of the monarch (who could not be a Catholic). But the Canadians said "if that point is raised by us they must go home at once. At a recent provincial election a Liberal Government was swept out of office in a Liberal Province by a Ku Klux Klan performance on a religious issue, of less importance than the religion of the King." The Canadians feared a political backlash at the next Federal election if religion became a Commonwealth issue, and Costello felt that as they "are so friendly and so intent on making constitutional advances we cannot afford to put them in a hole politically".[89]

The British too had their problems, and just over a week after the opening of the Conference, Passfield called an emergency meeting of Heads of Delegation. He warned that unless he received assurances on certain issues, he would have to advise his Cabinet the following week "that there was no likelihood of a unanimous report emerging from the main Conference". His intervention was sparked by discussions that convinced him he couldn't "join in the recommendations that were obviously in the minds of certain of the Dominion delegations". The key difficulty concerned the Crown—he wanted the report to confirm the maintenance of the existing legislative structure, and to promise consultation between all Dominions if any change was proposed.[90] The Irish delegation felt they should not jeopardise the report by "making trouble" on the issues involved, "provided the British proposals ... are not substantially altered for the worse", and this approach was approved by the Executive Council.[91]

Costello's main role was on the committee looking at the Colonial Laws Validity Act. The Committee was named after its chairman, Sir Maurice

Gwyer, the British Procurator General and Treasury Solicitor (a senior legal advisor to the Government). At the first meeting, the minutes recorded the general view that the parliament of a Dominion should not be given power to alter the fundamental provisions of its constitution. Costello wrote on the minutes that both he and the South African delegate had objected to this statement, but their objections were not noted.[92] Three days after this first meeting, Gwyer produced a draft of the law which would become the Statute of Westminster. He included a provision excluding Dominion Parliaments from amending their constitutions.[93] This was clearly going to be a major source of tension between the Irish and South Africans and the rest.

Diarmuid O'Hegarty reported to Dublin that progress on various issues, such as shipping, extraterritoriality and reservation, was "rather satisfactory". But in relation to the Gwyer Committee, he pointed out that while the Colonial Laws Validity Act would be repealed, three matters had not been settled: the reference to the Crown; the amendment of Dominion constitutions; and the suggestion of a Commonwealth Court. He explained the British worry that with reservation and the Colonial Laws Validity Act gone, the Irish "could repeal any law of the Imperial Parliament in so far as it relates to us, including the laws relating to the Crown". The British viewed the Treaty as being based on British law (a view the Irish did not accept, as they saw it as an agreement between two states) and therefore vulnerable to amendment in the new dispensation.[94] Costello, then, was in a central position, dealing with the most contentious issues facing the Irish.

On 12 November Costello flatly rejected a British proposal for a permanent Commonwealth Court to arbitrate in disputes between governments. To his fellow lawyers on the Committee, he poked fun at judges in general: "We must leave a Permanent Court out of mind. How would a Permanent Court consisting of judges set to work? We all know what judges are, how they spread themselves and deliver judicial homilies, but I cannot say judicious homilies."[95] However, he said he would consider an *ad hoc* body of at least five members.

Two days later, he raised the issue of the King's religion—which the Canadians had claimed would lead to them walking out of the conference and going home (it didn't). He explained to his colleagues that if his Government had to introduce legislation relating to the religion of the King it would "inevitably raise a religious discussion". He argued that instead of legislation, there should be a declaration of the Imperial Conference that the succession would not be altered without the consent of all the Dominions. The Australian delegate, Sir William Harrison Moore, objected that this would not be enough, as any Dominion could simply legislate to remove the Crown entirely. To which Costello replied, foreshadowing de Valera's introduction of the External Relations Act, and his own repeal of it, "Then you just walk out of the Commonwealth ..." The South Africans indicated their view that they already had the right to secede. Gwyer complained that Costello's proposal would create seven Crowns, one in each of the Dominions, rather than the "one undivided unified Crown" which the British believed existed for the whole Commonwealth.[96] This was precisely the principle the Irish were trying to establish—a "several" rather than a unitary Crown, to recognise the complete independence of the members of the Commonwealth.

At a further session, Costello claimed the Irish were taking "a big political risk in going into this question of an agreement relating to the Crown". In return, they wanted to be sure that there would be no exceptions to the repeal of the Colonial Laws Validity Act—that all of the Dominions would have the right to repeal any British statute which had been passed applying to them. He said the Free State could repeal its constitution in its entirety, but that the Treaty would remain, a document which had for them "a certain sacredness, as those who have followed events in the Irish Free State during the past few years must know" (which would not be much consolation to the British if the opponents of that document came to power). Rather than a "rigid" and "formal" legal approach, the Irish sought uniformity through agreement and reciprocal action. He had made a number of suggestions to Gwyer the previous evening about how the draft Bill (the future Statute of Westminster) should be drawn up. Gwyer said he "was impressed by his views, and I think we could put down something ... designed to meet points discussed between Mr Costello and myself last night".[97]

This co-operative atmosphere disappeared very quickly, however, after the publication of a document following a Heads of Delegation meeting on 17 November which stated that the report would be an experts' report only. At the following day's session of the Gwyer Committee, Costello claimed this meant they were precluded from considering political questions at all. "The Irish delegation were prepared to make agreements upon the Crown and any other matters that might call for an agreement. We were prepared to give way here and there for the sake of getting an agreed report. But if this is to be an experts' report merely, I will not take part in discussion of any single topic that is of a political character." The Canadian Oscar Skelton agreed that it was "a preposterous document, radically erroneous and impossible of acceptance by us".[98]

When Gwyer suggested continuing with the work, and allowing the conference to make the decisions, Costello testily replied, "We have met the British Government everywhere, and at every stage when an agreement seemed to be in sight something was done—I do not say deliberately—but something was definitely done which prevented agreement from being arrived at." He went on to accuse the British of "stirring up religious war ... I would not have it on the records of my Department that I had signed a document ... related to the Crown and yet did not raise the question of the religion of the King at all. Surely, Sir Maurice, you realise what would be said ..." He agreed to Gwyer's suggestion that they continue, in the legal phrase, "without prejudice", but observed that they were further away from agreement on certain issues than they had been a few days before.[99]

The Committee then moved on to consider a British proposal that the final report should contain an undertaking that the Free State regarded the terms of the Treaty (or "Articles of Agreement" as the British insisted on calling it) "as so fundamental in character as to be inviolable and beyond the scope of the ordinary law". Costello again dug his heels in, saying McGilligan would not be prepared to sign a report containing this provision. He was again supported by Skelton. Costello also objected to what he saw as a suggestion that the Free State Constitution derived from an Imperial statute. He said the relevant paragraph was unacceptable—and so the Committee agreed to defer discussion on its application to the Free State.[100]

The day's discussions ended with nationality—a question which Costello observed with commendable understatement "has been causing us a certain amount of difficulty for 700 years or so". He rehearsed the Irish case that they were "a mother country, an unadulterated nation". He referred to the difficulties they had with the British regarding passports. London wanted the expression "British subject" used; Dublin felt "Irish national" was sufficient. Costello insisted that separate nationality must be recognised, arguing that if someone qualified as an Irish national, then the status of "British subject" would be implicit in that. He also used the analogy of shipping. The Conference had heard suggestions of a common status of ships registered in the various ports of the Commonwealth—could something similar not be done for nationality?[101]

Gwyer returned to the paragraph relating to constitutional change two days later, asking Costello if he had any alternative to propose, but the Irish Attorney General stonewalled, saying the "time has not come for me to make any suggestion ... I have already indicated my views on that paragraph." However, despite what might have been seen as an obdurate approach, it was Costello who was asked by Gwyer to draw up a rough draft of the matters that had been agreed. He said he would, but took another pot shot at the British, claiming there had been a lack of clarity in previous drafts that caused confusion. When the British suggested there had been a moment when the delegates had been in agreement, Costello replied, "On which of the five drafts?"[102]

The final draft specifically excluded the right to amend the constitutions of Canada, Australia and New Zealand[103]—but crucially did not extend the exclusion to the Free State or South Africa, an omission that would later be challenged by Winston Churchill, as we will see below. On the proposed Commonwealth Court, the Gwyer Committee recommended further discussion, but again agreed with the Irish view that it should be an *ad hoc*, rather than permanent, tribunal, and that it should be limited to disputes between governments.[104] In other words, it would not be the Privy Council by another means. At the final session of the main conference, at which the report was agreed, McGilligan paid tribute to the work of the Gwyer Committee, which he said had the most difficult task of all those set up by the Conference. The Irish Minister also hailed the progress of equality and free association, saying the obstructions to co-operation "were removed as far as principles are concerned by the Report of 1926, and removed in detail by the Report we now have before us, and when that Report comes to be accepted next year at the Imperial Conference it will, I think, prove very definitely to be the last remaining obstacle to the freest co-operation with all the members of the British Commonwealth of Nations".[105] The report, according to David Harkness, "was both an end and a beginning. It marked the destruction of the old Empire as well as the creation of the new Commonwealth."[106]

As the 1930 Imperial Conference approached, the British circulated a detailed agenda, covering a wide range of issues, including trade, agriculture, research, statistics, transport, communications and overseas settlement. Joe Walshe noted with considerable suspicion that the agenda "is drawn up on a much more comprehensive scale than has ever before been attempted, and it gives the definite impression that some sort of centralisation on the economic side is to be attempted". He advised an urgent critical examination of the proposals.[107] As Attorney General, Costello was closely involved, with Walshe forwarding him an economic policy document from the Federation of British Industries before it was sent to ministers.[108] He was not, however, a member of the official delegation, which was made up of McGilligan, FitzGerald and Agriculture Minister Patrick Hogan.[109] Cosgrave's possible attendance was left open,[110] but in the event he was ill at the time of the Conference (he complained to McGilligan that he had been sick in bed for four days, although it appears he was suffering from nothing worse than a bad cold).[111]

The Irish were interested in constitutional, rather than economic, matters. Some weeks before the Conference opened, McGilligan wrote to Dominions Secretary Jimmy Thomas outlining the issues he wanted brought up. He was particularly forthright about the Privy Council: "The existence of an extra-State institution claiming without any form of democratic sanction to exercise jurisdiction in the ... internal affairs of the Irish Free State remains a menace to our sovereignty." The Irish were also concerned at the lack of direct access to the King for Dominions, believing that advice to the monarch should come direct from the government concerned, not through the British.

They wanted to clarify the *inter se* applicability of treaties to remove any misconception that the members of the Commonwealth constituted a single sovereign State. And they wanted direct communication with foreign governments, rather than having to go through the Foreign Office in London. McGilligan concluded that "the elimination of the foregoing difficulties at the Conference will allow the delegates to examine with freer minds the important economic problems which are listed for their consideration".[112]

A confidential briefing note from the Department of External Affairs for the delegates put direct access to the King at the top of their concerns, because "the defective channel of access is at the root of all the difficulties in the way of the external self-expression of the Dominions". Royal approval for diplomatic documents was only given after a British Secretary of State signified his agreement—which naturally led foreign governments to see the Commonwealth as "an organic unit" rather than a collection of independent, sovereign states. The obvious solution was to have such documents issued in the name of the Governor General rather than the King—but the Irish recognised this would "perhaps be too much to expect the British to accept", and suggested that the Dominion High Commissioner in London should convey his government's advice directly to the King, without going through the British Government. The briefing also highlighted nationality (the Irish wanted to eliminate the description "British subject", while at the same time ensuring that Dominion nationals obtained all the rights and privileges enjoyed by British subjects) and the Privy Council, "the only operative Imperial institution which can be said to make of the Commonwealth a legal and constitutional unit, as distinct from the Diplomatic Unit created by the unified control of the King's external acts ..."[113] Finally, the Irish wanted to ensure that when negotiating treaties, the British Government did not "purport to act for the nationals of all the members of the Commonwealth", as this would imply the Commonwealth was a single sovereign state.[114]

The South African Prime Minister, General Hertzog, believed the forthcoming Conference should, and would, confirm the right of Dominions to secede from the Commonwealth. He regarded such confirmation as a test of constitutional liberty—if the Dominions truly were free, they should be free to leave the Commonwealth. Joe Walshe believed such a declaration would be "the logical result of all that the Irish Free State has been urging" in relation to the Commonwealth. He also suggested that such a declaration "would enable the Irish Free State to get out of Articles 1 and 2 of the Treaty without laying herself open to the charge of having broken them". Article 1 gave the Free State the same constitutional status in the Commonwealth as the other Dominions, while Article 2 stipulated that it would have the same relationship to the Crown as Canada. However, Walshe went on to point out that even if Ireland was able to "get out" of the first two articles in this way, it wasn't clear whether the rest of the Treaty—for instance Article 7 on defence—would stand.[115]

The Conference opened on 1 October 1930, with British Prime Minister Ramsay MacDonald in the Chair. In his opening statement, McGilligan once again stressed the importance of constitutional issues. "For us the recognition of our position as a free and sovereign State comes before all other considerations ... While certain elements of the old system of Imperial control were maintained, even though it was only in form, the will to co-operate was correspondingly weakened ... I should not be frank with you if at this juncture I did not definitely place before you in what seems to my Government to be the proper perspective the considerations which should govern the proceedings of this Conference."[116]

Abolition of appeals to the Privy Council was to prove one of the most contentious of these items. McGilligan was ingenious in his arguments, suggesting that retention of the appeal helped opponents of the Treaty, negated the 1926 declaration of autonomy, and did nothing to help Southern loyalists. The latter, he argued, had eight years' experience of the Free State, and "have suffered no indignities and no injustice".[117] In response, the British claimed that Article 2 of the Treaty, which said the Free State's relationship to the Crown would be the same as that of Canada, meant that it would be the same as Canada's had been in 1921.[118] In other words, any advances secured by the Canadians after that date would not apply to the Irish.

It is difficult to believe the British actually meant this seriously, particularly as the Lord Chancellor, John Sankey, had the previous year delivered a landmark Privy Council decision in a Canadian case which established the "living tree doctrine". This holds that a constitution is organic and must be read in a broad and liberal manner so as to adapt it to changing times.[119] The British were attempting to establish one law for the Canadian goose, and another for the Irish gander. Costello was well aware that this trick had been tried before—the previous year, he had sought the advice of Chief Justice Hugh Kennedy on a number of matters raised at the Gwyer Committee. Kennedy had advised him that during the discussions in London on the draft Free State Constitution in May and June 1922, the British tried "to pin us to the old out of date Canadian text ... the result of our stand of Michael Collins' 'quality' was a complete climb down on their part and a ... full admission of our right to the benefit of every constitutional advance made by Canada ..." He added that the British also tried unsuccessfully to include in the Free State Constitution "the now purely technical limitations on the amendment of the Canadian constitution"—another issue that would be raised again in 1930.[120]

Costello accompanied McGilligan to a meeting of Heads of Delegations on 6 October, at which British Attorney General Sir William Jowitt argued that the Treaty meant the Irish were in a different situation to the other Dominions. "The matter was therefore one of contract, part of a bargain then entered into. He could not see how a contract could be derogatory to status ..." McGilligan pointed out that even if the Privy Council appeal was in the Treaty (which he didn't accept), it could be abolished in the same way as reservation was going to be abolished. Thomas rejected this view. If that was their position, Costello asked, why had the British not objected to the Irish Land Act of 1926 (which, as we have seen, circumvented a Privy Council decision) as also being contrary to the Treaty? Thomas weakly replied that the lack of protest didn't mean they acquiesced in either the Land Act or in legislation to remove the appeal.[121]

Other matters, meanwhile, had been referred to a committee under Sankey—advice to the King, the appointment of Governors General, and the issue of diplomatic documents.[122] As Desmond FitzGerald observed, "practically all the substantial points" were referred to it. "It is called a legal committee, no doubts because most of its members will not be lawyers."[123] In fact the initial name, the "Politico-Legal Committee", was changed to the more descriptive "Committee on Certain Aspects of Inter-Imperial Relations".[124] While McGilligan made most of the running on this committee as well as in the Conference, Costello played a useful supporting role. On the question of treaties, he attacked the existing practice, claiming it implied that the Commonwealth was "contracting as one party irrespective of the autonomy of the separate members of the Commonwealth ... unless and until that implication was definitely put on one side there would always be the liability of friction in the future".[125] When the protection of minority rights was raised as a reason for retaining the Privy Council appeal, Costello told Sankey that no-one in Ireland made that argument; it was only put forward in England.[126]

The Irish were less than impressed with the performance of the British. Desmond FitzGerald complained that MacDonald and Thomas "were badly briefed ... with myself and P. McG. [McGilligan] acting as technical advisers to the whole lot".[127] On another occasion, he observed, they "had (or pretended to have) the wrong end of the stick. I told them that I had dealt with the matter in 26 and what the circumstances were. MacDonald said I was wrong and proceeded to prove it by reading from the report—and landed on a sentence that proved what I said. That sort of thing happens constantly— and makes them irritable ..."[128] They took a particularly dim view of Jimmy Thomas, who was "legendary for his tactlessness, his indiscretion, his volatility and his bright, breezy vulgarity. He was also notorious for newspaper leaks, drinking, gambling and snobbery. In a prim, staid government where these qualities were in short supply, Thomas stood out, beloved by many (including the King) and loathed by others, including most of the dominion prime ministers."[129] After one conversation with the

Dominions Secretary, FitzGerald reported he "heard more blasphemy and general bad language than for a long time. 'Bloody' was general ..."[130] Thomas was incredibly tactless; Irish diplomat Freddie Boland recorded that he went up to Sir Samuel Hoare at a garden party in Buckingham Palace and asking him how "Lady W" was. The response, if any, was sadly not recorded.[131]

As well as the conference work, there was the usual round of social engagements, including a dinner at Buckingham Palace. Having recovered from the "bad shock" of a missing pair of breeches (which were found),[132] FitzGerald reported that the Irish delegation "ostentatiously fasted ... as we felt that it was bad form for them to have had it on a Friday". The fasting was purely for effect—they ordered up tea and rolls as soon as they got back to their hotel.[133] There were less formal pursuits too, including ice-skating, where FitzGerald amused himself by talking to a young woman. "Of course the others were all tickled. I should have preferred if she had been better looking and more amusing—brighter. But we got on terms that nearly produced her life history ..."[134] It is highly unlikely that John A. Costello spent his time chatting up young women—in any case, his wife joined him for at least part of the time in London. With a characteristic mixture of elitism and self-satisfaction, FitzGerald wrote home after a conversation with her, "Mrs Costello a bit of a bore—but I get on all right I think ..."[135]

As October drew to a close, Sankey prepared a draft report, to which the Irish vehemently objected. They rejected the suggestion that international conventions would not apply between members of the Commonwealth (unless they specifically agreed that they should apply), feeling it implied that the Commonwealth was "a single sovereign State".[136] But the most serious issue was nationality, which Costello later said "caused more bitterness between this country and the British Government ... than any topic discussed from 1926 to 1930".[137] McGilligan told a meeting of heads of delegations that Sankey's suggested formula was "politically impossible". The Lord Chancellor had proposed the wording "Every national of the Irish Free State is hereby declared to possess the common status of a subject of His Majesty by virtue of the allegiance which he owes to His Majesty as a national of the Irish Free State." The Irish were seeking a recognition that Irish nationality sprang from its own nationhood, but that it could be reconciled with common status under the Commonwealth. The British took a strong line against the Irish, with MacDonald accusing them of proposing to "sweep away the basis on which the common status rested ... if it became non-existent for one, it would become non-existent for all".[138]

Frustrated at the failure to deal with the Privy Council question, McGilligan and FitzGerald went to MacDonald to insist that it be raised, "as it was a matter of vital importance".[139] But at the following day's meeting of heads of delegations, MacDonald requested a postponement so that he could gauge opinion in the House of Commons. He observed that two of the key participants in the 1926 conference were now dead (i.e. O'Higgins and Birkenhead), and he asked McGilligan "to give him a statement which would strengthen his hand when he saw the leaders of the Opposition".[140] McGilligan duly wrote a letter, explaining that the Irish agreed not to pursue the Privy Council matter in 1926, after Birkenhead "urged strongly that we should not then press it to a conclusion, as he had already taken great political risks through the support he had given us and as a certain section of his party were filled with distrust of our every action ... If Mr O'Higgins would agree to that, he, Lord Birkenhead, would promise him the full weight of his support when the matter was brought up at the next Imperial Conference."[141]

The principals were dead, but there were two other witnesses who attended the breakfast meeting in Birkenhead's house. They were the English and Irish Attorneys General at the time, Sir Douglas Hogg and John A. Costello. The latter, of course, was still in office and at the 1930 Conference; the former, now Lord Hailsham, was in opposition. The Irish were convinced—correctly, it would appear—that MacDonald, Sankey and Thomas were "in constant consultation" with Hailsham. MacDonald even passed a note to McGilligan suggesting that Hailsham should be invited to join the discussion in Downing Street so that he could state what had taken place in 1926. The Irish Minister, believing the Conservative was being invited "for the purpose of arguing Article 2 of the Treaty against the Irish Free State delegates", rejected the suggestion.[142]

MacDonald reported the following day that he had met Baldwin and Hailsham, who insisted that the Free State had given guarantees to Britain about the rights of the minority, including the right to appeal to the Privy Council against a decision of the Irish courts. The Prime Minister said the Opposition would oppose the Statute of Westminster on the grounds that it would allow the Free State to abolish the appeal without agreement. McGilligan replied angrily that it was "monstrous" to suggest abolition of the appeal would break the Treaty. Sankey said nobody wanted to go back on what had been agreed in 1926, but equality of status did not entitle the Free State to break the Treaty. McGilligan pointed out that the cases so far referred to the Judicial Committee had nothing to do with southern Loyalists—one involved a Swedish paper company, another unemployment insurance (see Chapter 3). He said, "the acid test of the sincerity of the 1926 declarations was the question of appeals ... If they had not the freedom which had been given to all the rest, the consequences were going to be very serious."[143]

FitzGerald described the meeting as "appalling. Massed British guns directed on us ... Faced with dishonesty, treachery and cowardice." The one bright spot was the support of Australia's Scullin and Hertzog of South Africa. "Thomas completely dishonest and treacherous. Ramsay contemptible ... Tody [McGilligan] told off old Sankey so much in the morning that he did not appear in the afternoon. Probably told that his presence might annoy us."[144] Even more likely to annoy the Irish delegates was the Lord Chancellor's attempt to outflank them with an indirect approach to Cosgrave. At the opening of Parliament on 28 October he had met Lord Granard (who, as we saw in Chapter 3, was a member of the Irish Senate as well as the House of Lords) and asked him to convey a proposal to the President.[145] Sankey suggested that the Irish introduce legislation to abolish the appeal, "on the understanding that the British Government would not take any steps to oppose it". Cosgrave sent Michael McDunphy, the Assistant Secretary to the Executive Council, to London to confer with the delegation, who viewed the move as "a dishonest attempt to sidetrack the official delegation". McGilligan felt the Government would be bound to bring in legislation after the Conference, "irrespective of what action the British Government were disposed to take in the matter".[146] Cosgrave duly informed Granard that "he was very reluctant to interfere with Mr McGilligan, and that, if he did interfere, it would only be to stiffen the hands of the latter, that members of the Council at home held very strong views".[147]

Diarmuid O'Hegarty, in London with the delegation, evidently held very strong views too. He urged "an extremely stiff front ... Sankey is entirely untrustworthy." He added that the argument that the Treaty was "static" was "the most serious breach of faith with which we have yet been faced".[148] In Dublin, meanwhile, an aeroplane was put on standby in case of the need for "urgent personal contact with the delegation"[149]—a fairly dramatic move in the context of the times. In a letter to Granard, which he presumably expected to be passed on to the British, Cosgrave expressed his "amazement that Lord Hailsham's recollection of the meeting does not appear to coincide either with what Mr O'Higgins told me at the time or with the present recollection of our Attorney General ... I begin to see now what was in Mr O'Higgins' mind when he used the phrase—'I wonder will they keep their promise'."[150] This remark had been made to Costello a few days before O'Higgins left the 1927 Naval Conference in Geneva, shortly before his death.[151]

The performance of the Labour Government was quite extraordinary. As Costello was to point out later, the Irish got more help from "the representatives of a Conservative Canadian Government ... in striking contrast to the conservative attitude of the British Labour administration".[152] Sankey's attempt to outflank the Irish delegation in particular was badly judged, ill-timed and counterproductive, and left the British on the defensive. At a meeting of heads of delegation on 13 November, FitzGerald pointed out that the Treaty had been accepted on the basis of statements by Lloyd George that their status was not static. "If these statements were not made in good faith, the whole basis was altered and the Irish Free State was not a member of the British Commonwealth." Costello chipped in the observation that in 1926 the Colonial Laws Validity Act was still in force, and that the whole situation had now been altered in this respect. When Scullin of Australia asked if the repeal of the Validity Act would give the Free State the same rights as Canada, Jowitt said it would, "so far as *legal* rights were concerned, but there were also what might, for want of a better word, be called 'moral' rights".[153] In his concluding speech to the final meeting of the Conference the following day, McGilligan was distinctly frosty, saying it would take time for the results of their work to be seen, and it was only as they saw those results that they could decide whether Irish willingness to co-operate would increase or not.[154]

As we have seen in the previous chapter, Costello was asked early in 1931 to draft a Bill to abolish the right to appeal, but the legislation was not actually introduced until after the change of government. However, despite the failure to make progress on the Privy Council and related issues, the 1930 Imperial Conference did endorse the Statute of Westminster and the British agreed to put it through Parliament. They even agreed to McGilligan's request that the date for it to come into operation should be 1 December 1931. This was to allow the Irish Government to introduce the Merchant Shipping Bill and get it into committee before Christmas of 1931. McGilligan believed this would be "very important to them from a political point of view, having regard to the coming General Election".[155]

By the time the Statute came before the British Parliament, there had been huge changes in the British political scene. After the Labour Cabinet split over spending cuts in the midst of the Depression, MacDonald formed a National Government in August 1931, which won a massive election victory that October. Ironically, from the Irish point of view, the three British politicians they trusted least, MacDonald, Thomas and Sankey, retained their respective positions as Prime Minister, Dominions Secretary and Lord Chancellor. The Government had a huge majority, but was vulnerable to pressure from Conservative backbenchers, many of them deeply unhappy with the idea of loosening the bonds of empire. The Statute prohibited the parliaments in Australia, New Zealand and Canada from amending their respective constitutions. During the second reading in November 1931, Winston Churchill signalled an amendment which would add a prohibition on altering the Irish Free State Constitution. So far, so predictable. But in reply, Thomas said that "every consideration will be given ... to all that has been said here today, and ... the Government will be asked to consider the whole situation in the light of the Debate that has taken place".[156]

Given the experience of the 1930 Conference, it was not surprising that Dublin was seriously worried. Cosgrave wrote to MacDonald, warning that such an amendment "would be wholly unacceptable to us ... the interests of the peoples of the Commonwealth as a whole must be put before the prejudices of the small reactionary element in these islands".[157] McGilligan wrote in even more trenchant terms to Thomas: "I cannot conceive anyone except the most rabid reactionary desiring to reopen old sores and recreate the feeling of unrest and disturbance between our peoples all over the world. I do not believe that Mr Churchill has that desire. If he had he would not have signed the Treaty ... the Treaty will be observed by the people of this country so long as it is a free instrument. If it becomes overshadowed by the slightest suspicion of external legal restraint it loses its free character, is no longer the same instrument and must inevitably defeat its original purpose."[158]

Thomas told the Irish High Commissioner, John Dulanty, that he had been "playing for time", because "practically nobody was in the House except the Diehards and ... he was determined that ... the Bill should not be defeated on the second reading". In his defence, he also pointed out that he had said the Government would give consideration—rather than *favourable* consideration—to the proposed amendments.[159] Ramsay MacDonald told Dulanty he agreed with Cosgrave's letter, and said de Valera would be "jubilant" over Churchill's speech, which he described as "one of the most mischievous speeches ever made in the House of Commons".[160] His formal reply to Cosgrave said he would not alter the Bill "unless the Government itself is defeated".[161] After minor amendments, the Statute received the Royal Assent on 11 December 1931.[162]

The Statute has frequently, and fairly, been described as a triumph for the Cosgrave government. It implemented many of the demands pursued by O'Higgins, McGilligan, FitzGerald and Costello over the previous decade. The Colonial Laws Validity Act no longer applied; no Dominion legislation would be declared void because it conflicted with English law; Dominion parliaments had full power to introduce legislation with extra-territorial scope; laws passed at Westminster would not apply to Dominions unless they requested that they should.[163] In Costello's words, its passage "marked the final crumbling of the legal theory on which the Constitution of the Old British Empire rested ... The King, the bogey used by Anti-Treaty politicians, became a symbol of the fact that the states members of the Commonwealth were associated in that community ... by their own free will."[164]

Another tribute to the progress made came from an unexpected quarter. In the Seanad in June 1932, Eamon de Valera, then President of the Executive Council, acknowledged that "the 26 Counties ... as a result of the 1926 and 1930 conferences, had practically got into the position—with the sole exception that instead of being a Republic it was a monarchy—that I was aiming at in 1921 for the whole of Ireland ... I am prepared to confess that there have been advances made that I did not believe would be made at the time."[165] And while de Valera in office ignored the Statute of Westminster, there is no doubt that it cleared the path for his constitutional changes in the following years.[166] His Attorney General, Conor Maguire, advised him that the Government had the power to remove the Oath, because "from the British point of view ... the passing of the Statute of Westminster leaves it open to the Irish Free State to amend the constitution in any way it pleases".[167] Ironically, this view was confirmed in 1935—by no less a body than the much resented Privy Council.[168]

Costello's role in the development of the Free State's international status was significant of itself, but it is also of interest for what it tells us about the background to the Declaration of the Republic in 1948. Nicholas Mansergh argued that Cumann na nGaedheal, "while much preoccupied with the ending of all elements of continuing subordination, continued to think of Irish fulfilment within the Commonwealth".[169] This would seem to be supported by Patrick McGilligan's comments to the then Prince of Wales, later Edward VIII, at the 1930 Conference: "We don't object to the Monarch or the Monarchy, but we do object to the British Parliament using the Monarchy. The King advised solely by our Ministers is what we want, and we will then be strongly monarchic."[170] This was the problem for Cumann na nGaedheal. They had successfully transformed the Commonwealth, but in the process they had become—in the public mind as well as their own—identified as the party of the Crown. It was an image Jack Costello became determined to change.

Chapter 5 ~

THE BLUESHIRTS WILL BE VICTORIOUS

" ... the Blackshirts were victorious in Italy and ... the Hitler Shirts were victorious in Germany, as ... the Blueshirts will be victorious in the Irish Free State."[1]

JOHN A. COSTELLO, 1934

"It is ridiculous to talk about Cosgrave being a Fascist or James Dillon or myself or Tom O'Higgins or any of these people—it is absurd."[2]

JOHN A. COSTELLO, 1969

On 28 February 1934 John A. Costello made his most famous speech in the Dáil—which was unfortunate, as it was probably also his most ill-advised. He was responding to Fianna Fáil Justice Minister P.J. Ruttledge in a debate on the banning of uniforms. The ban was aimed squarely at the Blueshirts, a quasi-Fascist movement which formed part of the new Fine Gael party. Ruttledge defended his legislation by outlining similar measures in other countries, to which Costello replied, "The Minister gave extracts from various laws on the Continent, but he carefully refrained from drawing attention to the fact that the Blackshirts were victorious in Italy and that the Hitler Shirts were victorious in Germany, as assuredly, in spite of this Bill and in spite of the Public Safety Act, the Blueshirts will be victorious in the Irish Free State."[3]

It was deeply ironic that Costello, as wedded to democracy and the rule of law as any leading Irish politician, should come to make a speech comparing members of his own political party to Mussolini's Fascists and Hitler's storm-troopers. As he ruefully acknowledged 35 years later, the phrase went around his constituency at every subsequent election. But he claimed that it never affected him, because "my own constituents and everyone in Ireland knew that it was only a phrase". He insisted he only meant that the Blueshirts would ensure free speech, adding that "at that time Mussolini and Hitler had not reached the bad situation that they subsequently reached, and which brought them the odium of the world".[4]

It was true that the worst excesses of Nazism and Fascism were in the future. However, while the plight of German Jews may not have received a huge amount of coverage in the Irish media at the time, the treatment of the Catholic Church by the Nazis did. On the very day Costello drew his comparison between the Blueshirts and Hitler's Brownshirts, the *Irish Independent* reported Nazi attacks on the Cardinal of Munich, "whose sermons against paganism and in defence of the Old Testament have made him a target of attacks by Herr Rosenberg and other prominent Nazis. Stones were hurled though Cardinal Faulhaber's windows a few weeks ago."[5] Genocide may not have been apparent in 1934, but thuggery most certainly was.

As far as Jack Costello was concerned, it was "only a phrase". He did not wear a blue shirt himself, was not a fascist ideologue like some former Cabinet ministers, and did not subscribe to extreme views about anything. It was, as he put it, "absurd" to talk of him or Cosgrave or Dillon or Tom O'Higgins being fascists;[6] but his speech gave the Government the opportunity to do just that, as was shown during the Dáil debate.

The controversial passage was part of a very long speech, covering more than 12 columns of the official record, most of which was devoted to a defence of civil rights, and a claim that the Bill was a menace to democracy because it was aimed by the Government at the main Opposition party, which had been acting within the law. "It is going to set a precedent for anybody who wishes to stifle for all time ... the right of freedom of speech and the right of free association ... The actions of the Government have brought the law, as administered by the present Government, into disrepute."[7]

But Government speakers pounced on the comparison between the Blueshirts and the Nazis. Conor Maguire, Costello's former associate in the L&H, now his successor as Attorney General and bitter political opponent, described it as the "fatal slip" of the speech. "Here we have it plain and clear that the Blueshirt organisation is here to be the spearhead of an attack upon democratic and Parliamentary institutions."[8] Seán Lemass, the Minister for Industry and Commerce, said his speech "brings very forcibly before the Dáil another stage in the development of militarism in politics".[9]

Perhaps the main explanation, if not justification, for the speech was the belief on the Opposition benches that democracy was under threat from the Government, and in particular from its leader—a belief that would carry through to the debates on de Valera's new Constitution three years later. The fact that events proved these fears groundless does not mean that they were not genuinely felt. To understand how and why the speech was made, it is necessary to consider why Fine Gael felt this way, and how John A. Costello found himself in the Dáil in the first place.

As we saw in Chapter 3, W.T. Cosgrave was opposed to political involvement on the part of the Attorney General. However, Costello played an active role in the 1932 election. In later years he claimed he was "seduced from the path of righteousness"[10] by Ernest Blythe, who asked him to speak in his Monaghan constituency. In fact, before he went to Monaghan, he had already spoken to at least one election meeting, for the Dublin County candidates, in Rathmines Town Hall. In this, his first reported political speech, he said the happiness and prosperity of the people depended on the election result; that the Cumann na nGaedheal candidates represented all classes and creeds; and that the removal of the Oath would be "the clearest breach of the Treaty".[11]

The following evening he spoke at an election meeting for Blythe in the Diamond in Monaghan Town. It was a colourful occasion. Blythe was met by "a torch-light procession ... headed by Doohamlet warpipe band" as he entered the town, and the Cumann na nGaedheal speakers faced a rival Fianna Fáil rally a hundred yards away.[12] Judging by the account in the *Irish Independent*, Costello's speech was a rather dry recitation of the legal arguments on the annuities question.[13] The following morning, the Attorney General tried to address an after-Mass crowd at Maheracloone Lower without much success. "When the congregation came out from Mass, they more or less lined up beside the ditch while Senator O'Rourke and I were maintaining a very precarious standing. And having lined up, a whistle was blown, and the entire congregation ... walked away. And that was my first real entrance into practical politics ..."[14] It could have been worse—Cumann na nGaedheal speakers at an after-Mass meeting at another Monaghan village, Latton, faced scuffles which had to be broken up by Gardaí with drawn batons.[15]

It seems unlikely that the Attorney General's intervention made much difference to the outcome, which saw Blythe hold his seat fairly comfortably (he was defeated in the following year's snap election). But nationally, Cumann na nGaedheal didn't fare so well, winning just 57 seats to Fianna Fáil's 72, and losing office as de Valera was elected President of the Executive Council with the support of Labour. Cumann na nGaedheal's defeat was probably inevitable thanks to the depression which followed the Wall Street Crash. But the party leadership, with the notable exception of Dick Mulcahy, certainly didn't help matters by shunning the nuts and bolts of party organisation. W.T. Cosgrave told Garret FitzGerald in the 1960s that his Government had contained "a half-statesman, Kevin O'Higgins, but no politicians". The former President said Desmond FitzGerald was "too busy arguing about theology with Father Cahill" to worry about party organisation, while Patrick McGilligan refused even to go to Cork for a meeting.[16] Fair criticism, no doubt—though the party leader was even more to blame than his ministers.

While Jack Costello was dipping his toe into political waters, his father had already plunged in. Following his retirement, and the death of his wife in July 1929,[17] John Costello ran for a seat on Dublin Corporation, being elected on three occasions for the North City (Number 3) electoral area. At the time of his first election in 1930 Cumann na nGaedheal did not contest local authority seats, as councils were regarded as non-party political. He ran instead under the banner of the "Greater Dublin Constitutional Group", whose Chairman promised "to oppose all political discussion at Corporation meetings" in order "to secure the businesslike conduct of meetings, to enable the Corporation to concentrate on strictly Dublin affairs, and to avoid the introduction into local business of party bitterness and party wranglings, which has already done enough harm elsewhere".[18]

The new Councillor's political tone was moderate and reasonable—arguing the case for negotiations to reach a settlement in the Economic War with Britain in a letter to the *Irish Independent* in August 1932: "One does not need to be a politician to realise the value of negotiation as a means of overcoming obstacles and arriving at a basis for agreement ... Political parties might continue to express their opinions to very little purpose, unless the ordinary man in the street, who after all is the sufferer, stands up for his own rights and insists on immediate negotiations."[19] He was also active on behalf of his constituents—his work was still remembered in Dublin North West in the 1950s,[20] to the advantage of his grandson Declan, a TD for the area.

By the time the 1933 local elections came round, it was decided that the Constitutional Group candidates should run under the Cumann na nGaedheal banner. Party secretary Liam Burke explained that the Constitutional Group was "unequipped with the necessary political machinery ... to prevent ... threatened personation" (i.e. vote stealing). Burke promised that after the election, the candidates would revert to their traditional view, and resist Fianna Fáil attempts to use the corporations as a vehicle for party politics.[21] John Costello lived up to this promise after retaining his seat and being elected Chairman of the Joint Committee of the Grangegorman Mental Hospital (which was at the end of the street on which he lived, Rathdown Road). At his first meeting as Chairman he sent a message to Fianna Fáil, then abstaining from the Corporation, expressing "the hope that at the next meeting they would have their absent colleagues".[22] It was also on the Grangegorman Committee that he became friendly with fellow councillor Big Jim Larkin[23], a relationship which built bridges for his son with the Labour Party.

By 1936, John Costello was standing on the Fine Gael, or United Ireland Party, ticket. He had the backing of the Lord Mayor, Alfie Byrne, who included him on a list of candidates he urged the public to support. The Lord Mayor warned voters, "The Municipal council is not the place for politics. We have had too much politics in this country ... Bands will play; slanderers will get busy; personators ... will be active, and strenuous efforts will be made to make the Municipal Council a replica of An Dáil—a political machine where minorities must bow to force of numbers."[24] It was to be Councillor Costello's last election—in October 1936, a day after chairing a meeting of the Grangegorman Mental Health Committee, he became ill and died at the age of 74.

To return to his son's entry into politics: when Cosgrave and his colleagues lost office in 1932, they were firmly convinced that their exile on the Opposition benches would be a short one, because de Valera and Fianna Fáil would be unable to govern responsibly. Their worst fears appeared to be realised, as the new Government released all political prisoners, suspended Article 2A and lifted the ban on the IRA—although, in a "deliberately conciliatory gesture", de Valera appointed former Cumann na nGaedheal TD James Geoghegan as Minister for Justice.[25] So, when a new election was called in January 1933, Cumann na nGaedheal were confident of victory, a confidence boosted by what Costello later described as "huge demonstrations in Dublin and elsewhere".[26] A contemporary account, albeit in a pro-Cosgrave paper, described the former President addressing "one of the largest political meetings that Dublin has witnessed for a generation", with 500 Gardaí and "several hundred members of the Army Comrades Association" foiling attempts to disrupt it.[27] It was in this election campaign—"arguably the most bitter, turbulent and colourful in the history of independent Ireland"[28]—that John A. Costello first stood as a candidate.

He had already been selected to contest a by-election caused by the death of his friend and colleague at the Bar, Tom Finlay. Finlay had been in turn a District Justice, assistant secretary in the Department of Justice, practising barrister, and, from December 1930, TD for Dublin County. He had then won the by-election caused by the death of Major Bryan Cooper with a massive 35,362 votes to 15,024 for Fianna Fáil's Conor Maguire.[29] In the 1932 general election, Finlay was re-elected on the first count, but in November 1932, he died of paratyphoid. According to the *Anglo-Celt*, the local paper in his native Cavan, news of his death "came as a terrific shock, causing strong men to weep like children". No doubt the sorrow was genuine, although the fact that Finlay was a nephew of the *Anglo-Celt* editor may have affected the tone of the coverage.[30]

Costello had been friendly with Finlay, in Government and at the Bar, and their wives were also close—Mrs Finlay was godmother to one of the Costello children.[31] A selection convention chose John A. Costello to contest the expected by-election. Not everyone was delighted—the candidate later related the response of one north County Dublin senator to his selection: "he said with deep disgust: 'Another lawyer!'". Costello's election theme, he later recalled, was that Cumann na nGaedheal was a national rather than a sectional party.[32] He also stressed that W.T. Cosgrave would achieve "peace on decent terms with Great Britain ... Cumann na nGaedheal was going to win this election, but they wanted a large majority."[33] The eight-seat Dublin County constituency stretched from Balbriggan to Bray, and out as far as Tallaght and Firhouse. The new candidate "fell into every ditch in north County Dublin in the dark when I was trying to find my way round".[34] He evidently discovered a fair few votes in those ditches, being elected on the first count with 10,941 first preferences, 890 over the quota. He was in third place behind Seán MacEntee of Fianna Fáil and Cumann na nGaedheal's Henry Dockrell. Cosgrave's party managed to retain its four seats in the constituency, while Fianna Fáil won a seat from Labour. But nationally, Cumann na nGaedheal had a disastrous election, dropping 9 seats to just 48, while de Valera won his first overall majority with 77 seats.

In opposition after a second defeat, party discipline quickly fell apart. Mulcahy complained to Cosgrave that front bench meetings were "almost impossible. They start late—with bad attendance and decide little if anything at all."[35] A parliamentary party meeting chaired by Costello in June had to be abandoned "owing to the small attendance".[36] The former ministers who survived the election were faced with the need to pick up the threads of their careers and earn a living. Just as the First World War had given Costello a chance to break into the Bar, so the shattered state of the parliamentary party offered him an opening in Cumann na nGaedheal. He was quickly playing a significant role in the parliamentary party, chairing a committee on External Affairs, and also one on meetings, which was "to receive reports from each Deputy as to his intentions and to see that a scheme of meetings was carried out".[37] He was also to make an immediate impact in the Dáil chamber, thanks in large part to Fianna Fáil's decision to sack Garda Commissioner Eoin O'Duffy.

Emboldened by his overall majority, de Valera moved to stamp his authority on the justice area. The only change to his cabinet was the replacement of Justice Minister Geoghegan, formerly of Cumann na nGaedheal, with P.J. Ruttledge, "a republican hardliner whose IRA sympathies were well known".[38] On 22 February, the Executive Council decided to remove O'Duffy as Garda Commissioner. He was offered an alternative job, first as head of a new branch of the Department of Industry and Commerce dealing with mineral development, and after he rejected this, as Controller of Prices. O'Duffy rejected this offer too.[39] The curt letter of dismissal cited Section 2 of the Garda Síochána

Act, 1924 as the legislative basis for the sacking.[40] When de Valera was challenged by Cosgrave about the sacking on 1 March, he again mentioned Section 2 of the 1924 Act. The President said no charge had been made against the general; he was removed because the Executive Council felt a change of commissioner was in the public interest.[41] Had Cumann na nGaedheal stayed in power they would have sacked O'Duffy too; but things look different from the Opposition benches. Cosgrave told his parliamentary party that the dismissal "might well be indicative of a change of policy as well as a change in personnel",[42] and he put down a Dáil motion condemning the Government's action.

But as the debate began, John A. Costello lobbed a legal hand grenade into the Dáil chamber—his first contribution in the House. He pointed out that the section of the Garda legislation cited by the Taoiseach had been repealed, and that O'Duffy "is neither in fact nor in law removed". The Ceann Comhairle said he wasn't going to interpret legislation and the debate continued, but Costello kept de Valera under pressure. The President sniffily suggested that "the former Attorney-General ... should have known better" than to raise doubts over the legality of the dismissal. Costello in turn accused de Valera of making "an unworthy attack" on him.[43] It was an impressive debut for the new TD, an indication that his forensic legal skills would be a valuable addition to the Opposition. The next time a Garda Commissioner was removed, in 1978, officials duly noted the legal slip, pointing out that the incident "lends support to the wisdom of our present general practice of not quoting statutory authority for decisions taken by the Government".[44]

During his first year in the Dáil, Costello made sensible, if sometimes over-lengthy, contributions on matters including Road Traffic, National Health Insurance and Workman's Compensation Bills, where his legal background and knowledge of the Attorney General's Office stood him in good stead. Some of his most trenchant interventions concerned the Government's plan to cut Civil Service pay. Fianna Fáil in opposition had championed the cause of middle and lower grades in the Civil Service, with de Valera complaining that their pay was "in most cases ... barely sufficient to meet the costs of the maintenance of a home".[45] In Government, of course, it was a different matter. The 1933 election had been precipitated by a threat from Labour to vote against pay cuts—once returned with an overall majority, the Cabinet agreed to press ahead with reductions.[46]

The economies were billed as "temporary", but Cumann na nGaedheal strongly opposed them, with Costello taking a particularly strong line against the "immorality" of the proposal. He also had harsh words for James Dillon and Frank MacDermot of the Centre Party, who proposed that the reductions should apply to TDs as well as civil servants. He began his contribution by apologising for missing the start of the debate, as "unfortunately I am under the necessity of earning my own living"—not for the last time, he had been in the Four Courts when the debate began. He then claimed that the £360 per year allowance for TDs was too low, rather than too high, and that very few Deputies would have a profit out of such a sum, particularly after "the demands made upon him by his constituents and by others all over the country in respect of donations to charitable purposes and subscriptions to different objects". Costello accused the Minister for Finance, Seán MacEntee, of merely pretending to save money. He also admitted the previous Cumann na nGaedheal government had made mistakes in cutting the old age pension and the salaries of Gardaí and teachers, but had made a definite decision not to cut the pay of civil servants. He pointed out that the new ministerial salaries introduced by Fianna Fáil were after-tax figures, while the Cabinet had also given themselves free cars. "The man who holds the position that I held as Attorney-General has these perquisites in addition to £1,500 a year, free of tax, and liberty to get as much money as he can by private practice." But the core of his argument, to which he would return again and again, was that the previous government had agreed with the Civil Service unions a guarantee of their pay in 1929 as a solution of the Wigg–Cochrane case. Costello said the agreement he had reached with Bill Norton and other union leaders on the issue was "my greatest achievement as Attorney General". If the Government could now cut Civil Service pay, there would be no guarantee they could not double the cuts the following year.[47]

Costello put down a series of amendments at committee and report stages designed to protect the pay of transferred officers, those who had moved from the British to the Irish Civil Service after the Treaty, arguing that the Government was breaking a promise as well as a contract, which "is a wrong both legally and morally".[48] He even suggested that de Valera and his ministers should seek theological advice to "find out whether, according to Catholic principles and Catholic theology, the provisions of the Bill ... are not immoral".[49] Whether MacEntee looked into his soul or not, when the Bill returned to the Dáil to discuss amendments passed in the Seanad, the Minister introduced his own amendment to exclude transferred civil servants from the cuts. Costello expressed satisfaction at having "fathered this particular amendment", while MacEntee acknowledged that it had been "agitating my mind for a considerable time, an agitation which was brought into focus during a debate which took place here on Deputy Costello's amendment".[50] Costello was to continue his interest in Civil Service pay throughout the 1930s, supporting calls for an arbitration scheme—a fitting tribute to his father's early activity in the Civil Service Guild (see Chapter 1). His position drew favourable comment from the *Civil Service Journal*,[51] and also brought him into close co-operation with Labour leader Bill Norton, which was to prove useful in 1948.

But the main political issue of 1933 and 1934 related not to hair shirts but to blue shirts. The Army Comrades Association had been formed in February 1932 by Colonel Austin Brennan and Commandant Ned Cronin, ostensibly as a self-help group for ex-servicemen. In August Brennan was replaced as President by Dr T.F. O'Higgins, brother of Kevin and Cumann na nGaedheal TD for Leix-Offaly. The new President claimed the ACA was "a benevolent body, engaged primarily in efforts to alleviate the hardships that fall on unemployed and disabled ex-members of the Army". But he stressed too the organisation's opposition to communism and support for free speech, deprecating "the new fashion of branding as 'traitors' certain public men with whom we ... had the privilege of being associated in defence of the State".[52]

While some in the movement, such as Ernest Blythe and Desmond FitzGerald, may have been attracted to fascist ideologies, other leading figures stressed the defence of free speech as the main aim. Shortly after the ACA was founded, Mulcahy urged a non-violent approach, stressing that the organisation had nothing to do "with mob violence whether of the Communist or the Fascist type", having been established to save the institutions of the State "being overpowered from the outside or ... destroyed or rotted from the inside".[53] Half a century later, James Dillon said they had "fought a desperate battle for the preservation of free speech in this country. And let it never be forgotten that we could not have won that battle but for the Blueshirts ..."[54] As we have seen, the ACA was heavily involved in the 1933 election campaign, guarding political meetings against Republican attack. In March 1933, the blue shirt and Fascist-style salute were adopted. As John M. Regan has pointed out, while the shirt had an obvious association with Continental fascist organisations, it was also very similar to the official Garda shirt, and therefore "reinforced the self-perception that the association as a police auxiliary was an unofficial and voluntary arm of the state".[55]

The economic war with Britain, sparked by de Valera's withholding of the Land Annuities, helped both to increase support for the Blueshirts and to radicalise them. While British economic sanctions hurt large farmers, they still had to pay the annuities, which were now retained by the Irish Exchequer. Costello had been counsel in an attempt to have the courts decide whether the Government was bound to pay the annuities before the 1933 election, an attempt derailed by the re-elected Fianna Fáil government, which passed legislation, as Costello later indignantly recalled, "for the specific purpose of putting an end to that action".[56] The former Attorney General wasn't in much position to complain, as this was exactly the strategy he had recommended to deal with Privy Council decisions.

Legal action on the annuities was to continue side by side with political action, with Costello playing a leading role. In fact, the legal side of the struggle continued long after the demise of the Blueshirt movement. In 1935 Costello was lead counsel in a case taken by Louth County Council against the Government, which had withheld the Agricultural Grant because of the failure to pay annuities to the State.[57] The following year he won £400 damages against the Dublin County Sheriff for failing to secure an adequate price for seized goods. Costello won the case after exposing the ignorance of the official concerned of his legal duty to the person whose goods were seized—the judge said the sheriff was supposed to "hold the scales of justice evenly between both parties".[58]

As rural unrest grew in 1933, the Executive Council began to take the ACA more seriously. At the end of May it ordered the dismissal of Reserve Officers known to be members of the organisation, and requested a report on the strength, armament and activities of the ACA, as well as of the IRA.[59] But it was the appointment of sacked Garda Commissioner Eoin O'Duffy to lead the ACA on 20 July that made a confrontation inevitable. At the same time as O'Duffy assumed the leadership, the Blueshirts were taking steps to revive the annual commemoration of Collins, Griffith and O'Higgins, which had been abandoned when Fianna Fáil entered government. On 21 July, Ned Cronin, Secretary of the National Guard, wrote to Government officials seeking permission to lay a wreath at the Cenotaph in Leinster Lawn on Sunday 13 August. He explained that as well as relatives of the dead leaders, the ceremony would include "about fifty members of the ACA with buglers".[60] The Executive Council decided that admission to Leinster Lawn should be by ticket only, and that only individual applications would be accepted,[61] to make an organised Blueshirt attendance more difficult.

On 30 July, the Government revoked firearms certificates held by, among others, former ministers and leading supporters of the Opposition, including Patrick McGilligan, whose home had been raided by the IRA just a week before.[62] In the Dáil, Cosgrave put down a motion criticising the move, claiming the withdrawal of licences from "law-abiding citizens" was causing uneasiness in the public mind. Costello delivered a blistering attack on the Minister for Justice, claiming his "so-called explanation ... would not deceive a baby". He ridiculed the excuse that the guns had been withdrawn for stock-taking, pointing out that one TD had paid his five-shilling fee for a firearms certificate on Friday, only to have it withdrawn on the Saturday. He also criticised de Valera for his "smiles and sniggers" during the debate.[63]

The Government's next move was more extreme. On 11 August, two days before the planned parade, de Valera reactivated Article 2A of the Constitution and banned O'Duffy's march. While it seems unlikely that the General really intended to emulate Mussolini's "March on Rome", he had given the Government an excuse to take strong measures, allowing de Valera to resurrect emergency legislation without arousing opposition from militant Republicans[64]—who would later, of course, be its chief victims. Later in the month the Government used the emergency powers to ban the National Guard, which O'Duffy immediately renamed the Young Ireland Association. Believing the ban to be unjustified and politically motivated, the Opposition— Cumann na nGaedheal and the Centre Party as well as the Blueshirts—now had strong grounds for believing that the Government was intent on moving against them all. The impetus towards unity became irresistible.

On 9 September, agreement was reached on a merger between Cumann na nGaedheal, the Centre Party and the Blueshirts, with O'Duffy as leader. The new party was called Fine Gael, or the United Ireland Party—the latter name was used more in the early days, but was eventually supplanted by the former. The National Executive was made up of six nominees of each of the constituent parts, with Costello one of the Cumann na nGaedheal nominees, along with former ministers Mulcahy, John Marcus O'Sullivan, FitzGerald-Kenny and Blythe, and former Labour TD Dan Morrissey. Cosgrave was leader in the Dáil, and one of no fewer than six Vice-Presidents.[65] Costello later claimed to have been unhappy with the choice of O'Duffy, but said it was necessary in the interests of unity.[66] With the benefit of hindsight, he described the General as "the world's worst politician ... he was a man of great integrity ... but he had no conception of what the rough and tumble of political life meant".[67] He also blamed the leaders of the Centre Party for insisting on O'Duffy as leader instead of Cosgrave.[68]

It was understandable that MacDermot and Dillon didn't want to serve under Cosgrave, whom they had opposed when he was President of the Executive Council. They actually wanted former Agriculture Minister Patrick Hogan, rather than O'Duffy, to take the leadership, but Hogan rejected the offer. In any event, while MacDermot and Dillon "could be forgiven for not fully appreciating O'Duffy's pedigree ... the former Ministers could not plead such innocence".[69] Why did Cumann na nGaedheal agree to be led by the man they had planned to sack as Garda Commissioner? O'Duffy's biographer has pointed out that from the perspective of the Opposition, "Fine Gael represented a defensive merger against a government which was assaulting its political and economic liberties." It later transpired that Fianna Fáil was not planning to outlaw political opponents—but that wasn't how it appeared at the time.[70]

O'Duffy also regretted the merger in later life, but at the time it made sense for him too, as it would be more difficult for de Valera to ban the Blueshirts if they were part of the main Opposition party. While Blueshirts automatically became members of Fine Gael, the opposite was not the case.[71] Some Fine

Gael TDS were enthusiastic wearers of the shirt, with 14 having their names taken by Gardaí when they wore them in the Dáil—including Dr T.F. O'Higgins, Desmond FitzGerald, Gearóid O'Sullivan and Patrick Belton.[72] Costello was notably not among their number.

The first meeting of the newly formed Fine Gael parliamentary party was held on 28 September, with Costello among the 42 TDS and 10 senators in attendance.[73] The following day, Frank MacDermot moved a Dáil motion accusing the Government of being "unjust and oppressive" in its use of the Public Safety Act. The motion followed the arrest of four prominent Blueshirts (including Cronin and Belton) after disturbances at a sale of cattle seized for the non-payment of annuities. They were the first to be tried by the reconstituted Tribunal (all were found guilty).[74] In his contribution, Costello criticised de Valera's public comments about the case as potentially prej-udicial, and said the only justification for the use of the Act would be that "the very foundations of the State are being menaced in such a way that the ordinary institutions of the State are not able to cope with the menace". He pointed out that the Government had not moved against the ACA, or the blue shirt, until General O'Duffy took over the leadership. And, the former Attorney General insisted, there was no law in the country to prevent him, or anybody else, from wearing a blue shirt on a public platform or anywhere else.[75]

In the course of the debate, Seán Lemass indicated that this situation might change, with a prohibition likely on the wearing of blue shirts. More dramatic was a claim by de Valera that Richard Mulcahy had met the British Minister for War, Lord Hailsham, in Glasgow. This allegation was immedi-ately denied by both men.[76] Mulcahy's visit to Glasgow had in fact been a holiday with family friends, and the allegation astonished him.[77] He indignantly rejected the implication that he had been seeking arms for the Blueshirts and demanded that de Valera establish a tribunal to inquire into the matter. The following week de Valera had to tell the Dáil that the source of his information (apparently a journalist with the *Irish Press*) had admitted that the story wasn't true. He apologised to Mulcahy, but Costello badgered the President, asking if the source would be prosecuted for criminal libel.[78]

In November, Fine Gael finally got round to formally agreeing its policy at a Standing Committee meeting attended by Costello.[79] The 25 points included the voluntary reunion of Ireland as a member of the British Commonwealth; direct negotiations with Britain to end the Economic War, with complete remission of Land Annuities and Agricultural Rates pending a settlement; "unconditional opposition to Communism"; abolition of Proportional Representation; organisation of "agricultural and industrial corporations with statutory powers ... under the guidance of a National Economic Council"; a Reconstruction Corps to put able-bodied unemployed people to work; a

Ministry of Housing; encouragement of sporting activities, as well as "the awakening of a spirit of self-reliance, dignity and discipline in the rising generation, and the inculcation through the Young Ireland movement of the ideal of voluntary disciplined public service"; maintenance of free speech; and the preservation of the Irish language.[80]

The document was a compromise between the various constituent parts of Fine Gael, and while there were echoes of Mussolini—such as the emphasis on sports and voluntary disciplined public service, as well as the agricultural and industrial corporations—it was certainly far from fascist. Costello later downplayed the influence of corporatism on Fine Gael. "I don't know very much about it, never did, but that was the thing that was hung on to by O'Duffy and some—only some—of his followers ... I didn't stand for it, Cosgrave didn't stand for it, the bulk of the party didn't stand for it, and certainly there wasn't two per cent of that amalgamated party would have anything to do with Fascism."[81]

Meanwhile, O'Duffy's increasingly intemperate speeches were causing concern in the ranks of the new party. According to Costello, "he had been causing us tremendous trouble by speeches around the country, you never knew what he was going to say". In Ballyshannon, Co. Donegal, on 9 December, he gave the Government its chance with a particularly incendiary attack: "I say as a Republican myself that ... whenever Mr de Valera runs away from the Republic and arrests you Republicans, and puts you on board beds in Mountjoy, he is entitled to the fate he gave Mick Collins and Kevin O'Higgins. He does not understand the people of this country because he is a half-breed." The detective inspector who served a summons on O'Duffy reported that in his opinion "the General was under the influence of alcohol". As John Regan observed, "to elect to the leadership of the new party either a covert republican or a drunk would have been unfortunate. To elect both was carelessness."[82] O'Duffy defiantly insisted that he would address his next scheduled meeting, at Westport on Sunday 17 December, where he was arrested, complaining later that members of the force he had created dragged "their former commissioner ignominiously through the streets".[83]

On the Monday, Costello made a late-night application at the home of High Court Justice Johnston for an order of Habeas Corpus to secure O'Duffy's release. The judge wouldn't give the order, but did give the legal team (which included McGilligan as well as Costello) leave to appeal to the High Court.[84] Mr Justice O'Byrne found, in effect, that O'Duffy had been arrested for wearing a blue shirt, which was not a crime, rather than anything specified under Article 2A, and ordered his release.[85] As his biographer has pointed out, it was "the sort of technical decision that had infuriated O'Duffy when commissioner".[86] But it was a major propaganda victory for the Blueshirts, and a legal triumph for Costello, who after all knew better than anyone the intricacies of Article 2A. His successor as Attorney General, Conor Maguire, noted that the Public Safety Act was "a very unwieldy instrument save for the one purpose it was designed, viz. to deal with the IRA".[87] But the Government was determined to take action, and two days after his release, O'Duffy was arrested on five new charges.

The summons, issued on 22 December, ordered him to appear before the military tribunal at Collins Barracks on 2 January. The first two charges related to membership of an unlawful association contrary to Article 2A—the association in question being the National Guard between 22 August and 8 December, and the Young Ireland Association between 8 and 17 December. The other charges related to his speech in Ballyshannon—he was charged with sedition, incitement to murder President de Valera, and attempting to incite murder.[88] In an affidavit, O'Duffy pointed out that the Young Ireland Association had been dissolved on 14 December after a Government ban (it was immediately replaced with a new organisation, the League of Youth), that the National Guard ceased to exist in September, and that at the time of swearing his affidavit he was not a member of either organisation (which was hardly surprising if they had ceased to exist). He further denied sedition or in any way inciting or attempting to incite anyone to murder de Valera at Ballyshannon or anywhere else.[89]

On New Year's Day, his legal team won a conditional order from the High Court, which gave the tribunal 10 days to show why it should hear the charges. The tribunal suspended its case against O'Duffy pending the outcome of the High Court case. On 21 March, the High Court ruled that O'Duffy could be tried on the first two charges but not on the other three, which should have gone before the ordinary courts. Mr Justice Sullivan, President of the High Court, said it would be "a revolting absurdity" to suggest that the tribunal could try any offence of any description, or that it could not be held to account by higher courts. While the charges of illegal membership were within the scope of the tribunal, because they were based on Article 2A, the sedition and conspiracy charges were not. The Justice said those offences could only be dealt with by the tribunal if a minister certified that the offences were aimed at impairing or impeding the machinery of government or the administration of justice.[90] O'Duffy appealed the decision to allow the first two charges to the Supreme Court, where Costello was again on his legal team, along with A.K. Overend, Vincent Rice, Cecil Lavery and Patrick McGilligan.[91] As it happened, the appeal was not pursued, being overtaken by events.

Costello scored another significant legal victory in the case of Captain Patrick Hughes, who had been sentenced to two years in jail by the tribunal for the attempted bribery of a detective. The High Court accepted Costello's argument that the tribunal did not have jurisdiction to convict him for the offences stated.[92] As a result, the Executive Council had to release 33 prisoners convicted by the tribunal as they were liable to successful challenge in the High Court.[93] In fact, the legal onslaught on the Blueshirts was remarkably unsuccessful (partly because of the way legislation was worded, partly because of an absence of illegal behaviour). Of the total of 38 Blueshirts charged with membership of an unlawful association after August 1933, 13 had a *nolle prosequi* entered, seven were found not guilty, 13 received non-custodial sentences, and just five were jailed.[94] As Costello put it later in the Dáil, "We found a way ... to meet the injustices meted out to some of our supporters ... We found gaps through which people could creep."[95]

In an effort to close some of those gaps, the Government introduced legislation banning the wearing of uniforms on 23 February—the Bill on which Costello made the infamous speech quoted at the start of this Chapter. When the Seanad refused to pass the Bill, thereby delaying its enactment by 18 months, de Valera published legislation to abolish the upper house. This action "illustrated why de Valera's commitment to democracy was genuinely doubted by the opposition".[96] Costello played a prominent role in opposing the abolition of the Seanad, claiming that it was "really the only safeguard which the Irish people have at the present moment for the safeguarding of their rights and liberties". He claimed de Valera had introduced it in "a fit of Presidential pique", and that if the upper house was abolished the Constitution could be amended in any way the Executive Council saw fit. "A decree of the Executive Council will be law in an hour if they like, and a resolution of a Fianna Fáil club will be law in half-an-hour ... We believe that the Government ... will be hitting the death blow at democratic rights in this country."[97] He also opposed the abolition of university representation in the Dáil, taking the line that equal opportunities, rather than equal rights, were the essence of democracy. Everyone had the opportunity of going to university, and therefore "the person who has idled around as a corner-boy" should not have the same rights as he, who had "worked hard all the years of my life".[98]

Following the successful legal challenges to the military tribunal, the legal wing of Fine Gael initiated another case, seeking a High Court direction that the League of Youth was not an unlawful organisation. The effect of this was to put a stop to the Government's serial banning of each new identity adopted by the Blueshirts. Costello was one of the plaintiffs in the case, as well as a member of the legal team. The argument advanced was that the League was "an integral part of United Ireland and subject to the control of the National Executive", adding that the party was "the recognised constitutional Opposition party". The statement of claim set out the objectives of the organisation, and pointed out that while the Executive Council had declared both the Young Ireland Association and the National Guard unlawful, it had not given "any indication of acts alleged to have been done for either of the said Associations grounding or justifying the opinion of the Executive Council". The Government's defence was based on Article 2A, arguing that the declaration by the Executive Council that the League of Youth and the National Guard were unlawful was by definition proof that they were; and that if the League of Youth was similarly declared unlawful, the courts had no power to interfere in the Executive Council's action. The Attorney General argued that the plaintiffs were seeking "judicial declarations of an academic character ... upon a matter as to which jurisdiction to pronounce an opinion, conclusive for all purposes, is by the Constitution conferred upon the Executive Council".[99] By the time the court finally ruled in favour of Costello and the other plaintiffs, the League of Youth had ceased to exist[100]—but the tactic had succeeded in preventing another Government ban.

Costello was also one of the counsel in an unsuccessful attempt to have Article 2A declared unconstitutional, after leading Blueshirt Jerry Ryan was charged with shooting with intent to murder. A Department of Justice memorandum on the case noted that Costello had been Attorney General when the article was introduced in the first place. "Making all allowances for the latitude allowed to politicians and lawyers there is something very strange and distasteful in this extraordinary *volte face*: it certainly makes it very difficult to believe that the persons concerned are guided by any principles."[101]

De Valera's attempts to put the Blueshirts on the wrong side of the law met little success. Luckily for him, the spur of the hardship caused by the Economic War led O'Duffy into increasing extremism which caused the movement to implode. Urging farmers to withhold annuities and rates in protest at the Economic War made sense to many in the party's grassroots, but it greatly alarmed the constitutional wing of the party, including Costello, Cosgrave and Dillon. O'Duffy's rhetoric was equally disturbing. According to Costello, Dillon upbraided the general, telling him that he was magnificent as long as he stuck to a script, "but let any old woman in the crowd shout 'Up de Valera' and God only knows what you will say!"[102]

With O'Duffy encouraging the Blueshirts to withhold annuities and resist the seizure of cattle, clashes with the Gardaí increased. On 13 August 1934, a young member of the organisation, Michael Lynch, died during an attempt to disrupt a sale at Marsh's Yard in Cork. The Blueshirt annual conference in the Mansion House the following weekend adopted a motion calling on farmers not to pay their annuities unless the Government agreed to suspend collection for the duration of the depression. Michael Tierney pointed out the choice facing Fine Gael: "Reject the resolution and weaken O'Duffy, or accept it and take part in an organised campaign of resistance to payment which I don't think any responsible political party could dream of standing over ..."[103] When the National Executive of Fine Gael met on 30 August, a compromise proposal was put forward, declaring that members should only resist cattle seizures in ways "consistent with the moral law". Costello, along with Tierney and Patrick and James Hogan, strongly argued that the word "moral" should be deleted. This would have kept Fine Gael within the law of the land, rather than the less easily defined moral law. According to Tierney, Cosgrave resisted this change because "he is keen on morality!"[104]

In a letter to Seán MacEoin, O'Duffy complained that the National Executive meeting "shattered all my hopes" for the National Guard, particularly "all the talk we had about the moral law ... I had two letters today from bishops, advising me of the position—neither even referred to the *moral* side, and I *do* know that the bishops will keep us safe on this ..." He added that he was still undecided about "what is best to do in the interests of the organisation—to get out quietly, or to try to carry on for another while".[105] James Dillon attempted to broker an agreement that would keep the General under control, with weekly meetings between him and the Vice-Presidents "to discuss all matters arising from the activities of the League of Youth", written scripts for all speeches, and written rather than oral replies to press queries.[106]

O'Duffy's letter to MacEoin indicates he wasn't happy with the arrangement; a letter to Costello shows that Cosgrave wasn't happy either. He complained that O'Duffy regarded party policy as "elastic", to be changed as circumstances dictated. "He objects to the strait jacket and apparently has little thought for the strait jacket he puts on others." Cosgrave saw himself at odds with Dillon, who would be happy with "a patch up", while he believed they were faced with "a vital and fundamental difference of opinion". Cosgrave said that "so far as I am personally concerned the Government political policy is safer than the General's". He thought it might be possible to reach a temporary accommodation with O'Duffy, but that rehabilitating him in the public mind would be "an almost insuperable job", that he was quite likely to break his word, and that "on a platform with others he may at any time precipitate a controversy".[107] On 20 September O'Duffy submitted his resignation after failing to reach agreement with the three Vice-Presidents he had been dealing with, Cosgrave, Cronin and Dillon.[108] Ned Cronin took over as head of the League of Youth, but was in turn asked to resign in September 1936.[109] He emigrated to England, having ruined himself financially through his involvement in the Blueshirts. Costello later invited him to return to Ireland to act as an advisor to his first Government, but he died on his return to Dublin.[110]

In a front bench reshuffle following O'Duffy's departure, Cosgrave asked Costello to "accept a roving Commission over certain ... general matters".[111] He fulfilled this commission, speaking on a wide range of subjects, including external affairs, finance, and of course legal matters. He also addressed other issues—such as the teaching of Irish. While he supported the aim of restoration, he accused the Government of attempting to "ram the Irish language down the necks of the Irish people", saying that an exclusive concentration on the language "will reduce the people of this country to nothing less than a set of ignoramuses". He accepted that the policy of teaching through the medium of Irish had been followed by the Cumann na nGaedheal government as well, but argued that it was "going to kill the Irish language".[112] In contributions foreshadowing his establishment of the Arts Council as Taoiseach, he stressed the importance of teaching art in primary and secondary schools "with a view to its subsequent application to industry".[113] He also wanted the School of Art to take up this aspect, pointing out that "the biggest industrial firms in England pay huge salaries to the best artists they can lay their hands on for designing the goods which they hope to put on the markets of the world".[114]

His Dáil speeches revealed a genuine concern for his poorer constituents, particularly regarding their housing. In 1934, he said he had "seen pretty bad slums in the City of Dublin—I know them fairly well—but I have never seen anything to equal the housing conditions in the village of Dundrum".[115] A year later, he spoke of the difficulty of dealing with constituents from Ringsend seeking houses—"it is a heart-breaking experience for a public representative to have to tell the people who come up with genuine stories of housing conditions, which are appalling to listen to, that he is unable to do anything for them ..."[116]

He showed an interest in foreign affairs, which Cosgrave recognised at the start of 1936, when he appointed Costello and John Marcus O'Sullivan as front bench spokesmen on External Affairs.[117] Costello had already criticised de Valera (as Minister for External Affairs) for not giving a fuller exposition of the international scene each year on his Department's Estimates. "I shall continue to press as long as I am on this side of the House, that the Department of External Affairs should be taken seriously."[118] He also repeatedly stressed his belief in the importance of Commonwealth membership, which he believed gave Ireland "an opportunity of exercising a very deep, wide and beneficent influence in international affairs".[119] There were also, he argued, "solid practical advantages for our people" in the Commonwealth, especially when abroad.[120] As he put it in an address to the National University branch of Fine Gael: "I have no objection to being what is called a British subject, but I am quite certain that I am not going to lose my Irish nationality, and the two things are not incompatible."[121] He accepted that "if we had a Republic it would be another matter", but while Ireland was in the Commonwealth "we have very practical rights which can be obtained as a business proposition for the citizens of this country".[122] He also urged de Valera to send representatives to a planned Commonwealth Economic Conference, arguing that it would allow him to "put his hands as deeply as he possibly could into the pockets of John Bull and extract as much British gold as he could extract".[123]

Costello also argued that Commonwealth membership was "the only possible method of achieving ... the unity of Ireland ... [as] a free and independent sovereign ... state ... the outstanding political problem in the country at present was not the question of separation, or to be or not to be a Republic, but the unity of our native land in one nation and under one flag".[124] Those comments were made in the course of a by-election campaign. At other times, Costello advocated a more circumspect approach, calling in the Dáil for a policy of silence, "broken only very occasionally, merely to show that we have not forgotten our brethren in the North ... The less that is said about it the better ... Discreet work behind the scenes is the way to end Partition."[125]

As a leading barrister, he was a knowledgeable contributor to debates on legislation affecting the practice of the law, admitting that he did so at least partly as "a member of a trades union".[126] He occasionally explicitly stated that he was giving the views of the Bar Council, as when urging that the Court of Criminal Appeal should be made up of three High Court judges, instead of the existing composition of two High and one Supreme Court judge which was favoured by the judiciary.[127]

Costello objected vociferously to the Courts of Justice Bill which provided among other things for the appointment of two extra Supreme Court justices, on the grounds of cost and the lack of work for the new judges to do. His explanation of the terms of the legislation, and the £3,000-per-year cost of the new judges, convinced the Fine Gael parliamentary party to oppose the Bill.[128] In the Dáil, he pointed out that much of the ordinary work of the courts had been farmed out by government to the military tribunal, or the new Land Commission Tribunal, or to County Registrars (who had taken over land annuities cases). He complained that "there never was, certainly not in the last twenty years, a period when there was so little business doing. The Bar is feeling the pinch and ... there never was so little business in the Supreme Court in my time." He also made a heartfelt case for the provision of stenographers in all High Court cases, rather than having to rely on the judge's notes, and objected to provisions for disciplining district justices, arguing that it would compromise their independence.[129] He later claimed that the extra appointments would give the Government "a blank cheque to raid the taxpayers' resources and also to rob litigants", who he argued would face higher costs. The Attorney General, Conor Maguire, dryly observed that "Deputy Costello is carried away by his own oratory, and I doubt if his belief is as deeply seated as his words would suggest."[130]

As the Courts of Justice Bill made its way through the Dáil, the Chief Justice, Hugh Kennedy, urged the Minister, P.J. Ruttledge, to make the wearing of wigs by judges and barristers optional, as well as abolishing the practice of addressing judges as "My Lord"—he suggested either the Irish "A Bhreithimh" or "Sir". Ruttledge agreed in principle, but Maguire warned that the abolition of wigs would "arouse a storm of protest amongst members of the Bar and would be likely to give rise to fierce controversy".[131] In the Dáil, Costello sought an assurance from the Minister that the representations he had received "about robes and modes of address do not affect members of the Bar"—indicating he was siding with tradition rather than with Kennedy, his former mentor.[132] In a debate during the war on the effect of clothes rationing, he raised the plight of newly qualified barristers whose "coupons are all swept away buying wigs and gowns ... They are as necessary for us in earning our living as a knowledge of law is."[133] His traditionalism on legal matters was also evident when a High Court judge suggested Ireland might adopt the Continental system of examining magistrates. Costello told the *Irish Times* that the existing system, derived from Britain, was "the finest in the world. Anything that is wrong with the system arises from abuse and non-adherence to its fundamental rules."[134]

One constant theme pursued by Costello was the question of arbitration in the Civil Service—a question that was to cause (or at least give de Valera an excuse to call) the 1938 election. In July 1935, he closely questioned the Minister for Finance, Seán MacEntee, on the details of an arbitration scheme which had been put to, and rejected by, the staff associations. The exchange, incidentally, is a very good example of Costello's cross-examination technique, and of MacEntee's evasive style. The Minister rejected Costello's suggestion that a deadlock existed between him and the associations, and declined to give any of the relevant details that were sought.[135] Two days later, Costello raised arbitration on the adjournment, recalling de Valera's promise in January 1932 to set up an Arbitration Board and adding, "That specific promise was given, and I think it is incumbent on every party in this House to see that this promise is kept."[136]

As a practising lawyer, he also made substantial contributions to technical pieces of legislation, including the marathon debates on the Insurance Bill. There was at least an element of conflict of interest in his contributions. According to the *Irish Times*, he had been one of a number of leading barristers engaged by the five Irish insurance companies "to look after their interests ... It is understood that the lawyers will be asked to advise as to the reactions of the Bill on the interests of the companies concerned, and presumably to suggest amendments when the Bill reaches the Committee stage."[137] During the debate, Lemass accused him of arguing that "insurance law should be framed to meet the desires of the insurance companies".[138]

This was slightly unfair—Costello made many sensible suggestions, some of them accepted, and spent a great deal of time on the legislation. At one point, he tormented Lemass over his proposal that life and other insurance should be separated, a legal requirement in other countries according to the Minister. Along with McGilligan, he rather unkindly pressed Lemass to give details of the legislation in other countries, details which were clearly not in his brief and which he couldn't supply.[139] The next time the Bill was before the House, the Minister was able to quote chapter and verse of the foreign legislation, but it had been an embarrassing lapse for the normally well prepared Lemass.

There was certainly an element of self-interest in his opposition to the proposed tribunal to arbitrate insurance claims. He said such matters should be dealt with in court, rather than in "bastard tribunals that would be held in a hole-and-corner way by non-lawyers and behind closed doors".[140] According to a legal colleague, passage of the Bill led Costello to lose cases from Irish Life, but he apparently accepted the loss philosophically, observing that "God never closed one door but He opened another."[141]

Another bugbear was the powers of the Revenue Commissioners, which he urged should "be exercised reasonably ... not ... used as an instrument of tyranny." He argued against the reopening of tax returns by the Revenue, citing the legal principle that "it is better for the law to be certain than just. It is better that there should be some finality to these transactions even though a fraudulent person gets away with it occasionally, and it is not very often that a fraudulent person gets away with anything very substantial ..."[142] On another occasion, responding to a charge by MacEntee that he was being unfair to the Revenue Commissioners, he argued that he was not interested in their "tender feelings", but in those of the taxpayer, "for whose very tender feelings the Revenue Commissioners have no feelings whatever, whether he is suffering any hardship or not".[143]

During Cecil Lavery's successful by-election campaign in Dublin County, Costello argued that "if Fianna Fáil retained power much longer it might be impossible for a future Government to save the country from the mess" it had caused.[144] His jaundiced view of Fianna Fáil was reinforced later that month with a controversy over alleged corruption involving mining leases in Wicklow. The allegations, made by Patrick McGilligan, were that two members of the Government party, Deputy Bob Briscoe and Senator Michael Comyn, had secured the leases through political influence with the Minister, Seán Lemass. In the debate on the establishment of a select committee to investigate the controversy, Costello objected to the limited terms of reference, accusing Lemass of "trying to side-track the real issues". Lemass confirmed that the Committee wasn't being established to try him or his department, but was "set up in the first instance to try Deputy McGilligan ... to find out if he had any foundation for these allegations".[145] Costello was appointed to the Committee, which was chaired by Labour leader Bill Norton. But a row was caused by Fianna Fáil's refusal to let McGilligan be a member—a refusal characterised by Costello as the first time in the history of the State that the Opposition had been denied the right to nominate whoever they wanted to such a Committee. The reason given was that McGilligan was the accuser—but as Costello pointed out, Lemass was "going to make him the accused".[146]

However, Costello did an effective job of making Department officials feel like the accused—R.C. Ferguson, Assistant Secretary of Industry and Commerce, "protested that the cross-examination of Mr Costello was very unfair". He had been under pressure as to whether he had treated the application by Briscoe and Comyn any differently because they were members of the Oireachtas, and of the Government party. He insisted that he treated it as he would from any member of the public, and that he had not consulted Lemass about the matter.[147]

Costello evidently found the Select Committee approach effective, for he sought to use it for an investigation into the sacking by the Government of the Secretary of the Department of Local Government, E.P. McCarron. There were a number of reasons for Costello's interest, apart from the obvious political advantage of embarrassing the Government. The first and most important was his long-standing support for the proper treatment of officials—as he said during the debate on his motion to appoint a Select Committee, his first speech in the Dáil concerned the sacking of another senior official (O'Duffy). Secondly, McCarron was also a former O'Connell School boy. And thirdly, the immediate cause of his dismissal was an appointment to Grangegorman Mental Hospital—an institution with which Costello's father had been involved. Costello argued that it was in the public interest "that public officials—both governmental officials and officials of local authorities—should be assured of the security of their tenure, and that they should feel that in exercising their functions they are entitled to exercise them irrespective of the political policy of the particular Government for the time being". He said ministers were entitled to receive independent advice, "otherwise the Civil Service is nothing but a corrupt political machine and the sooner it is got rid of the better".[148] The Government treated the motion as one of censure, and it was duly defeated, de Valera arguing that a Dáil committee could not review or revise the decisions of the Executive Council, because "on that day that Government has to disappear".[149]

In opposition, Fine Gael was very much in the doldrums. In January 1935, a meeting of the party's Standing Committee had to be abandoned for the third week in a row because of poor attendance. Costello was one of just four members to show up. Ned Cronin, who was in the chair, complained it "was impossible to have any work done either at Headquarters or in the country so long as members of the Executive Committee ... showed such apathy in attending meetings".[150] Costello played a prominent role within the organisation, serving on committees to prepare statements of the party's policy and to select by-election candidates.[151] He was also on a committee set up after "grave dissatisfaction was expressed at the poor attendance of the Party in the Dáil".[152] He himself couldn't be accused of not pulling his weight—he was a frequent, forceful and effective contributor to Dáil debates. But he was far from being a full-time TD, with his appearances in the Chamber largely limited to the late afternoons or evenings—he urged the Minister at one point during the debate on the Courts of Justice Bill to delay the resumption of the debate "until we are able to be here in the House when we come from court tomorrow".[153]

Behaviour like this understandably contributed to an image of Costello as something of a political dilettante. As a supporter of Noël Browne put it, he and his ilk were guilty of "turning up in the Law Library and earning your income down there and then strolling down to the Dáil and getting another job down there as part-time, which is what the John A. Costellos of this world were at—they were immensely rich people dabbling in politics".[154] In fairness, Costello never claimed to be a full-time politician—quite the opposite. He frequently said he would not like being a full-time TD. "One job helped the other, and politics helped to broaden attitudes. If you spend all your days at the law, you tend not to be able to talk about anything else."[155] In a letter to Seán MacEntee, proposing a system of pensions for former ministers (from which he excluded former Attorneys General—it was a completely altruistic proposal), he said such pensions should not be so high that they would create "a class of professional politicians with no interest to serve but their own".[156] After his retirement from politics, he said an election was unlikely in 1971 because at least 96 per cent of the Fianna Fáil TDs relied on their Dáil salaries for their livelihood. "It is an evil thing, which is a consequence of having full-time politicians in the Dáil."[157]

But Fine Gael's problems went deeper than the desultory approach to Dáil business by many TDs. In a thoughtful letter to Cosgrave in September 1935, Mulcahy reported on his impression of the views of the public, gleaned when giving lifts to people around the country (curiously, he said he was "totally unknown to most of these people", which even in a pre-television age seems a bit unlikely given his prominent role in recent Irish history). He said Fine Gael was not picking up support being lost by Fianna Fáil, partly because people thought they were the old Cumann na nGaedheal party "with a new name but without a new policy", partly because they were viewed as "a new imperialist grouping to defend England's interest in the Treaty".[158] The latter point tied in with Costello's experience during an election campaign in the 1930s. Waiting in Haddington Road for Mass to finish, he overheard two teenagers discussing the election, and one of them saying, "Sure that fellow Costello is only an old Englishman."[159]

Fine Gael had been well and truly lumbered with the reputation of being pro-British, and efforts by leading figures in the party, including Costello, to stress the benefits of Commonwealth membership added to that reputation. De Valera, on the other hand, largely ignored the Commonwealth. After the death of George v in January 1936, he refused to allow the Irish High Commissioner in London, John Dulanty, to sign the proclamation of accession for the new King as his counterparts had done. Dulanty still attended meetings of the High Commissioners, but confessed to his Canadian opposite number that he "felt like a whore at a christening".[160] De Valera was planning to clarify matters in his new Constitution, then in gestation, but his hand was forced by the abdication of Edward viii. He reacted by recalling the Dáil and introducing two pieces of legislation—one to remove all mention of the Crown from the Constitution, the other to authorise the King to act on behalf of the State in foreign affairs through the accreditation of diplomats and ratification of international agreements.

Costello made a forceful contribution on the proposed amendment of the Constitution. "This Bill creates a political monstrosity, the like of which is unknown to political legal theory ... we are to have this extraordinary and ludicrous position—a state of affairs which will make us the laughing stock of international jurists throughout the world—that for one purpose we have no head of this State and for another purpose we have a foreign King as the head of our State. What sort of State is that at all?" He criticised de Valera for not consulting the other members of the Commonwealth (ironic, in view of his own actions in Canada 12 years later), and said in an important passage, which would later be carefully attached to the file dealing with the repeal of the External Relations Act, "I do not care what the position is going to be in this country from a constitutional point of view, provided we know definitely where we stand. I can understand the position, constitutionally and internationally, of this country being a member, a full, recognised, decent member of the British Commonwealth of Nations. I can understand a decent declaration of a republic. But I cannot understand the indecency which is being perpetrated on this country by this Bill ... I want at least that it should be definite ..." He also suggested that the new legislation actually invested the King "with greater authority, greater force and greater prestige than he had when his Kingship as head of our State was a mere fiction".[161] Curiously, Canadian Prime Minister W.L. Mackenzie King made exactly the same point in the privacy of his diary, suggesting it would encourage a common policy on foreign affairs. "In trying to assert their nationalism, they have really made themselves more imperialistic than we who are retaining the Crown in internal as well as external affairs."[162]

When the External Relations Bill was introduced into the Dáil on Saturday 12 December, Costello criticised the first two sections, outlining that diplomatic representatives were appointed, and international agreements concluded, on the authority of the Executive Council. These were completely unnecessary, as they "merely express the existing practice, the existing state of affairs and the existing law of the country. Why then put them into a statute?" He also suggested that the effect of the Bill "which is to give us half a Crown is that it gives no Crown at all", because it only conferred authority on the King as long as he was recognised as the symbol of the co-operation of Australia, Canada, Great Britain, New Zealand and South Africa. The Crown, he argued, was never recognised as the symbol of co-operation, but as the symbol of free association. Therefore, the Bill could never come into effect.[163] He tried on the Committee Stage to change the wording to "free association" to match the reports of various Imperial Conferences and the Preamble of the Statute of Westminster. De Valera said he was prepared to accept "association", but not "free association", as he had doubts about how free Commonwealth association really was. He also argued that they should not import phrases into legislation—a suggestion which brought an indignant response from Costello, who pointed out that the words had been put in the Statute of Westminster by the Irish delegation. "Co-operation" stayed, and Costello voted for the Bill along with the rest of the Fine Gael TDs.[164]

He was to raise many of these issues again in the debates on de Valera's new Constitution. But before dealing with that, we should return to where this chapter began, with Eoin O'Duffy. The ignominious end to his leadership of Fine Gael had not exhausted his crusading zeal—and the outbreak of the Spanish Civil War gave him just the crusade he needed. While his intervention in Spain turned out to be a bit of a disaster for him, for those who went with him, and indeed for Franco, it was taken seriously enough at the time. When de Valera introduced a Bill to legislate for non-intervention in the Spanish Civil War, Costello claimed it was not designed to honour Ireland's international obligations, but to prevent O'Duffy bringing recruits to Spain. He added that some of those who went to Spain were strong supporters of Fine Gael, who had no sympathy with communism or fascism, but who "left good jobs for Spain in what they believed to be in the interests of their religion and not in the interest of Fascism". He pointed out that if the Bill was passed, those who were already in Spain could not come home for a holiday and then return to the fighting. With considerable indignation, he claimed that this provision would even apply to the Catholic chaplain attached to O'Duffy's brigade.[165] Some months later, he expanded on his views, saying that while they didn't have enough information to form a proper view of the situation in Spain, it was clear that the Spanish government "stands for Communism" and therefore Ireland should not send a representative to it. He also said that they were not opposed to the policy of non-intervention—a statement seized on by de Valera, who observed that Fine Gael's position hadn't been so clear initially.[166]

However, this was the last time O'Duffy would trouble Irish politics. New issues were looming—a new Constitution, a world war, a resurgent IRA—which would challenge the political elite, including John A. Costello.

Chapter 6 ∽

NO HOPE WHATEVER

"I know enough constitutional law to know how little constitutional law I know."[1]

JOHN A. COSTELLO, 1936

"We had men there who had apparently no future ... we had no chance of getting on and no hope whatever."[2]

JOHN A. COSTELLO, 1969

John A. Costello was one of the leading contributors to the debate on de Valera's new Constitution in 1937; he could also claim an indirect role in inspiring that document in the first place. As we saw in the previous chapter, he was severely critical of the proposed abolition of the Seanad in 1934, largely on the basis that it would allow a majority in the Dáil to change the Constitution without any other check. In response, de Valera agreed to examine the Constitution to identify "fundamental Articles dealing with the democratic foundations of the State. I do not mind if these are fixed so that they cannot be changed ... without some such provision as a Referendum."[3] The result was the establishment of a constitution committee[4]—which eventually led to the new Constitution.

The draft Constitution was published at the start of May 1937, and undated notes on Costello's copy show some of the concerns he would raise in the debates: provisions relating to the Irish language (in the name of the State, and in a proposal that laws could be passed to make the use of either Irish or English exclusive for certain purposes); the powers of the Taoiseach (to fire ministers and to seek a dissolution of the Dáil after losing its support); the method of electing the Seanad; and, above all, the new office of President of Ireland (he noted that proposals to give this official extra powers through legislation were "autocratic").[5] All these matters would be extensively debated, but the issue with which he raised the biggest initial storm was surprising.

Costello, the former opponent of female membership of the UCD Literary and Historical Society, now turned into a defender of women's rights.

Article 3 of the Irish Free State Constitution had stated that citizenship would be enjoyed by every qualified person "without distinction of sex" while Article 14 said the vote would be available to everyone over 21 who complied with electoral laws "without distinction of sex". It has been convincingly argued by constitutional lawyer Gerard Hogan that this "was not some sort of free-standing equality guarantee" but simply gave women the same citizenship rights as men. As proof, Hogan points out that much discriminatory legislation was passed while the Constitution was in force[6]—not least the Juries Act of 1927, passed by the Cosgrave Government of which Costello was Attorney General, which exempted women from jury service (although they could apply to serve).

However, the absence of the phrase "without discrimination of sex" in the draft was uneasily noticed by women's organisations. And in an article in the Irish Independent on 6 May, five days after the draft was published, Costello seized on the omission. He claimed that it affected the status of women "if not expressly, certainly by implication". Costello then pointed out that in other articles, the State was not to be prevented from having due regard to differences of capacity, physical and moral, and of social functions. He argued that this "allows a wide latitude" to introduce discrimination, adding that it "offers its Framer as a whole burnt offering to feminists and feminist associations".[7] This last phrase, recalling comments by Kevin O'Higgins at the 1926 Imperial Conference (see Chapter 4), caught de Valera's attention, as he referred to it several times during the Dáil debates.

The President responded to Costello's article in a speech in Ennis, saying he had deliberately left out the phrase "without distinction of sex". It had been used in 1922 because women had only just got the vote, and therefore it was "a badge of previous inferiority". There was no need to include the phrase in the new Constitution, because nobody was challenging their right to equal citizenship.[8] Maybe not, but it was arguable that they could—and Costello made that argument enthusiastically.

De Valera told the Dáil that women had equality "right through this document. There is nothing in it to suggest that they cannot vote for and become members of the Dáil, that they cannot vote for and be Senators, or that they cannot vote for and become President." He added that the mention of women in two Articles was "to give the protection which, I think, is necessary as part of our social programme".[9] He returned to this theme the following day. "My line of approach is not one of prejudice against women or women's rights. There is no truth whatever in it." Costello pointed out that Article 16 would enable a government to pass legislation to remove the vote from women.

De Valera responded with the not very reassuring observation that the provision "applies to other people as well as women". He said the provision was there to exclude certain classes of people—those of unsound mind, prisoners, and so on—but conceded, "you may strain that and say that the extraordinary thing could happen, and that half of the electorate was going to be disqualified".[10] But he eventually had to concede the point, and amended his draft to include the words "without distinction of sex" in relation to nationality and citizenship rights in Article 9.1.3.[11]

Having won this battle, Costello then turned his attention to the other provisions relating specifically to women—Article 40 on Personal Rights, which gave the State the power to take account of "differences of capacity, physical and moral, and of social function" in its laws, and Article 41 on The Family, which spoke about women's role in the home and said mothers should not be obliged by economic necessity to work outside it. He said the provisions "do not appear to have any really practical value in a constitutional instrument. They are headlines, if you like, statements of general principles, statements of high ideals, to put it at its highest." He agreed that there was nothing in the Constitution to prevent women getting work equally with men—but, he said, there was nothing to prevent a law being passed which would do so. It was, he said, "an incitement or an invitation to a future Legislature" to pass such a law.[12] Costello supported the removal of the phrase "by her life within the home" on the basis that it could be seen as a slight on women working outside the home, and indeed on single women. The promise to ensure that mothers wouldn't be forced by economic necessity to work outside the home was, he argued, unnecessary. The preceding article already committed the Government to support the family—and in any case the article didn't cover any other reasons why mothers might be forced to work, such as a drunken or lazy husband.[13]

In his obituary of Costello in January 1976, *Irish Times* Political Correspondent Michael McInerney wrote of his liberal attitude on some social issues, adding, "it is of interest ... that he was one of the very few who opposed the Constitutional ban on divorce in 1937".[14] Such opposition would indeed have been interesting, given Costello's reputation for loyalty to the Church. But in fact the point he raised—which was accepted by de Valera—related to a foreign registry office wedding that was subsequently dissolved. The case he cited involved a Catholic Irish girl who "married a Scotchman of a different religion in a registry office. Of course, that marriage was not in accordance with the views of the Catholic Church, was invalid and no marriage at all ... the marriage was never consummated, because the parties separated at the door of the registry office and never saw each other again. The girl came to Ireland and desired to marry. The case was submitted to me when I was Attorney General with a view to prosecution for bigamy. I need hardly say that I did not prosecute."[15]

He argued that the draft ban on the remarriage of people whose marriages had been dissolved under the civil law of any other state would affect such people. "It is no marriage, according to the Catholic Church. It is not a marriage, according to the law, because it has been dissolved in England, and this Article prevents either of the parties getting married here." De Valera promised to look into the matter, but warned that dealing with all possible exceptions might undermine the purpose of the clause, which was to ensure that a valid marriage would not be dissolved within the State.[16] The final article banned remarriage of people who had a dissolution abroad but whose marriage was "a subsisting valid marriage" under Irish law[17]—a provision that would exclude the registry office wedding.

But most of the debate was devoted to the new office of President of Ireland. Fine Gael "suspected that office might be a vehicle for the establishment of a de Valera dictatorship, either by his becoming President and being voted considerable powers by a compliant government or by installing a 'yes man' as president".[18] The former concern was prompted by Article 13.10, which stated that further powers and functions could be conferred on the President by law—the provision beside which Costello had written "autocratic".

Pointing out that the word "Taoiseach" had been translated on German radio as "Führer", he claimed that the office of President was a "scheme ... for dictatorial powers", whether it was occupied by de Valera or anyone else. Costello particularly objected to election by popular suffrage, which he believed would make the President "the centre of political activity in the future", either directing events himself, or through his "yes man", the Taoiseach. He declared, "I tell the House there is not a greater tyranny than the tyranny which masquerades under the cloak of democracy" (to which MacEntee rather wittily responded, "What about the tyranny that masquerades under a blue shirt?").[19] De Valera later picked up on the comment himself, saying that anybody can say that anything is masquerading. "I could say, for instance, that the lawyers over there who have been talking about this were only masquerading as lawyers and were really politicians."[20]

De Valera was to make this suggestion more than once during the debates on the Constitution. He complained that Costello, along with the other lawyers on the Opposition benches, was playing politics rather than giving considered legal opinions. "If I were asking the Deputy's opinion privately, I would listen to it with the greatest care. I am afraid, however, that when he speaks from the benches opposite, he goes half the way with his argument as a lawyer, and then you can see the turn around."[21] At another stage of the debate, de Valera said that at one time he was "innocent enough" to think that

Costello spoke in the Dáil strictly as a lawyer, but that "he has not his wig on here, and therefore I expect that he feels at liberty to make a case that he would not dare to make elsewhere".[22]

Costello also made an issue of the separation of powers, claiming to see danger to the independence of the judiciary in Article 37, which allowed non-judges to exercise "limited functions and powers of a judicial nature" in non-criminal matters. This, he claimed, would make civil servants judges and establish "bureaucracy in excelsis". He also linked the provision with the powers of the presidency, saying it could be used to pass a motion "providing that the President can decide anything he likes except matters of criminal law. He may issue letters of cachet lodging persons in jail without trial and there is nothing in this Constitution to prevent him ... This Draft Constitution allows the President to raise taxes on the people, on any and every article, without consideration by the Dáil."[23]

However, he appeared to be more fundamentally concerned about the reduction in the jurisdiction of the courts than about possible presidential transgressions. He proposed an amendment which would restrict non-judges to exercising judicial functions in "the exercise of administrative functions". De Valera promised to have the matter examined.[24] The Revenue Commissioners noted that Costello's proposed amendment would affect a large number of tribunals and commissioners exercising judicial functions not related to administration. In a memorandum sent to de Valera, they claimed that transferring these functions to the courts "would be disastrous from the point of view of the public as well as the State. The legal profession would be the only section of the community which would have reason to welcome such a change." The Commissioners speculated that Costello's real aim was the abolition of the Special Commissioners of Income Tax, which had been hearing appeals against tax assessments since 1853. "He has consistently shown hostility to this body ... The transfer of their functions to the Courts would mean a very considerable increase in expense to taxpayers, and, owing to the delays and confusion caused, would probably bring about a state of something approaching chaos in the administration of the Income Tax ..." The Minister for Finance, Seán MacEntee, suggested to de Valera that when dealing with the issue in the Dáil he should avoid mentioning the legal doubts which existed over the prevailing practice in Government departments, and that if the Opposition raised it, he should point out that nobody had felt confident enough to test the matter in the Courts.[25]

De Valera gave no ground on this issue, or on the presidency. Costello pointed out that the requirement to consult the Council of State was no check on the President's powers, claiming that he had devised the phrase "after consultation with" along with Kevin O'Higgins during the drafting of the

Court Officers' Act 1926 "for the purpose of meaning nothing". He returned to the problem he saw with direct election, complaining that the President "can claim the same authority for his actions, legal or illegal, as the Government of the day can for their actions. The source of both their authorities is the vote of the people." This, he believed, could lead to conflict between government and president, who could "resort to highfalutin' talk about his being the guardian of the Constitutional rights and liberties of the people ... and the direct appointee of the plain people".[26] One of the amendments proposed by Costello would restrict the President to a single seven-year term on the basis that if he were eligible for re-election, he might direct all his public actions towards that end. In any case, he believed, seven years was too long a term.[27]

He also wanted to remove the right of an outgoing president to nominate himself, saying he could not see the reason for treating him differently from other candidates. And, despite his suspicion of the new office, he opposed the provision for impeachment, saying it was a holdover from ancient British practice, and that if anyone was ever impeached, "all that will happen is that there will be an awful lot of talk either in the Seanad or in the Dáil, and in the end nothing will happen". However, he expressed the hope that "Providence and my constituents may spare me to witness this extraordinary trial by impeachment of some unfortunate President, as I think it will be a matter of considerable amusement."[28]

Costello strenuously objected to what he saw as curtailments of civil rights in the new Constitution. He claimed that the phrase "subject to public order and morality", which qualified the guarantee of certain rights, was "a grave menace" to freedom, because it gave the Government considerable latitude to define threats to order or morals. He made two suggestions to limit emergency powers, claiming that he would recommend them to any government he was advising—firstly, to allow the courts to certify whether or not there was a state of emergency, and secondly to provide for an appeal from special courts to the Court of Criminal Appeal. He said these safeguards would "go far towards calming the very reasonable fears that special courts would be used for subverting the liberties of the subject". The irony of such suggestions from a former Attorney General who had helped bring in emergency powers was not lost on de Valera. He pointed out that if Costello were still Attorney General, he would "be the first to enter a caveat" to personal rights in order to see peace and order preserved—an accusation that was not denied.[29]

In his initial notes on the draft Constitution, Costello described as "a patent absurdity" the provision that the Irish text would prevail if there was a conflict between it and the English version. He wrote that the Irish text was obviously a translation of the English, and that "the draft was conceived in English, will be debated in English, and, at least for many years must be construed by

Judges not learned in the intricate idioms of the Irish language".[30] During the Dáil debate, Costello successfully objected to de Valera's original intention to have the state called "Éire" in both Irish and English texts. He objected to the practice of mixing the two languages in one document (citing the practice of starting a letter "A chara" and finishing it "Mise, le meas", with the rest written in English). But he said his real reason for putting down the amendment to change the name to Ireland was to do with the State's international status. "In so far as we are known abroad as a nation internationally, we are known by the use of the word 'Ireland'. If you put in the word 'Éire', then foreigners may think that there is some distinction between the State that we have here and what has been known for centuries as Ireland." De Valera rather reluctantly accepted the argument, and the amendment.[31]

Costello took exception to the provisions surrounding the Government too. He strongly supported the idea of collective responsibility (an idea that would be severely tested in his own first government), saying a minister must abide by the majority decision in Cabinet "irrespective of his own particular views before the decision was come to". He objected to the provision that the Taoiseach could demand a Minister's resignation, saying this meant they "hold office at the will and pleasure of the Prime Minister".[32] He believed this would make the Taoiseach too powerful. In Costello's view, the holder of that office might be first among equals, but he should not dictate to the other members of the Cabinet. It was a view he would put into practice when he himself became Taoiseach 11 years later.

Ironically, given their later positions on the abolition of proportional representation, Costello urged de Valera not to specify in the Constitution the form of PR to be used. He said it should be left open, as it had been in the Free State constitution, rather than opting to "pin our faith" to the single transferable vote. STV would eventually lead, he argued, to a large number of small parties, leading to "instability in government". But de Valera warned that a simple commitment to PR could be abused by finding an electoral system which was ostensibly proportional but which was very far from being so in practice.[33]

Costello also made an effort to put protection for transferred civil servants into the Constitution, arguing that such a provision would prevent any future legislature repealing the 1929 Civil Service (Transferred Officers) Compensation Act, which he had drawn up as a solution to the Wigg-Cochrane case. He argued that he was not seeking a privileged position for these officers, but merely a position of safety. He pointed out that if the transferred officers hadn't had a guarantee in the Free State Constitution, the Wigg-Cochrane case would not have been won. His proposal was strongly supported by Bill Norton, but de Valera was not disposed to give way. He pointed out that

Costello had a special interest in the issue, and it would be unfair if other groups of people did not have their rights enshrined in the Constitution because they didn't have a similar advocate in the Dáil. De Valera acknowledged that he might be hard to convince. Costello said it wasn't hard to convince him—it was impossible.[34]

In fact, he had secured some concessions—copper-fastening the rights of women and securing Ireland as the official name of the state, as well as certain minor changes to other articles. In the main, though, de Valera proved obdurate on matters of substance. However, Costello looked on the bright side, saying there were advantages to the Government ignoring the advice of the lawyers on the other side of the House. "If this Constitution is persisted in, as it stands at the moment, we who expect to be making our living for some years at the Irish Bar can look forward to making a rich harvest ..."[35]

But before he could concentrate on reaping his expected rich harvest, he had to face a general election. He fought the 1937 general election in a new constituency, Dublin Townships—effectively the constituency later called Dublin South-East. It was a three-seater, and in 1937 Seán MacEntee topped the poll, being elected on the first count with 27.4 per cent of the vote. Fine Gael won just over 45 per cent of the vote, which was perfectly split between Costello and his running mate, Ernest Benson, ensuring that both were elected—Costello was ahead by just 105 votes.

Dublin South-East produced many prominent politicians over the years—apart from Costello and MacEntee, they included Noël Browne, Garret FitzGerald, Ruairí Quinn, Michael McDowell and John Gormley. Quinn reported the comment of one woman talking to a Labour Party activist: "Oh, we don't elect TDs here, we elect Ministers."[36] The constituency had—and has—the image of being very well-heeled. There was much talk during Garret FitzGerald's time as Taoiseach of the "Dublin 4 set", for instance. But it also had—and has—areas of significant social deprivation. In 1939, Costello told the Dáil that he spoke "as the representative of a ... constituency with poor people, with people on the border-line of poverty, with people on the border-line of comfort, and with very few rich people".[37] Costello spent a good deal of time dealing with constituents seeking housing, which he described as "one of the most disheartening and heart-breaking tasks" he faced.[38] On another occasion, he observed, "I hear stories that would wring the heart of a stone—and I can do nothing."[39] This was to continue even while he was Taoiseach.

The first contest in Dublin Townships in 1937 was marked by controversy involving Seán MacEntee—not for the last time. According to figures supplied to the returning officer, he and his running mate, Bernard Butler, spent £1,210 on their campaign, compared to the £106 reported by Costello and Benson.[40] After being challenged about these figures by Gerry Boland, the Minister for

Lands and Honorary Secretary of Fianna Fáil, MacEntee defensively replied that around £500 was spent on newspaper advertising, "mainly to make good the weakness of the Headquarters effort in that regard". He claimed that this expenditure helped the party in areas outside the constituency. Another £34 was spent delivering copies of the election bulletin to 13,000 houses, and of the Constitution to 3,500 houses. £100 was spent on letters to constituents, £73 on a constituency headquarters and a number of committee rooms, £22 on loudspeakers, £46 on bands, £91 on printing, £50 on "signs, streamers, flags, etc.". It was an astonishing amount of money in the context of the times, covered by a direct personal appeal for support which raised £1,115 and £100 from Fianna Fáil headquarters. But MacEntee argued it was justifiable due to the nature of the constituency, which was "an overwhelmingly middle-class, residential district, the residents of which do not come to public meetings".[41]

Perhaps MacEntee did need to spend this amount to get his message across, but he got a poor return for the investment. Not only did Fianna Fáil win only one of the three seats on offer, Dublin Townships also returned the highest No vote in the country in the Referendum on the Constitution. 59 per cent of valid votes in the constituency were cast against the Constitution. The only other constituencies to vote No were Cork West (55.5 per cent against), Wicklow (51.7 per cent) and Dublin County (51.7 per cent).[42] However, nationally, the Constitution was accepted by 56.5 per cent of voters, on a very high turnout of almost 76 per cent.

The general election left de Valera in a minority, but he managed to return to government. The new Dáil had to deal with a number of matters arising from the Constitution, including arrangements for electing the new Seanad. Costello was scathing about the proposals, pointing out that there was no basis on which to establish a functional or vocational upper house. There was no equivalent of the corporative system in Italy, nor was one likely to develop. "There is no use trying to set up machinery for something which has no proper foundation." He rightly observed that no matter how good a candidate was, he would not be elected without party political support.[43] How, he asked, was a Seanad with "specialised knowledge, independence of thought and action" to emerge when the electorate was made up of politicians, including councillors? He also warned of the danger of political corruption, of councillors "being subject to corrupt pressure, of being asked to vote for a particular person for a monetary consideration, because that is going to happen, and we had better face it".[44] This was a prescient observation—ironically, in 1945 Costello would himself be on the legal team of John Corr, who was convicted of bribing councillors to influence their Seanad votes.[45]

In a speech to a Fine Gael meeting in Dublin in December 1937, Costello claimed that the "so-called economic war has steadily poisoned the life stream of our body politic", and that "there can be no relief until that absurd conflict is put an end to". That much may have been true—but he also predicted that the Government, "under their present leadership at all events" would not have the courage to make an honourable and advantageous peace.[46] In fact, that was exactly what de Valera was working on, and in April 1938 he reached agreement on ending the economic war, as well as securing the return of the Treaty ports. It was a diplomatic triumph which he rightly recognised would be extremely popular with the electorate, if he could only find an excuse for appealing to them again. Luckily for him, just such an excuse was to be supplied by John A. Costello.

In March, Costello moved a private members' motion in the Dáil calling on the Government to establish arbitration for disputes on pay and conditions in the Civil Service. As he admitted when moving the motion, the subject had been before the House on several occasions already, and the arguments were predictable. He pointed out that arbitration machinery was already working well in Britain, and so "we are not taking any leap in the dark" with the proposals.[47] The Government claimed that binding arbitration would impinge on the Government's control of the public finances. When the debate finally wound up with a vote in May, Costello said it was clear that any scheme of arbitration would be "subject to the paramount right of control in the Dáil".[48] Then, to everyone's surprise, the Government was defeated in the vote, by 52 to 51. The result was greeted with cheers from Opposition TDs, who suggested it was time for the Government to resign. The Taoiseach was not present, having gone to Limerick for the funeral of his uncle, Patrick Coll.[49]

The Government spent two days considering its options after the first Dáil defeat under the new Constitution. These were broadly four—accept the vote and introduce arbitration; ignore the decision of the Dáil altogether; put down a motion of confidence to clarify if it still commanded a majority in the Dáil; or call an election. Given the favourable political situation, the last option was an attractive one to de Valera, so while his decision appeared to surprise observers, it shouldn't have. The decision to call an election was made at a Cabinet meeting on the morning of 27 May, and announced late that night. The Taoiseach said a Government with a precarious parliamentary majority "cannot do the nation's work as it should be done", and that it had to be able "to refuse sectional demands which it considers not to be in the general interest".[50]

MacEntee attacked his constituency rival with relish, telling voters that the election had been precipitated by Costello, claiming the issue was not arbitration, but the demand that "it should be applied without any safeguard for the taxpayer".[51] In fact, Costello's motion had specified that the Government's acceptance of any arbitration awards would be "subject to the overriding authority of the Oireachtas"[52], but that mattered little in the context of a heated election campaign. He later complained that his rival had gone round the constituency "raising the hair on the heads of the taxpayers about the amount of money and taxes" arbitration would cost.[53] MacEntee increased his share of the vote to just under 31 per cent, while the Fine Gael share also rose—but Benson benefited more than Costello, and was elected on the first count along with MacEntee. Though well ahead of the second Fianna Fáil candidate and elected comfortably, Costello was almost one thousand votes behind his running mate. He later claimed that the fall in his vote was due to attacks on his position on arbitration. "Every effort was made to deprive me of my seat ... because of the stand I took on behalf of civil servants."[54] But the figures were an indication that despite his high profile in the Dáil, he could take nothing for granted if there was slippage in the Fine Gael vote.

Costello continued to mix politics and the law, notably in arguing cases before the Civil Service Compensation Board, the body set up under the 1929 Act to hear compensation claims from transferred civil servants. The most significant case was that of Peter Hegarty of the Department of Local Government. In a decision delivered in August 1938, the tribunal agreed that, as a transferred civil servant, he was entitled to compensation because his position had been changed by the new Constitution—in effect, it held that he had been discharged from the service of the Free State because the Constitution had come into force.[55] As Costello noted with some glee, he had been in the position of arguing that "a great change had taken place by virtue of the Constitution, and the Minister's advisers were forced to make the case ... that really no change had taken place at all ... the Minister will forgive me if I got a certain amount of amusement out of the Hegarty case ..."[56]

With an estimated nine thousand civil servants who had transferred from the British to the Free State still working for the Government, the possibility of many more such claims was clearly a live one.[57] Legislation was introduced in October to clarify that anyone deemed to have been discharged from the Free State civil service on the coming into force of the new Constitution was deemed to have been immediately reemployed, on the same terms and conditions, in the service of the Government of Ireland.[58] Costello argued during the debate on the Bill that only around 40 civil servants had lodged claims based on the Hegarty decision, and that the Government was not faced with a "very serious financial embarrassment".[59] The Government wisely ignored this point of view and closed the loophole.

Another case involved a client who sued for libel after being referred to as a "hangman judge". Costello met one of the character witnesses, civil servant Leon Ó Broin, on the way into court, and asked him if he remembered Hempenstall, "a figure from the '98 period who had the ugly reputation of being judge, jury, hangman and all. I did, and when I was in the witness box Costello exploited that piece of Irish history to secure judgment and £3,000 for his client."[60]

Far more serious matters were on the horizon, though. In July 1938, with the Sudeten crisis brewing on the Continent, the Dáil discussed the Army Estimate. Costello made the point that Ireland would be attacked if it suited some big nation to do so—no matter what constitutional provisions or type of sovereignty she had. He also, equally realistically, pointed out that Ireland did not have the resources to pay for an adequate defence against these big nations. However, thanks to geography, it was in British interests to defend Ireland. He correctly foresaw that Ireland would supply food to a Britain at war, but wrongly believed this would make neutrality impossible as Irish ships and harbours would be attacked. The logic of his argument was that "we are going to be attacked if it suits another country to attack us ... we cannot afford to equip ourselves for modern warfare, and that therefore we shall have to depend on some nation which has a common defence policy with us to assist us". Specifically, he suggested Ireland should co-operate with "the other nations of the Commonwealth". Defence Minister Frank Aiken dismissed the suggestion of a defence agreement with Britain while Partition lasted.[61]

It may seem odd that at this late stage Costello still regarded Ireland as a member of the Commonwealth—but such she still was, despite de Valera's refusal to have anything at all to do with the machinery of the Commonwealth. Even the decision to remain neutral in the Second World War did not imply a final break with Dominion status, according to the distinguished scholar Nicholas Mansergh. He pointed out that South Africa only decided by a narrow vote in Parliament to enter the war, making abundantly clear that "the decision between peace and war rested with each dominion Parliament. If Éire be regarded as a dominion, there was no difference in principle between a South African Parliament deciding by a small majority against neutrality and the Dáil deciding virtually unanimously in favour of it."[62]

Neutrality, however, was not the policy of the IRA, which launched a bombing campaign against Britain early in 1939. De Valera's response was to introduce two pieces of legislation—a Treason Bill, which prescribed the death penalty; and the Offences Against the State Bill, which provided for the reintroduction of the military tribunal and internment without trial. All these powers were to be extensively used during the Second World War. Fine Gael reluctantly offered to support the legislation, subject to certain safeguards. Costello acknowledged that the Offences Against the State Bill was "practically verbatim copied" from legislation introduced between 1922 and 1932, especially Article 2A. But he wanted some sections removed from the Bill.[63] He objected to provisions putting the onus of proof on those accused of having illegal documents in their possession, and giving the State power to suppress an organisation—he claimed this was too drastic a provision to be included in ordinary law, and cited his own party's experience of having an organisation banned. He also insisted that there should be a right of appeal from the special tribunal to the Court of Criminal Appeal—saying that "if, God forbid, I had anything to do with anything like Article 2A again, I would certainly wish to have, from the point of view of any person prosecuting or defending before a special tribunal" such a right of appeal.[64] His amendment was accepted, and the right of appeal from the tribunal established in law.

On Saturday 2 September 1939, the day after the German invasion of Poland and the day before Britain and France declared war, the Oireachtas was recalled to pass two measures. The first was a constitutional amendment to give the Oireachtas power to declare that a state of emergency existed (to avoid the possibility that the courts would hold that emergency powers could only be used when the State was actually involved in a conflict). The second was a comprehensive Emergency Powers Bill. It was so comprehensive, in fact, that Costello claimed it caused him "profound shock". However, given the circumstances, Fine Gael was prepared to give the Government the powers it sought—on certain conditions. In particular, Costello was worried about the powers of delegation in the Bill, which would allow the Government to confer powers on various people without further consultation with the Oireachtas. "To me, with my legal experience and legal instincts, they are very objectionable indeed." He argued that the powers of censorship should be "exercised with the utmost tact and with the greatest possible leniency towards newspapers"; that the power of control over persons entering or leaving the State, or of moving freely about the State, should not apply to Irish citizens; and that the Government should use Orders under the legislation "as sparingly as possible and to allow no element of bureaucracy to enter into the administration of the measure"[65]—a theme he was to return to repeatedly during the war years.

He described the Offences Against the State Act as the "lineal successor to Article 2A. It is an improved copy of Article 2A, with the holes in Article 2A more or less stopped." But he made the point that Article 2A had only been brought in as a last resort, to meet a breakdown in the administration of justice, and he vigorously objected to the use of such powers to deal with lesser difficulties.[66] Following a judicial declaration that Part VI of the Offences Against the State Act was unconstitutional, the Dáil was recalled at the start of 1940 to deal with amending legislation. The Government wanted to allow for the internment of Irish citizens, the power left out of the original legislation because of objections from Costello and others. Now he repeated his arguments, saying that Fine Gael stood for two things—the maintenance of law and order, and the guarantee of constitutional rights to citizens. Costello said he didn't think legislation introduced to deal with an emergency created by a war outside the State was the place to deal with a domestic problem (i.e. the IRA).[67]

Costello continued to play a prominent role within Fine Gael, being elected by the National Executive as one of the 18 members of the party's Standing Committee.[68] He was in demand as a speaker, and his contributions were extensively covered in the media—the *Irish Times* reported his contribution to a party meeting in December 1941 more prominently than those of McGilligan and Mulcahy. He used this speech, at the Mansion House in Dublin, to point out that while Fine Gael had been criticised for not forming a National Government, they hadn't actually been invited to form one. And, while they were supporting the Government on defence, the party "had not sold its independence of thought".[69]

During the war years, he continued to speak on a wide range of issues. In 1940, he objected to a proposal to restrict the tax advantages of covenants, arguing that it would deprive charities like the St Vincent de Paul of much needed income, and referring to his personal interest in one of the Society's conferences.[70] He also objected to the level of income tax (which was 6/6 in the pound or 33 per cent), claiming that it was the result of Government extravagance over the previous eight years rather than being due to the war. He put forward the novel argument that high taxation caused unemployment, because "each individual has to do without one particular workman or one particular servant or perhaps, two more that they might keep on if the income-tax was not so high".[71]

Restrictions on the petrol ration following the sinking of a number of tankers on their way to Irish ports led Costello to deliver an impassioned speech on behalf of the private motorist. He argued there were "huge numbers" of people dependent on the motor trade—mechanics, petrol retailers, car distributors, chauffeurs, insurance clerks, and so on. "The owner of the private motor car should be given great consideration and not thrown on the scrapheap in this fashion. It is on the private motor car that many men and women depend for their business or trade." Costello was critical of the Government for not foreseeing that ships were liable to be sunk in the middle of a war and laying in extra emergency supplies.[72] His call for more petrol was both unrealistic and unreasonable in the circumstances—though no doubt popular with his constituents.

Costello returned to a related subject later in the war, when a number of doctors had their petrol ration reduced after being accused of trying to get official approval to use their cars to go to a golf course. He told the Dáil that they had never asked the Department of Supplies for permission to use their cars to go golfing—it appeared someone had made the request without their permission. Costello took particular exception to the fact that the story was given to the newspapers, despite the doctors having made it clear that they had not made the application. "There was never in the history of bureaucracy ... such an impudent performance, such an irresponsible performance, as the publication yesterday in the Press of this lie about these six professional gentlemen ..." According to Lemass, the doctors involved were members of Portmarnock Golf Club—and the request concerned whether one of them could take a car to the club at the weekend so that any emergency calls could be answered immediately.[73]

This was not at all unreasonable, because the journey to and from Portmarnock was something of a marathon during the war. For Costello it meant a walk down Herbert Park to catch a tram to Nelson's Pillar, then a walk down Amiens Street to board a train to Portmarnock, before taking a 20-minute ride in a horse-drawn victoria to the club. And, of course, the journey would have to be repeated in reverse in the evening.[74] Obviously, doctors trying to answer an emergency call would be in serious difficulty if they had to rely on such arrangements. Lemass agreed to restore their petrol ration, though warning that it was up to those receiving a ration not to abuse it, while his Department would withdraw the privilege if there was "any possibility" of it being abused.[75]

Quite apart from the principle of State interference, Costello had an obvious personal interest in defending the reputations of fellow members of Portmarnock. He also had a professional interest in the survival of private motoring. As he observed during a discussion of legal costs (he insisted the costs were largely for expert witnesses rather than "the legal gentlemen involved"), the curtailment of private motoring was causing a fall in personal injury cases, which he described as a "lucrative source of revenue for the members of my profession. At all events, let us hope there will be still some cases drifting into court and let us hope that the war will be over very shortly and that we will have our motor cars again on the road."[76]

Jack Costello retained an interest in wider issues of legal reform, having the reputation of being "the keenest law reformer in the Library".[77] In June 1941, he and Dillon introduced a proposed amendment to the Constitution to safeguard the independence of the judiciary.[78] They proposed a Supreme Court investigation into complaints against a judge before a vote was taken in the Oireachtas, as well as increasing the threshold for removal from a simple to a two-thirds majority in both houses. During the second stage debate, Costello made the rather startling admission that "I do not like the machinery that I have provided in my own Bill, but I had to provide something, merely for the purpose of initiating a discussion with a view to seeing if anybody could suggest a different or better machinery ..." But his point was that the existing system meant "there is nothing necessary to secure the removal of a judge but a vote of the Oireachtas, and if the Government recommends that a judge should be removed, that recommendation must be accepted by both Houses, otherwise the Government would have to fall ..."[79] De Valera said he didn't think the change was necessary, and it was duly defeated. Costello's fears of an overbearing legislature sacking judges proved unfounded. But the point he raised about how complaints against judges would be investigated was prescient—and still hasn't been resolved.

The other legal reform promoted by Costello, this time in conjunction with McGilligan, related to the more technical area of tort reform. Though the Bill was published in June 1941, it wasn't discussed in the Dáil until November. Costello explained that his aim was not simply to secure some (much-needed) reforms, but "to direct attention to the fact that there is quite a large body of our law at the moment badly in need of reform".[80] He gave as an example the absence of a law allowing for legal adoption.[81] Justice Minister Gerry Boland welcomed the raising of the issues involved, though he thought the middle of the Emergency was perhaps not the best time for such legislation. Still, he agreed to have the matters raised in Costello's Bill examined in his Department and to introduce his own legislation.[82] Nearly six years later, Costello was told the legislation had been drawn up, but the whole subject was to be referred to a new Law Reform Committee—as soon as it was set up.[83] He complained that "we neither have a law reform committee nor is my Bill to be brought in ... I was given what I thought was a promise by the Minister that the Bill would be introduced."[84] In office, he was able to have the Tortfeasors Act passed into law in 1951, as well as encouraging the establishment of a Law Reform and Consolidation section within the Attorney General's Office.[85]

But that was the future—during the war, he was in Opposition, and continuing a dogged campaign against the abuse of special powers. In July 1941, when a Bill to continue emergency powers came before the Dáil, Costello sought an assurance from Government that they would only use the powers for the purposes mentioned in the legislation—to secure public safety, maintain public order, and provide and control supplies and services. He pointed out that it was difficult to see how an Order freezing the Civil Service bonus could come under any of these categories. He also said the Dáil could have debated the measures contained in Emergency Orders, rather than have the House sit only a couple of days a fortnight. "It would be far better for public opinion, and for the security of the State, if the people had the safety valve of the Dáil and the Seanad, the Oireachtas as a whole, for the expression of their views in connection with the matters that were dealt with in these Orders ..."[86]

In January 1942, Labour introduced a Dáil motion to annul one of those Emergency Powers, No. 139 of 1941. As well as allowing unsigned statements to be admitted as evidence before the tribunal, it effectively put the onus of proof on the accused. As Costello pointed out, this meant that if someone was accused of murder or treason "if he does not prove that negative, without a single tittle of evidence being adduced on behalf of the person prosecuting him, he can be condemned to death and suffer death". The former Attorney General expressed some sympathy with Gardaí who believed people to be guilty of certain crimes but were unable to prove it. He said the provisions of the Emergency Order would be a dangerous temptation to them: "I fear the police official who is out to get a conviction ... There are many of them who will extract a statement at all costs ... But, in connection with these provisions, the man I fear most is the conscientious, truthful, efficient, zealous police officer who will convince himself on hearsay evidence that a person is guilty of a crime, and who will go all out ... to secure a conviction ..."[87] Costello was one of 20 TDs who supported the Labour attempt to have the Order rescinded, along with other prominent Fine Gael figures like McGilligan, O'Higgins and FitzGerald-Kenny. The party had allowed a free vote on the Order, and Cosgrave, Mulcahy and Dillon were among those who voted with the Government, who secured 71 votes.[88] Dillon left Fine Gael the following month, February 1942, because of his opposition to neutrality.

Fine Gael believed the 1942 School Attendance Bill to be unconstitutional. Costello prepared a lengthy opinion on the matter, going through the various arguments against and for it, and possible answers to the points likely to be raised by the Government. The Fine Gael criticism was that the Bill gave ultimate authority to decide on a child's education to the Minister rather than the parent, which appeared to be repugnant to Article 42 of the Constitution. The argument was set out in a letter to President Hyde requesting him to refer the Bill to the Supreme Court to test its constitutionality.[89] When he did so, Costello was the leading counsel arguing against the Bill.[90] The court found section 4 of the Bill unconstitutional, effectively killing it—proving that the new Constitution had its advantages for an Opposition with no hope of defeating legislation in the Dáil.[91]

Costello could have been forgiven for approaching the 1943 election with reasonable confidence. The Government was unpopular in the midst of wartime shortages, and Costello was a prominent member of the opposition, who had played a leading role in raising many of the issues of concern to his constituents, particularly (though not exclusively) the middle-class ones. His prominence was rewarded with extensive coverage in the newspapers—his opening and closing election speeches received front-page attention in the *Irish Times*, for instance. The opening address, in Leinster Square in Rathmines, made the case for "a National Government, representative of, and acting for, all sections of the community". He said no other party in the Dáil made such an offer to the people (which raised the question of how a national government was to be formed). He also claimed that Fine Gael had a constructive policy for national recovery, with increased employment, lower taxation, and a return to prosperity led by agriculture. He said nobody was challenging neutrality—an indication of the popularity of that policy—which had been made possible by the efforts of the Cosgrave government at Imperial Conferences and in Geneva.[92] His closing speech again stressed the virtues of a national government, and said unless Ireland had "prudent leaders capable of effectually participating" in post-war negotiations, she would become "the Cinderella of the nations".[93]

Before the campaign began, Costello's solicitor friend John Burke, a Fianna Fáil supporter, wrote to Seán MacEntee expressing his view that there was no chance of a second seat for the party in Dublin Townships. "I believe that if Dev and yourself were to go forward only one would get the quota. Benson will get the Protestant vote, you will get the weight of the Party backing and Jack Costello the balance. Jack gets a big personal vote and you must agree the Dáil would be very much the poorer were he not returned."[94] If the acerbic MacEntee responded to this last point, it has unfortunately not been preserved.

In any case, he was probably too busy engaging in Red-baiting against a resurgent Labour Party to bother about the effect on the Dáil of Costello's absence. So vociferous were his attacks that Lemass wrote asking him to tone them down, arguing that they were helping rather than hurting Labour. He concluded laconically, "I hope it won't cramp your style." MacEntee responded in wounded tones, observing that "elections are not won by billing and cooing at your opponents". He agreed to bear in mind the concerns that had been raised, but rejected the assertion that his constituency was so different to that of Lemass. "There is almost as large a proportion of working class voters in it as in the other city areas and the vast majority of our workers are of course working class people. They are not of the same mind as your workers in regard to this matter."[95]

The result in Dublin Townships was a triumph for Fianna Fáil, and more particularly for MacEntee, and a personal disappointment for Costello. The Fianna Fáil vote was actually marginally down from the 1938 election, from 47.7 to 46.2 per cent, but the Fine Gael share of the vote was down by 10 per cent, from 52.5 to 42.6 per cent. The difference was caused by the two Labour candidates, who between them took just over 11 per cent of the vote. Costello was clearly hurt more than the other candidates by the Labour intervention— his share of the vote, at 19.45 per cent, was the lowest he ever got in the constituency, and he lost his seat to the second Fianna Fáil candidate, Bernard Butler. Fine Gael activists believed Costello's shock defeat was the result of the alphabetical ordering of the names of the two candidates in all the election literature, which put Ernest Benson ahead of him. This order was reversed on party propaganda in the next election.[96]

If MacEntee expected praise for the result, which after all had deprived the main Opposition party of one of its most effective Dáil performers, he was in for a disappointment. De Valera criticised him at Cabinet for his anti-Labour diatribes, which were blamed for the loss of a number of Fianna Fáil seats. This led to the inevitable letter of resignation, in which he claimed that while "the campaign in Dublin Townships was by no means the only one which Fianna Fáil fought successfully, it was the only one in which to the general public at least the success was unmistakeable. It is usual to censure men for losing elections, but not for winning them." He said the improvement in the party's position in Townships had been due to his vigorous defence of Government policy against Labour attack in the working-class areas. "If the candidates in Roscommon had gone to the same trouble and pains as I did to make the case for the Government's policy, the Labour votes in that constituency might have been held for the Government as they were in the working class districts of Dublin Townships ... I thought I had succeeded, but apparently it would have been better to have lost than won."[97] Not for the first or last time, he was prevailed upon to withdraw his resignation, but the dispute must have soured the taste of victory. (MacEntee was a serial resigner; at a later stage, he even threatened to resign while in opposition, from the "Committee of the Party", in protest at what he regarded as the failure of the Irish Press to adequately support the efforts of Fianna Fáil in the Dáil and the country.[98])

Costello, of course, was not the only leading Fine Gael figure to lose his seat—Richard Mulcahy was also defeated, in Dublin North-East. At the first parliamentary party meeting following the election, W.T. Cosgrave noted that Fianna Fáil had only 67 seats, compared to a combined total of 71 for the Opposition. There was criticism from Wexford TD Sir John Esmonde of contacts with other Opposition parties about the election of a Taoiseach. Cosgrave said there hadn't been any negotiations, only informal contacts, and that any agreement would have to come back to the parliamentary party for final decision.[99] Whatever discussions there were came to nothing, and de Valera was re-elected Taoiseach as head of another minority government.

It was clear that Cosgrave would not remain leader for long—but his obvious successor, Richard Mulcahy, was now in the Seanad. James Dillon was approached to take on the leadership in the Dáil by McGilligan, but decided after some hesitation that he could not return to the party, whether as leader, deputy leader or front bench member, so long as the European war lasted, "gladly as I would serve in any of these capacities in different circumstances, under Dick Mulcahy's presidency". Dillon said he believed Tom O'Higgins must take on the leadership instead.[100] Cosgrave announced his resignation on 18 January 1944, telling the parliamentary party that "he found himself not capable of making the physical effort called for in the office of Leader of the Party". Dr T.F. O'Higgins was elected chairman and leader of the Party in the Dáil, Seán MacEoin having refused nomination.[101] Mulcahy was president of the party.

Dillon's biographer, Maurice Manning, has pointed out that Dillon could have accepted the offer, as the Treaty ports were no longer an urgent issue, but "he felt that his views, so strongly expressed, were incompatible with leadership of Fine Gael and he could not in honour accept". Manning goes on to argue that the decision was a costly one. "Had he been party leader or even deputy leader after Mulcahy returned to the front bench it is very likely that he and not Costello would have been the compromise choice as Taoiseach when the first inter-party government was being formed."[102] This was certainly more than possible—after all, Dillon had been to school with Seán MacBride, so he could have had some claim on Clann na Poblachta support. As against that, nobody appears to have considered O'Higgins, who had been leader in the Dáil and deputy leader after Mulcahy's return, as a possible Taoiseach. Perhaps his family connections, Army service and prominent role in the Blueshirts made him less acceptable than Costello was, or Dillon might have been.

As leader, Mulcahy adopted a strong pro-Commonwealth position, both at the Fine Gael Ard Fheis in January 1944 and in a speech to the Literary and Historical Society in UCD the following month. He told the students that there should be closer co-operation between Ireland and the other members of the Commonwealth. "At no time have we severed our connection with the Commonwealth." The Canadian High Commissioner in Dublin noted that this pro-Commonwealth policy was seen by Mulcahy's friends as "courageous but politically risky".[103] He also took a more proactive approach to party organisation than W.T. Cosgrave had—which was not saying much. Mulcahy travelled the country on an autocycle, a bicycle powered by a small engine, trying to build Fine Gael into an effective fighting force.[104] The lack of progress made by the party certainly wasn't due to lack of effort on the part of its leader.

The youngest Costello child, John, recalled the war years as a time of "a marvellous traffic free town, a fine public park and excellent swimming in easy cycle distance". His father's leisure time was limited, as he worked to midnight every night, but what spare time he had was devoted to his wife (Saturday mornings), his children (Saturday afternoons), and of course golf (Sunday afternoons). He took the children riding at Dudgeon's stables on the Stillorgan Road (where UCD now stands). The dachshund, Slem, came too, and Jack would walk around "in a state of huge anxiety for the safety of his children, his dog and the horses". Grace, Eavan and Declan rode—John and Wilfie didn't enjoy the sport, the latter complaining that it was "like knives going through you".[105] During this period Eavan studied art with the Dublin painter Mainie Jellett. Jack and Ida wanted to support Jellett, and their daughter was very happy learning to paint.[106]

The war years also saw change in the Costello household, with the arrival of Ida Costello's niece, a war orphan. Ida's brother, Major Victor O'Malley, had died in Aden during service there with the British Army; his wife was killed in one of the early air-raids on London. Their daughter, Mildred Patricia O'Malley (always known in the family as Patricia), then came to live in Herbert Park.[107] Patricia, who was only 13 or 14 at the time, had to travel over from wartime London to Dublin on her own, but on arrival became one of the family, going to school at Sacred Heart in Leeson Street, where Grace and Eavan had been, and then to UCD. Her arrival must have added to the financial burdens of a family with five children to care for already, but the experience appears to have been a happy one for all concerned, with Patricia remaining "very close" to her adopted family.[108] After she graduated, Patricia got a job in the RDS Library, before marrying quantity surveyor Gerald MacCarthy and moving to Pennsylvania. When Costello visited the United States as Taoiseach in 1956, Irish Ambassador John Hearne ensured that she and her husband were invited to as many of the official functions as possible.[109] The couple had three children, but Patricia died tragically young in 1967.[110]

Another major, and worrying, development in the family came when Declan contracted TB of the kidney, an unusual form of the disease which led to him losing a kidney. He had to go to a clinic in Switzerland for 10 months in 1946. At the time, Swiss mountain air was regarded as a cure for the disease—for those who could afford to go there. Declan was fortunate that his bout with the disease came just as new drugs like streptomycin were becoming available. He benefited from the new drugs, but a relapse meant he had to go back to Switzerland, staying in a hotel this time, at the end of 1947 and start of 1948—which meant he missed out on some significant political developments at home.[111]

The other change in family life came just after the war, when Grace Costello married solicitor and economics lecturer Alexis FitzGerald,[112] who was to have great influence on his father-in-law. Grace had qualified as a barrister in 1943, quite a rarity for a woman. Female participation in the legal professions was increasing, but very slowly. The number of female solicitors and barristers increased from just 1 per cent in 1926 to a still tiny 4 per cent in

1951.[113] Her daughter believes Grace didn't really enjoy the law, and only pursued it to please her father. In one of her early cases, she was presenting her brief when the judge asked her a question. Not knowing the answer, she simply paused and then continued without acknowledging the question. The judge later told a colleague that young Grace Costello was very impressive in court, but that the poor girl seemed to be a bit deaf![114]

During his enforced absence from Leinster House, John A. Costello continued his legal work. He served as the nominee of the Irish Bank Officials Association on an arbitration board established to decide on whether the officials should receive a bonus.[115] He also continued his close association with the Electricity Supply Board. Dick Browne, his golfing partner, was chairman of the Board, while his old friend Arthur Cox was its law agent.[116] Throughout his professional career, he was "unswervingly loyal to the ESB", and would "fight back like mad" if opposing counsel tried to do down the board.[117] He also had many cases of workmen's compensation, in which he almost invariably acted for the worker rather than the company—a bias which was to stand him in good stead in his dealings with the Labour Party. However, his time in the political wilderness was not to last long.

In a carbon copy of 1938, de Valera used defeat on a Transport Bill as an excuse to call a snap general election in May 1944. Costello campaigned vigorously, determined to win back his seat. He said the country had been "thrown into turmoil for the sole purpose of safeguarding the political fortunes of a political party ... They have no policy for peacetime problems. They have, however, full determination to obtain security of tenure in their jobs." Recognising that the election had been turned into a referendum on the question of whether the next government would be formed by Fianna Fáil or by a combination of other parties, he stoutly defended the principle of coalition. It was not coalition but "corruption and inefficiency" that had led to the fall of democracy on the Continent. "National Government in England and America has been found to be a source of strength. Why should it not bring unity and strength to this country?"[118] He returned to the coalition theme frequently, as did Mulcahy, who said a coalition would ensure that "policies affecting the whole country could be brought about in the most open manner, and would put an end to half-thought-out polices conceived in secret".[119]

The focus on coalition was understandable, and necessary if Fine Gael was to hold power again. The party didn't even nominate enough candidates to form a government—it ran 57 candidates for a 138-seat Dáil.[120] Again, neutrality was not an issue. The Fine Gael election ad for Dublin Townships stressed Costello's role as Attorney General in negotiating the Statute of Westminster, which it claimed had made neutrality possible.[121] His energetic campaign paid off—he won just over 26 per cent of the vote, only 500 fewer than MacEntee, and was elected on the first count. His running mate, the sitting TD Ernest Benson, didn't fare so well, securing just over 19 per cent of the first preferences, which wasn't enough to overtake the second Fianna Fáil candidate for the last seat. Both major parties had improved their position since the previous year—Fianna Fáil had 49 per cent of the vote, compared to 45 per cent for Fine Gael. Labour secured just under 6 per cent—the party was never in contention for a seat in the Townships constituency, feeling the squeeze on smaller parties normal in a second election.

Back in the Dáil, Costello was also back on the front bench. In June he was named spokesman on External Affairs—however, Mulcahy carried out a reshuffle just three months later, making Costello spokesman on Justice, as well as assistant to himself as spokesman on External Affairs.[122] Whatever his precise title, Costello soon resumed some of his favourite themes—objecting to the lack of an appeal to the courts from a decision by the Revenue Commissioners, to the politicisation of presidential and local elections, and to delays in bringing cases to trial.[123] He also continued his strident opposition to the emergency powers assumed by the Government. When a bill to amend and continue these powers came before the Dáil in July 1945, he claimed that it would leave almost all of them intact—with the exception of those dealing with censorship. He argued that "the Government should be divested as quickly as possible of all the powers that were vested in them under the peculiar conditions and dangerous circumstances that existed in 1939". De Valera insisted that Costello's assessment of the powers that would remain was not accurate,[124] and told the Dáil that the advice from the Government's legal advisers was different to Costello's.[125] Four years later, Costello as Taoiseach would sponsor the revocation of the remaining Emergency Powers Orders.[126]

Some of the themes raised during the earlier controversy over the Schools Attendance Bill, and opposition to Emergency Orders, surfaced again in Fine Gael's attacks on the 1945 Public Health Bill. Costello told the Dáil that his party "look with extreme suspicion upon such a measure ... the provisions in their general tendency are fraught with possible public danger and in particular instances in the Bill the dignity of the human person is insulted and the liberty of the individual set aside ... this Bill is nothing less than a monstrosity". While characteristically overblown, his rhetoric was prompted by genuine concerns. He pointed to the failure to consult the medical profession and the provisions for detaining people with TB, even claiming that the Bill gave the Minister power to ban perms and decide what swimming costumes could be worn. "Instead of dealing with the fundamentals, providing decent food, proper wages, decent houses, employment for the people, giving them education in washing themselves, and providing them with baths and a proper water supply with which to wash themselves, teaching them that the simplest precautions will be far better than any number of prosecutions, you are bringing in a measure the cost of which to put into operation will be colossal. Such a Bill cannot command respect, and can do nothing else but bring the law into complete contempt."[127]

He returned to many of these points during the lengthy committee stage of the Bill. He warned the Parliamentary Secretary, Dr Con Ward, that while Fine Gael would support legitimate powers, "we are not going to give him a blank cheque to exercise his inventive medical skill on the public".[128] The point of most of his amendments, he said, was that public opinion "must be informed and educated, not coerced", warning that the use of criminal sanctions in such legislation would ensure its failure as it would not have public support.[129] He returned in particular to the provisions for the forced detention of infectious persons, insisting that "a person afflicted with disease has still some rights left", adding that the provisions of the Bill were "entirely unjustified by the moral law and, I think, possibly unjustified by the provisions of the Constitution".[130] On one day he accused Ward of fascist tendencies, asserting that his claim that the rights of the community were superior to the rights of the individual was "widespread on the Continent of Europe a few years ago".[131] The following day, he complained about "the socialistic tendency of present Government policy". He claimed Fianna Fáil was invading "even the most private aspect of the lives of individual citizens", and infringing the personal rights and personal dignities of the individual. The measures would, he claimed, lead to more bureaucracy, more staff, and therefore more taxation.[132]

At a fairly late point during the committee stage, Ward introduced two new provisions to allow the Government to deal with expectant and nursing mothers and with children—provisions which would later become famous (or notorious) as the basis for the Mother and Child Scheme. Costello was not impressed, believing that the proposals would allow the Department "to do anything it likes regarding their subject matter". He objected to the compulsory inspection of schoolchildren, and pointed out that Ward had said that mothers who could afford their own doctors were not subject to similar compulsion.[133] The Health Bill was delayed, however, by the resignation of Dr Ward after allegations of tax evasion and malpractice at a bacon factory he owned in Monaghan. Costello pointed out that the whole matter had become public because of a falling-out of two members of Fianna Fáil after one of them (Ward) fired the brother of another, and suggested the Dáil should not be led into a similar situation again. He also said, fair-mindedly, that Ward's case had been prejudiced by the establishment of a tribunal without any preliminary investigation into the charges against him.[134] Despite this charity towards a political opponent, he later vociferously objected to the State paying Ward's costs, as he "has been found guilty of a grave public scandal" and had "to leave a public position by reason of the findings of the tribunal".[135]

When the Health Bill was reintroduced in 1947 by the new Minister for Health, Dr Jim Ryan, the provision for compulsory inspection of school-children again proved a focus for opposition, particularly from James Dillon. On 3 December 1947 he took the Minister for Health to court to test the constitutionality of the Bill, with Costello, Lavery and McGilligan as his legal team. As Dillon's biographer, Maurice Manning, has noted, the court challenge allowed de Valera to play for time in his reply to (secret) objections to the Bill from the Catholic hierarchy—with the result that "the entire problem was handed over to the new government in February 1948".[136]

The conviction that the Government was amassing more power at the expense of the individual citizen informed many of Costello's contributions to the Dáil in the early post-war period. He objected to the 1945 Land Bill because it would restrict appeals to the courts against Land Commission decisions;[137] he objected to wage control without price control, claiming it had depreciated wages and purchasing power;[138] and he continued his campaign against legislation by Emergency Order. Costello admitted that it wasn't just an Irish problem, as in all parliaments there was a tendency "to derogate from the powers of the representatives of the people and shift the centre of gravity of the constitutional structure away from parliamentary institutions to that of the executive". He claimed the Dáil was becoming "a machine merely for registering Government decisions" rather than a deliberative assembly.[139] His claim that legislation by order was excessive was given force in April 1946, when Finance Minister Frank Aiken disclosed that a total of 7,846 orders and amendments to orders had been made since the start of the Emergency.[140]

Costello raised a particularly serious legal lapse by the authorities in the Dáil in May 1946, during a discussion of a supplementary estimate to cover law charges. He began by complaining that cases were being sent to the military tribunal when the ordinary courts were working well, with trained lawyers available to oversee them and properly assess the evidence. He questioned how the Attorney General decided which cases to send to the tribunal, suggesting that "a particular individual is selected to be 'rail-roaded' to a conviction". He then produced an example of a case in which he was involved. The defence team hadn't been given a copy of a witness statement— but they took the risk of demanding it be produced. When it was, they found that it directly contradicted the evidence the witness had give to the tribunal. And, of course, counsel for the prosecution had the statement in their pos-session all along and knew that it conflicted with the evidence given in court.

Costello conceded that this was the only case of its kind that he knew of, but insisted it should never happen again, and that counsel for the State should be directed by the Attorney General "not to win a case but to see that justice is done".[141]

The following month, he criticised tribunal procedures again, claiming that a man had been executed on foot of an Order which his counsel and his solicitor could not procure and which the accused had not seen.[142] This assertion was viewed within the Department of Justice as "untrue and ... irresponsible to the last degree". The case involved the murder of Gardaí by Patrick McGrath and Francis Harte; they had been sentenced to death for murder, and the Order to which Costello referred dealt only with the manner of trial and the method of execution.[143] With considerable bitterness, an official wrote that Costello appeared to be motivated by "irritation at any step which tends to emphasise that the important question in a criminal trial is whether the accused person is guilty or not. That sound doctrine is not agreeable to lawyers who, like Deputy Costello, are making a lot of money by getting convictions quashed on purely technical grounds ... It is a serious misfortune that the main speaker of the Opposition on such matters should be a lawyer whose professional interests are so frequently at variance with the public interest."[144]

The 1946 debate on the estimates for External Affairs provided an opportunity for the Opposition to explore Ireland's relationship with the Commonwealth. Dillon said he wanted Ireland to be a member, but in any case she should make up her mind as to whether she was a Commonwealth member or a Republic. "Is there not something contemptible and rotten about pre-tending to be one thing when we are, in fact, something else?" Costello said "nobody but the Taoiseach knows what the present position is". He believed useful results could be achieved from the Commonwealth association, "which I gather that the Taoiseach in some obscure way still says exists". He argued that "our head of State, in so far as there is a head of this State, resides in Buckingham Palace", because an international treaty between Ireland and the USA would be signed by the American President and the King of England. But he said he had no interest in the form of government, whether Ireland was a Commonwealth state, a kingdom or a republic—what concerned him was the State's international standing. "The form of government makes no difference, provided we have freedom, that we are an independent State, and a fully fledged member of the family of nations. I do not care whether the head of State resides in Buckingham Palace or Phoenix Park, provided we are a sovereign State and that we are nationally and internationally free."[145] The logic of that argument was irresistible—the only way to achieve clarity about the State's international status was to declare the connection with the

Commonwealth, already dead in practice, to be dead in law as well. Patrick McGilligan made a similar point in the following year's External Affairs debate: "If I have to make a choice between living a lie and some trouble arising in our international relations, I would rather have the trouble in international relations ..."[146] He, and Costello, would soon have that trouble in spades.

However, Costello in opposition displayed about as much consistency on this issue as he would display in government. Just a month after arguing the importance of clarity of status, he stressed during a debate on potential Irish membership of the UN that Ireland still belonged to the Commonwealth, "however tenuous at the moment that association may be". He spoke of the advantages of an association which "Fianna Fáil and all other parties" recognised existed and would continue to exist. Costello would adopt a different position as Taoiseach. He would also reverse his views on neutrality, which dominated his speech on the UN. "Whether or not we were neutral in the last war, there can never be any question again of this country being neutral in any future war." He believed United Nations membership would impose obligations making neutrality impossible, and appealed to all Deputies to admit this "and to see that there is no flapdoodle and tosh-talk throughout the country about our neutrality". He said he supported the Irish application to the UN because "we must either join some combination of big nations which will protect us against aggression in future wars, or else leave ourselves open to become the plaything or the pawn of any big nation, or group of nations, in future world conflicts".[147] By the time he became Taoiseach, the logic of that argument would imply membership of NATO, but he managed to ignore that logic.

A long-running legal case with political ramifications concerned what were known as the Sinn Féin Funds—a sum of money vested in the High Court in 1924 by the two joint treasurers of the party (both pro-Treaty) in an effort to stop de Valera getting his hands on it. By the late 1940s, the money had accumulated to around £24,000—or about half a million euro in today's values.[148] In April 1947, de Valera brought in the Sinn Féin Funds Bill, to pre-empt the decision of the courts. Costello strenuously argued against the attempt to usurp the authority of the courts. He acknowledged that his first official act as Attorney General in 1926 had been to bring in a Land Bill dealing with the Lynam v. Butler case. But he made the point that the aim of that legislation had not been to overturn a decision of the Irish courts, but to prevent that decision being appealed to an outside body (the Privy Council). The decisions of the courts must, he said, "be regarded as sacred". Costello also objected to de Valera's claim that there was a difference between equity and law, claiming it was a "very dangerous doctrine for the head of Government to declare".[149]

Costello was to appear for Sinn Féin President Margaret Buckley, along with Seán MacBride and Charles Casey. When the case came to court in February 1948, Casey plaintively complained that his co-counsel were now Taoiseach and Minister for External Affairs respectively. Another barrister in the case, Cecil Lavery, was now Attorney General. The case was deferred to allow for new counsel to be briefed.[150] Inside government, Lavery argued that the State's case should be changed—it had originally objected to giving the funds to an organisation pledged to use unlawful means to achieve its aims. But Lavery asked whether this would include "residents of the 26 Counties organising a riotous assembly in ... Belfast in pursuance of the object of destroying British authority in the Six Counties". The Government decided that this aspect of the case should not be relied on, and that the Government should simply argue that it wanted a decision on who owned the money.[151] Despite this change of tack, the judgement went against Sinn Féin—while the High Court accepted that the party in 1948 was the same as that of 1923, it was not the legal successor of the party of 1917–22, largely because when de Valera moved to resurrect Sinn Féin in 1923, he had ignored its existing officers and standing committee, thereby breaking the continuity of the movement.[152] Not that it mattered greatly—by the time legal costs were paid, just £1,700 was left out of the original £24,000.[153]

That was in the future, though—in 1945, Fine Gael looked to be a long way from power. Liam Cosgrave, by far the most able and active of the party's newer TDs, criticised irregular Dáil attendance at the start of that year. According to figures compiled by the Chief Whip, P.S. Doyle, Mulcahy managed to attend on 22 of the 25 sitting days between June and December 1944 while Cosgrave was present on 19. Costello managed just 12—although this was considerably better than MacEoin and McGilligan (eight each) and Dan Morrissey (just four).[154] It was agreed to add a note of Dáil attendance to the parliamentary party minutes, and to circulate the figures for January and February to Deputies' home addresses. Costello managed to attend on eight of the 15 sitting days in the first two months of the year, but voted in only three of the 13 divisions.[155]

The party was not, then, in particularly good shape as it faced a number of by-elections, as well as a presidential election. Mulcahy canvassed the other Opposition parties to see if an agreed presidential candidate could be found. He suggested Alfred O'Rahilly, a suggestion received with lukewarm enthusiasm by Joe Blowick of Clann na Talmhan and outright rejection by Labour. Some in the parliamentary party felt they should not contest the election at all, but deputy leader T.F. O'Higgins said failure to do so would leave Fianna Fáil "rampant". "It was essential to keep the Party in existence and ... no matter what chances the Party might have either in the Presidential or by-elections, they could not act otherwise than throw down the gauntlet every time". Seán

MacEoin, the chosen candidate, compared his situation to his experiences in the War of Independence. "The shortage of ammunition was a great worry then ... it was even worse now, but the sacrifice demanded was not so great."[156]

In the event, MacEoin won 31 per cent of the vote. Seán T. O'Kelly of Fianna Fáil was just under a quota with 49.5 per cent. The Independent Republican candidate, Patrick McCartan, later a major figure in Clann na Poblachta, won 19.5 per cent. McCartan had been supported by Labour, Clann na Talmhan and some Independents. Significantly, his transfers favoured MacEoin over O'Kelly—more than 55 per cent went to the Fine Gael man, 13 per cent to O'Kelly, and 32 per cent were non-transferable.[157] Clearly there was potential for co-operation among the Opposition parties.

Costello later recalled the long years of Opposition as a period of "hard, arid, arduous work under conditions of no hope".[158] The understandably low morale within the party was demonstrated by the continuing poor attendance in the Dáil. A more serious portent was a letter from Liam Cosgrave to Mulcahy in May 1947. "A party working under such conditions cannot have confidence in itself, let alone expect public confidence ... While I do not wish to embarrass yourself or the party, in view of the pending Tipperary by-election, I must say that I cannot any longer conscientiously ask the public to support the party as a party, and in the circumstances I do not propose to speak at meetings outside my constituency."[159] Coming from one of the few rising stars in Fine Gael, this was an extraordinary vote of no confidence in the party.

If there were good reasons for believing that Fine Gael's future was bleak, there were also indications that the Government was more unpopular than ever—particularly the formation and initial success of Clann na Poblachta, the new radical Republican party led by the exotic Seán MacBride. The new party won two of the three by-elections in October 1947, leading de Valera to call a general election for the following February. The Fianna Fáil government also faced an embarrassing political controversy over the sale of Locke's Distillery to some foreign gentlemen who turned out to be crooks. The issue was raised by Opposition TDs, particularly the colourful Independent Oliver J. Flanagan, and a tribunal established. Costello's contributions on the scandal concentrated on the constitutional point that Deputies had legal privilege for what they said in the Dáil. In an echo of points made in relation to the Wicklow Gold mining inquiry, Lemass had said deputies would have to give evidence of allegations they had made. Costello said such a move would infringe the Constitution, and that any Deputy would have to resist such a request. "Once a Deputy is obliged to give to any court other than this Dáil ... his source of information, the independence of every Deputy and in particular of Opposition Deputies, is gone for ever and democracy is uprooted in this country."[160]

An election loomed; and Fine Gael's only chance of escaping from the Opposition benches lay in reaching agreement with the other Opposition parties. O'Higgins and Dillon had both been involved in attempts to form an alliance between Fine Gael, Clann na Talmhan and some of the Independents.[161] These came to nothing, but there were other indicators that an alliance might be possible. Given Fianna Fáil's implacable opposition to coalition, all other parties knew their only hope of office was through combination. Transfer patterns in the presidential and by-elections indicated that voters understood this logic. And in the Dáil, a long period in opposition inevitably led to greater co-operation among the parties. As Costello pointed out in April 1947, it was becoming increasingly obvious in the House that "every single Party, and Independent Deputy, are lining up against the Government, whatever the differences between themselves may be ..."[162]

During the 1948 election campaign, he criticised Fianna Fáil's record, claiming that "if the Irish people prove themselves incapable of choosing a substitute, democracy here cannot survive ... If given a dominating influence in the new Dáil, Fine Gael would co-operate with any constitutional Party which would tackle the vital problems of poverty, disease, the cost of living and production."[163] The Fianna Fáil organisation in Dublin South-East put out a leaflet pointing to his admission that such a government would have to refrain for some years from dealing with issues about which "acute party differences exist".[164] Fine Gael's new-found enthusiasm for coalition was a result in part of hard-headed calculation about their level of support, in part of understandable frustration at their inability to unseat Fianna Fáil. It was about to produce very surprising results—not least for John A. Costello.

Chapter 7 ～

| PLAYING WITH FIRE

*"Now remember boys, if a government is formed,
I won't take any office, and I certainly won't be
Attorney General".*[1]

JOHN A. COSTELLO, 13 February 1948

*" ... a fear amounting almost to terror that I would be
a flop as Taoiseach ... "*[2]

JOHN A. COSTELLO, 29 February 1948

On 15 February 1948, as on practically every Sunday morning for 40 years, Jack Costello played golf at Portmarnock. With him were the other members of his regular four-ball—his former school friend Dick Browne, then chairman of the ESB; Dick Rice, Chairman of the Revenue Commissioners; and Dublin City Sheriff Seamus O'Connor. He played well, as he told his son Declan, getting "a beautiful drive and a glorious second at the first hole, landing on the green and nearly getting a three".[3]

Portmarnock was then, as now, a golf links "with a national and international reputation",[4] and Costello was captain of the club, a position he regarded as a great honour.[5] But if more attention than normal was paid to the quality of his game—which was even noted in the *Irish Times*[6]—it wasn't because of his position in the club. It was because this regular round of golf was played in far from ordinary circumstances. For John A. Costello was wrestling with the biggest decision of his political career: whether to accept the entirely unanticipated and unwanted chance of becoming Taoiseach of Ireland's first coalition government.

Although he banned discussion of the subject as they played, it must have been on all their minds. Seamus O'Connor had already given his view—when they called to collect him, "he came out towards the car doubled up in two laughing at my predicament ... and explaining, when I told him that I hadn't yet accepted, that I had no choice". After their round, his other companions agreed. Costello was surprised to get this advice from Browne in particular, "as I fully expected that with his non-political and very hard-headed outlook he would advise me against it".[7]

But there was one more advisor he wished to consult before making his decision, his old university friend and rival Arthur Cox. At a quarter to five, he arrived in Cox's office along with Rice and Browne, and they discussed the matter again. Cox observed that by entering politics, Costello had been "playing with fire", and he had to expect to be burned at some stage. Having accepted what taking the job would mean to Costello, and praising his work as a senior counsel, Cox "finally produced the argument which finished the matter as far as I was concerned. He said that if I refused the nomination and the thing did not come off as a result of my refusal I would regret it for the rest of my life. That convinced me as I felt that I could not refuse."[8]

The die was cast for Costello, though he spent the next three days hoping that something would happen to derail his election. While his agreement was crucial to the proposed coalition government, others had done the ground-work to make it possible. That groundwork really began with the increased co-operation on the Opposition benches noted in the previous chapter. This included transfer patterns in the 1945 presidential and 1947 by-elections, and a greater confluence of views in the Dáil, as the Fianna Fáil government became increasingly unpopular.

The wind of change was blowing too in the newly renamed constituency of Dublin South-East, where for the first time Jack Costello topped the poll, taking almost 29 per cent of the vote, while MacEntee was just under the quota with slightly less than 25 per cent. MacEntee would not regain his pos-ition at the top of the poll until 1961. The second Fianna Fáil TD, Bernard Butler, had moved to Dublin South-West, and the party lost its second seat in South-East to a new candidate, Dr Noël Browne of Clann na Poblachta, who won just under 17 per cent of the votes. None of the other candidates broke the 10 per cent mark.

The size of the Dáil had been increased as part of MacEntee's attempt to secure Fianna Fáil's position, from 138 to 147, the maximum allowed by the Constitution. Despite this increase, Fianna Fáil dropped one seat to 68; Fine Gael gained one seat to 31 (although, as this was a larger Dáil, the party's *percentage* of seats actually fell), while its vote dipped below 20 per cent for the only time, to 19.8 per cent; Labour gained six seats to 14, while their separated brethren in National Labour gained one to five; on its first outing, Clann na Poblachta took 10 seats (a bitter disappointment to MacBride, who had expected to win many more); Clann na Talmhan lost four seats, returning with a total of seven; and there were 13 Independents.

The final result of the election was delayed due to the death of Fine Gael candidate Eamonn Coogan in Carlow-Kilkenny. The vote in that constituency having been deferred for one week, leading figures in all the parties descended to canvass. Prominent among them was Seán MacEoin, whose presidential campaign in 1945 had demonstrated that a Fine Gael candidate could attract support from Opposition voters. In Carlow-Kilkenny he met leading figures from the other parties, including Jim Larkin of Labour and James Pattison of National Labour, and concluded that an inter-party government could be formed, that the onus was on Fine Gael and its leader to make the first move, but that Mulcahy would not be acceptable as Taoiseach to Labour or Clann na Poblachta because of his Civil War record (although MacEoin, strongly in favour of Mulcahy's leadership himself, formed the impression that the other parties would relent if no acceptable alternative was obtainable).

MacEoin reported his findings to Mulcahy the day after the vote in Carlow-Kilkenny, and found that his leader was already thinking along similar lines. However, Mulcahy pointed out that National Labour held the balance of power, and that the party's National Executive was strongly inclined to support Fianna Fáil. MacEoin agreed to meet them behind the scenes to see what could be done.[9] Meanwhile, Mulcahy consulted Fine Gael colleague Dan Morrissey, a former Labour TD, about his options. Morrissey said that even if a coalition could be formed it would probably only last six months, "but that I had to do it". On 11 February he wrote to the other party leaders, inviting them to a meeting in Leinster House (Mulcahy evidently wasn't superstitious—he set the meeting for Friday the thirteenth). All except National Labour attended.[10]

But while National Labour was publicly remaining aloof, MacEoin had travelled to Cork to meet local TD James Hickey. The National Labour man agreed that a coalition should be formed, subject to the proviso that Paddy McGilligan would be Minister for Finance. A number of other TDs—Spring, O'Leary and Everett—were also contacted and gave their approval. They naturally didn't want their position made public in advance of their official meeting on the day before the Dáil assembled. However, MacEoin later recalled, they gave him an assurance that "if their confidence was maintained they would support the formation of a new Government".[11] Clearly, this was less than cast-iron—but it gave Mulcahy reasonable grounds for believing that an alternative government could be formed, if agreement could be reached on a Taoiseach.

At the meeting of the other four parties on 13 February, there was broad agreement on the desirability of forming an alternative government, and on the allocation of portfolios among the parties. But Mulcahy later recalled that Labour leader Bill Norton told him that his party would not agree to "serve in a government under the leadership of one who had been the leader of another party. My reply ... was that ... while the Fine Gael party might feel that I should be the leader of the Government ... I would not stand between them and the setting up of such a government."[12] This has sometimes been interpreted as an attempt by Norton to ease Sean MacBride's path into government; in fact, Labour were just as opposed to Mulcahy as Clann na Poblachta, and for the same reasons.

Crucially, at this point Norton suggested to Mulcahy that Costello should be brought to the next meeting the following night, "for the purpose of your advice and help. There was a general feeling that you should be so asked."[13] If not an explicit suggestion of Costello as a potential Taoiseach, the request certainly had that implication. Norton had known Costello for a long time, and had, as we have seen, negotiated with him a successful conclusion to the long-running dispute over the rights of transferred civil servants. Costello was also friendly with another leading Labour figure who would be a Minister, T.J. Murphy. He later recalled that they had frequent conversations in the Dáil. But he felt that the main factor making him acceptable to Labour was his father's friendship with Big Jim Larkin from their joint service on the board of Grangegorman Hospital.[14] Larkin's son, also Jim, was overheard by Mulcahy at the time of the formation of the Second Inter-party Government saying to Costello, "Don't you know that we would do anything for you?"[15]

Costello also knew Seán MacBride from the Law Library, later claiming to have invested considerable time in trying "to persuade him to bring his gun-men colleagues within the framework of the constitution and legality—into the Dáil".[16] The other salient point is that while Costello had been Attorney General, he only took up that post in 1926, and had played no part in the Civil War. As Liam Cosgrave put it, he "had not been so prominent in politics that he had incurred any enmity".[17]

It was, then, only on the evening of Friday 13 February that Costello entered the picture. His first involvement in the discussions was to meet Patrick McGilligan along with Richard Mulcahy and the latter's election agent, Paddy O'Reilly. O'Reilly took the view that they could persuade the other parties to accept Mulcahy as Taoiseach if they "stood firm", but Costello disagreed.[18] It seems Mulcahy was also realistic about the chances of getting support from the other parties—while some members of the front bench wanted to offer their potential partners a choice of Mulcahy or the return of de Valera, the General disagreed.[19] For Mulcahy, with his memories of the Civil War split, the removal of de Valera took precedence over any ambitions of his own.

While Costello shared this analysis, he clearly had no inkling that he would be the alternative choice. As he walked down the steps of McGilligan's house on the Friday night, he later recalled, he said, "Now remember boys, if a government is formed, I won't take any office, and I certainly won't be Attorney General."[20]

Blissfully unaware of what was about to befall him, Costello did some legal work on Saturday morning, before playing four holes of golf at his local course, Milltown. He was anxious to break himself in after the election campaign before his regular game at Portmarnock the following day. But shortly after he arrived home, he had a caller, Senator James Douglas, an old friend who had some unsettling news for him.

Douglas reported that Seán MacBride had mentioned Costello as a possible Taoiseach, and wanted to see him. Costello was at first disposed to treat the idea lightly, dismissing it as absurd, but agreed to meet his fellow barrister. According to Costello's letter to his son Declan in Switzerland, MacBride called at 3.30 on the Saturday afternoon. "We had a frank talk during which he told me that his people would accept me and would not accept any of the others whose names I suggested. I pressed Dan Morrissey very strongly but to no avail. He left shortly after five with my refusal but asking me to re-consider it." It is curious that this encounter was not mentioned anywhere else by either of the two men. The only other source which mentions it (briefly) is Patrick Lynch's "Pages from a Memoir", which is based in part on the letter to Declan.[21] Given that the letter was written within a fortnight of the events described, it seems highly unlikely to be incorrect. Perhaps with the passage of time, all concerned were anxious to downplay MacBride's role in putting the Government together.

However, Costello was not MacBride's first choice as a Fine Gael altern-ative to Mulcahy. According to his own account, the Clann leader suggested Sir John Esmonde, who he described as "then one of the leaders of Fine Gael".[22] MacBride appears to have been the only person who considered the Wexford baronet a leading figure in the party—his name was immediately ruled out by the Fine Gael negotiators, who, according to MacBride's memoirs, then suggested Costello's name. The Clann leader readily agreed, as he "had great respect for him; he was businesslike and capable. He had not really been much involved in bitter civil war politics."[23]

Curiously, MacBride continued to hold Esmonde in high regard, telling Costello's secretary, Patrick Lynch, over dinner in October 1949 that he was thinking of having Esmonde replace him as Minister for External Affairs, so that he could take up a new Department of National Development. The conversation was reported to Costello, who evidently didn't take it too seriously.[24]

In any event, on the evening of Saturday 14 February Costello went to meet his Fine Gael colleagues in Mulcahy's house, Lissenfield, in Rathmines. He came under "intense pressure, having been at the outset informed that I was the only one to whom Labour and Clann na Poblachta would agree". Among those at the meeting were Mulcahy, Morrissey, McGilligan, O'Higgins and

MacEoin, all about to become ministers, Liam Cosgrave, Gerard Sweetman and Liam Burke, the General Secretary of Fine Gael. Burke provided the only light relief for Costello, as he "emotionally likened the situation to the unanimous election of a Pope"! The putative pontiff did his best to claim his "complete unfitness for the job", but was overruled by his colleagues.[25]

MacEoin later recalled that persuading Costello to accept the responsibility presented "the greatest difficulty ... He resisted for a long time and he said amongst other things that his practice at the Bar was of a high order and that his emoluments and briefs brought him in a high salary, that he had responsibilities to himself, his wife and family and that it was unreasonable to ask him to accept the great responsibilities at a much lower salary. This was waved aside by his colleagues who felt that he must make the sacrifice for the sake of the country." His plea for more time to consider his position was rejected, as "it was felt that if he got time he might refuse so he was pressed to give provisional assent".[26]

Costello finally found himself with little option but to agree—he was particularly moved by the appeal from Dr Tom O'Higgins, who had lost his father and brother to Republican violence. As he wrote to Declan, "I had to realise what a tremendous tribute it was to me and how my friends and colleagues looked to me to complete for them what they had all worked so hard and sacrificed so much to bring about." Having given his provisional agreement, he went home to Herbert Park to break the news to his family. Bizarrely, he told his wife, Ida, that his new job would be less stressful than his existing career as a barrister. "I said that it would mean less night work and worry."

Then yet another meeting later that evening in the Mansion House. All the parties to be involved in the Inter-party Government were represented, except National Labour. James Dillon was there too, as the representative of a group of six Independents who had agreed to support the government (the others were Alfie Byrne and his son Alfred Byrne junior, Patrick Cogan, Charles Fagan and Oliver J. Flanagan). Costello was faced with his future Cabinet, chosen without reference to him. He again tried to argue his unsuitability for the job, as well as his financial worries. But his potential coalition partners dismissed his concerns. "William Norton said that they were wasting their time unless I agreed as his group would have nobody but me. Seán MacBride said the same ..." He asked to be given until Monday to think about it—they gave him until eight o'clock the following day, Sunday. "They then proceeded with the discussions of plans based on the assumption of my acceptance. They allotted ministers and settled procedures. I intervened from time to time as if I were forming the cabinet always with guarded references—'If I do accept'. It was close on midnight when I got home and I didn't sleep much that night."

What were the concerns playing on Costello's mind that night, and the next day as he played golf and consulted Cox and the others? One aspect was financial—he was making a very good living at the Bar, and he still had a family to support. Only Grace had left the family home at this stage, Declan was receiving presumably expensive treatment in Switzerland, and Wilfrid's care would have to be paid for indefinitely. He also had a fairly elaborate domestic staff, with a cook, two maids and a gardener.[27] Critics have pointed to his evident reluctance to make financial sacrifices—Eithne MacDermott, for instance, referring to the "whinging note" he adopted on this issue.[28]

But while money was certainly an issue, it seems to have been more of an excuse than a deciding factor. As he wrote to his son some days later, "I think I can honestly say that it was not the financial loss or even the parting from my life's work as an advocate ... that made me fight so hard against acceptance but a fear amounting almost to terror that I would be a flop as Taoiseach and bring discredit on the new administration if it was formed. I felt that such a new departure would be looked upon with distrust and be subjected to severe criticism. If I proved unfit it would be disastrous for them all."

After receiving Cox's unwelcome advice, he finally told Mulcahy on Sunday evening that he would accept, and went to another meeting in the Mansion House with his future Cabinet. "The meeting was quite informal—sitting around the fire as I refused to take the chair or have any formality." Of course, while the alternative government now had a Taoiseach, it did not yet have a majority, and Costello spent the next three days hoping that something would prevent it getting one.

There had been little difficulty in reaching agreement on policy. Seán MacBride laid down three conditions for the Clann's participation—the planting of a minimum of 25,000 acres of trees a year; the provision of money from the Hospitals Trust to build hospitals and sanatoria; and improvements in old-age pensions and health benefits. He later claimed there were "visible signs of relief" around the table when he didn't insist on constitutional change, such as the repeal of the External Relations Act. "I did mention in private conversation with them afterwards that I would naturally be very glad to see the External Relations Act repealed, but I realised that I hadn't got a mandate for that ... All the other things I had asked for were things that they had campaigned for as well, and therefore it was reasonable to ask for them ..."[29]

The parties agreed a 10-point programme of policy points on which they agreed: increased agricultural and industrial production; a housing drive; a reduction in the cost of living; taxation of "unreasonable" profits; a comprehensive social security plan; the removal of the Supplementary Budget taxes on tobacco, beer and cinema tickets; facilities for TB patients; the establishment of a Council of Education; a National Drainage Plan; and modifications to the means test for old age, widows' and blind pensions.[30]

Costello, meanwhile, "immersed" himself in his legal work, including "a difficult licensing case which in fact proved to be my last" in the Circuit Court on the Monday. But that evening, as he drove through the gates of Leinster House, he received "the shock of my life" when Michael Donnellan of Clann na Talmhan stopped his car. "He nearly pulled the arm off me and addressed me as 'our Taoiseach' telling me that he knew for certain that the five National Labour were voting for us." (If MacEoin's account of his previous negotiations with National Labour is accurate, it seems strange that he didn't prepare Costello for this shock.)

His colleagues having confirmed the news, he met the five National Labour TDs, led by Jim Everett. "I spoke plainly. I told them I didn't want the post and that if there was agreement it had to be absolute agreement, no formulas designed to cover but not get rid of difficulties." The only concrete point raised by National Labour concerned the right of representation at the International Labour Organisation in Geneva, from which the Irish Transport & General Workers' Union had been excluded. Costello said he couldn't make any promises, except that if a government was formed, he "would see that their party got a square deal".[31] Such was Costello's reputation that this was enough for Everett and his colleagues, who resisted heavy pressure from their party executive to support Fianna Fáil and announced they would back a change of government.

Bonfire celebrations greeted him in Donnybrook that night—the following afternoon he received "a tremendous ovation" from the first meeting of the new Fine Gael parliamentary party. Characteristically, he pointed to Mulcahy and said, "There is the man you should be applauding, not me." He had to address his constituency supporters again that night, who he said were as enthusiastic as he was depressed. Fianna Fáil too were depressed—they had fully expected National Labour to vote for de Valera, as the party's executive had instructed. Seán Lemass recalled that "up to the night before the Dáil met we did not realise there was going to be a majority against us. Even then, we did not believe it was going to last very long because it was such a makeshift sort of government."[32]

On Wednesday morning, after Mass in the Pro-Cathedral to mark the new Dáil term, Costello had his "first experience of the battery of cameras which pursued me for days after. I went down to court after Mass still trying to convince myself that something would happen to prevent the inevitable." After lunch in the Stephen's Green Club with Ida, Grace and Alexis, he went down to Leinster House with his son-in-law. With a change of government on the cards after 16 years, there was intense public interest. "The Chamber itself was packed to capacity and a big crowd filled Kildare Street some hours before the Dáil sat."[33]

The incoming Taoiseach, meanwhile, "was feeling like nothing on earth. I had the feeling that the whole thing was a fantasy." He was nominated by Mulcahy, who praised him "for the character and ability that has pointed him out so clearly to a number of groups in the House and in the country as the man to hold together and to bind that spirit and to lead it to achievement"— a handsome tribute given that Mulcahy had been passed over by those same groups. He added that Costello "by making sacrifices of various kinds ... is stepping in to encourage men of various parties to sit down together and face whatever difficulty arises, politically, socially or economically in Ireland these days". His nomination was seconded by Norton, who said Labour was willing to give inter-party government a trial, and "to give to our people something of the fullness and sweetness of life which inter-party government has given democratic people in other countries with which this country is comparable".

MacBride accepted that his party had not received a mandate to repeal the External Relations Act "and such other measures as are inconsistent with our status as an independent republic. These, therefore, have to remain in abeyance for the time being." He added that Costello was "a man of honour, of integrity and of ability, well fitted to fill the high position for which he has been proposed". Dillon said Costello was "a decent man and he comes of decent people". He added that he was "more optimistic" than MacBride about achieving his objectives—on the basis that Ireland would soon be called upon to "take her place with those nations who seek to defend the liberty of the world from the greatest threat that has ever challenged it ... In accepting that invitation, we may see a sovereign, independent and United Ireland delivered from the nauseating frauds of a dictionary republic sooner than we anticipate."[34]

De Valera was defeated by 75 votes to 70, and then Costello's nomination was approved by 75 to 68. Two independents who supported de Valera— Thomas Burke, the Clare bone-setter, and Ben Maguire of Sligo-Leitrim—did not vote against Costello. He was supported by five parties (Fine Gael, Labour, Clann na Poblachta, Clann na Talmhan and National Labour), as well as eight Independents—the six put together by Dillon as well as Patrick O'Reilly and William Sheldon. When the result was announced, Oliver J. Flanagan called out, "Thanks be to God that I have lived to see this day," and was rebuked by the Ceann Comhairle. Costello confided to his son that this annoyed him, as he was about to speak and he felt the Ceann Comhairle was motivated by his dislike of Flanagan. The new Taoiseach's acceptance speech was made off the cuff—he admitted that he "couldn't bring myself to think of it" beforehand, another indication of his deep reluctance to accept the inevitable.[35]

For once, he was brief. He expressed his appreciation of the honour that had been conferred on him, but pointed out that the position "was not sought by me nor wished for by me in any way", and that he had not been part of any political manoeuvre. "I will have to shoulder serious responsibilities for which I am in no way fitted. At the same time I am quite confident, from my contacts and knowledge of the men who are joining in this Government, that everybody will work for one purpose and one purpose alone, namely, the good of all sections of the people." He also urged the "men of patriotism, honesty and courage" on the opposite benches to offer the new Government help and support.[36]

Two new members of the Dáil—Noël Browne and Tom O'Higgins junior —later wrote separately of the simplicity of the change of power. After the vote, the Dáil was adjourned to allow the new Taoiseach go to Áras an Uachtaráin to accept his seal of office from the President. The Ceann Comhairle announced that when they returned, Fianna Fáil and Opposition TDs would swap sides in the Chamber. "Thus was marked in the Dáil the fact that all the powers of government had passed from one side of the House to the other."[37]

Immediately after the vote, Costello was met at the exit from the Dáil Chamber by Maurice Moynihan, Secretary to the Government, and J.J. McElligott, Secretary of the Department of Finance, who knew him.[38] The two officials accompanied Costello, "feeling very forlorn", to the Taoiseach's room at the back of the chamber, where he met de Valera. They had "a few frosty words" before the outgoing Taoiseach left. Costello told Declan that McElligott "was delighted at the change though officially he was correct. He gave me in a few minutes a lurid picture of what was facing me and I then proceeded to go out to the car for the journey to the Park."[39] He was accompanied in the car by Moynihan, by Alexis FitzGerald, and by Captain Mick Byrne, a prominent constituency worker who later became his aide-de-camp.[40]

Then it was back to Leinster House for the debate on the nomination of the members of the new Government. Costello, of course, had had little or nothing to do with their selection, or the distribution of portfolios. The team was generally well regarded—the US Minister, for instance, suggested that the Cabinet was "an impressive group—more able, I should say, than its predecessor". However, he added that it was "chosen from six [sic] political parties whose ideas and policies are contradictory".[41]

The Tánaiste and Minister for Social Welfare was Labour leader Bill Norton, on whom Costello was to rely greatly, recalling often in later years how his advice had been sought whenever a difficulty arose.[42] Patrick Lynch noted the two men's mutual sympathy and understanding, describing the Labour leader as "very able, very practical, very hard-headed". He was also "utterly devoid of sympathy" for Noël Browne and for progressive politics in general. Lynch believed Norton was "essentially a conservative"[43]—an assessment with which Browne would have entirely agreed. The Tánaiste played a key role in keeping the coalition together, thanks to his experience as a negotiator and feel for issues likely to cause the Government trouble—he "exhibited a high degree of the skill that consists in making the rough ways of government smooth". While he had no sympathy with the old guard in Fine Gael, "he was shrewd enough to see that his mistrust was shared by that party's newer elements".[44]

Fine Gael leader Dick Mulcahy had initially been pencilled in for Finance and then External Affairs,[45] but ended up in Education—a "backroom" role in which he was happier than he would have been in a more prominent Department, or as Taoiseach.[46] Although MacEoin claimed National Labour had insisted on Patrick McGilligan in Finance, Patrick Lynch believed it was MacBride who demanded he got this key role—a decision that disappointed McGilligan, who wanted to be Attorney General as there was too much work involved in Finance.[47] Labour too were keen on McGilligan, having "half an idea that he was nearer to them than to his own party".[48] In any event, McGilligan was a key figure in Cabinet, both because of his portfolio and because of his character—which even Noël Browne was prepared to compliment, calling him "easily the brightest intellectual in the coalition Cabinet".[49]

MacBride took External Affairs, and began his Cabinet career in a highly influential position. He had, after all, played a key role in the formation of the Government and in the choice of its Taoiseach. He contributed on a wide range of issues, most of them outside his own departmental brief, and was taken seriously by his colleagues—initially, at any rate. Mulcahy later recalled how he and Dr Tom O'Higgins reacted to MacBride after the first Cabinet meeting—"Another de Valera".[50] Coming from these two, this was not in any sense a compliment. But it did indicate a certain stature, a stature that MacBride was to lose over the lifetime of the Government.

MacBride nominated his inexperienced party colleague Noël Browne to the Department of Health (of course, *any* Clann nominee would have lacked experience of parliamentary politics, as did MacBride himself). As well as believing that a doctor would be best placed to take on the "job of work" in Health (particularly, although MacBride didn't mention it, one so prominently associated with the fight against TB), he also thought the appointment of a young man not associated with the Republican movement would widen the Clann's appeal and remove the criticism that it was "only a group of old IRA men, parading under a new façade". MacBride later claimed that he faced a lot of criticism on the party executive over this decision. "I had to throw my weight heavily onto the scales to get them to agree. It was a reluctant agreement on the part of the majority of the Standing Committee ..."[51]

While MacBride suggested it was the nomination of Browne that caused the opposition, it seems more likely to have been prompted by distaste at the idea of entering government at all, a move which was only narrowly adopted after a marathon meeting of the National Executive, by 18 votes to 16.[52] Concerns about Browne were also raised by Fine Gael's Seán MacEoin, who asked MacBride if he was wise taking on the "young fellow" Browne. "You don't know very much about him. You'd be much better off with somebody like Con Lehane, an experienced republican and politician."[53] MacBride would have cause to regret his decision, as would the Clann and the Government.

Clann na Talmhan leader Joe Blowick became Minister for Lands, a position in which he did little damage and little else. National Labour's Jim Everett took Posts and Telegraphs, while T.J. Murphy of Labour was in Local Government (after his death in April 1949, he was succeeded by Michael Keyes). The other Fine Gael ministers were MacEoin in Justice, O'Higgins in Defence, and Morrissey in Industry and Commerce. James Dillon became the first Independent to be appointed to an Irish Cabinet, achieving his long-time ambition of becoming Minister for Agriculture.

Liam Cosgrave had a key role as Government Chief Whip—speaking of the difficulties of that job, he quoted Wellington's reported remark about his own troops: "I don't know about the enemy, but they certainly frighten me."[54] At Costello's retirement dinner, he spoke of the contradictory aims of some of the Government's supporters—one believed the Taoiseach was a Republican, others that he would preserve the "tenuous link with the Crown"; one wanted an increase in the price of milk, another would withdraw his support if the cost of butter went up; and yet another would bring down the Government unless a ban on taking sand from the foreshore in his constituency was lifted. As Cosgrave wryly commented, "For all I know they're still drawing sand from the foreshore!" Much as they differed, though, all were "united in their dedication to John Costello as a man of the very highest integrity".[55]

This dedication to the Taoiseach was particularly evident among members of the Cabinet. Everett told his Departmental Secretary "more than once, with obvious approval, that the Taoiseach was a saint".[56] Cosgrave recalled Costello in Cabinet as being patient, adding that he was "highly respected by Labour and Blowick and of course Fine Gael members".[57] Even Noël Browne said Costello "was a most fair-minded chairman of the Cabinet, most honourable in every way, he gave us plenty of time to debate everything, and gave every-body the same opportunity to discuss". Browne characteristically qualified this praise by adding, "but that is not important". He believed that "on basic fundamentals and important social and economic and financial issues the dominant policies that come out of a multi-party situation are those of the biggest party in that ... government".[58]

As the *Irish Press* sourly noted, there were 13 in the Cabinet, compared to 11 in the outgoing government. "In a team of 11, sufficient places could not have been found to reward all those who had a claim to office as a result of their contribution towards coalition making." The paper also noted that all the key posts had gone to Fine Gael, which wasn't strictly accurate but was close enough to the truth.[59]

The change in status for the Costello family was immediately evident, as an unarmed Garda patrol was placed on 20 Herbert Park.[60] Costello's absence from a meeting of the Irish Council of the Society of St Vincent de Paul was noted by the Chairman, Brother E.J. Duffy. Another attendee later told Costello, "Your deputy explained your absence was due to the fact that you were busy forming a new Government for the country ... Even with the rank of Taoiseach you were just a member to Ned and no matter what pleas your deputy put up he was shot down and eventually told 'it was no excuse.'"[61] As for the new Taoiseach, once the initial shock wore off he took to his new duties with the same determination and focus he had shown for the law. He assured Declan in Switzerland that he was "perfectly and supremely happy and contented, and face the future and what it holds with resignation, and with confidence and hope".[62]

On the Tuesday after his election, Costello broadcast to the nation, claiming that in the formation of the Inter-party Government "the Irish genius for democracy has asserted and proved itself". He said the participating groups would maintain their separate policies and individuality, but that agreement had been reached "over a wide field of action". If the new Government was a novelty, he said, it was "a refreshing and timely" one, which brought together "men of different groups who have been colleagues and friends for many years and who have learned to know and respect one another without necessarily seeing eye to eye on every detail of every subject". Warning against frequent elections as neither desirable nor necessary, he said the Dáil would become "a deliberative assembly rather than a machine for registering the will of a majority party".[63]

He cited national freedom and unity as "chief of these fundamental objectives upon which there is complete agreement"—but then went on to say that "economic considerations must take priority over all political and constitutional matters". The Government's aims were to increase national income to pay for adequate health and social services, reduce the cost of living, increase exports, establish a Council of Education to remove educational matters (including the revival of Irish) from party politics, and action against the "twin evils" of TB and emigration. He recognised the right to a fair return for those who put capital into Irish industry, saying that "no decent Irish industrialist has anything to fear from this Government. Obviously, however, unreasonable profits acquired at the expense of the consumer will be scooped for the common good."

Costello also outlined a lofty ambition for Ireland to act "as the interpreter of Europe to the New World and as the interpreter of the New World to Europe, intending thereby to further peace among men, to strengthen that culture of which we all are a part and to extend the dominion of the Christian religion". In his peroration, the new Taoiseach recognised that difficulties lay ahead. "The members of the Government, for whom I speak tonight, are more than willing to do their share. With the willing help of our people and under the providence of God we have no doubt that we will fully succeed."[64] According to the *Irish Independent*, he was applauded by a crowd in Henry Street as he left the radio studio after eleven o'clock that evening.[65]

Press reaction to Costello's election was predictably mixed. In an editorial, the *Irish Independent* said the majority of citizens would welcome the form-ation of the government, noting that it was led by a Taoiseach "who not only stands in the highest rank in his own profession, but whose profound knowledge and experience of public affairs admirably fit him for his office".[66] The *Independent's* headline was "Mr Costello is Taoiseach". Clearly, this would not do for the *Irish Press*, which hilariously opted instead for "Mr de Valera is no longer Taoiseach". In an editorial, the *Press* thundered that the new ministers had been chosen not for their ability, "but simply and solely because their party had to get its reward in representation for its help in making the Coalition Government possible. The fantastic nature of some of the appointments indicates how fierce the bargaining must have been and how desperate must have been the efforts to reach an agreement." The paper's political correspondent sniffed that the atmosphere was that of a "commercial deal".[67] This dismissive attitude on the part of Fianna Fáil extended to the new Taoiseach. Years later, Todd Andrews described Costello as "a lawyer of no political distinction ... a survivor from the Irish Parliamentary Party. He was regarded by Clann na Poblachta as innocuous and malleable. In fact, in government he did not know whether he was coming or going."[68]

Others were naturally more enthusiastic, and the new Taoiseach received a huge number of congratulatory letters and telegrams. Former Finance Minister Ernest Blythe sympathised that he had been "elevated to something more like a bed of thorns than a bed of roses", but said that didn't take away from the honour.[69] Fellow barrister Kevin Liston congratulated him on his own appointment, and on that of Cecil Lavery as Attorney General. "You will both be sadly missed from the library—but I need scarcely add that the lowering of the standard will make it a bit easier for the rest of us who are lower down in the class!"[70] But perhaps the most welcome letter for Costello personally came from a medical consultant, who advised him to look after his health—"more than ever, I think your relaxation at golf will be helpful".[71]

For many supporters of the Opposition parties, news of Costello's election seemed almost miraculous after 16 years of de Valera. In his memoirs, barrister and future minister Patrick Lindsay described his desperate hunt for news while out of touch on circuit on the day the Dáil met. He finally found a guard in Tuam who informed him with evident emotion of Costello's election. The two agreed on a celebratory drink, but when Lindsay suggested he should park his car properly the garda responded, "Leave it where it is. We have freedom for the first time in sixteen years."[72]

The new Taoiseach, responding to a letter of congratulations from diplomat Michael MacWhite, wrote on 10 March that "the honour was thrust upon my unwilling self but now that I have accustomed myself to the radical change ... I am extremely happy. I believe we are going to do a great deal of good. The volume of support is increasing daily and I hear from all parts of the country of a widespread feeling of relief brought about by the change."[73]

It would be imagined that the British would have been happy to see the back of de Valera. But in fact the British representative in Dublin, Lord Rugby (formerly Sir John Maffey), wrote what appears to have been a sincere note of commiseration to the outgoing Taoiseach. He told de Valera "how deeply I felt today's swift closing of the chapter". Rugby thanked him for his accessibility, patience and frankness over the previous eight years, and wrote of his "deep and warm ... regard ... for you as a man and a fellow-traveller through anxious times". The new leader of the Opposition responded philosophically that he naturally regretted "being no longer able to do things or to get things done" but that "not having the power I have not the responsibility".[74]

American diplomats were somewhat more enthusiastic about the change. Vinton Chapin, in charge of the legation during the absence of US Minister George Garrett, informed Washington before Costello's election that he was a prominent member of the Irish Bar who was a "strong supporter British Commonwealth. He is friendly disposed to the U.S. and ... little change international policy expected." A month later, Garrett himself described Costello as "Dublin's outstanding lawyer", adding that he was "generally considered the best selection that could have been made". And in July, the Legation's Second Secretary said Costello's emergence as a national figure had given Fine Gael "a tremendous shot in the arm ... He is a marvellous individual personality and enjoys the respect of everyone. It is significant too, I think, that he does not have any great record, particularly during the Civil War. Thus, the Fianna Fáil Opposition finds it difficult to work up popular feeling against him."[75]

James Dillon had a high regard for Costello. But, alone among ministers, he was critical of the Taoiseach's chairing of Cabinet. Costello's lengthy anecdotes held things up, "to the extent that one would sometimes despair of doing any business. But he was so good a man, and everyone was so personally devoted to him, that when the chips were down no one would bring him to order." As

Dillon's biographer, Maurice Manning, noted, this may have missed the point—Costello was quite capable of using delay as a way of avoiding contention at Cabinet.[76]

Patrick Lynch described the lengthy and indecisive Cabinet meetings as "one of the weaknesses" of the Inter-party Government. Many meetings ended without any decisions being taken—but he blamed this on McGilligan rather than Costello, believing that the Minister for Finance deliberately missed meetings where MacBride wanted to criticise his Department. This led to issues (like preparations for devaluation, for instance) staying on the Cabinet agenda for months with no decision taken.[77] This view was supported by Dr T.K. Whitaker, then a senior official in Finance, who recalled that his minister was something of a "Scarlet Pimpernel", seldom seen in the Department, as he didn't want to get embroiled in unseemly day-to-day rows, particularly with MacBride.[78] In October 1949, MacBride complained to Lynch that McGilligan had been "too ill" to attend a Government meeting, but two days later was able to go to Longchamps, outside Paris, for the Arc de Triomphe race.[79]

McGilligan, while undoubtedly brilliant, was something of a hypochondriac. Both he and his wife were constantly convinced that he was in danger of serious illness, which no doubt explains how he lived to the age of 90. In March 1949, Costello wrote to his friend Tom Bodkin that McGilligan had been ill since Christmas, "and finally went into a nursing home whence he emerged with the 'depressing' news that there was nothing wrong with him". Bodkin replied that McGilligan "must be a very tough man for, in the fifty years or so that I have known him, he has always looked delicate and worked furiously".[80] In mid-1950, the British Ambassador was told McGilligan had considered resignation because of ill-health, but had been prevailed upon by Costello to change his mind because MacBride had "put in a claim to the succession".[81] The source of this story was the banker Lord Glenavy—the suggestion of MacBride moving to Merrion Street would have been enough to frighten the financial establishment, and may have been made for precisely this reason, as it is not mentioned anywhere else.

MacBride felt that the people who mattered most in Cabinet were Costello, Dillon, McGilligan, O'Higgins and Norton. He and Dillon had been in school together in Mount Saint Benedict; the Clann leader regarded Dillon as "active and efficient", with views that "were always amusing and interesting and reasonably sound".[82] By contrast, the Agriculture Minister was not impressed by MacBride's contributions in Cabinet, describing him as having "the judgement of a hen".[83]

Dillon was a colourful and controversial figure. The US Legation noted in December 1948 that Fianna Fáil was expected to continue attacking the Minister for Agriculture, and that his "tendency toward overstatement may damage coalition".[84] These views, curiously, were echoed the following month at a meeting of the Fine Gael parliamentary party. Costello said Fianna Fáil was making Dillon "the object of attack with a view to discrediting him and thereby bringing down the Government and forcing a General Election". He urged TDs and senators to go on the offensive, speaking to meetings at least every second weekend to get the Government's message across. Other speakers, while they paid tribute to Dillon's good work, "felt that he was talking too much and in somewhat exaggerated terms at times".[85]

The Minister for Agriculture caused tensions with some of the Independents supporting the Government too. William Sheldon, the Donegal Independent, wrote to Costello the day before his election as Taoiseach to make it clear that while he would be voting for him, he could not "accept the position of having anyone 'lead' or speak for me and therefore cannot consider myself represented in any way by Deputy Dillon".[86] Both Sheldon and Wicklow Independent Patrick Cogan later wrote to Costello complaining about Dillon's attitude towards farmers, particularly regarding the provision of credit facilities and the de-rating of agricultural land. Sheldon told Costello that he was "still prepared to give my support to your government generally, but I should be disingenuous if I were to disguise that I am disturbed by some tendencies in agricultural matters".[87] Costello's replies were polite, but supportive of his minister. Cogan secured the Taoiseach's full attention with a letter in May 1950 seeking a discussion on credit for farmers, "as I feel that I cannot support the Government on any issue while they take up such an un-reasonable attitude on this question".[88] Costello replied immediately, agreeing to a meeting. Keeping the Independents sweet was a time-consuming process for the Taoiseach, but one he couldn't afford to ignore.

Both Costello and Browne later recalled differences of opinion at the Cabinet table between members of Fine Gael. Browne said the hostility between individual Fine Gael ministers "dissolved when faced with outside opposition in the Cabinet",[89] although he didn't specify what led to this hostility. Costello said there was no disagreement between Fine Gael and Labour, and that any trouble "would be more between Fine Gael members, or between the Department of Industry and Commerce who wanted to put tariffs on for the benefit of Irish industry, and James Dillon who wanted to keep them off for the benefit of agriculture".[90]

But while there may not have been disagreements between Fine Gael and Labour Ministers, the wider parties were another matter. In May 1948, after three months in Government, the Fine Gael parliamentary party was con-gratulating itself on "the rising tide of enthusiasm and willing support which is everywhere in evidence", and planning more party meetings around the country to take advantage. But these were to be resolutely Fine Gael occasions—the minutes of the meeting, chaired by Mulcahy, note that "the organisation of Inter-Party meetings are often a snare and must be treated cautiously".[91] Two months later, however, a change of emphasis was apparent, with Gerard Sweetman and Michael O'Higgins reporting on exploratory talks with the party's coalition partners. These talks had suggested a series of inter-party meetings, designed "to review, explain and support Government policy and to solidify inter-party strength". The parliamentary party supported the creation of a permanent Inter-party Committee to oversee such events.[92]

The following year Sweetman, the party's Honorary Secretary, reported the Taoiseach's request that every deputy and senator should submit a monthly report "stating what Meetings they had addressed either on behalf of the Party or of an Inter-party nature so that he, the Taoiseach, could get a picture of the manner in which propaganda was moving throughout the country".[93] He also urged branches of the party to counter "mendacious propaganda" being spread about the Government and to ensure that people were properly informed about what the Government and party were doing.[94] An interesting insight into the real views of people in the party is given in the minutes of the Fine Gael Advisory Committee, a body containing a number of senators and other influential figures. In January 1949, it complained that "Labour doctrine and false philosophy, social and economic, is being imposed on the Government. Fine Gael is strongest party and should not be afraid to make its weight felt ... Supporters shocked to find Fine Gael so out of touch with economic realities and industrial relations and highly impregnated with Socialism."[95]

This view would have come as something of a surprise to left-wing members of Labour and Clann na Poblachta (including Noël Browne) who regarded the Government as being dominated by Fine Gael, and in particular by the more reactionary elements within that party. Costello was called upon once or twice a year by delegations of Labour deputies anxious about particular matters—the cost of living, unemployment, housing, worker representation on State and semi-State boards, and so on.[96] Again, smoothing ruffled feathers was time-consuming, but necessary, and the Taoiseach was generally regarded as being good at it.

A more crucial issue for Labour in government was Norton's proposed social security scheme. Costello knew how important making progress was for Labour—but he had doubts about the scheme. His own copy of the Social Security White Paper was clearly well read, with copious marginal notes and underlining. He also highlighted a sentence in a memorandum by McElligott, presumably because he agreed with it: "While some reform of existing insurance schemes may be necessary, the improvements proposed go much too far."[97]

His economic adviser, Patrick Lynch, was extremely critical of Norton's plans: "In its present form the draft White Paper contains disincentives both for work and saving; in short, it tends to undermine the Government's policy of securing more productivity ... and more investment ... Redistribution of a low national income as proposed in the White Paper would impose a flat direct tax indiscriminately on rich, not so rich and poor alike. It would have the effect of dampening the spirit of enterprise and discouraging saving ..."[98] McGilligan was even more critical, describing it as "a centralised bureaucratic type of scheme following the well known lines of doctrinaire socialistic teaching ... I think the community will have to be very careful of not being fooled by words as they certainly are being fooled in England ..."[99]

However, whatever his private thoughts, Costello was head of an inter-party government, and he defended his government's agreed policies in public. At the February 1950 Fine Gael Ard Fheis he stoutly supported Social Security, claiming "it is nonsense to suggest, as a few people have suggested, that the White Paper proposals represent the first step on the road to total-itarian socialism. This attitude represents a confusion of thought that refuses to distinguish between genuine social security and the totalitarian Welfare State."[100] Given McGilligan's views quoted above, it would be interesting to know what he thought of this statement.

"Jobbery", or the filling of jobs in the gift of the Government on the basis of political bias, had been one of the sins of Fianna Fáil in the eyes of the Opposition. Once they were in power themselves, of course, their perspective changed. Noël Browne claimed to be shocked by an example of "Fine Gael jobbery" early in the lifetime of the Government, when Seán MacEoin pro-posed to appoint someone who had left school at 12 or 13, despite there being a number of better qualified candidates. Browne suggested that he was only being appointed because he knew MacEoin or was a Fine Gael member. "Unperturbed, MacEoin smilingly replied, 'That's not a bad way to make an appointment, Noël!'"[101] This may or may not have been an accurate report of MacEoin's behaviour, but the Minister for Justice did write to Costello in November 1949 strongly urging the appointment of a non-civil servant (by inference a party supporter) to the post of Controller of Government Publications.[102]

After 16 years in opposition, it was only natural to give what patronage was available to party supporters. For instance, in March 1949, the Fine Gael Advisory Committee agreed to draw the attention of Costello and McGilligan to vacancies on the Boards of State companies "with a view to making Fine Gael appointments to replace those directors who retire annually".[103] Costello and his colleagues were no worse than Fianna Fáil, or indeed their coalition partners, in this regard. But, as Patrick Lynch pointed out, while Costello "was personally the epitome of integrity", he was willing to change policy where necessary for short-term political advantage. "In the longer-run the totality of these apparently trivial day-to-day expedients may compromise the possibility of adhering to principles earlier formulated."[104]

The result was the most notorious example of jobbery from the period, the Battle of Baltinglass in 1950. This involved the transfer of Baltinglass Post Office in County Wicklow from Helen Cooke, whose family had run it since 1880, to Michael Farrell, a supporter of Jim Everett, the local TD and Minister for Posts and Telegraphs. Local protests generated huge media interest at home and abroad, and led to the Independent TD Patrick Cogan withdrawing his support for the Government, and the resignation of Noel Hartnett from Clann na Poblachta. Costello backed his minister, although Everett eventually had to back down in the face of public outrage. The Battle of Baltinglass was to prove a potent weapon for Fianna Fáil in the 1951 general election.

One Fine Gael member for whom a job was found under the new government was Costello's leading constituency activist, Mick Byrne, who was given a temporary commission as a commandant and appointed his aide-de-camp.[105] Then aged 56, he had been a member of the Volunteers, a collector for the Irish Republican Prisoners' Dependents, and a captain in the National Army up to 1924.[106] Later he worked for the gas company. Following an accident there he had an artificial steel hand shaped like a hook, and was known as "Steeler" Byrne. The hook was reputed to be very useful during attempts to disrupt election meetings.[107] Noël Browne was in awe of his brilliance as a tallyman (he was able to predict Browne's election early on the day of the 1948 general election count).[108]

While formally serving as ADC, Byrne's role was more that of a personal assistant to the Taoiseach. It was a job which evidently only he could fill, for when Costello returned to office in 1954 he was decidedly lukewarm about having an ADC at all.[109] This reluctance was castigated by his son-in-law, Alexis FitzGerald, who said he should always be accompanied by an ADC. "I don't mind you writing yourself down. You shouldn't write your office down. Every time you go out at the moment you do. It should stop. Of this, I am convinced."[110] There were no such problems during Costello's first term as Taoiseach, as Byrne filled his ceremonial role enthusiastically, being described by a British journalist as "the smartest man in the Irish Army—beautifully polished tan boots, buff breeches, olive-green tunic and Sam Browne".[111] On the day before the first Inter-party Government left office, Byrne was appointed Inspector of Supplies in the Office of Public Works.[112] Costello remained very close to him—the Mass card from his funeral was one of a number kept in the former Taoiseach's bedroom in later life.[113]

Two days after the formation of the Government, the British newspaper the News Chronicle confidently predicted that MacEoin's appointment as Minister for Justice "has dashed the hopes of unrepentant followers of the new IRA. He has a fine battle record in the revolution, a shrewd outlook, and is not likely to grant any amnesty to IRA firebrands now in gaol."[114] At about the time this was being written, MacEoin was informing Seán MacBride that the prisoners would in fact be released. According to MacBride's own account, the Minister for Justice told him he appreciated the fact that the Clann leader hadn't raised the issue, but had decided to take immediate action. "This is exactly what I was hoping would happen ... If they were really genuine about cooperation they would do this without my having to say it. And it worked ..."[115] Given MacBride's difficulty in persuading the Clann to enter government such concessions were important—already in March the US Minister in Dublin was advising Washington that while MacBride "is a charming individual and will probably prove to be a good Minister ... his party Clann na Poblachta is a dead duck ..."[116]

There was naturally a suspicion that the release of the prisoners was part of the Clann's price for entering government. This was, equally naturally, vehemently denied by ministers. The archival evidence is not conclusive. The first written reference is a letter from Stephen Roche, Secretary of the Department of Justice, to Maurice Moynihan, Secretary to the Government, seeking formal confirmation of a decision to release Liam Rice and Eamon Smullen from Portlaoise Prison. MacEoin had told Roche that the Government had decided on 24 February that the two men should be released, and they were duly set free.[117] The fact that Justice had to seek formal confirmation of this decision from the Department of the Taoiseach is an indication of the somewhat chaotic arrangements surrounding Government meetings at the time, but doesn't shed any light on the question of who originally suggested the releases. Although the initiative was clearly political rather than depart-mental, that doesn't rule out MacEoin as the originator. In any case, the release would have appealed to Costello, given his long-standing aversion to emergency powers.

The following month, the remaining three prisoners, Tomás MacCurtain, Henry White and James Smith, were also released (both MacCurtain and White had originally been sentenced to death for murdering gardaí, although White's sentence had been reduced to manslaughter on appeal).[118] In August, the Government agreed to the reburial of the remains of six IRA men who had been executed during the Second World War and whose bodies were buried on prison grounds.[119] (While this was of course welcome to Clann na Poblachta, it is perhaps significant that it was Labour Deputies James Larkin and Roddy Connolly who lobbied MacEoin on this issue.)

In April 1948, Costello outlined in the Dáil his position on the inclusion of Republicans in government. He had been tackled by Fianna Fáil's Gerry Boland over MacBride's attendance at an Easter Rising commemoration at which volunteers had been sought for the IRA. With some passion, Costello said that his chief reason for becoming Taoiseach was his belief that bringing Clann na Poblachta into government would lead to "the end of the gun as an instrument for furthering political theories or wishes ... we will see the end of the gun in politics in this country".[120]

But the most important concession to Republicans was "a general easing of pressure on the republican movement",[121] and "the end to police harassment and intimidation".[122] In this more benign atmosphere, Republicans like the newly released MacCurtain began rebuilding the IRA.[123] By the middle of 1950, this was being noted in Government circles. Maurice Moynihan was told by Daniel Costigan, an official in the Department of Justice (later appointed Garda Commissioner) that "the IRA are getting more active—drilling, instructing in explosives, but [he] thinks the police may be playing it down".[124]

Coalition led to changes in the way government worked. One aspect was the increased use of Cabinet committees. These were not unknown in single-party governments, but were far more prevalent under Costello. A summary of the number of outstanding Cabinet committees shows there were eight in February 1938 and 10 in January 1940. But the First Inter-party Government established 57 of these committees, and the Second Inter-party Government 33. By contrast, in de Valera's government of 1951–4 there were just 15. The most important of these committees in the First Inter-party Government was the Economic Committee, established on 27 February, made up of Costello, Norton, Mulcahy, MacBride, Dillon, McGilligan and Morrissey.[125]

There was change, too, in the approach to collective responsibility. A strict interpretation of collective responsibility and Cabinet confidentiality had been laid down even before the formal establishment of the Irish Free State. In August 1922, the Provisional Government decided "that all decisions of the Cabinet should be regarded as unanimous, and should be treated as strictly confidential".[126] There were a number of cases of ministerial dissent being recorded in the minutes of the Executive Council, all of them in 1923—Joe McGrath's opposition to the appointment of the Commissioner of the Dublin Metropolitan Police; W.T. Cosgrave objecting to the deletion of a number of sections of the Civic Guard Bill; and Kevin O'Higgins' attempt to have allegations against army officers in Kerry properly investigated.[127] But in the main both Cumann na nGaedheal and Fianna Fáil stuck to a rigid inter-pretation of collective responsibility.

This interpretation was set out by W.T. Cosgrave when he refused to give the Army Inquiry Committee a copy of his Attorney General's legal opinion. " ... I must point out that the Executive Council acts collectively, and that its proceedings are necessarily of the most confidential description. When it arrives at a decision to do or abstain from doing any particular act, the decision is the decision of all its members. Previous divergence of views, individual opinions, arguments pro or con, all become merged in the decision which becomes, not the decision of a majority, but the decision of all binding every member of the Council equally whatever may have been his previous attitude ..."[128]

As a former Attorney General, Costello was well aware of the established practice; but as head of a diverse coalition government, he had to recognise a changed reality. In November 1948, he answered questions about remarks made by Dillon and by MacBride, and whether they contravened Government policy. In both cases, he said the ministers were speaking in a "personal capacity", and therefore the question of Government policy didn't arise. Lemass derisively asked if the Taoiseach could "arrange to have some signal given, such as the flying of a flag over Government Buildings, whenever a Minister is speaking in a manner in which he is expected to be taken seriously".[129]

McGilligan expressed the new approach in the Dáil in 1950, after a public divergence of view between himself and MacBride: "Have we got to the stage when men, just because they join the Government circle, must all ... when they go out of the council chambers speak the same language?"[130] The answer to that question, according to the theory of collective responsibility, was yes; but a more flexible approach was part of the price of coalition government. The British Ambassador noted in March 1950: "Cabinet responsibility is not marked. Members of the Government criticise in public the policy of their colleagues ... 'Free votes' on contentious subjects have shown differences of approach between Ministers on which the Opposition has not been slow to seize. But the Government as a whole shows every sign of intending to remain in office for the balance of three years needed to complete its full term; the ranks are closed at once against any real threat to its stability."[131]

There was change, too, in relations with the Civil Service. One of the first decisions of the new government was to exclude officials from cabinet meetings—a move described as a "disaster" by Patrick Lynch.[132] MacBride objected to the presence of the Secretary to the Government, Maurice Moynihan, as a representative of "the establishment in excelsis".[133] More importantly, Moynihan had worked closely with de Valera for 11 years. The Government's suspicion of him was not unprecedented—when Fianna Fáil entered government in 1932, the Secretary to the Executive Council, Diarmuid O'Hegarty, was removed. The difference, however, was that O'Hegarty, who was appointed a Commissioner of Public Works, was replaced by someone the new Government trusted.[134] Moynihan wasn't, continuing as Secretary to the Department of the Taoiseach and carrying out his existing duties, with the exception of attending Cabinet meetings. The result was that Liam Cosgrave ended up taking minutes and deciding what should be recorded as decisions.[135] If Cosgrave wasn't there, Costello had to do the job himself.

But while Moynihan was excluded from the Council Chamber, he still fought a battle to ensure proper procedures were followed, and that ministers did not trespass beyond their departmental responsibilities. The main offender was MacBride, who frequently attempted to express his views on matters beyond External Affairs. Moynihan warned Costello that this "would open the way to the creation of chaos in the arrangements for the transaction of Government business".[136] Costello, however, was reluctant to confront MacBride on this issue just a year into the lifetime of the Government. On two occasions in January 1949 he told Moynihan that he agreed with the rule that memoranda should be submitted by the responsible minister, but that MacBride's contributions should be circulated anyway, due to "unusual circumstances".[137] However, as time went on MacBride's influence declined and order was restored to Government business.

One of the key battlegrounds in Cabinet was over economic policy. It was not clear at first how much change the Inter-party Government would introduce. The initial emphasis was on cutbacks rather than extra spending. Costello wrote to each minister in March that "the Government is definitely committed to economy and retrenchment in the public service" in order to pay for the lifting of extra taxes imposed by Fianna Fáil in the previous year's supplementary budget. Savings were "essential ... to check inflationary tendencies resulting from excessive State expenditure and to lessen the impact of taxation on the cost of living ... It is not too much to say that the fate of our government depends on the success or failure of the economy drive by individual Ministers ...".[138] The following month, the new Taoiseach told the Federation of Irish Manufacturers that a change of government "hardly causes a momentary interruption in the economic life of the people". However, he went on to suggest that it was impossible to have decent industries "if we bolster up inefficiency at the expense of the consumer". In what was a clear criticism of tariffs, he called for an emphasis on positive encouragement of "Irish initiative, skill and craftsmanship rather than on negative steps to discourage fair and reasonable competition".[139]

The issue of protection, and specifically the restrictions on foreign investment imposed by the Control of Manufactures Acts, became a major source of disagreement between External Affairs and Industry and Commerce. The disagreement was brought to a head during the negotiation of a Treaty of Friendship, Commerce and Navigation with the United States. MacBride was keen to reach agreement with the Americans, but the negotiations dragged on well into 1949 because Industry and Commerce opposed change. Costello revealed his views on the subject to Vinton Chapin of the American legation in October 1948, describing the Act as "outmoded and outdated and ... as much humbug as the External Relations Act". He added, from his experience at the Bar, that the restrictions were easily circumvented.[140] Costello knew what he was talking about—one of the main architects of ways to get round the Acts was his old friend Arthur Cox, who "drove a coach and four through the legislation".[141]

However, while Costello may have thought the Act "humbug", he had to take political realities into account. The American Minister in Dublin, George Garrett, reported in December 1948 that the Government would be reluctant to repeal the Acts because of strident opposition from Lemass and from the Federation of Irish Manufacturers.[142] In a speech in New York the following month, Dan Morrissey repeated the Industry and Commerce view—industrial policy was based on the maintenance of protective tariffs and retention of control by Irish nationals in new industrial undertakings.[143]

Garrett tackled both Costello and MacBride on these remarks, suggesting that they must be taken on their face value as an indication that the Government was not going to change the rules. However, "both Costello and MacBride were inclined to deprecate the importance of Morrissey's statements, suggesting that they had largely been made for political effect".[144] Norton, meanwhile, delivered a speech suggesting the establishment of an Industrial Development Commission which would foster new industries and examine tariffs (an idea which bore fruit in the Industrial Development Authority). The *Irish Times* in an editorial suggested Norton had helped "to correct any misguided impression that might have been left by ... Mr Morrissey ... Mr Norton has introduced the necessary safeguards. The government ... will not follow blindly the policy of its predecessor."[145] The Treaty was eventually finalised in 1950, giving the Americans some but far from all of what they had been seeking. It is an indication of the strength of protectionist feeling in Industry and Commerce that the Department was able to hold out against the Taoiseach and the Minister for External Affairs so successfully.

Disagreements over free trade were also reflected in the Irish delegation to the Anglo-Irish trade talks in London in June 1948. As head of the delegation, Costello had to conciliate a range of departmental interests. Industry and Commerce wanted the power to protect more industries; Agriculture wanted to secure better prices for farmers' products on the British market; Finance wanted to ensure Ireland could still draw dollars from the sterling area pool. This last point was complicated by the forthcoming Marshall Aid allocations. MacBride and External Affairs were determined to refuse any offer of a loan, on the basis that Ireland should hold out for an outright grant. But Finance felt dollars should be accepted, even if they had to be repaid, to help ease the pressure on sterling.

Costello initially backed MacBride, telling the Dublin Chamber of Commerce in May that "we are not prepared to take American aid at any cost. We are as proud of our economic independence as we are of our political independence and we are determined that we will not incur foreign liabilities and commitments which are not within our power to meet ..."[146] But the matter was made much more urgent at the talks on 18 June, when the British Chancellor, Sir Stafford Cripps, announced that Ireland would no longer be able to draw dollars from the sterling area pool from the end of the month. Costello accurately described this announcement as "a bombshell"—it would severely restrict Ireland's ability to import vital goods. A late-night negotiating session with Cripps two days later in Costello's suite in the Piccadilly Hotel finally reached a compromise—Ireland could continue to draw down dollars pending the receipt of Marshall Aid, on the understanding that she would do her best to get the maximum aid. It was a "vindication of Finance's belief in the pre-eminence of the sterling crisis in Anglo-Irish economic relations".[147]

The Anglo-Irish talks were also the scene for one of James Dillon's more colourful phrases, his promise to drown the English with eggs. In a memoir quoted by his biographer, Maurice Manning, Dillon revealed that he had come up with this phrase at a press conference after the "hot-tempered" Costello "found some question which was addressed to him peculiarly provocative and proceeded to reply to the Press man with considerable emphasis. I thought that was an excellent moment to relieve the situation ..."[148] His comments grabbed the headlines and diverted attention from Costello's belligerence.

But if the Taoiseach was rescued by his Minister for Agriculture on this occasion, it was more often the other way round. After his retirement from politics, Costello recounted an incident from the early days of the Government, when Dillon sought, and received, his agreement to a scheme of land reclamation. He took the Taoiseach's approval as sufficient sanction (or pretended he did), and announced the scheme in a speech in Mullingar. James McElligott, Secretary of the Department of Finance, first read of the plan in his newspapers, when he was heard to say (according to Costello), "It can't be true! It can't be true!"[149] While somewhat embellished for an after-dinner audience, the anecdote was essentially accurate; Dillon had gone on a solo-run which caused "a state of upheaval" in Finance. The incident "showed that his observance of cabinet procedure could be cavalier, if not completely out of order".[150] It also rather neatly illustrates the problems Finance faced with this new government.

Part of McElligott's problem was his own minister. McGilligan had started out in the approved manner, severely pruning the estimates left behind by Fianna Fáil (the most spectacular victim of this pruning was the proposed transatlantic air service, cancelled just a month before it was due to start). And he frequently sent memoranda to colleagues appealing for reductions in spending, arguing in December 1948, for instance, that unless spending was cut, there would have to be "crippling increases in taxation", adding that while "some redistribution of incomes is necessary in the interests of social justice ... the redistribution of incomes has already proceeded so far that Ireland is probably one of the most egalitarian countries in the world".[151]

But McGilligan, and Costello, were reluctant to impose the sort of Cabinet discipline found in single-party governments. In February 1949, McElligott complained about public announcements by ministers of expensive schemes "without any prior consultation with the Department or, as far as we know, with the Minister for Finance".[152] The implication of the phrase "as far as we know" was extraordinary—McElligott was suggesting that his political superior might be keeping things from him. Later in the same year, he warned that Finance "has lost its power to control the situation ... the Minister for Agriculture ... cherishes ambitious schemes ... the Minister for Health is equally ambitious ... We have also confronting us the issue of a White Paper on Social Security, the cost of which, if implemented, would run into staggering figures ..."[153]

As well as extravagance in the spending departments, he also had to contend with McGilligan's equally strong desire to cut taxes. In the run-up to the Budget of 1949, the Secretary advanced an ingenious argument against a 6d in the pound tax cut, which would cost £1 million to implement. He said it "will not please Labour. There is nothing, it will be said, in the Budget for the working man—nothing off beer and 'baccy ..."[154] Given that McElligott's concern for the working man had not been particularly evident before, his argument was presumably a sign of desperation in his dealings with his minister.

If Finance resented the other departments, that resentment was more than returned. Dillon complained to Costello that Finance had become an "intolerable octopus", observing that officials in other departments spent their time "carefully composing lies for submission to the Department of Finance on the principle that if you want X the only hope of getting it is to ask for 10X + 3Y ..."[155] Costello, displaying his customary sympathy for a colleague, described McGilligan in March 1949 as "immersed in the preparation of the Estimates and ... vigorously pushing aside the gloom of his officials".[156] McGilligan's efforts in that regard had evidently failed by the end of the year, when Costello complained that a memorandum he had submitted to Government "creates an unnecessary atmosphere of gloom, which is scarcely justified by the facts stated ... we are both very acutely aware of the far-reaching decisions which must soon be taken by the Government on matters of public finance and budgetary policy ... A negative or unduly pessimistic presentation of the facts will not provide the kind of atmosphere in which I propose to have these Cabinet discussions take place."[157]

Finance also found itself under siege over the devaluation of sterling (or "the sterling" as MacBride always referred to it) in September 1949. As early as June of that year, having been tipped off by the French Foreign and Finance Ministers,[158] MacBride submitted a memorandum to Government on the possibility of devaluation, arguing that it was "essential to consider the steps which can be taken at this stage to minimise the disastrous consequences" devaluation would have for the Irish economy. Specifically, he wanted Government action to repatriate assets invested in Britain and their use for "national development projects" in Ireland.[159] The Department of the Taoiseach noted that this memorandum appeared to be out of order, as it should have been submitted by Finance rather than External Affairs, but that Finance was not objecting to its circulation.[160] But while the memorandum was circulated, it wasn't actually discussed—the subject was postponed at no fewer than 14 Cabinet meetings, until MacBride's prescient warning was overtaken by events.[161]

On Saturday 17 September, Costello received a message from Attlee confirming the British were about to devalue. In his memoirs, MacBride recalled that the resulting Cabinet meeting was held in Iveagh House, headquarters of the Department of External Affairs. This was the only time the Government met there, and MacBride implied that the meeting was held on his turf in recognition of his interest in the issue.[162] In fact ministers met for two hours in Government Buildings before resuming in Iveagh House from 11 p.m. to 4.45 a.m.[163] Iveagh House was chosen because most ministers were due there anyway for an official reception in honour of Archbishop Cushing of Boston. MacBride, supported by Browne, argued against devaluation; McGilligan and Dillon opposed them. Finance official T.K. Whitaker later described "MacBride sitting astraddle on a chair in the middle of the room (with other members of the Government sitting around the sides) and relentlessly crossexamining his senior Finance colleagues".[164]

Not for the last time, Norton's attitude proved crucial; once he sided with Finance the decision was made.[165] The Government agreed to follow the British example, with a statement declaring that devaluation was "the course of least disadvantage". However, MacBride refused to let the issue go, insisting on further discussion of the implications of devaluation and recommending a drive to increase dollar earnings, particularly through encouraging tourism and moving away from reliance on the British market. "The Minister for External Affairs strongly urges that in this situation the trade policy of the government should be to purchase our imports in the cheapest markets and to sell our exports where we will get the best prices possible."[166]

The Government agreed to set up a special committee including outside experts to consider the various points raised by MacBride. It was to meet when memoranda had been received from various interested Departments. However, in February 1950, Moynihan noted that Finance and Agriculture had still not submitted their observations. After discussing this with Costello, he noted "there is no need to remind the Ministers for Finance and Agriculture further in this matter".[167] This strongly suggests that while Costello was prepared to humour MacBride, he was happy to let the matter drop as soon as he decently could—an interesting insight into his management style. MacBride—correctly—dismissed the committee as "a mere sop" in a conversation with Costello's assistant, Patrick Lynch. In the same conversation, on 8 October 1949, MacBride complained that only Browne, Dillon and himself were getting results, and that he would have to leave Government within two months "unless there was a material improvement and the atmosphere ceased to be clouded by what he called Fine Gael conservatism".[168]

The fall-out from devaluation included an attempt by MacBride to block the reappointment of Joseph Brennan as Governor of the Central Bank in 1950. Brennan had already clashed with the Government over his report for 1949. Summoned to a meeting with Costello, McGilligan, Mulcahy and McElligott on 18 November, he was told by the Taoiseach that "he considered its general tone and tendency contrary to Government policy". Costello was careful, however, to stress that it was up to Brennan to decide how he should frame his report. The Governor put up a spirited defence, arguing that the Central Bank was "anxious to understand what the monetary policy of the Government was ... they were bewildered by reading the various speeches of Ministers". In reply, Costello "stated that the Monetary Policy comes from the Taoiseach and the Minister for Finance" (in other words, not from MacBride). At one point, he accused the Central Bank of wanting to interfere with Government policy. He also argued that the need for housing outweighed the threat of inflation—"inflation has to be chanced as against social betterment".[169] Brennan later said that he "merely abbreviated a passage to which the Taoiseach had taken particular exception (on the ground that it was not in accord with Government policy) while leaving the substance unchanged". The "banshee of Foster Place", as the bank was known in political circles, was left to wail on.[170]

MacBride, who significantly was not at the meeting, had meanwhile criticised the Central Bank, and the commercial banks, in a widely reported speech to the Catholic Commercial Club: "The time has come when our banking system and our financial authorities should cease to look upon themselves as mere money lenders who treat money and credit as a commodity to be exploited, irrespective of the needs of the community as a whole."[171] This speech led to complaints from Brennan, from the Government stockbroker, and the Governor of the Bank of Ireland. Brennan sought a statement from McGilligan that MacBride had not been speaking on behalf of the Government.[172] No such statement was made, although Costello did give Brennan to understand that in an inter-party government "it was considered permissible for a Minister in an individual or party capacity to give public expression to views which might not necessarily be those of the government as such".[173]

MacBride and Brennan did agree on one thing, though—neither wanted the Governor reappointed. The Clann leader argued that Brennan's "views, policy and acts ... are in direct conflict with the policy of the Government", and that in an inter-party government the position should be filled by an agreed nominee.[174] Brennan meanwhile told McGilligan he did not want to be considered for reappointment, only to be summoned by Costello to be told he already had been. The Taoiseach spoke about co-operation between the Bank and the Government. "I told him that cooperation had to be two-sided, and the Minister for Finance was not doing his part."[175]

Brennan's reappointment was a clear victory for financial orthodoxy over MacBride. The Clann's standing committee issued a statement deploring the reappointment "as being indicative of a decision to continue the disastrous policy of the export to Britain of our men and money".[176] Costello's decision was presumably taken in the interests of maintaining the confidence of financial circles in his government. Allowing the Governor to resign would have led to an even bigger row over its investment strategy. However, Costello had already demonstrated that he was open to new economic thinking—but on his own terms, not MacBride's.

There were many disadvantages in becoming Taoiseach without having been party leader; but there were advantages too. One of these, as Ronan Fanning has pointed out, was that Costello "was unencumbered by the baggage of advisers and henchmen who ordinarily surround a party leader in opposition".[177] He was free to choose his own advisors, and turned first to his son-in-law, Alexis FitzGerald, who in turn recommended an economist in the Department of Finance, Patrick Lynch. Lynch was transferred to the Department of the Taoiseach three days after the formation of the Government "for the purpose of preparing economic data" for Costello. In July 1950 he was promoted to be Assistant Secretary to the Government and of the Department of the Taoiseach[178]—a very rapid rise which showed his value to the Taoiseach.

Independent economic advice had been offered before—notably by Professor Timothy Smiddy to de Valera—but the formal appointment of Lynch was unprecedented. The historian of the Department of Finance has suggested that it was a recognition both of the increasing importance of the economy in political debate in the postwar years, and of Costello's view of his role as Taoiseach, as "the mouthpiece of the Inter-party Government on major issues which might split the coalition—a role he also assumed, for example, in the direction of the government's foreign policy. In short, the capital budget was too important a decision to be entrusted to the Department of Finance alone."[179]

Lynch found Costello "very quick on the up-take" when it came to economics. His knowledge of the area was minimal when he became Taoiseach, but with Lynch and FitzGerald he would insist on a detailed discussion of economic issues. "He never made a speech about any aspect of economic policy without understanding the implications of what he was talking about. It is possible to convert Keynesianism ... into fairly easily defined issues concerning investment and so on, and this he understood and could defend in Cabinet."[180]

Costello's new interest in economics was noted by Lemass, who in July 1949 suggested his "knowledge of the elementary principles of national economic policy was acquired within the past year or year and a half. If, however, we have, in courtesy, to assume that it is of longer standing that that, I can only say that we would never have suspected it."[181] Costello replied by recalling the words of his UCD French professor at his last lecture. "He told us that we then knew enough French to learn French. I have never forgotten that ... The longer I have lived and the more experience I have gained in law, politics or economics, the more I realise how little I know and how much there is still to be learned ... I do not suffer the illusion that I know everything. When I was charged with the responsibility of my present post last year I took the precaution of gathering around me the best men and the best advice available here on Irish economic affairs so that I might be the better able to discharge the task this House placed upon me."[182]

The influence of these "best men", Lynch and FitzGerald, was not necessarily welcomed by his political colleagues. In later years, Mulcahy described them as being "a hard crust of intellectualism around him", believing that by relying on their advice, Costello's contact with his Cabinet colleagues was weakened.[183] (Criticism of intellectualism may be more of a comment on Mulcahy than on Costello.) McElligott was unhappy too—meeting Lynch on the steps of Government Buildings on the day after Costello's speech on the Capital Budget, he said, "You are a very young man, I want to give you one piece of advice. The more politicians know, the more dangerous they are!"[184]

It was Lynch who suggested at the start of 1949 that "a clear distinction should be made between the capital and current budgets, thus making Keynesian policies explicit". If capital investment was separated from other spending, the need to balance the budget would not be a constraint on borrowing for capital purposes. Like MacBride, Lynch believed that part of the Irish economic problem was chronic underinvestment while sterling assets accumulated in Britain, all the while declining in value. A balance of payments deficit would in effect repatriate these sterling assets—although he stressed that "Keynes rejected inflation as much as he abominated continued deflation". Along with FitzGerald, he drafted a speech for Costello to deliver to the Institute of Bankers in November 1949, making sure to clear it with McGilligan in advance. The Minister "made no changes of substance" to the draft.[185]

In his speech, Costello said the Government accepted its responsibility to reduce poverty and unemployment, and "to create economic conditions within which it will be possible to provide a high level of employment and ... arrange our economic affairs [so] that no resources of land or labour which can be usefully employed should be allowed avoidably to remain idle ..." He blamed Ireland's poor economic performance on a lack of capital investment, particularly in agriculture, and said it was "the complete acceptance of this view by all the groups represented in the present Government" that made possible its formation. While some investments would earn revenue, others, such as housing, would "bring social and economic benefits ... just as indispensable to the national well-being".

Costello said the need for investment was so great that past national savings would have to be drawn upon to pay for it. This would be done by repatriating some of the money invested in sterling assets—although it must be made "as sound and secure as anything which can be obtained ... abroad". He said the Government was determined to extirpate evils such as infertile land, lack of housing and shortage of hospital accommodation, and that this would "even justify short-term economic loss for the sake of social and long-term economic gain ... There are greater evils ... than a temporary deficit in the Balance of Payments." Care would have to be taken to use the money for investment rather than consumption, to balance the projects properly between sectors, and to increase savings to pay for investment. The new strategy would be signalled by a division of the Budget into current and capital sides. "Our aim is to enrich the country by augmenting the national capital and increasing productivity, by means of a comprehensive long-term programme ..."[186]

How significant was the introduction of the Capital Budget? Brian Girvin has pointed out that if the Capital Budget heralded the arrival of Keynesian economics, "it was remarkably short lived. Subsequent budgets were deflationary, emphasising a continuing commitment to the balanced budget and a fear of balance of payments crisis." He also observed that the Capital Budget was important, "but only if part of an overall process to facilitate growth in the economy".[187] And the increase in capital investment was only possible because of Marshall Aid—once it ran out (and until Ireland joined the World Bank and the International Monetary Fund in 1957), government simply didn't have the access to outside capital that would allow for significant State investment.[188]

Even its architect, Patrick Lynch, admitted that there was "an element of charlatanism in this initiative", since Finance already made a reduction from the current budget in respect of capital items which were deemed "proper to meet from borrowing". But while the concept was there before Costello's speech, afterwards "the scale increased very greatly".[189] As Ronan Fanning has pointed out, Costello had in effect taken "personal charge of the direction of budgetary policy in a manner never before attempted by a head of government since independence".[190]

While Costello was telling bankers publicly of the virtues of investing capital at home, he was also putting pressure on them in private. On the day before his speech to the Institute of Bankers, he chaired a meeting with representatives of the banks in an effort to secure funding for public housing in Dublin. The Government wanted the banks to take up a £5 million bond issue from Dublin Corporation. Costello began by appealing to the better nature of the financiers, relating his experiences of "the terrible housing conditions in which many people lived", and pointing out that the best the Corporation could do for that year was to provide a new house for families of seven living in a single room. "The Government were determined that all possible steps would be taken to improve those horrible conditions."

This appeal was by way of preamble; Costello quickly moved on to threats. He pointed out that British banks were required to put 40 per cent of their resources at the disposal of the Treasury through Bills and Treasury Deposit Receipts, and suggested that "if the Irish banks were un-cooperative on this question of investment some Irish Government would be compelled by pressure of public opinion to adopt measures ... to ensure that the Banks worked in the national interest". For the bankers, Lord Glenavy asked "whether the present transaction would be an isolated one or whether ... further demands would be made on the banks". Costello said it would not be an isolated incident, and the bankers went off to consider their options.[191] Ten days later they returned for another meeting, and haggled over the interest rate to be paid— Costello warned them, "The Government had public duties and responsibilities to the community and they were determined to discharge them ...".[192] The Taoiseach's threats worked—the banks agreed to take up the Corporation loan.

But the main source of new capital investment was Marshall Aid, which financed nearly half of all state investment from 1949 to 1952.[193] The impact of the aid on the Irish economy was questionable—for instance, almost one quarter of all ERP funds were used to purchase tobacco[194] and the projects were of long-term rather than immediate economic benefit. Local authority house-building increased dramatically—from 744 house completions in 1947 to over 8,000 by 1950; there was also the massive investment in hospital-building under Noël Browne; and of course there was James Dillon's Land Project, which aimed to reclaim four million acres through increased fertilization and better drainage.[195] This investment, as Finance pointed out repeatedly at the time, would not show a return for many years, if at all. On the other hand, the imports and dollars involved allowed a higher standard of living than would otherwise have been the case.[196] This had important political consequences—for it allowed Costello and McGilligan to satisfy the competing demands of the constituent parts of the coalition.

There were three by-elections during the life of the government. The first two saw Fianna Fáil and Labour holding their seats in Donegal East and Cork West respectively. But in November 1949, Fine Gael won a seat from Fianna Fáil in Donegal West. The contest became known as the "Platypus" election, because during it de Valera said that every time he looked at the Government in the Dáil he was reminded of an animal he had seen in Canada with "web feet, powerful claws, the bill of a duck and the tail of a lizard".[197] The by-election victory was a personal triumph for Costello, who received a "prolonged round of applause" from the Government benches in the Dáil in recognition of his achievement.[198] However, the gain of a seat in Donegal was offset for Fine Gael by the resignation of Sir John Esmonde from the party in September 1950, and from the Dáil the following May, and by the death of Galway West's Josie Mongan in March 1951.[199]

Just over a year into his first term as Taoiseach, the British magazine *News Review* described Costello's typical day. He frequently went to early morning Mass in Donnybrook, and walked the family dachshund, Slem, in the nearby park. The Taoiseach generally spent two hours after breakfast dictating correspondence in his upstairs study, "lined ceiling to floor with books—most of them on law. Working to a background of radio music (he listens a great deal), and using a Dictaphone, he ... will reel off with lucidity and speed three to six cylinders ..." At 11, his car would arrive with whichever of his two drivers was on duty, along with Mick Byrne, his ADC.

In Government Buildings, his first-floor office "is the same as it was in Dev's time. The sage green Dun Emer carpet with mauve and gold border has been down nearly 25 years ... There is a map of Ireland in a vivid blue sea, a safe, indifferently open, a cupboard of rolled maps and plans, a globe, a small radio. There are two ordinary black phones on the brown desk: an internal Dictagraph, and a private switchboard on which he can call any Minister, any time." The Cabinet met on Tuesdays and Fridays in the ground floor Council

Chamber in Government Buildings, "round an oval polished mahogany table with six great brass ash trays running like a centre-piece down the middle".

Lunch was sometimes taken with MacBride in Iveagh House, but more usually the Taoiseach went home to Herbert Park. Official entertaining at lunchtime would be in a private room in the Gresham or Russell Hotels, or for more formal occasions at Iveagh House. After lunch, Costello would return to Government Buildings until seven or eight in the evening (three o'clock on a Saturday). Speeches were drafted at night, at home in his study.

According to the *News Review*, the Taoiseach regularly attended weekly recitals at the RDS. "He is also fond of dancing, likes the cinema and the theatre, but doesn't go often now. 'People make a fuss; you can't slip in quietly.'" But most of his leisure time was spent at home, reading (he told the *News Review* he liked biography, economics and thrillers; in reality he mainly read the latter). The family also played bridge, although Costello admitted, "They're all better than I am."[200] And of course, while he was Taoiseach, he was still the TD for Dublin South-East, and continued to deal with a wide range of constituency matters (some of them utterly trivial, such as a request from a hairdresser in Haddington Road to have him excused from jury service).[201]

One of the perks of the job appears to have been privileged access to new films—there are several references in his appointments diary to morning visits to the Film Censor's Office, presumably for an advance viewing of the latest release.[202] He also continued to pursue other cultural interests. He collected paintings by a number of Irish artists, presenting friends and relatives with wedding gifts of small works by Nathaniel Hone, Evie Hone, Grace Henry and William Leech. He was influenced in his collecting by his friend, John Burke the solicitor,[203] who also encouraged him to collect furniture by the Dublin cabinet-maker Hicks. He had a good eye for silver, much of it bought at Weldon's antique shop.[204] He was also for many years a patron of Weir's jewellers on Grafton Street, where he bought presents for his grandchildren. As one of them remembered, "he liked beautiful things".[205]

Costello's interest in the arts had practical implications for Government policy, as he drove developments in the area in both of his administrations. This can be seen in the attempt to secure the return of the Lane Pictures, and the establishment of the Arts Council. As Attorney General, he had been involved in the long-running dispute with Britain over the Lane Pictures. These 39 paintings—including works by Manet, Monet, Renoir and Degas— were originally left by Sir Hugh Lane to the National Gallery in London after controversy over his plans for a gallery in Dublin. Lane, a successful art dealer and nephew of Lady Gregory, had founded the Dublin Municipal Gallery of Modern Art in 1908, but had been severely disappointed by the Corporation's opposition to his plan for a permanent home for the collection. £40,000 had been raised towards the cost of building a museum on a bridge across the Liffey, and Lane had promised that he would cover any extra cost—but the Corporation still opposed the plan "in very strong language".[206]

His biographer considers that Lane's "intractability appears to have been responsible for the failure of his art gallery plan in Dublin". His refusal to compromise on the site and architect for the project led to the Corporation's rejection.[207] After this row, he made a will leaving his paintings to London, but the British failure to exhibit them greatly annoyed him, so he wrote a codicil leaving them to Dublin instead. After his death in 1915 on the *Lusitania,* the codicil was found. But crucially it had not been witnessed, and was therefore legally invalid. A battle began between Dublin and London—neither of which had shown much interest in the paintings while Lane was alive.[208]

Thomas Bodkin was a friend of Lane and, as we saw in Chapter 1, an acquaintance of Costello's in UCD. He practised as a barrister as well as dealing in art, before becoming Secretary to the Commission on Charitable Bequests, and later Director of the National Gallery from 1927 to 1935. Even before taking up the latter post, he was widely regarded as an expert in art, and submitted a memorandum to the Provisional Government in January 1922 proposing that it should restore the recently abolished independent Ministry of Fine Arts.[209] Bodkin was friendly with W.T. Cosgrave, writing speeches for him, as well as a comprehensive history of the controversy over the Lane Pictures.[210]

He was also Honorary Professor of Art at Trinity College, which led to "sustained attack" from "some of the less respectable Catholic journals".[211] An example comes from the *Catholic Bulletin* of February 1931, which criticised a speech made by Bodkin: "[T]hese Catholic Friends of Trinity College, entrenched within the Central Catholic Library Organisation, persist in purveying Papist 'rats' for that Protestant rat-pit." Bodkin was sufficiently concerned at this attack to send a copy of what he had actually said to Cosgrave. His speech suggested that Catholics confronted with "heresy" had a twofold duty: "We have first to protect ourselves: but we are also bound to try to do something for the heretics"[212]—by which he meant, of course, Protestants. It is illuminating that these far from ecumenical sentiments could be attacked as too liberal—and an indication that the similar views about Protestants of his friend Jack Costello were closer to the mainstream than might be realised today.

Whatever about his religious views, Bodkin's political opinions meant he was not consulted by de Valera about arts policy as he had been by Cosgrave, and in 1935 he moved to Birmingham to become the first Director of the Barber Institute of Fine Arts, which opened in 1939. When Costello became Taoiseach in 1948, he sought Bodkin out to help pursue two pet projects—the Lane Pictures, and "our old and forgotten scheme of art in Industry and the possibility of developing artistic schemes in country districts".[213]

De Valera had displayed no great concern about the Lane pictures—when he mentioned it to Lord Rugby in February 1947, the British Representative said it was "the first time that Mr de Valera has brought up this 'injustice to Ireland' and I do not know why he is now moved to take an interest in it".[214] A month after Costello became Taoiseach, the British Cabinet was assured that the controversy was not likely to be revived by the Irish, and that no effort should be made to try to reach a settlement.[215] Bodkin, however, had other ideas, writing to Costello in April that he had "a feeling in my bones that you are the man who will, at last, get these pictures back".[216]

The Taoiseach had an opportunity to raise the matter directly with the British Prime Minister, Clement Attlee, during the Anglo-Irish Trade talks in London. He found Attlee "a difficult man to get to know. He was very reserved and laconic, but after ranging over many aspects of Irish problems we came to that of the Lane Pictures." Costello suggested that Attlee should recognise Ireland's "strong moral claim" and make a gesture on that basis.[217] He wrote to Attlee the following month, suggesting that the British people should "give the pictures to the Irish nation as a free gift and invaluable token of goodwill ... The Irish people would then formally undertake to make liberal loans of the Pictures to English Galleries and to the North of Ireland."[218] Rugby informed London that the renewed Irish effort was due to Bodkin, as members of the Government "take little or no genuine interest in the topic on cultural or artistic grounds. Politics provides the main factor in keeping the question alive with them."[219] Politics, specifically the furore over the declaration of a Republic, also prevented further progress. In November, Attlee decided it was not the time to pursue the matter "while other and wider issues are under consideration".[220]

In January 1951, following the theft of the Stone of Scone from Westminster Abbey by Scottish nationalist students, Lord Rugby advised London that "special precautions" should be taken to protect the Lane Pictures.[221] One of the paintings, Jour d'Eté by Berthe Morisot, was stolen in 1956 by two Irish students, but returned undamaged to the Irish Embassy two days later.[222] One of the students was the son of Sarsfield Hogan of the Department of Finance, who wrote a note of apology to the Taoiseach for "a folly which has put trouble on you and the Government".[223]

Costello continued to raise the Lane Pictures, both in government and opposition. In 1958, he strongly advised de Valera against accepting a suggestion from Professor Lionel Robbins, chairman of the board of the (British) National Gallery, of a loan of the pictures to Dublin, provided the Irish Government agreed "formally to abandon any claim to the legal ownership of the Lane pictures ..."[224] Costello advised de Valera that this condition was "so insulting as to be unacceptable", although on the basis of previous experience with the British it might be regarded as an opening offer which would lead to discussions which could reach a reasonable settlement.[225] He was right, and an agreement was eventually reached on a long-term loan of the pictures to Dublin.

However, Costello, like the good barrister he was, spotted a change in a revision of the draft agreement which would prejudice the underlying Irish claim. The original draft suggested that the agreement "would settle <u>for a considerable period</u> the question of the Lane Pictures". The underlined words were left out of a later draft,[226] but reinstated after Costello spotted their omission. By the time final agreement was reached a new Taoiseach—Seán Lemass—was in place; he wrote to Costello thanking him for his "unfailing co-operation" in the matter.[227] These thanks were repeated in a Dáil statement by Lemass in November. In his own statement to the House, Costello singled out Bodkin for praise.[228]

The other issue on which Bodkin and Costello collaborated was the establishment of the Arts Council. Fianna Fáil Minister P.J. Little had proposed the establishment of a Cultural Institute or Council of National Culture in November 1945,[229] but nothing was done about it. Costello, however, was personally interested in the arts, both for their own sake and for their applications to industry. The first step was to commission Bodkin to write a report on the arts. This was submitted to Government on 4 October 1949, and was scathing of existing cultural institutions, and of the neglect "amounting almost to contempt" for art in the education system. The report recommended the establishment of an Arts Council.[230] There was no doubt about who Bodkin—and Costello—envisaged in charge of the new body. Bodkin told the Taoiseach that if he was offered the post of Chairman "I shall accept it promptly". He was not going to come cheap, however, suggesting a salary of £3,000 per annum.[231]

A lengthy correspondence ensued between the two men, with Bodkin not unreasonably insisting on a firm offer before giving up his job in Birmingham.[232] He became alarmed at reports that the new Council would include in its aims the fostering and development of the Irish language, as well as music, literature and drama. Bodkin confessed he didn't speak Irish, and wasn't an expert in the other subjects either. "The work which I want to address myself to, and which alone I consider myself quite competent to do, is that connected in some way, however slight, with the visual arts."[233] Costello reassured him that these aims had only been included "to forestall criticism if they had been omitted".[234] Having finally received a formal job offer in January 1951, Bodkin now baulked, claiming that the terms of the Arts Bill "[reflect], to my mind, the old bureaucratic spirit of the Department of Education that so effectively frustrated the work I might have done when I was Director of the National Gallery of Ireland".[235]

With commendable patience, Costello claimed he "was not wholly disappointed" at Bodkin's refusal. While his aim had been to secure Bodkin's services, he felt he couldn't press him unduly given the difficulties of the job he was asking him to do. He initially considered dropping the whole matter, but after "a breathing space" he decided to have the Bill redrafted. The Taoiseach confessed that he was at fault because "owing to pressure from the storms that were blowing on me in all directions I didn't examine the Bill as closely as I should". Among the storms he mentioned were "strikes—milk, bread, Railways, Banks—Estimates, Price Orders and a succession of ... problems". He also admitted that he had been "unduly influenced" by the advice of his Department's Secretary and Assistant Secretary (Maurice Moynihan and Nicholas Nolan) that the Council should be under the remit of the Minister of Education rather than the Taoiseach.[236]

The redrafted Bill met with Bodkin's approval, and he suggested that he might be allowed to withdraw his refusal to accept the Director's post.[237] But the delay cost him the job—by the time the Arts Council was up and running, Fianna Fáil were back in power. Costello made an effort on his friend's behalf, advising the new Taoiseach that he had intended to appoint Bodkin, that the legislation had been redrafted to meet his wishes, and that he would still be prepared to act.[238] These representations evidently cut no ice with the new government, which appointed Paddy Little to the post.

Bruce Arnold criticised the manner in which the Council was set up. "Without real power, direct ministerial responsibility, direct involvement within the civil service, a proper vote with political decisions about the spending of money, the Arts Council from its inception was set adrift on a course that left it to the mercies of its members and, more importantly, its director." He argues that the establishment of the Council "was seen as a kind of absolution for the politicians".[239] This implies that once the Council was set up, politicians could ignore the arts. But, of course, they had been happily ignoring the arts for decades; at least now someone was *obliged* to pay some attention to the area.

The historian of the Council offers a more balanced assessment, suggesting that Costello's government "had taken the soft option in establishing an Arts Council without attempting to place it within an overall defined arts policy. But it is also true that the measure was the most significant step since independence towards the development of an official arts policy."[240] At the launch of the Council in January 1952, de Valera generously pointed out that its establishment "was due to the initiative of Mr Costello when he was Taoiseach". Costello stressed the economic benefits of the arts and of the application of art to industry, adding that "there could be no nationality without art".[241]

Costello's personal interest in the arts allowed him to use his position to secure real advances. His interventions in the field of foreign policy were to have more mixed results.

Chapter 8

MR COSTELLO WAS RARIN'
TO GO

"Jack Costello had about as much notion of diplomacy as I have of astrology."[1]

FREDDIE BOLAND

"Mr Costello was rarin' to go and, almost like a child with a secret, could not hold it ..."[2]

JOSEPH CHAPDELAINE, CANADIAN EMBASSY, 1950

For more than a quarter of a century, a large statue of Britain's Queen Victoria dominated the entrance to the parliament of independent Ireland. The Queen remained undisturbed on her plinth on the Kildare Street side of Leinster House during the decade of W.T. Cosgrave's government, and the 16 years of de Valera's first administration. It was significant that it was the government of John A. Costello which finally moved her.[3]

The statute of the Famine Queen had considerable symbolic importance, but little artistic merit. Tom O'Higgins described it as a "work of intense, although no doubt unintentional ugliness ... popularly known as 'Ireland's revenge'".[4] Even the British Representative in Dublin, Lord Rugby, admitted that the statue "is in itself not a beautiful object".[5]

At the end of June 1948, Costello informed the Dáil that the statue was to be removed to provide more car parking spaces.[6] Rugby admitted that there may have been something in this, but that the Government was probably glad to find an excuse.[7] Sir Eric Machtig of the Commonwealth Relations Office said it was "difficult to repress one's feelings of indignation at this step". But he thought there was little London could do about it—a view shared by King George VI, who agreed that "for the present, it would be better to take no action".[8] An attempt to purchase the statue by the Northern Ireland-based National Union of Protestants was rejected on the basis that MacBride didn't want it re-erected "on Irish soil".[9] The statue eventually ended up outside the Queen Victoria Building, a shopping centre in Sydney, Australia.[10]

The removal of the statue was symbolic—it showed that Costello, for whatever reason, was prepared to do things which de Valera had considered, but hadn't quite got round to. That symbolism was marked in a cartoon in *Dublin Opinion* (used by Ronan Fanning on the cover of his seminal book *Independent Ireland*). The cartoon showed Victoria saying to a startled looking de Valera, "Begob, Eamon, there's great changes around here!"[11] The move outflanked de Valera and annoyed the British—and so was a perfect portent of what was about to happen to the External Relations Act.

As we saw in Chapter 5, Costello had expressed doubts about the External Relations Act when it was brought in at the time of the abdication crisis, and his view hadn't changed in the meantime. De Valera himself had had enough of the Act; he told Lord Rugby in October 1947 that "it had done no good and had involved him and his Government in difficulties and humiliation".[12] A Bill had in fact been drafted to transfer to the President the powers exercised under the Act by the King.[13] During the 1948 election campaign, Rugby noted similar sentiments from MacBride and from Fine Gael deputy leader T.F. O'Higgins, and reported to London that "it is quite plain that the annulment of the External Relations Act will not be long delayed. No party has left the door open for any other course."[14]

However, the situation was complicated by lingering pro-Commonwealth sentiment within Fine Gael. The day after the despatch quoted above, the newspapers reported a speech by Mulcahy saying his party "would not alter the present position which has been accepted by all members of the British Commonwealth as being in consonance with membership". Rugby noted that Mulcahy's speech, coming so soon after O'Higgins had taken the opposite line, was "indicative of the way in which the Fine Gael party mismanage their affairs".[15]

Most Fine Gael supporters would presumably have taken Mulcahy's views as definitive. Garret FitzGerald later recalled reassuring the inhabitants of Waterloo Road that the party supported Commonwealth membership.[16] But of course, Mulcahy did not become Taoiseach; and Fine Gael was not in government on its own. Costello, however, had a long record of involvement in the Commonwealth, and in his election address he told the voters of Dublin South-East that if Fine Gael were in government, "it will not propose any alteration in the present constitution in relation to external affairs".[17] After his election, Rugby reported to London that he had learned "from a wholly reliable source that Mr Costello takes the line that though he does not like the Act he does not propose to interfere with it".[18] And the Taoiseach told journalists that the Government was "not making any change in the political structure of the State".[19]

As we saw in the previous chapter, MacBride said on the day the new Government was elected that he wouldn't be pushing for the repeal of the Act. In his memoirs, he said it would have been "grossly unfair" to do so, given the problems it would cause for Fine Gael (and also for Clann na Talmhan— MacBride said Joe Blowick was "extremely conservative himself and was always terrified of anything that might possibly injure ... our cattle trade"). As a result, by his own account, MacBride "decided not to bring it up at cabinet meetings".[20]

However, he did push out the boundaries of Ireland's constitutional position, with Costello's full agreement. This was most marked in the case of the presentation of credentials by the new Argentinian Minister in Dublin. These were addressed not to King George, as was the practice under the External Relations Act, but to President O'Kelly. Both Costello and Cecil Lavery, the Attorney General, approved this new procedure,[21] which amounted to a significant undermining of the External Relations Act. This undermining would presumably have continued even if the Act was not repealed, thereby making it a dead letter.

On the related issue of partition, the summer of 1948 saw considerable speculation about a possible breakthrough. For this, Costello must take some responsibility, as he was prone to loose and unrealistic talk on the subject. In July, he told the Dáil that "for the first time since 1922, this Cabinet will, by its policy and its actions, give some hope of bringing back to this country the six north-eastern counties of Ulster. I must speak on that subject ... with restraint and responsibility, but I do make that assertion with all the confidence that I have in me."[22]

Although there appears to have been absolutely no basis for his confidence, journalists and diplomats naturally thought there must be something behind it. Vinton Chapin, the Counsellor in the US Legation, said to Costello's son-in-law Alexis FitzGerald that he presumed the comments "are uttered because he knows they are to be followed by deeds". FitzGerald, knowing that this was not the case, advised his father-in-law to stress "the inevitable gradualness of any possible solution".[23]

The British and Americans believed Costello was forced to adopt a robust position on partition as a result of de Valera's stridency on the issue during a world tour which took in the US, India and Australia.[24] This seems to be borne out by Costello's assertion in a private letter that he believed de Valera "is doing great damage by his Partition speeches but, of course, they serve as the one method by which he can now publicise himself".[25] However, some of those who knew the Taoiseach believed he was "very bitter about the North", and therefore needed little encouragement to adopt a strong line on partition. Risteárd Mulcahy accompanied Costello on a trip to Donegal, during which their car became stranded on a flooded road near Omagh. They were rescued by the RUC, to whom Costello was "very rude" as a result of his hostility to the regime they represented.[26]

But while his government pursued a "sore thumb" policy on partition—raising it at every opportunity in every international forum, no matter how inappropriate—it also co-operated with Stormont. The two governments reached agreements resolving difficulties over the Foyle fisheries, the drainage of the Erne, and the financial problems of the Great Northern Railway. At the 1951 Fine Gael Ard Fheis, Costello said these agreements "have given some grounds for the belief that friendly relations can do much to achieve eventual unity more certainly than threats of bloody warfare".[27] In this he was absolutely right. But Northern Unionists were to perceive his government as more likely to break connections than to build them, thanks to the repeal of the External Relations Act.

Unionists were certainly concerned at talk in the summer of 1948 about moves on Irish unity. This talk was given added impetus by the "remarkable" number of visits to Ireland by leading British politicians, including Prime Minister Clement Attlee, Lord Chancellor William Jowitt, and Common-wealth Secretary Philip Noel-Baker.[28] In advance of his visit, Jowitt wrote to Costello that his visit to London for the trade talks had left "a host of friends behind you", and that what had been done "may prove to be the foundation of a happier relationship more advantageous to both of us".[29] MacBride played the main role in pushing discussions with the various visitors, to no apparent avail. However, the contacts led to a sensational story in the London *Observer* that Attlee was involved in talks to end partition.

When he arrived at the Border the next day, Attlee was presented with a copy of the story, which he hadn't seen, by the young journalist John Cole. "He took a suck at his pipe, and enquired in his usual staccato tone: 'Got y' notebook?' He then proceeded to dictate a statement of about 400 words, without hesitation or amendment, contradicting the *Observer* story, point by point."[30] The story was also dismissed by officials at External Affairs, who told the American Minister, George Garrett, that they knew nothing about any talks, and that the story was "journalistic whimsy". However, Garrett con-cluded that while it was unlikely that partition was in fact being discussed seriously, "one must not disregard the fact that in recent weeks the attitude of Prime Minister Costello has been one of calm assurance that progress was being made along this line".[31]

To return to the question of the State's constitutional status, we have a perfect indication of Costello's view in June 1948, thanks to the ever meticulous Nicholas Nolan, Assistant Secretary of the Department of the Taoiseach. He pointed out to his boss, Maurice Moynihan, that various Yearbooks asked them for information on Ireland, including its constitutional status. In January 1947, the then Minister for External Affairs (de Valera) had agreed that the description should be "an independent Republic associated with the States of the British Commonwealth". But what was the new Taoiseach's view? It turned out that Costello favoured a different designation: "Ireland is a sovereign, independent, democratic State, associated with the States of the British Commonwealth."[32] These conflicting definitions were utterly con-sistent with the views each man had taken of the External Relations Act and the Constitution—de Valera believed the Constitution had in effect created a republic; Costello insisted that a republic could not exist while the Act was in force. But if Ireland was not quite a republic, was she a member of the Commonwealth? Costello's definition suggests not—like de Valera, he said Ireland was merely "associated" with the Commonwealth.

Costello believed that Ireland had left when she stopped attending Commonwealth meetings.[33] He put his view on the public record in answering Dáil questions from Captain Peadar Cowan, by then a former member of Clann na Poblachta.[34] "The process by which Ireland ceased formally to be a member of that Commonwealth has been one of gradual development ... It has ceased to be formally a member, but is associated with the other members ..."[35] Cowan continued to ask awkward questions—was Ireland a republic? Costello said this question was "purely one of nomenclature" which he wasn't prepared to discuss. How did Ireland become associated with the Commonwealth? "Matters of history", according to the Taoiseach, which it would serve no useful purpose to deal with.

Cowan also wanted the Taoiseach to define the precise nature of the association. Precision, of course, was something de Valera had avoided, but Costello was not one for evasions, and on 5 August he gave the Dáil the following definition: "Ireland's association with the Commonwealth of Nations depends on the factual position. This factual relationship ... depends on the reciprocal exchange of concrete benefits in such matters as trade and citizenship rights, the principle of consultation and cooperation in matters of common concern and on the many ties of blood and friendship that exist ... Our association with the nations of the Commonwealth is a free association, which, by virtue of its very freedom, could be determined by unilateral action."[36]

In other words, Ireland was, in Costello's opinion, already outside the Commonwealth, although it retained an association with it. That association was governed by practical links, not by legislation, and in particular not by the External Relations Act. However, the Canadian High Commissioner in Dublin was not impressed with Costello's idea of "association". "Since he made this statement I have been trying to ascertain what particular association might be said to subsist between Éire and the British nations now that the Commonwealth link has been broken. I have not found any ... It takes at least two to form an association and its nature and objects, its mutual rights and obligations, must be ascertained and defined. There may be good reasons why such an association should be formed, but its formation has not yet taken place ..."[37]

So did Ireland enjoy trade and citizenship rights in Britain and the other Commonwealth countries because of her association with the Commonwealth, or was she "associated" with the Commonwealth because she enjoyed trade and citizenship rights? On this point, which of course was crucial to any move to make changes in the formal relationship between Ireland and the Commonwealth, Costello appeared to be slightly confused. In the Dáil debate on the Anglo-Irish trade agreement, he stated that Ireland's right to preferential treatment in trade with Britain and the other members of the Commonwealth would remain "so long as we are associated with the league of nations known as the British Commonwealth of Nations".[38] But in fact, the Agreement gave Ireland trade advantages which were not specifically dependent on membership of, or even association with, the Commonwealth. The same was true of the British Nationality Act of 1948, which said Irish citizens who were not British subjects would be treated in the same manner as British subjects. Ironically, then, by concluding these agreements the British had already cut the ground out from under the position they would later adopt to try to prevent the repeal of the External Relations Act.

Three developments brought matters to a head in the summer of 1948: repeated difficulties on the question of official toasts; the prospect of an invitation to the Commonwealth Conference in October; and further awkward questions in the Dáil.

The question of after-dinner toasts may seem arcane, but it had a bearing on the developments which led to the repeal of the External Relations Act, and was one of the issues which annoyed Jack Costello when he was in Canada. The point was that the British did not recognise the President of Ireland as a head of state, holding that King George VI was still Head of State of Ireland by virtue of his position as head of the Commonwealth. At a lunch in Downing Street for the Irish delegation to the trade talks, Costello noted that Attlee "proposed one Toast and one Toast only, namely, The King". The Taoiseach had expected that he would propose the toast to the King, and that Attlee would reciprocate by toasting the President. "That this protocol was not followed by the British Prime Minister was significant as demonstrating the attitude of the British ... [and was] a striking confirmation of the views we held as to the confusion and difficulty created in our international relations by the External Relations Act."[39]

The British were aware of the Irish sensitivity on this point—Rugby told London that Lord Chancellor Jowitt had been inveigled into proposing a toast to the President of Ireland at a dinner in his honour in Dublin in August. It was the first time he had heard such a toast, and he put the new development down to Irish resentment at what he called "the London contretemps".[40] His Canadian counterpart, William Turgeon, felt it was "part and parcel of the general scheme to substitute the President for the King in Ireland's External Affairs".[41]

While Rugby was inclined to fall in with the new Irish practice, the Commonwealth Relations Office held that it would be impossible to toast the President "without an admission that Éire was in relation to the United Kingdom a foreign country and the President of Éire in the same position as the Head of a foreign State".[42] With Attlee's approval, the CRO advised the High Commissioner in Canada about the potential difficulties in advance of Costello's visit, asking him to informally draw the attention of the Canadians to the issue.[43] As we shall see below, the resulting confusion over toasts strengthened Costello's determination to clear away the ambiguities surrounding Ireland's constitutional status, and was another British contribution to the repeal of the External Relations Act.

The second factor leading to a reappraisal of links with Britain was the forthcoming Commonwealth Conference, to be held in London in October. Ireland had not attended a Conference since the change of government in 1932; the British felt that this might change now that a new administration was in place, particularly given the important role Costello (and McGilligan) had played on the Commonwealth stage. Attlee raised possible Irish attendance with Costello during the trade talks in London in June. However, the British Prime Minister's roundabout way of raising the subject was obviously a bit too roundabout for the Taoiseach, who did not interpret it as a definite invitation.[44] When no response arrived from Dublin, Lord Rugby was asked to raise the matter with MacBride.[45]

The Clann leader duly submitted a memorandum to Government, arguing that there were matters which they might want to discuss at the Conference—such as partition, eliminating Ireland from the King's title, and replacing High Commissioners with Ambassadors. However, it would have to be made clear that Ireland was not a member of the Commonwealth—and MacBride concluded that it would be better not to be represented.[46] On 19 August the Cabinet agreed that Ireland should not be represented as a member of the Commonwealth, but left open the possibility of attendance "otherwise than as a member of the Commonwealth, for the purpose of discussing any particular subject", pending the receipt of further information by MacBride.[47] As Patrick Lynch pointed out, this wording "suggests that, on the day before the

Taoiseach left Dublin for Canada, the government did not consider Ireland a member of the Commonwealth".[48] This did not, though, necessarily imply any immediate repeal of the External Relations Act, which referred to Ireland being "associated" with the Commonwealth.

This Cabinet meeting—which also approved the text of Costello's speech to the Canadian Bar Association—may have been the one recalled by MacBride in his memoirs. He claimed to have suggested that the time had come to say "straight out that we are not members of the Commonwealth". He said his suggestion was backed by Dillon and Norton.[49] Whether this is an accurate report of the discussion will never be known. But it does appear that, as with the question of toasts, the British query about the conference had pushed Costello's government towards clarifying Ireland's position and removing ambiguity.

Curiously, possible Irish attendance at the October conference was still being discussed even after Costello's Canadian press conference confirming that the External Relations Act was to go and that Ireland was no longer a member of the Commonwealth. On 6 September (the day after the *Sunday Independent* reported that the Act was to go), Rugby phoned MacBride to see if Ireland would be represented, and if so, by whom.[50] On the morning of the seventh (before Costello's news conference) the two men met to discuss the Conference. Rugby reported that MacBride "stated specifically that the Éire government intended to do away with the External Relations Act". Despite this, Rugby expected Ireland to be represented at the Conference.[51] The government in Dublin took a similar view, deciding that "subject to Ireland's position in relation to the British Commonwealth being made clear, a representative of Ireland should attend for the purpose of taking part in the discussion of certain items".[52] But after Costello's Canadian announcement, the British had other ideas. Commonwealth Secretary Philip Noel-Baker told the Irish High Commissioner in London that the meeting was "exclusively one of Commonwealth Prime Ministers, and I don't see how in these circumstances we could possibly have issued an invitation to your Prime Minister".[53]

The third factor pushing the Government towards making a decision was the continuing pressure in the Dáil on the External Relations Act. Following a "pretty stormy debate" on the estimates for the Department of the Taoiseach, Bill Norton suggested that he could take the Adjournment Debate before the Dáil rose for the summer to give the Taoiseach a break. Costello was more than happy to agree. However, "before anybody knew what had happened, the whole thing, the Republic and the External Relations Act and whether we were in or out of the Commonwealth was being debated all round the place".[54]

Norton told the Dáil that "it would do our national self-respect good both at home and abroad if we were to proceed without delay to abolish the External

Relations Act". De Valera responded, "You will get no opposition from us."[55] According to Costello's later account, these exchanges led him to raise the matter with his Government colleagues. "My clear view was that a decision to repeal it should be taken by the government before they might appear to be forced to do so by, for example, the introduction of a private member's Bill in the Dáil to repeal the Act. I had myself arrived firmly at the conviction that it was nationally desirable that the Act should be repealed."[56]

The Government viewed Captain Peadar Cowan as the most likely source of a private member's bill to repeal the Act. They would no doubt have been surprised to learn that de Valera, the architect of the Act, was presented with a draft Bill to repeal it on the day after the Adjournment Debate. The draft Bill was sent by his former Attorney General, Cearbhall Ó Dálaigh, who said it was more complete than the one he had prepared some time before (i.e. at the end of 1947—see above), and there might be a need for it "if what you say comes to pass".[57] It is not clear if the initiative came from the former Taoiseach or the former Attorney General. What is clear is that if de Valera had introduced this Bill in the Dáil in the autumn, it would have been politically devastating for the Government, seizing the initiative from Costello and his colleagues and possibly provoking a split with Clann na Poblachta.

In any case, according to Costello's account, he felt it was better for the Government to act before it was forced to, and "an express decision was taken by the government that the External Relations Act should be repealed and the necessary legislation introduced immediately the Dáil reassembled".[58] The only problem with this account is that there is absolutely no evidence in the Government archives to back it up. We saw in the previous chapter that civil servants were excluded from Cabinet meetings at this time, so it is perhaps believable that a decision would not have been recorded; but as Noël Browne pointed out, it was usual before a decision was taken to prepare a memorandum and circulate it to all other Departments for consideration and observations. This clearly didn't happen in this instance, which left Costello open to the accusation that his announcement in Canada that the Government was to repeal the Act was taken on a whim and without proper authorisation.

Eithne MacDermott, author of a history of Clann na Poblachta, counted five sources where Costello admitted he wasn't sure if the decision was properly minuted. These were Brian Farrell's *Chairman or Chief, Ireland Since the Famine* by F.S.L. Lyons, an interview with Vincent Browne in *The Citizen*, the John A. Costello Remembers series in the *Irish Times*, and Costello's own memorandum on the repeal of the External Relations Act. To this might be added his "Seven Days" interview with David Thornley. She concludes that "such guilty hints imply that Costello seems to have known perfectly well that this decision was never actually committed to writing".[59] The number of repetitions may appear significant, but probably isn't—he used his own memorandum as a brief for all of the other interviews, and like the good barrister he was, he stuck to his brief doggedly. Rather than five separate sources, there was one source repeated several times. It may also be significant that in 1959, responding to Fianna Fáil taunts in the Dáil, Costello said that if they looked up the Government records, they "will find there that the decision of the Government to repeal the External Relations Act was taken in August, before I left for Canada at all".[60]

Freddie Boland, Secretary of the Department of External Affairs, told Nicholas Mansergh that "the Cabinet itself while it had discussed the desirability of repealing the External Relations Act had reached no conclusions when Mr Costello went to Canada. His announcement ... came as a 'bomb shell' to his colleagues ..."[61] In an interview with journalist Bruce Arnold, later broadcast in a radio documentary, Boland said the issue had been discussed twice in Cabinet and there was a consensus that the Act would go, "but there was no decision as to when and how the job would be done".[62]

This view was backed by James Dillon. In his memoir, he accepted that proper procedures were not followed—there had been informal discussion and agreement round the Cabinet table, but no formal decision.[63] However, as noted above, MacBride told Rugby some hours before Costello's news conference that the Government intended to do away with the Act,[64] which implies a rather more definite decision had been taken. The Minister later told Rugby that he hadn't brought the matter up in Cabinet—it had in fact been raised by Fine Gael, "who had had such a grim time in the period of the Cosgrave government defending what they did not really believe in that they had decided this time not to find themselves in that position against a virulent Opposition".[65]

This seems to be a fair assessment of the situation—the matter had clearly been discussed at Cabinet and consensus reached, but without a full consideration of the implications, and without consulting other interested parties, most notably the British. It is significant that the Cabinet approved the drafting of a Bill to repeal the External Relations Act on 9 September— just two days after Costello's press conference. On the form seeking urgent consideration of the matter, MacBride said that "recent developments have made it imperative that a decision should be arrived at immediately".[66]

The British were later to make much of the failure to consult them; but here Costello's unorthodox approach arguably paid off. The British knew that the External Relations Act was to be repealed soon after the Dáil returned in the autumn. They had considered warning Dublin that repeal "would be regarded by the older members of the Commonwealth as ending her membership of the club", but accepted that such a warning "would probably have no effect" and that "unilateral action by Éire will force the issue whatever the argument may be".[67] Rugby later complained that Costello had crashed "the delicate fabric" of the Act, with "not one word to me as to the desirability of re-examining the difficult procedure of the External Relations Act, no suggestion of any discussion in London".[68] However, it is clear that if Costello had broached the subject with London, he would have been confronted with endless warnings about the difficulties involved; presenting a *fait accompli* had its advantages.

Here the story moves across the Atlantic to Canada. Costello had been invited to Montreal to speak at a meeting of the Canadian Bar Association. The Taoiseach told his friend Michael MacWhite, the Irish Minister to Rome, that all his colleagues thought he should accept the invitation; in fact, Richard Mulcahy had earlier told MacWhite that "both our national and international affairs will ... be better served by his being at home".[69] Despite Mulcahy's reservations, the invitation was accepted; once it was, the Canadian Government offered Costello hospitality, including the use of a Government railway carriage.[70] The Prime Minister, William Lyon Mackenzie King, was less than enthralled at the prospect of the visit, which was one of many official visits at around this time, as he prepared for his retirement. He complained in his diary, "It is just appalling the number of engagements connected with this visit and other social events next week ... All involving more preparation of speeches, days in the city etc and this at a moment when the last hours of the summer are flying so swiftly by."[71]

In advance of the visit, the Canadians worried that Costello might say something which would cause controversy. William Turgeon, the High Commissioner in Dublin, on his own initiative suggested to the Taoiseach that "he should consider his mission to Canada as one of a lawyer speaking to lawyers and speaking only of subjects in which members of the profession are interested". He also informed him that "the Irish Catholic people in Canada are not at all anti-British, that the great majority of them hold about the same views on Empire and Commonwealth questions as other English-speaking Canadians. I think he was surprised to hear this." Lester Pearson, the under-secretary of state for External Affairs, welcomed Turgeon's "gentle warning" to Costello, saying it "should prevent him from making statements which might cause embarrassing controversies in Canada".[72]

The Irish Department of External Affairs was also concerned about what Costello might say, with Secretary Freddie Boland writing a personal letter to the Irish High Commissioner in Ottawa, John Hearne, setting out in detail MacBride's views. He said it was generally recognised that the "days of the External Relations Act are numbered" and that they should proceed on the assumption that it would be repealed in the near future. "In the meantime, it is very important that any statement made about our relations with the

Commonwealth should emphasise the undesirability and inappropriateness in our case of *any* constitutional arrangements of the kind which Britain and the overseas dominions maintain between themselves as symbols of their association in the Commonwealth ..." Boland advised that Costello should avoid "any public statement which had too 'Commonwealthish' a flavour".[73] Which, as it turned out, was not to be a problem.

Costello left Government Buildings for Cork on the afternoon of 20 August, embarked on the *Mauritania* from Cobh on the twenty-second, and arrived in New York five days later. He was accompanied by his wife, Ida, by Patrick Lynch, and by his ADC Mick Byrne (who received permission from the Canadians to bring his revolver with him).[74] They travelled in some style— first class on the *Mauritania* on the outward leg, and the *Britannic* on the return; staying in the landmark Château Frontenac in Quebec and the Waldorf-Astoria in New York. The weather in New York was extremely warm, with temperatures of 104 degrees (40 degrees Celsius),[75] and the party had to buy extra summer clothes in New York at their own expense.[76]

On his arrival in Montreal on 30 August, Costello was met by Hearne and John T. Hackett, President of the Canadian Bar Association (he was at this point still a guest of the Association rather than the Canadian Government). At a press conference, he told journalists that as he was a guest of the Bar Association, he did not "propose to express any views at present on controversial political matters".

On Wednesday 1 September, he delivered his lunchtime address to around one thousand lawyers at the Bar Association lunch. His theme was "Ireland in International Affairs". The text of this speech had been considered and approved by Cabinet before Costello left Dublin—the only time a speech was so approved, according to MacBride.[77] Despite his injunction to Hearne about avoiding Commonwealth themes, Boland drafted a speech which concentrated on the development of the Commonwealth, and was in line with Costello's views as expressed at various Imperial conferences which Boland had attended. He avoided references to the External Relations Act (in line with MacBride's wishes). But when he showed it to Costello, the Taoiseach remarked, "It's fine, but there's too much of the smell of Empire about this."[78]

Whether or not Costello made many changes to Boland's original draft, the final speech traced the well-trodden path of the constitutional development of the Commonwealth under Irish, South African and Canadian prompting. He explained why Ireland in the 1920s could not accept the Crown as enthusiastically as the other members of the Commonwealth (except South Africa). "The harp without the Crown symbolised the ideal of Irish independence and nationhood. The harp beneath the Crown was the symbol of conquest."

In dealing with the External Relations Act, he repeated many of his criticisms of 1936, pointing out, as he had then in the Dáil, that according to the Statute of Westminster the Crown was the symbol of free association, not the symbol of co-operation as de Valera's text had it. He said the Act ignored the formalities of the issue of full powers to negotiate or sign treaties; and it dealt with the appointment, but not the reception, of diplomatic representatives. The most quoted sentence of his speech said, "The inaccuracies and infirmities of these provisions are apparent." However, he then went on to ask, "is it fruitful ... to enquire too legalistically into the nature of Ireland's association with the Commonwealth?"[79] The implicit answer was no—so his audience could be forgiven for thinking that the speech signalled no new departure. Certainly the British High Commissioner in Canada didn't think much of the address, saying it "lasted an hour and a half and went into details of Irish politics with which most of the audience were unfamiliar and considerably bored".[80]

Whatever about the speech, the next few days saw a series of events that formed a controversial backdrop to Costello's confirmation at a news conference that the External Relations Act was to be repealed. He later wrote that he was subject to "the most extraordinary, fantastic and completely unfounded" allegations as to why he had said what he had. These stories suggested that "in a fit of pique ... I on my own responsibility 'declared the Republic in Canada' ... [that] I got annoyed, summoned the representatives of the press, and on my own initiative proceeded to declare the intention of my colleagues and myself to repeal the External Relations Act".[81] Costello's indignation was obvious, but misplaced. While he had very good reasons for what he said at the press conference, as we will see below, he was also the main source of suggestions that he had been annoyed at his treatment at the hands of the Governor General of Canada, Lord Harold Alexander, a distinguished British soldier with family connections to Northern Ireland.

The first point of friction occurred the day after Costello's speech to the Bar Association, when the Taoiseach and his wife attended a garden party in the grounds of McGill University in Montreal. In his official diary of the trip, Patrick Lynch noted, "Atmosphere rather chilly ... Governor General ... very cool and reserved. Suspect he was displeased by some passages in Taoiseach's address to the Bar Association. In general he appears to be either anti-social or somewhat hostile." Costello later complained to President Seán T. O'Kelly that while he and his wife had been asked by an aide to join the Governor General's party for tea in a special marquee, Lord Alexander did not greet them or speak to them when they were there.[82] The Canadian *chargé d'affaires* in Dublin commented that while Costello "is a very genial person usually ... there is a touch of sourness about him ... He would pass lightly on the fact that the Governor General had sought him to come and have tea under his tent, a gesture of great courtesy, and would brood over the fact that there was no conversation between the two ...".[83]

On Saturday 4 September, the Taoiseach's party left Montreal for Ottawa. He was met on his arrival by Prime Minister Mackenzie King, who recorded the Taoiseach's gratitude in his diary: "He was so appreciative of my being at the station and I felt happy that I had given up the morning to this end."[84] After his visit, Costello "spoke feelingly of his meetings with Mr Mackenzie King and of the honour done him in Mr King ... having met him personally on his arrival in Ottawa".[85] But his satisfaction at his treatment was not to last.

That evening, the Costellos attended a dinner hosted by the Governor General and Lady Alexander. As guests of honour, Jack and Ida Costello were seated on the right of Lady and Lord Alexander respectively.[86] Two problems arose—the question of toasts and, bizarrely, the table decorations. Hearne believed he had received a promise from W.H. Measures, the Head of Protocol of the Canadian Department of External Affairs, that both the King and the President of Ireland would be toasted. But the latter toast was not given.[87] Measures later claimed that while Hearne had raised the issue with him, he had advised him to contact Government House about it.[88] (It may be significant that Measures did agree to have a toast to the President on the menu card for a later dinner given by Mackenzie King, much to the annoyance of the Prime Minister, as we shall see below. Hearne may have gained the impression that Measures had agreed to a toast on both occasions.) Officials at Government House denied hearing anything about the toast, so Lord Alexander certainly didn't know about it.

More famously, on the table in front of Costello was a replica of Roaring Meg, one of the cannon used in the defence of the Siege of Derry. This ornament had been presented to Alexander when he was made a Freeman of the City of Londonderry some six months previously. When questions were later raised about its use, Canadian officials pointed out that it was "constantly used by the Governor General as a centrepiece on the dining room table at formal functions at Government House ... the placing of this ornament on the table at the time of the Costello visit was quite a routine proceeding and ... it did not occur to anyone that it should not be used".[89] Costello "considered the matter as being in very bad taste", but decided not to make any comment so as not to embarrass Mackenzie King, who was seated on the other side of Lady Alexander. The Canadian Prime Minister evidently didn't notice any awkwardness, writing in his diary that it was "a very pleasant party. I much enjoyed the talks with the different guests present."[90]

In his memorandum, Costello admitted that he thought at first that the failure to honour the toast was a deliberate action on the part of Alexander, but that he had later come to the conclusion that he would not have been guilty of such conduct. "It would certainly have been an extraordinary action for the Governor General to take on his own initiative ... It seems to me to be inconceivable that Lord Alexander would deliberately take a step which would be an insult to this country ... I therefore acquit Lord Alexander of any complicity in omitting to propose the Toast of The President of Ireland, as had been arranged with the Chief of Protocol of the Canadian Department of External Affairs."

However, this considered account was written in the 1960s—the significant point is that at the time, Costello believed he, and Ireland, had been deliberately snubbed. And on his return to Dublin he relayed his indignation—both at the omission of the toast and the presence of Roaring Meg— to at least two independent witnesses, President Seán T. O'Kelly and Frank MacDermott, who gleefully passed it on.

MacDermott, the former Centre Party leader and founding Vice-President of Fine Gael, was then living in Paris, where he was the *Sunday Times* correspondent. He interviewed Costello about the repeal of the External Relations Act, and was given a full (and, no doubt, vivid) account of the "insults" he had received from the Governor General. This part of the interview was off the record, which didn't stop MacDermott telling Lord Rugby, who in turn informed the Canadian High Commissioner, Turgeon.[91] MacDermott also relayed the story directly to Lester Pearson, Canada's new Minister of External Affairs, when the latter was in Paris.[92]

The second source was President O'Kelly, who told Rugby in December that he had asked Costello why he had made his announcement in Canada, and that the Taoiseach replied, "Because I was stung into it," then relating his complaints about the garden party, the toasts, and Roaring Meg.[93] O'Kelly was so taken with the story that he was still repeating it a year later, this time to the new Canadian Ambassador, David Johnson.[94] After receiving all these reports, the Canadians looked into the matter, but concluded that while the alleged incidents may have prompted an earlier than anticipated announcement, they certainly did not cause the decision to repeal the Act and to leave the Commonwealth. As the *chargé d'affaires* in Dublin, Joseph Chapdelaine, commented, "Mr Costello was rarin' to go and, almost like a child with a secret, could not hold it ..."[95]

Costello also repeated the same story to Senators William Bedell Stanford and William Fearon, both representatives of Trinity College, who had raised questions about the timing and location of the announcement during the Seanad debate on the Republic of Ireland Bill. They were called to the Taoiseach's room in Leinster House, a call Stanford compared to "being summoned to the Headmaster's study". Costello again went through the way he was treated—the absence of the toast, Roaring Meg, and so on—leaving the two Senators with the clear impression that "the immediate cause of his precipitate announcement in Canada had been indignation rather than calculation—and, as we know, he was by nature rather irascible—understandable indignation in the light of what looked like insults".[96]

While Stanford and Fearon didn't spread the story to diplomats as MacDermott and O'Kelly did, they presumably weren't the only people Costello told the story to. He was later to complain about the "legend" that he "declared the Republic" because he was insulted. But the legend originated with Jack Costello, who only had himself to blame for the widespread belief that his press conference performance was prompted by these incidents. As his assistant Patrick Lynch pointed out, the Taoiseach, as an experienced constitutional lawyer, was unlikely to have been influenced on such an important issue by perceived insults, "whatever their later utility as conversational material". However, by repeatedly making use of this conversational material, Costello had "gradually ... created a mythology that grew with repetition and, for some people served as a substitute explanation for the reality of the press conference".[97]

One other incident should be mentioned, a typical example of Costello's rather careless choice of words on occasion. On the evening after the Government House dinner, he recorded a broadcast for the CBC National Network. In it, he claimed that "the virus of atheistic Communism is poisoning the bloodstream of nations and peoples. The Irish nation is anxious to cooperate with all nations in creating the conditions of a just and permanent peace ... We cannot but feel that Canada and Ireland might fruitfully share the task of laying the foundations of a citadel of freedom which may shelter all free democracies in this threatened world."[98]

These sentiments, while admirably anti-communist, were also admirably vague and non-committal. However, in an interview with journalists after the broadcast, Costello was reported to have become considerably more bellicose, saying that Ireland would come to Canada's aid if she were ever threatened by war from communists. This promise, given Ireland's military strength, did not overly impress the journalists, one of whom "asked the rather pointed question whether Ireland was spending much money on defence. Mr Costello replied that not much money was being spent since the government was trying to improve its system of social security."[99]

Costello denied making the comments attributed to him—the *Irish Independent* incorrectly reported that he had made the comments during the radio broadcast rather than after,[100] so he was able to point to his script, which of course didn't mention the promise of aid. The Taoiseach told Bill Norton that "some of the Canadian papers are really beyond everything. It was impossible to read into anything I said what they said I said."[101] But MacBride evidently agreed with the Taoiseach's reported comments, rather bizarrely telling the American Minister, George Garrett, "If any country is attacked by Communists, we're in it."[102] The report of Costello's promise of aid was also accepted as accurate by the Canadians (who were not overly impressed by it). Fianna Fáil would make great play of his comments, with Seán Lemass even claiming his press conference announcement was an attempt to distract attention from them.

But while conspiracy theories about Roaring Meg or threats of war are entertaining, they are entirely irrelevant. For as Costello told Norton in his letter, "it was really the article in the *Sunday Independent* that decided me ... to state publicly that we intended to repeal the External Relations Act".[103]

On 5 September, the *Sunday Independent* splashed on its front page the news that the Government had decided to repeal the Act, quoting various statements by Cabinet members and declaring that "it must be taken for granted that the change that honour demands will be made". In particular, it pointed to Costello's "very important" speech to the Canadian Bar Association; Norton's statement in the Adjournment Debate in the Dáil; MacBride's speech on the External Affairs estimate; and Dillon's statements in opposition. It also quoted an article by Nicholas Mansergh predicting the demise of the Act. The paper's editor, Hector Legge, wrote the story, and always denied claims that it was based on a leak from a Cabinet Minister. It is certainly believable that the repeal of the External Relations Act could be predicted on the basis of "journalistic intuition" as he claimed. However, he went further, pointing out that both Costello and MacBride had said Ireland was no longer in the Commonwealth. The story continued, "honesty of purpose may soon find the present Government declaring that we are a Republic".[104] Legge's certainty suggests that he had been given a clear steer on the story—the question is by whom. Legge was friendly with both Dillon and MacBride, either of whom might have had a motive for wanting this particular kite given a test flight.

Two decades later, Costello told Michael McInerney of the *Irish Times* that the story "worried and surprised me. It seemed to me to be quite obvious that the story was not just 'intelligent anticipation' but was the result of a 'leak' from some person with inside knowledge." He refused to tell McInerney which minister he believed was responsible "although he seemed to have a shrewd idea who it was".[105] In fact, he indicated to Nicholas Mansergh that he believed MacBride to be responsible for a deliberate leak.[106]

However, on the day after the story appeared, MacBride sent a telegram urging the Taoiseach not to comment on the *Sunday Independent* story.[107] As MacBride's biographer points out, this was "a strange response if Seán had been the leak".[108] But what is on the written record may not have been the only advice offered by MacBride. Louie O'Brien, his personal secretary (who also believed he was responsible for the leak), claimed that he phoned Costello and said the easiest thing to do was to confirm the story, even offering to consult other members of the Cabinet to secure their approval.[109]

The only other supporting evidence for this story comes from Patrick Lynch, who along with John Hearne was trying to persuade Costello to avoid commenting. The Taoiseach said he was expecting a telephone call from Dublin. "I have no record of that call, but I do remember his referring later to a telephone conversation he had with Seán MacBride before his press conference."[110] It may also be significant that on the morning of the news conference, MacBride met Rugby and "stated specifically that the Éire government intended to do away with the External Relations Act".[111] It is possible that he may have done so because he was anticipating that Costello would confirm the *Sunday Independent* story later in the day. The evidence is far from conclusive, but if there was a telephone conversation between the two men, it might explain why Costello suspected MacBride of leaking the story in the first place.

The question became more urgent on the Sunday evening, with a phone call from a Canadian journalist looking for a comment from the Taoiseach on the *Sunday Independent* story. Costello's reply, delivered by Hearne, was a simple "no comment". However, he had already agreed to a request from the press gallery of the Canadian parliament to hold a news conference on the Tuesday morning.[112] Clearly he would be asked about the External Relations Act. Costello felt he had four options—decline to make any comment (which would have been "at least a qualified admission of the truth of the report"); deny the story; confirm it; or say that the matter would be dealt with on the return of the Dáil (which would also be seen as "an implied admission"). Costello concluded that as the report was in fact true, "there was nothing in honesty and decency open to me but to admit the truth".[113]

A "no comment" might have been seen as an implicit admission that the story was true, as Costello surmised; but it would have saved him a lot of criticism, then and later. The slights he believed he had received at the hands of Lord Alexander didn't lead to the decision to repeal the External Relations Act; but they may well have influenced Costello's choice to confirm this decision to the media. He decided to do so despite the strong urgings of Hearne and Lynch. "He said that if I'm asked the question I'm not going to prevaricate ... if I'm asked a direct question I'll say yes." This he did, confirming that it was his government's intention to repeal the External Relations Act. But he also answered in the affirmative when asked if this meant Ireland was leaving the Commonwealth. Lynch was surprised at this, asking the Taoiseach later if it was wise to have done so. Characteristically, Costello replied, "No qualification."[114]

After the news conference, he rang his son Declan, asking him to tell both MacBride and Mulcahy what had transpired. MacBride, who didn't seem surprised, said, "That's very good news." Mulcahy also thanked Declan for informing him.[115] This appeared to be the first either had heard about it, which undermines Freddie Boland's claim that MacBride was "knocked out" by the news when he told him about it while he was having dinner with Rugby.[116] Rugby's impression was that MacBride was "not a little surprised—indeed perturbed—by this sudden unconventional development".[117] When this account appeared, MacBride claimed he was only surprised because anyone was surprised at what Costello had said, "in view of the speeches made for some months and of the banner headlines which had appeared in one of our leading newspapers only four days before. I certainly was not 'perturbed' in any sense that could be construed as indicating disapproval ..."[118]

However, two days after the press conference, Rugby reported to London that MacBride had told him "as a personal confidence that neither he nor any member of the Cabinet here had any idea that Mr Costello was likely to make any statement in Canada on the subject of the External Relations Act ... I am sure that Mr MacBride is sincere in this."[119] Boland, meanwhile, was telling anyone who rang him up to inquire about the news that "our Prime Minister has simply made an awful gaffe".[120] It seems clear from all these accounts that nobody disputed the accuracy of Costello's statement that the Government intended to repeal the External Relations Act. The surprise was caused by the fact that he actually admitted this when asked. Clearly, it was felt that the more diplomatic approach would have been to evade the question.

Costello's announcement also came as a surprise to Mackenzie King. "I had known that this question was coming up at the meeting of Prime Ministers but had not anticipated anything of the kind would be announced in Ottawa, and certainly not on the day of the government giving the Prime Minister a dinner." At that dinner—in the Ottawa Country Club—Costello explained what he had said at the press conference, and regretted that the newspapers "always make heavy headlines". Mackenzie King, meanwhile, was more concerned about the printed menu cards, which contained two toasts—to the King, and to the President of Ireland. Mackenzie King was appalled, as he realized that this "was equivalent to regarding Ireland as an entirely separate country with a President as head of state. A state as much independent of the British Crown as the USA." He held Measures, the head of protocol in the (Canadian) Department of External Affairs, responsible.

With a certain amount of hyperbole, the Prime Minister claimed in his diary that this situation was "filled with dynamite which might have occasioned an explosion which would have been far reaching indeed". However, when he raised his problem with Costello, the Taoiseach said he didn't want to embarrass him in any way. The compromise was that while Costello would propose the toast to the King, the Canadian would respond by toasting the President of Éire, as opposed to Ireland. The change of name avoided upsetting those at the function with links to Northern Ireland, including Lady Alexander. But Costello would have been well pleased, as the toast to the President, however he was described, confirmed independent Irish status. Mackenzie King was happy too, noting that in his "very pleasing and helpful" speech, Costello "spoke of the Commonwealth of Nations as if he was still a member of it" and "did not go into any controversy".[121]

On 9 September Costello and Hearne went for lunch to Mackenzie King's home at Kingsmere outside Ottawa. During the three hours he was there, Costello outlined (at what was obviously considerable length) his position on the repeal of the External Relations Act. John Hearne recorded the conversation, although he pointed out that "no summary could adequately record the Taoiseach's objective and masterly presentation of the historic Irish case against the Crown. He was superb."[122]

In his diary, Mackenzie King was less fulsome: "It seemed to me that Costello was quite sincere in his whole argument and that his statement was logical enough." King recorded Costello as saying that Ireland would like to continue as a nation associated with the Commonwealth, but not on the basis of allegiance to the Crown. He also said Costello "wanted to bring about a situation where Irishmen wherever they were, would be prepared to fight to maintain a Christian civilization".[123] This latter statement didn't appear in other records of the conversation.

Costello believed he had persuaded Mackenzie King of the validity of the Irish position, which would lead to Canadian support in the future. Specifically, he told Norton that the Prime Minister was "a very good friend ... who will advocate us when he is in London next month".[124] In fact, Mackenzie King had already discussed the matter with his Cabinet, where a number of Ministers including St Laurent were "pretty strong on the idea of no severance, with allegiance part of the Crown". But after discussion they came round to his view that "it might perhaps be better for peace loving nations of the world to hold together on some kind of basis that would not, for the present, be too clearly defined".[125]

Given the invaluable support the Irish received from St Laurent during the Paris and Chequers talks, Costello's discussions with Mackenzie King were not without value. The Taoiseach was also clearly impressed to be presented with a copy of the Prime Minister's book, *Industry and Humanity*, noting that Mackenzie King inscribed a message on it "in his own writing".[126] Luckily, he didn't appear to notice that, as the Canadian Prime Minister recorded in his diary, "it was not the latest edition".[127]

On Friday the tenth, Mackenzie King attended a lunch at the Canadian Club, where Costello made a speech praising him. While the Prime Minister affected to find the compliments a bit over the top, he made sure to record them all in his diary anyway.[128] That afternoon, the Irish party left for Quebec, later travelling to Toronto (where a side trip took them to Niagara Falls), before visiting Boston and New York. They sailed home on the *Britannic*, which flew the Tricolour in honour of the Taoiseach, the Captain having explained that "his grandfather was a Fenian". According to Costello, the party were so tired after their busy schedule that they slept through a hurricane.[129] A storm of a different kind was waiting for them at home.

The *Britannic* arrived in Cobh at 6 a.m. on Friday 1 October,[130] and a number of ministers went out by ferry to greet the Taoiseach and have breakfast with him, after his eventful month away. Mulcahy commented to Patrick Lynch that "the Taoiseach has been drinking some very heady wine in Canada". But if this was an indication of irritation at Costello's performance abroad, no such irritation was displayed by MacBride. Lynch drove back to Dublin with him, stopping off at Abbeyleix for lunch, where they discussed events thoroughly. According to Lynch, the Minister for External Affairs "queried nothing, he just began commenting on the favourable impression that Costello had given in Canada".[131]

On his return to Dublin, the Taoiseach addressed an enthusiastic crowd of several thousand, who gathered in the rain outside the Mansion House to hear him. He told them that the repeal of the External Relations Act would lead to the end of bitterness and the removal of "all causes of strife between every section of the people". His ministers were reported to have greeted him warmly[132]—but was this merely a public show of affection masking irritation at his Canadian adventure? The acting Canadian High Commissioner, Priestman, noted the absence of Dillon from the Mansion House, and drew the conclusion that "all is not well in the pro-Commonwealth wing of the Government ... I have seen Mr Dillon in town recently and there would not therefore appear to be any substantial reason for his absence ... particularly as he is known to be fond of the public platform ..."[133]

This, however, showed a misunderstanding of the position of the Minister for Agriculture, who had been one of those pushing for repeal, believing the External Relations Act amounted to "living a lie".[134] If any minister had qualms about Costello's comments, they evidently decided that jettisoning the Commonwealth was preferable to jettisoning the Taoiseach, which it quickly became obvious were the only alternatives on offer.

Here we come to yet another controversy—this time over a claim by Noël

Browne that at a caucus meeting of ministers held shortly after Costello's return, the Taoiseach offered to resign because "he deeply regretted his unconstitutional action" in announcing a decision which the Cabinet had not yet authorised.[135] Browne claimed the meeting was held in Costello's house. All surviving members of the Cabinet (Costello was dead by the time the claim was made) denied that any such meeting took place and that any such resignation offer was made. Declan Costello and Patrick Lynch also denied all knowledge of such a meeting. Given Browne's tendency to exaggerate, and his sometimes casual approach to the facts (particularly evident in his autobiography), his account was treated with some scepticism.

However, Government records contain conclusive proof that a meeting was in fact held in Costello's house at around the time Browne claimed it was, and that the Taoiseach's actions in Canada were discussed. A note by the Assistant Secretary in the Department of the Taoiseach, Nicholas Nolan, on Thursday 7 October said that a meeting was to be held in the Taoiseach's house that evening,[136] as does an entry in Costello's appointments diary.[137] A further note by Nolan on a Cabinet decision, approving Costello's actions while in Canada and the United States, asked if it is to be dated 7 October (the day of the meeting in Herbert Park) or the eleventh (the date of the next formal Cabinet meeting).[138]

So Browne was right about the meeting. Was he also right about the offer of resignation? In an interview for an RTÉ Radio documentary, Browne said that Costello "blurted out this thing, if you want I'll resign". He said Seán MacEoin dismissed the idea out of hand, saying there was no need for Costello to resign, a position backed by Browne himself.[139] This suggests the idea of resignation had not been fully thought through—and a slightly defensive, emotional and ill-considered remark like this would not have been out of character for Jack Costello, particularly given the fact that he had just hours before received a rather disturbing communication from the British Government (a factor which was not highlighted by Browne, but which would explain why Costello might have thought it proper to at least offer his colleagues a way out of a potentially sticky situation).

The message from London (undated, unsigned, and on un-headed note-paper) was handed to him by Lord Rugby in Government Buildings on Thursday 7 October at ten past one. It warned that if the repeal of the Act meant that Éire became a foreign country, there would be "important consequences, particularly in the field of preferences and nationality". The UK had treaty obligations to offer Most Favoured Nation treatment to a number of foreign countries "which would preclude us from according to Éire that special treatment which on other grounds we would wish to accord her". The note suggested talks on these issues before Dublin took further action. Rugby reported to London that Costello "was rather on the defensive in regard to his recent pronouncement and repeatedly stressed the firm intention to strengthen the friendship underlying the steps he was about to take. I said that we had been and still were rather in the dark about it all ..."[140]

This British approach may well have brought home to Costello the potential difficulties he had created for himself, and if he did in fact talk about resignation this was probably the reason, rather than a guilty conscience over acting without Cabinet sanction. But the meeting of ministers in Herbert Park backed him, and the formal Cabinet minutes record that "the action taken by the Taoiseach during his visit to Canada and the United States was approved".[141]

However, it appears his colleagues kept a close eye on Costello's public statements from then on. When MacBride found out that the Taoiseach was planning a press conference, he intervened to make sure there would be no questions. Rugby observed that here "on a smaller scale we see reproduced the Marshall-Truman pattern in the management of affairs of state".[142] And while most of his 3-hour speech on the second stage of the Republic of Ireland Bill was delivered off the cuff, the section relating to trade and citizenship rights was read from a text supplied by External Affairs.[143]

It is clear from Rugby's reports to London that he held Costello personally responsible for developments, saying the Taoiseach had "conducted this business in a slapdash and amateur fashion". He later added that Fine Gael "had a sudden brainwave that they could steal the 'Long Man's' clothes ... They are all somewhat bewildered by their own sudden illogical iconoclasm and must now find high sounding phrases to justify it."[144]

This resentment was returned with interest by Costello, who by the end of October had developed "a curiously truculent bitterness towards the British", according to Vinton Chapin of the American legation. Costello told Chapin that the External Relations Act was "a humbug arrangement", adding that if the British wanted to treat them as aliens "that's all right with us, we've been trying to establish that status for seven hundred years". He appeared confident that the trade and nationality questions could be resolved—the British had already given commitments on both these matters, and trying to escape from them would risk their relationship with India. Chapin observed that Costello's attitude "may result from emotional reaction as well as from stress of official responsibilities, plus advice received on grounds of political expediency".[145]

A similar assessment of Costello's attitude was made by the British, after the Irish suggested a conference involving the main Commonwealth countries to discuss the implications of repeal[146] (involving Canada, Australia and New Zealand was smart politics, as they acted as a restraining influence on the British). A memorandum for Attlee suggested that Costello should be "pressed to come himself. But should he be asked to bring Mr MacBride as well? My information is that Mr Costello is very emotional on this question and cannot easily be made to look at the facts. There is apparently some reason to believe that Mr MacBride would be more calm ..."[147]

The irony of the British looking to the former Chief of Staff of the IRA to restrain the former delegate to Commonwealth conferences is striking. But Costello did not take part in the discussion. MacBride and McGilligan met the British and Commonwealth representatives, first at Chequers and then in Paris. The Taoiseach's absence is curious. While not on a par with that of de Valera from the Treaty negotiations in 1921, it does suggest that either he or his colleagues agreed with the American and British assessment of his emotional state.

McGilligan and MacBride, with the strong and crucial support of the Australians, Canadians and New Zealanders, reached agreement with the British that neither side would say anything to make it more difficult to maintain that they were not foreign countries; Ireland and the Commonwealth countries would exchange reciprocal citizenship rights; and the Irish would co-operate with the British to fight claims based on Most Favoured Nation status.[148]

While his political judgement when speaking in public may have been suspect, there was no doubt about Costello's legal skills. MacBride's draft of the bill to repeal the External Relations Act was titled "The Executive Powers of the State (International Relations) Bill", and included the following as Section 1(2): "In any instrument relating to the executive power of the state in or in connection with its external relations, the state may be referred to as the Republic of Ireland (or the Irish Republic)."[149] As well as being extraordinarily wordy, it was rather unclear and unduly permissive ("*may* be referred to ..."). On his copy of the Bill, Costello redrafted the section to the far simpler and more direct "The description of the State shall be the Republic of Ireland." He also changed the title to "The Republic of Ireland Bill".[150]

Ronan Fanning suggests that these changes "bear out the interpretation that it was Costello's ... impatience with the ambiguities of the External Relations Act and a determination that there be an end to ambiguity which gave the legislation its shape and substance".[151] MacBride's version would have added ambiguity; Costello's removed it. Costello also showed his determination to assert ownership of the legislation by deciding to bring it through the Oireachtas. His officials had assumed MacBride would do so.[152]

This decision was interpreted by Noël Browne as a slight to MacBride—in fact, it was urged on Costello by his son-in-law, Alexis FitzGerald, as a way of explaining to Fine Gael supporters how and why he decided on repeal. FitzGerald admitted that "my own reaction to the announcement ... was one of unhappiness, until I grasped what had been done and what the possibilities of the situation were". However, he pointed out, "there are serious Unionists who seriously support Fine Gael on the grounds that the party could be relied on more than the others to support the British connection ... I think these people deserve the attention of a well thought out argument."[153]

Well thought out arguments were not going to restore Costello's relationship with the *Irish Times*, though—the paper claimed, "the standard of political honesty in Ireland has been lowered grievously by the action of Mr Costello and his Fine Gael colleagues".[154] During the 1951 election campaign, the paper badly misquoted the Taoiseach in a headline, which read, "Fine Gael Glories in break with Commonwealth—Mr Costello". In fact, as the body of the story made clear, Costello said Fine Gael "gloried in the fact that the severance of the link with the British Commonwealth brought peace to the country and took the gunplay out of Irish politics". His son-in-law wrote to the paper the following day to point out the distortion, adding that "fair accounts" were given in both the *Irish Independent* and—more surprisingly—the *Irish Press*.[155]

Despite the attitude of the *Irish Times*, Costello always denied that the declaration of the Republic lost the Protestant vote for Fine Gael. He insisted to John Kelly (later a Fine Gael Attorney General) that that vote had been lost in 1932—Protestants had all expected to be murdered in their beds when de Valera got into power, and had been voting for him since out of gratitude that they weren't![156] And of course, while the pro-Commonwealth vote may have been alienated, Costello's move had widened his party's appeal, as his son-in-law observed: "By one stroke of genius politically, you have placed Fine Gael back in the centre of the national tradition right where Mick Collins had it. No longer will young Fine Gael politicians have to engage in the hopeless task of defending the Commonwealth association."[157]

Fianna Fáil—particularly Frank Aiken—made a point of highlighting Costello's unlikely credentials as a Republican, particularly as he had for years described himself as a King's Counsel. As the Taoiseach admitted to Aiken in the Dáil, those called to the Inner Bar since 1924 were called Senior Counsel. Aiken pointed out Costello was described in the telephone book and in various directories as a K.C. and said that "some people have grave doubts as to whether he is a Republican masquerading as a King's man or a King's man masquerading as a Republican".[158] In Aiken's papers is a copy of a ballad lampooning "Jay Cee the S.C. from Dublin Town [who] described himself as K.C. to win favour for the Crown".[159] Aiken raised the issue a number of times in the Dáil—Costello eventually suggested in exasperation that he should see a psychiatrist.[160]

Costello's speech introducing the second stage of the Republic of Ireland Bill was a marathon, lasting three hours. He said the Bill would "end forever, in a simple, clear and unequivocal way this country's long and tragic association with the institution of the British Crown and will make it manifest beyond equivocation or subtlety that the national and international status of this country is that of an independent republic". He claimed the measure would be "an instrument of domestic peace, of national unity and of international concord and goodwill". The Taoiseach added, with more than a hint of self-deprecation, that over the previous quarter century, we "have had rather too much ... of constitutional law and constitutional lawyers".

But how could he explain the apparent change in Fine Gael's approach to the Commonwealth? Ingeniously, he blamed the British. His party had attempted to honour the Treaty; but once the British tamely accepted de Valera's undermining of the settlement of 1921, "those who were under an obligation to maintain that Treaty were released".

He admitted that when answering questions from Peadar Cowan in July and August he had "walked very warily" and hadn't expressed his personal opinion; but now he did—Ireland had not been a member of the Commonwealth since 1936. But while clearing up ambiguities was important, it was not the Government's main reason for introducing the measure. The most important factor in the decision was, he insisted, to "put an end to the bitterness and conflict between sections of our people".

"It has been my lot to assist at the birth of two Constitutions of this State. It has been my misfortune, if I may put it that way, during the six years when I was Attorney-General, to devise and put into operation here measures which were and which were admitted to be oppressive in order to try to combat acts of violence of one kind or another ... I took no pleasure in carrying out the functions thrust upon me at that time. But the experience that I had then left its mark upon me ... I was determined that never again would I take any part in a Government that had to enforce order by extra-judicial processes. I never will ... I ask for a verdict on this measure which will put an end to violence, bring into being domestic peace and concord amongst Irishmen so that never again will an Irish Government have to execute an Irishman because he wants a republic ... We are going to put an end to that here once and for all."[161]

Many thought the speech a *tour de force*; not surprisingly, Lord Rugby was not one of them. He felt that Costello's "painfully prolonged exposition did not ring at all true ... Not being altogether happy in his own soul, Mr Costello abandoned the quiet tone which suits him best, and frequently broke into the traditional style of the flamboyant Irish orator. Since the substance was not convincing these efforts did not produce a ringing echo ... there was too much humbug about it all for supporters as well as opponents."[162]

As the new year dawned, Jack Costello had cause for satisfaction—preparations for the declaration of the Republic were well under way, and none of the dire consequences threatened by the British were going to transpire. It appeared he and his government would be none the worse for his adventure in diplomacy. His daughter Eavan, in a post-Christmas letter, noted that "Daddy is not quite so busy now that we are all safely Republicans!"[163] But the repeal of the External Relations Act was to have unwelcome effects north of the Border.

In November, Northern Ireland's Prime Minister, Sir Basil Brooke, met Attlee at Chequers to seek ways to compensate for the change in Dublin's status.[164] Officials from London and Belfast got to work, but the British were intent on introducing "minimal" legislative changes. Brooke's priority was to strengthen Northern Ireland's constitutional position to head off pressure from Dublin on partition, as well as "to eliminate the possibility of interference by any government in Whitehall now or in the future".[165] The latter desire, which reflected Unionist distrust of Labour, was achieved all too well—the absence of "interference" from London was a contributory factor in the outbreak of the Troubles in 1969.

Feeling themselves under threat, Unionists rallied round Brooke. A meeting of the standing committee of the Ulster Unionist Council in December passed a vote of confidence in the Prime Minister (and concluded by singing "For he's a jolly good fellow"). "The proceedings throughout were most enthusiastic, reminiscent of the old days when the Ulster Volunteer Force was formed."[166] Sensing the mood, Brooke told the following month's meeting that he was "perfectly satisfied" with the negotiations in London on the constitutional position, and believed the time was right for a general election "so that it may be made clear beyond doubt that the decision of Northern Ireland is to remain part of the United Kingdom".[167]

In response, Costello invited the leaders of all parties in the Dáil to a meeting in the Mansion House to consider how to help anti-partition candidates in the election.[168] MacBride may have been the original source of the idea—he had proposed an all-party committee on partition in April 1948, to avoid the issue being used "for party purposes, which is manifestly undesirable".[169] The committee agreed to take up a collection to raise funds for anti-partition candidates the following Sunday—in line with tradition, the collection was taken up outside Catholic churches as people left Mass.

Demonstrating his lack of understanding of the North, Costello told an American diplomat that the parish had been selected as a matter of convenience, and that the Church "would remain strictly on sidelines avoiding possible ... secular controversy".[170] In fact, a more efficient way of raising Unionist indignation could scarcely have been found; and what became known as the "Chapel Gate Election" proved a triumph for Brooke. The collection was of no use to sitting nationalists, as none of them were in marginal constituencies. But it was a disaster for the Northern Ireland Labour

Party, which was wiped out by the Unionists as Protestant voters concentrated on constitutional questions rather than social policy.

The interference from Dublin also gave Brooke greater leverage with London. Attlee told him that a formal protest against the propaganda campaign would be counterproductive. But he reminded him that forthcoming British legislation, the Ireland Bill, would affirm Northern Ireland's constitutional position and territorial integrity. "I feel that the most effective action that we can take is to make a clear and firm statement on the subject of partition in the proceedings on this Bill." But this statement would have to wait until after Easter, as the British "consider that it would be inexpedient to introduce the Ireland Bill until the Republic of Ireland Act has been brought into force by the Éire government."[171] Dublin had to be seen to be responsible.

Costello was anxious that the coming into force of the Republic of Ireland Act on Easter Monday "should be marked by fitting national celebrations". But de Valera was dismissive, writing to the Taoiseach that "public demonstrations and rejoicings are out of place" while partition lasted.[172] Fianna Fáil boycotted the celebrations, which centred on the General Post Office. In a radio broadcast, Costello said they had "put ourselves apart but not cut ourselves adrift from our former associations with the great nations of the Commonwealth ... We hope for a closer and more harmonious association based on community of interests and common ideals than could ever have existed from formal ties."[173] Two weeks later, the British published the Ireland Bill.

While the Bill recognised the Republic, and stated that it and its citizens were not to be treated as "foreign" under the terms of British legislation, it also gave a guarantee to the North: "In no event will Northern Ireland or any part thereof cease to be part of His Majesty's dominions and of the United Kingdom without the consent of the Parliament of Northern Ireland." Brooke was delighted, writing in his diary, "We have got what we wanted ... Ulster is safe."[174] This—entirely predictable—gesture to Unionism was seen in London as an equitable balance to what the British thought was generous treatment of the new Republic. Irish nationalists regarded it as a base betrayal.

De Valera pushed Costello for an immediate statement against "the British Bill intended to confirm Partition"; Costello replied that he wanted to wait until MacBride reported back on his discussions with Attlee.[175] The Taoiseach suggested another reason for delay to US Minister George Garrett—"he wanted to cool off before issuing statement".[176] On Saturday 7 May, the Cabinet met to agree the terms of an *aide-memoire* to be sent to the British. It recorded the Government's "emphatic and solemn protest against the re-enactment by the British Parliament of legislation purporting to confirm the unjust partition of Ireland ... the Government of Ireland can only regard the enactment ... as an unnecessary, provocative and gratuitous reassertion of the claim of the

British Parliament to intervene in Irish affairs".[177] This was, MacBride told the British Representative, Sir Gilbert Laithwaite, "much milder and more restrained in tone than had at one time seemed likely". Laithwaite said he was "astonished that there should be so much disturbance over the reaffirmation in a statute of a declaration which has stood on record since last October"[178]— a reference to Attlee's statement in the House of Commons, in similar terms to the proposed legislation.

Costello now led the political response, opening a Dáil debate on a motion criticising the British with a "vigorous and bitter" speech which lasted for an hour and a half. There was an "air of crisis" about the meeting of the Dáil, with packed public galleries and a full attendance of TDS. The Canadian diplomat David Johnson thought the Taoiseach "probably feels that he has to speak in this way to maintain the leadership of the nation".[179]

Costello stressed the united response of the Dáil, as the motion was to be seconded by de Valera. He accused the Labour Government of "purporting to annex permanently portion of our country, to fasten and to clamp down upon our people the wrong of Partition which was initiated 29 years ago ..." He said it was important that members of the Dáil should speak "calmly and coolly". This sentiment was rather undermined when he went on to say that while he didn't believe Attlee and his colleagues were being vindictive, he did think they were "guilty of stupidity". Ironically, in view of his own Canadian pronouncement, he complained bitterly of the lack of advance warning given by the British, which he claimed was due to their desire "to get it into the House of Commons so that it would be too late for the protest and too late for examination ..." Finally, to applause, he said that while Ireland had no great strength as a nation, "we can hit the British Government in their prestige and in their pride and in their pocket".[180]

The outrage continued at a large public meeting in O'Connell Street on the evening of the following Friday, addressed by all the party leaders. Laithwaite complained that Costello's speeches "were intemperate in tone and designed to work up feeling through the country ... His petulance, his refusal to see the arguments for the other side, his readiness to appeal to prejudice, his disposition to labour a weak point, his anxiety to play on the feelings of his audience, are all, it is said, part of his normal Court manner."[181] One of those in the crowd, the young Fine Gael activist Richie Ryan, was equally biased, if in the other direction. He thought the speech demonstrated Costello's ability as an orator. He remembered that it "evoked repeated enthusiastic applause but de Valera's whining voice bored the crowd".[182]

So why was Costello so put out? George Garrett observed that the Taoiseach had claimed repeal of the External Relations Act would improve relations with Britain, and had also predicted a solution to partition. Now he and his colleagues found the "carpet ... pulled out from under them".[183] David Johnson asked him privately why the terms of the Ireland Bill had caused such a commotion, when Attlee's verbal commitment in the House of Commons in October had not. "He treated in an airy manner a declaration of policy by a Prime Minister. He was of course right in saying that a declaration of policy by a Minister is more easily changed than a declaration enshrined in a statute." But there were other factors at play—Johnson pointed to Costello's "sense of betrayal" at the British failure to inform him in advance.[184] The irony, given his own behaviour over the External Relations Act, is breathtaking.

Johnson believed another reason for the intemperate language used by Costello and others was the fear that a more restrained approach would leave an opening for those who believed in the use of force. Johnson perceptively observed that this vigorous leadership could "boomerang" after the Taoiseach told him there was a real danger of violence. "What are their followers to say and think if all the brave words used over the last two or three weeks produce nothing tangible?"[185] This, of course, was exactly what happened. "Combined with the heady rhetoric of 1948–49, what the Ireland Act ... did was convince a number of young men that the only way to make progress against British arrogance and unionist intransigence was through violence."[186]

Far from taking the gun out of Irish politics, Costello's actions had arguably helped plant the seeds for the Border Campaign of the 1950s. In claiming that the declaration of the Republic would reduce violence, Costello was demonstrating the formative experience of the Civil War. Having lived through that conflict, which was mainly caused by the dispute over constitutional status rather than partition, it was natural for people of his generation to view the demand for "the Republic" as the cause of IRA violence. Now that he had helped close that question, it brought into sharp focus the remaining, and more intractable, issue of the Border.

In October 1949, at a function in Áras an Uachtaráin, Costello spoke to the British Ambassador about the tensions that had arisen over the Ireland Act. Referring to the "very close and friendly relations that had been maintained at a personal level", he said his government had no choice but to take the line they had. Had they done otherwise, "there would have been acute internal difficulties". The situation had now eased, he said, and things were quieter. Ambassador Laithwaite added, however, that "despite this somewhat surprising statement, there was nothing in the remainder of our conversation to suggest the slightest weakening on the part of the Taoiseach on the partition issue".[187]

Costello's approach to the other main foreign policy challenge in his first administration—the formation of NATO—was also heavily influenced by partition. Just two months after the formation of the Government, heavy hints were received from the Canadians that Ireland would soon be asked what her attitude would be to a regional defence agreement.[188] The anti-communism of the Government was not in doubt; but even at this stage Washington anticipated that Dublin might try to link the question of partition to that of defence. The overriding strategic importance of bases in Northern Ireland meant that there was no prospect of American encouragement for a united Ireland. In May, John Hickerson of the State Department wrote to George Garrett in Dublin contrasting British help during the war with Irish neutrality. "We do not propose at this point to take up the battle for Ireland against a valuable friend and partner. Furthermore, if the Dublin Government were to gain control of Northern Ireland, facilities in that area might be denied us in the future."[189]

A CIA assessment in April 1949 noted that denial of Ireland to an enemy was "an inescapable principle of United States security", because of the danger it could pose to the UK. As an ally, Ireland would be a "positive asset" as a potential site for naval and air bases. Neutrality "would probably be tolerable" because of the availability of bases in Northern Ireland, but the CIA believed Dublin was unlikely to remain neutral "in spite of military weakness and the Partition issue". And it added that the end of partition would only be conceivable if Ireland joined NATO[190]—turning Costello and MacBride's strategy on its head. The significance of Ireland in Washington's eyes is indicated by a 1950 list of outstanding serious and lesser problems between the United States and Britain—which doesn't contain a single mention of Ireland.[191] MacBride's strategy—backed by Costello—of seeking concessions on partition in return for joining NATO was thus dead in the water before it had even been tried.

In December 1948, Garrett was advised by Hickerson that it had been agreed at the Washington Security Talks (involving Belgium, Canada, France, Luxembourg, the Netherlands, Britain and the US) to invite a number of countries to join the proposed Atlantic Pact if they were willing—Iceland, Norway, Denmark, Ireland and Portugal.[192] On 7 January, an *aide-memoire* from the United States government asked what Ireland's view would be of an invitation to join the pact. Washington assured the British that they would treat any mention of partition as an indication that "the Irish were not seriously interested in the Pact and that they would not be consulted further about it".[193]

Freddie Boland, Secretary of the Department of External Affairs, told Neil Pritchard of the Commonwealth Relations Office that he was doing his best to keep as many doors open as possible. The Government were bound by many statements ruling out commitments as long as partition existed, but he would "try to get the Éire Government round the table with the other participants. It would in any case be some time before any Éire Government could enter into a Defence Pact entirely without reservation, but participation in the discussions would be a long step in the right direction." While Ireland would not take on commitments that would automatically involve her in hostilities, Boland suggested she might take on lesser commitments. Rugby observed that even if this did not happen, "we need shed no tears. If and when the Soviet menace becomes immediate, this country will not be able to stand out."[194]

The Irish reply, agreed by Cabinet on 8 February, was more definite than Boland had hoped. While Ireland agreed with the general aim of the proposed treaty, "any military alliance with, or commitment involving military action jointly with, the State that is responsible for the unnatural division of Ireland ... would be entirely repugnant and unacceptable to the Irish people".[195] As anticipated, this was taken by the Americans as "an impossible condition as the price for its signing the North Atlantic Treaty ... all the signatory powers are agreed that the issue of partition was irrelevant to the organisation and the intention of the Pact".[196]

Professional Irish diplomats disapproved of the Government's approach. Michael MacWhite privately advised Costello that a mistake had been made. "Had we adhered to the Pact we would be in a position to achieve far more ... Outside, nobody will listen to our pleas for the ending of Partition."[197] Boland thought MacBride's attempt to secure progress on the Border through NATO was "rubbish", and later received reports that Ireland's friends in Congress believed the Irish were making fools of themselves. He fell out with his minister after MacBride implied he had been keeping Dillon informed about opinion in Washington. MacBride backed off when Boland vehemently denied this,[198] but their relationship was clearly coming to the end of the road, and shortly afterwards he was transferred to the London Embassy.

The Government, then, clung to formal neutrality. But this didn't prevent some secret defence co-operation with the British and Americans, just as had happened during the Second World War. At the end of 1948, the US Legation reported to Washington that a British-sponsored survey of beaches between Dundalk and Dublin was to be carried out, to assess their suitability for landing craft. The survey had been arranged by Sir Reginald Denning, the British GOC in the North, and Liam Archer, the Irish Army Chief of Staff, and cleared with the Minister for Defence, T.F. O'Higgins. In order to avoid "embarrassing questions", the project was to "be given the largest measure Irish front possible", with the British to be described as acting in an advisory capacity.[199]

There were limited talks with the British about actions in the event of hostilities, under the rather unhelpful title of "War Book matters". MacBride was concerned about any leak of the talks, which he said would be "very embarrassing". Boland told the British that the Cabinet was divided on the issue. But he said the British "should be wrong to think that Mr MacBride was the strongest advocate of neutrality. The strongest advocate of neutrality was, in fact, Mr Norton." Boland added that he had no doubt that if war broke out, Costello, O'Higgins, Dillon and McGilligan would be in favour of implementing whatever understandings were reached with the British.[200] Denning and Archer appear to have had reasonably regular meetings to discuss defence—in May 1951 the British general said he had read the Dáil debates on defence and had not been impressed. He said he "failed to understand why we were not making a stronger effort to strengthen our defences" and asked about the extent of communist influence and the dangers of sabotage. Archer replied that communist influence was negligible and that "no fifth column could be said to exist".[201]

But despite such secret moves, Ireland remained to all intents and purposes isolated. A State Department policy statement on Ireland in August 1950 said it was "desirable that Ireland should be integrated into the defense planning of the North Atlantic area ... but this cannot be done upon the terms at present advanced by the Irish Government ... The Irish Government should concentrate its attention upon better Anglo-Irish relations and should not be allowed to believe that it can play off the United States against Great Britain."[202]

Chafing at this situation, Dillon wrote to Costello in January 1951, strongly urging the signing of a bilateral defence pact with the Americans. He accepted that the policy of not joining NATO while partition lasted was "politically inescapable", but suggested that since Spain had managed to join the pact, Ireland's isolation "is more marked and more incongruous in a world situation of Communism versus the Rest". He suggested that the Americans would welcome having an alternative to Britain as their "Atlantic Pearl Harbour".[203] There was a major problem with this approach—the Americans had never shown the slightest interest in a bilateral defence arrangement with Ireland, despite suggestions by Garrett. In fact, in March 1951, MacBride suggested such an approach directly to Truman, who gave a non-committal answer. MacBride's meeting with the President was something of a waste of time. He stressed that Ireland wished to join NATO, but "could not do so because of political difficulties which he was sure the President knew about". Truman brushed the issue aside, saying that while the NATO nations hoped Ireland would join, "outsiders intervening in family issues always suffered and the issue was rarely settled".[204]

Costello appeared to adopt the same line on military alliances, and on partition. Towards the end of 1950, Laithwaite complained that while the Taoiseach was "personally very friendly and approachable, he appears to feel bound from time to time to make speeches ... on the Partition issue, which are uncalled for and unhelpful".[205] Questioned about the Government's policy by an American diplomat, he "'blew his top' ... and gave ... a long lecture, the effect of which was that the policy of the Irish Republic was neutrality and nothing but neutrality".[206]

But there were limits to how belligerent he was prepared to be on the issue. On the same trip to Washington as his unproductive visit to the White House, MacBride compared what Britain was doing in Northern Ireland to what the Soviets were doing in eastern Europe. Liam Cosgrave made a speech critic-ising these "extravagant statements"; MacBride sent a message to Costello saying the effect of Cosgrave's speech was "unfortunate" in the United States, and asking the Taoiseach to correct the "false impression" it had created.[207] But Costello did nothing, suggesting rather strongly that he agreed with Cosgrave on the matter. In fact, he intimated to Cosgrave that he planned to appoint him rather than MacBride to External Affairs if returned to govern-ment (as he did in 1954). According to Cosgrave, "he accepted that the views given by me were realistic".[208]

If Costello had come to see that the "sore thumb" policy of dragging part-ition into every international arena was counterproductive, he was still stuck with the consequences. As was Ireland. Staying out of NATO may have been a good thing—it certainly was as far as advocates of strict military neutrality were concerned. But it was not the result that Costello and his government aimed for. Their goal had been to use NATO membership as a bargaining chip to secure progress on partition, and by that yardstick the policy was a failure.

As for the more dramatic decision to repeal the External Relations Act and confirm that Ireland was no longer a member of the Commonwealth, the aim here had been to "take the gun out of Irish politics", as well as to clear up ambiguities and develop a better relationship with Britain. It certainly didn't remove violence from politics in Ireland, at least not in the long term. But Costello's move did clarify Ireland's status, and arguably helped in the development of a more mature relationship of equals between Dublin and London.

But the manner of his Canadian announcement, and his repeated com-plaints about the "slights" he had received before making it, left Costello on the defensive for years afterwards. He was accused of "declaring the Republic" in a fit of temper, without Cabinet authorisation. As we have seen, this is not fair—it was clear that a decision, at least in principle, had been taken to repeal the External Relations Act, and the British and other governments were aware of this. However, Costello did not handle the controversy well.

In the late 1960s he drew up a memorandum on the subject, which he sent to various people including Archbishop McQuaid and John Hearne, as well as journalists and academics researching the subject. He insisted the memorandum was "in no sense intended as a justification of, or apologia for, the action of the First Inter-party Government, or my own part" in repealing the Act. To justify, or to apologise, would have implied that he had done something wrong. In his own eyes, it all came down to his belief that at his press conference, "there was nothing in honesty and decency open to me but to admit the truth".[209] This approach to international diplomacy is not one that has caught on.

Chapter 9

A VERY HAPPY SUCCESS FOR THE CHURCH

"Dr Browne has had the start of a whole day to make his allegations, and no matter what I do I shall never catch up with him to the end of my public life."[1]

JOHN A. COSTELLO, APRIL 1951

"That the clash should have come in this particular form and under this Government, with Mr Costello at its head, is a very happy success for the Church."[2]

JOHN CHARLES McQUAID, APRIL 1951

If the removal of Queen Victoria from her perch outside Leinster House was an early indication of the controversy that would surround the repeal of the External Relations Act, the new Cabinet took an equally symbolic step at its first meeting which presaged the other great controversy that would affect its reputation—the Mother and Child crisis.

This was to agree a message from Costello to Pope Pius XII. The Taoiseach told the Pontiff that he and his colleagues "desire to repose at the feet of Your Holiness the assurance of our filial loyalty and devotion as well as our firm resolve to be guided in all our work by the teachings of Christ and to strive for the attainment of a social order in Ireland based on Christian principles".[3] Costello told his friend Michael MacWhite, the Ambassador to Rome, that he received "a wonderful letter from the Pope signed by his own hand" in reply, adding that "it was worth while for that alone becoming Taoiseach". He said he had "an intense desire to go to Rome" while in office, "particularly to see the Pope".[4] This did not look like a government likely to cause problems for the Church.

During the Mother and Child Crisis, Cardinal D'Alton commented that, in contrast to the "unreliable" Browne, the bishops could be thankful "that the

Taoiseach is so sound on the matter".[5] Historian Ronan Fanning has written that "it is almost impossible to exaggerate the near-feudal deference of Costello and his Ministers to the Hierarchy in general and to the Archbishop of Dublin in particular".[6] But it is important to recognise that John A. Costello's deference wasn't the result of expediency, lack of courage or absence of principle. He sincerely believed that deference and obedience were not only right, but required.

Even 20 years later, in his "Seven Days" television interview with David Thornley, Costello became extremely exercised on being challenged about his acceptance of the ruling of the bishops. "We believed ... that you must have in politics and in statesmanship and in legislation and in the conduct of all affairs of the State the principles of Christianity put into operation and ... we were told by an authoritative body in the Catholic Church that a measure if brought into operation would be contrary to morals and the teaching of the Church ... I would do the same again, and any other Government would have to do it."[7]

One can disagree with Costello's actions, but he cannot be accused of inconsistency—unlike, for instance, Noël Browne, whose public stance in the Dáil, when he accepted the ruling of the bishops, differed from his later position. Costello may well have been wrong, but he was acting out of principle, principle he adhered to throughout his life.

There have been suggestions that Costello was a member of the secretive, ultra-Catholic organisation the Knights of Columbanus. Evelyn Bolster, the historian of the Knights, claimed that Costello, along with Seán T. O'Kelly, was a member of the Columbians, an offshoot of the Ancient Order of Hibernians which merged with the Knights in the 1920s. But, importantly, she did not suggest that he was a member of the Knights while Taoiseach. In fact, she named the members of the organisation who were in Cabinet as Mulcahy, MacEoin, Norton and Blowick.[8]

The new Taoiseach's obsequious attitude to McQuaid is well demonstrated in their correspondence. While Costello was usually polite in letters, the tone he adopted with McQuaid was of quite a different order. Replying to an invitation to a special Mass to celebrate the anniversary of the Pope's coronation, Costello wrote, "I accept the invitation as I am sure will each member of the Government to whom I will have it immediately conveyed." Acceptance of a similar invitation the following year was "not merely our duty but a privilege". It is important to note that McQuaid occupied a more exalted position than other churchmen. When Cardinal Griffin of Westminster wrote to the Taoiseach seeking a grant for the Irish Centre in Kilburn, Costello immediately sought McQuaid's advice. McQuaid noted the Cardinal's proposal to have the centre "open to all denominations", a development he evidently viewed with concern.[9] This was enough to kill the initiative from Costello's point of view.

The Government's ostentatious Catholicism was not just for home con-sumption; in November 1949, MacBride stressed the importance of ministerial pilgrimages to Rome during the Holy Year of 1950. In particular, he considered it "essential that the Taoiseach ... should pay an official visit to Rome ... in the middle of the month of January ... as a means of encouraging other Catholic Governments to follow the Irish example". Costello duly travelled to Rome in January, accompanied by his wife, Ida, and two of his children, Declan and Eavan (whose travelling expenses he paid). During his visit, he met Monsignor Giovanni Montini, the future Pope Paul VI.[10] On a later trip commemorating the fourteenth centenary of Columbanus's birth he met Archbishop Angelo Roncalli, later Pope John XXIII. This occasion saw Costello, MacBride and de Valera united, with McQuaid, in a celebration that saw 20,000 pilgrims converging on Luxeuil in the French Alps.[11]

As was only natural in a graduate of the National University of his era, Costello was suspicious of Trinity College—in fact, he was also suspicious of the only Trinity graduate in the Cabinet, Noël Browne.[12] His attitude towards Protestants has already been noted in the introduction. This of course was before the ecumenical era, a period when Catholics were forbidden to enter Protestant churches, never mind Trinity College. This caused difficulty at the funeral of former President Douglas Hyde, where the Cabinet waited outside St Patrick's Cathedral rather than attending the service. Poet Austin Clarke, who did go inside along with at least one other Catholic, the French Ambassador, scornfully depicted

> Costello, his cabinet
> In Government cars, hiding
> Around the corner, ready
> Tall hat in hand.[13]

Given the prevailing attitude, it is not perhaps surprising that the bishops didn't just expect deference from politicians; they expected submission. In December 1948 Noël Browne wrote a perfectly polite letter to Archbishop Joseph Walsh of Tuam, explaining that he didn't want Castlebar Hospital to be entirely staffed by nursing sisters, as it was to be a training centre and he wanted to provide promotional opportunities for lay nurses to discourage emigration to England. But he respectfully added that in other circumstances and other hospitals "I would be delighted to see an all-religious staff."[14]

This innocuous reply led to a vicious response from the hierarchy, directed to Costello rather than to Browne. Having drawn attention to the fact that the Minister was a Trinity graduate (no more needed to be said, evidently), the letter accused him of seeking to impose conditions which would effectively exclude religious from nursing or supervisory positions in regional hospitals. "We protest against the Minister's action as a slight on the religious vocation and as savouring of secularism."[15] Costello's handwritten reply regretted that Browne's letter "should have been interpreted in such a way as to cause misgivings in the minds of the Irish Hierarchy", stated that "any policy savouring of unfair discrimination against religious sisters ... is something that was never intended and which it is our fixed determination to avoid", and promised to continue to use the services of the sisters.[16] This response indicates why the bishops expected immediate capitulation from Browne over the Mother and Child Scheme: it was what they were used to.

One example of a policy that was effectively dictated by McQuaid was on adoption. Costello had supported the introduction of legal adoption during the 1948 election campaign; but in office things were different. Justice Minister Seán MacEoin told the Taoiseach that he had concluded "that it would be extremely difficult to frame a practical proposal that would not be likely to lead to a very undesirable controversy".[17] MacEoin didn't specify the source of the "undesirable controversy" and denied at a meeting of the Fine Gael parliamentary party that opposition was coming from the Church.[18]

But others believed differently. James Dillon recalled MacEoin telling the Cabinet after consulting McQuaid on proposed adoption legislation that "he won't have it!" As far as MacEoin was concerned, that was the end to the matter. Dillon, with evident disapproval, noted of his colleague, "It would never have occurred to him to cross the Archbishop."[19] Patrick Lynch described MacEoin as "greatly influenced by the Church, by the Knights of Columbanus. Reactionary in all his views, a most conservative Catholic ... He was the spokesman for the Hierarchy at the Cabinet table."[20] Those conservative views were reflected in MacEoin's account of a visit to Spain: "I met a Christian gentleman in General Franco, and I could see why my colleague General O'Duffy RIP (who was my best man at my wedding in Longford) was prepared to support him in his efforts to break the Communistic Red Government of Spain."[21]

MacEoin was eager to follow Catholic principles in his Department. After the Vatican requested an amnesty for prisoners to mark the 1950 Holy Year, MacEoin recommended to his colleagues a remission of one-quarter of all sentences. He acknowledged that this might be seen as excessive, but pointed out "that the Vatican have asked for a significant gesture". This appeared to be a clinching argument for him, but the Cabinet disagreed, finally approving a maximum remission of three months for lesser offences and six months for those sentenced to penal servitude.[22]

After he moved to the Department of Defence, he approved (without consulting the Cabinet) a proposal by the head chaplain of the Army that the Defence Forces should be dedicated to "Our Lady, Queen of the Most Holy

Rosary". After the change of government, de Valera raised concerns about "giving to citizens belonging to non-Catholic denominations grounds for feeling offence to their conscience". It was agreed to call the ceremony an invocation rather than a dedication, and that non-Catholic members of the Defence Forces would not be compelled to attend the ceremonies. The invocation went ahead in October 1951.[23]

Dillon himself was a staunch Catholic, but as his biographer points out, "he also had a very clear sense of the boundary between politics and religion: he would not have been his father's son if he had not".[24] Patrick Lynch recalled Dillon giving Noël Browne the benefit of his insights into the way the Church operated. "My family have been identified with politics for a very long time, and we know how the Black Brigade works. Never challenge the Black Brigade on an issue of principle. That's the mistake you are making Noël, if you approach them with practical proposals you can't lose."[25] Dillon disapproved both of MacEoin's supine attitude on adoption and Browne's confrontational approach to the Mother and Child scheme.

When the crisis broke, Browne believed that he could appeal to public opinion, and he had good grounds for this belief, after three successful years in the Department of Health, particularly in tackling TB. He arrived in the Custom House at a good time—plans for improving the treatment of TB had been put in place by Fianna Fáil, new drugs were coming on stream, and MacBride had insisted on the provision of funding from the Hospital Sweepstakes for capital investment in health. But he also brought to the job a crusading zeal, and an enthusiasm for publicity which broke down social taboos about the disease. By 1950, the number of TB deaths had fallen to 2,353, the lowest ever recorded at that time, compared to an annual average of 3,649 in the previous decade. He had also overseen the provision of 7,000 new hospital beds, the Cancer Council, the Blood Transfusion Service, the National Rehabilitation Organisation, and BCG inoculation. But the Mother and Child Scheme was to prove a step too far.

The roots of the scheme lay in the 1945 Health Bill, which after extensive amendment became the Health Act of 1947. In October of that year, Bishop James Staunton wrote to de Valera on behalf of the hierarchy, raising concerns about the Health Act and the powers it gave to the Minister. The hierarchy believed these powers interfered with the rights of "the individual person, the family, the professions and voluntary institutions". Interestingly, it did not mention the absence of a means test, but concentrated on the powers to detain people who were a probable source of infection, the sections dealing with health education, and the requirement on doctors to notify certain diseases.[26]

The letter and memorandum were read out to the Cabinet. De Valera then asked his Minister for Health, Dr Jim Ryan, to look into the points raised.

Ryan prepared a memorandum, which pointed out that ministers tended to put more powers than they intended to use into legislation, in order to avoid court challenge, and that many Acts could be said to "enable them to violate Catholic principles". But in practice, these powers had not been abused, so there was no reason to fear the Health Act. De Valera was not impressed with this argument, saying he would not transmit Ryan's memorandum as it stood, as it required "considerable revision". He eventually sent a version of the memorandum to Staunton two days before the change of government, but avoided giving his own views on the basis that there had been a legal challenge to the Act in the meantime.[27]

This legal challenge was the one launched by James Dillon, with Costello and McGilligan among his counsel, which was mentioned in Chapter 6. As we saw then, Fine Gael in general, and Jack Costello in particular, had been severely critical of the Government's health proposals, both in 1945 and in 1947. This criticism had been aired during the election campaign. More surprisingly, Noel Hartnett of Clann na Poblachta also criticised the Act because it "interfered with the Catholic principles governing the rights of the State and of the family".[28] But in government, once some amendments were made to the Fianna Fáil proposals, Costello and his colleagues were prepared to continue with them—although there were rumblings within Fine Gael. Mulcahy forwarded to his party colleagues in Cabinet (including Costello) a letter from a party supporter criticising the proposals. Mulcahy noted that the supporter, a Dr Sheehan from Kerry, "was publicly very active against the Health Bill which we opposed. We have to take some notice of his criticism ..." In his letter, Sheehan complained that "the Fine Gael Ministers have turned a complete somersault" and were supporting the proposals "which they opposed when Dr Ward was Medical Gauleiter". He added that Browne "appears to be the worst Pink Totalitarian of them all ... genetically un-Irish, upbringing un-Irish".[29]

In fact, Browne had proposed some significant changes to the scheme, including the repeal of the section allowing compulsory medical inspection of children, clarification that health authorities were not being given compulsory powers, and the establishment of a medical appeal panel to hear the cases of people detained as probable sources of infection.[30] But the most significant amendment proposed by Browne in a memorandum for Cabinet in June 1948 was not accepted. Browne suggested that the Minister should be given power to charge for services under the Mother and Child Scheme. Under the 1947 Act, the service would have been free to all sections of the community. Browne's memorandum for government noted that the Irish Medical Association objected to the provision of free services to people who could afford to pay for them. He "does not propose at this stage to commit himself to the acceptance or rejection of the point of view of the Association". But his proposed amendment would allow him to decide later whether or not to charge for the service and in the meantime would "lessen the opposition of the medical profession to it".[31]

This was a sound enough tactic. But at the Cabinet meeting on 25 June, Browne was outflanked by Norton, who, "in the proletarian voice which he affected on such occasions … shouted down to me, 'Yer not goin' to let the doctors walk on ye, Noël?' Before I could answer him, the Taoiseach asked, 'What would you prefer, Doctor?' I replied that I would prefer to keep the existing proposals, free of direct charge, and with no means test, already included in the Fianna Fáil Health Act."[32] Browne's biographer has pointed out that this was all very embarrassing for him, as Norton had "depicted him in cabinet as cautious and fearful … and had put him unexpectedly … on the defensive on an issue which was critical to his understanding of his own mission".[33] Browne now went off to draft the scheme, under the impression that he had the full support of his Cabinet colleagues.

The text of Browne's Bill to amend the 1947 Health Act was approved by Cabinet on 4 November 1949. However, at no point did Cabinet approve the actual introduction of the service, or the regulations setting it up. This point was seized on by Costello to show that the Mother and Child Service *per se* did not have Government approval. Intriguingly, he asked his officials in February 1950 to check on what decisions had been made by Cabinet on the scheme— the only one they could find was that of June 1948. He was reminded of this finding in March 1951 when the situation was coming to a head.[34]

A more experienced minister might have been expected to cover his back by gaining such formal approval. However, the terms of the 1947 Act strongly suggest that Browne was not required to have his regulations approved— Section 28 empowered the Minister for Health to make regulations as to how health authorities were to exercise their powers under Part III of the Act.[35] John Horgan has pointed out that a more experienced government might have insisted that the regulations, which would inevitably have cost implications, should be brought back for approval.[36]

There were two main sources of opposition to the Mother and Child Scheme, medical and episcopal, and it is a mistake to underestimate the importance of either. While the bishops were to prove the final straw for Browne's Cabinet colleagues, the doctors made the initial running, in public at least. The entrenched power of the medical profession was not a uniquely Irish phenomenon: in Britain, the opposition of doctors to the National Health Service led to "the most important, most difficult domestic fight of the post-war Labour Government's life".[37]

Worries about the centralising power of the State may seem overblown to modern eyes, but in the late 1940s and early 1950s they were real enough.

Those opposed to increased State involvement had the recent example of totalitarian regimes in mind—Neil Farren, the Bishop of Derry and a UCD contemporary of Jack Costello, explicitly made the link, claiming that "the power and spirit behind practically all social legislation is ... taken from the worst principles of Nazi and Soviet materialism".[38]

A further complication was the situation within Clann na Poblachta. Browne's biographer John Horgan has pointed out that the Minister and his associate Noel Hartnett were "indisputably operating a dual strategy. One strand had as its objective the creation of a free-for-all Mother and Child Scheme; the other had the implicit, and increasingly the explicit, aim of forcing the Clann out of government in order to preserve its ideological purity."[39] This conflict within the party was being openly discussed in the newspapers by February 1951,[40] as was Browne's "inclination to withdraw from the present Government".[41] MacBride claimed that Browne set out his aim of breaking up the party and the Government at a dinner in the Russell Hotel in November 1950—he circulated Cabinet colleagues, including Costello, with a memorandum of their conversation.[42] The Taoiseach was therefore well aware that Browne was isolated within his party, as well as within the Cabinet.

The Taoiseach was also well informed of medical opinion. Dr Tom O'Higgins remained a committee member of the Irish Medical Association while he was a minister. Costello himself was greatly influenced by Alexis FitzGerald's brothers, Oliver and Paddy, both of whom were prominent and influential in medical circles.[43] Oliver's son, Alexis, remembers Costello being in their house while he was Taoiseach, probably around the time of the Mother and Child controversy, and that Costello was accompanied by Dillon and possibly Norton.[44] In any event, as a barrister, Costello would have been sympathetic to the views of fellow professionals. He became steadily more convinced of the case against a free Mother and Child Scheme, telling Patrick Lynch on 23 March 1951 that he was totally opposed to it, and would not be a member of a government that implemented it.[45]

While Fine Gael links with the medical profession were well known, one of Browne's fellow Clann na Poblachta TDs was also warning Costello against the scheme. Dr J.P. Brennan, TD for Dun Laoghaire, was the Master-General of the Irish Guild of St Luke, SS. Cosmas and Damian, an organisation for Catholic doctors. "The Guild is concerned essentially with the traditional application of Catholic principles in the practice of medicine, and nothing else. There is no doubt that these appear to be endangered by the 1947 Act."[46]

Medical opposition, then, was partly informed by the same concerns bothering the bishops, about excessive State interference with the rights of the family (and the medical profession, of course). But it was also driven by concerns over the financial position of doctors, and Browne seems to have seen this as the primary motivation in the opposition to him. He may have been right too. But his handling of his fellow doctors was less than diplomatic. He told an IMA deputation in October 1950 that his personal preference would be for "a whole time salaried service", but he accepted that the public and the profession would not accept such a development for many years. He also insisted that while the scheme could be improved, "the decision regarding abolition of a Means Test was immutable and the Association must recognise this fact".[47] Such a hardline approach inevitably stiffened the IMA resistance, prompting Costello to try to negotiate a solution himself.

The Taoiseach had made a point of making conciliatory noises in a number of speeches to medical bodies. He told a meeting of the IMA that improvements in health services could only be achieved if there was "full understanding and complete co-operation between the medical profession and the Government ... Anything in the nature of unfriendly relations or intractable misunderstandings can only bring difficulties and frustration in their train for all of us."[48] He told the annual dinner of the Royal College of Physicians that while some friction might arise between the Government and the medical profession, "there is absolutely no reason why the causes of this friction should not be removed by amicable discussion and friendly co-operation".[49] No reason, except for an obdurate Minister and an equally obdurate profession.

On 25 November 1950 the Medical Secretary of the IMA, Dr P.J. Delaney, wrote to Costello asking him to receive representatives of the Association to discuss health developments. He said he was acting on a suggestion by Dr T.F. O'Higgins, the Minister for Defence.[50] The Taoiseach immediately agreed, and along with Norton met an IMA delegation four days later.[51] Costello later told the Dáil that he put forward Browne's view "as an advocate, a view with which I did not agree. I put it forward as strongly as ever I could ..." He claimed that Browne was furious, accusing himself and Norton of selling him down the river, and refusing to allow them to negotiate any further on his behalf.[52]

The written record bears out Costello's version of events, although it is more temperate than the fury Browne allegedly showed in a face to face meeting. A letter from Browne rather stiffly thanked Costello for sending him a report on his meeting with the IMA. He hoped that once they had considered what the Taoiseach had said, "they will realise that the Mother and Child Scheme cannot be changed in its fundamentals and that accordingly the way will be open for me to continue negotiations". On the same day, he wrote to the Association asking if they had made up their minds on his scheme, "as he is anxious to be in a position to introduce the Scheme early in the New Year".[53] He later explained to Costello that he had done this to avoid the spread of any impression that future negotiations would be conducted by the Taoiseach and the Tánaiste, rather than himself. "I would be very much obliged, therefore, if you would be good enough to communicate with the Association making it clear to them that any future negotiations about the Mother and Child Service will be conducted with the Minister for Health."[54]

The IMA set up a special committee on the strength of its meeting with Costello "in the hope of bridging the difficulties which presently exist".[55] This produced an alternative scheme which was rejected out of hand by Browne as it compromised the principle of not having a means test. At the beginning of March 1951, Browne wrote again to Costello saying he was "still willing and anxious to negotiate with the Association and to consider any reasonable proposals which they may put forward. As, however, its latest letter leads me to believe that it has no sincere desire to reach agreement except on its own terms, I have decided to proceed without further delay with measures for the introduction of a Mother and Child Service, and I enclose a copy of a letter which I am sending to the Association today conveying this decision."[56] This rather rash action by Browne now brought the second strand of opposition to his·plans to the centre of the stage.

As we have seen, the hierarchy had raised concerns about the 1947 Health Act with de Valera before the change of government. After some publicity about Browne's plans in the summer of 1950, the issue was considered by the bishops at their meeting on 10 October. On their behalf, Bishop James Staunton wrote to Costello once again raising concerns about the powers taken by the State under the proposed scheme. The bishops complained that these were "in direct opposition to the rights of the family and of the individual and are liable to very great abuse ... If adopted in law they would constitute a ready-made instrument for future totalitarian aggression."

Significantly, the first concern now mentioned by the hierarchy related to the absence of a means test. While the State had the right to intervene in a subsidiary capacity, it did not have the right to supplant the duty of parents to provide for the health of their children. The State "may help indigent or neglectful parents: it may not deprive 90% of their rights because of 10% necessitous or negligent parents".

The letter also complained about the State taking over provision of physical education and education in regard to motherhood. There were concerns, too, about gynaecological care, which in some countries was taken to include contraception and abortion. "We have no guarantee that State officials will respect Catholic principles in regard to these matters." It added that "doctors trained in institutions in which we have no confidence" (a reference to Trinity) might be employed under the scheme and provide care "not in accordance with Catholic principles". Curiously, despite the fact that the letter was dated 10

October, a note on Costello's copy states that it was handed to him by McQuaid on 7 November.[57] The Taoiseach told the Dáil that the letter was "personally handed" to him on that date, after McQuaid's return from a visit to Rome.[58] The delay seems rather strange, but it would appear to explain why Costello only mentioned the letter to Browne on 9 November.[59]

In the meantime, Browne had met three bishops—McQuaid, Staunton and Browne of Galway—on 11 October, the day after the hierarchy's meeting, but before Costello received the resulting letter. Browne believed he had resolved his difficulties; in fact, according to McQuaid's later version of events, he had actually made a very poor impression on the prelates (mainly, it would appear, because he was prepared to argue his case, rather than accepting their ruling).

Browne later recalled that he had told Costello that he had satisfied the misapprehensions of the bishops; further, he even claimed that the Taoiseach, after meeting McQuaid on 12 October, had been "in a position to corroborate His Grace's and Their Lordships' satisfaction with the explanation which I gave in relation to their misapprehensions concerning the Scheme". Costello flatly denied that he had said anything of the kind. "In view of what I had been told by His Grace at my interview with him I certainly could have given you no such assurance."[60]

Costello gave the Staunton letter to Browne in November, asking him to draft a reply. In this reply, Browne claimed that the only "fundamental difference in principle" between the existing Public Assistance system and the Mother and Child Service was the absence of a means test. Browne ventured to suggest that the objections of the hierarchy might be based "on the misapprehension that there will be compulsion on mothers or children to avail of the Scheme ... There is no such compulsion." Parents would retain the right to provide for the health of their children if they wished.

He insisted that the "education in respect of motherhood" contemplated under the Scheme related to diet during pregnancy and the avoidance of smoking, and care would be taken to ensure that "its operation will include nothing of an objectionable nature under this head". Responding to the concerns about medical personnel, Browne (himself, of course, a Trinity graduate) said that "this country is predominantly Catholic, the medical profession is predominantly Catholic and there is an adequate and zealous clergy which will be quick to detect any practices contrary to Catholic teaching and to instruct its flock appropriately".[61]

This draft was given to Costello. Browne later said he believed it had been sent, and as he heard no more about it, he assumed the "misapprehensions" had been laid to rest. Costello told a very different story. He said he had told Browne he had not sent the reply, that he had, "out of consideration for you and in an earnest desire to help you in your difficulties with the Hierarchy ...

offered my personal help to you as intermediary with the Hierarchy to try to smooth their difficulties and resolve their objections, which I felt could be done by appropriate amendments of the Scheme ..."[62] Given that the Taoiseach was taking a similar approach with the doctors, this seems reasonably plausible. But in fairness to Browne, he may well have been misled by the date on the hierarchy's letter. He must also have misinterpreted whatever Costello said to him after the latter's meeting with McQuaid on 12 October.

In parallel with his talks with the IMA, the Taoiseach was in close consultation with McQuaid. The Archbishop later told Bishop Browne that he had met Costello immediately after their meeting with Noël Browne, and again on 7 and 25 November. He had also met Norton twice, and MacEoin and the Attorney General (Charles Casey) once each. As a result, he believed the possibility of the Mother and Child proposals being accepted by Cabinet "is not even to be considered".[63]

In mid-January, the Archbishop outlined to the hierarchy's standing committee what he had been told by Costello. "The Bill is not Government policy. Not a single Minister wants it, except Dr Browne ... [The] Taoiseach ... has given me the assurance that whatever the Church declares to be right in respect of the Mother and Child Health Service will be unequivocally accepted by him, *even if* the Minister had to resign or the Government fall. In fact, the Minister is the greatest single embarrassment that the Government endures ... I have, by arrangement with the Taoiseach, dealt with the Taoiseach as head of the Government. I have allowed the contest to be fought between the Doctors and Minister. The Taoiseach foresees and fears that Dr B. may resign and carry away the support of the Clann: that would mean the fall of the Government. The Taoiseach proposes to have Dr Browne answer the Hierarchy's letters, to send to us that answer, to await our decision as to whether Dr B's answer is in accord with the Bishops' desires, and thus to put the Hierarchy's answer squarely to Dr Browne ... I do not consider it advisable to give Dr Browne and the Clann the chance of going to the country on the basis that the bishops destroyed the Mother and Child Scheme for *poor* women and children. But I am convinced that, even at that risk, we may yet be obliged to break the certain introduction within our country of Socialist State medicine."[64]

McQuaid's mention of the political dimension is interesting, as it is usually overlooked in accounts of the Mother and Child crisis. As we have seen, Browne's biographer John Horgan argues that he had a dual strategy—on the one hand, he wanted to implement the Mother and Child Scheme; on the other, he wanted to force the Clann out of Government on an issue which would restore its radical credentials. Whatever happened, he would win.[65] From what Costello told McQuaid, the Taoiseach was clearly aware of this strategy, and determined to try to outflank Browne. There was little he could do about the Minister resigning if he didn't get his way on the Mother and Child Scheme. But he could do something to lessen the impact of the resignation—and one way was by enlisting the help of the hierarchy. It might be a stretch to say that Costello was using McQuaid as much as McQuaid was using Costello. But certainly the two men were using each other.

This, then, was the explosive situation into which Browne tossed his Molotov cocktail by deciding at the beginning of March 1951 to press ahead with the introduction of the scheme. McQuaid was "surprised to read in the daily press of the sudden determination of the Minister for Health to implement the Mother and Child Health Service". He was even more put out to receive a pamphlet from the Minister "which purports to explain the principles of the Mother and Child Service which the Minister is about to introduce". McQuaid wrote to Browne setting out his concerns, and copied the letter to Costello. He pointedly thanked the Taoiseach for "the immediate understanding and cooperation I have on every occasion received from you ... in all that concerns the provision of a sane and legitimate Mother and Child health service".[66] McQuaid reminded Browne that he had withheld approval from the scheme in October. "Now, as Archbishop of Dublin, I regret that I must reiterate each and every objection made by me on that occasion and unresolved, either then or later."

On 15 March, after returning from the funeral in Connemara of Fine Gael T.D. Josie Mongan, the Taoiseach was told Browne was looking for him. The Minister wanted an extra £30,000, saying if he got that sum he would "have the doctors killed on Sunday". Costello asked Browne about McQuaid's letter, but the Minister said there was "nothing in that", an assessment based on his own theological advice. By his own later account in the Dáil, Costello said, "Whatever about fighting the doctors, I am not going to fight the Bishops and whatever about fighting the Bishops, I am not going to fight the doctors and the Bishops. It may come to a point where either you or I will leave the Cabinet on this, unless we can settle the matter with the Bishops."[67]

Costello subsequently wrote to Browne, chiding him for not responding to McQuaid's letter. "I am afraid you do not appear to realise the serious implications of the view expressed in that letter since you have, by advertisement and otherwise, continued to publicise the Scheme to which objections have been taken. Such action might well seem to be defiance of the Hierarchy ... I have no doubt that all my colleagues and, in particular, yourself, would not be party to any proposals affecting moral questions which would or might come into conflict with the definite teachings of the Catholic Church." He urged Browne to come to an agreement with the hierarchy to remove their objections, adding that any financial problems in relation to the scheme would be immediately resolved "once the larger issues raised in the correspondence from members of the Hierarchy are settled".[68]

An increasingly testy correspondence between the two men ensued. On 19 March, Browne denied that the hierarchy were opposed to the Mother and Child Scheme. He pointed out that he had sent the brochure to each bishop, but only McQuaid had raised objections. He also said he had been in contact with a member of the hierarchy who assured him that "so far as he is aware the Hierarchy as such have expressed no objection to the Mother and Child Scheme whatsoever on the grounds of Faith and Morals". He then asked a pointed question of the Taoiseach: "I would be interested to know whether your withholding of approval to the M&C Scheme is due either to the supposed opposition of the Hierarchy to the Scheme or to the possible opposition of any individual member of the Hierarchy."[69] Browne's approach not only challenged Costello's position as leader of the Government, but McQuaid's as leader of the hierarchy.

Relations between Taoiseach and Minister were now close to breaking point. On 21 March, Browne requested the Government Information Bureau to release to the press a letter from the Secretary of his Department to the IMA. Tipped off by Maurice Moynihan, Costello had the publication stopped, as the letter claimed the Mother and Child Scheme was Government policy, a claim with which he disagreed. Costello later told McQuaid that Browne had demanded to know why his statement had been stopped. Costello replied, "Because I am Taoiseach." Browne then accused Costello of using the hierarchy to defeat the Mother and Child Scheme.[70]

As the sense of crisis mounted, Costello was joined by Norton, Mulcahy, Dillon, O'Higgins, Cosgrave and Patrick Lynch, and sent a telegram to MacBride in Washington, requesting him to return at once. He wrote a letter to Browne which was sent by despatch rider to the Custom House. The Minister had left his office, but returned at around 8.40 to receive it.[71] Costello's letter responded to the points raised by Browne two days previously. The Taoiseach pointed out that the October letter came from the entire hierarchy "and must be regarded as still expressing the Hierarchy's views until a contrary expression has been received from the Hierarchy". He reminded his minister that he had already requested him to have their objections resolved.[72]

Browne felt it necessary in his reply to stress his religious credentials, saying he had been concerned from the beginning to ensure that the scheme contained nothing contrary to Catholic moral teaching. "I hope I need not assure you that as a Catholic I will unhesitatingly and immediately accept any pronouncement from the Hierarchy as to what is Catholic moral teaching in reference to this matter." He then attacked the Taoiseach, noting that he hadn't mentioned any difficulties with the Church during his negotiations with the doctors. "It seems strange that at this late hour when the discussions with the IMA have reached a crucial point that you advance, as the only remaining objection to the Scheme, the one which of all possible objections ... should have first been satisfactorily disposed of ..."[73]

The air of crisis subsided somewhat the following day. The request to MacBride to return home was withdrawn, in view of his success in arranging a meeting with Truman[74] (discussed in the previous chapter). Costello wrote in more conciliatory tones to Browne, stressing that he was motivated solely by "a friendly desire to help a colleague and I take it somewhat amiss to find misconstrued my endeavours". He added that he had explained to McQuaid why he had delayed responding to Staunton's letter, and this had been communicated to the hierarchy. "I need hardly say that I accept unreservedly your statement that you would abide by any pronouncement from the Hierarchy as to what is Catholic moral teaching in reference to this matter."[75] That afternoon, Browne rang to report on a meeting with McQuaid, at which he agreed that the hierarchy should adjudicate on the matters arising, and undertook to accept their decision. He also asked the Archbishop to try to secure an early decision "in view of the importance of the matter to him, as it might mean his leaving the Cabinet".[76] This is confirmed by McQuaid's account. The Archbishop claimed the Minister "apologised abjectly", and, when McQuaid said he personally believed the scheme to be contrary to Catholic teaching, added that "that was for him the end".[77]

Thus, Browne was exactly in the position Costello had said in January he wanted him; waiting for the hierarchy's ruling on his scheme, and in no position to argue with that ruling. Or so it appeared—Browne was to prove less obedient to the hierarchy than he indicated at this stage. At around this time he also rejected a compromise proposal from Norton that would have required households with an annual income above £1,000 to pay for services. Browne remained wedded to the free scheme, while the Labour leader had come to the conclusion that some scheme was better than none.[78]

Costello, meanwhile, told McQuaid that even if the hierarchy approved the scheme, he was determined not to implement it, as he "was convinced of its impossibility and of the impossibility of fighting the Doctors, who were intensely opposed to the Scheme".[79] This account ties in with Patrick Lynch's recollection that on the same day the Taoiseach said he would not be a member of a government that implemented such a scheme.[80] Again, this raises the question of Costello's motivation: was he simply following the dictates of his church (the usual interpretation), or had he reverted to traditional Fine Gael policy on State control of medicine? Conor Cruise O'Brien seems to have advocated the second interpretation, saying that Costello, "in an effort to quash Browne's scheme, called in the help of the Catholic Church".[81] The truth in all probability lies in a combination of the two factors. Joe Lee suggested that "the strength of Costello's position was that while his piety was absolutely genuine, it also happened to coincide with the material advantage of the interests he represented".[82]

In any case, the Taoiseach's resolve not to go ahead with a scheme even if the Church approved it was most unlikely to be put to the test. On 4 April, the hierarchy met and followed McQuaid's advice to reject Browne's scheme. The Archbishop told his colleagues that if they did so, they would have "saved the country from advancing a long way towards socialistic welfare. In particular, we shall have checked the efforts of Leftist Labour elements, which are approaching the point of publicly ordering the Church to stand out of social life and confine herself to what they think is the Church's proper sphere."[83]

The following evening, McQuaid delivered this decision to Costello at Government Buildings. It was, the Archbishop was careful to put in writing, "the unanimous decision of the General Meeting of the Archbishops and Bishops". While declining to enter into a detailed examination of the points raised by Browne, the reply stated, "The Hierarchy must regard the Scheme proposed by the Minister for Health as opposed to Catholic social teaching."[84]

The different responses of Costello and Browne are instructive. As McQuaid later recorded after discussing the hierarchy document with the Taoiseach for an hour and a half, he "at once accepted fully the decisions of the Hierarchy [and] expressed great relief at the decision which would terminate the enormous worry and waste of time occasioned by Dr Browne's actions".[85] Browne, however, after reading the letter in the presence of Costello, Norton and Brendan Corish, said, "It's all right. The Bishops have not condemned the Scheme on grounds of morals." According to Costello, Corish was shocked at Browne's attitude: "If I had not heard the remark, I could not have believed it to be possible."[86] After seeking theological advice, Browne put a great deal of store in the distinction between moral and social teaching (the first had to be obeyed by all Catholics; the latter could in conscience be rejected). Clearly, others in the Government were less impressed by this distinction.

McQuaid took a similar view, asking Costello to tell his Cabinet colleagues that "the letter was a definite condemnation of the scheme on moral grounds. Catholic social teaching meant Catholic *moral* teaching in regard to things social." This dubious theological gloss was welcomed by the Taoiseach, who said he was pleased to have this statement in advance of the Cabinet meeting to be held later that day, 7 April. McQuaid also pointed out the number of times the bishops had used the phrase "this particular scheme"—in other words, an alterative could be acceptable.[87]

Leabharlanna Poiblí Chathair Bhaile Átha Cliath
Dublin City Public Libraries

Browne has left a vivid, though obviously one-sided, account of the three-hour Cabinet meeting. He described Costello reading McQuaid's letter. "Clearly, for him, it was holy writ ... He then looked at me and said 'This must mean the end of the mother and child scheme." The Taoiseach agreed "grudgingly" to allow Browne to ask each of his colleagues if they accepted the ruling. All did, although Labour's Michael Keyes demurred slightly, saying, "They shouldn't be allowed to do this," before nodding his agreement with the others. Browne, completely isolated, left the meeting.[88]

That evening, Costello and Norton agreed the terms of the formal Government decision, which was sent by despatch rider to Browne's home.[89] This said the Government had decided, after considering McQuaid's letter (Moynihan advised against citing this letter in a formal government decision),[90] that the scheme should not be pursued, but that a new scheme should be brought forward that would be "in conformity with Catholic social teaching", and that would provide the best modern facilities for those who couldn't afford to pay for them—in other words, it would include a means test.[91]

Given Browne's consistent refusal to consider a means test, this decision left him in an untenable position. Costello told McQuaid that Browne must leave the Cabinet.[92] A letter was drafted in the Department of the Taoiseach seeking Browne's resignation, in which the Minister was to be berated for lack of discretion in leaking to the press that he was considering his position. It also pointed out that if he continued in office, the Government "could feel no confidence that effect would be given to their desire for the early introduction of an acceptable Mother and Child Service", given his fractious relationship with the IMA.[93]

However, the letter was not sent. Costello still harboured a hope, unrealistic as it now appears, that something could be salvaged from the wreckage. Nearly two decades later, he claimed that if things had been handled differently by MacBride, "the whole situation might have been very well resolved".[94] This would, obviously, have required compromise from Browne, and also from the doctors. Neither was very likely. In any event, MacBride had by now had enough. Despite the Taoiseach's suggestion that "possibly we should hold off", he wrote demanding Browne's resignation.[95]

Browne complied, in a terse letter, on 11 April. Costello, characteristically, was more generous in his reply, saying he and his colleagues appreciated Browne's work in the Department of Health, "and regret that circumstances should have arisen that have made your resignation unavoidable".[96] Costello invited Browne to accompany him to Áras an Uachtaráin when he went to advise President O'Kelly to accept the resignation; the outgoing Minister declined, going to the Park on his own an hour and a half later.[97] Presumably the conversation would have been a little stilted had the two men travelled

John and Rose Costello with their children May, Thomas and John Aloysius (holding his father's watch).

"The only boy wearing a watch-chain …" Young John Costello with fellow Junior Grade Exhibitioners at O'Connell School in 1906. He is second from the left in the middle row. Behind his left shoulder is Seán Heuston, later executed after the 1916 Rising. (*Allen Library*)

The Attorney General at the side of the President of the Executive Council, 1928. *Left to right*: Diarmuid O'Hegarty (Secretary to the Executive Council); Patrick McGilligan (Industry and Commerce, and External Affairs); James FitzGerald-Kenny (Justice); John Marcus O'Sullivan (Education); JAC; W.T. Cosgrave (President of the Executive Council); Ernest Blythe (Vice-President, Finance, and Posts and Telegraphs); Desmond FitzGerald (Defence); Richard Mulcahy (Local Government and Public Health); Patrick Hogan (Agriculture); Fionán Lynch (Fisheries). (*Irish Times*)

"A famously dapper dresser." The young Costello on the verge of a glittering career.

Costello watches as Patrick McGilligan signs the Optional Clause of the Permanent Court of International Justice, 14 September 1929. *Left to right*: JAC, John Marcus O'Sullivan, Seán Lester, John Hearne, a Spanish official of the League of Nations, Patrick McGilligan. (*Irish Independent*)

"I said that it would mean less night work and worry." The new Taoiseach with his wife, Ida, who is holding the family dog, Slem, 20 February 1948. (*Irish Times*)

Costello's first Cabinet. Seated, *left to right*: Noël Browne (Health); Seán MacBride (External Affairs), Bill Norton (Tánaiste and Social Welfare); JAC; Richard Mulcahy (Education); T.F. O'Higgins (Defence); T.J. Murphy (Local Government). Standing, *left to right*: Dan Morrissey (Industry and Commerce); Jim Everett (Posts and Telegraphs); Patrick McGilligan (Finance); Joe Blowick (Lands); Seán MacEoin (Justice); James Dillon (Agriculture). (*TopFoto*)

"Lined ceiling to floor with books—most of them on law." In the study at home in Herbert Park.

The Taoiseach turns waiter, helping serve meals at the annual dinner for residents of St Patrick's House, Kilmainham, 14 April 1948. (*Irish Independent*)

The Irish delegation arrives at Northolt in London for the Anglo-Irish trade talks, 16 June 1948. *Left to right:* Morrissey, Dillon, McGilligan, Norton, MacBride, John Dulanty (High Commissioner to London), JAC. (*TopFoto*)

Making a point. The Taoiseach gestures during a news conference to mark the opening of the trade talks. Norton and MacBride seem amused. (*Associated Press*)

Jack and Ida Costello arrive in New York on board the *Mauritania*, 27 August 1948. (*AP/Press Association Images*)

"The inaccuracies and infirmities of these provisions are apparent." Costello explains the External Relations Act to the Canadian Bar Association, 1 September 1948. Canadian lawyer P.H. Bouffard and Ida Costello listen.

The Taoiseach explains his decision to repeal the External Relations Act to a British journalist, as MacBride looks on. (*Corbis/Hulton-Deutsch Collection*)

The British weren't impressed, as this cartoon by David Low indicates. From the *Evening Standard*, 19 October 1948. (*The British Cartoon Archive, University of Kent*)

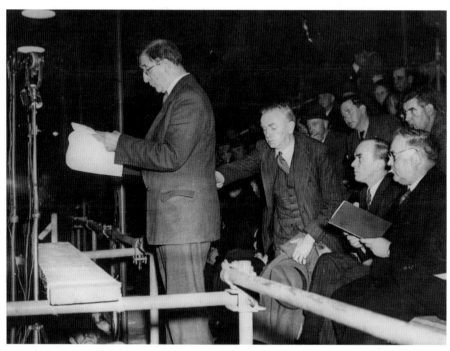

Costello pushes de Valera closer to the microphone as he addresses the mass meeting in O'Connell Street to protest against the Ireland Act, 13 May 1949. MacBride and Norton sit beside the Taoiseach. (*AP/Press Association Images*)

"Near-feudal deference"? The Taoiseach with the Archbishop of Dublin, John Charles McQuaid. Costello's ADC, Mick Byrne, is behind. (*Irish Independent*)

"His most successful period as a barrister." Costello at the Four Courts while in Opposition again. (*Associated Newspapers/Solo Syndication*)

Back in power, Costello receives his seal of office from President Seán T. O'Kelly, 4 June 1954. Secretary to the Government, Maurice Moynihan, looks on. (*TopFoto*)

A second Government. *Left to right* (seated): Seán MacEoin (Defence); Brendan Corish (Social Welfare); Bill Norton (Tánaiste and Industry and Commerce); JAC; Richard Mulcahy (Education); Joe Blowick (Lands); Michael Keyes (Posts and Telegraphs); James Dillon (Agriculture). Standing: Gerard Sweetman (Finance); Liam Cosgrave (External Affairs); Tom O'Higgins (Health); Pa O'Donnell (Local Government). Not pictured: Jim Everett (Justice). (*Lensmen Photographic Archive*)

"We must have friends." President Eisenhower welcomes Costello to the White House, 14 March 1956. (*Corbis/Bettmann*)

"An immense fillip to national self confidence." Acknowledging enthusiastic American crowds on St Patrick's Day, 1956.

A private audience with the Pope, 2 September 1959. *Left to right*: Monsignor John Ryan, Pope John XXIII, JAC, Ralph Sutton. (*Pontificia Fotografia, Felici*)

Golden jubilee at the Bar, 23 November 1964. *Left to right*: son Declan, daughter Grace, JAC, Thomas A. Doyle (Chairman of the Bar Council), son-in-law Ralph Sutton. (*Irish Times*)

"A perfectly happy man."
The former Taoiseach in
old age. (*James G. Maguire
Studios*)

Two Freemen of Dublin in their last public appearance together. De Valera laughs at one of Costello's jokes, 7 March 1975.

together. But Browne was about to give everyone in the country plenty to talk about.

First, he gave the correspondence to the morning newspapers, ensuring the widest possible publicity for his viewpoint. Then he made a scathing attack on his former Government colleagues in the Dáil, forcing Costello in turn to make a lengthy contribution setting out his own position and that of his government.

Browne said he "had been led to believe" that his insistence on the exclusion of a means test had the full support of his colleagues, but now knew that it had not. "While ... I as a Catholic accept unequivocally and unreservedly the views of the Hierarchy on this matter, I have not been able to accept the manner in which this matter has been dealt with by my former colleagues in the Government." He repeated the claim that Costello had led him to believe that the hierarchy had been satisfied by his October meeting with McQuaid and his colleagues, and complained again that the Taoiseach hadn't forwarded his letter to the bishops. "This conduct ... is open, it seems to me, to only two possible explanations—either that he would not oppose the scheme if agreement were reached with the Medical Association on the means test or that, in the light of his knowledge of the objections still being made by the Hierarchy and withheld from me, he intended that the scheme without a means test must never in fact be implemented."[98]

Costello said that he had "seldom listened to a statement in which there were so many—let me say it as charitably as possible—inaccuracies, misstatements and misrepresentations". He had attempted to act as peacemaker, and had given Browne every help, even after the crucial Cabinet meeting. "I wanted him to know that we still were willing to help him and did not want to turn the corkscrew on him. My attitude during all those frightful months received the thanks embodied in the document read here today by Deputy Dr Browne."

He pointed out that it was Browne who had sought to amend the legislation to allow for the charging of fees, but the Cabinet rejected the proposal because "we were young as a Government at that time, and we thought we could not put the provision he suggested through the House". Costello criticised the former Minister for making public matters that were "to be adjusted behind closed doors and ... never intended to be the subject of public controversy". But, with the permission of Archbishop McQuaid, he read further documents into the Dáil record which, he claimed, showed that Browne was wrong to suggest that he had "deluded him and tricked him". Costello claimed it had been clear all along that he hadn't replied to the hierarchy's letter because he was attempting to reach a solution.

Browne's criticisms of his former colleagues were repaid in full by the Taoiseach, who said he had reached the conclusion that Browne "was not competent or capable to fulfil the duties of the Department of Health. He was incapable of negotiation; he was obstinate at times and vacillating at other times ... I regret my view is that temperamentally he is unfitted for the post of Cabinet Minister." On the vital question of Church–State relations, Costello said that a government which was "given advice or warnings by the authoritative people in the Catholic Church, on matters strictly confined to faith and morals ... will give to their directions ... complete obedience and allegiance ... I, as a Catholic, obey my Church authorities and will continue to do so, in spite of the *Irish Times* or anything else, in spite of the fact that they may take votes from me or my party, or anything else of that kind."[99]

Costello's speech was a carefully constructed defence of his position, and was effective in the context of the Dáil. But his problem was reaching the wider public. As Browne's biographer John Horgan has noted, "few people would have read all the densely packed columns [of the Dáil debates] ... More, on the other hand, would have read at least a large part of the voluminous correspondence which Browne released to the newspapers ... reading other people's letters, after all, is far more fun than reading Dáil debates."[100]

While he was speaking in the Dáil, there was yet another twist. McQuaid had rung up demanding to speak to the Taoiseach. Patrick Lynch, who was in the "bull-pen", the section of the Dáil where officials sit, was summoned to take the call. The Irish News Agency, one of MacBride's pet projects, had asked the Archbishop to write a 1,000-word article explaining the bishops' point of view on the controversy. McQuaid was outraged at this request, and vented his anger on the unfortunate Lynch. When Costello returned to his office, Lynch passed on the message. The Taoiseach put his head in his hands, exclaiming, "Dear God! This is the end."[101]

It was far from the end; Costello would be pursued by questions about the Mother and Child crisis for the rest of his life. The *Irish Times* was particularly critical, both at the time and later. Costello professed not to care, telling a meeting of UCD's Literary and Historical Society that he was "around long enough not to be particularly upset by what John Masefield would call the flung spray and the blown spume of the Pearl Bar".[102] As Noël Browne's iconic status was burnished in later years, Costello's image was tarnished (although not as much as MacBride's). But what was the effect, apart from ending Browne's ministerial career and giving Unionists ample evidence to claim that the Republic was a theocratic state?

McQuaid rated the crisis as the most important event in Irish history since Catholic Emancipation in 1829. "That the clash should have come in this particular form and under this Government, with Mr Costello at its head, is a very happy success for the Church. The decision of the Government has thrown back Socialism and Communism for a very long time. No Government, for years to come, unless it is frankly Communist, can afford to disregard the moral teaching of the Bishops."[103]

But it wasn't quite as straightforward as that. Conor Cruise O'Brien pointed out that the government which obeyed the hierarchy was defeated, the party that chose bishops over Browne was shattered, Browne himself was comfortably returned to the next Dáil, and the following Fianna Fáil government introduced a Mother and Child Scheme.[104] This is true, although Browne, while he voted for his successor's scheme, later disowned it. And there were clearly limits to anti-clericalism in Fianna Fáil. In 1953, when the new health scheme was being criticised by the hierarchy, Dan Breen told a parliamentary party meeting, "It's a terrible pity that 30 years ago, when we had the chance, we didn't shoot a few Bishops." His novel approach to Church–State relations was greeted with silence, "although Eamon de Valera looked glum".[105] In the long run, the controversy damaged the Church's image, and certainly couldn't be seen as a success, happy or not.

To return to the immediate aftermath of Browne's resignation, Costello took over as Minister for Health himself. The move was supposed to be temporary,[106] but he remained in the post until the change of government—one reason may have been that a new appointment would have required a Dáil vote, which the Government had no guarantee of winning.

James Deeny, the Department's Chief Medical Officer, was then on secondment to the National Tuberculosis Survey, but was told that the Taoiseach "worked only with the medical staff, whom he saw all day every day. When he had decided what he wanted to do, he sent for the Secretary of the Department and in the presence of the medical people gave him his orders. As he was Taoiseach as well as Minister for Health and had a positive determined manner, no one dared to say anything, but the administration did not like it."[107]

The dislike was returned with interest. Costello held senior civil servants in the Department partly responsible for the crisis that had been allowed to develop. Dr J.D. McCormack, a senior medical adviser in the Department, was also a fellow member of Portmarnock. He claimed to the Taoiseach that there was "a prejudice against the medical profession among the lay administrators".[108] This confirmed Costello's suspicions about attempted State control of medicine. He later told the Dáil that he took away from his short time in the Department "one paramount impression ... there was, in the course of the day-to-day administration of this Department, being done ... something which was ... steadily and surely leading to socialised medicine".[109]

The Taoiseach proceeded to sideline the civil servants and put the Department's medical staff in charge of negotiations with the IMA. Nothing came of this approach before the general election.[110] The joint committee he had set up was dissolved by the new Minister, Dr Jim Ryan—Costello blamed the decision on the need to placate some of the Independents supporting the new government[111] (principally Browne). Given time, Costello's approach might have led to a compromise, although one that would have suited the medical profession.

But time was something the Inter-party Government no longer had. Discussions of the Mother and Child issue, for the sake of clarity, usually ignore the other pressing matters facing the Government, almost as if it was the only problem facing Costello and his colleagues. But of course this was very far from the case, and while the difficulty with Noël Browne may have been the most important factor in triggering the 1951 general election, it certainly wasn't the only one. As early as January, the Canadian High Commissioner in London was reporting a prediction by Boland, now the Ambassador to London, that there would be an election in May. "Rising costs and increasing shortages were making life difficult for the people and government. The recent country-wide strikes of railway and bank employees had pointed up the strains under which the Irish economy was suffering. I got the impression that the wear and tear of the last couple of years had taken something out of Costello's coalition which is not likely to go to the country in quite the solid phalanx he foresaw when he was in Ottawa three years ago."[112] Current affairs journal *The Leader* noted at around the same time that "the situation in industry has taken a serious turn for the worse over Christmas" with strikes threatening national paralysis, while the Government had "given the impression of weakness all along the line in its handling of the Baltinglass issue". It added that the absurdity of the latter situation "often brings govern-ments down except in a country which enjoys comedy in politics".[113]

Costello was, occasionally at least, able to enjoy the comedy himself. He told a meeting of the Literary and Historical Society in UCD that being in government "brought neither power nor enjoyment", although some people seemed to believe he was omnipotent. This he denied, exclaiming, "Power! Why, we could not even cook up a job in a village post office!"[114] A sense of the pressure the Taoiseach was under is given by a letter to his friend Tom Bodkin in February (before the healthcare situation reached crisis point). Costello apologised for delays in dealing with the Arts Bill. "The spirit was willing but the insanity that swept through the country before and after Christmas and the illness of practically all my colleagues threw such a burden on me that a 24 hour day wasn't long enough to provide time to deal with everything ... Again strikes—milk, bread, railways, banks—Estimates, Prices Orders and a succession of problems delayed me ..."[115]

Similar sentiments were expressed by James Dillon, who wrote at the start of the year to congratulate Costello on the resolution of an ITGWU strike. "When I behold you battering away Christmas Day and every other day, while your colleagues collapse around you, I must confess to a sentiment for which awe is not too strong a word!"[116] *The Leader* agreed, saying that "the Taoiseach has been called upon to do too much. He has been in the centre of things amid the Cost of Living crisis, the Bank Strike, the Rail Strike and the Health debacle, and has often performed functions that otherwise would have been attended to by the respective Ministers in the Departments of Industry and Commerce, Finance and Health."[117]

Dillon himself would contribute to the Taoiseach's problems. His policies had already led to the loss of the support of Independent TDs Patrick Cogan, Patrick Lehane and William Sheldon. At the end of April, Patrick Finucane and Patrick Halliden resigned from Clann na Talmhan in protest at the way he had treated milk producers. As Dillon's biographer Maurice Manning has written, the collapse of the Government's support had far more to do with agriculture than it did with the Mother and Child Scheme—which explains why Fianna Fáil made the Agriculture estimates "the battleground for its showdown with the government". The Independent farmer TDs who had supported the Government in the past were prepared to continue doing so—if the price paid to milk suppliers was increased. Dillon flatly refused. As Manning states, his attitude "is astonishing given what was at stake. Neither did his colleagues in government put him under any pressure to change his stance ... There was ... nothing inevitable about the collapse of the government after the Mother and Child crisis. It had the wherewithal to stay in office, at least in the short to medium term, had it so chosen. It chose otherwise, and in so doing was not helped by Dillon's handling of matters under his political remit."[118]

The other factor agitating the rural Independents was Norton's Social Security scheme, which was felt to discriminate against farmers, who weren't covered. In March, Costello told Bodkin that "the Opposition thought they were sure of defeating us on it but I think they have now changed their minds".[119] However, with certain defeat looming on the Agriculture estimates, the Government had run out of road, and Costello asked his officials on Tuesday 2 May to advise on possible dissolution dates. The next day, he agreed to seek a dissolution for the following Monday, the seventh, with polling on Wednesday 30 May and the assembly of the new Dáil two weeks later.[120] He told the British Ambassador, Sir Gilbert Laithwaite, that he "found it impossible to carry on in face of attitude of Independents, and was certain that right course was to appeal to the country which he was confident would support his Government". Laithwaite did not share his confidence. In London, officials noted that this would mean de Valera's return—"but at least one might then count on a new Irish Minister for External Affairs".[121]

Costello's annoyance at the Independents was reflected in his statement announcing the election, when he accused them of having "irresponsibly sought to embarrass the Government by exploiting petty grievances. The Government, however, is responsible to the people as a whole. Its sole consideration has been for the common good of all our people which must at all times take precedence over sectional interests." He also pointed out that his government remained undefeated[122]—which was true only because a vote had been avoided by the dissolution of the Dáil.

In an address to his own constituents in Dublin South-East, he pointed out that resignations were not unique to inter-party governments. He added that his government had lasted "for a year longer than the average life of a Fianna Fáil Government", and claimed there was "as much, if not more, harmony in the Inter-party Government as in the single party Government of which I had experience". He also cautiously addressed the Browne situation, saying his criticism of his constituency rival had been "appropriate in the circumstances of his final actions in office. But I did not, nor do I now, intend to detract from his achievements in those years when he co-operated with us."[123]

If he was nervous of a groundswell of support for Browne in his own constituency, he had good reason. More than one hundred people had to be turned away from a Browne meeting in the Mansion House because it was full.[124] When the Taoiseach addressed a meeting in Ringsend, in the working-class end of Dublin South-East, a group of women came up to the platform waving placards, remaining there for his entire speech. The slogans left no doubt as to which side they were on: "No means test", "Healthy mothers, healthy children, healthy nation", "Equal rights to happy motherhood", "Mothers must have the best care".[125] In later years, his Director of Elections, Tommy Doyle, made light of their intervention, telling Costello's retirement dinner of the "solid phalanx of somewhat forbidding and unprepossessing spinster ladies, who were equipped with placards and made a great deal of trouble about the Mother and Child situation, and really, without any disrespect to them, you would have gauged from their age that this was a topic that shouldn't give them any personal concern!"[126]

The Taoiseach undertook a fairly punishing schedule, speaking in most major towns over the course of the campaign, although he made sure to spend time in Dublin South-East as well—of the final 18 days of the campaign, no fewer than four were devoted entirely to his own constituency.[127] He was reported to have travelled 2,100 miles and spoken at 27 meetings, compared to de Valera's 40 meetings. The Taoiseach's meetings were marked by "over long" speeches, which left him with a bout of laryngitis at a critical point in the campaign.[128] He had to cancel visits to Carrickmacross and Cavan on 23 May as a result, while at the start of the campaign he appears to have had dental trouble, visiting the dentist on 9 and 10 May.[129]

His speeches concentrated on what he saw as the achievements of his

government. A hand-written conclusion to one summarised his interpretation of the previous three and a half years: "Peace, order, stability and
prosperity: these we have given you. You can secure their continuance by
having the Inter-party Government returned to office."[130]

Costello argued that the peace to which he referred was a product of the
repeal of the External Relations Act and the declaration of the Republic. This
had closed "a chapter of sustained political uncertainty ... and an era begun in
which undistracted attention can be given to social problems".[131] His government, he claimed, had removed "the last source of constitutional difference
from the politics of the twenty-six counties".[132] To complaints that the election
was marked by apathy, he pointed out that in previous campaigns the worry
had been caused by too much enthusiasm: "What has in the present campaign
been described as apathy might more accurately be described as peace."[133]

Stability had been established through coalition government, which put into
"practical effect the democratic principles of Proportional Representation
and adult suffrage in such a way as to guarantee full representation of every
section of the community, not merely in the Dáil, but in the Government as
well".[134] He pointed out that the Fianna Fáil need for an overall majority
invariably led to two general elections in quick succession. "The people then
only gave it to them to protect themselves from a third general election."[135]

Prosperity he ascribed to his government's economic policy, which he
contrasted to that of Fianna Fáil, who "like certain kings of old, have learnt
nothing or forgotten nothing".[136] He said Fianna Fáil were pessimistic about
the economic development of Ireland, and were "the last political party in
Europe standing steadfast in defence of a system of finance which died with
Montagu Norman." If they objected to the amount the Government had
borrowed, they had two choices—"curtail development or increase taxation".[137]

Costello claimed that in 1947 Fianna Fáil had planned to reinstate the
wages standstill policy, and that everyone who had received a pay rise since
then should remember that fact. But the Taoiseach admitted that the
Government was not yet satisfied with "a society in which there still remained
so many social evils ... Much has been done but much more has yet to be
done."[138] And he rejected (accurate) claims by Fianna Fáil that his own party
were unenthusiastic about social welfare plans, saying that if the Government
was returned, "the Social Security proposals will be enacted without delay".[139]

He returned to his themes—peace, stability, prosperity—in a final speech
in Bray on the eve of polling, in which he stressed that the choice facing voters
was between the Inter-party Government and Fianna Fáil. The bitter divisions
over the Treaty feud had been removed, he claimed, while the inter-party
innovation had introduced institutional flexibility which allowed politics
to escape from the "arthritic rigidity which single-party domination had

imposed". And in case that wasn't enough, he used the opportunity to announce that the Government had decided to accept the pay rise recommended by the Civil Service Arbitrator.[140] The campaign overall was dominated by economic, rather than constitutional, issues, and for that reason was seen as "unquestionably the opening of a new era".[141]

The election proved to be a triumph for Fine Gael, and for Jack Costello personally. He received almost a third of the vote, 31.4 per cent, the highest share received by a candidate in Dublin South-East or its predecessor, Dublin Townships, up to then. Most unusually, the other two seats were also filled on the first count, with Noël Browne pipping Seán MacEntee for second place by 139 votes. The new Clann candidate, Dr Patrick McCartan, got less than 2 per cent of the vote. Costello's son Declan was also elected to the Dáil for Dublin North-West. In his first electoral outing, which came shortly before his twenty-fifth birthday, he topped the poll, winning 22 per cent of the vote.

Nationally, Fine Gael came back from the brink of oblivion, increasing its share of the vote to 25.7 per cent, six points more than in 1948, with the most significant rises in the more agricultural areas—7.6 per cent in Connaught-Ulster and 7.8 per cent in Munster. It also won an extra nine seats. The reunited Labour Party won 16 seats, three fewer than the two parties took in 1948; Clann na Poblachta was reduced to just two, Clann na Talmhan had six, and there were 14 Independents. Fianna Fáil, meanwhile, added 4.5 per cent to its vote, but won just one extra seat, giving the party a total of 69. Inter-party transfers were relatively effective—the Government parties missed out on four seats they could have won with better transfers, but another eight were won on transfers, particularly from Clann na Poblachta.[142]

The result was, to say the least of it, indecisive. It is important to stress that it was not seen at the time as a rejection of the Inter-party Government and an endorsement of Fianna Fáil; quite the opposite. Most newspapers expected that a majority of the Independents would vote for Costello, making him Taoiseach again. The British Ambassador briefed London that the result was a "moral defeat for Fianna Fáil", but observed that whatever government was returned would face difficulty because it would lack an effective working majority.[143] On 4 June, Lemass confessed that what would happen when the Dáil met "is still a very open matter", as the balance of power lay with the Independents. "The position cannot be satisfactory no matter what happens, but the only prospect of some effective work being done is if FF can succeed in forming a government. Another Coalition, dependent on the support of nearly all these Independent deputies, offers a very depressing prospect." [144]

Of the 14 Independents, Dillon and his group—Alfie and Alfred Byrne, Charles Fagan and Oliver J. Flanagan—would vote for Costello. So would Patrick Lehane, Patrick Finucane and William Sheldon, despite their differences with the Minister for Agriculture. This gave Costello 72 votes to the 69 of Fianna Fáil, and left the balance of power with six non-aligned Independents—Browne, Cowan, Cogan, McQuillan, Michael ffrench-O'Carroll and John Flynn. Flynn had supported de Valera in the past, ffrench-O'Carroll was a new TD, and the other four had voted for Costello in 1948. Those Independents now found themselves wooed by both sides. Ffrench-O'Carroll, a follower of Noël Browne, found himself in Costello's house, as the outgoing Taoiseach and Tánaiste tried to sell him the idea of a health scheme based on social insurance. But he wasn't convinced. He agreed to act with Browne, who wanted absolute loyalty from those around him, telling ffrench-O'Carroll, "I want people who will go with me all the way."[145]

MacBride tried to make things easier for Costello, saying he would not accept a post in a new Inter-party Government as his presence would "be availed of by some Independents for motives of their own, to create additional difficulties for the government". In any case, as he acknowledged, the election result was "a repudiation of the policies I have been advocating and of my actions in the course of the last three years".[146]

The Cabinet met on 5 June "on the understanding that they will be staying in office".[147] But Fianna Fáil were also making a pitch for Independent support, publishing a programme for government which included the continuation of many of Dillon's policies in Agriculture, new legislation on social security and a mother and child scheme. It was "a shopping list to attract the Independents",[148] and it worked. Flynn, Browne, Cogan, Cowan and ffrench-O'Carroll were all to support de Valera this time. Only Jack McQuillan of the unaligned Independents decided to support the outgoing Taoiseach.

On the morning the Dáil was due to meet, Industry and Commerce Minister T.F. O'Higgins told the British Ambassador they now expected to be voted out. "Some soreness is clearly felt that the Speaker [sic] who was re-elected without contest should not be seeking re-election as Speaker but rejoining Fianna Fáil as a voting member. As new Speaker would be a Fine Gael supporter, this gives de Valera his bare majority."[149] This duly happened— when the Dáil met, de Valera announced that Frank Fahy, who had held the position since 1932, would not be seeking re-election as Ceann Comhairle. Labour's Patrick Hogan was elected instead. The result was a gain of one vote for de Valera, and the loss of one for Costello, a swing of two votes. As Maurice Manning has noted, this raises the question of why an Independent who was likely to vote against the Government was not chosen instead of Hogan, but it appears this wasn't even considered.[150] Costello told the Dáil he felt it was his duty to nominate a Ceann Comhairle, "even in the peculiar circumstances in which we find ourselves in this House today".[151]

Costello's nomination was defeated by 74 votes to 72, the appointment of Hogan as Ceann Comhairle having made the difference. De Valera was elected by 74 to 69, as three of the Independents who supported Costello—Finucane, Lehane and Sheldon—abstained. Dillon quickly christened the five Independents keeping de Valera in power the "busted flush". Costello said he had "no doubt that the vast majority of the electors desire an Inter-party Government. I have equally no doubt that some of the Independent Deputies who voted against the Inter-party Government were voting against the very people who elected them to this Dáil ..."[152] But such complaints, merited or not, could not disguise the fact that the inter-party experiment was over—for the time being.

Chapter 10 ～

TRUMPET-TONGUED DENUNCIATION

*"The country will now have a chance of seeing
whether the present crowd can do any better."*[1]

JOHN A. COSTELLO, JULY 1951

*"If that bloody fellow had been working for me,
I'd have won me bloody case!"*[2]

PATRICK KAVANAGH

In June 1953, Jack Costello characterised a series of by-election results as a "trumpet-tongued denunciation" by the voters of the Fianna Fáil administration.[3] The phrase could equally serve as a description of his political approach as leader of the Opposition. During the three years he was out of power, he kept up a constant and comprehensive critique of Government policy, and in particular the austerity introduced by his constituency rival Seán MacEntee in the 1952 Budget.

But while politics played a huge part in Costello's life in these years, so too did the law, in what was arguably his greatest period as a barrister. The aura of having headed a government added to his legendary status in the Law Library, and he was regarded as being at the height of his powers.[4] This was demonstrated in the Patrick Kavanagh libel trial, discussed below.

He very quickly returned to the routine of spending most days working in the Law Library until five o'clock or after.[5] But political work took up more time than it had before 1948, mainly because Costello was the recognised leader of the Opposition in the Dáil. While Richard Mulcahy remained leader of Fine Gael, Costello "would certainly have been seen in the country as the 'real' leader".[6] This had political implications. Costello's pre-eminence was an indication that the inter-party arrangement remained in place, waiting for a chance to return to government. This may explain, as Cornelius O'Leary suggested, why de Valera did not attempt to solidify his position with a snap election, as he had in 1933, 1938 and 1944. This time was different, because "a viable alternative government was in the offing".[7]

It is significant, too, that it was Costello, rather than Mulcahy, who approached Dillon in May 1952 with a suggestion that he should rejoin Fine Gael.[8] Dillon took up the suggestion, bringing Oliver J. Flanagan into the party as well. Costello acted as a focus, organising meetings of "the Heads of the various groups which form the combined Opposition",[9] ensuring that the unity forged around the Cabinet table was not lost while on the Opposition benches. He told his constituency executive that Fine Gael would continue the work it did in the Inter-party Government "in an Inter-party Opposition". He said the Opposition's role was "to protect the people against the preponderant power of a mammoth party which by its very nature threatens the liberty and integrity of the citizens in a small country."[10] Observers recognised his strong position within Fine Gael "by virtue of the ascendancy he acquired as head of the former Government and of his role as formulator of policy since becoming leader of the Opposition".[11]

One of the key tasks facing Costello was to defend the record of the Inter-party Government. As his close friend Senator James Douglas wrote in early August, Fianna Fáil, "especially MacEntee, is trying to put over the idea that the Inter-party was reckless and irresponsible in its financial policy ... it seems to me that the game is to create a general impression that the country has been left in a serious financial position, and then to claim later that it was saved from financial ruin by Fianna Fáil".[12]

Costello tackled these suggestions head on in a speech to his constituency executive later in the month. He claimed the Inter-party Government's policy of capital development had led to an unprecedented expansion in agriculture and industry. "It is still our policy and one which we believe should, in spite of the difficulties of the times, and particularly because of the uncertainties of the future, be pressed forward with all reasonable speed." He defended his government's record on inflation, pointing out that it had refused to sanction increased milk prices, despite the political advantages of doing so. "We left the finances of the State in a sound and healthy condition, and the continuance of the bold and courageous policy of capital expenditure to develop the resources of the State ... will best secure the maintenance of employment, financial stability and economic security."[13]

This speech, which was fully reported in the newspapers, was seen by The Leader as the start of "real controversy" on the question of whether a financial crisis was looming. Costello's emphatic denial of such a disaster was to dominate his political activity in the coming months.[14] At this time, and throughout this period in opposition, he was heavily reliant on his son-in-law, Alexis FitzGerald, who acted "as a kind of one-man research centre and as speech writer".[15] FitzGerald's ideas on economics, particularly on capital investment and the repatriation of sterling assets, dovetailed with Costello's own views. They were also politically useful—there was a need to respond to Fianna Fáil's policy of austerity.

The Costello family had their summer holiday in Italy,[16] as they were to do for several years around this time. On his return to the political frontline, he told his friend Tom Bodkin that reports from the country "indicate dissatisfaction with the present government and a general expectation of an early election". He was particularly critical of Lemass for making speeches full of "gloomy prophecy and indications of bad times ahead. He has cast himself for the role of the politician who will tell the people the facts no matter what the political consequences. The fact, of course, is that he has found himself enmeshed in his own promises which he can't fulfil."[17] He told Dillon that he would "deal with some of Lemass's major misrepresentations" in a speech in his constituency.[18]

This speech, delivered at the opening of Fine Gael rooms in Rathmines in October 1951, made fun of Lemass for his "Dunkirk manner". Costello pointed out that the Tánaiste "only dons his mantle of heavy statesmanship when the burdens of Government press upon and dismay him. The perception which he now displays of the problems of Irish economics did not after all come to our assistance during the trials of last winter." He apologised for "striking a disharmonious note of cheerfulness", but said, "I don't think that things are so bad and I doubt if the Tánaiste does either. After all, this is a technique that has been used before—prophesying the arrival of evil days and claiming credit if they do not come ... the only reason they talk as they do, is to injure at the cost of the nation the reputation of their predecessors ..."[19]

This reputation was about to suffer another injury, this time from the Central Bank, which issued its report for the 1950/51 financial year in October. With some understatement, the Irish Times described it as a "gloomy review of financial tendencies".[20] The Central Bank complained that Marshall Aid "was expended largely on consumer or near-consumer goods"; that "the constantly increasing scale" of State spending had pushed up costs; and that the public works programme was "disproportionate". The economic position, it complained, "is one of high consumption, high investment (with insufficient early output of the character most needed) and low savings".[21]

A few days after the report's publication, Dillon sent a memorandum to Costello, criticising the Central Bank's views as "crazy, damnable doctrine". He summed up the report as saying that "it is economically criminal to spend money on building houses or hospitals for our own people in Lifford or Monaghan, but economic virtue and vision to lend the money to the British Government at 1.25% to build houses and hospitals 100 yards down the road in Strabane and South Armagh ... If this report is accepted, the wisest thing young people could do would be to fly this country as quickly as possible."[22]

Costello didn't need any encouragement from Dillon to reject the report. He had evidently criticised the Governor of the Central Bank, Joseph Brennan, to his friend Tom Bodkin. The latter said that, in the light of their earlier conversation, he was "not surprised to read what I can only describe as Poor Joe's diabosterous report. He seems to have ossified, though even when we were boys together at Clongowes he showed signs of a reactionary temperament despite his academic brilliancy."[23]

MacEntee added to the controversy by publishing a White Paper on the country's external trade and payments on 29 October. This claimed Ireland was unique in Europe, with only Greece among the OEEC nations approaching its lack of balance in international trade. The White Paper forecast an adverse trade balance of £70 million, prescribing reduced spending on consumer goods and cuts in imports as the only solution.[24]

In a speech in Cork at the start of November, Costello attacked the Central Bank's economic diagnosis, "which has since been supported by the tendentious and misleading White Paper ... An atmosphere of crisis has been created and maintained to the point where real damage may be done to our people and our economy unless immediate steps are taken to restore public confidence ..." He recalled his forecast in his speech to the Institute of Bankers in 1949 of a "temporary disequilibrium in the Balance of Payments" caused by the repatriation of sterling assets to pay for capital investment. "What I foretold has happened, but it is not 'crisis' ..." He also noted that neither the Central Bank report nor the White Paper had mentioned that the monthly figure for the adverse balance of trade had been declining since June.[25]

In fact, while the balance of trade for 1951 turned out to be the largest ever recorded, it was lower than MacEntee forecast, at £61.6 million.[26] The Minister claimed the lower figure was due to the corrective measures taken by the Government.[27] Others weren't so sure. A series of articles in *The Leader* in August and September 1952 strongly supported Costello's argument that imports reached their peak in April 1951, and that the problem was caused by increased import prices rather than volumes. In other words, it wasn't extravagant consumption that caused the problem, but international price inflation due to the Korean War. Not surprisingly, perhaps, Costello preserved the series in his private papers, underlining the conclusion that the White Paper had used "selected statistics to support a preconceived thesis".[28]

When the Dáil resumed in November, the dispute over the two documents was centre stage, and Costello led the fight for the Opposition. He said that "when a lie is started it is very difficult to catch up on it. I doubt if we will ever be able to get it out of the heads of the people that this gap in the balance of payments ... has been brought about by some sort of profligacy and unnecessary spending on luxury goods by the last Government." This, naturally, he denied, adding that "the suggestions and tendentious information, or misinformation I should call it, contained in this White Paper are utterly without foundation".[29]

In his contribution, Lemass said that there was a problem, but not a crisis—a remark which became the headline for the following day's *Irish Times*.[30] As Costello pointed out, this description had been "borrowed" from his own speech in Cork.[31] He was later to claim that by winning the argument over whether there was a crisis, the Opposition had headed off the threat of an autumn supplementary budget.[32] However, while Lemass may have downplayed the seriousness of the situation in the Dáil, MacEntee was sticking to his guns within government, and in the long run was to win the argument in favour of austerity. The divisions within Cabinet were highlighted by Costello, who contrasted the expansionist policy of Lemass with the restrictive policy of MacEntee. The Minister for Finance was, according to Costello, "suckled in a creed outworn since the day when Gladstone died".[33]

In his Ard Fheis speech in February, he noted that MacEntee "has recently resurrected the crisis ... from the Limbo of Governmental errors to which it was consigned" by Lemass. While the Tánaiste had described the situation as a problem rather than a crisis, MacEntee was now claiming it was "difficult almost to the verge of desperation". Costello accused his constituency rival of "striving for dramatic effect" but achieving only melodrama. "We decline to accept the view that the country is on the verge of economic disaster."[34]

The Budget built on MacEntee's gloomy view of the economy was presented to the Dáil on 2 April 1952. It removed subsidies from tea, butter and sugar, and reduced subsidies for bread and flour, while increasing welfare payments in partial compensation. The subsidy cuts saved £6.67 million, while the welfare increases cost £2.75 million. Other measures included a one-shilling increase in income tax, and a swingeing £10 million increase in excise duties on tobacco, beer, spirits and petrol.[35] It was massively unpopular, and "contributed significantly to both the reality and the atmosphere of depression".[36]

In criticism which he would repeat frequently in the coming years, Costello claimed the Budget was cruel, unnecessary and unjust. Lemass appeared to agree, at least in part: "It is an easy matter to describe the Budget as brutal and cruel; we are dealing with a brutal and cruel situation; there is no easy way out of it."[37] Later, when the Finance Bill introducing the Budget measures came before the Dáil, Costello claimed he would not be a party to such measures in government. "I would not stay one second in office, nor would I be associated with anybody in office who would be responsible for a Budget or a Finance Bill of this kind."[38] This promise was to be forgotten in the crisis year of 1956.

One of MacEntee's economy measures was the withdrawal of Costello's State car. The bad news was broken by de Valera, who must have wondered when he went into opposition in 1954 if the favour would be returned.[39] In fact, not only did Costello not try to withdraw de Valera's car when their roles were reversed, he insisted that his predecessor should keep his Packard as "he was accustomed to it and found it comfortable". Later, in response to a query from de Valera about insurance, Costello said the car should be available to him on exactly the same terms as when he was Taoiseach.[40] Deprived of his car in 1952, Costello wrote to the Garda Commissioner to thank him for the four years of "devoted service" he had received from his drivers.[41] He reverted to driving his own car, a Humber, which he did with care but considerable speed—he claimed to never look at his speedometer, so if anything ever happened he could honestly say he didn't know what speed he was travelling at.[42]

MacEntee's biographer has argued that the 1952 Budget was not quite as severe as is commonly thought, as current and capital expenditure both rose slightly in real terms compared to the previous year, and the capital investment plans of the Inter-party Government remained largely intact. In fact, the Government rejected MacEntee's proposals to cut capital investment, opting to raise taxation instead.[43] This contradiction was noted at the time by Costello, who pointed out that the Government's planned capital programme was "as great if not greater than the capital programme we had". He accused MacEntee of secretly planning a Budget surplus, through unnecessary increased taxation, in order to pay for this programme. This was being done, he alleged, because Fianna Fáil had criticised Inter-party Government borrowing, and so could not follow a similar policy.[44]

In any event, the result of MacEntee's policy was deflation, which led to increased unemployment. Ken Whitaker, then a rising star within the Department of Finance, later rejected the view that there was an alternative policy of expanding demand through fiscal action. He argued that while the 1952 Budget may have been too severe, there was no way of pursing an expansionary policy when there were virtually no sources of foreign borrowing available.[45] Whitaker insisted that in the absence of Marshall Aid, the Inter-party Government would have had to pursue a similar course if it was still in power.[46]

Whitaker may well have been right, but it would have been too much to expect the Opposition leaders to admit this. Costello in particular kept contrasting his government's "system of productive capital expenditure based on the system of the double budget" with Fianna Fáil's "adoption of a system of taxation".[47] Rising prices and taxes would particularly hit "those sections of the community for whom ... Fine Gael as a party has always been concerned ... the sections described for want of a better terms as the 'white collared workers' ..."[48]

Costello claimed he wasn't opposing for opposition's sake; rather he was setting forth a realistic alternative, the policy of capital investment followed by his government, "which, if continued, would have saved the country from the spectre of increased unemployment and emigration which is now haunting the land". He said this programme would have been funded by national loans (rather than foreign borrowing, which as we have seen was virtually unobtainable at the time). Instead, he said, the Fianna Fáil government introduced a Budget "which is not merely calculated but deliberately designed to depress the standard of living of the Irish people ... what is being attempted is tantamount to a fiscal revolution or rather counter-revolution, calculated to assault and deflate the incomes of the people and their standard of living".[49]

These attacks, allied to the evident unpopularity of the Budget measures, had their effect within Fianna Fáil. Senator Michael Yeats (a former candidate in Dublin South-East) put down a parliamentary party motion criticising the Government's economic policy, which attracted 35 signatures. De Valera and MacEntee made it clear there would be no change; but after the leadership won the vote, Lemass said in Yeats's ear, "Never mind, Senator, you were 98 per cent right."[50]

As the Dáil limped towards its summer recess, tempers were evidently stretched beyond breaking point, with a number of physical altercations between Deputies. Fine Gael TD Seán Collins so enraged Fianna Fáil's Mark Killilea that the latter crossed the Dáil chamber in an effort to strike him; the following day, Collins was in fact struck, by Education Minister Seán Moylan. Moylan having admitted the assault, de Valera conceded that a "simple apology" was not enough to close the incident. But he suggested the cause had been the personal remarks made within the Chamber. His proposed solution was a committee to draw up rules to deal with "this whole question of privilege, abusive personal remarks and personal imputations" so that the targets of such invective would not have to take "the law into their own hands". Not surprisingly, Costello wasn't happy; de Valera's proposed solution completely ignored Moylan's assault, which he characterised as "one of the gravest which has occurred in the history of this Parliament". The Taoiseach responded by saying that if someone insulted him, "and I have no redress other than to knock him down, and I am fit to knock him, I will do so".[51]

Within hours of this exchange, another altercation took place, when Dillon was jostled on the stairs leading from the Dáil chamber by Fianna Fáil's William Quirke, the Leader of the Seanad, who knocked the cigarette from his mouth.[52] In the course of a debate that evening on the Moylan incident, Costello claimed that such assaults were occurring "all too frequently", pointing out that in each case a member of Fianna Fáil had assaulted a member of Fine Gael.[53] Moylan apologised in the Dáil, while Quirke did so in the Seanad. Dillon remained unmollified, claiming there was "a careful Fianna Fáil organised conspiracy" and calling for extra gardaí to be deployed in Leinster House "to restrain Senators or others who go rambling through our corridors looking for drink and fight".[54]

By October 1952, Costello was able to point to improving balance of trade figures. These, he claimed, showed the Government's diagnosis of the situation was wrong—as was the "cure which it so roughly administered ... the cure of gloomy talk, pessimistic outlook, credit restrictions, severe taxation, high interest rates and progressively increased unemployment ... Because the Government took an incorrect view ... every section of the community has been made to suffer."[55]

In his February 1953 Ard Fheis speech, Costello set out what *The Leader* described as "the most complete and detailed statement of policy which has been heard from any Irish political leader within living memory ... it was a programme prepared by a party confident of being concerned with responsibility for government in the near future and staking its claim to office on positive proposals rather than on generalised bromides or pious aspirations". It was, the journal said, part of a process Costello had engaged in since becoming leader of the Opposition. "He has consistently dedicated himself to the difficult task of laying down ... a new economic policy for Fine Gael ... He has succeeded in persuading the public that Fine Gael have no intention of being a party of the past."[56]

The speech, which was later published by Fine Gael as a pamphlet, *Blueprint for Prosperity*, again criticised the Government's deflationary policy. Costello argued that it must be replaced by "a policy of financial easement and economic expansion ... We cannot be content with mere exhortations to harder work and increased production, but must instead take steps to change the conditions of production in such a way as to lead to that greater creation of wealth which alone can bring a greater measure of prosperity."

Investment would be funded by "prudent" repatriation of sterling assets through "deliberately planned and controlled deficits" in the balance of payments; by some foreign capital; and by savings at home. Costello stressed the importance of maintaining financial confidence, ruling out a break with sterling. It was also vital to restore public belief in the future of the country. Among his concrete proposals were the establishment of a domestic money market (following the example of the Reserve Bank of India) so that banks could secure at home the liquidity they sought in London; changes to the Control of Manufactures Acts to attract risk-bearing foreign capital; a central savings office; and a Capital Investment Board.[57]

This was, as *The Leader* noted, an ambitious statement of policy; it contained many ideas which would later have a significant impact on the Irish economy. MacEntee evidently recognised the appeal of the speech, for he had officials in the Department of Finance and the Revenue Commissioners draw up memoranda on various points raised by Costello. The officials were predictably critical (Whitaker, for instance, suggested it was "obviously absurd to set up Indian credit arrangements as standards to be followed by this country"), especially of the proposed Capital Investment Board.[58]

Inside government, Lemass was pushing a rather similar agenda to that set out by Costello, arguing in July 1953 that continuing unemployment and emigration were caused by the low level of capital investment by private enterprise. Therefore, he argued, "there appears to be no practical alternative to an enlarged programme of State investment". He wanted £10 million per year invested in road development and other labour-intensive projects. MacEntee rejected this proposal, arguing that "work for work's sake" would be created "at the cost of heavier taxation and great risk to the country's financial stability". However, MacEntee was overruled, with the Government agreeing to the establishment of a National Development Fund of £5 million per year. MacEntee attempted to reopen the question, arguing that this extra sum would make a Budget deficit a certainty, and that the decision would signal "that 'the lid is off' and that economy is no longer to be seriously thought of". His appeal for further consideration appears to have gone unanswered.[59]

Costello was predictably unimpressed, dismissing the Fund as "a new machine for distributing political benefits", and claiming that the Government was attempting to repair the damage it had caused to the economy with "works of an impermanent, and probably of an uneconomic character, which are little better than temporary Relief Schemes". Capital investment, he said, "does not consist in pulling weeds out of the river Dodder, nor in wiping out villages for the sake of impatient road hogs ... This is not Capital Investment, but rather rehabilitation of the victims of disaster—the disaster of FF finances ..."[60]

MacEntee's policies on borrowing, and on Ireland's sterling assets, were also the subject of criticism from Costello. He pointed out that despite the austerity policy introduced by the 1952 Budget, the banks' sterling holdings actually increased. "The Irish people have to suffer austerity, to eat less and live less well in order that the Irish banking system should increase its holding of sterling assets." The money, he insisted, would have been better used at home, especially as the value of sterling was depreciating.[61] To make matters worse, MacEntee had held off seeking a loan in the autumn of 1951, when Irish credit was good. When he finally launched a loan the following year, the air of crisis he had generated meant a much higher level of interest was needed to attract investors.[62]

Apart from the economy, health was also a controversial issue during the lifetime of the Fianna Fáil government, inevitably given the Mother and Child crisis. Costello nailed his colours to the mast early on—everyone accepted the need for improved health services, and the challenge now was to agree a scheme "which will conflict neither with moral principles nor with the just social requirements of the community".[63] When Health Minister Jim Ryan published his White Paper at the end of July 1952, it "accepted the principle of the No Means Test, but its application is circumscribed. Dr Browne had envisaged care of the children up to 16, it is now cut down to 6 weeks ... He has won a formal point of principle, but is it the shadow as opposed to reality?"[64] Many would argue that that was exactly what Browne got—but it was enough to allow him to vote for the Fianna Fáil scheme and continue supporting the Government.[65]

The Fianna Fáil scheme also (after much negotiation) satisfied the hierarchy; but the doctors remained implacable. It is instructive that Fine Gael opposed the Bill, and was the only party to do so. This lends support to the view that medical, rather than episcopal, influence was the main motivating factor in Fine Gael opposition to the Mother and Child scheme. On Costello's prompting, Sweetman wrote an indignant letter to the *Guardian*, after that paper's Dublin correspondent suggested that Fine Gael had only objected to the Health Bill when they "got wind that the Hierarchy was intending to issue a statement attacking the Bill as contrary to Catholic social teaching". Sweetman pointed out that the Fine Gael opposition was "based on principles consistently advocated by the Party since 1945, when it violently opposed the objectionable proposals then introduced by Mr de Valera's Government".[66]

In a vociferous speech, accompanied by much thumping of the bench in front of him, Costello denounced Ryan's scheme as "unjust to the middle classes", a mere "extension of the dispensary services", which offered no real benefit to anyone. The proposal to take a £1 "contribution" from those outside the scope of the Bill to allow them to participate was, he claimed, "a fraudulent subterfuge to get over a moral objection which was put forward to the free-for-all scheme". The Bill, he said, was "incapable of amendment", and he vowed to "oppose it as vigorously and with every possible means lawfully and constitutionally within my power and at my disposal". He insisted that Fine Gael remained committed to a "proper" health scheme, and criticised Ryan's decision to disband the expert committee Costello had established within the Department.[67]

Noël Browne claimed what was really irritating Costello was that "his friends were kicked out of the Custom House". The former Minister claimed that the former Taoiseach had given this expert group "*carte blanche* to bring in whatever scheme is acceptable to the Medical Association". Ryan accused

Fine Gael of political expediency, saying he had never heard "a more unreasonable ... or a more vigorous speech against any measure introduced in this House".[68] With some justice, Costello could be accused of going over the top. As Captain Peadar Cowan said at a later stage in the debate on the Health Bill, "Deputy Costello always suffers here from the serious defect of grossly exaggerating his point."[69] In any event, the 1953 Health Act became law—but its actual implementation was to be left to a new Costello government.[70]

The first electoral test since the general election, and the Budget, came in June 1952, with no fewer than three by-elections, in Mayo North, Limerick East and Waterford. The latter seat had been held by Fine Gael's Bridget Redmond; the other two were Fianna Fáil's. Opening the by-election campaign in Limerick, Costello urged Opposition co-operation to ensure the Government didn't win the seat. The Opposition had called for a general election to seek the voters' views on the Budget—now the people had their chance. He promised that if returned to power, his government would immediately restore the food subsidies removed by MacEntee.[71] In Waterford, he said a vote against the Government "will be a clear signal to halt the present drift towards economic stagnation before it has gone too far ... Finance must be made the servant and not the master of the nation."[72] In Mayo, he accused the Government of being solely concerned with balancing the budget. "With what happens to the rest of the economy they are not concerned ... We are in favour of a progressive financial policy, but with the traditions of our party we can be relied upon to maintain the fundamental soundness of such a policy."[73]

Given the Dáil arithmetic, three Opposition victories could have led to a change of government. It was, Costello told Tom Bodkin, a time of "great alarums and excursions—hopes and fears. Hopes on the part of my colleagues that they would win the three by-elections—fears of the consequences to me personally on my part." However, while Fine Gael won Limerick East—a "first class miracle", according to Costello—Fianna Fáil took the seats in Mayo North and Waterford, leaving the overall numbers in the Dáil unchanged. "They are a tough ... crowd that will not be easy to beat but will be beaten ... Business is stagnant here, unemployment increasing, taxes and prices rising. And still they hold grimly on ..."[74]

The first test of opinion in the capital came with the death of Independent TD Alfred Byrne of Dublin North-West. Fine Gael didn't contest the election, agreeing to support Byrne's brother Thomas, as did Labour.[75] Clann na Poblachta ran The O'Rahilly, while the Fianna Fáil candidate was Lord Mayor Andrew Clarkin. MacEntee's Budget was the main target of opposition attack, with Costello saying that a Fianna Fáil victory "would be taken as an endorsement of their actions in removing the food subsidies".[76] He again accused the Government of misinterpreting the situation, and therefore adopting the wrong policies. "The fruits of Fianna Fáil policy have been so bitter that I think it can reasonably be said that its policy has been disastrous."[77]

The result was a triumph. Byrne was elected on the first count, with a massive 61 per cent of the first preferences. Fianna Fáil's Clarkin got 31 per cent, while The O'Rahilly received just 8 per cent. The British Embassy reported to London that the result, while not affecting the position in the Dáil, was "generally regarded as a major setback to Fianna Fáil", who had put up a strong candidate and campaigned hard in his support.[78] Costello claimed that no government since the establishment of the State "received such a strong rebuff or such an unmistakable demonstration of public mistrust". He pointed out that Fianna Fáil didn't win a majority of the votes in any of the three previous by-elections either. "After such a crushing defeat any self-respecting democratically elected government would dissolve the parliament and submit themselves and their policy to the people ... An alternative government is available to them with a forward progressive policy that is based upon confidence in the people and in their capacity to develop the resources of the country."[79]

The next opportunity for the Opposition came in June 1953, after the deaths of a Labour TD from Cork East and a Fianna Fáil deputy in Wicklow. The economy again proved the dominant theme, with Costello telling voters in Cork that the Government's "policy of enforced austerity and ... restrictionism which has caused decline in industry and business prospects must be abandoned".[80] In Wicklow, he complained of the "disgracefully false charge" by Fianna Fáil that the Inter-party Government "engaged in a wild spree of borrowing". He claimed his government's record was better than that of Fianna Fáil, further accusing de Valera of securing the support of Independents with a programme "which sounded more like a Deed of Purchase than a policy".[81]

In Wicklow, Fine Gael candidate Mark Deering was in third place on the first count, which was headed by Fianna Fáil's Paudge Brennan, son of the deceased TD, followed by Labour's Senator James McCrea. However, Deering pulled ahead on transfers and managed to take the seat. In Cork East, Richard Barry of Fine Gael topped the poll, and took the seat with the transfers of Labour's Sean Keane Junior, whose father had held the seat before his death. Costello told a correspondent in England that the results "were very encouraging and we are in full swing in preparation for a General Election which cannot be long postponed".[82]

The Fine Gael gain from Fianna Fáil in Wicklow narrowed de Valera's majority, but the Taoiseach opted to meet the challenge head on. On the Monday after the by-elections, the Government decided to put down a confidence motion for debate in the Dáil on Wednesday 30 June. The

Taoiseach spoke for 55 minutes, the leader of the Opposition for 15 minutes longer.[83] Costello claimed the motion was "a ragged cloak for the Government's political shame", saying that with a "meagre majority" it planned to continue in office "in defiance of the will of the people ... in the hope that something may turn up at some time in the future to save them from the wrath of the electorate". He claimed the six constituencies which had seen by-elections were a "perfect microcosm of the whole country", and that the Fianna Fáil vote had fallen from 46 per cent in the general election to just 39 per cent. However, he forecast that the Independent deputies "whose political existence depends on their maintaining the present Government in power [would] continue to do so".[84] Of course, he was right—the Government won the vote by 73 to 71, and also regained the political initiative.

Two weeks later, former Ceann Comhairle Frank Fahy died. De Valera quickly moved the writ for the Galway South by-election, which was held on 21 August. Fianna Fáil was always likely to do better in this constituency than in some of the urban areas, and the quick campaign allowed the party to build on the momentum generated by the confidence vote. The Fine Gael candidate, Brendan Glynn, described Fianna Fáil's "terrifying organisation, as thorough and frightening to many in this constituency as its counterpart behind the Iron Curtain". But he said they had been "quite shaken" in the few days before the vote, and that Costello's "wonderful meeting in Ballinasloe on Wednesday night nearly finished them".[85] In fact, the Fianna Fáil candidate was elected on the first count with 54.5 per cent of the vote; however, Glynn increased the Fine Gael vote from 29 per cent in the 1951 general election to 33 per cent, a reasonable though not dramatic performance in a difficult constituency.

At the end of November, Costello appealed for the co-operation of supporters of all Opposition parties "to bring about the final break up of the Government which has wrought such havoc".[86] But most observers felt that the Government had actually consolidated its position, especially since three of its Independent supporters—Noël Browne, Michael ffrench-O'Carroll and Patrick Cogan—joined Fianna Fáil in October.[87] While Galway wasn't in itself particularly important, the by-election "acquired almost national significance by the fuss with which it was surrounded".[88] As 1954 dawned, the Government looked relatively stable—but within a few months, Jack Costello would be back in office as Taoiseach.

Before looking at how that came about, we should consider Costello's other preoccupation in these years, the law. As was pointed out at the start of the chapter, this was arguably his most successful period as a barrister. He was at the height of his powers, had the status of being a former Taoiseach, and was one of the most sought-after senior counsels. When Arthur Cox was asked to act for Winston Churchill in a libel action being taken against him by Brigadier Eric Dorman-O'Gowan,[89] he asked Costello to lead the legal team. Churchill's British lawyer, Hartley Shawcross, told his client that "Costello is said to occupy easily the leading position at the Irish bar and he impressed me as being undoubtedly a fighter."[90] However, the former Taoiseach did not get an opportunity to defend the Prime Minister, as the matter was settled out of court.[91]

A libel action which did go to trial involved two Irish institutions—*The Leader* magazine, and poet Patrick Kavanagh. Kavanagh took exception to a profile of him published in *The Leader* in October 1952, and sued for libel. Among other things, the profile referred to Kavanagh holding court in McDaid's pub, surrounded by younger artists: "The great voice, reminiscent of a load of gravel sliding down the side of a quarry, booms out ... With a malevolent insult, which, naturally, is well received, the Master orders a further measure ... 'Yous have no merit, no merit at all'—he insults them individually and collectively ... His observations on contemporary city life are shot through with a superficiality and lack of perception." However, the profile also acknowledged that Kavanagh was "our finest living poet", that he had been "harshly" treated by the State, and that his poem *The Great Hunger* was "probably the best poem written in Ireland since Goldsmith gave us *The Deserted Village*".[92]

According to his biographer, Kavanagh didn't expect the action to come to trial, anticipating that *The Leader* would agree an out of court settlement.[93] Curiously, Costello indicated at the time that it was Kavanagh who wouldn't settle. He told Tom Bodkin that he had "a certain amount of sympathy with the Plaintiff though I think he was very wrong in bringing the action in all the circumstances and particularly in not giving us an opportunity of doing something before the Proceedings were instituted. However, I suppose he knows his own business best."[94]

The trial was a public sensation—future Chief Justice Ronan Keane, who attended as a law student, recalls members of the public queuing out the Round Hall of the Four Courts and down the quays trying to get in. The level of public interest was only matched by the Arms Trial almost 20 years later.[95] The Kavanagh action opened on Wednesday 3 February 1954, before a newly appointed judge, Mr Justice Tommy Teevan. Kavanagh's legal team was led by former Fine Gael TD Sir John Esmonde; Costello led for the defence.

The offending profile was read in full, and Kavanagh's counsel claimed that he had been "gravely injured in his character, credit and reputation and in his profession as a writer and journalist, and had been brought into public hatred, scandal and contempt". Kavanagh told the jury that "a wild life is total anathema to me".[96] In his cross-examination, Costello demonstrated a detailed knowledge of Kavanagh's writings, and compared the relatively complimentary tenor of the profile in *The Leader* with Kavanagh's own published criticism of other people's work, which according to his biographer was "far more vicious and personal".[97] Observers were struck by Costello's effective way of appealing to the jury, contrasting his "plain man of the people persona with Kavanagh's profession of himself as an artist".[98]

The profile had referred to "the ceiling of his Pembroke Road flat on which his friend Brendan Behan has woven such delicate traceries of intermingling colour to suggest a London sky at evening".[99] During the second full day of cross-examination, Kavanagh vehemently denied being a friend of Behan, becoming quite heated on the subject. One of Behan's brothers, Seamus, wrote directly to Costello after reading newspaper reports of this evidence. He said that Kavanagh had perjured himself. "I have frequently seen Mr Kavanagh in my brother's company, and I have been myself introduced to Mr Kavanagh by my brother in McDaid's of Grafton Street (Harry Street). You may make what use you wish of this letter."[100]

However, Costello didn't need to use the letter, for on the day it was written he was able to produce in court a copy of Kavanagh's novel *Tarry Flynn*, signed by the author: "For Brendan, poet and painter, on the day he decorated my flat, Sunday 12th, 1950" (the month was not included in the inscription). As Kavanagh's biographer noted, this badly damaged his credibility with the jury, "who may have had difficulty in following the heavily literary content of the cross-examination, but who could recognise what appeared to be a palpable lie on his part as to his relations with Behan". The book had been given to Costello by Rory Furlong, a half-brother of Behan's, who had also been annoyed by Kavanagh's evidence.[101]

Costello's cross-examination was relentless, forensic, and devastating for Kavanagh. The poet spent a total of 13 hours in the witness box, answering 256 questions from his own counsel, and no fewer than 1,267 from Costello. At one point his return to court was delayed for 20 minutes as he was examined by a doctor. Kavanagh referred to his tormentor as the representative of a "small, pernicious minority", but then apologised. Costello brushed off the comment, saying he took no offence from it.[102] This exchange took the venom out of the cross-examination—but by this stage, Costello had done what he needed to do.[103]

It took the jury just an hour and a quarter to decide that Kavanagh had not been libelled. He was "stunned ... and dreadfully upset" by the verdict. There was some criticism of Costello's cross-examination, then and later, as being unduly aggressive. But Kavanagh evidently didn't feel that way—he voted for Costello in the 1954 election.[104] The poet was also reported to have said of Costello, "If that bloody fellow had been working for me, I'd have won me bloody case!"[105]

As well as recognising Costello's legal skills, he also recognised that the new Taoiseach might feel—or be made to feel—a sense of obligation towards him, and that he would therefore be a soft touch. Costello did in fact have a great respect for the poet, and spoke of his sympathy for him as he faced serious poverty (although of course as a barrister his first responsibility was to win the case for his client).[106] By the time the case was appealed, he was Taoiseach and therefore played no role in the proceedings. The Supreme Court granted the appeal, but the case was settled before coming back to the High Court. Kavanagh let it be understood that he had got nothing out of it because *The Leader* had no money, but in fact he did receive an undisclosed lump sum.[107]

A more immediate prospect of some financial gain was through the Taoiseach, who he proceeded to hound in search of a job. For Christmas 1954, he sent Costello a copy of a new poem, "Prelude". The Taoiseach responded that he wished he could "acknowledge more gracefully and more substantially the grace and substance" of the poem.[108] In February, Kavanagh wrote to "the man who of all people in Ireland probably knows me most intimately", saying his economic position was "impossible" and he would have to emigrate. He suggested a number of solutions to his plight, which he indicated had first been suggested by Costello himself "though I failed to take up the cue at the time". These were a grant from the Arts Council, or a job in the Radio Éireann newsroom, or in the publicity department of Aer Lingus.[109]

The Taoiseach set to work, trying to persuade the President of UCD, Michael Tierney, to provide Kavanagh with a job, while also putting pressure on the Arts Council to do something for the poet. He told Paddy Little, the Director of the Council, that "the underlying idea is to give assistance to a person of literary achievements who is in need of encouragement perhaps more than financial aid".[110] Kavanagh may have disputed the latter observation, as he was at this time recovering in hospital after having a lung removed. The Taoiseach visited him in hospital, spending over an hour with the poet.[111]

At the end of May, Costello wrote with good news—Tierney had arranged for Kavanagh to deliver lectures in UCD. He also believed the Arts Council would be prepared to "sponsor" him in some capacity. Costello suggested a commission for a volume of poetry, a critical study, or a book of essays.[112] Kavanagh replied that he "would like very much to put into book form my arguments regarding the nature of the poetic mind; this could be a very interesting book ... This would not be essays but a loosely continuous argument under a generic title."[113]

The Council agreed to this suggestion, but predictably the promise of money in the future wasn't enough for the poet. At the start of July he wrote to Costello to announce that his landlady was threatening to evict him by the end of the month because he owed over a year's rent. He asked the Taoiseach to see if the Council would give him £100 up front.[114] This Costello did, telling Little that "it would all be part of the effort to help one of our great living poets to survive and would, I believe, be within the competence of the Council even if no return were ever received for the expenditure".[115] Not surprisingly, the Council didn't agree, especially as "Mr Kavanagh has let it be known that he is to receive a grant from the Council and that he feels entitled to spend any such money that he may receive on any purpose that he himself thinks fit."[116] However, under strong pressure from the Taoiseach, the Council gave in and agreed to commission Kavanagh to write the book, with a £100 advance.[117] As an indication of how the Council members felt about this, they adopted at the same meeting a standing order banning all future individual applications for financial assistance.[118]

This wasn't the end of the matter, as was usual where money and Patrick Kavanagh were concerned. He wrote to Costello in June 1956 sympathising on the death of his wife—and also seeking an appointment to talk to the Taoiseach about his financial situation.[119] At around this time, the poet had sought the payment of the remaining £100 from the Arts Council, which was only due when he finished the book, "and became abusive when he met with a refusal".[120] This was presumably what he wanted to talk to Costello about, but the balance of the money doesn't appear to have been paid.

There is no doubt that Kavanagh had found a very powerful patron in Jack Costello. It is possible that the Taoiseach's support was due to a guilty conscience after their court encounter, but it is far more likely that it was another example of his humanitarian instincts. He collected various hard-luck cases throughout his life, and did his best to help them. He continued to do this after he left office—for instance, he frequently gave Kavanagh lifts in his State car.

On one such occasion, the irrepressible poet asked Costello's Garda driver, Mick Kilkenny, to buy him a half-bottle of whiskey in the Waterloo House on Baggot Street (the inference being that he was barred from that establishment at the time). Costello said a Garda on duty couldn't go into a pub and offered to go in himself, but the driver insisted on doing it to save the former Taoiseach the embarrassment of being seen in a pub. Characteristically, Kavanagh complained about the price, as the whiskey was sixpence more than other places. Equally characteristically, after Costello was dropped home he asked his driver to take Kavanagh wherever he wanted to go. The poet told Kilkenny that Costello was a "wonderful man", who was never too busy to pass the time of day with him.[121]

As well as a very busy professional life, the period as leader of the Opposition between 1951 and 1954 also saw an increasing volume of constituency work. Costello was now a national figure, and had to deal with correspondence from all over Ireland as well as from Dublin South-East. He spent a lot of time dealing with requests from constituents seeking help getting jobs or housing. As he wearily told a Dublin Corporation official some time later, "notwithstanding abundant evidence to the contrary, my constituents have a child-like belief that I am able to get houses for them ..."[122]

Not every request, though, was so mundane. In September 1952 he got a letter from Michael Gallagher of Gort, who complained that his neighbour "has got an unlicensed bull for his seven milch cows, which is danger to us next the wall outside. If he break out, our heifer is in danger. See to him please." Costello's secretary, Ita McCoy, wrote that he "considers this the prize letter of his political career, and therefore does not want to part with it". He did, however, want the local TD to look into the matter.[123] After all, every vote counts.

Politics was allowed to intrude as little as possible into domestic life. In 1953, *The Irish Home* magazine sought to do a feature on his home life, following a similar article on President O'Kelly. Positive coverage was assured by the promise that the text and the photographs would be submitted to him for approval before publication, but he declined anyway, as "my wife and myself do not wish the privacy of our home to be the subject of public comment".[124] Family life continued to be important to him, especially now that grandchildren were arriving. He was known to his grandchildren as 'Pampam', while Ida was called 'Nangie'—a result of the inability of their first granddaughter, Jacqueline FitzGerald, to pronounce Grandpa and Granny properly as a small child.[125]

At this time, the youngest Costello daughter, Eavan, went for a medical examination before taking up a job as a librarian in UCD. A heart problem was discovered, which needed surgery to insert an artificial valve. She had to go to London for this pioneering surgery, being one of the first people to have it.[126] However, by March 1953 she had recovered enough to take up her job.[127]

Wilfrid's troubles continued, and it appears that he was in residential care at this time. The Abbot of Glenstal, Dom Bernard O'Dea, wrote in February 1952 to say he had received "an excellent letter from him ... in which he admitted his unreasonableness to the family". In reply, Costello said, "Wilfrid is continuing to make progress. He is quite settled down and writes very cheerfully."[128] This may have been a reference to his time in a psychiatric hospital in Scotland.[129]

In the Dáil, Costello continued to be influenced by his professional background. In July 1953, he supported a Courts of Justice Bill, despite concerns that some of its provisions would impinge on judicial independence, because it also provided for increases in judicial salaries. He claimed that judges had been hit by the economic downturn just as the unemployed had, and that salary increases were needed to ensure they could continue "to keep themselves free from not merely the actuality of corruption, but from the possible breath of corruption". Intriguingly, he denied a personal interest, saying that "not merely have I no ambitions and no desires but I rather think I have no opportunity of ever finding myself upon the Bench".[130] Whatever about ambition and desire, he was about to be offered an opportunity for a place on the highest bench of all.

The offer came from an unlikely source—Eamon de Valera. Following the death of Supreme Court Justice John O'Byrne (Costello's predecessor as Attorney General) in early 1954, the Cabinet agreed that the Taoiseach should approach the leader of the Opposition to see if he was interested in the vacancy. According to his own memorandum of the conversation, de Valera phrased the offer in a rather indirect way. "I said I didn't know whether he would under any circumstances consider it, or whether in the present circumstances he would feel at liberty to consider it." Costello replied that "he had burnt his boats and realised the consequences. He had given up hopes of an easy life and he could not give the opportunity for charges of the Sadlier and Keogh type to be made against him."[131]

The latter reference was to two Irish MPs who in 1852 took office under Lord Aberdeen, breaking their pledge to remain in independent opposition at Westminster. The fact that their names were still common political currency just over a century later shows the damage to their reputations. Clearly, this leader of the Opposition felt it would be impossible for him to take a judicial appointment offered by the Government, though de Valera was at pains to stress that the offer was due to "his position at the Bar, and our duty to get the best Supreme Court possible". But the political implications of acceptance must have been clear to both men.

Political principle played a part—but so did personal preference. Jack Costello frequently said he had no interest in being a judge, saying he preferred "to be fighting my cause, either as an advocate or a politician ... A Judge has to be aloof, living in a rarefied atmosphere of seclusion."[132] He also felt he wouldn't have been able to stop being an advocate from the bench—like Cecil Lavery, who was notorious for interrupting counsel's argument to summarise in a more succinct way the point being made.[133] Most who knew him agreed that he wouldn't have suited, or enjoyed, life on the bench.[134] After his refusal, the appointment went to Martin Cyril Maguire, who had been called to the Inner Bar on the same day as Costello in 1925, and who was already a judge of the High Court. The Minister for Finance, Seán MacEntee, must have had mixed emotions at this result. He had, on cost grounds, argued that a High Court judge, who would not be replaced, should fill the £3,700-a-year place on the Supreme Court bench, rather than appointing from outside the judicial ranks.[135] But he had missed an opportunity of getting rid of his most formidable constituency rival.

And electoral considerations were about to become critical again, with two poor by-election results pushing de Valera into a general election. The vacancies were caused by the deaths of two Fine Gael TDs, Dr T.F. O'Higgins of Cork Borough, and James Coburn of Louth. The significance of the result was not the double Fine Gael victory in the 4 March polls, but the scale of the swing towards the main Opposition party. In Louth, the Fine Gael vote increased from 35 per cent in the 1951 general election to 43.4 per cent. The swing in Cork was even more pronounced, from 30 per cent to 44.3 per cent. Costello later told the American Ambassador that the "landslide" in the Cork by-election had been a "great surprise" to Fine Gael.[136]

On the evening the results were announced, the Government met in Leinster House. Shortly before 11 p.m., the Director of the Government Information Bureau, Frank Gallagher, announced that the Taoiseach was "of opinion that it is necessary that a general election should be held as soon as the financial measures required to provide for the public services have been completed".[137] This was taken to mean a quick election after the Vote of Account was put through the Oireachtas. Newspaper reports suggested that this statement "came as a surprise even to prominent Fianna Fáil deputies".[138]

Lemass, who was in London at the time, later told Fine Gael's Patrick Lindsay that he disapproved of the announcement, as he felt there was really no need for an election.[139] Many backbenchers were said to be "distressed by the prospect of campaigning immediately under the impact of two very heavy defeats" and brought pressure to bear on the Cabinet to delay polling day.[140] In this manoeuvre, de Valera was helped by his customary ambiguity of phrasing—precisely which "financial measures" was he referring to? Costello submitted a parliamentary question the day before the Dáil was to resume after the by-elections to try to get an answer to that question. In the face of this prompting, de Valera phoned Costello to tell him the election would be held on 18 May, after the Budget, making for a very long campaign indeed.[141]

The Taoiseach claimed that delaying until after the Budget would allow voters "to be presented with all the essential facts concerning the State finances", as well as allowing for the use of the latest register of electors.[142] Costello accused him of bowing to political expediency, putting the country "to the trial and the expense of an unnecessarily long drawn out election", and pointing out that if the Government was calling an election because it had lost public support, "it can have no authority to bring in a Budget".[143] That Budget would also, presumably, be designed to appeal to the voters.[144]

MacEntee's last Budget did indeed contain a reduction in income tax, as well as an increased subsidy for wheat and flour. Costello characterised it as "a recantation" of the policies introduced in 1952. "The proposals in the Budget as a whole are an admission of the failure of those policies and in many respects they furnish striking justification of the charges that we made ... that the [1952] Budget ... contained wholly unjust and unnecessary over-taxation."[145]

Two issues dominated the campaign itself: the economy, and the relative merits of coalition and single-party government. Labour was intent on driving a hard bargain if it was to participate in government again. In 1952, it had determined that a special delegate conference would have to approve any proposal to enter government. As the campaign opened, the party leadership stated that they would only enter a coalition that was "publicly committed in advance to an agreed programme of economic and social measures in broad conformity with Labour policy". In particular, the party was insisting on the reintroduction of the food subsidies abolished by MacEntee in 1952. The British Ambassador observed that they were attempting to entrench them-selves so deeply that "Fine Gael ... would have to advance nearly all the way to meet them".[146] De Valera agreed, accusing the party of demanding the right to veto government policy. "Even as a small minority it is the will of the Labour Party that must prevail."[147]

Fine Gael clearly had to stake out its own position, without alienating Labour. Costello stated that while his party would do its best to maximise its own support, it would "invite those other parties especially representative of important sections of the national life to join with it and participate in the creation and conduct of the vigorous, courageous and constructive govern-ment which the country so urgently requires. In such a Government there would be neither domination by a majority nor dictation by a minority, but co-operation for the common good." He added that collective responsibility would be observed in the same way as in a single-party government[148] (which would be a change from his first administration). He went further towards the end of the campaign, insisting that it would be "contrary to the national interest for Fine Gael to govern on its own" even if it had a majority.[149]

Costello responded to attacks by Lemass on the alleged instability of the first coalition by pointing out that it had lasted longer than the outgoing Fianna Fáil government. He added that the public conflicts between Lemass and MacEntee "suggest that all has not been heavenly harmony" over the past three years.[150] He insisted that the one difficulty of the Inter-party Government was Dr Browne, "a personality whom the public have had in the last three years a far better chance of understanding". He added with satisfaction that Browne had "now become the difficulty of the Fianna Fáil party".[151]

Despite his airy dismissal of Noël Browne, he evidently felt slightly defensive about the fall-out from the Mother and Child affair. At the opening of the campaign, he assured a Fine Gael constituency meeting that "Ireland has always been jealous of its reputation for fair treatment of the minority."

However, he quickly added that despite this, he could not accept "the secularist view that would suggest that the Church and the leaders of all religious persuasions are to play in our life but a small and isolated part".[152] A month later, he accused Fianna Fáil of mounting a whispering campaign claiming that Fine Gael were intent on "persecuting the Protestants". To disprove this, he pointed out that his party had the highest number of candidates from "the minority".[153]

During the campaign, Costello made sure to supply a script for all his speeches to the newspapers "so that there could be no possibility of mis-representation or, rather, no really effective possibility of misrepresentation or distortion of what I said". But he believed that no matter what he said "my speeches would be misrepresented and words would be put into my mouth that I had never uttered".[154] He made a virtue of his refusal to set out a detailed policy for government. "Policy ... cannot be based on the flimsy structure of extravagant promises made during election times, but on the calm consideration of all available facts ... when, being restored to Office, we have learned as only a Government can the full story and the full state of affairs." He said Fianna Fáil demands for specifics were "designed merely in the hope of embarrassing us in the coming election campaign, and in an effort to divert public attention from their own misdeeds ..."[155]

Costello told voters that election promises "would dishonour you as much as they would dishonour us. We do not believe that the Irish people are to be bought ..."[156] The Opposition was "refusing to tie its hands for the sake of electoral gain. It is a curious position for a Government to have got itself to that it descends to taunting an Opposition for not making dishonest promises ..."[157] In particular, he refused to give a commitment to restore food subsidies. At the final Fine Gael rally in O'Connell Street in Dublin, he said Fianna Fáil had been reduced to asking if he was going to reduce prices to 1951 levels. This, he said, was impudence. "It is as if a motorist, who had knocked down and injured some people, were to question the competence of those who were seeking to bind up their wounds and to criticise the general behaviour and driving of other users of the road." Given the Government's unpopularity, it was perhaps wiser to avoid promises, and stick to criticism. This he did with relish. Accusing MacEntee of mounting "a flesh creeping campaign", he noted acidly that "there is a great deal less flesh on the people to creep than there was three years ago ..."[158]

The British Ambassador observed that the Opposition's "main attack, since the Budget of 1952, has been upon the scale of taxation and state ex-penditure. They do not commit themselves, despite repeated invitations from the Government, to how they would reduce them: they are content to exploit popular dislike of Fianna Fáil's comparatively austere policy ... Mr Costello is not committing himself to a thing yet."[159] However, it is not true to say that the Opposition, and the potential Taoiseach, ran an entirely negative campaign.

Costello dusted down his *Blueprint for Prosperity*, first outlined at the 1953 Fine Gael Ard Fheis, for the campaign trail: no break with sterling, the creation of a domestic money market, a Capital Investment Board, encouragement for domestic saving and foreign capital.[160] Industry would be developed "under the stimulus of Capital investment, and through increased agricultural exports, whose economic effect on the country is even more beneficial than Capital investment". He tentatively expressed a preference for encouraging industry through tax relief rather than increased protections, "which tend to raise prices and thereby put up the cost of living".[161] And he said the proposed Capital Investment Board "would indicate in what field any liberation or relaxation of restriction [on foreign capital] might not be to the advantage of the Irish community".[162] This cautious sidling towards a more open economy was seized on by Fianna Fáil, and the *Irish Press*, which accused Fine Gael of being unpatriotic.[163] Costello responded by promising "the continuance, as a permanent feature of our economy, of the protection of industry with a view to its progressive expansion".[164]

While he had been forced to backtrack, Costello had given an important, if muted, pointer towards future policy developments. In fact, he had already cautiously hinted at dissatisfaction with protection in the Dáil. In the course of a lengthy speech criticising Lemass's Restrictive Trade Practices Bill (which he claimed would be ineffective, counterproductive, and also possibly unconstitutional), Costello also criticised protectionism. He said Ireland had more restrictive practices than other countries, which had been "bred in the atmosphere of restrictionism which has unfortunately been associated with the national policy of industrial development". However, he was careful to stress that he was referring to "the intensified campaign or policy of protectionism which was inaugurated in 1932 ... Irish industry was protected and encouraged long before 1932."[165]

The elections results revealed a stunning victory for Fine Gael in Dublin South-East. The party took a second seat at the expense of Noël Browne, running for Fianna Fáil for the first and last time. Fine Gael activists had been targeting this second seat since 1951. As the secretary of the Sandymount Branch advised Costello in November of that year, "The votes are there ... it is really a matter of hard work—and I'm not particular whether it's MacEntee or Browne we oust."[166] Hard work was certainly put in—the Sandymount members were so enthusiastic they organised a branch meeting for New Year's Eve, 1953.[167] The constituency organisation was comparatively well funded too, thanks to a number of "large subscriptions" collected during the 1951 campaign by then Attorney General Charles Casey for Costello, which hadn't been spent in the earlier campaign.[168]

Costello won his highest ever share of the first-preference vote, at 42 per cent. His surplus was large enough to bring in his running mate, economist John O'Donovan. The Minister for Finance, Seán MacEntee, with 22 per cent of the vote, was fewer than 500 votes ahead of Noël Browne, a gap reduced to just 108 before he took the last seat. MacEntee had been extraordinarily generous to his running mate, allowing Browne to distribute personalised election literature, despite the reservations of his election workers, who feared his seat could be in danger.[169] Characteristically, Browne didn't remember this generosity in his autobiography, where he claimed MacEntee's "people dominated the party organisation in the constituency ... I knew I wouldn't be allowed to win."[170]

In any case, MacEntee had a very close shave. At Costello's retirement dinner in 1969, the Fine Gael Director of Elections for the constituency, Tommy Doyle, recalled MacEntee "standing at one end of the room [in the count centre in Bolton Street], a worried man and not in good health. He got there by the skin of his teeth. John Costello walked up to him, he took him by the hand and he congratulated him warmly. He [MacEntee] was visibly moved." Evidently perturbed by this image, Costello dryly observed that MacEntee was "a redoubtable warrior, with whom I made many a struggle in the Dáil chamber and on practically every street corner, notwithstanding what Tommy Doyle says, in my constituency".[171]

Constituency activists were naturally overjoyed at the result: Fianna Fáil in disarray, Costello topping the poll, O'Donovan elected on his first attempt, and Browne defeated. The annual report of the Sandymount branch rated "the smashing up of the Fianna Fáil party in the constituency as our Number One achievement".[172] Nationally, the results were equally good for Fine Gael, as the party continued the revival begun in 1951. Its share of the vote rose to 32 per cent and it gained 10 seats on the last general election result, to give a total of 50 (although this included Dillon and Flanagan, returned as Independents in 1951). Fine Gael was now just 15 seats behind Fianna Fáil. Labour had 19 seats (including the outgoing Ceann Comhairle, Patrick Hogan, who was returned unopposed), Clann na Talmhan had 5, Clann na Poblachta 3, and there were 5 Independents.

There was no doubt that there would be a new government, and no doubt either that Jack Costello would be at its head. On the face of it, this is slightly surprising, because Richard Mulcahy was still officially the leader of Fine Gael. His son later wrote that the reasons for him standing aside in 1948 were no longer relevant, but that the question of him replacing Costello never arose.[173] Presumably the question was settled in 1951, when Costello was recognised as leader of the Opposition, and during the election campaign, when he was clearly seen as de Valera's rival for the office of Taoiseach. In any case, Labour would have been as reluctant to serve under Mulcahy in 1954 as they were in 1948. Costello's return to the office of Taoiseach wasn't universally welcomed within the family—both his wife, Ida, and his eldest daughter, Grace, were upset at the prospect.[174]

The identity of the next Taoiseach may not have been in doubt, but there was plenty still to be settled in terms of policy. There followed intensive negotiations between Fine Gael and Labour on a coalition agreement. The British Embassy noted that Fine Gael needed Labour support to form a government, "and it remains far from clear whether Labour will reduce its price or if not how Fine Gael can pay it".[175] The smaller party demanded four Cabinet seats—including Industry and Commerce, to give it an input into economic policy. Labour also insisted on a detailed policy programme. As the party's historian observed, "Labour ... had learned from experience that if the devil is in the detail, it was best to summon these demons and deal with them at the outset."[176]

One of the key issues was food subsidies, given Labour's election campaign focus on their reinstatement, and Costello's refusal to commit Fine Gael. The initial Fine Gael draft of the programme offered an examination of the facts and an "early" announcement by the Government of measures to reduce the cost of living. This vague aspiration clearly wasn't going to satisfy Labour, who countered with an alternative draft, promising a 6d decrease in the price of a pound of butter from 1 July, as well as a reduction in the prices of flour and butter from 1 October. Costello drafted the compromise which was eventually accepted: as an indication of the Government's determination to reduce the cost of living, there would be an announcement within a fortnight of a reduction in the price of butter, while the prices of other commodities would be examined with a view to reducing them as soon as possible.[177]

Given the respective party positions during the election campaign, this was clearly a victory for Labour. However, Costello claimed (unconvincingly) to the American Ambassador that it was his idea, not Norton's. "Everywhere he went during the campaign ... people had asked him not so much to bring down the price of tea or bread, but rather to bring down butter prices ... he is convinced that Mr de Valera's Government made its fatal mistake by destroying the subsidy on butter all at once."[178] He later repeated much the same thing in the Dáil—he had been asked about reducing the price of butter "by the women and the children at every meeting I addressed throughout the country ... I did not say I would, but I made up my mind that if I were ever in a position to do it, I would do it."[179] Costello claimed that when he got back into the Taoiseach's office he consulted the Director of the Central Statistics

Office, who said that "butter was a staple and necessary article of diet ... of every section of the people, rich and poor". A butter subsidy would also, perhaps not incidentally, give "some little relief to the dairy farmers".[180]

On welfare, another key issue for Labour, the original Fine Gael draft simply promised to improve Social Welfare services. Labour countered with specific promises—pension increases, improved payments under the Workmen's Compensation Act, and retirement pensions for men at 65 and women at 60. All the Labour demands were included in the final draft of the programme.[181] Whatever about the more conservative elements within Fine Gael, Costello had committed himself to pensions at 65 and 60 during the Dáil debate on Fianna Fáil's Social Welfare Bill in 1952: "I am in favour of such a provision and always was in favour of it when it was put into Deputy Norton's Bill."[182]

Health might have been expected to provide more difficulty—after all, Fine Gael had been alone in its opposition to Jim Ryan's Health Act. The initial Fine Gael draft promised to improve the organisation of the health services, to expand them so that no-one would be denied medical or surgical aid because of lack of means, and to provide better hospital and dispensary accommodation. Labour called for the removal of health "from the field of acrimonious political discussion", the fullest and most effective use of the provisions of the existing Health Act in consultation with Local Authorities and other interests, and on the basis of the experience gained to determine "what further measures may be necessary to ensure proper provision of modern health services for the people". Fine Gael could hardly be expected to accept the reference to the "existing Health Act" they had so vociferously opposed. The final compromise took its beginning from Labour (removing health from "acrimonious discussion", consulting with Local Authorities and other interests) and its end from Fine Gael (improving and expanding health services, with no-one denied treatment because of their means). The Fianna Fáil health legislation was tactfully not mentioned.[183]

Fine Gael agreed to a number of other Labour demands, including an Agricultural Wages Tribunal and a specific commitment to continue the protection of Irish industry.[184] The statement was issued simultaneously by Fine Gael and Labour Party headquarters on 31 May.[185] Labour didn't get all it wanted, but it certainly drove a hard bargain, considering that it had not done nearly as well in the election as had Fine Gael. The latter party had, according to the British Ambassador, "gone a very long way indeed to meet Labour's demands".[186]

Clann na Talmhan also decided to support the new government, and on the morning the new Dáil met a party meeting confirmed that Blowick would once more join the Cabinet as Minister for Lands, while Clann na Poblachta offered the coalition external support. When the Dáil met on 2 June, Costello was nominated by Mulcahy, with Norton seconding and Blowick also speaking briefly in support. By far the longest speech was made by MacBride. He repeated his preference for a national government, then explained why he would be supporting Costello as the best alternative to such an arrangement—because it reflected the will of the people as expressed in the election, and because inter-party government was superior to the single-party variety. MacBride added that he would have voted for Costello anyway as "a man of integrity, honour and ability ... I am satisfied that he is a man fitted to occupy the position of Taoiseach and that he is the man whom the people desire to have as Taoiseach."[187]

De Valera's nomination was defeated by 66 votes to 78; Costello's was supported by 79 votes to 66. The difference in the totals was due to Jack McQuillan, who abstained on the vote for de Valera but then voted for Costello. Of the other Independents, Alfred and Thomas Byrne supported Costello, Ben Maguire voted for de Valera, and Donegal Independent William Sheldon (who had supported the First Inter-party Government) abstained. The Ceann Comhairle, Labour's Patrick Hogan, did not, of course, vote. Costello's election was greeted with applause from the TDs supporting him, "in which some people in the public gallery joined".[188] The new Taoiseach-elect thanked the Dáil for the honour conferred on him, while recognising "the serious problems that have to be faced".[189]

Later, after receiving his seal of office from the President, he announced his Cabinet. Norton was Tánaiste again, as well as taking the Department of Industry and Commerce; his party colleagues Brendan Corish (Social Welfare), Jim Everett (Justice), and Michael Keyes (Posts and Telegraphs) were also in Cabinet. Blowick of Clann na Talmhan was back in Lands. Mulcahy returned to Education and MacEoin to Defence, while Dillon went back to Agriculture—he later claimed to have been offered a choice of Justice, Finance or Agriculture, but said he had no interest in being a minister if it wasn't in the latter Department.[190]

Finance was a difficult portfolio for Costello to fill. He wanted McGilligan to take it again, but his old colleague pleaded ill-health, and became Attorney General instead. When Dillon also declined, he turned to Gerard Sweetman, who had made himself invaluable in opposition as the energetic and efficient Fine Gael Chief Whip. He may have been less popular with some of the rank and file deputies, who were said "to regard him as heifers must regard the man who is driving them to market".[191] The British Ambassador reported to London that Costello "obviously places much reliance" on Sweetman, who he described as a "glutton for work".[192] But Sweetman was also a conservative on economic matters—he was described by *Hibernia* magazine in 1969 as "one of the keenest minds of the nineteenth century".[193]

Costello appears to have offended him by saying that he would always have available the advice of McGilligan and John O'Donovan, the economist who was appointed Parliamentary Secretary to the Government. According to Cabinet colleague Tom O'Higgins, Sweetman was "extremely annoyed. He was determined to be his own man and did not feel the need for help from anyone else."[194] O'Higgins suggested the remark was made in private, but it was evidently widely known, as Seán MacEntee referred to it in the Dáil. In 1955, he congratulated his successor on having "shaken himself free, not only of the Attorney-General but also of the Parliamentary Secretary to the Government ... He [Sweetman] is, I think, one of the ablest men in the Government and I think ... one of the most tenacious and courageous."[195] Tenacious and courageous he certainly was—but he had reason to be resentful as well.

The other difficulty was what to do with Seán MacBride. Freddie Boland, the Irish Ambassador in London, told British officials that Costello "felt under some obligation" to MacBride, but that the younger generation in Fine Gael "had refused to accept his inclusion in the Government".[196] This seems extremely unlikely. In fact, MacBride was offered a Cabinet position, but declined. It appears the Clann executive was not in favour of him taking a post,[197] but in any event he believed that with only three TDs, his party was not in a strong enough position to take part. As he put it in a public statement on the eve of the Government's formation, "With all the good will in the world on the part of all concerned, I would ultimately find myself in the position of a lodger who was not paying for his keep." He stressed that there was no policy difference, nor was there disagreement on the portfolio he would occupy. The Clann simply didn't have enough TDs.[198]

MacBride's decision may have been a relief to many in Fine Gael, but Costello appeared to regret it. Replying to a letter of congratulation from MacBride's wife, Catalina, the new Taoiseach wrote, "We are sorry that Seán will not be more closely associated with us than he is."[199] But, as he told the Dáil, the new Government would have "his full support and ... his experience and his knowledge and goodwill".[200] Events were to show that MacBride was not quite as reliable or supportive as Costello expected.

Instead, Liam Cosgrave, just 34 years old, became Minister for External Affairs. Other young ministers included Corish (35) and Tom O'Higgins (37) in Health, which left the average age of the Cabinet at 52.[201] Costello made the job offers himself[202]—there is no indication of whether he consulted with Mulcahy as party leader before doing so. He only told Tom O'Higgins at one o'clock on the day the new Dáil was to meet that he wanted him to be Minister for Health. The two men met in the Law Library. Costello had just finished a court appearance and was on his way to change before going to Leinster

House. He told the younger man he wanted him to join the Government. "I am sure I must have looked as astonished as I felt, because I remember his saying something like: 'Do you want to?' to which I stammered an affirmative answer and asked: 'What post?' He then said, quite formally: 'I want you to become Minister for Health in my Government, and furthermore, I want you to take health out of politics'. And that was that."[203]

The other new face in the Cabinet was Pa O'Donnell, victor of the Donegal West by-election in November 1949, who became Minister for Local Government. The Parliamentary Secretaries appointed by the new government were Michael Donnellan of Clann na Talmhan, who was given responsibility for the Office of Public Works; Labour's William Davin, who was appointed to the Department of Local Government (after his death in 1956 he was replaced by Dan Spring); and four members of Fine Gael: Denis O'Sullivan, who was Chief Whip, Oliver J. Flanagan, who was Parliamentary Secretary to Dillon in Agriculture; Patrick Crotty in Industry and Commerce; and Costello's newly elected running mate, John O'Donovan, who took the new post of Parliamentary Secretary to the Government.[204]

O'Donovan's position was so novel that questions were asked about it in the Dáil. Costello explained that he was not given any executive functions— he was instead to devote his experience as an economist "to assisting the Government and myself in the formulation of economic and financial policy and in the examination of particular economic and financial problems as they arise ... it is this way that his special ability, knowledge and experience can, at present, be best utilised in the national interest".[205]

In his Dáil speech on the nomination of ministers, Costello said the country had suffered in the previous six years because of the political instability of both the Inter-party and Fianna Fáil governments. This government, he insisted, "has stability and it is going to last".[206] His old friend Arthur Cox—who was one of the Taoiseach's 11 nominees to the Seanad, where he sat as an Independent—was perhaps more prescient: "You have a tough time before you—but at least it will be interesting!"[207]

Chapter 11

GIVING THE PEOPLE QUIET

"We have given the people quiet over the last nine months and we want to maintain that situation."[1]

JOHN A. COSTELLO, MARCH 1955

"We have done reasonably well despite the many bewildering problems with which we were confronted."[2]

JOHN A. COSTELLO, NOVEMBER 1955

As the Dáil prepared to break up early in July, Costello was pleased with progress. "I believe that the new Government has got off to a good start. I felt it was vital to secure from the start public confidence in the new administration and to make it clear that there was no longer any political instability. I believe both objectives have been attained. The personnel of the new Government—particularly because of the number of young Ministers in it—has given satisfaction."[3]

This point was frequently mentioned in commentary on the new government. *The Leader*, for instance, praised "the weight given to members of the younger generation" in the Cabinet. An editorial considered that the new Taoiseach "envisages a radical revolution of previous fiscal policy", although it claimed this would have been easier if the Government hadn't committed itself to restoring the butter subsidy.[4] As well as a (relatively) youthful image, the new government also enjoyed a solid majority in the Dáil. And the Cabinet seemed likely to be more harmonious without Clann na Poblachta. As Liam Cosgrave put it many years later, there was "less nonsense talked with MacBride and Browne missing".[5]

Shortly after Costello was elected Taoiseach, he received a courtesy call from the American Ambassador, William H. Taft III. Grandson of a president, and son of an influential senator known as "Mr Republican", Taft was very well connected indeed. He was also friendly with Costello already, which may in part explain his flattering comparison between the new Taoiseach and his predecessor. "He does not retain the formal approach and aloofness of Mr de Valera. His manner is pleasant and unassuming. He listens to others with much greater interest and attention than his predecessor does." However, Taft went on to observe, "I have noted that he is somewhat impressionable and that his temper is easily aroused by what he considers unreasonable."[6]

Jack Costello would have to confront much that he considered un-reasonable in his second term as Taoiseach, but for the moment things were going smoothly. Maurice Moynihan, excluded from Government meetings during the First Inter-party Government, carried out his normal duties as Secretary to the Government in the Second, making things considerably easier for Costello. The Taoiseach also had a car at his disposal again, and two Garda drivers—Sergeant Paddy Byrne, who had driven him before, and Mick Kilkenny, who found Costello to be "a thorough gentleman" who never uttered an evil word and always showed charity to others. Unlike some others over the years, he didn't keep drivers hanging around for hours outside the house, and always ensured they had a meal.[7] Costello rejected a Garda offer to put an unarmed patrol at his house, as had been done in 1948; in fact no special police protection arrangements were made for any of the new ministers.[8]

Ironically, the first potential crisis the Government faced concerned the same issue which helped sink the First Inter-party Government—health. As we saw in the previous chapter, Fine Gael and Labour had differed in their views on the 1953 Health Act. Now, a Fine Gael Minister for Health, Tom O'Higgins, had to implement it. During the election campaign, his Fianna Fáil predecessor, Jim Ryan, had signed a regulation requiring health authorities to provide certain services from 1 August. But according to O'Higgins, the authorities simply weren't ready to provide the services. And if the regulation remained in force it would mean the existing limited right to hospital accommodation for dispensary patients and insured workers would in effect be abolished.[9]

That, at least, was his view. But he also realised that his Labour Party colleagues, who had supported the Act, "would not take kindly to an apparent postponement of its operation at the behest of a Fine Gael Minister". After briefing Costello and Norton, O'Higgins went on a charm offensive with Labour TDs, culminating in an address to a meeting of the Parliamentary Labour Party. He must have been persuasive, because his position was endorsed, with Jim Larkin proposing a vote of confidence in his handling of the issue.[10] Legislation postponing the implementation of the 1953 Act went through the Dáil before the summer recess. To ensure it became law before 1 August, the new Seanad was "exceptionally" summoned to meet on the earliest possible date, 22 July.[11]

The "ticking time-bomb" left for O'Higgins by his predecessor had been defused; but the new Minister proved to have more fundamental changes to the health system in mind. An advisory body he set up in January 1955 recommended an insurance-based approach, rather than the State-funded service envisaged by both Noël Browne and Jim Ryan. Costello made his preferences clear in the Dáil some months later, when he lauded a Budget provision to give tax relief for medical insurance. "We want our people not to have their hands out to the taxpayer for their health service but rather to be enabled, out of their own resources, to establish and maintain their own independence by providing against their own ill-health ... We feel that this line offers the best approach both from the point of view of the individual and of the moral law."[12] It also fell in with the wishes of the medical profession.

The political implications of health insurance were not lost on his son-in-law, Alexis FitzGerald, who urged Costello to have O'Higgins "go to town" on the issue, as "it is desirable and would attract the middle classes".[13] Legislation establishing the Voluntary Health Insurance Board was introduced in 1956;[14] in the words of historian Dermot Keogh this measure, which was continued by the new Fianna Fáil government in 1957, "effectively put pay to 'socialised' medicine in Ireland".[15] This was a victory for Fine Gael, in line with the approach championed in opposition by Costello. In particular, it showed adroit handling by O'Higgins, one of the real stars of the Second Inter-party Government, and one of the Fine Gael politicians who retained a relationship with Labour in the long years of opposition after 1957.

More fundamental than health for relations between Fine Gael and Labour was the economy. As we saw in the previous chapter, one of the first decisions of the new government was to reduce the price of butter. The new Minister for Finance, Gerard Sweetman, pointed out that this would cost £1.25 million for the year, while increased Civil Service pay sanctioned by the new government would cost another £900,000. He demanded new economies "at once" to offset this extra expenditure. "No time should be lost in pruning services and personnel regardless of the criticism which any worthwhile economies will inevitably provoke." On 26 June, the Government agreed that each minister would examine his estimate along with Sweetman to reach agreement on economies, with disagreements being submitted to a newly established Estimates Committee, made up of Costello, Norton, Dillon and Sweetman.[16] Thanks to the work of this committee, the 1955 Estimates showed a decrease of £2.75 million—as Costello pointed out in the Dáil, this was *after* £2 million had been spent on the butter subsidy, so the reduction on the previous government's spending was close to £5 million.[17]

Clearly, if it had been up to Sweetman, the Government would have been following a more conservative economic programme. He had quickly demonstrated that he had "the strength of character and independence of outlook necessary for a Minister who hopes to maintain the ascendancy of the Department of Finance over all other Departments".[18] This did not, of course, make him popular with his colleagues. But at the end of 1954 he was still on good terms with the Taoiseach, writing a letter of thanks to Costello on Christmas Eve "for your kindness and understanding ... over all the past six months. At times I fear I must have sorely tired your patience." He concluded by referring to himself as "the most explosive member of your Cabinet".[19]

Sweetman was to have cause for combustion early in the New Year. In the Dáil, he had insisted that the butter subsidy would be the last concession during the 1954/55 financial year.[20] But in January, the Government decided that the Exchequer should absorb an increase in the price of tea, at an estimated cost of £1.2 million. The decision was made after a special 4-hour Cabinet meeting, which also discussed the wider Exchequer position.[21] The cost of living had been one of the main issues in the election campaign, so there was considerable pressure on the Government, especially the Labour Party, to keep prices down. As *The Leader* commented, "Mr Norton at least will be able to reassure Mr Larkin that the Labour tail is wagging the dog. No more unfortunate method could, however, have been chosen ..."[22] British Ambassador Walter Hankinson agreed, saying "this curious Conservative-Labour alliance" had struggled to reconcile its promise to reduce both the cost of living and taxation. The tea situation had intensified this difficulty "to a degree almost pathetic". The end result "served to support the guess that Mr Norton ... was being awkward to his majority colleagues". Hankinson also pointed to the curious torpor of the Government, saying it had "transacted the minimum of essential business before the long summer recess, produced nothing of much interest during the autumn session, and adjourned ... for the longest permissible Christmas recess".[23]

In February 1955, Costello told the Fine Gael Ard Fheis that on entering government, they had "no illusions as to the magnitude of the effort that would be required to repair the ravages of ... three wasted years and to revitalise the Irish economy ... I think I am entitled to say that we have not done too badly ... the economic barometer is now steady with at least a tendency to rise ..."[24] With some understatement, the British Embassy described the speech as "not particularly inspiring".[25] In truth, it was an extraordinarily downbeat assessment, particularly for an Ard Fheis. The Government had very little to show for its efforts, apart from a reduction in the price of butter and a stabilisation of the price of tea. What had happened to Costello's *Blueprint for Prosperity*, his new thinking about capital investment and the attraction of foreign capital?

During the election campaign, officials in the Department of the

Taoiseach had looked at Costello's proposal for a Capital Investment Board. A memorandum for de Valera concluded that while the proposals bore some similarities to those advanced by J.M Keynes, Costello had "given very few details". He hadn't, for instance, made any distinction between public and private investment. Whoever wrote the memo appeared unimpressed with the concept.[26] However, that was while Costello was leader of the Opposition. Once he became Taoiseach, officials dutifully began exploring the idea, seeking information from the London Embassy about how the British National Investment Council had operated. The answer was: not very well. Freddie Boland reported the impression that the Council was "purposeless and unnecessary" and had been allowed to lapse.[27]

Costello doesn't appear to have pushed the idea any further at this point. Instead the running was taken up by Sweetman, who proposed a "survey" of the State capital programme to find out whether "this large expenditure is contributing to national wealth and productive employment", and whether it was correctly balanced between productive and non-productive investment.[28] A committee of officials, chaired by Ken Whitaker, was established, but it worked slowly. After two years, it had completed a general review and a chapter on rent control, and had done preliminary work on the ESB and housing.[29] The general survey suggested that "works of social benefit and works of inferior productivity which entail a redistribution rather than an increase of incomes should ... be kept within bounds and a better balance struck in the State capital programme as between economic and social objectives".[30] Given Costello's vocal support for social investment in housing and hospitals, this was hardly what he was looking for. In any case, a committee of officials was emphatically not what he had advocated in opposition.

In 1956, the Commission on Emigration recommended the establishment of an Investment Advisory Council; Sweetman argued that this would serve "no useful purpose".[31] A similar demand from a trade union delegation in June of that year provoked a defensive response from the Taoiseach. He said he had advocated the establishment of a Capital Investment Board, and he hadn't changed his mind. But, he added rather lamely, "the Government could not do everything at once".[32] Costello did manage to include the Capital Investment Committee as part of his landmark economic speech in October 1956 (see Chapter 13). But the fact that it took two and a half years, and a desperate economic situation, before he could get his idea adopted as Government policy, speaks volumes about the limits on his influence, even as Taoiseach.

It was the same story with his other big idea, that of opening up the Irish economy to more foreign investment. As we saw in Chapter 7, he had in 1948 described the Control of Manufactures Act as "outmoded and outdated" and "humbug".[33] But little had been done during the term of his first government to address this issue. Second time around, he appeared more anxious to act. On 25 June 1954, the Taoiseach asked the Department of Industry and Commerce to examine possible changes to the Control of Manufactures Acts, which ensured factories were Irish-owned and Irish-financed. He wanted to know if the legislation should be amended "so as to permit, subject to any necessary safeguards, a greater inflow of external capital into Irish industry".[34]

A powerful head of steam was building up for change; in January 1955, the State investment bank, the ICC, called for relaxations to the Control of Manufactures Act.[35] The Central Bank and the Department of Finance also called for changes to the restrictions on foreign capital, although they thought the Act was so "outmoded and unsound" that it should be repealed rather than amended.[36] Change was also urged by two members of the Commission on Emigration, economist James Meenan and Costello's son-in-law Alexis FitzGerald. The latter argued that "no other well-intentioned legislation has so retarded the progress of industry". FitzGerald pointed out that if capital was important, then "intelligent experienced capital, i.e. capital in the control of experienced entrepreneurs, is most vital".[37]

But Industry and Commerce was having none of it. In September 1954, Norton said his Department did not believe amendment was necessary, while repeal would be "a breach of faith towards those who have set up factories here on the basis of the existence of the Acts". The memorandum warned that allowing uncontrolled access to foreign capital would lead to "the danger of exploitation for selfish purposes [which] would constitute a grave threat to existing and future industrial development". Norton suggested instead that the Government should indicate it wanted to encourage external capital with "some form of brochure dealing generally with the opportunities offered by this country to foreign investors".[38]

When, some months later, Costello's private secretary mentioned that nothing had actually been done about restrictions on foreign capital, "the Taoiseach referred to the evident reluctance of the Department of Industry and Commerce to amend the Acts and stated that, in these circumstances, no further action was called for ..."[39] It was an extraordinary admission of helplessness by the Taoiseach.[40] As with the Capital Investment Board, further moves on foreign capital would be included in Costello's October 1956 speech, but in the meantime, some progress was made in attracting investment from abroad, even without fundamental changes to existing legislation.

Norton's brochure, *Window into Ireland*, was produced in August 1955. The Tánaiste managed to generate considerable interest among investors in visits to Germany and the United States.[41] The Government also accepted an Anglo-American oil company's proposal to build an oil refinery in Cork. These moves led to criticism from de Valera and other supporters of the traditional policy.[42] Costello vigorously defended the attraction of foreign investment in a speech to the Federation of Irish Manufacturers in February 1956. He insisted that foreign industrialists were being encouraged to establish factories to produce goods not already produced in Ireland, or produced in insufficient quantities, and in particular goods for export. The view that complete national control of industry must at all costs be preserved was, he argued, "incompatible with our large scale emigration, our substantial unemployment and our expressed determination to provide a decent livelihood here for our people". Adequate powers remained to protect the national interest. But it was clear that Ireland was "in danger of missing the tide if we do not press ahead vigorously now with our policy of accelerating industrial development by inducing foreign industrialists to invest in this country".[43]

In the meantime, the economic situation had begun to worsen. In July 1955, Costello told the Dáil that the balance of payments would be kept under review, but he didn't believe "we need fear any crisis before the end of the present year". He added that credit restriction and import controls aimed at controlling a deficit tended to "bring other evils in their train". Prevention, he said, was better than cure.[44] However, his optimism proved unfounded, and prevention ineffective. The balance of payments deficit increased from £5.5 million in 1954 to £35.6 million at the end of 1955. A number of factors were blamed—agricultural and other exports to Britain had fallen because of the deflationary policy being followed by the Government there, while consumer spending at home rose after a national wage increase.[45]

But there may have been another factor—the Government's decision in February 1955 not to follow an increase in British interest rates. This was the first time an Irish government had followed such an independent course, and Costello explained that it did so on the basis that "adjustments of this kind should be dictated by our own interest rather than by events and conditions elsewhere".[46] It also helped to keep the cost of living down, and was politically popular.

But Cormac Ó Gráda and Patrick Honohan have argued convincingly that the decision to hold interest rates down was a major factor in the balance of payments crisis. Of the £50 million deterioration they calculate in net foreign assets in 1955, they estimate that £10 million was due to a fall in exports (largely in cattle), £17 million to extra imports, and no less than £22 million to a turnaround in private non-bank capital flows. This they mainly attribute to firms repaying loans from British banks by borrowing from Irish banks at lower interest rates. The decision to delay interest rates was, they argue, "a policy blunder. The authorities simply failed to observe the implied interest rate discipline of the fixed exchange rate and integrated financial market with Britain."[47]

This connection between interest rate policy and the balance of payments wasn't fully recognised at the time. For Sweetman, it was 1952 all over again. Like MacEntee, he believed the main problem was consumer spending, and that deflation was the way to choke this off and restore the balance of payments. His colleagues, particularly Norton and Costello, were inclined to follow the policy they had advocated in 1951/52—do nothing, and wait for the imbalance to work itself out. Eventually, though, Sweetman had his way, introducing curbs on consumer spending at the start of 1956, including import levies and new taxes on consumer goods. Predictably, these had the same effect as MacEntee's Budget of 1952—increased unemployment and emigration—while the balance of payments was already sorting itself out unaided.[48] The Government also backtracked on its interest rate policy. Costello announced at the start of 1956 that a "temporary" increase in rates was needed, because the problems in the balance of payments were "no mere self-regulating deficit, but a deficit which if left unchecked might well grow out of hand".[49]

Despite the problems with the balance of payments, there were some grounds for optimism about the economy. As Costello told the February 1956 Fine Gael Ard Fheis, unemployment was just 6.8 per cent, the lowest recorded up to then. Although this may have been due to increased emigration rather than job creation, the Taoiseach could also point to an extra 7,000 people in industrial employment over the 1953 figure, while 1955 had seen a 3.5 per cent increase in manufacturing production over the previous year. "The economy in general is sound. It may be that our people desire the Government to go too quickly towards the achievement of their aims. We have always insisted that we cannot do everything and certainly we cannot do everything at once."[50] Costello and his colleagues seem to have believed that if the balance of payments problem could be resolved, they would be set fair to resume a policy of economic expansion. That view may have been unrealistic, given the underlying problems in the Irish economy and society revealed in the 1956 census. In any case, the Suez Crisis was about to fundamentally change the economic outlook.

Economic tensions were naturally evident at Cabinet. According to Patrick Lindsay, who joined the Cabinet in late 1956, the three most influential people around the table were the Taoiseach, Attorney General Patrick McGilligan, and Sweetman. Another strong influence was James Dillon. According to Lindsay, if Dillon spotted a potential difficulty, he would begin by saying he wanted to sound a "Three Bell Warning". "When James sounded the 'Three Bell Warning', we all listened with respect and in the majority of cases accepted his judgement."[51] Dillon of course was now a Fine Gael minister, rather than an Independent, and he found the change not to his liking. He complained in his memoir that he had to bring his proposals to the parliamentary party first, "where every jealousy and cross-current could be manifested, and every mischief-maker and pest busied himself to make difficulties. One had to fight one's way through the party, and then go through the whole procedure again in cabinet. So I did not so much enjoy being a Fine Gael Minister."[52]

The feeling was reciprocated by some of his party colleagues. John O'Donovan told the American Embassy in March 1955 that Dillon might be sacked, as he was proving an embarrassment and had alienated farmers. "He said that when Dillon agreed to receive a farmers' delegation he would first insult them collectively and before the audience was over would usually insult each member individually." O'Donovan observed that Dillon would only listen to two members of the Government: "He would do what Mr Costello told him to do, and Mr McGilligan had at times the power of persuasion over him." O'Donovan believed either Sweetman or Cosgrave might replace Dillon: "They both were quiet, would listen to delegations and reason with them, and did not 'blow off steam' in public." He also believed he might be considered for the position himself.[53] O'Donovan's comments may have been wishful thinking, but they indicate a certain disquiet about Dillon that is understandable given his contribution to the collapse of the First Inter-party Government.

The other major figure in Cabinet was Norton, the Tánaiste and Labour leader. Lindsay believed him the best speaker in the Dáil—not excluding Dillon and Costello—saying he was "incisive, sharp and devastating in debate". He recalled Norton persuading the Cabinet not to lay off turf workers. "Look, the difference between their wages and what you get on the dole is about a pound or thirty shillings. Why cause an upheaval of this kind when it's not going to cost the country that much?"[54] Not that Norton and his colleagues could ever be described as radical. As *The Leader* dryly noted, the Government was conservative, and while some ministers were described as Labour, a stranger "would be unlikely to pick them out from their colleagues on the strength of their public utterances". The same piece also asked whether Labour's main achievement in government, the retention of food subsidies, was really the best way limited public funds could be used to help the less well off, claiming that if the money had been used to boost social welfare payments instead, benefits would have been increased by 60 per cent.[55]

However, the retention of food subsidies was vital if wage claims were to be kept under control. In February 1955, the Congress of Irish Unions gave notice to the employers' body that it was terminating the 1952 wage agreement. Unions claimed wages had fallen behind prices; in fact, according to statistics prepared for the Taoiseach, earnings had gained slightly against prices between 1951 and 1954.[56] However, perception is more important than statistical reality, and the perception among workers was that they had fallen behind, which was a problem for the Government, particularly Labour.

When the Dáil resumed after the 1955 summer break, Fianna Fáil sought to take advantage of this perception. Lemass put down a motion of no confidence in the Government, on the grounds of its "failure to prevent the increase in the cost of living".[57] The Government argued that it had done all it could to control inflation, and that the effect of increases in the cost of living had been mitigated by increased industrial and agricultural earnings, and by the restoration of public confidence in the economy.[58] Costello indignantly denied promising to reduce prices during the general election, comparing Fianna Fáil "lies" on this issue to the propaganda techniques of Hitler and Goebbels (how this was not found to be "unparliamentary" language is not clear). He said his government had said it would try to control the cost of living—and, if this proved impossible, to allow incomes to rise. He also claimed that the Government had kept the cost of living down by not following the British interest rate increase. And he pointed out that unemployment in the third quarter of 1955 was the lowest recorded up to then, at 5.4 per cent.[59] The Government comfortably won the vote. In a subsequent by-election campaign, Costello claimed the no-confidence motion had had the effect "of demonstrating the unshakeable unity and strength of the present Inter-party Government, and of consolidating the Parties behind the present Government".[60]

Unions and employers were unable to reach agreement on a general wages policy, and in mid-1956, the employers sought Government intervention. When representatives of the two sides met Costello, Norton and Sweetman, they rehearsed their grievances. Costello adopted a hands-off approach, advising them to hold direct negotiations, and "if necessary" come back to the Government. However, it was clear that there was something the Government could do to help keep a lid on inflationary pressure. One of the union representatives made it clear that "any interference with food subsidies would certainly be followed by a demand for wage increases".[61] Despite the parlous economic situation, the Inter-party Government left food subsidies alone, and in October the trade union movement decided not to begin a campaign for a national wage increase.[62] However, when the new Fianna Fáil government abolished the subsidies, unions announced they would be seeking higher wages to compensate their members,[63] thus sparking another wave of industrial unrest.

The only change to Costello's second Cabinet was the appointment of Patrick Lindsay as Minister for the Gaeltacht in October 1956. According to Lindsay, he was approached about the move a year earlier by Costello, who was "clearly worried about the way in which the Government was operating and by a lack of energy in some areas". Costello told Lindsay that he was to be appointed Parliamentary Secretary to Mulcahy, and that when the new

Department was set up, he would take over at Education while Mulcahy became head of the new Department of the Gaeltacht. Whether or not that was the original plan, it didn't work out that way; Mulcahy remained in Education, and Lindsay was appointed the first Minister for the Gaeltacht.[64]

In his second government, as in his first, Costello frequently had to act as referee between feuding ministers. For the obvious reason that he was in charge of the purse strings, Sweetman was frequently one of those involved; Norton was frequently his sparring partner, as the interests of Industry and Commerce and Finance clashed.[65] But where did the Taoiseach stand on the conflict between Finance and the other Departments? A very good indication is given by the serious row between Norton and Sweetman in 1956 over the future of the railways. In June of that year, the Board of CIÉ appealed to the Government to take action to "prevent the collapse of public transport" and save the railways. A committee of investigation, chaired by Dr J.P. Beddy, was established to report on the future of public transport.

A Finance memorandum was sent to the committee, arguing that "railways have outlived their economic utility"; that investment in railways "can no longer be regarded as capital expenditure which could properly be met by borrowing since the railways cannot be made solvent"; and that rail should be replaced by road transport as quickly as possible. Norton was furious, writing to Beddy to assure him the memorandum did not represent Government policy. Separately, he accused Sweetman of "an unpardonable breach of propriety", saying the more he thought about it, the more appalled he became. He complained to Costello that it was "simply outrageous that one Government Department, irrespective of the Government's views, should seek to accomplish the abolition of the railways". Sweetman argued that the committee was supposed to hear the views of all interested parties, and Finance was obviously interested as it would have to come up with whatever funding was needed.

Getting wind of the memorandum, Seán MacBride wrote a strong protest to Costello, warning that he would publicly oppose any move to destroy the railways, adding that such a policy was "tantamount to political suicide. The Government is already unpopular enough without, on the eve of a by-election in the one 'railway constituency' we have [Louth], advocating the scrapping of the railways." Costello assured him the Government "have not entirely lost all political sense! ... You may take it that this ... is merely a Finance memorandum. The Government ... are not bound by it in any way ... The memorandum was sent by the Department as an expression of an extreme orthodox financial view."[66] What is perhaps most significant about this episode is the evident distaste Costello felt for the "extreme orthodox" views of Finance as the Government headed into its final months.

It also demonstrated that MacBride, unsurprisingly, was not content to silently support the new government. Despite his decision not to take a Cabinet seat, he had an elevated view of his own importance. When a committee was set up to represent backbench members of Fine Gael, Labour, Clann na Talmhan and Clann na Poblachta, he quickly became its leading light, acting as liaison between the committee and Costello. In April 1955 he wrote to the Taoiseach, expressing the hope that the committee "will be able to do useful work. There is a wide field of policy and administration over which there is little or no controversy but which ... receives but scant attention." He attached a list of the matters the committee members would like to raise with ministers—a very comprehensive list indeed, and one which reflected many of MacBride's own obsessions, such as forestry.

His suggestion that the committee should have a chance of discussing these matters directly with the ministers involved was underlined by Costello—he clearly felt MacBride had to be humoured and kept on side. And the Clann leader was not disposed to be trifled with. He asked Costello to ensure that ministers were "as co-operative as possible in their relations with the Committee". After all, he pointed out, the members had the "task of allaying the criticism of their own organisations and friends ... Where a committee of this kind unanimously makes a suggestion which is not contrary to Government policy, it is essential that they should be satisfied."[67] Seán MacEntee suggested that MacBride had acted as "the fixer" for the Government on this committee, the aim of which was "to persuade the doubtful and to silence critics among the rank and file ... He had invariably succeeded in securing acceptance of the Government's programme and it was very largely due to his talent for equivocation that the Coalition had held together."[68]

MacBride also urged new economic thinking on the Government, suggesting to Costello in November 1955 that Italy's Vanoni Plan "is well worth looking at. Many of Italy's problems are similar to ours." MacBride had prepared a report on the Plan as rapporteur to a committee on economic questions of the Council of Europe.[69] The Plan proposed the creation of employment through investment in "impulse sectors" such as agriculture, public utilities and public works. It had also attracted the attention of Seán Lemass, who used it as the blueprint for proposals he prepared with the help of Todd Andrews and outlined in a speech to a Fianna Fáil meeting in Clery's Ballroom in October 1955.[70] The Taoiseach dismissed Lemass's plan, claiming that because it ignored agriculture, it had "no more solid basis than a froth of words".[71]

MacBride also maintained his interest in foreign affairs, urging Costello in October 1956 to send food and medical supplies to help the people of Hungary "in their heroic struggle for national liberty and religious and political freedom". He (immodestly) added that he would "willingly place myself at the Government's disposal" if his services could be of use. After all, he "personally knew" Austrian Foreign Minister Dr Figl and the Hungarian exile leaders.[72] The following month he wrote to Liam Cosgrave, in New York for the UN General Assembly, advising him that he had been asked by the Greeks to travel to New York to advise them on Cyprus. He told his successor that he had asked US Ambassador Bill Taft to find out what the State Department's view was, and suggested rather imperiously that Cosgrave or Freddie Boland "may have an opportunity of putting out some feelers about it too".[73] Cosgrave mordantly observed to Costello that MacBride's ideas on Cyprus "are quite impracticable and unlikely to appeal to anyone, even Greece ... I need hardly say that his presence here would be no assistance ... but, if he has decided to come, I suppose there is little we can do about it."[74]

Shortly afterwards, the Government would be wishing MacBride had remained distracted by foreign affairs. In fairness, MacBride must have felt at least a twinge of jealousy at the role being played on the world stage by Cosgrave. This role was made possible by Ireland's admission, after a 10-year wait, to the United Nations, and will be examined in the next chapter. Like O'Higgins, Cosgrave was one of the successes of this Cabinet, another astute appointment of a young man to an important portfolio.

The Republic's admission to the United Nations was viewed with some apprehension north of the Border. In Belfast, Prime Minister Lord Brookeborough felt it was inevitable that the Irish delegation would attempt to raise partition. In that event, the Northern Cabinet felt that the British delegation should include a representative of Northern Ireland to counteract such propaganda.[75] This view was understandable given the record of MacBride in Costello's first government. But Costello, like Cosgrave, was determined not to try to repeat the "sore thumb" policy of MacBride.

Shortly after the election, the new Taoiseach discussed the North with Vincent MacDowell, who had unsuccessfully contested Dublin South-East for Labour. MacDowell knew what he was talking about. A former IRA activist, he was interned in Belfast Jail during the Second World War, but had since adopted a more peaceful approach—he was later to be a founder member of the Northern Ireland Civil Rights Association (and later still a Green Party councillor in Dun Laoghaire).[76] His advice to Costello was simple: do as little as possible. "If the Irish Government plays a waiting game of caution and inactivity, it will be speeding the process of change in the North ... openly encourage the maximum amount of economic co-operation and public friendship. At all times strive publicly to reduce the tension and promote goodwill between the Unionists and ourselves, and lower the intensity of feeling on all sides. Avoid flamboyant gestures and inflammatory speeches like the plague. On an unofficial level, they merely irritate, on an official level they provide the badly-needed rallying point for disintegrating Unionist sentiment ..." MacDowell pointedly referred to the Chapel Gate election of 1949 as an example of counterproductive campaigning.[77]

But other elements had different ideas. Just 10 days after the new government took office, the IRA carried out a daylight arms raid on Gough Barracks in Armagh. Fifteen men, some of them in British Army uniform, got away with nearly 300 rifles and automatic weapons without firing a shot.[78] The drift towards violence in the North was accelerated by the actions of Liam Kelly, who, after being expelled from the IRA, founded a breakaway Republican paramilitary group, Saor Uladh, with a political wing, Fianna Uladh. In 1953 he was elected to Stormont for Mid-Tyrone, but his victory speech was judged to be seditious and he was sentenced to six months in prison. However, Seán MacBride had plans for Kelly, and in the summer of 1954, he and the other Clann na Poblachta Oireachtas members nominated him for the Seanad. His address on the ballot paper was given as Crumlin Road Jail. Perhaps as a consequence, he was elected on the first count on the Labour Panel.[79]

The publicity attracted by Kelly—and in particular his election to the Seanad—caused disquiet among mainstream Nationalists in the North. Shortly after his election, Cahir Healy wrote to Costello, advancing the old appeal for admission of Northern representatives to the Dáil. In addition to the usual arguments, he now had a new one: if constitutional nationalists were excluded, while Kelly was a senator, "it may well be assumed in the North that the physical force policy is the only one which meets with approval down here".[80]

In advance of Kelly's expected release from prison in August, Costello was invited by Fianna Uladh to attend the welcome home celebrations in Pomeroy. The Taoiseach politely declined, but expressed his "pleasure that Mr Kelly will shortly regain his freedom and that he will be available to take his place as a member of Seanad Éireann ... after the summer recess".[81] The homecoming, addressed by MacBride, degenerated into a riot when the RUC tried to seize Tricolours under the recently introduced Flags and Emblems Act.[82] 40 people, including nine policemen, were injured.[83]

IRA arms raids continued. In October, five soldiers were shot during a raid on a depot in Omagh, leading to what was described as "the most intensive man-hunt ever undertaken in Northern Ireland".[84] The Gardaí reported that this was an official IRA action (as opposed to Liam Kelly's escapades), with a strong input from the Dublin battalion. The report added that the Dublin IRA had in recent times concentrated on training in "commando" tactics—"it now seems obvious why this kind of training was so dominant".[85] In response, Costello convened a meeting with the Garda Commissioner and the

Secretaries of the Departments of Justice and Defence, along with the Tánaiste and the Ministers for Justice and Defence.[86]

Costello explained his Northern policy to the Dáil later that month, during a debate on a motion put down by Jack McQuillan calling for the admission of Northern representatives. The result was never in question, as Fianna Fáil joined Fine Gael in opposing the motion. However, Clann na Poblachta and Labour (including Norton and the other ministers) voted in favour. Costello didn't seem too bothered by the lack of Inter-party unity. Although Fine Gael didn't allow a free vote, he acknowledged that others might take a different line. "On this matter, I have said that each individual is free to do as he liked." More important, he said, was his statement of Government policy on partition and the use of force. In this, he passionately defended the elected government's Constitutional monopoly of force, and argued that coercion of Unionists would not only be wrong, it would be counterproductive. "Let us have a united nation, but let it be a union of free men and not a united nation in which a fifth of the population have been cowed by force or fear and feel themselves enslaved ... There are some people who are prepared to die for Ireland; I want to appeal to the youth of Ireland to live and work for Ireland. That is the best contribution they can give to the solution of Partition."[87]

The next day's *Irish Times*, which deplored Norton's vote, strongly praised Costello's "statesmanlike" speech: "both his own and his party's prestige has been enhanced as a consequence"[88]—although it should be remembered that Costello had said similar things before. The *Irish Times* may have been impressed; the Army Council of the IRA was not. In a statement issued in November, it attacked both Costello and Kelly without naming either. No Republican, it insisted, could give allegiance to either of the states established by the British; by implication, becoming a member of the Seanad was a betrayal. The IRA also dismissed the declaration of a republic. It had done "nothing more than make confusion more confounded, and the glib use of such terms as 'freedom in this part of Ireland' has served only to lull the youth of the country into a false sense of national well-being". By using one of Costello's favourite phrases, the Army Council made it clear who it was talking about. The statement then went on to promise a "carefully planned and progressive policy of opposition to the British occupation forces in the Six Counties", adding that the campaign would be conducted "with charity towards all, with malice towards none"[89] (except, presumably, Britain).

The British Ambassador praised Costello's "important and forthright attack upon the use of violence by unconstitutional bodies", but said Labour's attitude "must be regarded with concern", even thought the motion in question did not deal directly with the IRA.[90] A very different picture was being presented to the Commonwealth Office by Freddie Boland, the Irish

Ambassador to London. He told Sir Percival Liesching, Permanent Under Secretary, that while the Labour ministers "had been rather half-hearted in the discussions of anti-IRA policy ... the issue had been thrashed out most firmly by the Prime Minister [sic] and others". He added that the most important part of Costello's speech had been approved by Cabinet and "was therefore a definite declaration of considered Government policy". Boland then went on to assert that the Government "meant business" and was determined "to take extremely strong action against the IRA". Speaking in confidence, he told Liesching that the Gardaí were preparing for a "swoop" designed to forcibly suppress the organisation. "Mr Boland said that when the time came there could be no half-measures. Ordinary judicial processes would have to be suspended and military courts set up and wired camps installed for the detention of several hundreds who would be arrested." In these circumstances, he argued, it would be counterproductive for Dublin to receive demands from London to take action against the IRA.[91]

The British then waited—in vain—for the promised action against the IRA. In mid-December, Boland was summoned back to the CRO to explain. Liesching pointed out that he had been led to believe that action would be taken within weeks, but was obliged to admit that the Irish Ambassador had never actually committed himself to a timescale. Pressed further, Boland indicated that the Government was worried that public opinion would not support drastic action, that there was still some Labour sympathy towards the IRA, and that in any case there had been no further violence since Costello's Dáil statement. Liesching recorded two impressions—that the Irish Government was anxious to avoid taking extreme measures, and that Boland himself "would prefer to see the more drastic course taken".[92]

In January, Commonwealth Secretary Lord Swinton told his Cabinet colleagues that the Dublin Government "were evidently apprehensive that there would not be a sufficient body of public support in the Republic for drastic action to suppress the IRA". He raised the apparent change of heart with Boland some days later. The Ambassador "deprecated the notion that his Government had got cold feet or had failed to carry their Labour colleagues with them ... the Government had felt they were taking a more statesmanlike course". Swinton, however, was not convinced. "I have little doubt myself that the Government did get cold feet, that they had trouble inside their Cabinet, and that they felt they were not strong enough to carry out their original intention."[93]

In public, meanwhile, Costello was reiterating his more conciliatory policy towards the North. In an important interview with the *Yorkshire Post* in January, he expressed his willingness to meet Brookeborough "at any time to discuss matters of common interest", hoping that such discussions would engender goodwill, preparing the ground for "the ultimate eradication of the root of all evil—Partition".[94] In Brookeborough's absence his deputy, Brian Maginess, said his government had no objection to discussing matters of common concern—so long as Éire was prepared to accept that partition was "a matter which has been finally determined".[95]

Costello, of course, was not prepared to accept any such thing. In a reply to Maginess, he pointed out that there had been no precondition about accepting partition during discussions on the River Erne, the Great Northern Railway or the Foyle Fisheries. No Irish government could accept such a position, he said, adding for good measure that the only way that partition could be finally determined "will be by its ending".[96] On the surface, the spat strengthened divisions. But, as *The Leader* perceptively pointed out, Costello's original statement implied that improved relations would have to precede discussion of partition. This, it suggested, was a welcome change "from policies which tended to stress the main point of disagreement rather than the many points of contact which exist between the divided parts of the whole country". The magazine also pointed out that Maginess had annoyed the Orange Order (as Minister for Home Affairs he had banned a number of marches through Nationalist areas)—as an aspirant to party leadership he had "seized the opportunity presented by the Taoiseach to demonstrate his 'Ulster' patriotism".[97]

In the long run, this stand did Maginess no good—Brookeborough demoted him to Attorney General under pressure from right-wingers. But Costello's approach arguably laid the groundwork for a friendlier relationship with Belfast. It also encouraged a more conciliatory attitude from Fianna Fáil. In his 1957 Ard Fheis speech, de Valera suggested the best way to solve the problem of partition was to have the closest possible relations with the people of the Six Counties, "and get them to combine with us in matters of common concern".[98] Lemass has—rightly—received much credit for his opening to the North, but he was building on foundations laid by his two predecessors. And, of course, the policy could not succeed until Brookeborough was replaced by Terence O'Neill.

In April, a group of Six Counties nationalists asked for a meeting with the Taoiseach. Faced with a challenge from Sinn Féin, they were looking for financial support for the Westminster election to be held the following month. Costello told the Secretary to the Government, Maurice Moynihan, that financial support was already being given to the Anti-Partition of Ireland League in Britain, apparently out of the confidential Secret Service vote.[99] Before meeting the nationalists, the Taoiseach suggested to MacBride, a trustee of the Mansion House Fund, that the balance in the Fund could be used to help nationalist candidates. But the Clann leader refused, as his party and Kelly's Fianna Uladh "could not oppose 'the boys in jail'".[100] Deprived of this potentially useful source of funding, Costello set up a Cabinet committee of himself, Norton, Mulcahy, Everett and Cosgrave to keep the matter under review and take any necessary action.[101]

MacBride had managed to scupper the attempt to support non-violent methods in the North—an ominous portent for future Government policy. The American Embassy referred to MacBride's "affinity for the IRA and his apparent ability to obtain 'protection' for the IRA from the Irish Government". This led the Embassy to believe "that MacBride's present connection with the IRA may be much more active and direct than is generally believed".[102] This was undoubtedly an overstatement of MacBride's involvement—the same could not be said of some other members of the Clann. And MacBride remained closely allied to Liam Kelly, the senator whose anti-partition activities were about to escalate.

Over the summer of 1955, the IRA raided two Army barracks in Britain for arms; British Cabinet Secretary Sir Norman Brook drafted a note "in friendly terms" to Dublin seeking improved police co-operation, arguing that if they wanted Irish co-operation, the letter "must not be too stiff". Prime Minister Anthony Eden, however, "toughened up" this draft. "I know that we have to take account of Irish feelings, but one day this message may be published, and there are British feelings to be considered too."[103] But the latest IRA activities were once again overshadowed by Liam Kelly's activities.

In November 1955, Kelly led members of his Saor Uladh organisation in an attack on Roslea RUC barracks in County Fermanagh. One of the attackers was killed in the raid; his body was brought back across the Border and buried after an inquest held in secret in the middle of the night.[104] The Secretary of the Department of Justice said the "police on the spot ... adopted an attitude of extreme reserve so that their investigation of the affair might not be hampered ... [but] they seem to have carried caution too far ..."[105] At a by-election meeting in Limerick, Costello indignantly denied that the Government or senior Gardaí had ordered the inquest to be held in secret. He also pointed out that those who wished to use violence to coerce Unionists into a united Ireland "are repeating the error the British made with us ... What kind of unity would be established as the result of unlawful force causing civil war—even if successful?"[106] But the bizarre nature of the inquest was only a detail; the real significance of Roslea, according to the *Irish Times*, was that gunmen believed the Republic was "a place of sanctuary for them ... That attitude is based on the obvious unwillingness of the Government to adopt a strong and realistic policy in dealing with illegal organisations ... words are not enough ..."[107]

But words were all the Government was prepared to offer. On 30 November Costello made a major statement in the Dáil on partition and the use of force. The lines of his speech were approved in advance by Cabinet.[108] The roots of the violence, he insisted, lay in partition; those who created and sustained partition therefore bore the "primary responsibility" for the existence of violence. But, "in stating where the responsibility for the evil lies, I do not condone the evil itself". For the use of force *was* evil, and would lead to civil war with Unionists. The men of violence were guilty of "unpatriotic conduct [which] dishonours the national institutions established with so much difficulty over so many years and challenges the Constitution freely enacted by the people". If the men of violence did not respond to his appeal, he said, "then the duty of the Government is clear ... We are bound to ensure that unlawful activities of a military character shall cease, and we are resolved to use, if necessary, all the powers and forces at our disposal to bring such activities effectively to an end."[109]

It was, Archbishop McQuaid told him, "very well done indeed, clear and temperate".[110] Too temperate, according to US Ambassador Bill Taft, who questioned "whether the Government's warning words will deter the fanatical members of unlawful Irish militant organisations from perpetrating further acts of violence in Northern Ireland". His scepticism seemed to be endorsed by a report later in the month from the Embassy's Second Secretary, who reported that "the Irish police do not plan to take any action to stop the recruiting, drilling or the possession of illegal arms by the IRA or other militant groups in Ireland".[111] The British Ambassador urged on Liam Cosgrave the need to take action to prevent the south being used as a sanctuary by terrorists. While he reported that Cosgrave "showed some uneasiness on this score", he got no promises of action.[112] This attitude gravely disappointed the Stormont government, which urged London to apply pressure "to ensure that the authorities in Dublin would take effective steps to put down the IRA".[113] That organisation, meanwhile, seems to have believed that an absence of violence in the Republic would save it from the threatened crackdown. As one supporter put it, "no member of the IRA was engaged in subversive activities against the 26 Counties, and ... the Government of that State had no right whatsoever to dictate policy in the northern State, which was outside its jurisdiction".[114] The irony of this partitionist attitude didn't seem to occur to the author.

Costello's approach of threatening rather than taking action was widely attributed to the need to keep Government supporters on side—not just in Clann na Poblachta, but in Labour too. *The Leader*, for instance, suggested that the Taoiseach's difficulty in drafting his statement was "to ensure that it would have the full approval of all his Inter-party colleagues as a formal statement of Government policy". The writer added that the solid support given to Costello by Labour TDs made it "a much more telling declaration than would have been a verbally more sweeping one from which there might have been an element of Labour dissent".[115] The difficulty of keeping MacBride on side was obviously even greater.

Such political considerations must have played a part; but Costello's approach was entirely consistent with his views on the use of emergency powers. As we saw in Chapter 3, he believed such powers were only useful as a deterrent, and said of Article 2A, his own contribution to emergency laws, that "every person that went to prison under that Article was a monument to the failure of that Article".[116] Despite his reluctance to resort to emergency powers, he reminded newspaper editors at the beginning of December that the Offences Against the State Act was still in force—and that they were prohibited from publishing certain matters.[117] Section 2 of that Act banned the use of "words, abbreviations, or symbols referable to a military body in reference to an unlawful organisation", and every copy of a newspaper breaching this provision was a seditious document.[118] He had strong views on media responsibility in this area, later saying it wasn't just the teaching of history which glorified the use of arms "but the action of many newspapers in featuring and emphasising this facet of our history, even at times when the use of arms was being advocated for the solution of the problem of Partition".[119] But while those prepared to use arms had been given a stark warning by the Government, they were also under increasing pressure to take action because of the activities of Liam Kelly.[120] Their decision to launch the Border Campaign in late 1956 would prove a military disaster; but by calling Costello's bluff, they indirectly caused the fall of his second government, as we will see in Chapter 13.

If Costello's approach to the North was more nuanced in his second term, so too was his approach to the Catholic hierarchy. He remained, of course, highly deferential to the bishops, particularly to Archbishop John Charles McQuaid, but he was also prepared to show some independence when it suited him, the most notable example being the Agriculture Institute. However, there were limits to this independence, and Costello was usually careful to ensure he had McQuaid's support.

In July 1956, the Bishop of Killaloe sent a blistering letter of complaint to Costello after attending the trial of a priest and nine laymen accused of assaulting two Jehovah's Witnesses. Bishop Joseph Rodgers bitterly attacked the Attorney General for allowing a case to proceed against a priest who had been "upholding and defending the fundamental truths of our treasured Catholic Faith" against blasphemy. The court evidently agreed, because while the charges against the assailants were dropped, the two victims were bound to the peace! Given Costello's reputation for supine acceptance of clerical dictation, a conciliatory reply might have been accepted. Instead, the Taoiseach told Rodgers that the law must take its course once a complaint was made, and that anyone believing blasphemy to have been committed should report it to the Gardaí. "I do not need to remind Your Lordship of the grave evils that would ensue if it came to be accepted that persons who are roused to indignation by the conduct of others—however just that indignation might be—were entitled to take the law into their own hands and to give expression to their feelings and enforce their views by violent means. If such a situation were to arise, not only would the public peace be threatened but the true interests of religion and morality would inevitably suffer." However, Costello took the Bishop's complaint seriously; he took the precaution of reading the letter to the Cabinet and clearing his reply with ministers. He also sent a copy to McQuaid, who described it as "admirable in its clarity and moderation".[121]

McQuaid, by virtue of his close control over his various clerical networks, had considerable information at his disposal which could be of use to the Government. For instance, in November 1956 he reported to the Taoiseach on "the investigations I have made" concerning four youths arrested for Republican activities. "They are certainly not bad young fellows, but misled by youthful idealism. I shall have them followed up quietly."[122] The flow of information went both ways; when Seán MacEoin supplied Costello with a memorandum on a new socialist political grouping involving Noël Browne he suggested that "it would be no harm to let His Grace of Dublin have a copy".[123] The Archbishop reaped more practical benefits from Costello too—when petrol was scarce following the Suez Crisis, the Taoiseach arranged for him to receive supplies. McQuaid was "very grateful", adding pointedly that "it is a consideration which was not shown me during the war".[124] Costello, then, was far more solicitous of the Archbishop than de Valera had been. But on occasion, he was prepared to take a line independent of McQuaid, and of the wider hierarchy.

In September 1955, the Taoiseach holidayed in Rome with his wife. The couple had a private audience with Pope Pius XII—the Taoiseach received a gold medal commemorating the proclamation of the Dogma of the Assumption, while Ida Costello was presented with a rosary blessed by the Pontiff. Pius was reported to have "expressed fervent wishes to the Irish President and Government and imparted a special blessing to 'Our beloved people of Ireland'".[125] Later, Costello met a senior Vatican official, Monsignor Domenico Tardini, the Pro-Secretary of State in Charge of Extraordinary Affairs. Tardini pointed out that the Irish Government accorded "very favourable" treatment to non-Catholics, which contrasted with the way Catholics were "persecuted" in the North. Costello explained that the Government gave "fair treatment to non-Catholics both on general principles and also in the interest of future unity". Tardini said "the favourable treatment accorded ... to non-Catholics is to him a source of some anxiety". According to the minutes of the meeting, Costello made no further reply, an indication he was not prepared to meet the Vatican's concerns on this issue.[126] To say the least of it, this is at odds with Costello's image as "ever loyal to the precepts of the church".[127]

McQuaid was accustomed to having his views accepted by the Government. For instance, when the Yugoslav soccer team played Ireland in 1955, the Archbishop had a private conversation with the Taoiseach, after which the Government advised President O'Kelly not to attend the match.[128] However, Costello resisted the Archbishop's wishes over the appointment of Seán Ó Faoláin as Director of the Arts Council (discussed below), and over the Censorship Board.

Two of the five places on the Censorship Board became vacant in mid-1956, but the Government took their time in filling them. The reason is revealed in a memorandum to Costello from the Secretary of the Department of Justice, T.J. Coyne. To meet growing criticism of the censorship regime, Coyne suggested the appointment of "broadminded persons, including perhaps one of the Protestant faith". However, McQuaid had "let it be known" that he was willing to nominate a priest to act on the Board (one of the vacancies was due to the resignation of the Chairman, Monsignor Deery). As Coyne pointed out, "His Grace ... may well nominate some priest of the diocese who is anything but broadminded. On the other hand, it is difficult not to invite him to make a nomination."[129] Finally, in December, the Government appointed Robert Figgis (a Protestant) and Andrew Comyn,[130] the latter on the recommendation of Alexis FitzGerald.[131]

However, the existing members and Costello's appointees could not work together, with the result that the chairman, Professor John Piggott, refused to call further meetings. After the change of government, he was sacked by the new Minister for Justice, Oscar Traynor.[132] The Knights of Columbanus, with the tacit encouragement of McQuaid, waged a campaign against Traynor as a result. The Minister complained to de Valera that the campaign was started because "His Grace was not consulted by the former Taoiseach or by me about recent appointments to the Board." Traynor suggested that de Valera should make an effort to secure Costello's support "so that the Hierarchy may be led to see at the outset that this Government and those which preceded it were carrying out their duties faithfully in accordance with the powers conferred on them".[133] After a private conversation with de Valera, Costello "expressed confidence in the Board as now constituted".[134]

He could hardly do otherwise, as two of the members had been appointed by him. But his position is completely at variance with the accepted image of Costello as bowing to the demands of the Church at every available opportunity. One recent writer has suggested that the dominance of the

Church "was not to be challenged for the first time until the 1980s. The state was anxious not to come into conflict with the Church on any matter, but certainly not on those considered to be of primary importance to Catholic faith and morals."[135] As we have seen, this was something of an exaggeration—control of the Censorship Board would have been seen by McQuaid as an issue "of primary importance to Catholic faith and morals", and Costello appears to have ignored his wishes. And there was certainly a clash over a matter which would not normally have been seen as concerning religion—the proposal to set up an Agricultural Institute.

The Agricultural Institute had been approved by government as far back as 1950. It was strongly backed by the Americans, who would pay the capital costs through Marshall Aid grants. However, delays in congressional approval, as well as jockeying for position between the various third level institutions, meant that little progress was made until Costello and Dillon returned to government in 1954.[136] While the various universities had somewhat grudgingly approved the plans, a new problem arose at the start of 1955, when the hierarchy suddenly expressed concern at the involvement of Trinity in the Institute. Bishop Michael Browne of Galway and Bishop Cornelius Lucey of Cork—two of the more hardline prelates, and each with a university in his diocese—were despatched to talk to Costello after a meeting of the hierarchy's standing committee. The bishops explained that they would object to involvement by Trinity "if the result would be to impair or diminish the National University, deprive its Colleges of the Faculties of Agriculture and Dairy Science, or allow Trinity to have a say in the teaching of Agriculture in the new Institute". Costello countered, with evident exasperation, that the involvement of Trinity had been agreed for some time, and no objection had been raised. Why, he asked, had the hierarchy not brought their concerns to the attention of his predecessor? "Their Lordships did not give any specific explanation ..."[137]

It is difficult to disagree with the conclusion reached by Maurice Manning: the bishops felt Costello would be a soft touch in comparison to de Valera.[138] However, they were to be sorely disappointed. Costello told Browne and Lucey that it was important not to give ammunition to those who might accuse the Government of discriminating against Protestants. He said they would be kept informed of developments, "and that every opportunity of conferring on difficulties would be given". But he certainly wasn't as accommodating on this issue as he had been on the Mother and Child Scheme—perhaps because he didn't share the concerns of the Bishops, or believe agricultural instruction to be a matter of "faith and morals".

As in the Mother and Child controversy, one of the main stated objections was the danger of increased government control, with the State accused of attempting to do what independent bodies, in this case the universities, were capable of doing themselves. In response, the Government stressed the consultations they had and would continue to conduct with the interested parties, and the Institute's autonomy from government, with a majority of the governing body being non-State nominees.[139] These assurances were of little avail, though, because the real objection was to Trinity involvement, and to the perception of the universities that they would lose prestige (and money) if they lost their Agriculture faculties.

If the controversy can be seen as a re-run of the Mother and Child affair, then the heads of the various universities played the role of the IMA. Like the doctors before them, they must have been delighted when the bishops weighed in on their side with "moral" arguments. Given Costello's views on Trinity, he might have been expected to be as open to persuasion on this issue as he had been on medical matters. But when the President of UCD, Michael Tierney, wrote expressing concerns about the surrender of his Faculty of Agriculture, the Taoiseach merely promised to pass his observations on to Dillon, adding that while the Minister would "no doubt ... consult with you ... he may not accept your suggestions".[140]

Costello had decided to fight for his government's policy, and he began a charm offensive on the hierarchy. He visited Archbishop Joseph Walsh of Tuam in July and went through the issues involved at some length, writing to him afterwards, "My justification for taking up so much of Your Grace's time must lie in the conviction that our discussion helped to remove many misconceptions as to the Government's proposal in relation to that Institute." He sent Walsh a copy of a memorandum by Dillon setting out the background to the Institute, assuring him that all interested parties had been promised "that nothing final would be determined until they had been given an opportunity of expressing their views".[141] He had also, crucially, discussed the controversy with McQuaid.[142]

Walsh was impressed by the memorandum, which "enables one to see all sides of the case", and predicted that the Institute "is going to do a great deal towards the uplifting of the country". But he warned that the facts should be made known to the public "before certain interested or prejudiced people spread false propaganda and do a great deal of harm". Armed with the memorandum, he promised "to discuss the matter fully with some people who might take a wrong view owing to want of knowledge".[143] It is possible he was thinking of his colleague from Galway. But Bishop Browne dismissed the memorandum, arguing that as the proposed institute "violates the University settlement of 1908, not even the agreement of yourself and Mr de Valera can heal its fundamental defect".[144]

Costello had been careful to keep de Valera on side;[145] now he decided to take Archbishop Walsh's advice and try to persuade the public. The occasion was a speech opening Muintir na Tíre's Rural Week in Navan, County Meath. His speech was drafted by Jack Nagle, an Assistant Secretary in the Department of Agriculture, although Costello, through Moynihan, made important suggestions, including the inclusion of a passage dealing with the religious and moral welfare of students. He also brought forward the publication of details of the Bill by two weeks, so they would be issued the day after his speech[146]—which he clearly expected to prepare the ground for greater public support for the legislation.

The tone of the speech, delivered on 14 August, was reasonable and concili-atory. The Taoiseach stressed that the proposals were a "basis for discussion" and were not inflexible. He utterly rejected suggestions that "the Institute is to be Government controlled, that it will be run by a majority of Government nominees, or that it will enjoy anything less than the academic autonomy at present possessed by the Universities". In fact, the governing body would be made up of one-third each of university representatives, agricultural organ-isations, and Government nominees. He insisted the State had no intention of interfering with the research programme of the Institute, nor did the Government intend to use the annual grant "to control the Institute in any way or to upset the accepted principle of academic autonomy".

Then he turned to "a point which is of the utmost interest to all of us, namely, the need for providing sufficiently for the religious and moral welfare of students of the Institute". For the first two years of their course, they would be at the university of their choice, completing the foundation course in science and related subjects. When they transferred to the Institute, he insisted, "every facility will be afforded for, and due precautions taken to ensure, the provision of equal care for students". He concluded by stressing that the Government's only aim was to establish an institute which would equip its students with the most up-to-date knowledge, to the benefit of agriculture and the country as a whole. And he called for "disinterested co-operation and goodwill" from those concerned.[147]

Two days later, he received a clear indication that co-operation and goodwill were unlikely to be advanced by his opponents. Bishop Browne and Monsignor Pádraig de Brún, President of University College Galway, called on him to discuss plans to open a new Agriculture Faculty in UCG. The Taoiseach expressed understandable frustration at this "somewhat strange" develop-ment. Why, he asked, had UCG not mentioned this desire before? Clearly, at a time when the Government was attempting to rationalise and (to an extent) centralise agricultural education, the creation of yet another faculty would create further difficulty. The discussion soon moved on to a philosophical debate on the merits of a central institute. Bishop Browne criticised what he termed "something resembling a factory for ... the mass production of

Agricultural graduates in one centre". He claimed the students would miss out on the advantages of university life, and in one central faculty might miss the benefits of personal attention. This was nonsense, and Costello was quick to point out the weaknesses in the prelate's arguments. After all, the students would have two years in their various universities before going to the Institute. And no one complained about medical students doing their practical training in hospitals.[148]

Bishop Lucey of Cork was also still vocal in his opposition. In September, he told a meeting at UCC organised by Macra na Feirme and the National Farmers' Association that a centralised institute wouldn't work, owing to the varied nature of Irish agriculture; that the proper function of the State was "to help the private citizen and his organisations rather than to edge them out with its own agencies"; and that while the people would vote down a government committed to socialisation, a gradual process of creeping State control could "nibble more and more from the field of private enterprise, until finally little worthwhile remains outside Civil Service control". He then criticised various aspects of the proposed institute, claiming that the Government-appointed director would be the real power, not the governing body, and criticising the Bill for putting Trinity on an equal footing with the NUI colleges.[149]

Ralph Sutton, who had married Eavan Costello in April 1955, and who lived at the time in Cork, sent a lengthy commentary on this speech to his father-in-law. Sutton pointed out that much of what the Bishop said was unfair criticism. For instance, Lucey claimed the governing body would only meet three times a year, when the draft legislation required it to meet *at least* three times a year. Sutton agreed with Lucey that Trinity was "no place for Catholics" but argued that this was irrelevant. Many of the more progressive farmers were Protestant, he said, and they had a right to send their sons to the Institute through Trinity. Anyway, Trinity was a university and its right to equal representation with the NUI "is recognised in the Constitution" (in the provisions on Seanad representation). Costello's other son-in-law, Alexis FitzGerald, had apparently advised writing a confrontational letter on the subject; Sutton counselled against this as it "would blow up the entire assembly of Bishops which is not what anyone wants".[150] This advice was astute; so were his answers to criticisms of the Institute. Costello evidently agreed with what he had to say, because he passed the letter on to Dillon, who used it as the basis for a speech to the Agricultural Science Association a few days later.[151]

In October, the secretary to the hierarchy, Bishop James Fergus of Achonry, forwarded a formal statement by the bishops—which was not being published, he said, as "Their Lordships do not wish to cause any embarrassment to the Government." After going through the concerns about academic independence and State incursion into higher education, the real reason for opposition emerged—"under the Draft Proposals, the National University is seriously injured, while Trinity College not merely loses nothing but gains a position of advantage out of all proportion" to its number of Agriculture students. Because Trinity would have representatives on the governing body of the Institute, and because the Institute would be a recognised college of the NUI, Trinity would have "an influence on the Board of Studies of the NUI, while the NUI would not have any similar voice or control in any of the councils of Trinity College". The establishment of the Institute would, the hierarchy statement continued, "involve the forcible injection into that University of extraneous and hostile elements".

The bishops stated they were concerned about damage to the NUI because it was "the only centre of university education that is acceptable to Catholic principles". Fergus said the bishops had never opposed giving Protestants "their just rights and due proportion of State endowments in accordance with their numbers". But he claimed the State had in recent years given Trinity a subsidy "out of proportion to the number of Protestants in this State ... It is a serious matter for the Irish Catholic tax-payer that he should be asked to endow an institution which is prohibited to Catholics as intrinsically dangerous, and it raises issues of very serious importance to us who are charged with the defence of Catholic Faith." The hierarchy's alternative was an institute with "effective academic freedom and autonomy ... which would have the function of co-ordinating and developing agricultural research".[152]

This was a serious challenge to the Government, couched in terms of "defence of the Catholic Faith", the approach which had proved so effective in the Mother and Child controversy. And control of higher education was just as serious a matter for the bishops as medicine—arguably more important. Given his performance in the earlier controversy, Costello might have been expected to buckle; he didn't. Notes written a few days after the hierarchy's letter arrived showed him in determined form. Up to now, the Government had not responded to charges made by individual bishops. Now, he thought, the Government must do so as the charges had been repeated. "It is essential to put on record our repudiation of certain charges explicit or implied in the memo, particularly that of State control." Given the Government's "repeated assurances", he felt it was "a little difficult to understand the repetition of the charge of the desire of the Government for State control". He also noted that there had been no objection to Trinity's role until January 1955, even though it had been involved since the scheme was first mooted five years before. Anyway, Costello argued, "justice requires that Trinity get some say in the Institute", because it already had a Faculty of Agriculture and there were Protestant farmers who should have access to the Institute. The proposed

Trinity representation on the governing body was, he added, "the very irreducible minimum".[153]

Costello ensured great secrecy over his reply, which was approved by Cabinet on 4 November. A draft had been circulated to a meeting of ministers in Leinster House two days earlier. Each copy was headed "Secret and Personal to Minister", enclosed in an envelope with a similar heading, and then put in the normal circulation envelope used for Cabinet documents.[154] Clearly, the Taoiseach felt any leak of the contents of his letter would be very damaging. It's easy to see why.

He began by repeating that the draft proposals could be changed, and were only a basis for discussion. It would be a matter of "deep concern" to the Government if the proposals had any unfavourable repercussions on Catholic university education—but they trusted that the letter "will effectively remove the Bishops' apprehensions in this respect". So far, so deferential. But Costello then went on to demolish the hierarchy's arguments point by point.

The Government, he said, would have expected the bishops "to accept without question" the assurances he and Dillon had given on State control, and "they regret that Their Lordships have thought it proper to disregard those assurances". He dismissed complaints about the appointment of the Institute's director by the President on the advice of the Government by pointing out that this was how judges were appointed. The bishops had claimed the governing body would be largely nominated by the State, when only 10 of the 34 members would be so nominated. Their assertion that the governing body had no control over the Director was even worse—Costello said it showed "a most regrettable lack of advertence to the actual terms of the draft outline". Recalling his commitment in his speech in August that the Government would not attempt to control the Institute through the grant, Costello regretted that "Their Lordships have, evidently, not given to this assurance the weight and importance that properly attach to such a declaration by the Head of the Government." Again, on the question of the moral welfare of students, there had been "a regrettable disregard of the relevant public declarations by the Taoiseach".

On alleged Trinity influence—"the forcible injection ... of extraneous and hostile elements"—Costello said the Government had been "unable to follow the reasoning" of the hierarchy. He said Trinity's representation couldn't be based on the number of Protestants in the Republic; they made up 34 per cent of the population of the island as a whole, and the ending of partition was "a primary aim of national policy". The Government did not feel obliged to respond to the point about State subsidies to Trinity, as it was not relevant to the issue at hand. He suggested the bishops should have raised it when the subsidies began in 1947, or when they were increased in 1952 (in both cases, by a Fianna Fáil government). He concluded in a conciliatory tone again; his comments were designed to remove misapprehensions, and the proposals remained open to amendment. The Government would bear the hierarchy's views in mind, "to the utmost extent compatible with the general interest of the community as a whole".[155]

It was an extraordinary document, showing a hitherto unsuspected independence of mind on the part of the Taoiseach and his government towards the hierarchy. Why did the Costello who enthusiastically bent the knee to the bishops in 1951 now stand up to them? Most importantly, of course, he believed in the Institute, while he had disapproved of the Mother and Child Scheme. Secondly, in contrast to 1951, the Government was solidly behind the scheme, while the hierarchy was split. As we have seen, Archbishop Walsh favoured the Institute, while McQuaid was at least neutral. When Costello sent him a copy of his reply to Fergus, the Archbishop replied that he would give the Government's views his "very careful consideration".[156] The official response from Fergus following the next meeting of the hierarchy's standing committee was distinctly chilly. It expressed "deep regret at the tone and contents of the document which the Government thought well to address to us". He added that the committee felt that none of its objections had been answered by the Government.[157] Costello brought the letter to Cabinet; the Government decided that "the letter does not call for any reply".[158]

However, despite this tough response to the hierarchy, the Government's plans were in serious trouble. The determined opposition from the universities was having its effect. In May 1956, Dillon wrote to Costello insisting that the proper use of the Marshall Aid funds "demands the establishment of an independent Agricultural University", though he suggested it could have a Faculty of Sociology and Philosophy under clerical control. He warned of "the danger ... that in order to avoid treading on anybody's toes we shall end up with a milk and water kind of research institute established at great cost ... which will add little or nothing to the resources of which we dispose already".[159]

But the academic opposition continued, which delayed the establishment of the Institute. And by this stage, Costello was becoming increasingly desperate for concrete achievements in a range of areas. In the course of a memorandum setting out ideas for his October 1956 policy speech (see Chapter 13), the Taoiseach suggested the Institute should be established without taking over the existing Faculties of Agriculture. "I believe that by conceding the claim of UCD and UCC to retain their existing position it would be likely to be accepted, and I think also would cost less."[160]

In the draft heads of a Bill finally approved by Cabinet in October, the Institute's scope had been reduced to that of a research body, aiming "to review, co-ordinate and facilitate agricultural research in progress and to promote additional research".[161] Costello told de Valera the plans had been changed as a result of the "considerable amount of criticism, on various grounds, from the interests concerned". The Government, he said, was now anxious to proceed and wanted the Bill introduced in the Dáil before Christmas.[162] More significant than his consultations with the leader of the Opposition were those with McQuaid. Having sent the Archbishop of Dublin an outline of the legislation, he received a prompt and cordial reply. McQuaid wrote that "the Institute that can be constructed on this basis ought to satisfy all the elements of the nation ... by reason of the fairness of representation and the specific functions of the Body. The number of times that the word research occurs in the draft—if I am not mistaken, 21 times—ought to let any person see the purpose of the Institute."[163] The American Ambassador also gave his approval; the Bill was introduced in the Dáil on 5 December, but fell with the Government. The legislation was finally steered through by de Valera, who had the name of the Agricultural Institute changed to An Foras Talúntais.[164] Later still, it became part of Teagasc.

Two postscripts might be mentioned. Given how much he resented Browne's publication of the correspondence with the hierarchy during the Mother and Child crisis, it is not surprising that Costello was sensitive about his own bad-tempered exchange with the bishops. Most unusually, he instructed his officials to remove the correspondence from the official Government files. This move was so irregular that it was noted on the file by Nicholas Nolan, who observed that the papers "should be treated as especially confidential".[165] Which was all well and good until October 1957, when the joint secretaries to the hierarchy wrote to the new Taoiseach, de Valera, seeking an assurance that he would take account of their representations.[166] Puzzled, de Valera asked Moynihan about it. On being told of his predecessor's action, de Valera rang Costello, who agreed that "in the circumstances, the papers would have to be made available" to the new government, and they were placed back in the file.[167]

The other addition to the story concerns James Dillon, who shortly after the defeat of the Second Inter-party Government met Pádraig de Brún of UCG in Dublin. De Brún said it was "a great pity" that Dillon hadn't stuck to his original proposals for a separate agricultural university. When Dillon pointed out that de Brún had lobbied against the plan, the UCG President said he had been obliged to do so, but thought the Minister should have ignored him! He thought the hierarchy were wrong in their opposition, but he couldn't say so as he had seven bishops on his governing body, and "they were bad enough as it was without adding fuel to the flames". According to his later account to Costello, Dillon "expressed astonishment that a Catholic Priest could be guilty of such conduct", and walked off.[168]

One Department in which Costello took a very direct interest was Justice. The Minister, Jim Everett, was in and out of hospital with stomach trouble when the Government was formed, so Costello was acting Minister for several months.[169] He arranged for the young Fine Gael activist and solicitor Richie Ryan to become private secretary to Everett, who had no legal background. The Taoiseach also handled the legal reform end of the portfolio, and brought most of this legislation through the Dáil. Ryan got the impression he enjoyed this work, and did it for relaxation as much as anything.[170] Costello's influence on law reform was clear. When Everett submitted a memorandum to government on a proposed Bill on the status of married women, he specifically stated that he did so "at the instance of the Taoiseach".[171] Costello also brought the Solicitors Bill and the Mortmain (Repeal of Enactments) Bill through the Dáil.[172] And despite being Taoiseach, he remained active as a Bencher of King's Inns—he was by this stage the Senior Bencher, and helped organise a visit to Ireland by the American Bar Association.[173]

He also continued to show an interest in the arts. Costello's return to power in 1954 presented a potential difficulty to Paddy Little, de Valera's appointee as Director of the Arts Council. Little moved to inform the new Taoiseach of the Council's work, with particular stress on Costello's pet projects. Little wrote that "at least 50% of our funds goes to the visual arts", adding that the Industrial Design Exhibition "was a great success, but our own people are very backward in these matters and we are attempting to hold an exhibition of purely Irish products in the course of the next year".[174] If this was meant to satisfy the Taoiseach, it failed. In 1955, Costello arranged for Tom Bodkin to be taken on as a consultant to the Council—an appointment that was not surprisingly viewed as a "coup" against them by the members.[175]

In a letter to Bodkin, Little said of Costello that "he wants to do big things, and so do we, and I do believe there are indications that a public appetite has been whetted for culture".[176] Costello, meanwhile, was assuring Bodkin that he intended to keep "in fairly close touch" with the work of the Council and, without appearing to interfere, to "endeavour to see that your advice is sought when necessary or expedient".[177] Three months later, the Taoiseach told Bodkin the Council "are feeling 'touchy' about my alleged interference with their functions". He added that he wanted "to shift the emphasis away from drama to the visual arts", as well as possibly starting lectures on industrial design.[178]

As always, he stressed the practical advantages of investment in the arts. He pointed out to Sweetman that a visit by French author Henri Daniel-Rops led to an enthusiastic article about Ireland which appeared in 12 French newspapers. The Taoiseach told Bodkin, with considerable satisfaction, that "the Minister for Finance ... agreed that such a visit followed by such an article receiving wide publicity was worth more than large sums spent on tourist advertising and that culture does pay practical dividends".[179] However, as the economic situation deteriorated, the battle to maintain support for the arts became tougher. In December 1956 he told Sweetman that he wouldn't comment on his categorisation of the Arts Council as a non-essential service "for the sake of my blood pressure". He pointed out that a new Council was about to be appointed. "I am particularly anxious to give the new body a fair opportunity of doing effective work. I am afraid I could not agree to change the decision, and I must ask you not to press me on the matter."[180] Later, in opposition, he suggested that tax relief for exports should also apply to works of art. "If we have here a man who is, say, a painter, or a writer, and if he as a result of his talent, genius or artistry sells the produce of his brains, or of his talent or genius abroad, why could we not have an incentive for that particular type of thing?"[181] The idea was rejected by the Fianna Fáil Minister for Finance, Dr Jim Ryan[182]—his successor, Charles Haughey, later deservedly received plaudits for introducing tax exemption for artists.

In December 1956, he secured the appointment of the author Seán Ó Faoláin as Director of the Arts Council—as Patrick Lynch noted, this was "the first official recognition he had ever received—apart from having his excellent novels banned".[183] Ó Faoláin himself said Costello was "the first person in authority to recognise that an Irishman is not necessarily, by being an artist, a fool or an irresponsible citizen".[184] The author's name had been suggested to the Taoiseach by his son Declan and Alexis FitzGerald, and was supported by Bodkin.[185]

The appointment was strongly opposed by Archbishop McQuaid because the writer was seen as something of an anti-establishment figure, and had clashed with the Archbishop in the past.[186] McQuaid "spent over one hour with Taoiseach and Dr Bodkin trying to prevent Ó Faoláin's nomination, by persuading Bodkin to take the post". Bodkin, however, turned down the offer, much to Costello's own disappointment—the Taoiseach told McQuaid "it had been my life's dream that he would work for Ireland in connection with the promotion of the Arts and particularly the application of the Arts to Industry in Ireland". He added that he considered Ó Faoláin's appointment as a way of giving Government support to artists and writers. "While I cannot expect Your Grace's blessings I feel sure that I will have your prayers." McQuaid replied that he "can only hope that the nominee will not let you down".[187]

One of the responsibilities of Cabinet was to decide whether to advise the President to commute capital sentences. In his autobiography, Noël Browne suggested that the First Inter-party Government routinely decided to have such sentences carried out, over-ruling the objections of the two Clann ministers. In fact, as John Horgan pointed out, only one person was hanged during that government's term—five capital sentences were commuted.[188]

The most notorious capital case to confront the Second Inter-party Government was that of Nurse Cadden, a backstreet abortionist who accidentally killed a patient. She was sentenced to be hanged, and the Court of Criminal Appeal dismissed her appeal.[189] The matter then came before Cabinet. Everett informed his colleagues that the Prison Medical Officer found that she "is quite amoral, and in that sense I would consider her abnormal".[190] The Minister told his private secretary that Cadden was "unrepentant in a state of mortal sin, but if given life imprisonment there was hope that she would see the error of her ways".[191] The sentence was duly commuted.[192]

This was in line with Costello's general approach: he disapproved of capital punishment and was an advocate of civil liberties. In fact, he had been an early supporter of the Irish Council for Civil Liberties, which was established in March 1948. In advance of the founding meeting, the *Irish Independent* reported that the Taoiseach was among the sponsors of the new organisation, along with Gerard Sweetman, Lord Killanin, and Owen Sheehy Skeffington.[193] A letter writer to the *Irish Independent* accused the new group of being a communist front organisation, comparing it to similar organisations in Britain and America. There was official suspicion too, with a Garda report being prepared, noting the names of the sponsors. Justice official Peter Berry noted beside Sheehy Skeffington's name, "This is the only left-wing agitator in the group."[194] Berry sent the Garda report to Maurice Moynihan, the Secretary to the Government, who raised it with the new Taoiseach. Costello explained that he had agreed to attend the inaugural meeting before he became Taoiseach; now he had decided not to attend.[195] Presumably, the official disapproval of the new organisation played a part in his decision, but as we shall see, he continued to oppose the use of special powers, even when the IRA began its Border Campaign at the end of 1956.

So how did the public view the Government? Perhaps the best gauge is by-election results, which indicate that up to the first quarter of 1956, Costello and his colleagues were viewed relatively favourably by the voters. By-elections were particularly important for this government. Defeats would not only have the usual effect of reducing its majority; they would also undermine its democratic legitimacy. While in opposition, Costello had claimed that government defeats in by-elections signalled a withdrawal of confidence by the voters. Perhaps foolishly, he continued to make this argument while in government, offering a significant hostage to fortune. For instance, in July 1956, during the Cork by-election campaign, he said the Fianna Fáil government had in 1954 "finally accepted the result of a whole series of by-elections adverse to them [as] the real wishes of the people and gave up Office".[196]

The first test of opinion didn't come until December 1955, after the death of Fine Gael's David Madden of Limerick West. Opening the campaign, the

Taoiseach gave a less than ringing endorsement of his government's performance: " ... we have done reasonably well despite the many bewildering problems with which we were confronted".[197] He later added another strangely lukewarm assessment of the progress the Government had made: "The balance between success and failure, though perhaps not spectacular, is well on the credit side."[198] During the campaign, Costello made the best of his government's record on prices, insisting that it was outside the power of any Government to control "the prices paid to workers on Ceylon tea plantations or to British coal miners". He pointed out that increases in the price of food produced in Ireland would increase farm incomes—presumably a resonant argument in this mainly agricultural constituency. And the Taoiseach reminded voters that the only general election promise he had made was to "give good government to the best of his ability".[199]

The Fianna Fáil candidate, Michael Colbert, won on the first count with 56 per cent of the vote, which was 2 per cent up on the party's general election result. Fine Gael's vote was marginally up, from 34 per cent to 35 per cent. Despite the fact that this had been a Fine Gael seat, Labour contested the by-election, a curious breach of the usual inter-party procedure in by-elections. The party's vote was down three points to just under 9 per cent. The loss of a Government seat was a blow, but in the circumstances it certainly wasn't a bad result. The Fianna Fáil victory gave that party all three seats in the constituency—the defeated Fine Gael candidate, Denis Jones, went on to top the poll in the 1957 general election, restoring the traditional balance of 2 Fianna Fáil and 1 Fine Gael.

Early in 1956, there was a more impressive show of inter-party solidarity— in favour of Clann na Poblachta, which was of course only supporting the Government from outside. Despite this, Costello threw his full support behind the Clann candidate, Kathleen O'Connor, who was attempting to hold the seat of her late father in North Kerry. He spoke at public meetings, and signed a newspaper ad urging voters to support O'Connor to "send a message of encouragement to the government".[200] This they did—O'Connor held the seat with 53 per cent of the vote, while the Fianna Fáil candidate received 47 per cent. A comfortable victory, although Fianna Fáil's vote had increased by seven points since the general election, at the expense of the combined inter-party total. Costello hailed the result as "a significant victory" and "a decisive vote of confidence to the Inter-party Government".[201]

The Leader was less complimentary, observing that "Mr de Valera wrung his hands in horror at the Coalition's financial ineptitude, but Mr Costello offered everybody factories ... Instead of escaping into the sugar-candy world of make believe, Mr Costello should have come out and told the electors in an adult way what they have to expect in the next twelve months and what his

Government proposes to do. A little less parish pump and more national politics would have increased public confidence in his Government."[202] Such sour comments could not dent the coalition's satisfaction. Two by-elections had resulted in one win and one loss, a reasonable record. However, it was to be the last political success Costello and his government would enjoy as they headed into a miserable year, which would end with the victor in the North Kerry by-election helping to remove them from office. But first, John A. Costello would enjoy a stimulating and diverting interlude away from the burdens of office.

Chapter 12 ᕧ

ⅼ WE MUST HAVE FRIENDS

*"In existing circumstances we cannot have formal
alliances. Because we cannot have alliances we must
have friends."*[1]

JOHN A. COSTELLO, APRIL 1956

*" ... your chivalry is so beautiful, and I am deeply
moved by it."*[2]

JACQUELINE KENNEDY TO JOHN A. COSTELLO, 1967

John A. Costello's visit to the United States in 1956 was a personal
milestone for him. It brought him into contact with the highest levels of
the American political system, saw him honoured by a prestigious
university, and gave him an opportunity to put his stamp on Irish foreign
policy. It was also emblematic of his private life, and his capacity for friendship, which brought into his circle an elderly priest, an eccentric American
scholar, and the widow of an assassinated president.

He had been to the United States twice before—in 1948, on his way to
Canada, and in October 1953, when he attended an Inter-Parliamentary Union
conference in Washington (at which the Irish, inevitably, tried to bring up
partition).[3] He liked Americans—his son John remembered him as being
"charmed" by them, as he loved their "informality and their old world
courtesy".[4] In both his terms as Taoiseach, he received a constant stream of
visitors from the United States. He went out of his way to be helpful too—one
visitor in 1949 mentioned that he had two elderly aunts living in Roscommon.
The Taoiseach personally phoned the Garda sergeant in Ballaghadereen,
asking him to drive out to let the ladies know that their nephew would be
down to visit them a few days later.[5]

Costello's American connection began with Father Joseph Leonard, a
Vincentian priest with an international reputation as a scholar and author on
the life of St Vincent de Paul. Costello came to know him at the start of the

Second World War, when he was living in semi-retirement in All Hallows on the north side of Dublin. Leonard had been a chaplain in the First World War—possibly as a result, he was rather deaf.[6] Their friendship was an important feature of his later life, with Costello taking him most weeks for a Saturday afternoon drive in the Dublin Mountains, where the elderly priest enjoyed the scenery. A mutual friend said after his death that the drives "meant everything to him".[7] Fr Leonard was, according to one of Costello's Garda drivers, a "saintly, jovial old man with a great sense of humour".[8]

After the priest's death, Costello wrote warmly of "a valued and rewarding friendship with a man older and wiser than myself". Fr Leonard had either given or recommended to him a long and varied list of books, from the theological works of Pierre Teilhard de Chardin and his own translation of a life of St Vincent de Paul, to D.W. Brogan's "The American Political System", to the novels of Henry James, to paperbacks by P.G. Wodehouse and detective stories by Rex Stout. As Costello remarked, "It is certainly not Father Leonard's fault if I have not gained much and varied fruit in my post graduate course under his guidance!"[9]

The reference to the Jesuit Teilhard de Chardin is interesting—he was a liberal and controversial theologian whose work was banned by the Vatican. In 1960, Archbishop McQuaid proudly informed the Nuncio that he had forbidden students at Clonliffe College from reading de Chardin several years before the official ban.[10] It is unlikely that Costello was greatly influenced by these works. According to his son Declan, he was "a practising Catholic, rather than an intellectual one", and wouldn't have read a great deal of theology.[11] Whatever about Teilhard de Chardin, Father Leonard was credited by some in the family for softening Costello's approach to religion, which had been rather rigorous.[12]

Before his return to All Hallows in 1939, Fr Leonard had been Vice-Principal of St Mary's, the Vincentian college at Strawberry Hill outside London. Strawberry Hill was built in the eighteenth century by Horace Walpole, son of Prime Minister Robert Walpole and in his own right a politician, art historian, and literary figure. It was because of this connection that Fr Leonard was introduced (by Lady Hazel Lavery)[13] to Wilmarth Sheldon Lewis, an American expert on, and collector of, Walpole's work. "Expert" is probably too mild a word—his autobiography reveals him as something of an obsessive. Lewis had the good sense to marry a wealthy wife, Annie Burr Auchincloss, whose fortune allowed him to amass an unrivalled collection of Walpole's voluminous correspondence. This was brought to the couple's home in Farmington, Connecticut; both house and collection were eventually donated to Yale. Costello had visited Farmington in 1953, when he was in Washington for a meeting of the Inter-Parliamentary Union, and no doubt was given a full tour of the collection.[14]

Lewis was known to his friends (including Costello) as "Lefty",[15] a nickname which quite unjustifiably implied a certain raffish quality. In fact, he had been given the nickname in honour of a gangster called Lefty Louie. He was grateful to the gangster, because, as he wrote later, "the possession of a nickname is a gift beyond rubies".[16] He may have been no gangster, but he was extremely well connected. He was one of the trustees of Yale, serving alongside such luminaries as former Secretary of State Dean Acheson (who had been a classmate at the college) and leading Republican senator Robert A. Taft[17] (father of the US Ambassador to Dublin).

The Lewises met Father Leonard on a visit to Strawberry Hill in 1928. Characteristically, the visit was part of their honeymoon trip to Europe— whether she liked it or not, the new Mrs Lewis was to find much of her life taken up with Horace Walpole. The couple became close friends with the priest, who introduced them after the war to his circle in Dublin, including Costello. In return, they "sent him friends they knew he would enjoy, Jackie Bouvier among them".[18] Jackie, the future Jacqueline Kennedy, was the step-daughter of Hugh Auchincloss, Annie Burr's brother, and spent time with the couple while at school near their home. She was reportedly "fascinated" by her step-uncle's Walpole collection.[19]

In 1949, Jackie and her stepbrother Yusha Auchincloss visited Ireland, where they met Father Leonard. The three visited Costello, then Taoiseach, at his office in Government Buildings, where he presented them with seven signed books on Ireland.[20] He later described her as "full of youthful vivacity, charm and great delight at what she found in Ireland".[21] She also became very fond of Father Leonard, asking him to officiate at her marriage to Jack Kennedy in 1953, and later to christen their first child, Caroline. He was too ill to travel to the United States on either occasion.[22]

Jackie had met the then Congressman Kennedy in 1951, and after a "spasmodic courtship" they married two years later in what was described as "the social event of the year".[23] They visited Ireland at the end of September 1955.[24] The Taoiseach was out of the country (in Rome), but in his absence the couple were entertained by Declan and his wife, Joan. Over dinner in the fashionable Jammet's restaurant, the Senator asked the TD to explain Irish politics to him. Declan found him "very agreeable, highly intelligent and anxious to learn".[25] In turn, Jackie Kennedy remembered the young couple, telling Jack Costello in 1966 that she had "never forgotten you, Declan and Joan's kindness to us".[26]

Jack and Declan were both in the Dáil chamber on 28 June 1963, when John F. Kennedy addressed the House. Later, at a reception in Áras an Uachtaráin, the President asked Declan how he could get in touch with Father Leonard, as he didn't want to leave Ireland without contacting him. A phone call to All

Hallows ensued, which gave the priest "great joy".[27] After the priest died, Costello wrote to Jackie Kennedy, by then a widow, seeking permission to quote from one of her letters to Father Leonard in an appreciation he was writing. He later sent her copies of her other letters to Leonard. She was effusive in her thanks for the confidence with which her correspondence with Leonard had been treated by Costello. "In the strange world I live in now, where privacy barely exists, and where I spend all winter in New York holding my breath and wondering which old letter of mine will come up for auction next!—your chivalry is so beautiful, and I am deeply moved by it."[28]

It was this American connection, through Father Leonard and Lefty Lewis, which led to Costello's trip to the United States in 1956. In November 1955 the President of Yale, Whitney Griswold, wrote to the Taoiseach inviting him to deliver a lecture to the School of Law, and to take part in informal conferences with faculty and students as a Chubb Fellow—for all of which he would receive an honorarium of $1,000.[29] Lewis, who was responsible for the invitation, urged his friend to accept. "You would have an interesting experience, I think—one that, so far as I know, no other Prime Minister has ever had, certainly no other Taoiseach! We would do everything we can to protect you from ambitious politicians and allow you full opportunity to meet and talk with students and faculty."[30]

Costello jumped at the opportunity. He told Griswold it would be "refreshing intellectually to pass a few days in the legal and University atmosphere and away from the political atmosphere", although he admitted to "some misgivings in view of the world-wide reputation of the Yale Law Faculty". He added that he wouldn't expect an honorarium, suggesting the payment could be described as a contribution towards expenses, as "I would not like it to be thought that I wished for reward for what I regard as an honour and a pleasure."[31] He told Lewis that he felt the invitation to be "of high significance", adding that Father Leonard was delighted and had "sent me a book to prepare my education. He thinks, evidently, that I must do a lot of 'home-work' in preparation for the Yale Law Faculty."[32]

The Taoiseach's visit was to coincide with Saint Patrick's Day, which sent the major Irish-American organisations into a frenzy of excitement. The Friendly Sons of Saint Patrick in Philadelphia had been inviting him since 1950; New York organisations were anxious that he should attend their parade.[33] But he had also been invited to attend functions by the authorities of New Haven, where Yale was situated. This invitation, he told John Hearne, the Irish Ambassador in Washington, "came as a surprise to me but in view of the fact that the Yale invitation is such an unprecedented and invaluable one I could not refuse to agree to their wishes".[34]

Hearne, however, had other ideas. He cabled the Department of External

Affairs urging them to "advise Taoiseach of absolute necessity of keeping his Saint Patrick's Day engagements open. Consensus of opinion here is he must not attend proposed banquet New Haven under the auspices of Yale University. Yale regarded as heart of American Protestantism and Yankeeism ... it would be impossible to explain to Catholics all over United States."[35] Despite this strong advice, Costello assured Lewis that he would attend the New Haven dinner, after his friend advised him that extensive arrangements had been made. Hearne told Seán Murphy, the Secretary of the Department of External Affairs, that this "would obviously cause great disappointment", adding that Archbishop O'Boyle of Washington had warned him that if the Taoiseach went to New Haven "they might as well close down the Irish Embassy in Washington so far as the American Hierarchy was concerned".[36] Further pressure was applied by Norton, then on a visit to Washington, who sent a telegram warning Costello of the "grave perturbation" that would be caused if he went to New Haven on St Patrick's Day. The Tánaiste said he would "strongly advise" him to change his plans, saying it had been mentioned to him "by religious and lay friends".[37]

The situation was further complicated by an invitation from the American Government to pay an official visit to Washington. Costello had told Ambassador Taft, who first suggested a visit to Washington, that "I would go where I was invited and to no place where I was not invited."[38] Within a fortnight, Taft had secured an official invitation to Washington, to arrive on 14 March and depart on the morning of St Patrick's Day. Taft told Costello that the State Department had specifically mentioned the morning of 17 March "because of a possible farewell call which it is hoped can be arranged".[39] This was clearly meant, and understood, to involve President Eisenhower, and therefore could not be ignored. But it added to Costello's difficulties—he wrote to John Hearne that he had been "in great distress over all this matter and I rely upon you to do what is possible and best".[40]

On the same day he informed his friend Lefty Lewis that he was "in a sea of trouble and difficulties and I want to appeal to your friendship to rescue me". The engagements in Washington meant he couldn't go to Farmington as planned. Even worse were "the clamant demands of Irish Societies for my presence on the night of St Patrick's Day". Apart from New Haven, Philadelphia and New York, these now included Chicago, Boston and Buffalo among others. "[S]o strong was the feeling that I should be in one of the bigger centres and not in a comparatively small one like New Haven that the suggestion was made that if I did not adhere to this advice the Irish Embassy in Washington would have to close down."[41] As we have seen, it wasn't the size of the New Haven gathering that led to the objection. In any event, the Mayor of New Haven agreed to change the date of the event there to 18 March. Lewis wrote to Costello saying he was glad everything was sorted out, but regretting "that what began as a quiet academic excursion should have turned into a Donnybrook Fair".[42]

The battle over St Patrick's Day having been settled, the rest of the programme was quickly filled in. Costello, accompanied by Charlie Murray, his private secretary, and by Alexis FitzGerald (whose airfare was paid by his father-in-law),[43] was to arrive in Washington on 14 March. He would go to New York at noon on St Patrick's Day and review the parade, before travelling on to Philadelphia for the annual dinner of the Friendly Sons of St Patrick. On the following day he would go to Yale, where he would stay until 21 March, followed by a couple of days with Lefty and Annie Burr Lewis in Farmington. The trip would end with engagements in New York.[44] He stayed on in the United States for a few days after his official visit ended, but at the request of the State Department he kept a low profile to avoid protocol difficulties,[45] telling journalists that he wanted some time to himself for "looking around".[46]

Costello arrived in Washington to be greeted by "a Dublin-like mist" and Vice-President Richard M. Nixon.[47] This was not a snub by Eisenhower— protocol dictated that the President only personally greeted heads of state, and that rarely.[48] Costello made a joke of the weather, telling reporters that "even the great American nation, which has achieved so much, can as yet not control the weather".[49] His first engagement was a private lunch in the White House with the President. Eisenhower's welcome was described as "significantly cordial"; he introduced his visitor to his wife and her mother, and showed him over the private part of the White House. There were 22 guests at the lunch itself, all men, including the Secretaries of the Treasury, Commerce and Labour, as well as a number of senators and congressmen.[50] The lavish menu featured clear turtle soup, fillet of flounder and T-bone steak.[51]

Unusually for such a private lunch, Eisenhower made an impromptu speech "which was marked by particular friendliness in tone and content".[52] In total, the President spent one hour and 40 minutes with his Irish guest, which seems like quite a substantial chunk of time—although it should perhaps be noted that he later found time to spend an hour on the South Lawn hitting golf balls.[53] As we shall see, Costello was to make much of the friendly reception he received. Eisenhower was reported to be pleased by his visitor too—particularly Costello's comment that one of the things he liked about the President was that he was "a good and not a great golfer". It was, according to one of his aides, most unusual for tributes to be paid to the President's golf. An Irish journalist based in Washington reported that the two men played a similar game[54]—which was not much of a tribute to either, by all accounts.

The journalist, Muriel Bowen, had formerly worked with the *Irish Independent*, but was at the time working her way round the world in an effort to improve her chances of getting elected to the British House of Commons for the Conservative Party. She told Costello her editor was eager for her to get an interview with him, particularly to get his impressions of the United States. As Bowen commented condescendingly, "I find the Americans love praise in any shape or form. Despite their cocksureness they think most things in Europe are just that little bit better."[55] As well as explaining Americans to Costello, she told her readers something about the Taoiseach. "Being Prime Minister has meant trying to overcome one of the basic difficulties of his personality: a loathing for the limelight. In private he is just as quick as is Sir Anthony Eden to tell one how much he hates cocktail parties."[56] This may have given some insight into the Taoiseach's personality; it also gave Ms Bowen's readers to understand that she was on intimate terms with not one but two prime ministers.

Costello's visit was also attracting attention from other newspapers, notably the *New York Times*, which devoted an editorial to his arrival. We are now used to Taoisigh using St Patrick's Day to promote Ireland in the United States; then it was a novelty, as the *New York Times* recognised: "St Patrick's Day this year will be special", it said, because of Costello's presence. The editorial praised Costello's "integrity, courage [and] high principles", before wrongly claiming that "as a young lawyer he gained fame in defending the leaders of the 1916 Easter Rebellion against the British".[57] The widespread publicity was clearly a boost for Ireland's image. Costello's presence was even noted by some enterprising cadets at West Point, who invited him to visit the military academy—largely because they had been confined to barracks for two months for a misdemeanour, and prime ministers were entitled to grant amnesty to cadets. After discussing their letter with Hearne, Costello wisely decided to ignore it.[58]

The first official speech of the trip, at the National Press Club in Washington, turned into a comedy of errors. Shortly after he began reading his script, his private secretary, Charlie Murray, realised to his horror that he had given him the wrong speech—Costello was reading the script he was supposed to deliver to the Senate a couple of hours later. Murray passed a note up to Hearne, who was sitting beside Costello; the Ambassador, however, had forgotten his glasses, and had to get the note read for him by one of the journalists, who had difficulty making himself understood as Hearne was rather deaf. By this time, however, Costello had discovered the error himself. One of those present wrote, "Few of us have ever seen a world figure so discomfited. But he made no attempt to cover up. He confessed what had happened and begged our pardon ... he couldn't have done anything calculated to appeal more to our sense of humour. He completely won our hearts, and we practically knocked ourselves out giving him an ovation. We even cheered when he started his speechmaking all over again."[59] Another witness told Costello he had turned a mistake "into a personal triumph. Some of our members even suspect the whole thing was arranged that way."[60] As at his Canadian news conference eight years before, Costello had decided the best policy to follow with journalists was to tell the truth—though this time with less spectacular results.

More formal speeches followed later in the afternoon, to the Senate and the House of Representatives. He was the first Irish head of government since W.T. Cosgrave to make such an address (though Cosgrave had addressed only one House). Some of his successors as Taoiseach (Liam Cosgrave, Garret FitzGerald, John Bruton and Bertie Ahern) were to address a more formal joint session of Congress, but the invitation was still a significant honour. He told the House of Representatives that the world's future would be in good hands as long as the United States continued to use her power "in an honest and forthright manner". In the Senate he expressed the hope that ties between the countries would be nourished and would continue to see "full community of sympathy and interest".[61] He received a standing ovation from senators on arrival and again after his speech.[62] As a gift, he brought five letters written by Richard Fitzpatrick, a captain in the British Army during the American War of Independence, which had been held in the National Library.[63]

Naturally, a visit to the Capitol was marked by partisan politics—particularly as this was an election year. Costello had confessed to Hearne before the trip began that he was "oppressed with the notion that because it is Presidential year there may be strange forces at work and I don't want to put a foot wrong".[64] The "strange forces" turned out to include a green china donkey (the donkey, of course, being the symbol of the Democrats) presented to him by Democratic congressmen. Appearing slightly embarrassed, Costello protested as he was photographed with the donkey, "You'll have me ruined here!" The (very) Republican Ambassador to Ireland, William H. Taft III, laughed along with the joke, but declined to join the group for a photograph.[65]

The official memorandum of the trip noted that "it was very evident that it was not desired [presumably by the Eisenhower Administration] that the Taoiseach should appear to be closely identifying himself with figures prominent in the Democratic Party. Equally it was obviously incumbent on him not to seem to neglect such people in view of the traditional support of the Irish-Americans for the Democratic Party. The tight rope was, it is believed, successfully negotiated."[66] It wasn't just good manners that made the tightrope walk necessary. Costello believed Irish prestige in America had grown because the Irish there had moved up the social scale—in the process losing their automatic loyalty to the Democrats. Many of them had voted for Eisenhower in 1952: " ... both parties are now fighting for the Irish vote and are, therefore, more conscious of the importance of Ireland".[67]

This added to the potential political significance of Costello's visit during a presidential election year. The Irish vote may or may not have been swayed by pictures of the Taoiseach with Eisenhower. But the fact that the possibility existed meant the administration felt it was worth making an effort to extract the maximum potential advantage. There were advantages for Ireland too, of course. The very fact of access to the White House was important. And Costello's visit included a new departure that was to be significant in future years, the presentation of a bowl of shamrock to the President. This ceremony has now become a regular feature of St Patrick's Day in Washington, giving Ireland unparalleled access to the Oval Office once a year, access that is the envy of other countries.

Boxes of shamrock had been presented to members of the US Cabinet and Congress for a number of years, but in 1952, External Affairs came up with the idea of presenting some to the President.[68] Ambassador John Hearne left a bunch at the White House for Truman. The President was on holiday in Key West in Florida at the time,[69] but every tradition has to start somewhere. The following year, Eisenhower was in the White House on St Patrick's Day. This time the presentation was more elaborate, with the shamrock in a cut-glass bowl (which had been supplied free of charge by Waterford Glass, then trying to break into the American market).[70] The President was clearly taken with the idea, writing that the bowl "graced my desk all day, and each visitor to my office took away with him a small bit of the emblem of your country".[71] This was good publicity for Ireland (and for Waterford Glass).

The presentation became a tradition, which was highly valued by Irish diplomats in Washington because of it gave them "the unique privilege ... in being admitted to a private audience with the President ... on our national feast day".[72] An audience for an ambassador was obviously of benefit—but far more important was the potential for a political engagement. John A. Costello was the first to take advantage of this potential (although, despite Taft's insistence that he should remain in Washington until the morning of St Patrick's Day, the presentation actually took place on the sixteenth).

Rather than Waterford Glass, Costello chose an antique Irish silver bowl for the presentation. The newspapers reported that he "took a sprig of shamrock from the bowl and put it in the President's lapel".[73] Eisenhower, according to the Irish memorandum of the visit, "was obviously touched by, and grateful for, the gift". The Irish record of the visit said the President and the Taoiseach had a half hour's discussion. However, the detailed White House record of Eisenhower's day shows that Costello's visit lasted just 10 minutes, from 9:02 to 9:12 a.m.[74] No matter how long the visit lasted, at the end the President "bade a cordial farewell to the Taoiseach and his party". The memorandum noted that Eisenhower later sent a personal letter to the

Taoiseach: "The terms of that letter and, indeed, the fact that such a letter was sent are significant."[75] The President thanked Costello for his "kindly gesture" in bringing the shamrock and the bowl, which was "a fine example of the work of Irish silversmiths of the eighteenth century. I am taking the bowl with me up to our farm so that Mrs Eisenhower can see it at once."[76]

Costello was much taken by the friendly reception he received, particularly from Eisenhower and Nixon. "In private relations ... they spoke in terms which might almost suggest they were concerned to flatter me ... As these were ... private occasions they cannot be explained simply by reference to the fact that this was a Presidential election year." Apart from the fact that the Republic of Ireland Act had made it easier for the Americans to treat him as the representative of the Irish people, he identified three reasons for his warm reception. The first was his belief that the Americans were impressed by his invitation to speak at Yale. "I believe that Washington became extremely interested in an Irish Catholic Statesman who was chosen to be honoured by one of their two most important non-Catholic Universities." This seems rather doubtful—Costello greatly overestimated the importance of the Chubb Fellowship. His other reasons seem more likely explanations—his own efforts in his speeches to stress Irish understanding of American difficulties, and the Republic's new membership of the United Nations (Irish membership had been vetoed by the Soviets, but she was admitted after a 10-year wait at the end of 1955 as part of a "package deal" which saw 16 countries from both sides of the Iron Curtain admitted).[77] In any case, Costello was prone to mistake courtesy and friendliness from foreign leaders for signs of deep affection—his reaction to Mackenzie King in Canada in 1948 being a prime example.

Still basking in the warm glow of his meeting with the President, Costello then had an equally congenial visit to the Supreme Court, where the Chief Justice and Associate Justices had come in specially to meet him. They had "an interesting and informal talk on various matters mostly of legal concern or reminiscence".[78] This was followed by a lunch given by Vice-President Nixon at the Capitol, the conferring of an honorary degree by Catholic University, a reception hosted by Hearne in the Mayflower Hotel, and finally a speech at Georgetown University. Costello later told Government colleagues that "as a matter of deliberate policy, I adopted in my speeches throughout a concili-atory attitude and tried to make the American people aware of our appreciation of their difficulties".[79] He certainly fulfilled this aim at Georgetown, telling his audience that Irish neutrality did not "spring from indifference to the outcome" of a war. "In the battle of ideas we are firmly committed ... And we hope to work with you in your Atlantic partnership and in the wider framework of UNO towards maintaining the peace."[80]

Costello's forthright anti-communism and expressions of support for the United States were welcome to Washington, but not surprising. Background information on the Taoiseach from the State Department said he had "always shown a friendly and cooperative attitude towards the United States and the United Kingdom" (although it was noted that he believed that partition prevented Irish membership of NATO).[81] Former US Ambassador George A. Garrett told Eisenhower that Costello was "a brilliant man, a first class administrator and a great friend of the United States".[82]

On St Patrick's Day, after Mass in Washington, Costello travelled to New York to review the parade. Heavy snow had fallen the night before, although the sun made an appearance during the parade itself. It remained bitterly cold, however, which reduced the estimated size of the crowd to below one million. Even still, 110,000 people took part in the parade, described as "heart-warming if not foot-warming" by the *New York Times*. Costello told the newspaper that St Patrick's Day at home was more of a religious occasion, with small and quiet parades, and "not such a big day in Ireland as it is here".[83] But he was suitably impressed by the event (the first to be viewed by a Taoiseach). "To stand as I did on the Reviewing Stand at the New York parade and to watch contingent after contingent of Irish groups pass the Stand in the most bitterly cold New York weather is to receive an immense fillip to National self confidence."[84] As historian Joseph Morrison Skelly has pointed out, Costello's impression of Irish-American support for the old country was overblown, the result of being in New York on St Patrick's Day. "Costello erred in assuming that Irish Americans sustained this high level of interest in Ireland all year long. They did not."[85]

Even before the parade had ended, Costello was on his way again, to Philadelphia for the dinner of the Friendly Sons of St Patrick. The following day, Sunday 18 March, he finally arrived at New Haven for his visit to Yale. College President Whitney Griswold met him at the station. As they were escorted through the traffic by police motorcycles with sirens screaming, Costello dryly observed, "We'd only have to try this once at home and we'd be out of office the next morning!"[86] That evening he addressed the annual dinner of the Knights of St Patrick, which was held, for the first time, in the University. It was, according to Costello's memorandum on his trip, a "friendly gesture by an important and predominantly Protestant University to a Catholic Irish-American Society" and "evidence of the goodwill towards Ireland created by the visit".[87] The Irish had entered the heart of "American Protestantism and Yankeeism" described by Hearne. Costello told the Knights that while Ireland did not have the "big divisions" spoken of by Stalin, the Irish "have created somewhat of a stir not to say noise in the world ... It is true that the nation is small in size and lacks material wealth but we have abundant recompense."[88] It was a theme he mentioned frequently during this trip, particularly in the context of Ireland's new membership of the United Nations—"while we cannot muster big battalions our moral influence is, or at least could be, considerable".[89]

On Monday he got down to the reason for his visit, the Chubb Fellowship. This was designed to bring "distinguished men in public life to the campus for three or four days to talk informally with groups of undergraduates, graduate students, and members of the faculty". There were up to six fellows a year. Costello's predecessors included Connecticut Governor Abe Ribicoff, ACLU co-founder Roger Baldwin, writer Arthur Koestler, and former Secretary of State Dean Acheson.[90] Later fellows included Presidents Harry Truman, Ronald Reagan and George H.W. Bush; Israeli Prime Ministers Shimon Peres and Moshe Dayan; authors Toni Morrison and Norman Mailer; and actor Robert Redford.[91]

Acheson advised that Costello's Chubb lecture should be "very informal" and that it should concentrate on life at the Irish Bar. "He said that he could not imagine a more fascinating story for American law students ... The theme would be the contribution of the legal profession in Ireland to building modern Irish national institutions."[92] The students had other ideas, though— Costello later reported that on every occasion he was expected to speak on Irish foreign policy. "In Yale University the students and faculty did not desire to hear anything of an academic character but insisted on ... matters relating to Ireland." Even his Sherrill Lecture to the Law Faculty, which he was prepared to devote to "natural law and social justice with particular reference to the provisions of our own Constitution and the decisions of our courts on those topics", was changed to a discussion on foreign policy.[93] The tone of his memorandum suggests he was rather disappointed.

Costello's stay coincided with the heaviest snowfall of the year, disrupting some of the planned events, but Yale's *Alumni Magazine* reported that the visit was a success. It said Costello had been "an attentive listener as well as a vigorous talker, and his full and candid expositions of Irish foreign and domestic policy held the enthralled attention of all who heard him".[94] This was, no doubt, something of an overstatement—although Costello was never short of vigour in his conversation, and could usually be relied upon for a "full exposition" of issues. In keeping with the informality of the fellowship, he stayed for a couple of nights in one of the student residential houses, having dinner with the undergraduates, after which he had a question-and-answer session with 20 students in the sitting room. Postgraduate student Robert Quinlan, who was appointed as a guide for the Taoiseach during his stay, told the *Evening Press* that he had made "a real impression on the student body, not only because of his academic background, but also because he succeeded in selling Ireland to the students without apparently trying to do so". He added that Costello "had maintained a very definite point of view on subjects of Irish policy, while being, at the same time, objective in his explanations of that policy".[95]

As we saw above, Costello believed the American Government had been impressed that he had been awarded the Chubb Fellowship, and attributed Eisenhower's friendly reception partly to this factor. His record of the trip for his Cabinet went on to claim that "it would be difficult to exaggerate the importance of the effect of the visit to Yale ... Apart from the personal honour bestowed on the Taoiseach, the visit had the effect of evoking in Yale a lively interest in Ireland."[96] This was undoubtedly hyperbole. The Fellowship may have been something of a personal honour, but it was mainly due to Lefty Lewis, with whom Costello spent two days after his time at Yale, most of it no doubt devoted to discussion of Horace Walpole.

Another outcome of Costello's Yale excursion was the creation of a fellowship for an Irish postgraduate student to spend a year at the University. The funds for this were donated by the Lewises (or, to be more accurate, by Mrs Lewis) and the recipient was to be chosen by Costello. The fellowship was worth $2,500, from which the tuition fee of $600 had to be deducted. In May, Costello wrote to UCD, UCC, UCG and Trinity seeking nominations, stating that the fellowship "should be awarded for a course in Economics with, possibly, Public Finance and Public Administration included". After an interview with the Taoiseach, the first fellowship was awarded to Noel J. Farley of UCD. The relationship which began in the warm glow following Costello's visit to Yale (President Griswold told him he wished "that in your case the Chubb Fellowship were a permanent appointment") did not endure. By 1965, Costello found that Yale was "tending to disregard" his role in choosing the recipient, and he had to write reminding them of the terms of the original arrangement.[97]

The official part of the visit resumed on Friday 23 March in New York, where the Taoiseach toured the nuclear research centre at Brookhaven National Laboratory and had lunch with officials of the Atomic Energy Commission. The Americans had offered co-operation on the use of atomic energy the year before, and the Irish had indicated that they considered nuclear energy as "a likely and feasible electric power source". While Costello was in Washington, an Atoms for Peace Agreement was signed, under which the United States was to supply enough enriched uranium to fuel a research reactor. Back in Ireland, an Atomic Energy Committee was set up "as the first step in introducing Ireland to the atomic age". After describing his visit to Brookhaven, the Taoiseach told the first meeting of the committee that atomic power presented a challenge and an opportunity. As native energy resources in water and turf became fully developed, and demand increased, "it appears nuclear energy must come into consideration and may offer many advantages ... [but] the technology of nuclear energy is complicated and difficult, and ... will require a substantial programme of education and training".[98]

In New York City, Costello again stayed in the Waldorf-Astoria. On the night of his arrival, a dinner in his honour was given by Horace Flanigan, the President of Manufacturers Trust bank. According to Hearne, he was a friend of Eisenhower and outgoing Secretary of State Dulles, as well as being "of our own Faith, of Irish descent (Limerick) ... his wife is a convert".[99] He was entertained to lunch by Cardinal Spellman, and received an Honorary Doctorate of Law from St John's University of New York. Just before his departure, the Taoiseach also met General Douglas MacArthur. According to the Irish record of their informal conversation, the general "commented favourably on Ireland's neutrality in the last World War", and foresaw a "gradual rapprochement between the USA and Russia—the one becoming more Socialistic, the other more Capitalistic—and thought that neutral countries like Ireland might help to bridge the gap".[100] But his most important business in New York related to the United Nations.

On Saturday 24 March he toured the UN headquarters, where the General Secretary, Dag Hammarskjold, entertained him to lunch. That evening, the United States representative to the UN, Henry Cabot Lodge, gave a dinner for him. Costello also addressed the United Nations Correspondents' Association. He told the journalists that Ireland was not neutral in the war of ideas, despite military neutrality. She would take a "militantly anti-Communist" line at the UN. And while the Irish would raise partition if a favourable opportunity presented itself, Soviet support on this question would be rejected. The Taoiseach added that "we are not going to be a sore thumb. We are not going to raise it at every opportunity."[101] This may have come as a relief to the correspondents, who presumably were all too familiar with member states using the United Nations to air their pet grievances.

Costello's comments were later criticised in the Dáil by Independent Jack McQuillan, who claimed they were at variance with an earlier statement in the Dáil in 1948, when Costello said that if Ireland became a member of the UN, the Government would "miss no opportunity of seeking to undo the unnatural division of our country". The Taoiseach denied that there was any conflict between his two statements. While no opportunity to undo partition would be missed, "this does not mean that our purpose would be advanced by raising the issue at inopportune times or on inappropriate occasions or by giving the impression that we are blind to all issues of international policy save that of Partition alone". He added that Ireland's influence at the UN "may be far from negligible", and that the best way of enhancing national prestige and serving the cause of national reunion was to make as useful a contribution as possible to the work of the United Nations.[102]

Costello had made plain his pro-American sentiments—as well as stressing that partition still trumped anti-communism when it came to NATO. He believed the United Nations provided Ireland "with a new stage upon which to exert our influence and impress ourselves as a force for good ... In existing circumstances we cannot have formal alliances. Because we cannot have alliances we must have friends."[103]

The same thought had occurred to the Americans, who were anxious to test the limits of Costello's friendship. Scattered through the papers relating to his trip are intriguing references to an approach from Ambassador Taft on a highly confidential matter. Frustratingly, the subject of the approach was never committed to writing—on the Irish side. But the Americans were less cautious, and a letter from the State Department to the White House spells out exactly what was involved. According to this document, the Americans were anxious to get wartime transit rights at Shannon for military transport. Taft, therefore, had "made a very secret and informal approach to the Irish Prime Minister with a view to obtaining permission for a United States civil air carrier to expand certain facilities at Shannon and to handle the transit of transport aircraft under military control in the event of the United States being involved in hostilities". The Americans noted that Costello had agreed to "think it over", but urged the strictest secrecy about the matter because "publicity of any kind would damage whatever slight chance we may have of obtaining the desired rights". The State Department didn't expect Costello to mention the matter when he met Eisenhower, and advised the President not to raise it himself.[104]

Here, then, was a test of Costello's sincerity, on an issue which had been politically sensitive for more than a decade. In 1944, while still a neutral in a world at war, Ireland had been invited to join the International Civil Aviation Organisation by the Americans, who were looking for alternatives to Britain as points of entry to Europe for postwar aviation.[105] The British were annoyed they hadn't been consulted, and even more annoyed that the Americans approached the Irish delegation at a conference in Chicago seeking unlimited landing rights at Shannon. They were aware of the approach because they were intercepting and decoding Irish diplomatic telegrams—this one was seen by Churchill.[106] Early in 1945, the British Prime Minister found out that the Americans were asking Dublin to sign a bilateral Civil Aviation Agreement. Churchill sent a petulant complaint to Roosevelt, pointing out that the Irish had been excluded from Commonwealth aviation talks "because of their behaviour in the war", and that he had already complained to Roosevelt in person about the previous approaches. "The War Cabinet have very strong feelings on this episode and we all earnestly hope as good friends that you will consider the matter personally yourself."[107]

Roosevelt sent a soothing reply, saying Washington's attitude to Ireland hadn't been changed by the agreement, any more than a similar agreement with Spain had indicated a change in attitude towards Franco.[108] But the Americans pressed ahead with the agreement—so anxious were they, in fact, that they agreed to the inclusion of the Shannon stop-over, which required aircraft to land there rather than flying straight to Dublin. Within a couple of years, by the time of Costello's first term as Taoiseach, the US airlines were lobbying for the removal of the stop-over, and protracted negotiations ensued over direct flights to Dublin. At the same time, there were informal indications that Shannon might be available for use by the American military in the event of war with Russia. The US Consul in Limerick reported to Washington that "high Irish airport officials as well as local political leaders have said ... that if the United States wishes to use the airport or any other facilities for military purposes they may as well feel free to do so". The Consul, William Moreland, admitted that these comments "border on the extravagant and are not entirely authoritative", but felt they were worth reporting.[109]

There was a less co-operative attitude evident at the talks on the stop-over, but the tension between the Irish and the Americans was nothing to that between the staff of the US legation in Dublin and the Washington-based officials who made up the delegation to the talks. The two groups quickly fell out, with George Garrett complaining of the "high pressure tactics" being used by the negotiators, including press leaks.[110] Garrett reported to Washington, with some evident satisfaction, that the talks over the Shannon stop-over had descended into farce when the head of the American delegation, J. Paul Barringer, "unfortunately got tight [drunk] at a dinner given by MacBride". In the course of a speech "his gratuitous remarks were insulting to the Irish and embarrassing to us ... Barringer continued at table to pay his respects in similar vein, mostly to John Leydon [the Secretary of the Department of Industry and Commerce] ... the following morning ... Leydon terminated this conference after a one-hour session."[111]

One of the press leaks Garrett complained of appeared in the *New York Times* in September 1949. It suggested that Marshall Aid funds were to be used to extend the runway at Dublin to allow for the landing of the largest transport planes—as well as bombers. The story suggested that Ireland would not be able to remain even formally neutral in another world war, so Dublin Airport could be used by the US military. When the story was reprinted in the *Irish Press* a fortnight later, it was immediately denied by MacBride,[112] but it was significant in that it linked the questions of civil and military aviation—precisely the question to be presented to Costello in 1956.

Given the political sensitivities involved, Costello's response to Taft was cautious, telling the American he would think it over. When the Taoiseach discussed the approach with John Hearne and Alexis FitzGerald in New York, his son-in-law advised against taking on any commitments, and Hearne agreed. The Ambassador told Costello he could "easily put the matter on the long finger" rather than turning Taft down abruptly. The Irish were getting "splendid official co-operation" with their investment programme, and "we should avoid any risk of word being sent down the line to go slow on investment in Irish industry". Hearne thought there was a prospect later on of agreeing "a clear-cut arrangement between the two Governments to be ratified after approval by Dáil Éireann. That would be the safest course, should you then decide that such an arrangement should be made."[113]

Characteristically, Costello continued to put the approach on "the long finger". Taft apparently pursued the matter in writing later in 1956. His letter does not survive, but Costello replied that he would be happy to have a further discussion about its (unspecified) subject. "I have mentioned the matter very confidentially to Mr Norton and I would like that the three of us should have a further talk."[114] There the initiative seems to have run into the sand, as there was a change of government shortly afterwards. The Americans can't have been too surprised—despite Costello's pro-American leanings, the State Department had accepted that there was only a "slight chance" of agreement. However, it could be argued that Costello missed an opportunity. After all, his first government had sought bilateral defence arrangements with the Americans, outside the NATO framework, but had been rebuffed. And an agreement with Washington on the use of Shannon by the US military in 1956 would hardly have led to the type of controversy seen in recent years. On the other hand, such an agreement would surely have led to Ireland rising on the list of Soviet nuclear targets.

Despite his reluctance to offer the Americans facilities for military use, Costello was enthused after his visit, and anxious to build on the good relationship he felt he had developed with Eisenhower. He sent a telegram to the President just before he left New York, thanking him for the "gracious and warm hearted welcome" he had received, and stressing that the Irish people "appreciate the efforts and sacrifices which the American nation is making in the cause of world peace".[115] Eisenhower's reply said Costello's visit had "certainly increased the depth of affection held by my countrymen for the Irish".[116]

How to build on this apparent diplomatic triumph? In a memorandum to Government, he proposed the appointment of a separate full ambassador to the United Nations, as well as the promotion of Irish consuls in Boston, Chicago and San Francisco to the status of consul general. The Minister for

Finance was, predictably, not impressed, and responded to Costello's suggestions in terms that were little short of insulting. Sweetman began by casting doubt on the Taoiseach's belief about future Irish influence, saying his warm official reception "was due to the fact that this is election year" (he was almost certainly right). He then dissected the failure of the Government, and more particularly Fine Gael, to develop a proper foreign policy since 1948, having another cut at Costello on the way. "The public were not sufficiently prepared for the announcement of the repeal of the External Relations Act; there was no prior build up ... the establishment of the Republic of Ireland was, without question, of inestimable value ... but without a clear and positive external policy it appears to lack logical effect. The action of India accentuated this apparent void."

Having skilfully denigrated Costello's proudest diplomatic achievement, Sweetman then rubbished his latest grand plan. "I do not believe we can play such an important role [in the UN] as that which seems to emerge from the Taoiseach's memorandum, but I do feel we can play a dignified role which will add to the nation's prestige." That dignified role, however, would have to be done on the cheap. The country could not "possibly hope to afford" wide-spread diplomatic and consular representation, and could hardly achieve Civil Service economies at home if the reach of External Affairs was to be greatly expanded.[117] The fact that Sweetman was by and large right can't have made his words easier for Costello to read. It is little wonder relations between the two men were frosty by this stage.

However, when the matter came before Government, Costello got much of what he wanted. The Cabinet agreed that Ireland should "play a prominent role in the United Nations Organisation and that everything must be done to ensure that our contribution is effective and likely to bring credit and dis-tinction to the country". Specifically, there was to be an ambassador accredited solely to the UN, with "appropriate staff (including a Press Officer) and a suitable residence". Cosgrave was to formulate "the principles and, so far as possible, the details" of Irish foreign policy. The question of upgrading consuls to consuls general was referred to the Cabinet Estimates Committee, while Cosgrave was to consult with Sweetman over increasing the allowances of diplomats in the United States. Cosgrave was to consider further Costello's proposals on strengthening links with Irish-Americans and increasing public interest in foreign affairs. And Norton was to prepare a plan for attracting more American investment in Irish industry. Finally, in an indication that the Taoiseach had been impressed by the pomp surrounding his official reception, Seán MacEoin, the Minister for Defence, was to look into "the question of Army ceremonial and of an improved and more extended use of the National Flag and the National Anthem".[118]

It was a comprehensive and fairly well thought out plan for capitalising on the good feeling evident towards Ireland in the United States. Perhaps the most important part of his report to Government dealt with future policy at the United Nations. In a draft of his memorandum, Costello suggested Irish influence should be "wielded so as to strengthen the Christian civilization of which Ireland is a part ... it is an important duty of Ireland not to take any action which by subtracting from the power of America and Britain would relatively strengthen the power of Russia". As a concrete example, he suggested that rather than instinctively supporting the Cypriot claim to independence, Ireland should act "in a responsible manner based on and informed by the fullest details available so that we should not take or recommend any action merely because it was politically easy for us to do so". For a small and practically undefended nation world peace was "of ultimate and vital importance. In the absence of world peace the defeat or containment of Russia is paramount. I am personally completely convinced that the United States has no aggressive aims and is sincerely anxious for peace."[119]

Costello's son-in-law Alexis FitzGerald pointed out that a public interest in foreign policy "won't come about by breaking a wishbone but by action". He suggested that if the Taoiseach himself wouldn't make a series of speeches to educate public opinion, he should get Cosgrave to do so. "Not merely would this be useful for its own purpose but be politically good, showing the people he was doing his job."[120] This Cosgrave did in a speech to the Dáil in June 1956, in which he outlined the three principles of his foreign policy. The first was adherence to the principles of the UN Charter, the second independence and non-alignment with any of the main power blocs. In case anyone could misinterpret the second point, the third made it clear once again where Ireland stood in the Cold War: "to do whatever we can as a member of the UN to preserve the Christian civilisation of which we are a part and with that end in view to support whenever possible those powers principally responsible for the defence of the free world in their resistance to the spread of communist power and influence".[121] The third guideline was "the foundation upon which the inter-party government built its United Nations posture", and it mirrored Costello's memorandum.[122] Just as Ireland had been neutral in favour of the Allies during the Second World War, she was now "non-aligned" in favour of the Americans.

During the Dáil debate on the External Affairs Estimate, Costello spoke at length on the threat of "atheistic Communism", a speech which drew favourable comment from Archbishop McQuaid. This was welcome to the Taoiseach, as there had been criticism of Irish entry into the UN from what he described as "ultra-Catholic sources".[123] He was able to tell one such critic, who referred to his "lame apologia" for Ireland's entry to the United Nations, that the Papal

Nuncio had called on him "to convey to me the gratification of the Holy See" with his speech on the External Affairs Estimate.[124]

Costello, then, had set the ground rules for Irish foreign policy, being the real author of the three principles outlined by Cosgrave. But in matters of detail, as was his practice, he left the Minister to get on with running his own Department. "Mr Costello never interfered in any way ... He left the decisions to me but I kept him and the Government fully informed of all major matters."[125] This was obviously sensible when the Minister attended his and Ireland's first UN General Assembly in November 1956. The Taoiseach assured the American Ambassador that the Cabinet received regular updates from the delegation in New York, although he appeared "a bit vague from a lack of knowledge on several points". Taft would have been more reassured by Costello's statement that "he had urged Mr Cosgrave to ascertain closely the US view on all difficult points".[126] When Cosgrave was asked by the Americans to support them on refusing to debate the admission of communist China, he readily agreed.[127]

The indications from New York were that Cosgrave had made a success of his first outing on the world stage. Freddie Boland reported to Iveagh House that no other speech had received such a positive response. "The volume of applause at its conclusion was really remarkable and delegates crowded round the Minister from all sides to congratulate him and express approval of his speech."[128]

The Cosgrave/Costello approach was in stark contrast to that pursued in later years by Fianna Fáil's Frank Aiken, who aroused considerable controversy by supporting calls for a debate on the admission of communist China to the UN (he stressed he wasn't supporting the admission, only a debate about it, but was lambasted by anti-communists for his trouble). Declan Costello put down a Dáil motion condemning Aiken's actions; his father said the Minister had contravened "one of the fundamental principles that we laid down" to direct policy in the United Nations. "We object to the policy advocated and to the action taken because it gave comfort to our enemies, the enemies of peace, and disturbed our friends who are the bulwarks of peace and the bulwarks against war."[129]

Costello clearly enjoyed his visit to the United States, and was greatly impressed by the courtesy shown him by Eisenhower and Nixon—and by his experiences at Yale University. But on his return to Ireland, he was to be engulfed by a sea of troubles—economic, political, but most importantly, personal.

Chapter 13 ～

SOMETHING IS WRONG
WITH THE COUNTRY

"My children and I have suffered a grievous loss ... a wife who gave me a lifetime of devotion and love."[1]

JOHN A. COSTELLO, APRIL 1956

"There has emerged a feeling of malaise, a feeling that something is wrong with the country ..."[2]

JOHN A. COSTELLO, SUMMER 1956

The most important and distressing problem facing Costello on his return to Ireland was the illness of his wife, Ida. He told Archbishop McQuaid that "unfortunately, I do not find my wife at all well on my return".[3] The Archbishop expressed his sympathy, and promised to "get very many prayers for her".[4] The Taoiseach also had spiritual support from his Labour colleague Jim Everett, who lent him a relic of Saint Pius X.[5]

Ida Costello, who was 65, had suffered from high blood pressure for some time, but while her husband was in the United States she was diagnosed with chronic bacterial endocarditis, an inflammation of the lining of the heart. She was admitted to Saint Vincent's Private Nursing Home in Leeson Street in Dublin.[6] On 19 April, Costello wrote to Eisenhower, once again thanking him for the reception he had received in the United States, and saying it had been "a very great pleasure to me to describe to my wife the generous cordiality which you extended to me".[7] The following morning, Ida Costello suffered acute heart failure and died.[8]

She was, Costello sadly wrote to McQuaid, "a wife who gave me a lifetime of devotion and love", and her death was "a grievous loss" to him and to their children. He told the Archbishop that the family had "been greatly comforted by the kindness of so many friends, by the many Masses that have been offered for the repose of her soul and by the conviction of our Faith that God has her now in His kind hands".[9]

The Taoiseach received a huge number of sympathy cards and messages of support, including a personal message from President Eisenhower, which he greatly appreciated.[10] There was also a massive turnout for the removal and funeral. As the coffin was being brought out of the nursing home followed by Costello and his family, out of the crowd stepped Patrick J. Burke, a Fianna Fáil TD for North Dublin, popularly known as The Bishop because of his frequent attendance at funerals. He pushed himself forward to shake hands with the Taoiseach, in full view of the press cameras. "A groan from the watching crowd indicated what was thought of this lapse of good taste."[11]

The loss of his wife of almost 37 years was, naturally, a terrible blow for the Taoiseach, then just two months short of his sixty-fifth birthday. He had always been a devoted family man, always anxious to get home rather than attend parties or official functions,[12] and he and Ida had enjoyed a "very affectionate" married life together.[13] A moving tribute was paid to Ida by James O'Brien, a friend who was then aide to the Mayor of New York. He wrote to Costello that "she left a legacy of sweetness and understanding to all who met her".[14]

During his period of mourning, Costello avoided formal parties, and declined an invitation from the Irish Ambassador to the Vatican, Con Cremin, to return that summer to the Villa Spada in Rome, where he and Ida had spent time in 1955. "I have very precious memories of our stay with you last year. I have, however, decided not to go away anywhere at all this year, and I am sure that Patsy and you will understand this."[15] He was still refusing social invitations by the following February.[16]

His family rallied round, particularly his eldest daughter, Grace, married to Alexis FitzGerald. As he told one correspondent, he took "refuge in my daughter's house on Sundays"[17]—her house on Nutley Road was not just a source of family comfort, but a place to escape the burdens of office. His other children also offered support. Eavan and her husband, Ralph Sutton, came up from Cork to spend Christmas with him. "Between them all they made it, if not a happy one, at least a peaceful and untroubled one."[18] In an effort to help fill his evenings, the family presented him with a television set that Christmas.[19] He was to become a keen television watcher in later life—and, just as he used to work with the radio on in the background, was able to combine his viewing with work on his legal briefs.[20] As might be expected of someone of his conservative social views, he would criticise anything which he regarded as vulgar, but kept the set on anyway for the company.[21]

Ida Costello's death was a bitter blow to her husband—but he seemed to deal with it as well as could be expected. Just how shattered he was became a matter of some political debate. James Dillon suggested in his memoir that "his heart was no longer in the business after that". In fact, he suggested that the Taoiseach had "become weary of the business of governing", and that his wife's death was a factor in his decision to call a general election early in 1957.[22] Not surprisingly, Declan Costello rejected such suggestions, which also surfaced when his father was removed as leader of the Opposition in 1959. Declan said his father carried on "absolutely normally", and that he did not become moody or depressed.[23] However, it is difficult to believe such a deep personal loss didn't have a profound effect on him. Another witness who saw the Taoiseach at close range at the time perhaps put it best, saying Costello "lost a bit of his bounce" after his wife died.[24]

And as Taoiseach, he needed every bit of bounce he could manage, as the economic situation turned from difficult to desperate. His wife's death also came as two by-elections were being fought—Fine Gael suspended its campaign as a mark of respect.[25] The inter-party candidates were facing an uphill battle in any event. Partly this was due to Sweetman's introduction of import levies in March to try to choke consumer demand in an effort to address continuing balance of payments problems. The levies covered a wide range of goods, from cutlery to musical instruments and from tinned fruit to umbrellas,[26] and were widely unpopular. They did what they were designed to do—the current account deficit was reduced in 1956 and turned into a surplus in 1957, while the net foreign assets of the banking system also began to turn around. But they had a devastating effect on the economy, reducing employment and increasing emigration to an unprecedented figure during 1957 of 1.8 per cent of the *entire* population.[27]

Sweetman's austere approach was enthusiastically encouraged by the Governor of the Central Bank (and former Secretary of the Department of Finance), J.J. McElligott. He had written to the Minister at the start of the year, arguing that Ireland was "suffering from a prolonged and deep-rooted excess of demand in relation to home produced supply ... Unless something positive is done to relieve materially this constant pressure of excessive demand which has permeated the whole economy, we are bound soon to receive a rude shock." The public must have the facts placed before them, so they could consider "the full implication of living on capital, a way of life we have been indulging in for eight years". He suggested the situation could be retrieved with "judicious adjustments" in economic and monetary policy—but the room for manoeuvre was now so limited that action must be taken soon, as it "may be about our last chance". Increased production was, in the long term, the answer; but in the short term there must be a reduction in demand, through the control of non-productive capital spending. This was traditional Central Bank policy. McElligott also added a new criticism: the Government's policy of keeping interest rates lower than in Britain, "which regrettably was much publicised as an achievement along the road of an independent monetary policy has done a lot of damage in boosting the feeling of prosperity which we have artificially built around ourselves".[28]

Whatever about the economic effects (see Chapter 11), lower interest rates were a positive for the Government from a political point of view. About the only good thing the import levies did politically was to help persuade the banks not to follow an increase in British interest rates, at least temporarily, at the start of 1956. Just before he left for the United States, Costello met the bankers along with Sweetman, and persuaded them to hold rates steady.[29] A few days before the by-elections, he wrote to thank the chairman of the Irish Banks' Standing Committee, saying he hoped that "the national interest will continue to have the benefit of co-operation between the Government and the Banks in matters of common concern, based on mutual confidence and candid exchanges of opinion".[30] This was only putting off the inevitable—the banks were to increase in interest rates a couple of months later. But would the decision have any impact on the two by-elections?

The short answer was no, as both contests showed a swing towards the Opposition. In Dublin North-East, Independent Patrick Byrne took 57 per cent of the vote and retained the seat of his late father, Alfie, while Fianna Fáil's Charles J. Haughey received 43 per cent. But this was a large increase over the Fianna Fáil vote in the constituency in 1954—then, the party had only managed to win 32 per cent of the vote, while the Inter-party candidates between them took 59 per cent (other Independent candidates took 9 per cent). In Laois-Offaly, Labour's William Davin had won just 11.3 per cent of the vote in 1954, compared to 43 per cent for Fianna Fáil and 45.6 per cent for Fine Gael (boosted by Oliver J. Flanagan's huge personal popularity). When Davin died, Labour had the right to nominate the inter-party candidate, choosing the late Deputy's son Michael. He boosted the Labour, but not the inter-party, vote, winning 44 per cent, and losing to the Fianna Fáil candidate, Kieran Egan.

These results, particularly the swing towards Fianna Fáil of 11 per cent and 13 per cent respectively, were the first real sign that the Inter-party Government was losing support. As we saw in Chapter 11, Government candidates had done reasonably well in by-elections up to then. Now the pressure was on, and Labour in particular was restive.

As early as February 1956, US Ambassador Bill Taft was speculating on an early election, suggesting that Labour could pull the plug on the coalition if austerity measures were taken. He thought Norton could keep his party in line "so long as things were going along fairly quietly, but the odds were that they would bolt if anything controversial like a new economic programme came up". His British counterpart, Alexander Clutterbuck, thought an immediate collapse unlikely, predicting a compromise over the Budget which "may tide things over for a while".[31] Clutterbuck was right. Sweetman's budget at the beginning of May increased taxes to further tackle the balance of payments problem, including a heavy rise in duty on petrol and cigarettes, and cut £5 million from spending. But it also increased welfare benefits. In Costello's words, the Government had "carried out a difficult task in difficult times in this Budget in the most humane way possible".[32] In the assessment of Labour's most recent historian, the Budget "did not lead to Labour losing much face, but neither did it provide anything for those who wanted the government to adopt a positive policy to halt the economic crisis".[33] There was more gloom to come.

On 1 June, preliminary results from the census carried out in April were released—and those results were devastating. The population was 2,894,822, the lowest ever recorded. The natural increase in the population was the highest recorded since 1881, but was more than wiped out by increased emigration of over 200,000, or more than 40,000 people in each of the five years since the previous census. Since 1951, the population had declined by 65,771.[34] It was, according to the Provisional United Trade Union Movement, "a great shock to our people ... The future of the nation is at stake and it is against this background that all economic questions must be judged." In a memorandum to the Government, the unions argued that the "alarming trends" revealed by the census should put the "temporary economic problems" of the balance of payments into their proper perspective.[35]

In the midst of this gloom, the death of Fianna Fáil TD Pa McGrath of Cork Borough precipitated another by-election, which was held at the start of August. Fianna Fáil had moved the writ with unusual speed, in order to "seek profit from the Government's difficulties", as Costello put it when opening the Fine Gael campaign. The Taoiseach said the country was suffering from "a serious but not an incurable disease". Complete recovery was certain "if the patient himself co-operates in the efforts to cure him". That co-operation, he suggested, should start with a vote for an inter-party candidate in the by-election. He appealed to voters "to strengthen the hands of the Government to deal with our very serious problems and difficulties, and not to weaken them in these critical times". He accused MacEntee of having deliberately caused the cost of living to rise when he was Minister for Finance. By contrast, the Inter-party Government had "adopted every device, orthodox and unorthodox, in an endeavour to keep down the prices of essential commodities, and allowed them only to rise where such increase was inevitable and beyond our control".[36]

The Dáil debate on the Taoiseach's estimate came in the middle of the campaign. During that debate, in the words of the *New York Times*, both Government and Opposition "faced up to the fact that the country was in a critical situation".[37] Costello spoke of a "trinity of problems" facing the country—emigration, unemployment, and the balance of payments deficit. "Any one of these problems would be formidable by itself; taken together, they are both a warning and a challenge to the country." He said there were two dangers—that of overestimating the difficulties, thus causing "panic and despair at home and a lack of confidence abroad", or of underestimating them, which could lead to apathy and a failure to take corrective measures.[38]

Among those measures was another dose of austerity. Sweetman complained on 20 July that despite the earlier introduction of import levies, "virtually no net improvement has so far been achieved. It is essential that further reductions in imports be effected." He urged colleagues to review their departmental purchasing programmes to reduce or defer any imports.[39] And on the twenty-fourth, just over a week before polling day, the Government agreed to increase import levies and extend them to new items, and to cut a further £5 million from Government spending.[40] *The Leader* noted the Government's promise "that if this shirt is not hairy enough to make the citizen itch into economic virtue a still more penitential garment will be provided".[41]

It was not, to say the least of it, an ideal background for a by-election. Costello made a virtue of necessity in his eve-of-poll speech. The fact the Government had taken such measures in the middle of an election campaign showed "its confidence that the people want the truth and won't be frightened by it ... Recent events have demonstrated the unity and strength of the Government and their resolution to do what is right even at the risk of losing support." He admitted some hardship had resulted, but said it was nothing like that caused by the 1952 Budget. He claimed his Government had "tried to temper the wind to the shorn lamb" by taxing inessential, or less essential, expenditure.[42]

His confidence in the voters was somewhat misplaced. The Fianna Fáil candidate, John Galvin, won 53 per cent of the vote, up 10 percentage points since the general election. Fine Gael was down 12 per cent to 29 per cent, and Labour down 2 per cent to 11 per cent. Costello put a brave face on the result, observing that it was based on "the smallest poll possibly ever recorded in Ireland", and merely showed that "the Opposition has obtained a temporary electoral advantage" from the country's economic problems. "The result does not dismay the Government. It will continue to perform the duty of carrying out those policies which cannot be popular but which are demanded in the national interest."[43]

If the domestic economic and political situation was parlous, it was about to get a whole lot worse, thanks in large part to international factors. In July, Egypt nationalised the Suez Canal. In response, Britain, France and Israel cooked up a fairly disreputable—and transparent—plot to get rid of the Egyptian leader, Colonel Nasser. At the end of October, the Israelis invaded; a week later, the British and French landed, ostensibly to keep the warring sides apart, in reality to seize the canal. The operation was a military triumph and a political disaster. Eisenhower was having none of it, forcing the British into a humiliating climbdown which destroyed the health and the career of Prime Minister Anthony Eden. The other consequences included an oil shortage which threatened to paralyse the western world. The British Embassy advised that oil supplies would be about 60 per cent below normal for some months, because the canal and the Iraq pipeline were both out of action.[44] The result was an intensification of the economic problems facing Costello.

There was already significant discontent within inter-party ranks, expressed forcefully by the Taoiseach's son Declan. At a meeting of inter-party TDS, the younger Costello directly challenged Sweetman's policies, calling for a much more radical approach. Declan was applauded by many of the Labour TDS—Sweetman was not amused. He told Declan privately that his speech was "shocking and unfair", and a breach of his responsibilities as a Fine Gael TD. At the next party meeting, he made those criticisms public. Jack Costello had been due to chair the meeting, but tactfully absented himself when Sweetman warned him of what he was going to say. It was an awkward situation for all concerned, especially as the Taoiseach and his Minister for Finance were not getting on at this stage[45] (although it should be noted that Ken Whitaker, the Secretary of the Department of Finance, was not conscious of any friction between the two men[46]—presumably they didn't parade their differences in front of civil servants).

Labour backbenchers were also deeply disaffected by now. Jim Larkin, in many ways that party's conscience while it was in government, was severely critical of the coalition in September 1956. He told a meeting of Labour's Dublin Regional Council that the economic situation was a warning to the Government, but a "danger" to Labour. "It is contrary to Labour's whole trad-itional policy to pursue and support negative measures, such as the curtailment of capital investment, reduced housing activities, and economies through disemployment. Labour has a positive policy, and before it is too late Labour must declare for progress and against retrogression and decline."[47]

But as far as Sweetman was concerned, the only realistic policy was further austerity. At the beginning of October, he got Government approval for yet more import levies, although he held off actually introducing them when the trade figures for September showed some improvement. But he publicly warned that Ireland was "not out of the woods yet. Let us behave like adults and not like children ... We must keep our heads. We have no cause or excuse for relaxing our efforts until we have closed the fatal gap in our Balance of Payments."[48] In private, Sweetman warned colleagues of the need to keep spending under control. "To ignore that need must make for a disastrous worsening of an already serious economic and financial situation. Present difficulties will be aggravated if decisive action ... is not taken immediately to limit public expenditure."[49] In later years Costello was to state his belief that his government "went too far and too quickly" with austerity measures, that they could have sought alternative economic advice "and we might consequently have taken the chances and let matters right themselves and let the balance of payments right itself without all those remedial measures".[50]

It was not, to put it mildly, a good time to be in government. After a particularly depressing Cabinet meeting, new Minister Patrick Lindsay recalled feeling "thoroughly dejected". Brendan Corish tried to cheer him up, telling him it wasn't always like that. Lindsay, ever the realist, replied, "Well, I'm afraid it's going to be like that for my time anyway, because we're going out the next time."[51] That was certainly likely as long as the only thing the Government could offer the public was more of Sweetman's austerity. But was there any possible alternative, along the lines suggested by Declan Costello and Jim Larkin, that could offer the country—and the Government—some hope?

In fact the Taoiseach had been working on just such a policy for some months, and was to make a major speech outlining his *Policy for Production* in October. Because it was announced after Larkin's criticism of the Government's economic policy, many assumed it was a reaction to those comments. Others have credited Health Minister Tom O'Higgins with the original suggestion for a policy initiative. In his memoirs, O'Higgins said he called for a fresh declaration of aims and a new policy for development in a memorandum to Government.[52] This memorandum doesn't seem to have survived, but is referred to in a later document by Costello, which quotes O'Higgins as saying they must give "evidence of a Government in action getting down to the job".[53] Even if O'Higgins was the first to formulate the idea, he was pushing an open door as far as Costello was concerned. It was clear that something needed to be done.

The pressure for positive action was increased by looming by-elections, in Dublin South-West and Carlow-Kilkenny, following the deaths of Fine Gael's Peadar Doyle and Fianna Fáil's Thomas Walsh respectively. In mid-August, Alexis FitzGerald urged his father-in-law that "everything from all over the country should be thrown into a desperate battle in Dublin and Carlow-Kilkenny". He offered a very comprehensive list of ideas for improving the Government's image, including moves on health insurance, developments in foreign policy, and economies in the Civil Service. He wanted to maximise the publicity surrounding the establishment of the Department of the Gaeltacht by holding a news conference in Irish—which would be the first ever held by any government. FitzGerald also suggested that Costello should announce a change to the method of electing the Senate. As he observed, this would "delight nine tenths of the people", although it would upset Fine Gael senators "who will feel that they wouldn't get in if the Senate were any good". FitzGerald also proposed a move on a National Concert Hall, more capital for agriculture, and the establishment of a Rent Tribunal. He warned his father-in-law that Fine Gael propaganda was "terrible", recommending the appointment of "some clever young person" such as "that young genius Garret FitzGerald" to improve it.[54]

All of this should be included in what he called Costello's "Queen's Speech", a reference to the British practice of outlining a government's legislative programme in a speech delivered by the monarch. FitzGerald advised the Taoiseach to get a strategy planned, and a timetable from ministers for the implementation of policy. "A spirit of siege warfare and urgency should be encouraged in the Government and party."[55] His father-in-law later said it was Alexis "who outlined and thought up the various schemes which were put into operation and which are now ... bringing benefit to this country by way of the export trade".[56] The "young genius" Garret FitzGerald also credited Alexis, along with Patrick Lynch, for the initiatives that "started the reorientation of the inward-looking post revolutionary Irish economy to the world outside", a process later "brought to fruition" in the *First Programme for Economic Expansion*.[57]

Certainly, many of Alexis FitzGerald's ideas were reproduced in a memorandum by Costello (unfortunately undated) which outlined the economic and political necessity for a major initiative. "Positive steps must be taken without delay to bring about a radical cure." He stressed that the restrictive measures which had been taken were "temporary and palliative"; now it was time to try something else, specifically an attempt to promote exports. "A clear and bold policy must ... be announced ... Such a policy would give hope, show that the Government is alert and alive to the necessity not merely of restriction but of expansion which they appreciate is the real and only permanent remedy for present difficulties ... In my view the public ... are really groping for signs of hope, and some positive action to give grounds for relief for the future. I am convinced that if a plan ... for increased production were now put before them the public would react very favourably." He observed that Fianna Fáil were accusing the Government of making false promises of early prosperity. While this was not true, it was true that Costello's own speeches before and during the election had led people to believe "that changes of a constructive nature would follow the formation of the new Government. It is no answer that these constructive proposals were honestly made. None of them have been followed up. This is what matters."

Costello followed this bleak assessment of his government's performance with an analysis of the political difficulties facing them. Far from being exaggerated, he believed, "they are insufficiently appreciated". There was no guarantee the Government could survive two more by-election defeats, and if it fell without having introduced at least a number of constructive measures "distinctively not Fianna Fáil in character", the whole idea of inter-party government would be discredited. Therefore, the Government must be bold and decisive. "The people will forgive mistakes. They will not forgive inactive caution." He wanted the new policy to be announced in a major speech, by him, around 20 September. This would set the scene for the raising of a new national loan, as well as preparing the ground for the by-elections. Legislation would be required, and this should dominate Dáil business in the weeks before the by-elections, so the Government could recapture the political initiative. The Taoiseach wanted one piece of legislation, "which should be given some striking title like the Expansion of Exports and Productivity Bill".[58]

The Taoiseach wanted as many decisions as possible, even on minor matters; he wanted them to "comprise new ideas, show originality, create public interest, and be different from Fianna Fáil policy"; they should also relate to what had been said while they were in opposition, so they wouldn't be seen as panic measures. "The object must be ... to garner for the Government the psychological advantages of making the public feel that this is the beginning of a new chapter ... The people want a tonic and unless we can give it to them there can be nothing but disaster." One of the more important suggestions was a tax break for extra exports. He also wanted the Government to finally establish the long-promised Capital Investment Board. Significantly, the Taoiseach accepted that much of what had been called capital spending could not really be described as such. While "desirable and necessary ... it has not added to the income-producing power of the community". He drew a distinction between building a hospital, which would lead to expenses rather than income, and establishing a factory which yielded incomes for workers.[59] This was something of a reversal of his previous attitude to capital spending.

Costello's blunt memorandum struck a chord with his ministers. Liam Cosgrave complained that the Government was failing in its propaganda, and hadn't explained to the public why the import levies had been imposed. Many people thought they were a revenue raising device, rather than an attempt to correct the balance of payments. "Finally, this Government lacks originality and is in effect merely administering the affairs of State with varying degrees of efficiency." He strongly endorsed Costello's proposals, which should be pursued vigorously. "Otherwise, we will continue to lose public support because we have failed to show the public that we are capable of giving the leadership which the Nation requires."[60] McGilligan warned of the "danger that Fianna Fáil may come back not because the public really desire them but because those now in power have failed to come up to popular expectation".

He believed there was still time to win back public support, but the budgets of 1957 and of 1958 ("if the Government last out to the latter date") were pivotal. The people must be made to understand the difference between the inflationary Fianna Fáil proposals and the Government's "selective remedial measures". There must be action on the cost of living, taxation and rates, the cost of government and local services—otherwise "defeat for the present Government is inevitable and inter-party collaboration in Government is doomed".[61]

On 5 October, Costello delivered his speech to a meeting of inter-party TDS and senators at the Engineers' Hall in Dawson Street (the text had been approved by Government the day before).[62] The overall tone was optimistic, suggesting trade figures had "taken a turn for the better and there is good ground for hope that the immediate measures found necessary by the Government are proving effective". Now it was time to introduce a pro-gramme for economic expansion. "These decisions are calculated to expand our production, both for home use and for export, and enable the country to balance its international payments even without any need to call on our external assets. They are also calculated to increase savings, and increase investment at home so that we may develop this under-developed country."

He stressed the importance of agriculture, saying that increased agricultural exports would pay for the imports of capital goods and material needed for industrial development. In the previous year, the export of cattle and beef was worth £42.5 million, or 40 per cent of Ireland's total export trade. Given that Britain was to ban the import of cattle which were not certified to be tuberculosis free, he committed the Government to spending up to £1 million a year on a scheme to eradicate bovine tuberculosis. But while there was an emphasis on agriculture, Costello said, "Government encourage-ment of industrial development will continue to be given as vigorously as ever." There would be a 50 per cent tax remission on profits from extra exports; grants for new factory buildings and tax relief for hotels; a campaign to encourage savings; and a Capital Investment Committee. Significantly, he stressed that Ireland would continue to welcome foreign capital investment.

The Taoiseach concluded on an upbeat note. "The Balance of Payments problem is a short term problem which can be and is on the way to being solved ... Pessimism is not warranted and is not helpful. Faint hearts will contribute nothing either to the solution of our immediate problems or to planning the measures required to ensure future prosperity. We are justified in pointing with pride to what has hitherto been achieved, and, in contemplating those achievements, we may well take courage and face the future with calm resolve, with confidence and with hope."[63] His 2-hour speech was greeted with an ovation, and was "reckoned to have restored inter-party unity, which seemed to be in jeopardy in recent weeks". James Larkin and Seán MacBride, described in the media as the two chief critics of the Government, both welcomed the programme. Larkin praised the "new positive constructive programme" and urged early implementation to reduce unemployment. MacBride's main complaint was that the programme had been delayed so long, but he said it was better late than never, and it gave some evidence of "positive, constructive planning". A vote of confidence in the inter-party leadership was proposed by Labour's Tom Kyne, seconded by Dan Morrissey of Fine Gael, with MacBride and Thomas O'Hara of Clann na Talmhan speaking in support.[64]

The British Embassy found it difficult to judge the probable effectiveness of the plan, given the lack of detail, but reported that "moderate opinion seems to be that, although it has been left very late, the plan may prove reasonably effective, if it is implemented with speed and energy".[65] Press reaction was mixed. The *Irish Independent* felt Costello was over-optimistic about the economic situation, and that his proposals were long-term, when "what the country needs at the moment is an immediate short-term policy to meet the present grave crisis". The *Irish Press* found little to disagree with in what the Taoiseach said. "The statement would be reasonable and even brave were it not so threadbare, not to mention the woeful record of Mr Costello's Government since it took office ... No promises can hide the failure of the Government ... more than fine words and promises based on past failures are needed." The *Irish Times* was more positive. "The plan Mr Costello announced yesterday is the one that ought to have been put before the country thirty years ago. The pity is that we have had to wait for it until a moment of 'crisis.'"[66]

But it was precisely because of the desperate economic situation that Costello had been able to secure agreement to his proposals. As we have seen, the Capital Investment Committee and changes to the Control of Manufactures Acts had been resisted by Finance and Industry and Commerce respectively for more than two years. As Tom Garvin noted, "it took the crisis of 1956 to finally unblock residual resistance to wide-ranging policy shifts".[67]

Arguably the most important development was the tax break for exports. Similar measures had been suggested twice before—in the Foreign Trade (Development) Bill of 1945, and on the recommendation of the Dollar Exports Advisory Committee in 1950—but had been blocked by the Revenue Commissioners.[68] Tax relief for exports, as well as for industrial buildings and coal mining, was introduced in the Financial (Miscellaneous Provisions) Act in December.[69] It was, according to Patrick Lynch, the first significant departure from the system of company taxation introduced in 1842. While it took some years to become effective, he wrote in 1967, "it is now the most important single spur towards improving efficiency in Irish industry and extending our trade abroad".[70] Lynch was hardly a neutral observer, but he was right to stress the importance of export tax relief. If nothing else, it was an important step on the road towards an outward looking, export driven economy—and one which is rarely credited to Costello and his government.

Another area where change was signalled in Costello's speech was on the Control of Manufactures Acts. As we saw in Chapter 11, the Taoiseach had been trying unsuccessfully to reduce restrictions on foreign investment. In his 5 October speech, he noted the number of developments "made possible by the personal and financial impetus and the technical help of industrialists from other countries". He said he was sure the public would welcome Norton's campaign to attract more foreign investment. Norton later told the Taoiseach that the IDA was to follow up all American industrial contacts "vigorously and without delay, and that no opportunity will be lost of opening up new contacts with a view to the possibility of industrial development here". The Minister was also keen on "special tax concessions to industry so as to enable this country to compete with other countries which are also trying to attract foreign industrialists".[71] It was to be left to the new Fianna Fáil government to actually amend the legislation, a move signalled by Lemass in May 1957.[72] It is certainly arguable that Costello had prepared the ground for this change, as well as others. However, the amount of credit he could take in this case was limited by the failure to actually take action.

The Capital Investment Advisory Committee was also an important development, although perhaps not in the way Costello would have expected. The terms of reference outlined in his policy speech gave the Committee the brief to advise government "on the volume of public investment from time to time desirable, the general order of priority appropriate for the various investment projects, and the manner in which such projects should be financed". It was chaired by John Leydon, former Secretary of the Department of Industry and Commerce, and included Lieutenant General M.J. Costello of Irish Sugar, Kevin McCourt of the IDA, economists Patrick Lynch and Louden Ryan, and Ruairí Roberts of the Irish Congress of Trade Unions.[73]

Despite Sweetman's opposition to the Committee (see Chapter 11), he managed to set its agenda, asking it to concentrate first on the expected deficit of around £12 million in the capital budget. Its first report, published at the end of January 1957, ruled out a cut in capital spending, as this would cause an unacceptable increase in unemployment. Borrowing was not feasible, so "the sole remaining method of finance is by way of reductions in current Exchequer expenditure". The Committee recommended abolishing the subsidies on butter and flour, saving £2.4 million and £6.4 million respectively, and ending the agricultural rate relief grants to local authorities, which would save £5.6 million. It also warned against allowing wages to rise to compensate for higher prices when the subsidies were abolished. The report argued that "the elimination of these subsidies would establish an indispensable condition of economic expansion by bringing prices and costs into a more realistic relationship". Not surprisingly, Ruairí Roberts of ICTU signed a minority report disagreeing with this line.[74]

In later years, Costello himself was critical of the Committee, accusing it of having "a bland unconcern for political practicalities".[75] Even at the time, it was clear that its proposals would have been unacceptable to Labour, while John O'Donovan claimed in a 1973 interview that when Sweetman told Fine Gael colleagues on 25 January 1957 that he intended to abolish food subsidies, four of them threatened resignation—Liam Cosgrave, Tom O'Higgins, Patrick McGilligan and O'Donovan himself.[76] The only surviving member of the group mentioned, Liam Cosgrave, has no memory of any such meeting, or of a threat to resign.[77] He does, however, confirm the depth of feeling on the issue of food subsidies at the time, so there may be some basis for O'Donovan's story. In any case, the general election meant it was no longer a problem the Inter-party Government would have to deal with. Not alone did the new Fianna Fáil government cut the subsidies, they also directed capital spending away from "social" to "productive" investment.[78] This was also to be a theme of the *First Programme for Economic Expansion*, an example of how decisions taken by the Inter-party Government informed the sea-change in economic policy spearheaded by Lemass and Ken Whitaker.

Another such decision was the appointment of Whitaker as Secretary of the Department of Finance. His promotion "contravened the hitherto sacrosanct principle of seniority", as he got the job ahead of the longer-serving Sarsfield Hogan. In his history of the Department, Ronan Fanning suggests that the decisive proponent of Whitaker's appointment was McGilligan.[79] Some believed Hogan was passed over because of his son's involvement in the (temporary) theft of one of the Lane paintings, mentioned in Chapter 7, others to the fact that his "undisguised passion for rugby had contributed to a somewhat distant relationship with the worlds of economics and high finance".[80] Whatever the reasons for not appointing Hogan, there were compelling ones for Whitaker's promotion. He was immensely capable, and more in tune with modern ideas about economics than many of his contemporaries. This is not, of course, to suggest that he lacked an appreciation of the economic perils facing the State. Three and a half months after his appointment, he wrote to Sweetman, saying he was "the only Minister who fully understands how narrowly we have avoided failure in recent months".[81]

The use of the word failure is significant. As Tom Garvin noted when quoting the above letter, "the rhetoric of the Republic as a failed state was quite noticeable at the time".[82] It's easy to see why. Between 1951 and 1958, GDP rose by less than 1 per cent per annum, and Irish GDP per head fell from 75 per cent of the western European average to just 60 per cent. As Gary Murphy has observed, "it was during the 1950s that Ireland went into relative decline against similar states in Western Europe".[83] Whitaker remembered the 1950s as "a very grim time—we were in the slough of despond, a time when people were asking if we had a future".[84] There is plenty of reason to see the 1950s as the dismal decade, the nadir of Irish independence. For this, political leaders on all sides must take much of the blame.

On the other hand, the 1950s were also the time when important decisions were taken which paved the way for the growth of the 1960s. The change in Irish fortunes is usually attributed to the *First Programme for Economic Expansion*, to the work of Ken Whitaker and to the leadership of Lemass. But it is wrong to ignore the important role of Costello and of the second Inter-party Government in broadening public debate and preparing the way for important initiatives on foreign investment and export led growth. As Whitaker wrote in 2006, "the foundations of new policies for economic growth were being laid and the appropriate institutions established" at this time.[85] Unfortunately for Costello's reputation, although he had sketched out an economic reform agenda in 1953, he only began making progress on it after his government had presided over an economic crisis; and he was removed from power before his ideas could be implemented. This is why Lemass and Whitaker get the credit for the Irish economic transformation.

The impact of Costello's October speech on Lemass's thinking was obvious even at the time. As we saw in Chapter 11, his Clery's Ballroom speech had signalled a new direction for Fianna Fáil, although Costello had dismissed it because it failed to even mention agriculture. In January 1957 he made another policy speech, which according to his biographer John Horgan was "calcu-lated to mend his hand in relation to certain elements of the plans recently announced by Costello's Government, which had been accompanied by specific proposals for both industry and agriculture. His recommendations for the improvement of the agricultural sector addressed an issue that had been conspicuous by its absence from his Clery's Ballroom speech, and his espousal of tax-free profits for exports, while it echoed speeches he had made as far back as 1948, was also an attempt to trump Costello's proposals."[86] *The Leader* commented favourably on Lemass's "thoughtful and painstaking proposals", which it said were sound and realistic, although they did not "differ all that much from the outline of policy made by the Taoiseach last October".[87]

As well as promoting a positive policy, Costello also made efforts to ensure his ministers didn't unnecessarily antagonise the public. In August, Alexis FitzGerald had suggested that he might tell ministers "to be particularly careful not to have rows with any groups for the moment and to turn away wrath with soft words in every instance".[88] It was a good idea, and Costello acted on it, telling ministers at a Cabinet meeting "to see that none of their Departments caused any further irritation among sections of the community which would do us political damage".[89] One minister who took this injunct-ion to heart was James Everett, who ordered Garda drivers of State cars to stop parking illegally, as this was "simply inviting adverse criticism from members of the public".[90]

A more serious matter was corporal punishment in schools, an issue which had become controversial after Owen Sheehy Skeffington raised it in the Seanad.[91] Mulcahy decided he should meet this "attack ... on our Clerical management and on nuns and brothers as teachers" by clarifying exactly what was permitted. Up to then, the only instruments officially allowed for corporal punishment were a light rod or cane. In view of the "existing and traditional position", Mulcahy added the strap (a heavy leather article) to this list. This was done "to remove doubt on the part of those traditionally using it and on the part of the public". Not surprisingly, though, the circular was interpreted by the newspapers as the Minister approving the use of the strap.[92] Sheehy Skeffington denounced Mulcahy's action as "cowardly and callous", claiming that instead of taking firm action against those who broke the rules, he had changed the rules to suit them.[93] Seán MacBride put down a Dáil motion calling for the regulation to be withdrawn.[94]

After the issue was raised at the inter-party meeting on 5 October, Costello reminded Mulcahy of the need to avoid controversy. The Taoiseach said he was "writing you this personally as I would not wish you to think that it is a direction to you in your own Department, but I think it is not a matter that we should allow to be the subject of public discussion which would divert attention from our constructive proposals". While he assumed the Department "has a good case for it nevertheless I urge you to withdraw the regulation". He added that he had heard an unconfirmed rumour that there was "almost something in the nature of a riot" at one Christian Brothers school "because of the undue use of corporal punishment".[95]

Mulcahy agreed to withdraw the offending circular. But he also made it clear that he felt he had no role in school discipline. Unless a teacher did something that could lead to criminal charges, there was no sanction available to the Minister against "a Clerical Manager or a Clerical teacher unrepudiated by his or her Religious Superior".[96] Like his predecessors and successors, Mulcahy was not inclined to interfere in how the Church ran educational facilities—a failure which contributed to the climate of secrecy surrounding serious abuses, particularly in residential institutions.

Of course, the immediate reason for avoiding public controversy, and for the 5 October policy speech, was the pending by-elections in Carlow-Kilkenny and Dublin South-West. In a speech in Mooncoin in Kilkenny, Costello said his government, after taking remedial action, was now putting forward constructive proposals, unlike the Opposition. He said the reason Fianna Fáil was not offering any precise policy was because "they cannot agree on one ... Nobody knows whether it is Mr Lemass's policy of free spending of money, to be got from nobody knows where, or Mr MacEntee's policy of heavy taxation even for Capital purposes that is to prevail."[97]

The Taoiseach stressed that Fianna Fáil had not said the Government's actions in trying to control the balance of payments deficit were wrong. Therefore, he suggested optimistically, "if the electors show now in a striking manner their approval ... the results will provide a salutary lesson for the future leaders of our democracy, and an encouragement to public men generally to act in a responsible manner".[98] Just in case this call for an endorsement of austerity didn't work, he also had an inducement for voters, in the shape of an extra £1 million for job creation in "productive employment".[99] He told a meeting in Dublin South-West that the "only thing we have to fear in these by-elections is apathy on the part of the electorate".[100] But he was clearly well aware that they had a lot more to fear than that.

Despite his policy speech, despite his efforts to avoid annoying the electorate, the results were as bad as could have been expected. In Carlow-Kilkenny, Fianna Fáil's Martin Medlar retained the seat of his late party colleague Thomas Walsh. His vote, at 58 per cent, was up 12 per cent on the last general election, while Fine Gael support was down 6 per cent and Labour dropped 1 per cent. Dublin South-West was much worse. The deceased deputy, Peadar Doyle, was a member of Fine Gael, so that party supplied the sole inter-party candidate, Edmond Power. He took 40 per cent of the vote—compared to the 53 per cent won by inter-party candidates in 1954. Fianna Fáil's Noel Lemass took 60 per cent, an increase of 20 percentage points.

Costello had aimed to change the political mood, and had failed. He put on a brave face, saying the losses were not unexpected and rejecting Fianna Fáil's clamour for a general election. The Taoiseach high-mindedly told an audience in Rathmines that "the Government of a country is not a game to be played by political Parties for Party purposes". He pointed out that Fianna Fáil had argued in 1953 and 1954 that no country could be governed if by-election defeats inevitably led to general elections. Of course, Fianna Fáil had only said that because Jack Costello had been arguing the exact opposite. But now, he suggested, there was a difference: while the inter-party Opposition had rejected the Fianna Fáil government's policy, and outlined an alternative, the same was not true now.[101] It was an ingenious if rather thin argument. It probably fooled nobody, least of all the Taoiseach. His private mood was revealed in a letter to Tom Bodkin, who had again declined an offer to take over the Arts Council: "I have had so many frustrating disappointments that one more does not make any difference."[102]

The voters may not have been particularly impressed, but at least Seán MacBride and his two colleagues appeared to be back on board after the October policy speech. In November, the Clann leader wrote to Costello with some "brief" (nine pages!) suggestions about economic policy in the light of the Suez Crisis. He concluded his letter with an offer to secure more information if required, telling the Taoiseach, "I shall be entirely at your disposal." A further "brief memorandum on the need for a ten year economic development plan"—which ran to 26 pages plus appendices—was prepared by MacBride for Costello at the end of November.[103] As late as 12 January, MacBride was sending advice to Costello on how to cope with the unemployment situation.[104] There was no apparent reason for Costello to have any fears about MacBride's continued support—but that was about to change, and the change had nothing to do with economic policy.

In Chapter 11, we saw Costello's restrained response to Republican violence, particularly the raid on Roslea barracks, and his warning that if such violence continued, the Government would take action. A subsequent report by Chief Superintendent P.J. Carroll noted that there was "a temporary setback" to the IRA following the Taoiseach's statement and a condemnation of violence by the Catholic hierarchy. However, these initiatives "had no lasting effect in deterring persons from joining the IRA or taking part in its militant activities". The Gardaí continued the policy of "observation" of IRA activities until May 1956, when the Government ordered a clampdown on IRA training camps and arms dumps. By then, though, "the IRA had changed their tactics ... and gave no opportunity for effective police action".[105]

The IRA had not made tactical changes simply to frustrate police action; the organisation was planning a major push against Northern Ireland, Operation Harvest, more popularly known as the Border Campaign. This opened on the night of 11 November with the destruction of six Customs posts, a raid on Gough Barracks in Armagh and the destruction of a BBC transmission station in Derry.[106] A month later, the campaign escalated, with attacks on RUC barracks. Unionists condemned the Dublin Government for failing to stop cross-Border attacks.[107]

On 14 December, the Government decided to use the Gardaí and the Army to deal with the IRA. A statement agreed at a Cabinet meeting referred to Costello's warning in 1955. "Since these organisations have again arrogated to themselves powers and functions that belong to the duly elected representatives of the people ... the Government have now determined to take ... such steps as the Government deem necessary and appropriate to prevent activities which, if they were allowed to continue, would inevitably cause loss of life and would involve the danger that civil war might ensue."[108] The *Irish Times* said there was no need to underline the gravity of the statement—but observed that it was now up to the Taoiseach and his government "to demonstrate the sincerity of their words by immediate and vigorous action".[109] This was done by deploying the Army to assist the Gardaí on the border. That weekend, 13 men were arrested at a farm outside Scotstown in Monaghan.[110]

Although the arrested men had to be released because no arms or incriminating documents were found,[111] it was at least an indication that Costello was prepared to take action. The American Ambassador reported to Washington that there was a "violent cleavage" within Cabinet, with Norton opposing the Government action. Ambassador Taft speculated that the IRA might have been prompted to challenge the Government's authority because of its "growing weakness ... resulting from economic crisis and losses in recent by-elections".[112] The American Embassy was not impressed with the Government's response, saying it was "still reluctant to arrest IRA leaders", and that what had been done so far "does not represent what the police could accomplish if given a free hand".[113]

The British were also sceptical of Costello's efforts. On 12 December the Ambassador, Alexander Clutterbuck, expressed his government's concern to Cosgrave. On the eighteenth, he followed up by delivering a formal communication from his government to the Taoiseach. This again expressed concern, and hoped that the promised action against the IRA would be effective and successful. Unusually, British Prime Minister Anthony Eden outlined the contents of this message in the House of Commons. Eden went on to stress that under the 1949 Ireland Act, Northern Ireland was "an integral part of the United Kingdom", and therefore the safety of its inhabitants was a direct responsibility of his government.[114] The Taoiseach told Clutterbuck that his Government "was making a mistake in delivering such a note and registering a protest ... such action exacerbated Irish Government annoyance at Britain's failure to treat partition as the point at issue, as well as giving rise to a resentful feeling that the British Government was interfering".[115]

A formal written response followed on Christmas Eve. It pointed out that the Government's attitude had been made plain in a number of public statements, and that the measures that might be required were "for determination by the Irish Government solely, in the light of their experience and judgment and in discharge of their responsibility to Dáil Éireann". It reminded the British of Costello's statement of November 1955, when he had pointed out that the root cause of violence was partition. "While fully sharing the desire of the British Government for a continuance of good relations, they find it a matter of the deepest concern that there has, so far, been no indication of any change of attitude on the part of either the British or the Six-County Government towards the problem of Partition." Eden's statement in the House of Commons that Northern Ireland was an integral part of the United Kingdom "is one that could never, in any circumstances, be accepted by an Irish Government ... The Six Counties are part of the national territory of Ireland, and it remains the profound conviction of the Irish Government that the evils attendant on Partition can be eradicated only by the removal of their basic cause."[116]

While this was fairly traditional nationalist fare, Cosgrave was also working on a new tack. In January, he sought Cabinet approval for an approach to the British Government to seek improvements in the treatment of nationalists *within* Northern Ireland. Cosgrave reported that, in the view of leading Nationalist politician Eddie McAteer, some senior Unionists recognised that the violence was due to the frustration of normal constitutional political activity. Therefore, he argued, the time might be right to ask the British to take action, although the approach would have to be made in secret to avoid encouraging the men of violence.[117]

Enda Staunton has argued that this concentration on reform within Northern Ireland rather than on the removal of partition marked "the genesis of a new policy which, with some relapses, was to continue to the present day".[118] If it was an attempt to change the parameters of debate away from the sterile concentration on the Border, it didn't work. London viewed the *démarche* as yet another attempt to remove partition, and rejected it on those grounds.[119]

Despite the lack of any encouragement whatever from London, Costello and his colleagues agreed to begin a study in each Department of the practical consequences of an end to partition.[120] The Taoiseach announced his "positive policy" towards the North at the Fine Gael Ard Fheis on 6 February 1957. The British thought there was "nothing new so far as a united Ireland was concerned" in the speech, but recognised that his idea of carrying out preparatory work was "novel".[121] When he returned to office, de Valera recommended that Departments should continue these studies. The Department of External Affairs, however, reported that most Departments didn't consider the matter urgent, and there are no further entries on the file, indicating that nothing was done about it.[122] De Valera attempted to put out feelers to London through the former British Representative, Lord Rugby, but the new Prime Minister, Harold Macmillan, wasn't biting. "I do not think that a united Ireland—with de Valera as a sort of Irish Nehru—would do us much good. Let us stand by our friends."[123]

While Costello was rejecting British pressure for more robust action, he was also facing criticism for the action his Government *had* taken.

Independent TD Jack McQuillan urged the Taoiseach to "discontinue immediately [the] use of Irish Army and Gardaí as instruments of British policy in helping to maintain Partition". Costello reminded McQuillan that the right to determine issues of peace and war, and to maintain armed forces, was vested in the Oireachtas. The Gardaí and the Army were not being used as instruments of British policy, but to safeguard the institutions of the State. "I trust that you will appreciate the ... magnitude of the evil that could ensue if any elected representative of the people were to lend his support to activities that are based on defiance of the democratic institutions of this State."[124]

But as the year turned, the situation got much worse. On 30 December a 23-year-old (Catholic) RUC constable, John Scally, was killed in a raid on the barracks in Derrylin in Fermanagh.[125] And on New Year's Day, two IRA men were killed in a raid on the RUC barracks in Brookeborough, also in Fermanagh.[126] The funerals of Seán South and Fergal O'Hanlon saw a massive show of public sympathy for the "martyrs", and Clare and Dublin county councils passed motions of sympathy for them.[127] Northern Nationalists reacted with even more emotion. As a 15-year-old from Tyrone, Austin Currie later recalled, "it was, in truth, satisfying to see someone putting the boot into the arrogant and dominating unionists".[128]

McQuillan, along with Patrick Finucane (who had left Clann na Talmhan), called for the recall of the Dáil, the sending of United Nations observers to the North, and the release of seven men arrested in Cavan on New Year's Eve.[129] The arrested men, who had been charged under the Offences Against the State Act, included a future Chief of Staff of the IRA, Ruairí Ó Brádaigh.[130] Costello rejected their demands out of hand,[131] but recognised the need "to steady public opinion in these matters".[132] On the evening of Sunday 6 January he addressed the Irish people on Radio Éireann.

Three young Irishmen (he included the RUC man, Scally) had died in the past week; the Government was resolved to prevent further attacks. He and his colleagues believed that Partition "cannot, and never will, be ended by force"; but "a small group, with no basis of legitimate authority, is seeking to embroil our country in war". He dismissed as a "wicked misrepresentation" the idea that the Gardaí and Army were being used to maintain partition. In fact, they were preventing actions which would make divisions between Irishmen permanent. "Neither appeals for sympathy with young men who have put themselves in danger nor natural sorrow for tragic deaths should be allowed to betray any of us into an appearance of encouraging these actions."[133]

The British Foreign Secretary, Selwyn Lloyd, told Ambassador Boland that Costello's statement was "extremely good".[134] The number of letters from Republican sympathisers, particularly in America, showed that it had greatly annoyed that constituency. But Costello remained defiant. One correspondent argued that "a lot of bloodshed" would be needed to end partition; the Taoiseach said bloodshed would "make the problem harder to solve and could very easily make it impossible to solve at all".[135]

But was Costello serious about putting a stop to the IRA? The answer was yes—up to a point. The private secretary to the Minister for Justice recalled that the Government was determined to use the ordinary criminal code rather than special powers and internment, to which Costello and Everett, as well as their colleagues, were "temperamentally opposed". Apart from anything else, Ireland didn't want to be the first country to seek a derogation from the recently signed European Convention on Human Rights.[136] However, the Offences Against the State Act *was* used, and two days after Costello's speech arrests of suspects began in earnest. Most of the IRA Army Council and GHQ staff were quickly picked up and convicted.[137] Responding to later criticism from MacEntee that the Government had used the ordinary courts to deal with the IRA threat, he said the fact that a military tribunal had not been needed was "a distinct contribution to the effective handling of a difficult situation".[138]

However, the day before Costello lost office, a Garda report indicated that the results had been limited. Chief Superintendent P.J. Carroll estimated the active strength of the IRA at 943, and predicted that "the increase in numbers will tend to continue, as the militant activities in the Six Counties will attract youths and the emergence of Sinn Féin as an active political party will help to secure members for the IRA".[139] After he returned to power, de Valera adopted a tougher approach, introducing internment in July. The difference in treatment under the two governments is indicated by the experience of one Republican activist, jailed for two months in January under the Offences Against the State Act, then interned for 18 months in July. The same activist observed of Costello that he had been "straightforward, and restrained and dignified ... Republicans could not complain that they weren't given fair trial."[140] Although the internees were released at the end of 1958, sporadic continuing violence led to the reconstitution of the Special Criminal Court in November 1961.[141] The Border Campaign was finally called off in February 1962.[142]

To return to the aftermath of Costello's broadcast condemning IRA activities, he gratefully acknowledged the support given to him by de Valera.[143] The leader of the Opposition was doing his best to be helpful, calling a meeting of the Fianna Fáil parliamentary party for 15 January which unanimously agreed a motion saying there could be no armed force except under the control of the Government. Less helpfully, the meeting also discussed the possible use of force by any future government to end partition. "While no definite decision was taken, the views expressed indicated that the employment of force at any time in the foreseeable future would be undesirable and likely to be futile."

The fact that "no definite decision" was taken on the future use of force indicates the underlying tensions in the party, as John Horgan has pointed out.[144] Costello, however, looked on the positive side of the motion, telling Fianna Fáil TD Dan Breen that "with the assistance of your leader, public opinion has been steadied and is now behind the effort to uphold the legality of the Constitution".[145]

If there was tension within Fianna Fáil over the Government's crackdown on the IRA, it was nothing to the tensions within Clann na Poblachta. MacBride and Con Lehane advised against pulling the rug from under Costello's government. The only alternative was the return of de Valera, who would be even tougher on the IRA. In the emotion of the moment, though, the Republican activists who dominated the Clann executive insisted that their three TDS should put down a vote of no confidence in the Government.[146]

On 28 January Clann na Poblachta announced that it was "impossible" to continue supporting the Government, and a motion of no confidence was put down in the names of MacBride and his two fellow TDS, John Tully and Kathleen O'Connor. The motion was carefully crafted to put economic problems first. The three reasons it gave for withdrawing confidence from the Government were the failure to produce a long-term economic development programme, the failure to anticipate the unemployment crisis and take effective measures against it, and finally the failure "to formulate and pursue any positive policy calculated to bring about the reunification of Ireland".[147] MacBride always insisted it was the economy which prompted the motion—a very lengthy statement to Dublin constituency representatives went into great detail on all the warnings he had given the Government on the subject, and doesn't mention partition or the Border Campaign once.[148] A statement by the party's Ard Comhairle was more forthcoming; after a lengthy diatribe against the Government's economic failings, it accused Costello and his colleagues of "acting as Britain's policeman against a section of the Irish people".[149]

On the day the Clann put down its motion, the Taoiseach happened to be discussing cross-Border relations with Trinity College senator William Bedell Stanford. He showed him MacBride's letter, and "spoke sadly about the 'dastardliness' of this manoeuvre ... he seemed greatly saddened by the ruthlessness of party politics, and disappointed at not having taken the gun out of politics as he had hoped in 1948. But he showed plenty of moral force and physical energy despite his rather slight build, and he still looked fit after his gruelling three years in office."[150] He wrote a rather hurt reply to MacBride, saying he had agreed to become Taoiseach with the aim of taking the gun out of Irish politics, and of helping to end "the bitterness between personalities and Parties that was poisoning the public life of the country. My first hope has not yet been fully realised. So far as the second hope is concerned, I do not intend, for my part, to permit recent events to add any further bitterness."[151] The British Ambassador reported to London that "to say that the Government are angered and disgusted at MacBride's behaviour is to put it mildly. Another six months would, it is felt, have made all the difference ... both on the political and economic fronts a new chapter might have been opened. To be compelled to go to the country at this moment, before they have had time to compete their work on either front, is hard enough; but to be forced to do so through the sheer opportunism of MacBride and his two followers is, they feel, the last word."[152]

Was an election inevitable? Some felt it wasn't. As we saw above, Dillon believed Costello could and should have tried to soldier on, but that he had lost heart after the death of his wife. Dillon thought that if MacBride had known that Costello would call an election, he would have withdrawn his motion of no confidence.[153] However, this seems unlikely, as it was not MacBride but the Clann executive that insisted on putting the motion in the first place. In any event, a hard-headed look at the numbers in the Dáil showed the Government's position was untenable. Fianna Fáil's Thomas Derrig had died in November, leaving the Dáil with 146 members, one of whom, Ceann Comhairle Patrick Hogan of Labour, would not vote unless there was a tie. Fine Gael had lost two seats and Labour one in by-elections, while Patrick Finucane of Clann na Talmhan had withdrawn his support from the Government in a dispute over milk prices and the failure to supply a factory for Listowel, as promised in the North Kerry by-election.[154] After the loss of Clann na Poblachta's three votes, this left the inter-party grouping with 71 seats (excluding the Ceann Comhairle), while Fianna Fáil, Clann na Poblachta and the Independents likely to vote against the Government had 74.[155] Any faint hope that Fianna Fáil might support the Government in an act of anti-IRA solidarity were dispelled when de Valera put down his own no confidence motion the day after MacBride's.[156] The British Ambassador described the Clann's sudden withdrawal of support as "a bombshell to the country", while the Fianna Fáil motion "finally dashed" any hope of Costello's government remaining in power.[157]

Determined to avoid inevitable defeat in the Dáil, Costello advised the President on 4 February that he would be seeking a dissolution on the twelfth of the month (the day the Dáil was due back after the Christmas recess). Polling day was to be Tuesday 5 March, with the new Dáil to meet on 20 March.[158] Announcing his plans nearly a week before the formal dissolution of the Dáil allowed Costello to use the Fine Gael Ard Fheis on the sixth to launch his election campaign. He acknowledged that an election at that time "must be gravely damaging to the national interest", but insisted he had no alternative. Responsibility rested with those parties who had put down motions of no confidence. These made an election inevitable, showed "a reckless and irresponsible disregard of the country's interests", and were "criminal and miserable acts of sabotage". He said the real reason for MacBride's action was, "to put it quite bluntly, because of Government action against the unlawful use of force".

The Taoiseach suggested a federal solution to the problem of partition, promising that minority rights would be respected in a united Ireland. "The spirit of peace cannot thrive in any community where there is discrimination against a particular category of people ... The object of our policy is a reunion willingly entered into and fully safeguarding the rights of all minority interests." He also again deplored the outbreak of violence and repeated his Government's determination to tackle it.[159] His speech was welcomed by the British Government, which saw it as containing "some of the most significant and moderate comment on the Partition issue to have come out of Dublin for some time past".[160]

The Government made some efforts to lighten the economic gloom. Even before the election was called, it had rescinded an earlier decision to restrict the public capital programme to £27 million. This decision had been made in November 1956, but at the start of the year Sweetman was complaining that Departments had submitted estimates for capital spending totalling £38 million. The Government avoided the hard decisions on cutting those estimates by deciding that the limit on capital spending should be increased to between £38 and £40 million, in order "to avoid a further deflationary effect on the economy".[161] On 16 January Costello announced a £4.5 million "mini capital budget" to bring relief to the unemployed. As he later pointed out, these moves were announced before MacBride's no-confidence motion precipitated the election.[162]

The same could not be said of certain other Government decisions. A few days before the election, it decided to reduce the price of tea. Lemass claimed there was no justification for this move[163]—except, presumably, possible political advantage. The Taoiseach also successfully interceded with CIÉ Chairman Ted Courtney (a contributor to his election fund) over the proposed dismissal of painters by the company. Costello wrote after the election to thank him: "It is a comfort to both of us that your action was not a mere political one but resulted in the saving of distress to a large number of families. That is your consolation and mine."[164]

There was some good economic news during the course of the campaign, with trade figures for January showing an increase of £3.7 million in exports, up 50 per cent on the same month in the previous year. Imports had fallen by £2.3 million on January 1956. In the light of these encouraging figures, Costello claimed the Government was "entitled to full credit for stopping the rot in the balance of payments and for producing a clear, definite and practical policy for increasing production".[165] However, he admitted that his Government's plans and policies were "only partially showing results" because of the unexpected timing of the election. The Taoiseach also stressed the scale and scope of the problems which had hit the country at the one time, and faced the Government "with difficulties which no other Irish Government ever has had to face".[166]

The campaign was marked by repeated Fianna Fáil attacks on the very concept of coalition government. Costello complained that "the phrase 'single party government' drums through all their speeches ... like the monotonous beat of an African tom-tom".[167] It was true that Fianna Fáil happily made hay of coalition differences. Frank Aiken said the members of the Government "spent most of their time double-crossing the people who voted for them and preparing to double-cross one another".[168] Jim Ryan said the country had suffered "not only the evils of a Coalition Government but the disaster of an incompetent Government".[169] Lemass said they were not going to simply find fault with the Government; he said they "did their best" but were "condemned to failure from the start" by the fact they were a coalition. "Each party in it was, for the past year, trying to judge the right time, in its own party interest, to get out of it, and in the end the smallest party beat them to it."[170] De Valera had a historical analogy. Recalling the "scurrying of the envoys that went from Party to Party when the first Coalition was being arranged", he said it was "sadly reminiscent to some of us of the scurrying of envoys that took place at another important juncture in our history".[171] He didn't actually mention the Treaty negotiations, presumably because his reference would have been understood by his audience.

But Costello didn't take these attacks lying down. He pointed to differences between senior Fianna Fáil figures. "It is impossible to reconcile ... Mr Lemass's plan which contemplates a large increase in public expenditure of approximately £20 million a year with the 'rigid economy' favoured by Mr MacEntee."[172] Lemass, with a cheerful disregard for the facts, dismissed this as "nonsense". He claimed that he and MacEntee "never had a fundamental disagreement on the aims of policy" (which of course is not the same as disagreement on the policy to achieve the aims). "Of course, we had arguments ... every Minister worth his salt has arguments with the Minister for Finance sooner or later."[173]

The Taoiseach criticised Fianna Fáil for not producing an alternative policy, in contrast to his own *Policy for Production* outlined the previous October. However, he acknowledged that the new policy had just commenced and had yet to take effect. "It has been like a machine which is at work but whose productive benefits have not yet reached the consumer—they are still along the assembly belt."[174] He also claimed that a sign of the "staleness of the political situation" was that the Fianna Fáil speeches "could all have been made ... at any one of the four elections which have been held since the War". The reason, he suggested, was that de Valera "refuses to discuss the real issues of policy".[175] He had evidently forgotten his own refusal three years before to commit himself on policy. In fact, speeches in this series of elections were somewhat interchangeable—not within Fianna Fáil, but between government and opposition. The speeches Costello made in 1951 and 1957 as outgoing Taoiseach could easily have been made by de Valera in 1954; equally, his criticisms of the Government in 1954 were echoed by Fianna Fáil in 1957.

One new issue was the IRA's Border Campaign. Former Fianna Fáil Justice Minister Gerry Boland claimed this was "a direct and inevitable result of Coalition policy. If carte blanche had not been given to this illegal organisation there would have been no Coalition Government in 1948 or 1954."[176] Costello took grave exception to this, indignantly denying that his government had turned a blind eye to the IRA. He pointed out that the raid on Armagh barracks took place 10 days after his second government took office, and the "arming, drilling, recruiting and planning" for that operation were clearly going on while Fianna Fáil was in office. The Taoiseach said he had no apology to make for his policy, which had been "temperate, but firm".[177] Following further criticism from MacEntee, he said the Government had accepted the challenge from the IRA "within 24 hours ... notwithstanding Clann na Poblachta, and the recognition of the temptation which would be presented to Fianna Fáil. This Election has come about, not because of any weakness in the Government but because of the Government's strength and devotion to principle, and because of its refusal in the national interest to make any compromise."[178]

The economic background music might have been dismal, but Costello remained upbeat, writing on 22 February that as he moved about the country, he found Government supporters "quietly confident of the result ... I always endeavour to avoid forecasting. I certainly feel, however, that the Government, particularly in the last ten days, have gathered considerable support."[179] Four days before polling, he predicted "a national rally" to the Government parties. "Such a rally would be a tonic not merely to the political system itself but to the national spirit generally ... I have no doubt of your support."[180] He should have.

In Dublin South-East, Costello still topped the poll—but his vote, at 28.4 per cent, was down almost 14 percentage points on 1954. That meant the end of John O'Donovan, whose seat was taken by Noël Browne, now running as an Independent. Browne's first-preference vote of 24.8 per cent was four points higher than three years before, when he was a Fianna Fáil candidate. The other seat was taken by MacEntee, who was also just under a quota with

24.3 per cent of the vote. It was, ironically, a small transfer from Costello which elected Browne to the Dáil again.[181] Nationally, Fine Gael lost the gains made in 1954, being reduced to 40 seats, the same number as in 1951. Labour slumped to 12 seats, and Clann na Talmhan to just three. The other Clann, which had precipitated the election, returned just one TD, John Tully; Seán MacBride would never be elected to the Dáil again. There were four Sinn Féin TDS, who were of course abstentionst. But the big news was the Fianna Fáil performance. In de Valera's last general election as leader, his party won 78 of the 147 seats on offer.

The British Ambassador was surprised at "a landslide of these dimensions ... since the whole campaign was deceptively quiet and even in its closing stages was marked by a discouraging lack of interest on the part of the general public".[182] But, as *The Leader* pointed out, "Circumstances were hard on the government. They had to apply unpopular measures, and Mr Costello had the great sorrow of seeing his policy of 'taking the gun out of politics' apparently thwarted ... Our gratitude to them is genuine, especially to Mr Costello who is patently a man devoid of personal ambition, and who has continued his disinterested service to the country when stricken with domestic sorrow."[183]

A typically pungent comment on the Government's plight was offered by Patrick Lindsay, who travelled to Áras an Uachtaráin to surrender his seal of office with Costello and Dillon. As they passed a pub on the quays, Dillon said he'd never been in a pub except his own in Ballaghaderreen, which he sold because "when I saw people going home having spent so much money on drink, I decided that they were depriving their families of essentials". Costello then chipped in the observation that he had only been in a pub once, in Terenure, "and was nearly choked by a bottle of orange". To Lindsay, the pub was "the countryman's club, where everything is discussed and where contacts are made". He was horrified by the attitude of his colleagues. "****. I now know why we are going in this direction today and why we are out of touch with the people."[184]

The Taoiseach was more philosophical. As he told Archbishop McQuaid, "there are many compensations in defeat", although he regretted that his Government had been "judged at the worst time and in the most adverse circumstances".[185] To another correspondent, he observed that "defeat was inevitable in the circumstances. It is distressing that we should be judged on incomplete work, but such is the nature of democracy." He added that he was "in no way discouraged".[186] He spent his final weekend as Taoiseach in Cork with his daughter Eavan.[187]

There was no suspense about the election of the Taoiseach in 1957, as de Valera was the only nominee. Costello opposed the nomination "in no spirit of animosity ... but in the firm conviction that in present circumstances the

Party to which he belongs is not equipped to provide the kind of Government which the country needs ... That Party has so far shown no policy which would justify a Government being selected from it." De Valera's nomination was approved by 78 votes to 53.[188] Later, in the debate on the nomination of the members of the Government, Costello promised that Fine Gael would be a constructive opposition, and claimed they left behind them a "solid contribution to some of the difficulties" facing the country. He pointedly said his party would try to forget that Fianna Fáil had not given them any co-operation in the previous Dáil.[189]

Despite his return to the opposition benches, Costello remained enthusiastic about politics, about Fine Gael, and about the inter-party approach. He told one correspondent that "so far as I have health and strength I will do everything possible to continue the fight and pass on the torch". To that end, he planned to continue his efforts to bring "young people and new ideas" into Fine Gael so as to revive the party and "make it a force not merely in politics but in ideas throughout the country". The former Taoiseach insisted that "we did a good service to the country by associating with the Labour Party"—they had been given an opportunity to see what government really involved.[190] But Labour were bruised by their experience, and by dealing with Sweetman in particular. Brendan Corish swore he would never again serve in government with the former Minister for Finance.[191] It did not point towards a happy or a productive period in opposition.

Chapter 14 ∿

A PERFECTLY HAPPY MAN

"Recent changes were ... rather a hurtful shock to me."[1]
JOHN A. COSTELLO, DECEMBER 1959

*"Put upon your banners the Just Society, that Fine
Gael is not a Tory party."*[2]
JOHN A. COSTELLO, 1969

"Am I a happy man? Yes, perfectly."[3]
JOHN A. COSTELLO, NOVEMBER 1974

The day after he lost office, Costello was back at the Bar, starting work immediately with a brief in Cork.[4] He was quite happy to return to the law after serving as Taoiseach—and there were plenty of people in the legal world happy to welcome him back.[5] The speed of his return to the law also demonstrated his priorities—as before, he would be a part-time Opposition politician.

The summer break was spent quietly. He told his friend Tom Bodkin that he was enjoying his first Long Vacation for four years. "I have done literally nothing—played golf and read and brought my grandchildren to the sea when the weather permitted." However, as a result of "a family conspiracy", he was persuaded to go to Cannes on holiday in September. He told Bodkin "my own honest desire was to stay at home but the conspiracy was too much for me".[6] Despite his reluctance, he was later reported to have had "a most enjoyable and particularly a most restful holiday in Cannes and looks very much the better for it".[7]

The loss of public office meant he had to deal again with the tax authorities, who seemed oblivious to his recent eminence. After receiving a tax assessment in September 1957 he had to complain that the inspector seemed unaware that he became a senior counsel 32 years before and was no longer "an ordinary Barrister-at-Law". Worse, the inspector had not adverted "to the position which I occupied until the 20th March last".[8]

Officialdom may have forgotten that Costello had been Taoiseach; but despite his return to active work at the Bar, he remained leader of the Opposition. One of his first tasks in that role was to respond to the first Budget of the new government. In a broadcast on Radio Éireann, he criticised Fianna Fáil's failure during the election to signal its intention of removing food subsidies. "It would have been better if the sacrifices now writ so large in the Budget had been writ even small in the election campaign."[9] In the Dáil, Costello rejected suggestions that the new government was following the advice of the Capital Advisory Committee in abolishing the subsidies. He pointed out that the Committee had recommended abolition in order to sustain the capital programme—not as a relief for general Government spending. "What they have done is not what the Capital Advisory Committee said they were to do—utilise the food subsidies for capital purposes because capital was so scarce—but they have done what the Capital Advisory Committee said that they were not to do at all—used them as current revenue."[10]

However, he was later to stress that Fine Gael's opposition to the Government was "moderate", because the party "could not honestly oppose much of the legislation proposed ... because they represented merely a continuance of policies which we had introduced when in Government". In the same speech (to the Fine Gael Ard Fheis in February 1958) he claimed Fine Gael had "placed the national interest before its Party interest" in 1956, introducing unpopular measures to tackle the balance of payments deficit and meeting the challenge of the IRA. Because of that, the party was in opposition. "We had no illusions as to its effects on our political fortunes, nor did we smugly console ourselves with the consideration that political virtue is its own reward. Our recompense is that we gave an honest headline for future politicians to follow and did something to increase the experience of reality by our democracy."[11]

There were some other pointers for the future in his early contributions from the opposition benches. Proposing a fact-finding committee to educate TDs and senators about the implications of the EEC and the Free Trade Area— he claimed that 80 per cent of Deputies didn't know the difference between the two—Costello firmly said Ireland could not leave itself outside their scope. He said the proposals for a Common Market presented a challenge, adding, "Personally, I think they also present us with an opportunity." But that opportunity could not be availed of unless politicians were fully informed.[12] His proposal was rejected by the Government. He also hinted that he realised his generation had nearly finished its time at the top in politics. "If we have not reached the end of a chapter in Irish history, at least we are nearing the end. You have only to look around you in this House and see that those people who bore the brunt of the effort to create the State, and subsequently to maintain it, are passing on."[13]

The most significant development under de Valera's final government was the publication of *Economic Development*, written by Ken Whitaker, in November 1958. In March of that year, Costello foreshadowed some of the themes of that document. He argued in the Dáil that "it is about time that a little bit of expansion was tried ... You cannot get that increase in business activity which can give its full and essential contribution to the ending of unemployment and emigration ... unless we can get foreign capital in here ... God only knows the amount of capital we have lost because of the Control of Manufactures Act."[14] John F. McCarthy has pointed to Ken Whitaker's support for foreign investment as one of the important differences between *Economic Development* and Costello's 1956 *Policy for Production* (the other difference he noted was the greater economic sophistication of the former).[15] Costello's Dáil comments, made before the publication of *Economic Development*, suggest there was less of a difference on foreign investment than McCarthy believed.

On the document itself, and the accompanying White Paper, Costello was reserved—but crucially, he and Fine Gael did not oppose the new direction. Ken Whitaker found the lack of criticism from the Opposition benches "quite extraordinary", and very welcome.[16] Costello told the Dáil in April 1959 that he didn't believe the documents contained schemes "which will come to any degree of fruition or will introduce any substantial increase in employment".[17] He claimed Fianna Fáil policies were like dud cheques. In this case, they had to get "a cheque which would not be accepted by the people ... marked good by the most distinguished civil servant we have in the service of this State".[18] And he pointed out that his government had put in place "two very valuable contributions to the building up and strengthening of our industrial fabric"—tax breaks for exports, and the attraction of foreign investment.[19]

The last point may have been stretching it a bit, but Costello could certainly claim that his government had started to pursue policies very similar to those in *Economic Development* before it left office. Costello's plan was based on the incorrect assumption that agriculture would be the main driving force of expansion—but so was Whitaker's.[20] Ronan Fanning suggested that "the larger historical significance" of Whitaker's initiative "was ultimately psychological ... [it succeeded] because so many so badly wanted it to succeed".[21] Had things worked out differently, perhaps Costello's *Policy for Production* would have been remembered as a turning point in Ireland's economic history.

Some of those closest to the former Taoiseach were trying to continue the process of modernising Fine Gael. The main movers were his son Declan, son-in-law Alexis FitzGerald, and the former Minister for Health, Tom O'Higgins. Alexis and Declan were the joint editors of a new party paper, the *National*

Observer. In his first editorial, FitzGerald suggested that "all the sacred cows may be chased around our pasture and we are not without hope that some of them will expire from the exhaustion of the exercise".[22] As could be expected, some of the owners of the sacred cows were less than enthusiastic about this idea. Tom O'Higgins, chairman of the paper, received a blistering complaint from party grandee Michael Hayes that "the *National Observer* is so busy belittling Fine Gael that it has no time for praise".[23]

In April 1959, Bishop Michael Browne of Galway wrote to Costello complaining about comments concerning him in an issue of the paper. The Bishop noted that the directors of the company were O'Higgins, FitzGerald and Declan Costello, and complained that the language used about him had "heretofore ... been associated with anti-clericals and Communists". Alexis— who had written the offending article—told his father-in-law he stood over the comments, and believed it was their duty to speak out with "a frankness, if not with an authority or a responsibility" equal to Bishop Browne's. Costello wrote a frosty letter to the Bishop, telling him the three individuals he mentioned "are exemplary Catholics. There is not a grain of either anti-clericalism or communism in any one of them, and I am surprised that Your Lordship should have thought it fitting to suggest otherwise. I am glad to have the friendship of Mr T.F. O'Higgins, and I thank Almighty God for my son Declan and my son-in-law Alexis FitzGerald."[24]

Their other initiative was the Fine Gael Research and Information Centre. The aim here was to generate discussion on new ideas, particularly on social and economic issues. As Declan Costello recalled, they felt they had to create public interest in Fine Gael if they were ever to get back into power.[25] Their work was welcomed by *The Leader*. "It has often been said that the one class of men who do not continue their education in after life are those who most need it, politicians."[26]

In opposition as in government, John A. Costello relied heavily on these close collaborators. For instance, in February 1958 he wrote to Alexis about a request from the *Irish Times* for him to contribute an article to a series about the present and future prospects for the country. "Needless to say my first reaction is not to turn myself into a journalist, and, in accordance with my practice, I am leaving the matter lie for the moment, but perhaps you would think about it and talk to Declan and Tom O'Higgins and any others you think proper ..." Predictably, FitzGerald was "very keen" that his father-in-law should write an article, which duly appeared under the very Costello-like headline "Pessimism throttles our progress".[27]

The other key figure in Costello's team was his secretary, Ita McCoy. A sister of Kevin and Dr Tom O'Higgins, she had been present when their father was murdered by the IRA during the Civil War. She had come to work for

Costello when he became Taoiseach, having previously been personal secretary to Dick Mulcahy. Later, she was secretary to her nephew, Tom O'Higgins, when he was deputy leader of Fine Gael, and then to Garret FitzGerald when he was Minister for Foreign Affairs.[28] Her efficiency was legendary—which was just as well as Costello juggled political, legal, constituency and personal affairs. She was also better able to decipher his terrible handwriting than most mortals. Enclosing a message for her to type in March 1958 he admitted that it was "indecipherable as usual".[29] On his retirement, he paid her a handsome tribute, describing her as "my guide, philosopher, and, I am glad to say, my friend. When I was dictating a speech or even in my legal work ... I know that I can't make a mistake because if I do she spots it at once."[30]

As we saw in the last chapter, Labour politicians were bruised and bitter after their experience in government, and determined to follow a more independent line. In July 1957 James Larkin objected to the Ceann Comhairle's description of Costello as leader of the Opposition. "I have a great regard for Deputy Costello's work as Taoiseach ... However, he is not my leader ..."[31] There were tensions, too, within Fine Gael. Liam Cosgrave held Gerard Sweetman personally responsible for the party's defeat at the polls, and told him so. He reportedly told the patrician Sweetman that Fine Gael "was no longer led by people living in big houses at the end of long avenues". For the next few years their communications were "strictly official".[32] Sweetman, meanwhile, was resentful of the way he had been treated by Costello, and implacably opposed to another coalition with Labour.[33]

Costello wasn't the only Fine Gael frontbencher who returned to a full-time career outside politics. The result was that much of the work in the Dáil devolved on those who *were* full-time politicians, principally Mulcahy, Cosgrave and Dillon.[34] Despite the Government's seemingly unassailable majority, Dillon did his best to keep Fine Gael on its collective toes, claiming in September that they had been waiting six months for de Valera to "get cracking", and the only result so far was "cracked" prices. "This Government may not last long, and it is of vital importance to this country that it should be succeeded by a strong Fine Gael Government, for which we should start organising now."[35] Costello, meanwhile, was proclaiming that he remained optimistic "because my faith in the country's future has never been shaken or dimmed ... Not even at the worst moments of last year's great economic stress did Fine Gael lose faith in the fundamental capacity of our people to overcome any problem that might temporarily thwart them."[36]

This declaration of faith in the people was made at the start of a by-election campaign in Dublin North-Central, caused by the death of Fianna Fáil TD Colm Gallagher. The result was a surprise—and comfortable—victory for Independent Frank Sherwin, who took just over a third of the first-preference vote. The Fianna Fáil candidate came second with 27 per cent while Fine Gael took just under 20 per cent. Sherwin had more than doubled the 15 per cent he received in the general election just seven months before, while Fianna Fáil had lost 21 per cent from its first-preference vote. By contrast, the Fine Gael vote was down by only 2 per cent, a reasonably acceptable result given the swing to Sherwin.[37]

There were five further by-elections during Costello's leadership of the Opposition. Fine Gael's best result was in Dublin South-West in July 1959, where Richie Ryan won a seat from Fianna Fáil. In three of the other contests, the party's vote was lower than in the general election—a 5 per cent drop in Dublin South-Central in June 1958, and 6.5 per cent in Clare and 1.4 per cent in Meath in July 1959. It wasn't disastrous, but it certainly didn't indicate that the party was recovering lost ground, particularly as the Fianna Fáil vote was substantially down in each of the five by-elections. In its commentary on the Dublin South-Central by-election, *The Leader* denied that any moral was to be drawn from the result. " ... as there is at the moment nothing very exciting happening, what people call 'apathy' gives the tone and result."[38]

But if by-elections failed to generate much excitement, a Fianna Fáil proposal to change the electoral system certainly did. As we saw in Chapter 6, Costello had advised de Valera not to specify the use of PR STV in the 1937 Constitution, arguing that the system would eventually lead to a large number of small parties and unstable governments; better, he argued, to leave the type of proportional representation open, as it had been in the Free State Constitution. De Valera rejected this advice, on the grounds that a government could find an electoral system that seemed proportional, but in fact wasn't.[39]

Twenty-one years later, de Valera had changed his mind. Not alone did he want to get rid of the single transferable vote, he wanted to abolish proportional representation altogether. The reason was the very one advanced by Costello in 1937, that the system led to a multiplicity of parties. When the Bill was introduced in the Dáil on 12 November 1958, Costello (along with Norton) opposed its first reading, normally a formal introduction without a vote. He acknowledged that this was an unusual tactic, but said it was "essential that we should at the earliest opportunity emphasise our implacable opposition" to the measure. Lemass's testy response indicated the Government's annoyance at his action.[40]

When it came to the substantive debate, Costello accused Fianna Fáil of arrogance in insisting that PR must go "just because they were beaten twice by the electorate under the most democratic system in the world". He accepted that he had argued that PR would lead to a multiplicity of parties, but now added the rider that if voters wanted a number of parties, they were entitled to have them. The impact of the alternative system could only be guessed at—the Irish Parliamentary Party had been wiped out in 1918 under the first-past-the-post system, even though it got a higher percentage of the vote than Fine Gael received in 1943, 1944 or 1948. "P.R., if you like to say so, saved Fine Gael at that time"—an argument, it might be thought, hardly likely to appeal to de Valera.[41] Costello believed that once the system was changed, it would be almost impossible to change it back, because Fianna Fáil would have an unshakable grip on power. "A dying generation such as we are has no right to impose its will upon young people ... They will never get a chance to change it by constitutional means and it will require something like a revolution to do so."[42]

The Government announced that the presidential election would be held on the same day as the referendum, claiming this would reduce costs. Nonsense, Costello told the Dáil: "it is the last effort to try to save the Referendum Bill from defeat by throwing the personality of the Taoiseach into the arena at the last minute ... they are asked 'Do not let the poor old man down; do not let him down now by voting against him on the Referendum Bill'".[43]

Outside the Dáil, Costello pointed out that the main argument for change was to ensure that governments had a strong enough mandate to give stability and achieve economic progress. But the current government had one of the largest majorities in the history of the State, and after almost two years in office "even the most optimistic cannot say that there has been anything other than a slight indication of recovery".[44] Without any public demand, the issue of electoral reform had been brought forward and was now dominating debate. "The Government appears to have lost all sense of perspective in its dealings with the affairs of the country ... the proposals involve a leap in the dark and a journey into the unknown".[45] In what was to be his last Ard Fheis speech as leader of the Opposition, he accused de Valera of being "obsessed with the fact that he has been twice defeated under the present electoral system". The Taoiseach admitted he had been wrong on this issue in 1937 and "now blandly states ... that he is right now radically to change the Constitution in a revolutionary manner without adequate examination or opportunity for calm consideration".[46]

In a speech in Cork in April 1959, Costello linked the two votes, on PR and on the presidency, saying voters had to "make decisions of grave import to the future of the country". He was confident that "the proper decision" would be made in the referendum. Evidently, he was less optimistic about the presidency. He suggested the holder of that office should have the confidence of every section of the community; he didn't mention de Valera by name, referring to him as "General Seán MacEoin's opponent", and pointing out that he was "a highly controversial figure".[47] In his final broadcast of the referendum campaign, he warned that "governments can be too strong". The aim of the change, he claimed, was "to secure the election of a government which can rule in the knowledge that it has an over-whelming majority in a subservient Parliament from which all effective Opposition is substantially excluded ... Hold fast to your own voting system. Have the courage to say NO ..."[48]

The voters did exactly that, though it was a close run thing—the proposal was rejected by 51.8 per cent to 48.2 per cent. Costello's Dublin South-East constituency had the highest voter turnout in Dublin, rejecting the Government's proposal by a thumping 64.4 per cent to 35.6 per cent. However, the voters were far more enthusiastic about the idea of a President de Valera— he defeated MacEoin by 56 per cent to 44 per cent. This, naturally, led to a change of Taoiseach, with Seán Lemass the sole candidate for the leadership of Fianna Fáil and therefore of the Government.

Costello told the Dáil he and his party opposed Lemass's appointment "not ... on the personality of the Taoiseach designate but on the fact that he and the Government ... have been guilty ... of grave dereliction of public duty and gross breach of confidence". He said they had been elected on the promise of dealing with the economy, but instead had wasted time by attempting to abolish proportional representation. The response from the Fianna Fáil benches was significant as it drew attention to Costello's less than exemplary Dáil attendance—Michael Davern jeered that he "was not two hours in the House in the past two years".[49]

Costello's part-time leadership was causing concern within Fine Gael as well. He generally attended the Dáil after court had risen for the day; and if the High Court was in Cork, he didn't attend at all. As well as being a lucrative source of cases, his work in Cork had personal attractions—he was able to stay with his daughter Eavan and her husband, Ralph Sutton, then living in the southern capital.[50] From the late 1950s on, the High Court sat twice a year in Cork for two weeks; there were also two one-week Assizes each year, when appeals would be heard from the Circuit Court. As in Dublin, most of Costello's work involved personal injury cases.[51]

His ability to attract briefs in Cork—where it was difficult for "outsiders" to break in—showed the high reputation which he had as a barrister.[52] In November 1958 he told Tom Bodkin he had "spent three continuous weeks in Cork with the High Court"[53]—missing two weeks of Dáil sittings as a result. Another example came the following March. The Dáil sat on Tuesday and Wednesday the tenth and eleventh; however, the High Court was on circuit in Cork that week. The leader of the Opposition did his best to be in two places at once, travelling to Cork on the Sunday evening, returning to Dublin on Wednesday evening for the only vote of the week (on the Budget), before travelling back down to Cork early on the Thursday morning so he could appear in court.[54] The business in the Dáil was not particularly vital on this occasion, but still it was no way to show the country, or Fine Gael, that he was serious about his leadership position.

In opposition, the usual problems of poor attendance by Fine Gael TDS resurfaced. Mulcahy complained to Costello about the running of front bench meetings and the attentiveness of the members: "they should sit to attention in an undistracted way ... one of the things that had been completely disturbing to the whole atmosphere and spirit of the Front Bench was the way in which, first, people came in late, secondly that they were not paying attention to what is going on, thirdly they take out a paper and begin to have a conversation about something or other ..."[55] There was, as the US Embassy noted, "bickering" within the party, particularly on the leadership question, and Dillon for one had been critical of poor Dáil attendances and the front bench's failure to give a clear lead on policy development.[56]

Frustrated by the situation, Mulcahy visited Costello at his home in Herbert Park in September 1959. Their discussion on the leadership was recorded in Mulcahy's typically verbose and convoluted style. What was crystal clear, though, was that Mulcahy held Costello responsible for many of the problems. Mulcahy said he would not lead the party after the next election, either in government or in opposition, and that the two of them had a joint responsibility to give a lead to the party. Costello replied that he had been anxious to avoid giving the impression that he was "ousting" Mulcahy. The party leader said this proved that the dual leadership was preventing Costello from doing things he should have been doing, as well as raising questions about his leadership capacity. " ... his line ... that he had been holding back in order not to appear to be ousting me ... was not at all an explanation of the difficulties that we had been experiencing with him about lack of attention ... The principal difficulty [was] ... that at no particular point did he show a sustained desire or attempt to wield a sustained influence in pushing ahead any part of the work."

Costello said he was prepared to assume the leadership of the party. But it wasn't at all clear to Mulcahy how he intended to mend his ways, although he acknowledged, "The fact that he says that he has been holding back because of my position contains the implication that he is prepared to come very definitely forward." Crucially, however, Costello said he would have to continue at the Bar for the next couple of years, as "he had very considerable expenditure for particular private and domestic reasons".

He also appeared to be worried about opposition to him within the party. He believed Liam Cosgrave was annoyed at being transferred from the External Affairs portfolio to Industry and Commerce. Costello said that

Industry and Commerce was "a more important position", but Mulcahy pointed to the lengthy list of legislation which Cosgrave would have to deal with in the Dáil in the coming session. "I suggested that this was a very heavy responsibility that might very well cool the ardour of anybody who had to deal with it."

Costello also "had certain difficulties in his mind about Sweetman". Mulcahy replied that Sweetman and Dillon "were the two people who were always there and always ready to step into the breach ... The only satisfaction they wanted was to be in the doing of things and to be feeling that they were done purposefully and effectively." The two men agreed to discuss the leader-ship with a small group (by inference, the two of them along with Cosgrave, Sweetman and Dillon) which had been set up to examine the recruitment of new party staff.[57]

Costello talked the situation over with two of his closest confidants, his son Declan and Patrick Lynch. The two younger men independently reached the opinion that Costello could take over the leadership on a part-time basis (this opinion was, according to Lynch, backed by a "similar opinion from Cork"—presumably from Ralph Sutton). Lynch argued that it was "surely wrong and even dangerous to attach decisive importance" to having a full-time leader. He said this was a "pretext", adding that the parliamentary allowance was so low that the best man could not be attracted "unless he is subsidized by his shop, his farm or his trade union". In any event, other attributes were more important, particularly "the qualities of judgement, experience and vision to inspire an organisation to follow him ... a part-time man with this essential ingredient of leadership is more valuable than a full-time chief who lacks it". He felt that Costello was in any event qualified by his 11 years as either Taoiseach or leader of the Opposition, which gave him international prestige and a following outside Fine Gael. In a dig at Dillon, closely associated throughout his career with the Ancient Order of Hibernians, Lynch pointed out that Costello had "never been associated with any sectarian organisation ... Personally I should be sorry to see the AOH exercise decisive influence in Fine Gael."[58]

On Saturday 17 October Mulcahy informed a meeting of the party's front bench that he intended to retire. Costello said the dual leadership structure should be abandoned; a number of others (Dillon, MacEoin, Mulcahy and Michael Hayes) agreed on a single leader, but insisted that that leader should be full-time.[59] Costello had apparently approached Liam Cosgrave about becoming his "managing director" in the Dáil while he became the formal leader.[60] Not surprisingly, Cosgrave rejected this suggestion; he also believed a full-time leader was needed. So too did Gerard Sweetman, who also had more personal reasons for opposing Costello, going back to their poor relationship in government. Declan Costello remained of the opinion that his father could contest and win a leadership election. But Jack Costello realised he was not getting the support of the people he needed, that Sweetman was doing his best to ensure that he was removed from control of the party, and that even if he won the vote, his leadership would have been difficult.[61] He told his driver he was standing down because "a lot of them don't want me and I think it's better to go".[62]

Accordingly, in advance of the meeting of the parliamentary party at which Mulcahy was to announce his resignation, Costello wrote to him setting out his views. He repeated his belief that it was "wrong in principle" to insist on a full-time leader. His own circumstances were such that he could not give up his practice. In order to avoid any misunderstanding that might arise from their joint resignation he had offered to take on the leadership part-time, with other front bench members taking up some of his functions. However, "some of our colleagues were clearly of opinion that a whole-time Leader was essential". Therefore, he had come to the conclusion "that I should not embarrass the Party in their choice"; he would stand down as leader of the Opposition, would not be a candidate for the leadership, and would occupy "the dignified, if unaccustomed, position of a back-bencher". He sought and received Mulcahy's agreement that he need not attend the meeting at which this letter was read out.[63]

The following day, James Dillon was elected leader of Fine Gael in a contest with Liam Cosgrave. An attempt by Michael O'Higgins to persuade Costello to change his mind was headed off by Mulcahy, who said his decision was final (as Costello had said in his letter). According to Dillon's memoir, he asked Mulcahy to give him the voting figures, and was told he had received 66 votes, against 26 for Costello and six for Cosgrave. As Dillon's biographer, Maurice Manning, pointed out, these figures couldn't be correct, as only 57 people were entitled to vote. But they do suggest "that a substantial section of the party still favoured a Costello leadership—even on his own terms".[64]

However, that was not to be. The British Embassy reported to London that Costello's leadership of the Opposition "had proved a disappointment to his party", and that while there were doubts about Dillon's ability, "he is certainly a great improvement on Mr Costello" (a judgement based at least in part on lingering resentment at the declaration of the Republic).[65] There was considerable surprise that Costello had ruled himself out of the running.[66] In Niamh Puirséil's brilliant, if rather unkind, phrase, he had been "firm ... that if there were no fees there would be no foal, so that was that".[67]

In public he was dignified, insisting that the decision was his own. But a letter to a priest friend in America showed his real feelings. The recent changes, he said, "were ... rather a hurtful shock to me ... In my view there had been a conspiracy, with a few only active in it ... I felt that I could have defeated it if I wished. After grave consideration and taking the best advice that I could I decided to clear out and abandon a position that would have inevitably brought me great trouble and worry, and would have entailed blaming me if political success were not achieved at the next Election. I did not want to cause a split ... The timing and the manner of procedure were hurtful to me, but I tried, not always with success, to take it as God meant it to be taken by me ... My personal relations with James Dillon continue friendly."[68]

An indication of this friendly relationship was Dillon's request for policy suggestions for his speech to his first Ard Fheis as Fine Gael leader. The former Taoiseach replied with a typically blunt assessment. He acknowledged that their ideas on policy formulation were rather different; Costello preferred to have a wider group than the front bench or even the parliamentary party involved, and suggested that every idea, even "cranky" ones, should be considered; he also suggested that expert advice should be sought from economists, as "politicians are not expert in the complicated problems that fall to be solved" (this of course was his own practice, when he relied heavily on Patrick Lynch and Alexis FitzGerald). He said the pursuit of an overall majority for Fine Gael was "illusory, will not be successful, may do damage and cause such disappointment as to break the spirit of Fine Gael supporters". He added that while it was understandable that those depending on the votes of farmers might be apprehensive of anti-Labour feeling among them, scorning Labour preferences would prevent Fine Gael gains.

The only hope for Fine Gael, he argued, was to attract the young people, and to avoid at all costs the label of "Conservatism or Toryism". He then went on to outline a relatively radical position. "I appreciate that the use of the word 'progressive' is rather futile and that Fine Gael, any more indeed than the country, can never become a purely Socialist Party, but there is a danger that it may be, or appear to be, something like a fading aspidistra in a Victorian drawing-room." As an alternative, he suggested "at least a hint of travelling some direction along the line of vocationalism", as well as "a scheme ... by which the workers could be given some share and interest in the business".

International isolation, he suggested, was a major cause of Ireland's economic failure, and he viewed Frank Aiken's policy at the UN as "the traditional Fianna Fáil policy of isolationism". The alternative, of securing the friendship of traditional friends, particularly the United States, would make Ireland more attractive for investment, and would not "necessarily, or inevitably, lead to joining such an organisation as NATO". On the North, he urged an approach to the British to pressurise the Northern Government to remove discrimination against Nationalists. "They should be forced to abandon the scheme of gerrymandering, to restore voting by proportional representation, and to take every step to give the Catholic minority their just rights." This would allow the government in Dublin to tackle the IRA with public support. "I had intended to take these steps had the Government not been changed in 1957." (This indicates that he was, as suggested in Chapter 13, interested in pursuing reform within Northern Ireland, rather than concentrating on partition.)

He harped once again on his old theme of developing culture and the arts. "If we could secure the manufacture of objects of art or goods with a distinctive design, devoid of leprechauns, shamrocks and shillelaghs, we might create a magnificent market." The former Taoiseach also suggested that an Irish television service was inevitable. "If we are not to have rubbish for our eyes as well as for our ears it is essential that our own musicians, artists and craftsmen should be encouraged, and others made welcome." And he called for an end to live horse exports, a move resisted by Dillon when he was Minister for Agriculture. "In loyalty to you I laid aside my personal opinion on this matter, and consequently suffered some political disfavour. It is not, however, for that reason that I recommend the adoption of this policy but from firm conviction ..."

The most interesting part of the memorandum deals with economic policy. Costello advocated a reduction in the number of departments and ministers to allow for the creation of a Department of Economic Planning. He disapproved of the creation of a Planning Section within the Department of Finance; he felt it should have been set up in the Department of the Taoiseach rather than in Finance, "the traditional role of which is not that of economic planning".[69]

Costello's views on economics, and particularly on getting control of planning away from the "dead hand" of Finance, were very much in line with the ideas his son Declan was pushing within the parliamentary party. They may not have been viewed as particularly helpful by James Dillon. And of course, it was much easier to advance such ideas from the backbenches than as leader—as Costello himself had found. But he continued to float what were, in Fine Gael terms, fairly radical ideas, suggesting in May 1961 that "there will be a break-up of the old political position here in the next ten years". He said it would no longer be enough to shout for one of the two big parties, or "Up Dev". In fact, he thought, the "left wings of Fianna Fáil and Fine Gael might unite with Labour" to form an alternative to the existing parties.[70]

Once he resigned as leader of the Opposition, he clearly wasn't going to be Taoiseach again, so arrangements were made to have his official portrait painted. A portrait of each former holder of the office is hung in Leinster House, in what is known as the Taoiseach's Landing, above the main stairs up to the Dáil chamber. To paint his portrait, he chose Seán O'Sullivan, a talented if somewhat wayward artist with an alcohol problem. Costello took the pre-caution of interviewing him in his studio, reporting to Finance Minister Jim Ryan that he "looked in good form and his Studio was in good shape, having all the appearance of work and attention".[71] The portrait was duly completed, but by convention not hung until the subject retired from the Dáil. It was to be another nine years before O'Sullivan's portrait of Jack Costello would join those of his predecessors. In fact, he served as a backbencher longer than any other former head of government. W.T. Cosgrave remained in the Dáil for a similar period after he left office—12 years—but most of that time was spent as leader of the Opposition.

As a backbencher, he often made the point that he was speaking for himself, not for his party. He was badly caught out during a debate on the 1967 Finance Bill when he criticised a provision which, as Finance Minister Charles Haughey pointed out, had actually been proposed by Fine Gael. Costello rather weakly replied that he knew of no party decision on the issue. "I am criticising this Bill and, if the Minister can answer my criticism, let him answer it by reasoned argument. It is no argument to say that somebody's spokesman said this, that or the other, and it shows that the Minister is in a parlous position indeed when that is the only thing he can say."[72] Ministers also criticised his Dáil attendance record. Under attack from Costello, Neil Blaney waspishly advised him not to get so worked up "for the little while he appears in the House".[73]

The law continued to conflict at times with politics. During a by-election campaign in Sligo-Leitrim in February 1961 he was asked by local TD Mary Reynolds to speak at a meeting but had to refuse as he had a consultation on the Monday, two "very important cases in Court on Tuesday", and then had to go to Cork on the Thursday.[74] In March 1960, he was lobbied by a number of Pioneer Associations to oppose extended pub opening hours. He told one correspondent that he too opposed the new hours, but "as the vote took place last Thursday at an hour when I had to be in Court I was unable to be present".[75]

When the new Minister for Justice, Charles Haughey, brought in legislation in 1962 to further reform opening times, Costello again opposed extended hours, though he insisted he was "not a killjoy or anything in the nature of a puritan in these matters". His view was that the shorter the hours, the better. "Anybody who has had experience of the evil effects ... of late night drinking in public houses cannot but feel appalled at the notion of giving any additional scope for those very terrible evils." However, as he acknowledged during the debate, in his legal practice he frequently applied for licences on behalf of clients. Later, in a Budget debate, he welcomed increased taxation on alcohol, though he added that he was not "in any way a confirmed pussyfoot or, I hope, intolerant in the matter of intoxicating drink".[76]

His busy legal career thrived. Costello was particularly proud of his role in the Educational Company case, which outlawed picketing to enforce a "closed shop". While unions were outraged by the decision, Costello regarded it as an extension of personal rights, as well as showing that the Constitution had some real vitality.[77] The case arose from a dispute involving the Irish Union of Distributive Workers and Clerks, which picketed the premises of the Educational Company after its 16 members there voted not to work with nine employees who had refused to join the union.[78] The union claimed this was a trade dispute, and the picketing was therefore legal under union legislation dating from 1906. Costello denied this, saying it was "fundamentally ... an effort of this particular trade union to organise its workers in the plaintiffs' employment". The Educational Company, he pointed out, had no dispute with anybody, and had a right to carry on its business without being picketed, unless there was some legal justification for it. Describing the union's action as "ruthless", he said the 1906 Trade Union Act must be interpreted in the light of the Constitution.[79]

He argued that it would be "in the teeth" of Article 40 of the Constitution for a group of people to be able to order other people to join a union, and say, "if you do not, we will force your employers to dismiss you". Citizens had a right to form associations, but unions didn't have a right to force people to join them. The Constitution, he said, guaranteed the citizen's personal rights, one of which was to dispose of his labour as he wished and not as he was dictated to by another individual or group of individuals.[80] In December 1961, the case finally came to a conclusion in the Supreme Court, and the judges agreed with John A. Costello. Union leaders claimed the decision threw unions back 60 years.[81] Costello dismissed this claim, saying the outcome of the case would be good for the unions and good for the country. "I cannot concede that it is necessary for trade unionism and its development that they should be in a position to want to achieve what they regard as justice by committing an injustice."[82]

Those who worked on cases with Costello remember his clarity of mind and expression, his directness, and "his total lack of any semblance of superiority which during his time some of his senior colleagues seemed to exude".[83] This last quality was demonstrated in the late 1950s or early 1960s. Tom Finlay was assisting him on a case, briefed by Alexis FitzGerald, and a complicated and esoteric point of law came up. Finlay told Alexis he didn't know anything about it, and while he could go and look up the references, he quite understood if he wanted to brief something else. Don't worry, came the reply—Mr Costello says he'll do it. And sure enough, the former Taoiseach very quickly produced "a document of precision [and] correctness ... he was interested in it, so he said he might as well do it".[84] No matter how eminent a barrister he was, he remembered the key to success—good preparation. He told his driver that winning a case depended on reading a brief properly—the barrister must know all the little details that are likely to come up.[85]

A solicitor who briefed John A. Costello in the late 1960s and early 1970s recalls that once he accepted a brief, "he presented his client's case fearlessly, with vigour and clarity". In later years he also benefited from the respect of judges, all invariably much younger than himself, who allowed him more latitude than most.[86] Two future chief justices, Tom Finlay and Ronan Keane, who knew Costello at this time, agreed that he was brilliant in front of a jury, especially in personal injury cases, which became much more common in the 1950s and 1960s. Costello almost invariably appeared for the plaintiff in these cases. They also agreed that while he loved being in front of a jury, he refused to get involved in bargaining to settle a case. Costello had the attitude that he was paid to fight cases, not settle them. If bargaining in the Round Hall of the Four Courts had to be done, the other senior counsel in the case would generally do it.[87] This frequently resulted in Costello being left in the courtroom while the talks took place, grumbling to himself that he couldn't see why the case shouldn't go on.[88]

One case which he did settle involved a well-known businessman who sued a trade association for libel after it circulated a negative credit reference on him. The businessman believed the source of the incorrect information was a neighbour who held a grudge against him; but the trade association refused to divulge its source. Costello advised that an application should be made to the Master of the High Court for an order allowing them to seek the information from the association. During the course of his argument, he asked a rhetorical question about how the association came to such a poor opinion of his client. "Did it look into its own corporate heart?" This reference to de Valera's famous remark brought a smile to the face of the Master (appointed to the office under an Inter-party Government), who granted the order. The association immediately settled to avoid the embarrassment of having to disclose its source.[89]

While much of his work concentrated on personal injury and motoring cases, he did take on at least one murder case as a favour to a solicitor friend. He was very pleased with himself when he succeeded in getting the charge reduced to manslaughter—until his client's mother started remonstrating with him for not getting her son off altogether. As he ruefully observed to his driver, "She *is* his mother, what else would she say?"[90]

He continued to travel to Cork, staying with Eavan and Ralph Sutton at their home in Sunday's Well. The Sutton children eagerly looked forward to the arrival of their grandfather, who would always bring a bag of lollipops for them.[91] Once, Isabelle Sutton, aged around four, asked what would happen if she planted one of the lollipop sticks in the ground; her grandfather told her to plant one and see. "The next morning I came rushing down, and lo and behold there was a lollipop tree growing in the garden! A tree had been literally covered in lollipops ... He had a wonderful way with children."[92]

Ralph Sutton took silk in March 1968[93] and the family subsequently moved to Dublin. After that, Sutton and his father-in-law would travel together to Cork and stay with Ralph's mother, Una Sutton, when the High Court was there.[94] As its longest-serving member, he was Father of the Munster Bar, and presided at the biannual dinners which were held on the Monday evening of the Assize week in Cork. All members were expected to attend, and a good excuse was required if the dinner was missed. Costello would speak after dinner—sometimes to admonish his brethren. For instance, he disapproved of the practice where the junior counsel in a High Court case might absent himself to appear in the Circuit Court. Costello took the view that if the client was being charged for the presence of a junior, the junior should be there.[95]

At the end of September 1960, Costello was the Fine Gael nominee to join Ceann Comhairle Patrick Hogan and Fianna Fáil TDs Philip Brady and Lionel Booth on a 10-day parliamentary delegation to Germany. He found the trip enjoyable and "highly informative ... on the international situation".[96] They met Chancellor Konrad Adenauer, who "looked bronzed and extraordinarily well, and with no apparent signs of his age"—he was then 84.[97] During a visit to the Bundestag, Costello noted that deputies were required to "clock in" each morning or pay a fine (half a century later, a similar system was introduced in the Dáil).

The TDs were treated extremely well by their hosts, not having to pay for anything. They were put up in what Costello described as "top-grade hotels", chauffeured around in Mercedes-Benz cars, with all expenses paid. Their entertainment included dinner in the Weinhaus Bruchenkeller in Frankfurt, where "somewhat embarrassingly the Orchestra surrounded our table and then 'discoursed' 'When Irish Eyes are Smiling' and 'Danny Boy'". They also attended the Opera in Berlin—Richard Strauss's Der Rosenkavalier, which Costello judged to be "magnificently produced and conducted", although he admitted it was not one that appealed to him.

While the visit may have seemed "rather of the nature of a joy ride", Costello concluded that there was a serious point to it, and the point was made in the city of Berlin. "I have formed the opinion that the real purpose of the invitation ... was to bring home to us, and through us to the Irish Parliament, the real significance of the City of Berlin in international affairs." While the building of the Berlin Wall would not begin until August of the following year, the emigration which precipitated that move was continuing. The Irish delegation was taken to a refugee camp where they were told that about 500 people a day were crossing the Border. They also met the Mayor of West Berlin, Willy Brandt, who according to Costello "would fill the cast of a ruthless gangster in an American film. This is not to take away in any way from his impressive appearance or his obviously dynamic personality." He was impressed, too, by Brandt's passionate commitment to the survival of West Berlin, which he believed was "essential to Western freedom".

But perhaps the highlight of their trip was a visit to East Berlin, where the staunchly anti-communist Costello had a glimpse behind the Iron Curtain. Like most visitors, he was struck by the contrast between the bustling West and the drab East of the city. With few people about and even fewer cars, he observed that East Berlin "presented to me the appearance of an Irish country town on a Sunday morning". The monument to Russian soldiers killed in the war was "rather striking", but the park in which it was placed was "cold and forbidding". However, as if to prove that human nature did not change, whatever the political system, their return across the Border was speeded up because "our young lady interpreter had given what is known as 'the glad eye' to a young Communist Policeman. She told us that she thought that was the easiest way to get through."

Costello's first election as a backbencher was in 1961. Perhaps because of his lower public profile, perhaps because of an attempt to split the vote with his running mate, Senator John O'Donovan, he lost his accustomed place at the head of the poll to MacEntee, who won 29 per cent of the first-preference vote, to Costello's 25.6 per cent. Noël Browne, running as an Independent, comfortably took the third seat.[98] It was, Costello later observed, "the most civilised election that has taken place in this country since the State was established ... There was absent ... the political excitement so beloved of political commentators ..." Costello took exception to suggestions in the newspapers that the result—a minority Fianna Fáil government—was a bad one. He argued that the previous government, with its large majority, had been overbearing and arrogant. "It was practically impossible to convince certain of the Ministers ... that the proposals they had put forward to the Dáil were capable of amendment. The Dáil was regarded as a machine merely for registering the decisions of the Government." Now was the time, he suggested, for the Government to engage constructively with the Opposition.[99]

He was himself constructively involved in a number of measures in the justice area. In 1961, he congratulated the Parliamentary Secretary to the Minister for Justice, Charles Haughey, on the Civil Liability Bill, which he said would benefit both the legal profession and the public at large, and on the Defamation Bill, to which he gave his "complete approval".[100] He was more critical of the Succession Bill, introduced by Justice Minister Brian Lenihan in 1964, which was designed to ensure that spouses were not left out of wills.

While Costello was supportive of the aim, he warned that the people were not ready for such a drastic move. "They have had this system by which they could leave their property or their money, big or small, to anybody they liked, for well over a century ... there is a big task in front of him to educate the people and to make them see."[101] When the Bill was reintroduced after the 1965 election, Costello played a key role in the committee stage, where the detail of the legislation was thrashed out and changed quite substantially. Lenihan accepted many of Costello's suggestions—at one point Michael O'Higgins, the Fine Gael spokesman, observed that he was sorry he hadn't had his assistance earlier when dealing with another section.[102] His influence on the legislation was widely recognised.[103]

The Government also sought his legal expertise to help with the review of the Constitution. He accepted an invitation to become a member of a group of legal experts chaired by the Attorney General which was to support the work of an all-party committee on the Constitution.[104] He was in distinguished company, joining Supreme Court judges Brian Walsh and John Kenny, leading barristers Niall McCarthy, Anthony Hederman, Liam Hamilton, and Donal Barrington, as well as John Kelly, law professor and future Attorney General.[105]

In 1964, Costello gave legal advice to Jack McQuillan, a TD who had at times been a thorn in his side. Despite this history, Costello refused to charge a fee for his advice, a decision for which McQuillan was grateful. "Your extremely generous action ... [was] something I didn't expect or deserve ... I want to say how deeply I appreciate what you have done both by giving so much of your very valuable time and attention to the preparation and conduct of my case and now by letting me off so lightly in the matter of costs."[106] However, while he won his libel case against the *Roscommon Herald*, it was a pyrrhic victory; he was awarded derisory damages, and the case was a contributory factor in his defeat in the 1965 election.[107]

In the Dáil, Costello spoke most years on the Budget, the estimate for the Department of the Taoiseach, and the estimate for the Arts Council. In discussing the latter, he stressed the practical economic benefits that could be gained through improved industrial design.[108] He frequently spoke of the need to abolish death duties, and in favour of some tax relief for the self-employed, those like himself who "get no allowance, as industrialists do, for depreciation in plant and machinery. His plant and machinery are his own physical capacity, brains and skill."[109]

Some developments didn't meet with his approval; he complained of "the era of the expense account ... the era of the expensive restaurant ... of the motorcar of a particular type as the status symbol".[110] He produced an example in 1965 of an "expense account" lunch in a city restaurant for four people which came to £27 (the equivalent in 2010 of €556).[111] "That was paid for by me and by the rest of us here in taxation and by the poor people when they buy cigarettes and drink."[112] He also stoutly defended the record of his two governments. Responding to criticism from Brian Lenihan, he said he would "allow nobody to say that either I or anybody concerned in Government with me was a reactionary". Costello added acidly that when it came to criticising the Inter-party Governments, "neither truth nor Christian charity has any place".[113]

Jack Costello remained on the progressive wing of Fine Gael. He always had a horror of the party being labelled "Tory", and did all he could to encourage progressive elements. The chief of those progressive elements in the mid 1960s was his son Declan, who was becoming increasingly frustrated at the party's conservatism. Declan considered leaving and joining Labour. However, fellow TD Michael O'Higgins suggested that rather than walking away, he should put his ideas before colleagues to give them a chance to accept or reject them. Declan Costello believed his father may have been behind the approach from O'Higgins;[114] curiously, Jack Costello apparently didn't discuss it directly with his son.

In any event, Declan Costello wrote to each member of the parliamentary party outlining his views, which he acknowledged were "not shared by the majority of my colleagues on the Front Bench". He asked colleagues for "a decision as to whether or not they are acceptable to the Party and, if necessary, I will ask that a formal vote be taken". He believed his ideas were not just right for the country, but would "have a dramatically favourable effect on the Party's fortunes". The principles were: full scale economic planning; targets for the private and public sectors; a Minister for Economic Affairs; government control of the credit policies of the banks; direct government investment in industry; increased social capital investment; direct rather than indirect taxation; and full and effective price control.[115]

His proposals—the foundation of the Just Society policy programme— were strongly supported by his father, and were endorsed by the parliamentary party (despite initial opposition from Gerard Sweetman). Jack Costello told his Garda driver he was delighted the policy had been accepted, adding that if it had been rejected "he would nearly have felt he would have to resign" from Fine Gael.[116] Political scientist Peter Mair has seen in the Just Society programme "a major watershed in the general political approach" of Fine Gael, and in particular a break with the policies put forward by Costello senior.[117] That was not how Jack Costello saw it; he later claimed to have had "quite a number of embryonic ideals which were not precisely articulated and they conform very much to those of the Just Society".[118] At his retirement dinner, he said he left the Dáil "satisfied that the Fine Gael party were on the right lines and walking in the right direction when they walked under the banner of the Just Society".[119]

The 1965 general election was the last to be contested by both Costello and Seán MacEntee, who between them had dominated the constituency of Dublin South-East since its creation. Costello ran a reasonably high profile campaign, with ads in the *Irish Times* and *Irish Independent*, 500 posters, 300 window stickers, and no fewer than 41,000 leaflets, at a cost of almost £300. Among the contributors to his campaign were his former Cabinet colleague Dan Morrissey, who gave the largest donation of £25, while smaller contributions were received from businessmen and legal colleagues. The balance was paid by Costello himself.[120] The result was reasonably satisfactory—Costello regained his place on top of the poll, with 28 per cent of the first-preference vote, 242 ahead of MacEntee. But Fianna Fáil's Seán Moore took the third seat from Noël Browne, running for Labour. The second Fine Gael candidate, James O'Connor, brought up the rear with less than 5 per cent of the vote.

As the 1966 presidential election approached, Fine Gael was casting about for a candidate. After two unsuccessful runs for the Áras, and now retired, Seán MacEoin had ruled himself out. Deputy leader Tom O'Higgins believed a contest was necessary to avoid a revolt among party members. He didn't think James Dillon would be suitable, and quickly found that Seán MacBride would be utterly unacceptable to his colleagues; he finally settled on Jack Costello. "He was highly respected in the party and throughout the country and, as the leader of two Inter-party Governments, would attract considerable support from other parties." Of course, he might be difficult to persuade, but O'Higgins decided to float the idea at a front bench meeting.

His suggestion was greeted by some nods around the table, before Gerard Sweetman intervened to shoot it down. He accused O'Higgins of following sentiment rather than practicality. "How, he asked, could we oppose, in the fiftieth anniversary of Easter Week, the oldest surviving officer of that Rising with a man who had been old enough in 1916 to have fought in the Rising and had not? He said that if we did so, we would expose John Costello to the most humiliating of defeats." O'Higgins was "astonished and hurt" by Sweetman's brutal intervention. Worse was to follow for him, though, as Patrick Lindsay proposed that O'Higgins should run instead. Having come to propose Jack Costello, Tom O'Higgins emerged from the meeting as Fine Gael's presidential candidate.[121]

Sweetman was undoubtedly influenced by his dislike of Jack Costello; but he was probably right. O'Higgins made a very good showing in the election, precisely because he was a (relatively) young candidate who offered a fresh approach to the office. Had Costello stood, he would certainly have been attacked for his lack of a "national record", and on that ground de Valera was unassailable.

The presidential election also prompted Garret FitzGerald, by then a senator and member of the front bench, to formally apply for membership of Fine Gael. He approached Costello to ask how he should go about doing so. "His response was, as usual, forceful, blunt and idiosyncratic. 'Forty years in politics; twice Taoiseach; never joined Fine Gael.' Somewhat timorously I suggested that times were changing ... With apparent reluctance and perhaps with a hint of disappointment at my conventional approach to politics," Costello gave him details of how to contact the constituency organisation.[122]

Within that Dublin South-East organisation, Costello was regarded with some awe—despite his personal modesty. The younger Alexis FitzGerald (nephew of Costello's son-in-law of the same name, and later a Fine Gael TD and senator himself) recalled that when the former Taoiseach entered a constituency meeting, the members would stand up. Costello would wear his grey hat until he arrived at the top table, where he would ceremoniously remove it. As in most political organisations, there was a certain amount of infighting in Dublin South-East; Jack Costello was one of the few unifying factors in the room. Even if he really wasn't a member of Fine Gael, Costello took the local organisation seriously enough. Whenever he had something he wished to say to a wider audience, he would either deliver a speech to a branch meeting or, if no suitable meeting was due, he would gather a group of constituency activists to his house, where he would read out his script before sending out the press release.[123]

The round of constituency work continued—much of it done by correspondence, though the house at Herbert Park remained a magnet for supplicants. There were "so many rather troublesome people calling at my house" that he had to insist on not seeing people unless they had a written appointment.[124] The search for houses remained one of the main issues for his constituents. As he told the Dáil, he advised them, "I can help you to get into Heaven but I cannot get you a house from the Dublin Corporation."[125] He continued to insist that he represented the ordinary voter, claiming his canvassers told him "if there was a big car outside a house, they did not call because it would have been a waste of time".[126]

In 1968, Jack Lynch's government attempted once again to get rid of Proportional Representation. Liam Cosgrave had privately supported the abolition of PR in 1959—this may have been a factor in his defeat by James Dillon in the leadership election of that year. Then he was a member of the front bench; when the question resurfaced in 1968, he was party leader. He attempted to persuade the parliamentary party to his point of view with an "emotional speech" described by one TD as "possibly one of [his] worst".

Cosgrave was immediately followed by John A. Costello, who gave "a brilliant address which set the tone of the debate".[127] The parliamentary party might well have rejected Cosgrave's approach anyway, but the force of the intervention by the former Taoiseach clearly helped.

Costello spoke forcefully and effectively in public against the proposal, which he characterised as "the government effort to resurrect the dead corpse of nine years ago". The proposed changes were, he claimed, "objectionable in principle, unsustainable in argument, productive of injustice and designed ... in the political and material interests of the members of the government and the Fianna Fáil Party".[128] Reviewing the speeches he had made on the subject in 1959, Costello confessed that he had been wrong. "On several occasions I did say ... that I believed that if the people turned down these proposals, that would be the last they would ever hear of the proposal to abolish PR. I misread my friends, the Fianna Fáil party ..."[129] The result was much more emphatic than in 1958, with the Government's proposal defeated by 60.8 per cent to 39.2 per cent. Once again Dublin South-East was even more opposed, voting against by 70 per cent to 30 per cent.

As his retirement from active politics approached, Costello became increasingly conscious of his place in history, and made a number of efforts to put across his side of the story. One saw him prepare a detailed memorandum on the events which led to the declaration of the Republic. This was circulated in the late 1960s to various influential figures.[130] Another was a series of interviews with the political correspondent of the *Irish Times*, Michael McInerney, published in five parts in September 1967 under the title "John A. Costello Remembers". McInerney described his interviewee as "impressive, with a resonant, slightly Dublin accent, of sturdy build and with a rough charm ... He has a straight direct manner, without any of the charisma of a Pearse, a Griffith, or a de Valera ..." The articles attracted considerable attention, not all of it positive.

Joseph Brennan, former Secretary of the Department of Finance and Governor of the Central Bank, objected to a suggestion that the Shannon hydro-electric scheme of the 1920s had "received fierce opposition from ... Department of Finance officials". Brennan rejected this claim, and urged Costello to "take proper steps immediately to withdraw it at least in so far as it may seem to concern myself". In his reply, Costello enlarged his claim, saying he believed that Brennan had threatened resignation unless the scheme was fully examined by Finance. In a not-so-subtle threat, Costello added that he didn't wish this to become public knowledge. Brennan demanded to know the source of his information; Costello refused to tell him. As Brennan probably guessed, the source was Patrick McGilligan, who as Minister for Industry and Commerce had defeated Finance objections to establish the scheme. In the final letter in the exchange of correspondence, Brennan repeated his criticism of Costello's "diatribe", adding that he particularly resented the "unfounded suggestion" that he had threatened resignation.[131]

As well as annoying former mandarins, Costello also helped a number of academics in groundbreaking research into Irish history and political development—David Harkness on the evolution of the Commonwealth, A.S. Cohan on the development of the Irish political elite, Brian Farrell on the role of the Taoiseach.[132] One researcher, looking at the office of the Attorney General, found him to be "a garrulous and entertaining man",[133] and this certainly comes across in one of his most important attempts to give his view of his career, a "Seven Days" television interview with David Thornley.

Costello was reluctant to do the interview, insisting that the programme's editor, Muiris Mac Conghail, come in to Leinster House so he could meet him. After 12 years in opposition, Fine Gael regarded RTÉ with suspicion, believing the station to be under the political influence of Fianna Fáil. Mac Conghail found the former Taoiseach "gruff", but evidently satisfied his concerns. The fact that the interview was to be conducted by Thornley was part of the attraction—he was highly regarded as a serious broadcaster. Apart from the historical interest of covering controversial topics like the declaration of the Republic and the Mother and Child scheme, Mac Conghail believed the interview could have contemporary political significance. Fianna Fáil had succeeded in "making 'coalition' a dirty word". He thought Costello, as the only head of a coalition government up to that point, might give a different view of the possibility of inter-party co-operation.

The interview was recorded before the 1969 election, but broadcast on 24 June, one week after polling. As it happened, Fianna Fáil had an overall majority, but had coalition been an option, the interview might have been influential in the process of Government formation.[134] Speaking before the results were known, Costello warned that if a second general election was caused by a refusal to co-operate in coalition formation, "the people would take a fierce vengeance on any party that doesn't carry out their will".[135]

By the time the interview was broadcast, Costello had left the Dáil and Thornley entered it (as a Labour Party TD). Costello, who had no experience of television, was uncomfortable, but with Thornley's expert guidance delivered a vintage performance. The encounter admirably demonstrated his belligerence when challenged on controversial episodes like the declaration of the Republic and the Mother and Child crisis. He and Mac Conghail became friendly as a result of the interview—Costello was later godfather to Marcus Mac Conghail.[136]

In March 1969, with a general election on the horizon, constituency activist Tony Keane had written to Costello "to request the honour of again proposing your name for adoption as a candidate. Needless to say we will do all in our power to ensure your rightful place at the head of the poll ..." However, the prospective candidate, just three months short of his seventy-eighth birthday, turned down the offer. "I think it would be a very bad headline for one of my age to put himself forward. It is a matter of very great regret that I must cease to be a Deputy for the Constituency which has done me the honour of electing me so consistently and for so long ... I assume of course that Senator [Garret] FitzGerald will be put forward and accepted as my successor."[137]

Fittingly, his final contributions in the Dáil were on a controversial Criminal Justice Bill. Costello declared himself to be against anything which prevented the right to free speech and free assembly. "We should not erode those principles and constitutional rights unless the public interest imperatively demands it." The final words he spoke in Leinster House were a warning that giving Gardaí the proposed extra powers would bring the force into disrepute "by reason of the fact that the people will not trust them and will be afraid of them. That would be a bad day's work for this House to do."[138]

At the selection convention for Dublin South-East at which he formally announced his retirement from politics (and which chose Garret FitzGerald and Fergus O'Brien as the Fine Gael candidates in the constituency), Costello made a lengthy speech. Acknowledging that co-operation between Fine Gael and Labour in Government didn't seem possible at that time, he observed that "this should not always be so". Coalitions were the norm in other countries using proportional representation, and the people had proved they wanted to retain PR. Through that system, they could choose a single-party government, or they could indicate that they wanted parties to co-operate. In a clear warning to the anti-coalitionists in Labour, he added, "The party which fails to heed the people's voice will do so at its peril."[139]

Costello also used this "farewell speech" to take a cut at Fianna Fáil. He claimed the Government was not just "bankrupt of ideas", it was "arrogant, divisive and harmful". He continued, "the Taoiseach has the unenviable task of trying to impose a code of conduct on his colleagues which is contrary to the traditions of his party, and which they do not understand. It is little wonder that he has failed. A party which has ruled as long as Fianna Fáil has may come to feel that it does so by divine right."[140] The Taoiseach, Jack Lynch, responded in a speech to a Fianna Fáil convention in Mallow a month later. It wasn't his party that didn't understand, he said—it was Fine Gael. "They have not understood for almost 50 years ... that is why Fine Gael have such a record in Opposition—a record unrivalled almost in any Western democracy." He advanced the intriguing argument that by criticising Fianna Fáil, John A. Costello was in effect criticising the Irish people, who had voted for them.

Lynch challenged Costello to prove his claim that businessmen viewed a subscription to Fianna Fáil as a good investment, and in turn criticised the record of the two Inter-party Governments. He concluded with the hope that "we might all be able to conduct this general election campaign on a higher and on a more responsible level".[141]

He may have been leaving the stage, but Costello obviously retained the ability to needle his opponents. He also played an active role in the election campaign in Dublin South-East. The younger Alexis FitzGerald was director of elections in the constituency. As a courtesy, he brought Garret FitzGerald's proposed election address to show Costello. The former Taoiseach took out a pen and started crossing bits out and adding amendments. Sadly, these were completely illegible, even to their author.[142] Of more benefit were his speeches, which stressed Fine Gael's emergence as "the party of national reform, of liberal belief and social and economic progress. It has through time developed into a party espousing the belief in social justice which I have throughout my career stood for." His support for "the doctrines of the just society" was of course particularly useful for FitzGerald, given his pronounced liberal views. Costello also observed that developing policy in opposition was "no good ... when the people are hungry for action in government now". He again criticised Labour's refusal to contemplate coalition. They were "caught in a mesh of socialist theorising", but would be forced to abandon this untenable position following the election.[143]

Dublin South-East was clearly in safe hands; his chosen successor topped the poll with 31.5 per cent of the first preference vote; Noël Browne (again running for Labour) was second and Fianna Fáil's Seán Moore, the only sitting TD contesting the election, came in third. Costello also campaigned for another FitzGerald, his son-in-law Alexis, who contested the Seanad election. Alexis asked him to write to a local councillor "saying, if you had a mind to, some nice things about me ... Sorry to bother you with this but there is no point in going in to the sea if you don't intend to swim and I find in me daily increase in ruthlessness."[144] The letter—saying very nice things indeed—was sent and Alexis was duly elected.

A gala presentation evening for Costello, put on by his constituency organisation in December 1969, illustrated the breadth of his career. No fewer than six speakers were required to cover the various facets of his life— Liam Cosgrave on the parliamentarian; Garret FitzGerald on his contribution to the foundation of the State; Tom O'Higgins on the Taoiseach and leader of the opposition; Tommy Doyle on the constituency campaigner; and Alexis FitzGerald on his contribution to Fine Gael. But the main event, undoubtedly, was the speech by Costello himself. He noted at the beginning that in his reply to a similar presentation, Seán Lemass had spoken for just two minutes; he said his reply, by contrast, "is going to last I'm afraid for a long time". He wasn't joking—his speech went on for no less than 51 minutes.

After covering his lengthy career in public life and paying tribute to many who had helped him along the way, he urged his audience to remember the achievements of the Inter-party Governments. "It's worth talking about, because we did something that hasn't been done since." And he urged the party to believe that Fianna Fáil could be beaten. "You can beat it if you go the right way about it ... I suggest to you, put upon your banners the Just Society, that Fine Gael is not a Tory party ... it's for all sections of the Irish people, but particularly for the poor and the weak and the distressed."[145]

One piece of unfinished business which occupied Costello's time was the Mansion House Anti-Partition Fund. Just under £55,000 had been donated in 1949, but not all had been spent. The remainder of the fund, invested in Government loans, increased from £4,900 at the end of 1964 to £7,700 a decade later. It was difficult to get all the members of the committee (Costello, Norton, MacBride, de Valera and Aiken) to agree on any course of action. Costello was clear—he wanted the Fund wound up. In August 1961, after some press comment about the fund, he wrote to the other members saying no useful purpose would be served by leaving the money unallocated. He believed it should be "expended for some anti-Partition purpose and the nature of that would have to be carefully considered".[146] Both de Valera and MacBride agreed that the money should be used[147] but nothing happened, possibly because the 1961 general election distracted the committee members.

Bill Norton's death in December 1963 further complicated the situation; now the surviving committee members had lost the power to direct the trustees to pay out funds. The Attorney General and the Secretary of the Department of the Taoiseach suggested legislation to clarify the membership so the money could be paid out and the Fund wound up. Costello suggested a simpler solution: the committee should assume it had the power to co-opt Brendan Corish in Norton's place, and then disburse the funds and dissolve.[148]

Again, nothing was done. In November 1968, the committee met in Áras an Uachtaráin—apparently the first meeting since 1955. It met again in December 1969, at the request of Seán MacBride, to "take stock of the position ... in the light of recent developments" (the outbreak of the Troubles). Costello supported the idea of holding a meeting. "I feel that we might be the subject of criticism if, having regard to the happenings in the North, we did not have a meeting ... It may be eventually decided that no action is called for but at least it could not be said that the Committee had not considered the position."[149] This meeting was again inconclusive, although in October 1971 the committee agreed to pay £500 to Father Brian Brady of Belfast to support a legal challenge to internment. It was also decided to pay for the production of two pamphlets outlining the case against partition, and the events leading up to the outbreak of violence in the North.[150] A note on the file in November 1974 stated that the preparation of the pamphlets had not been "pursued to fruition", and the committee hadn't met since.[151] Thus ended Costello's Northern initiative of 1949.

He remained an unapologetic and convinced nationalist, but also remained utterly opposed to the IRA. He was realistic about the situation— arguably more realistic than he had been when in power. In April 1972, after the parliament of Northern Ireland was prorogued and direct rule instituted, Seán MacEoin put forward the ingenious theory that the British Government had acted illegally. Under the Treaty, he argued, the Six Counties had the right to opt out of the All-Ireland Parliament, but not to return to direct rule by Westminster. He told Fine Gael leader Liam Cosgrave that the Government should apply to the International Court of Justice to have the relevant British Act declared illegal. Cosgrave turned to the most eminent legal adviser he could think of, Jack Costello. The former Taoiseach said the Treaty, as an international agreement, could only be regarded as binding while it was in operation; but, as he had pointed out when declaring the Republic, it had been dismantled by the Fianna Fáil government after 1932. "Because the British acquiesced in these fundamental breaches of the Treaty and because the Executive Authority (External Relations) Act 1936 did nothing to keep this country within the Commonwealth of Nations, even though the British pretended it did, the resultant position was that the Treaty no longer had any effect ... the Republic of Ireland Act 1948 put the issue beyond all doubt."[152]

The following August, Costello was chosen to deliver the main oration at the Michael Collins commemoration at Béal na mBláth. As well as being the fiftieth anniversary of Collins's death, the ceremony was also notable for the presence of the Minister for Defence, for the first time under a Fianna Fáil government. The Minister, Jerry Cronin, received "a surprisingly enthusiastic reception" according to the *Irish Times*, but "his welcome was pale compared to the thunderous applause" which greeted Costello.[153]

The former Taoiseach reflected on the progress made under an independent Irish government, remarking that "if everything has not been achieved, much has been achieved and it has been achieved through our own efforts and from our own resources and without our hands out to the British taxpayer". But the main thrust of his speech dealt, naturally, with partition and the use of force. He observed that there was only one legitimate army of the Republic of Ireland, the one founded by Collins. And he said that while the unity of the nation was "an article of our national faith" for Collins, the General was above all else a realist. "He knew the tactic of the limited objective, the deluding, narcissistic folly of extremism. He knew when force was legitimate and that it was immoral and illegitimate when employed against greater force and when the design did not include the ... objective of lasting peace based on the mutual recognition of community rights ... He wished to convert our northern fellow countrymen and not to coerce them."

This was not strictly accurate, given the plans Collins at one point pursued for armed attacks on the infant Northern state, but it was what the crowd wanted to hear. Costello was on safer ground when he returned to his own views on the North. He pointed out that the British people had a "serious responsibility" because their governments created the problem, and said no settlement could ignore the "just rights" of Northern Catholics. The eventual solution would require, he said, "idealism, patience, tolerance and a supreme exercise of the virtues of Christian charity". And, in a superb phrase directed squarely at those who supported violence in the cause of unity, he said "even Irish unity may be bought at too great a price if bought at the price of sin and shame".[154]

As an elder statesman in both politics and the Bar, he received many honours in his later years. His seventieth birthday brought congratulations from the Fine Gael parliamentary party, from President de Valera, and from Justice Brian Walsh, who observed that "in your case it is clear that the biblical three score and ten falls far short of the value of the case".[155] His golden jubilee at the Bar in 1964 was marked by a celebration in the Central Hotel,[156] while 10 years later both the then Taoiseach, Liam Cosgrave, and his predecessor (and successor) Jack Lynch attended a diamond jubilee event in the King's Inns, where a "huge attendance showed the esteem in which John A. Costello was held".[157] In 1962, he received from the Pope the Grand Cross of the Order of Pius,[158] a papal knighthood which is one of the highest honours bestowed by the Vatican.[159]

He didn't forget old friends, putting in a determined but unsuccessful effort to have Cecil Lavery appointed Chief Justice. He explained to the Taoiseach, Seán Lemass, that Lavery had "selflessly" declined a chance to be appointed President of the High Court by Costello's government, because of a technical point raised by the Department of Justice. "I myself felt that there was no substance to the point and that Mr Justice Lavery ought to accept the position ... The matter has troubled me very considerably ever since as I felt Judge Lavery had suffered an injustice ... He is, as you doubtless know, the outstanding legal personality of the last half-century in this country." Costello piously added that he had "never interfered in any way with any judicial appointment, nor endeavoured to influence it, except when it fell to my duty as a member of the government to do so". He did his best in this case, though, lobbying Cardinal D'Alton and Fianna Fáil minister Jack Lynch (through their mutual friend, the Fine Gael TD from Cork, Stephen Barrett).[160] After the failure of this effort, he was involved in an equally unsuccessful attempt to have Lavery elected to the United Nations International Court of Justice.[161]

Old rivals weren't forgotten either. As a former Taoiseach, Costello was a member of the Council of State, and in that context continued to have dealings with Eamon de Valera, who remained President of Ireland until 1973. Declan Costello recalled that while they were polite on a personal level, they did not have a particularly warm relationship,[162] which is understandable in the context of their political dealings over many years.

Against this, some in the Costello family remember a friendlier relationship. One of Costello's grandchildren recalls picking up the phone one day to hear the President on the other end of the line, ringing with an invitation to a Council of State meeting. The two men "chatted amiably" for some time.[163] There is even a suggestion—apparently emanating from the de Valera family—that the President used to call into Herbert Park for a cup of tea and a chat on occasion. It seems unlikely that civility went quite that far, although they certainly appeared to get on well at their last public appearance together, at the joint conferral of the Freedom of Dublin on them in March 1975, just five months before de Valera's death and 10 months before Costello's.

In his speech at the Freedom ceremony, the Lord Mayor, James O'Keeffe, said that de Valera and Costello were "without question the two most famous Irish statesmen alive today". While de Valera made a very brief reply of thanks, Costello was characteristically more verbose, recalling that he was Dublin born, but didn't have enough ancestry to be a "jackeen". He mentioned his father's service as a councillor, and his own work with the Corporation to get houses for his constituents. Costello observed that his fellow freeman did not like lawyers—but the profession had turned the tables on him while he was President by making him an Honorary Bencher of the King's Inns. "We fought many a fight, but I can say that never once did I hear him utter a single ungracious word or expletive about me. I received nothing but courtesy from him at all times."[164]

But despite this public conviviality, there was a reserve on Costello's part. In September 1970, he turned down a request to discuss Longford and O'Neill's biography of de Valera on RTÉ. "I have formed the very definite view that it would be quite inappropriate for me in all the circumstances to make any public comment. I may say that I have also turned down a request to review another biography of the same person."[165] Perhaps unfortunately, he did not keep his counsel in the immediate aftermath of de Valera's death in August 1975. Interviewed on television within hours of the former President's passing, Costello said "his influence was widespread in his life. I think his influence is now at an end. In my opinion he left nothing of permanent value."[166] The British Embassy noted that "virtually the only good thing he could say about Mr de Valera was the back-handed compliment that he had 'slavishly' adopted the parliamentary customs of Westminster".[167]

The remarks led to considerable public controversy, and were regarded as "disparaging" by the de Valera family.[168] Various explanations were offered: Tom Finlay, former Fine Gael TD and future Chief Justice, went to the funeral with Costello, who he said had a "fair hostility" towards his former rival. He felt the "rather dismissive" remarks on television were probably due to the fact that he hadn't had time to think of what he might diplomatically say.[169] De Valera's son Terry suggested that "the lawyer in him came out and he was simply speaking to what he regarded as his brief".[170] The truth is probably simpler. Jack Costello was asked a question, and gave his views honestly. It may not have been diplomatic, but it was a characteristic response.

In a newspaper interview in 1974, Costello said he was a "perfectly" happy man; the worst thing about his life was "that so many of my dear friends are dead and I am still here". His only pastime, apart from golf, was reading; the rest of his time was spent with his family, especially his 19 grandchildren.[171] Those grandchildren have fond memories of him, of the trips in the State car (even though it made some of them carsick), the half-crown coins he dispensed, and the gifts of Turkish Delight he would bring back from his trips to Cork.[172] One Christmas Eve, as he took a number of them round the shops, he remarked to his Garda driver that Seán MacEntee used to refer to him as "the nursemaid of Labour and Clann na Poblachta"; now here he was, acting as nursemaid to all his grandchildren.[173] For family occasions such as Communions and Confirmations, he would throw a big party in Herbert Park, and also had a Hallowe'en party for the grandchildren every year, as well as an afternoon party on his birthday.[174]

Grandchildren were frequently in and out of Herbert Park—Alexis and Grace's son Kyran stayed on and off in the house, partly to keep his grandfather company. Legal colleagues joked that the former Taoiseach had become an authority on a particular cowboy series on the television because his grandson kept putting it on.[175] He helped with the homework of any children staying in Herbert Park, but to the disappointment of at least some of them he declined to discuss his role in various historical events. He didn't want to "rake over the coals" of past controversies, although he did have a few favourite jokes, such as his assertion that he had been "out" in 1916—out on the golf course.[176] One granddaughter remembers spending hours in his study, "swinging around in his swivel chair, messing with his Dictaphone machine and trying on his wig". His influence was lasting—10 of his 19 grandchildren became either barristers or solicitors (although only one, Isabelle Sutton, entered politics—she was elected twice to Kinsale Town Council for the Green Party).[177]

He had well-entrenched habits: rising at 7.30, breakfast of bacon and eggs with freshly squeezed orange juice, then out of the house by 9 during the Law Term, for daily Mass in Donnybrook Church or in the Church of Adam and Eve on the quays on his way to the Four Courts. He would usually come home for lunch—he was an "avid" listener to the BBC "World at One" programme on radio.[178] In those days, Dublin traffic was much lighter, and it was possible for his driver to collect him at the Four Courts at 1.10, bring him home for lunch and drop him off again at 1.50.[179]

The two Garda drivers, Mick Kilkenny and Jack Christal (who succeeded Paddy Byrne in 1968), along with housekeeper Molly Ennis, formed "a small, very happy family" with the former Taoiseach. He included them along with the family in various celebrations (for instance, a seventy-seventh birthday dinner in the Burlington Hotel, or the celebrations after he was made a Freeman of Dublin) and was "generous and decent".[180] He remained addicted to golf, continuing to play well into his eighties, greatly enjoying the game (though his grandson remembers his progress round the course being punctuated by quiet grumbling about the quality of his shots).[181]

As well as going to the golf club and the King's Inns, he socialised at home, with dinner parties which featured Molly's excellent cooking, and legal and political reminiscences. The former Taoiseach drank wine, but very much in moderation, and the parties were quite traditional, with the ladies withdrawing after dinner, at which point the port would be produced for the men. When eating out, he was particular about the lights in the restaurant not being too dim, as he wanted to see what he was eating. He also disliked having his plate over-filled—if it was, he would send it back, asking for some of the food to be removed. And he hated picnics at the beach, as he didn't like sand in his food.[182]

At the weekends, Wilfrid, by then a permanent patient at St Patrick's Hospital, would come home to Herbert Park, making his own way there and being dropped home by one of his father's drivers on the Sunday evening. Wilfrid's care remained of huge concern to Costello for the remainder of his life—his eldest son was to die three years after him in 1979, of congestive heart failure.[183] On his visits home to Herbert Park, Wilfrid enjoyed playing his old 78 records up in his room; on Sunday evenings, the two of them would go to Grace and Alexis' house for supper.[184] Tragically, in 1972, Grace died of cancer at the age of just 50. The loss of his eldest daughter, the "apple of his eye", was a shocking blow to Jack Costello. Apparently he hadn't realised quite how sick she was when she was admitted to Saint Luke's cancer hospital.[185]

He was perplexed by some aspects of the modern world—for instance, he acted for a supermarket objecting to the rule that butchers' shops in Dublin should close at six o'clock. The supermarket didn't want to have to close its butcher counter at 6 while the rest of the shop remained open. But Costello had difficulty with the idea of having one shop inside another, having never been in a supermarket.[186] Costello remained a traditionalist on moral matters—when one of his grandsons (aged about 12) argued in favour of the importation of contraceptives, he became quite irate.[187] He was also a traditionalist on legal matters, opposing the suggested fusion of the two branches of the law. He believed that an independent Bar served the interests of justice, because it allowed the opposing parties, whatever their status or wealth, to be represented by counsel, and thus equalised before the Bar of the court.[188] In a newspaper interview to mark his sixtieth anniversary at the Bar, he stoutly defended the profession, describing it as "so completely independent that it is the greatest safeguard the public has against pressures from the State, big business or other sources. It is able to take up the cudgels in any fight."[189]

In those days, with no pension scheme at the Bar, retirement was not really an option for most barristers—in any case, Jack Costello would certainly have missed the activity.[190] But he remained sharp and alert into his eighties. In January 1975—when he was 83—he was lead counsel for Tara Mines in a complicated action in the Supreme Court involving the then Minister for Industry and Commerce, Justin Keating. The company was demanding an oral hearing on a particular issue, which it believed the Minister was anxious to avoid. One of the judges asked Costello how long such a hearing would take; he replied that it would be about forty days. "Forty days in the desert, Mr Costello?" "Yes, my lord, and no manna from heaven for the Minister." During the next recess, fellow counsel Kevin Liston commented on the alacrity of that exchange—and observed that none of the five judges had even been born when Costello was called to the Bar in 1914.[191]

Another prominent brief was at the moneylending tribunal, set up in December 1969 to inquire into an RTÉ television programme on that subject. The Government viewed the "Seven Days" programme as sensationalist and misleading; the RTÉ authority stood over it. The motion establishing the tribunal called for an inquiry into "the authenticity of the programme and, in particular, the adequacy of the information on which the programme was based and whether or not the statements, comments and implications of the programme ... amounted to a correct and fair representation of the facts".[192] As the current affairs magazine *Hibernia* noted, "if the Government was seriously concerned about money lending, the terms of reference of this enquiry would be very different indeed".[193]

Muiris Mac Conghail, the editor of "Seven Days", came to the same conclusion. He believed the Government was determined to clip the wings of RTÉ in general and "Seven Days" in particular. "It was the OK Corral—Fianna Fáil were not going to let me away with it." As the opening of the tribunal drew near, he received, out of the blue, a phone call from Alexis FitzGerald, who advised him that at some stage the interests of the programme team and those of the RTÉ authority would diverge. For that reason, "Seven Days" needed separate legal representation. Given the political context, FitzGerald felt he as a Fine Gael senator couldn't act as solicitor for them.[194]

If "Seven Days" couldn't have a Fine Gael politician as solicitor, it could have a former Fine Gael Taoiseach as lead barrister. John A. Costello was briefed to lead the "Seven Days" legal team, and made quite an impression during the 51 days the tribunal sat. "Dominating the daunting front row of the all-star legal line-up is the awe-inspiring figure of John A. Costello ... At 78 years of age, incredibly sprightly and endowed with immense intellectual acuity and drive, he is said to be working regularly into the early hours of the morning on the case. It could well be a fine and fitting climax to his career."[195]

Mac Conghail was impressed with Costello's physical fitness and mental sharpness, and wondered how he maintained his "baby faced glow". He kept a meticulous record of everything that was said, and could summarise the evidence of any witness after a quick look at his notes. He guided the "very young and very nervous" members of the programme team through their evidence, outlining the likely questions they would face. Costello also had the advantage of remembering how the Locke's Tribunal had worked, which was an advantage in the lengthy procedural wrangles which dominated the opening days. According to Mac Conghail, the members of the tribunal and the other barristers were "extremely rude" to the former Taoiseach, but Costello never responded to them. He was there to see that fair play was done; in Mac Conghail's view, he was "somewhat naïve in not understanding that the Tribunal was a political hatchet job".[196]

Predictably, the tribunal report was satisfactory for the Government. While it found that the programme-makers honestly believed that moneylending was widespread and violent, it said they failed to adequately check out sources. "The programme was found not to be authentic either in relation to the scale of the illegal money lending or in relation to associated violence."[197] The Attorney General, Colm Condon, subsequently rejected a recommendation from the Chief State Solicitor that the State should pay £7,500 of the "Seven Days" legal costs (it was recommended that RTÉ should be paid £13,500). Condon could "see no reason why any sum should be paid by the State in relation to the Seven Days team, nor did I at any stage see any reason why they should have been thought to require separate representation".[198]

In 1973, as the prospect of a new coalition between Fine Gael and Labour emerged and then became a reality, Costello's views were sought by the media. Like him, Liam Cosgrave found himself at the head of a coalition government after 16 years of Fianna Fáil rule. Costello said coalitions could be just as stable as single-party governments "provided you have good will and provided you have people ... of integrity and of courage and of persistent hope and belief in the country". Asked if he thought Cosgrave faced any real problems, he replied in typically direct fashion, "I do not."[199] In particular, he pointed out that Cosgrave only had to worry about two parties, and "to that extent his difficulties are enormously lessened from what I had to face in both Cabinets".[200]

However, while he was supportive of the new government, he was annoyed that Declan, after his contribution to the party over the years, was appointed Attorney General rather than being made a minister. The appointment was regarded by the liberal wing of Fine Gael as an attempt to contain his influence.[201] Declan Costello was disappointed; Jack Costello was furious. The younger Alexis FitzGerald, walking towards Leinster House, was offered a lift in the former Taoiseach's official car. On asking Costello how he was, he was told, "Terrible. Did you hear what they're making Declan?"[202] He also made his displeasure known to his friend Muiris Mac Conghail, who had been appointed Government Press Secretary by Cosgrave.[203]

By now he was not just a grandfather, but a great-grandfather. His great-granddaughter, Katie Armstrong, remembers a Ladybird book about puppies and kittens which he gave her. Her brother, Frank, was brought at six weeks old to meet his great-grandfather shortly before Costello died.[204]

As he got older, Costello had the usual run of illnesses, including a bad case of shingles in 1966.[205] But given his lifelong addiction to nicotine, his health was relatively robust. Eventually, he gave up smoking cigarettes and took up "evil-smelling" cheroots instead.[206] The cheroots may not have been quite as dangerous, but long-term smoking generally only has one result. Around the middle of 1975 he became ill. What was originally thought to be a chest infection turned out to be lung cancer.[207] During the summer law vacation he began to fail rapidly. At the Mass in St Michan's opening the Autumn Law Term that year many colleagues, shocked at his appearance, asked his Garda driver what was wrong with him.[208]

He went to Cork on circuit for the last time in October 1975—it was more of a token visit, as he didn't have much work on. While his visits to the Law Library became less frequent, he continued going to Mass in Donnybrook every day. Towards the end, he had to be helped up to Communion by one of his drivers.[209] He approached illness with his customary determination, insisting on coming down the stairs for breakfast no matter how ill he felt, with the help of his housekeeper Molly Ennis. Her devotion at this time was credited by some in the family for keeping him going.[210]

(Outside of family, she was the biggest beneficiary of his will, receiving a bequest of £1,000, as well as being allowed to live in the house in Herbert Park until she secured a new position. The will, drawn up in February 1975, also remembered his two drivers, various nieces and nephews, the Saint Vincent de Paul and the Bar Benevolent Society, all of whom received £100 each. Ita McCoy was left £500, and Costello's typewriter. The remainder of his estate, which was valued at £90,564.74 (just under €700,000 at 2010 prices)[211], was divided into five, one part each for Declan, John and Eavan, one fifth held in trust for Wilfrid, and the final fifth divided among Grace's children.[212])

His final illness was well known in legal circles. When Frederick Budd retired from the Supreme Court just before Christmas, he "expressed regret that his old colleague, Mr John A. Costello SC, was unable to be present and he wished him a speedy recovery to good health".[213] The end came suddenly. He was visited by the senior curate of Donnybrook parish on the evening of 5 January. There was no particular anxiety about his condition at the time, but the priest asked him if he would like to receive Holy Communion. "There is nothing that I would wish for better," Costello replied. One hour after receiving Communion, he was dead.[214]

There were many tributes. The Taoiseach, Liam Cosgrave, described him as "a true Christian gentleman"; Garret FitzGerald, then Minister for Foreign Affairs, said he was "unique in his loyalty, his vigour, his candour and his uncompromising honesty"; Tom Finlay, President of the High Court, said "he set in effect the standards of integrity and conduct for the Irish Bar probably for the last forty years or more".[215] British Prime Minister Harold Wilson wrote to Cosgrave recalling his contacts with Costello, most recently sitting beside him at a lunch in Dublin. "I know of the high respect in which he was held in the Irish Republic and among Irishmen everywhere, both as an eminent constitutional lawyer and as an upright and humane statesman and patriot." US President Gerald Ford said Americans would remember Costello "as a man of peace, as a statesman, and as a man dedicated to the rule of law".[216]

As a former Taoiseach, Costello was entitled to a State funeral, but the family declined the offer. It was, as an editorial in the *Irish Independent* pointed out, "entirely in keeping with the outlook of the late Mr John A. Costello ... In his private, political and legal life he was always the retiring man who never sought, although he often found himself in, the limelight."[217] The church in Donnybrook was packed for the funeral. A minor protocol problem arose because ministers were seated before members of the Diplomatic Corps, but a commonsense solution was found by mixing diplomats and members of the Government in the first four rows.[218] It was not, of course, the first time that Costello had ruffled diplomatic feathers. The homily was delivered by the parish priest, Bishop Joseph Carroll,[219] who paid tribute to Costello as a parishioner, as someone with an "unusually strong" sense of belonging to the parish community. "One of the most moving of our experiences here in the parish during the last few months, when his health began to fail seriously, was to see this distinguished man, so humbly making his way, with considerable difficulty, to the altar rails to receive Our Lord in Holy Communion."[220]

A week after his death, the legal profession paid its own tribute at the opening of the Hilary law term. The Supreme Court was crowded with judges, barristers and solicitors, the judges of the High as well as the Supreme Court assembled on the bench, and the Attorney General, Declan Costello, taking his place as leader of the Bar. The Chief Justice, Tom O'Higgins, a former Cabinet colleague of John A. Costello, said that many tributes had been paid over the past week to their former colleague; this was an opportunity to salute him as a barrister. He said Costello had in abundance the skills needed by a barrister—not only knowledge but wisdom and experience, not only rhetoric and skill but shrewdness, not only a quickness to appreciate facts but also a patience to discover the essential detail.

O'Higgins continued, "But he brought more—in addition to his natural talents and immense abilities went a sense of honour and an integrity which was unrivalled, an unassuming simplicity which caused him to shun the plaudits which his prowess evoked and in those cases where he felt that his client had been harshly treated or unfairly put upon, such a burning searing conviction of what ought to be or have been, that all opposition tended to crumble and disintegrate. He had no second best. For those for whom he appeared—the highest or the lowest in the land, those with vast riches and those with no means whatsoever—there was only one quality of service which he could give and that was the best he had it in him to give ... In this long period at the Irish Bar ... despite the demands of an enormous practice, despite the multiple other activities in which he was engaged, John Costello remained, essentially, unassuming and approachable—one to whose seat in the library any colleague could go knowing that he would get not only valued advice but also kindness, consideration and respect."

One of those colleagues spoke next. Francis Murphy, chairman of the Bar Council, paid a heartfelt tribute to Costello's devotion to the profession. "Of him, as a man and as a barrister, truly it could be said that he fought the good fight and ... by any standard by which he may be judged, it was agreed that not only did he fight the good fight but that he won."[221]

Chapter 15 ∿

∣ MEASURING UP

*"Possibly I'll get about two lines in ... history if I'm
referred to at all."*[1]

JOHN A. COSTELLO, DECEMBER 1969

*"The Taoiseach was indeed very much a dark horse
upon his entry into the highest office of State".*[2]

THE LEADER, FEBRUARY 1951

John A. Costello had no great illusions about his place in history. At the presentation evening to mark his retirement from politics, he spoke of himself as "small fry" compared to people like Seán MacEoin, Richard Mulcahy, Kevin O'Higgins, and Patrick McGilligan. Their names, he said, would be "written into the pages of Irish history ... in bright letters and letters of gold. Possibly I'll get about two lines in that same history if I'm referred to at all."[3]

His audience laughed at this suggestion, but in fact it wasn't too far off the mark. A quick scan of the index of most books dealing with the history of twentieth-century Ireland will show that the third man to head an independent Irish government is mentioned relatively briefly—if he's mentioned at all. It is perhaps significant that three of the ministers in his first Cabinet—James Dillon, Seán MacBride and Noël Browne[4]—were the subject of full-length biographies long before Costello himself. A postage stamp marking the centenary of his birth in 1991 is about the only official memorial he has received.[5]

Part of the reason may lie in Costello's own modesty, which appears to have been absolutely genuine. The nature of his appointment, as the least objectionable candidate to head the First Inter-party Government, and his evident reluctance to take the job may also have lessened his historical stature in many eyes. As Noel Hartnett observed in 1959, "There is no 'mystique' about John A. Costello ... He was never called the 'Leader' or any such grandiloquent title ... Costello is a simple, unsubtle man who has avoided arousing enmity in any of his opponents, even the most mean-minded."[6]

His personal qualities were of course the main reason why he became Taoiseach in 1948. Costello was trusted, and liked, by the other parties, and his diplomatic chairing of government was regarded as the main reason they were able to stay together.[7] By agreeing to become Taoiseach, Costello made the First Inter-party Government possible; by his conduct as Taoiseach he did more than anyone to make it work. That must rank as a very significant achievement.

That government set a template for politics in the following four decades; it was Fianna Fáil versus the rest. That dynamic, as well as the fact of getting into government in 1948, rescued Fine Gael from a slide to oblivion. After 16 years in the wilderness, the party was relevant again. Of course, a further 16 years on the opposition benches followed Costello's second government, but at least the possibility of coalition at some stage was on the horizon, and the party never again plumbed the electoral depths of 1948, when it received less than 20 per cent of the vote.

Costello did more than give Fine Gael a taste of power; he fundamentally changed its political direction as well. In 1948, the party was seen as very conservative indeed. That image changed over the following three and a half years, partly through coalition with Labour and Clann na Poblachta, but more fundamentally because of the economic ideas pursued by the Taoiseach. The most obvious sign of this was the introduction of the Capital Budget. As *The Leader* noted in 1951, "Mr Costello ... has introduced a fundamental change of policy and has for some time been steadily moving towards a radically new programme ... he has effected a minor revolution in the upper levels of the party."[8]

He also presented a more accessible face to the public than the somewhat austere Richard Mulcahy. Saving Fine Gael may well have been Costello's most significant political achievement between 1948 and 1951, but of course his first term as Taoiseach is better remembered for two controversial episodes: the declaration of the Republic and the Mother and Child crisis. Hopefully, this book has shown that both developments were more complex than is sometimes thought.

Contrary to popular myth, John A. Costello did not declare Ireland a Republic in a fit of temper while he was in Canada. However, he did confirm the truth of a report that his government intended to repeal the External Relations Act. His decision to do so was unwise, unnecessary and almost certainly prompted by annoyance. The wiser course would have been to stonewall—something he would have had no difficulty in doing. In the end, the whole affair worked out all right from the Irish point of view, but this was due to accident rather than design. Had it been otherwise Costello would have had to shoulder most of the blame.

The story about making a rash announcement while in a fury was believed because Costello was widely—and rightly—seen as a man with a temper. Ken Whitaker remarked that "he had a fieryness of spirit which he sometimes didn't control fully". Whitaker remembered there was a dynamism to him, but an impatience, a brusqueness and a dogmatic streak too.[9] In a letter to his friend John Burke in 1944, Costello wrote that "though I am emotionally somewhat tongue-tied I have a deep and abiding feeling of friendship and gratitude for you".[10] In fact, Costello was anything but "tongue-tied" emotionally; his emotions were very close to the surface, in politics and in life. This was seen in his temper, in his enduring loyalty to his friends, in his charity, and also in his tendency to read too much into gestures of courtesy, whether from Mackenzie King in 1948 or from Eisenhower and Nixon in 1956.

In the second great controversy of his first government, the Mother and Child crisis, the Taoiseach's behaviour, while overly obsequious to the Church in general and to Archbishop McQuaid in particular, seems to have been motivated by genuine concern about possible State control of medicine. He did his best to reach a compromise between the doctors and his young and inexperienced colleague Noël Browne. When this proved impossible, he attempted to reduce the threat to his government by using the Church to neutralise Browne. With any other politician, this probably would have worked. The failure of the stratagem put Costello on the wrong side of history, though this wasn't clear at the time. It is, of course, dangerous to judge Costello's attitude to the Church by the standards of today. As Tom Garvin succinctly put it, "the Irish democratic political process was heavily tinged with theocracy, for the overwhelming reason that the majority wished it to be that way".[11] On this question, John A. Costello was most certainly with the majority in Irish society.

His second period as Taoiseach was less successful than his first. Niamh Puirséil has suggested that the Second Inter-party Government "is a contender for the worst administration in the history of the state ..."[12] Perhaps, although there is stiff competition from the Fianna Fáil government which preceded it, and from any of the governments in the decade after 1977 (it is too early to reach a conclusion about more recent administrations).

The defining characteristic of the Second Inter-party Government was the curious torpor that seemed to grip it. Very little was done until economic crisis and the IRA Border Campaign forced it to act. Liam Cosgrave noted that there was "less nonsense talked with MacBride and Browne missing".[13] This was, no doubt, true; but their absence also removed the radical cutting edge which made the First Inter-party Government so unpredictable and so interesting.

The main charge which can be levelled against Costello is the failure to act sooner on the economic agenda which eventually led Ireland out of the dark days of the 1950s—policies which he knew were needed, such as the abolition of the restrictions on foreign investment, the shift towards more productive capital spending, and a greater concentration on exports.

However, while he was slow to move, he did move in the end, and his October 1956 *Policy for Production* was an important step on the road to a new economic dispensation in Ireland. The tax relief for extra exports signalled in the speech and introduced two months later was of major importance, as was the stated intention to attract more foreign investment, which implied the final demise of protection and the opening of the Irish economy to free trade. These were significant developments for which he was to get little credit, because he had hesitated too long and lost power before the new ideas could take effect.

Two things might be said in his defence. Firstly, we have seen at other times of economic crisis that drastic medicine only becomes acceptable when the depths have been plumbed—this was evident in the 1980s, when measures were introduced after 1987 that would have been unthinkable before. The same dynamic has been seen in more recent times, with Budget 2010 cutting social welfare rates and public service pay, developments that would have been impossible six months previously. Secondly, Jack Costello was not the only one to hesitate before pushing for change. Seán Lemass showed similar hesitation.[14] At least when Lemass returned to office and pursued a new course, he knew that Fine Gael was committed to very similar policies and would not oppose him.

Costello's role in foreign affairs, and in relation to the North, was also significant at this time. His pro-American views, set out during his visit to the United States and in a subsequent memorandum for government, set the tone for Ireland's first appearance at the United Nations. At the same time, though, he was wary of matching his words with action, and reacted cautiously to a top-secret American request for military facilities at Shannon Airport.

On the North, he pursued a more restrained and effective policy in his second administration. He eschewed the "sore thumb" tactics of Seán MacBride, stressing co-operation rather than confrontation with Stormont, and beginning the policy of seeking improvements for nationalists within Northern Ireland rather than constantly harping on partition.

There has been criticism of his failure to act sooner and with more severity against the IRA. Certainly a more proactive policy in 1954 or 1955 might have derailed plans for the Border Campaign. And, as de Valera's government would show, it took emergency measures to defeat the IRA. Costello's moderate response has usually been attributed to the need to retain the support of

Clann na Poblachta. But there was another reason. Adherence to the rule of law was a principle for him throughout his career. It can be seen in his reluctance to contemplate emergency measures as Attorney General; in his criticism of government by decree during the Second World War; in his desire to bring Republicans within the constitutional fold in 1948; and in his Declaration of the Republic, which he frequently characterised as an attempt to "take the gun out of Irish politics".

And it shouldn't be forgotten that the Second Inter-party Government did move against the IRA at the start of 1957. It may have been too little, too late, but Costello and his colleagues paid a high price for their actions, which caused an election at the worst possible time for the Government parties. Clann na Poblachta's withdrawal of support consigned Fine Gael and Labour to the opposition benches for 16 years. It also, of course, consigned MacBride's party to the dustbin of history.

His time as Taoiseach was only one aspect of Jack Costello's long and varied career. He was one of the nationalist students in pre-First World War Dublin who expected to come into their political inheritance under Home Rule; he lived through the War of Independence and the Civil War, though as an observer rather than a participant; he became Attorney General and was deeply involved in the development of the Commonwealth in the 1920s; a defender of the Blueshirts in the legal and the political sphere, he played a role in the development of the new Constitution; and he continued to influence legislation as a backbencher well into his seventies.

Above all, of course, he was one of the leading barristers of his day, and remained deeply involved in the profession until shortly before his death. Lemass, who like de Valera took a dim view of lawyer TDs, told a young colleague that legal training was the worst kind for a political career. He argued that lawyers reached a conclusion, and then considered how the facts could be used to support it; a politician should arrive at conclusions based on the facts.[15] On the other hand, barristers have a way with words, and this stood Costello in good stead in the political sphere—he was able to argue a case with force and passion, and this came through in his Dáil contributions. He also had a good grasp of the details of legislation and what the practical implications of changes were.

As a barrister, he tended to become utterly convinced of whatever case he happened to be arguing: " ... he threw himself into a case with immense zest, apparently utterly unable to conceive that his client might be in the wrong".[16] Once, he told his children about a case involving a nurse who was minding a baby when a hot water bottle leaked and the baby was scalded. The children immediately expressed sympathy for the baby, to the indignation of their father. "Poor baby? Poor nurse! The hot water bottle was faulty!"[17] No doubt his attitude would have been different had he represented the parents rather than the nurse.

Jack Costello's professional belligerence and desire to win an argument could at times be taken to extremes—even a guest appearance at a student debating society could see all the oratorical skills of the courtroom applied to demolish an auditor's inaugural paper. Historian Ronan Fanning was very unimpressed with such a performance in the mid-1960s when Costello "tore into the Auditor as if he was dealing with Dev in the Dáil. It was choleric, bad tempered and utterly inappropriate."[18]

Within the family circle, and with close friends, the belligerent pose of the advocate disappeared. His son Declan recalled his amazement as a child when he first saw his father on a political platform, hearing the kindly man he knew at home transformed into "a fierce orator".[19] Those who experienced the kindness which lay under his pugnacious manner always spoke well of John A. Costello. One of those was Noel Hartnett, the former Clann na Poblachta activist who fell out with MacBride, and by extension with Costello. In the 1959 profile of the former Taoiseach quoted above, Hartnett referred to Costello's reluctance to take on the job as Taoiseach, and commented, "Politically he had greatness thrust upon him. Future generations will discern that he fully measured up to his responsibility."[20] That seems like a fair assessment.

BRAINSE CABHAN CLOCH
DOLPHINS BARN LIBRARY
TEL. 464 0231

Leabharlanna Poiblí Chathair Bhaile Átha Cliath
Dublin City Public Libraries

REFERENCES

Introduction (pp 1–6)

1. Speech at retirement function, JACP, P190/350.
2. O'Higgins speech, ibid.
3. Keogh, Dermot, *Jack Lynch*, p. 474.
4. "Seven Days".
5. *News Review*, 14 April 1949, in JACP, P190/547.
6. JAC to Declan Costello, 29 February 1948, in possession of Declan Costello.
7. Ibid.
8. *IT*, 6 January 1976.
9. Interview with Mick Kilkenny.
10. Correspondence with Isabelle Sutton.
11. Parker to Costello, 17 March 1948, JACP, P190/376. Little Audrey was a fictional heroine of American jokes in the 1930s who found humour in unlikely situations.
12. *IT*, 6 January 1976.
13. See, for example, papers relating to his involvement in the Royal United Kingdom Beneficent Association, JACP, P190/348.
14. Lemass interview, *IP*, 29 January 1969.
15. Interview with Ronan Keane.
16. Lynch, Patrick, "Pages from a Memoir", in Lynch and Meenan (eds), *Essays in Memory of Alexis FitzGerald*, p. 40.
17. Interview with Declan Costello.
18. Undated memorandum from Alexis FitzGerald, JACP, P190/390.
19. Undated memorandum from Alexis FitzGerald, JACP, P190/390.
20. Interview with Declan Costello.
21. Fr J.J. Mathews to Costello, 26 February 1948, JACP, P190/372.
22. Interview with Declan Costello.
23. Address to University of Dublin Philosophical Society, 28 October 1948, JACP, P190/447.
24. Interview with Patrick Lynch, 1996.
25. Interview with Declan Costello.
26. *News Review*, 14 April 1949, JACP, P190/547.
27. DÉD, 16 June 1936, Vol. 62, Cols. 2436/7.
28. Interview with Jacqueline Armstrong.
29. "Seven Days".
30. *Irish Golf*, March 1948 JACP, P190/360. The fact that the then Taoiseach kept the magazine suggests it was of more than passing interest to him.
31. Interview with Declan Costello.

32. *Irish Golf,* March 1948.
33. Interview with Declan Costello.
34. Interview with Declan Costello.
35. News Review, 14 April 1949.
36. DÉD, 3 July 1935, Vol. 57, Cols 1635/6.
37. Interview with Muiris Mac Conghail.
38. 21 July 1948, Jowitt to Costello, NAI, Taoiseach's Private Office, 97/9/862.
39. Interview with Tom Finlay.
40. *News Review,* 14 April 1949, JACP, P190/547.
41. Interview with Richie Ryan.
42. Profile of Costello by Noel Hartnett, in *Development,* November 1959, JACP, P190/969.
43. Kingsmill Moore to Costello, 18 February 1948, JACP, P190/372.
44. The O'Mahony to Costello, 31 May 1948, JACP, P190/397.

Chapter 1 The value of practice (pp 7–24)

1. "The Old Order Changeth, Yielding Place to New" by John A. Costello, NS, July 1911.
2. NS, March 1912.
3. Interview with Ronan Keane.
4. He shared this lower middle class background with W.T. Cosgrave. Eunan O'Halpin has written, "It would be as unwise to ignore Cosgrave's modest background as to harp on it." Entry on Cosgrave in McGuire, James, and James Quinn, *Dictionary of Irish Biography.*
5. Birth Certificate, JACP, P190/959.
6. Information from Fran Leahy, Human Resources Manager, Property Registration Authority (the successor to the Registry of Deeds).
7. 1911 Census.
8. 8 March 1948, reply to Lord Rugby query, NAI, Taoiseach's Private Office, 97/9/823.
9. 31 January 1949, Brother Michael Garvey to Costello, NAI, Taoiseach's Private Office, 97/9/937.
10. Correspondence with John Costello.
11. Descriptions from Guy's Directory 1893 and Irish Tourist Association Survey, 1942/3, both accessed through the Clare Library website, www.clarelibrary.ie/eolas/coclare/genealogy.
12. Interview with Declan Costello. This slight connection was enough for Declan to be invited to write the foreword to a book marking the school's centenary.
13. Information from Fran Leahy.
14. *Thom's Directory,* 1898.
15. Information from Fran Leahy.
16. *Thom's,* 1913.
17. *Thom's,* 1927.
18. Interview with Declan Costello.

19. *IT*, 22 October 1936.

20. *FJ*, 6 June 1908.

21. *FJ*, 13 March 1909.

22. *II*, 13 October 1905.

23. *FJ*, 20 May 1914.

24. See Commander A.J. O'Brien-Twohig to JAC, 26 February 1948, JACP, P190/375.

25. Frederick Scales to Costello, 25 February 1948, JACP, P190/379.

26. See, for instance, JAC speech to the Irish Conference of Professional and Service Associations, 8 November 1958, JACP, P190/946. " ... as the son of a civil servant ... I have ... endeavoured to do what was possible to advance their interest ..."

27. Interview with Declan Costello.

28. Garvin, Tom, *Judging Lemass*, p. 41.

29. "Seven Days".

30. Interview with Jacqueline Armstrong.

31. Original purchase of house recorded in Registry of Deeds, 1890/60/210; memorial of indenture of assignment 1891/22/262.

32. Will of Bridget Callaghan, JACP, P190/958. Bridget appears to have been well off— she also had an interest in a house in Grosvenor Road, which was left to another sister and niece, as well as her own house in the upmarket Wellington Road, which she left to her nephew John A. Costello—provided he paid for her funeral, and spent £50 on having Masses said for her parents and siblings. He was also to receive any residue of her property. His father and brother, John senior and Tom, who were named as trustees, were not to receive anything.

33. School history from St Joseph's, Fairview, website, http://www.stjosephscbs.ie/.

34. See John Ryan to Costello, 20 February 1948, JACP, P190/378.

35. Interview with Declan Costello.

36. Brother J.A. Kean to Costello, 21 February 1948; JACP, P190/370.

37. *O'Connell School Centenary Record*, Dublin, June 1928, p. 11.

38. Ibid., p. 20.

39. Ibid., p. 21.

40. Patrick Judge, "The O'Connell School Museum", in Patrick Judge (ed.), *O'Connell School: 150 Years*, p. 72.

41. Frank O'Beirne to Costello, 20 February 1948, JACP, P190/375.

42. Judge (ed.).

43. Patrick J. Stephenson, "School and Environs: A Galaxy of Famous Names", in Judge (ed.), p. 121.

44. *O'Connell School Centenary Record*, p. 25.

45. *Results of annual examinations 1907*, published by O'Connell Schools (Christian Brothers), North Richmond Street, Dublin. Information from Darragh O'Donoghue, archivist, Allen Library, Dublin.

46. *O'Connell Schools and Mary's Place Register, 1904–1918*. Hours at Science were recorded for each student as they affected the size of the grant received by the school. Information from Darragh O'Donoghue.

47. *Results of annual examinations 1908*. Information from Darragh O'Donoghue.

48. Interview with Declan Costello.

49. Tom Fahy to Costello, 19 February 1948, JACP, P190/390.

50. See E. O'Mahoney to Costello, 26 November 1971, and undated reply, JACP, P190/918.

51. "Seven Days".

52. NS, November 1910.

53. Meenan, James (ed.), *Centenary History of the L&H*, p. 93.

54. Ibid., p. 108.

55. Ibid., p. 112.

56. Cox diary, Irish Jesuit Archives, Arthur Cox Papers, N3/5.

57. *FJ*, 30 July 1909.

58. *FJ*, 27 June 1910.

59. *II*, 11 January 1926.

60. *II*, 23 May 1955—Costello referred to first being in Salthill more than 50 years before on his way to Aran.

61. DÉD, 4 April 1935, Vol. 55, Col. 1980.

62. L&H Minute Book, general meeting, 9 March 1912, in UCDA, Soc 2/3.

63. Meenan, James, *George O'Brien: A biographical memoir*, p. 30.

64. Quoted in ibid., p. 29.

65. Ibid., p. 29.

66. "JAC Remembers", *IT*, 4 September 1967.

67. F.J. Wade to Costello, 19 February 1948, JACP, P190/381. Unfortunately this letter doesn't clarify what type of football was involved, whether soccer, Gaelic or rugby.

68. Frank Whelan to Costello, 24 February 1948, JACP, P190/381.

69. Mrs Deena Wallis to Costello, 21 February 1948, JACP, P190/381.

70. Interview with Declan Costello; correspondence with Georgina Sutton.

71. Information from John Costello.

72. De Vere White, *Kevin O'Higgins*, p. 9.

73. "The Old Order Changeth, Yielding Place to New" by John A. Costello, NS, July 1911.

74. McCague, Eugene, *Arthur Cox*, p. 28.

75. JAC memorandum on Tom Bodkin, for use by "This Is Your Life", 29 January 1960, JACP, P190/813.

76. George O'Brien in Meenan (ed.), p. 110.

77. JAC memorandum on Tom Bodkin, 29 January 1960, JACP, P190/813.

78. "Seven Days".

79. NS, May 1913.

80. Cahir Davitt in Meenan (ed.), p. 115.

81. L&H notes, NS, November 1910.

82. Cox in Meenan (ed.), p. 104.

83. Michael McGilligan in Meenan (ed.), p. 98.

84. *NS*, December 1911.

85. Bodkin in Meenan (ed.), p. 88.

86. JAC memorandum on Bodkin, 29 January 1960, JACP, P190/83.

87. L&H minute book, 18 February 1911, in UCDA, Soc 2/3.

88. L&H minute book, 25 February 1911.

89. *NS*, April 1911.

90. L&H minute book, 6 May 1911.

91. *NS*, April 1911. Those were the days when three children were regarded as a "small family".

92. *NS*, December 1911.

93. Michael McGilligan in Meenan (ed.), p. 100.

94. L&H minute book, undated but 2 December 1911, in UCDA, Soc 2/3.

95. L&H minute book, 2 June 1911.

96. L&H minute book, 2 March 1912 and 16 March 1912.

97. For instance, L&H minute book, 9 March 1912, JAC opposed the motion "That the Young Ireland movement was not politically effective", getting the second highest mark of 6.6, while Cox got just 6.44.

98. *NS*, March 1912.

99. L&H minute book, 4 May 1912.

100. *NS*, June 1912.

101. McCague, p. 7.

102. Arthur Cox in Meenan (ed.), p. 107.

103. "JAC remembers", *IT*, 4 September 1967.

104. Charles Lysaght in Callanan, Frank (ed.), *The L&H*, p. 58.

105. *NS*, June 1912.

106. Cox in Meenan (ed.), p. 106.

107. Ibid.

108. *NS*, June 1912.

109. Davitt in Meenan (ed.), p. 116.

110. Quoted in Meenan, 1980, p. 35.

111. George O'Brien in Meenan (ed.), p. 111.

112. L&H minute book, 25 May 1912.

113. Arthur Cox diary, 4 May 1913.

114. *NS*, February 1913.

115. L&H minute book, general meeting, 8 February 1913.

116. L&H minute book, general meeting, 1 March 1913.

117. L&H minute book, EGM for Inter-debate, 6 February 1913.

118. *FJ*, 7 February 1913.

119. Cox Diary, 1 March 1913.

120. Cox Diary, 4 March 1913.

121. Cahir Davitt in Meenan (ed.), p. 119.

122. Michael Tierney in Meenan (ed.), p. xxvi.

123. Cox Diary, 17 May 1913.

124. *EH*, 27 January 1951.

125. Callanan in Callanan (ed.), pp 3 and 8.

126. Eamon Delaney in Callanan (ed.), p. 253.

127. Callanan in Callanan (ed.), p. 8.

128. *ILT&SJ*, 20 May 1922.

129. NAI, S 3874 A.

130. Cox in Meenan (ed.), p. 106.

131. "Seven Days".

132. 8 December 1969, speech to Presentation evening at Jury's to mark his retirement, JACP, P190/350.

133. DÉD, 26 November 1958, Vol. 171, Cols. 1008/9.

134. *NS*, December 1913.

135. McCague, p. 17.

136. Cox Diary, 1 May 1913.

137. Cox Diary, 6 May 1913.

138. Cox Diary, 20 May 1913.

139. Cox Diary, 22 May 1913.

140. Cox Diary, 3 June 1913.

141. Cox Diary, 23 June 1913.

142. Cox Diary, 30 June 1913.

143. Cox Diary, 19 July 1913.

144. McCague, p. 17.

145. *FJ*, 31 October 1914.

146. Hogan, Daire, *The Honourable Society of King's Inns*, p. 7.

147. Ibid., p. 20.

148. Mackey, Rex, *Windward of the Law*, p. 23.

149. O'Higgins, T.F., *A Double Life*, p. 58.

150. Mackey, pp 23/4.

151. Mackey, pp 22/3.

152. *ILT&SJ*, 6 June 1914.

153. *ILT&SJ*, 31 October 1914.

154. *ILT&SJ*, 25 October 1913.

155. *Studies*, December 1913, p. 439.

156. 13 December 1913, Cox diary.

157. *ILT&SJ*, 7 November 1914.

158. Mackey, p. 25.

159. O'Higgins, p. 70.

160. *IT*, 2 November 1974.

161. Mackey, p. 25.

Chapter 2 An arduous road (pp 25–47)

1. Costello memorandum on Bodkin, 29 January 1960, JACP, P190/813.

2. Burke to Costello, 14 July 1949, JACP, P190/386.

3. Interview with Declan Costello.

4. "Seven Days".

5. "Seven Days".

6. *IT*, 10 March 1937—Kennedy was clearly something of an enthusiast for snuff, leaving other snuff boxes to W.T. Cosgrave and to solicitor John Burke.

7. O'Higgins, T.F., *A Double Life*, p. 74.

8. Interview with Ronan Keane.

9. Quoted in Kissane, Bill, *Explaining Irish Democracy*, p. 61.

10. Quoted in Callanan, Frank, *T.M. Healy*, p. 442.

11. Hogan, Daire, *The Legal Profession in Ireland, 1789–1922*, p. 5.

12. Ferguson, Kenneth (ed.), *King's Inns Barristers*, p. 70.

13. Healy, Maurice, *The Old Munster Circuit*, p. 43.

14. Quoted in Ferguson (ed.), p. 61.

15. Quoted in Meenan, *George O'Brien*, p. 44.

16. Mackey, p. 21.

17. Lindsay, Patrick, *Memories*, p. 97.

18. Ferguson (ed.), p. 77.

19. *ILT&SJ*, 26 February 1916.

20. Ibid.

21. *IT*, 12 March 1945.

22. *London Gazette*, 10 December 1915.

23. *London Gazette*, 23 June 1916.

24. Medal Card, TNA, 35895/23202.

25. *II*, 8 January 1918.

26. *IT*, 12 March 1945.

27. Ibid.

28. Website of Blackburn with Darwen Borough Council, http://195.8.175.10/server.php?show=ConWebDoc.16193&viewPage=2

29. *IT*, 12 March 1945.

30. 28 October 1948, speech to Trinity College Philosophic Society, JACP, P190/447.

31. *ILT&SJ*, 14 November 1914.

32. Hogan, p. 144.

33. *ILT&SJ*, 28 June 1919.

34. Note on Bodkin's life, in Bodkin Papers, TCD, MSS 7003/295.

35. Healy, Maurice, pp 175 and 179.

36. Ibid., pp 65 and 89.

37. "Seven Days".

38. DÉD, 27 November 1935, Vol. 59, Cols. 1456 and 1467.

39. JACP, P190/3, contains the original brief for the case.

40. Burke to Costello, 14 July 1949, JACP, P190/386.

41. Burke to Costello, 8 May 1949, JACP, P190/386. Declan Costello recalls Burke as being slightly eccentric, although he did do his father another favour, persuading him to invest in Hicks furniture for Herbert Park. Interview with Declan Costello.

42. Interview with Tom Finlay.

43. 8 December 1969, Tom Finlay speech at retirement dinner, JACP, P190/350.

44. De Valera, Terry, *A Memoir*, p. 205.

45. Interview with Tom Finlay.

46. "Seven Days".

47. Ibid.

48. *ILT&SJ*, 29 April 1916.

49. Typed extract from *II*, 23 July 1956, of Taoiseach's speech to military parade at Youghal, JACP, P190/660.

50. *ILT&SJ*, 15 July 1916.

51. Interview with Ronan Keane.

52. *ILTR*, 1916, pp 177/8.

53. Ferguson (ed.), p. 422.

54. *ILT&SJ*, 26 April 1919.

55. *ILT&SJ*, 4 February 1928.

56. *ILT&SJ*, 17 April 1920.

57. Hogan, *The Legal Profession in Ireland*, pp 149/50.

58. *IT*, 15 November 1966.

59. Quoted in Kotsonouris, Mary, *Retreat from Revolution: the Dáil Courts, 1920–24*, p. 23.

60. *IT*, 21 November 1966.

61. Quoted in Ferguson (ed.), p. 90.

62. Ferguson (ed.), pp 90/1.

63. Kotsonouris, p. 32.

64. *IT*, 2 November 1974: "The life and thoughts of a perfectly happy man; Saturday Interview: Henry Kelly talks to JAC".

65. *ILT&SJ*, 26 June 1920.

66. *ILT&SJ*, 6 November 1920.

67. *ILT&SJ*, 6 March 1920.

68. *ILT&SJ*, 20 November 1920.

69. *ILT&SJ*, 10 July 1920.

70. *ILT&SJ*, 17 July 1920.

71. *ILT&SJ*, 24 July 1920.

72. *ILT&SJ*, 25 September 1920.

73. Figures given by Sir Hamar Greenwood in the House of Commons; quoted in *ILT&SJ*, 21 August 1920.

74. *ILT&SJ*, 21 August 1920.

75. *IT*, 1, 8 and 27 November 1919.

76. 18 November 19, T.M. Healy to his brother Maurice, UCDA, P6/E/2: "I am going to London Saturday night for a court martial upon Father O'Donnell on Monday before the Australians. Lynch and a junior are also coming." Costello does not appear to have been mentioned again.

77. *IT*, 27 November 1919.

78. *ILTR*, 1920, p. 67, Riordan v. County Council of Clare, Ennis, 3 March 1920, before O'Connor LJ.

79. Laffan, Michael, *The Resurrection of Ireland*, p. 330.

80. Ibid., p. 269.

81. *ILT&SJ*, 10 July 1920.

82. *ILT&SJ*, 2 October 1920.

83. Note on Bodkin's life, in Bodkin Papers, TCD, MSS 7003/295.

84. Healy, p. 180.

85. 18 June 1955, Thomas Bodkin to Costello, JACP, P190/813.

86. Hopkinson, Michael (ed.), *The Last days of Dublin Castle: The Mark Sturgis Diaries*, entry for 29 September 1920, p. 48.

87. Ibid., entry for 12 August 1920, p. 89.

88. Ibid., entry for 17 January 1921, pp 111/2.

89. Macready, *Annals of an Active Life*, pp 586/7.

90. Sturgis Diary, p. 165.

91. Sturgis Diary, 27 August 1921, p. 165.

92. Macready, pp 586/7.

93. Affidavit of John B. Lynch, solicitor, 2 July 1921, JACP, P190/10. See also Foxton, David, *Revolutionary lawyers*, p. 288.

94. "Seven Days".

95. Judgment in Egan case, 26 July 1921, JACP, P190/6.

96. Hopkinson, p. 186.

97. JACP, P190/10, copy of Writ of Summons, 14 June 1921.

98. "Seven Days".

99. Healy, pp 149/50.

100. Hopkinson, p. 111.

101. Copy statement in JACP, P190/5.

102. O'Neill, Tom, *The Battle of Clonmult: The IRA's Worst Defeat*, p. 13.

103. Ibid., p. 29.

104. Ibid., p. 34.

105. Ibid., p. 38.

106. Macready affadvit, 11 July 1921, in JACP, P190/6.

107. See JACP, P190/6.

108. See JACP, P190/9.

109. See for instance Macready affidavit in Egan case, 27 June 1921, JACP, P190/7.

110. Copy of judgment, JACP, P190/6.

111. Macready, pp 588/9.

112. Undated *Daily Sketch* cutting, UCDA, P4/160.

113. "Seven Days".

114. *II*, 2 August 1921.

115. Macready, pp 590.

116. Ibid., pp 590–94.

117. Ibid.

118. *II*, 2 August 1921.

119. Macready, pp 590–94.

120. Kennedy note of appeal, 11 November 1921, UCDA, P4/147.

121. Hogan, Daire, *The Honourable Society of King's Inns*, p. 22.

122. See Ó Longaigh, Seosamh, *Emergency Law in Independent Ireland, 1922–48*, pp 25/6, and *ILT&SJ*, 25 November 1922.

123. Egan to Kennedy, 26 May 1924, UCDA, P4/147.

124. See correspondence in JACP, P190/389.

125. *FG Digest*, February 1956, JACP, P190/737.

126. *Ave Maria*, 4 January 1950.

127. Michael Hayes to Tom O'Higgins, 24 November 1959, UCDA, P53,270.

128. JACP, P190/6.

129. Costello to Secretary, D/F, 17 February 1927, in NAI, AG 18/27. The total fees for the three barristers were: Lynch £97.13.0; Kennedy £72.9.0; Costello £43.1.0. This did not include the fees for the appeal taken by the British.

130. *FG Digest*, Feburary 1956, JACP, P190/737.

131. "Seven Days".

132. *ILT&SJ*, 22 April 1922.

133. *ILT&SJ*, 1 and 8 July 1922.

134. *ILT&SJ*, 21 October 1922.

135. *ILT&SJ*, 20 January 1923.

136. Ferguson (ed.), p. 52.

137. Ibid., p. 104.

138. Ibid., p. 422.

139. Cronin, Patrick, *Boss Croker*, p. 4.

140. Ibid., p. 10.

141. *TIME* magazine, 22 August 1955.

142. Cronin, p. 10.

143. *IT*, 1 June 1923.

144. Tulsa World, 16 April 1933, available online at the Tulsa American Indian Resource Centre website, www.tulsalibrary.org/airc/

145. *IT*, 1 June 1923.

146. Cronin, p. 13.

147. Ibid., p. 14.

148. *IT*, 1 June 1923.

149. De Valera, Terry, *A Memoir*, p. 167.

150. Kennedy to O'Hanlon, 28 May 1923, UCDA, P4/134.

151. O'Hanlon to Kennedy, 24 May 1923, UCDA, P4/134.

152. O'Hanlon to Kennedy, 20 June 1923, UCDA, P4/134.

153. Kennedy to Henry O'Hanlon, 28 May 1923, UCDA, P4/134.

154. O'Hanlon to Kennedy, 20 June 1923, UCDA, P4/134.

155. Kotsonouris, p. 110.

156. *IT*, 2 June 1923.

157. *IT*, 2 June 1923.

158. *ILT&SJ*, 9 June 1923.

159. *IT*, 5 June 1923.

160. *IT*, 7 June 1923.

161. *IT*, 9 June 1923.

162. *IT*, 12 June 1923.

163. *IT*, 15 June 1923.

164. *IT*, 16 June 1923.

165. *IT*, 20 June 1923.

166. *IT*, 23 June 1923.

167. *IT*, 3 July 1923.

168. 12 November 1929, Diarmuid O'Hegarty to W.T. Cosgrave, NAI, S 5340/13.

169. *TIME* magazine, 19 August 1929—the magazine may not have been as accurate as could be wished—it referred to Mr and Mrs Croker living in "Iceland"!

170. *Palm Beach Daily News* website, photo caption by Augustus Mayhew.

171. *ILTR*, 1923, p. 21.

172. *ILTR*, 1923, p. 57.

173. Kotsonouris, p. 85.

174. Interview with Declan Costello.

175. Sheehy Skeffington, p. 248.

176. 28 February 1950, Costello to John Richardson, NAI, Taoiseach's Private Office, 97/9/1065.

177. Interview with Jacqueline Armstrong.

178. *News Review*, 14 April 1949.

179. Undated cutting from *Tuam Herald*, c. 1926, JACP, P190/48.

180. *IT*, 6 July 1929.

181. Interview with Declan Costello.

182. Interview with Declan Costello.

183. Interview with Declan Costello.

184. Thom's Directories, 1920 to 1924.

185. Wilfrid Costello doesn't appear to have suffered from a specific condition. Family members simply refer to him having a mental disability.

186. 20 February 1952, Very Rev. Dom Bernard O'Dea to Costello, JACP, P190/616.

187. Interview with Declan Costello.

188. "One to One: Declan Costello".

189. Ferguson (ed.).

190. Ronan Fanning, "Alexis FitzGerald" in Lynch and Meenan (eds), p 12.

191. *News Review*, 14 April 1949, interview with Costello, JACP, P190/547.

192. *News Review*, 14 April 1949.

193. Ibid.

194. Interview with Declan Costello.

195. Thom's Directory, 1924.

Chapter 3 He has done wonderful work (pp 48–74)

1. 8 December 1969, Costello speech at retirement presentation, JACP, P190/350.
2. 11 December 1969, Hugh Kennedy diary entry, UCDA, P4/41.
3. Letter to the author from Liam Cosgrave. Mr Cosgrave said he could say the same for Declan Costello, who "was always right and his opinion quickly given".
4. 18 May 1922, Kennedy to O'Higgins, NAI, S 1114 A.
5. "Seven Days".
6. Costello speech at retirement presentation, JACP, P190/350.
7. "Seven Days".
8. Regan, John M., *The Irish Counter-Revolution*, p. 252.
9. "Seven Days".
10. Thom's Directory, 1923.
11. 18 May 1922, Kennedy to O'Higgins, NAI, S 1114 A.
12. Costello speech at retirement presentation, JACP, P190/350.
13. UCDA, P4/624, P4/626, P4/629, P4/630 and P4/631.
14. 27 October 1922, Kennedy to Costello, P4/625.
15. Costello opinion, in P4/625.
16. 14 November 1923, Secretary, Department of Home Affairs, to members of the Executive Council, NAI, S 3400.
17. Ó Longaigh, Seosamh, *Emergency Law*, p. 58.
18. 9 November 1923, Kennedy to O'Higgins, NAI, S 3400.
19. 16 November 1923, Executive Council minutes, NAI, S 3400.
20. Costello memorandum in UCDA, P24/190.
21. 18 December 1923, Kennedy to O'Friel, NAI, S 3400.
22. 23 October 1924, O'Higgins to each Minister, NAI, S 3400.
23. Ó Longaigh, p. 59.
24. *IT*, 11 August 1923.
25. Garvin, Tom, *Judging Lemass*, p. 39.
26. *IT*, 16 October 1923.
27. 30 April 1924, Cosgrave to Kennedy, UCDA, P4/588.
28. 1 May 1924, Kennedy to Cosgrave, UCDA, P4/588.
29. 7 June 1924, warrant of appointment, NAI, S 9330.
30. 7 June 1924, O'Byrne to Cosgrave, NAI, S 3874 A.
31. Ferguson, Kenneth (ed.), *King's Inns Barristers, 1868–2004*, p. 407.
32. 5 July 1924, Executive Council minutes, NAI, S 3874 A.
33. 14 May 1970, Costello to Brian Lennon S.J., JACP, P190/921.
34. 29 April 1925, Costello to Secretary of the Executive Council, NAI, S 3874 A.
35. 30 April 1925, Kennedy to Secretary of the Executive Council, NAI S 3874 A.
36. NAI, S 3874 A.
37. *IT*, 7 May 1925.
38. 8 January 1926, extract from Executive Council minutes; 9 January 1926, McDunphy to Hugh Kennedy; 12 January 1926, A. McHugh, private secretary to Chief Justice to O'Hegarty. NAI S 9330.

39. *IT*, 11 January 1926.

40. *IT*, 19 January 1926.

41. J.P. Casey, *The Office of the Attorney General in Ireland*, pp 174/5.

42. Costello speech at retirement presentation, JACP, P190/350.

43. 22 March 1932, Minister for Finance memorandum, NAI S 9332.

44. See details of burial plots, JACP, P190/957.

45. *IT*, 23 January 1926.

46. 18 May 1922, Kennedy to O'Higgins, NAI, S 1114 A.

47. DÉD, 6 December 1923, Vol 5, cols 1551–1568.

48. 22 December 1930, Cosgrave to Costello, NAI, S 1114 A.

49. 30 December 1930, Costello to Cosgrave, NAI, S 1114 A.

50. Casey, p. 178.

51. 1 January 1931, Cosgrave note, NAI, S 1114 A.

52. 1 February 1932 unsigned memorandum, NAI S 1114 A; see also Casey, pp 55/6.

53. 5 July 1937, Costello to Hogan, JACP, P190/334.

54. 22 March 1932, Minister for Finance memorandum, NAI S 9332.

55. 10 March 1932, Executive Council minutes, NAI S 9332.

56. 22 December 1936, Government decision, NAI S 1114 A; 18 February 1948, notes for Taoiseach's discussion with the new Attorney General, NAI, S 14169.

57. 20 February 1948, note by Maurice Moynihan, NAI, S 14169.

58. 8 March 1948, note by Maurice Moynihan, NAI, S 14169.

59. 1 March 1948, note by Nicholas Nolan, NAI, S 14169.

60. 5 July 1937, Costello to Hogan, JACP, P190/334.

61. 6 January 1950, Moynihan note of discussion with the Taoiseach, NAI S 14169.

62. Casey, footnote, p. 216.

63. Regan, p. 153.

64. "Seven Days".

65. De Vere White, Terence, *Kevin O'Higgins*, p. 178.

66. *IT*, 2 November 1974.

67. Casey, p. 45.

68. *IT*, 2 November 1974.

69. "Seven Days".

70. Casey, p. 45.

71. Casey, p. 50.

72. British Cabinet Conclusions, 29 May 1922, quoted in Sexton, Brendan, *Ireland and the Crown, 1922–36*, note 44, p. 196.

73. 1 June 1922, Lloyd George to Arthur Griffith, NAI, S 4285 A.

74. 2 June 1922, Griffith to Lloyd George, NAI, S 4285 A.

75. 11 June 1922, extract from letter from Hugh Kennedy, NAI, S 4285 A.

76. 22 September 1922, O'Higgins to Johnson, NAI S 4285 A.

77. 26 July 1923, *The Times*.

78. *ILT&SJ*, 4 March 1922.

79. *ILT&SJ*, 3 March 1923.

80. 25 July 1923, notes of Privy Council sitting, NAI, S 4285 A.

81. 30 July 1923, Kennedy to Cosgrave, NAI, S 4285 A.

82. 7 December 1925, report of Privy Council hearing, NAI, AG 214/25.

83. 20 November 1930, McDunphy to Cosgrave, NAI, S 4285 A.

84. Bewley, Charles, *Memoirs of a Wild Goose*, p. 97.

85. No. 11/1926, Land Act, 1926.

86. 11 February 1926, Attorney General to Minister for Justice, NAI, AG 214/25.

87. Quoted in Harkness, David, *The Restless Dominion*, p. 114.

88. 16 April 1926, AG to Secretary, Department of External Affairs, NAI, AG 214/25.

89. 20 November 1930, McDunphy to Cosgrave, NAI, S 4285 A.

90. 31 October 1927, Minister for Finance note for Government, UCDA, P80/963.

91. Maguire, Martin, *The Civil Service and the revolution in Ireland*, p. 193. There is an excellent, detailed account of the Wigg and Cochrane case in Maguire, pp 184 to 193.

92. 17 June 1927, Walshe to O'Hegarty, NAI, S 5090.

93. 8 January 1931, O'Hegarty to Costello, NAI, AG 214/25.

94. 4 March 1931, Costello to O'Hegarty, enclosing alternative drafts, in UCDA, P24/96.

95. 10 March 1931, McDunphy to Costello, and 20 April 1931, McDunphy memo, NAI, S 6164.

96. 20 October 1931, Cabinet minutes, and 29 December 1931 McDunphy memo, NAI, S 6164.

97. "Seven Days".

98. For one of many examples, see "Seven Days".

99. 6 January 1976, 1330 News, RTÉ Radio.

100. MacBride, Seán, *That Day's Struggle*, p. 117.

101. Ó Longaigh, p. 74.

102. NAI, S 2257.

103. Ó Longaigh, p. 75.

104. Ibid., p. 76.

105. MacGarry, Fearghal, *Eoin O'Duffy*, p. 178.

106. 26 July 1927, counsel's opinion on High Court case no. 328 of 1927, JACP, P190/52.

107. 21 June 1927, counsel's opinion, in UCDA, P150/2033.

108. 19 July 1927, Cabinet decision, NAI, S 5485.

109. 20 July 1927, Costello to O'Hegarty, NAI, S 5485.

110. 10 August 1927, O'Hegarty to Healy, NAI, S 5486.

111. 17 August 1927, McDunphy to Ceann Comhairle, NAI S 5485.

112. 18 August 1927, Executive Council decision, NAI, S 5485.

113. 19 August 1927, Colm Ó Murchada, Clerk of the Dáil, to McDunphy, NAI, S 5485.

114. 12 October 1927, McDunphy to Costello, NAI, S 5485.

115. 7 November 1927, McDunphy to each Minister, NAI, S 5485.

116. 15 July 1927, Cabinet Decision, NAI, S 5486.

117. By the Constitution (Amendment No. 10) Act, 1928.

118. 17 July 1927, Cabinet decision, NAI S 5486.

119. 20 July 1927, Cabinet decision, NAI S 5486.

120. August 1931, D/J report on present position, NAI, S 5964 B.

121. DÉD, Vol 21, 10 November 1927.

122. DÉD, Vol 23, 24 May 1928.

123. Ó Longaigh, p. 85.

124. 8 December 1969, Costello speech at retirement event, JACP, P190/350.

125. Note dated August 1928 [clearly a mistake by Blythe], in UCDA, P24/1690.

126. DÉD, Vol. 20, 16 August 1927.

127. *The Leader*, Christmas number, 1958, article on PR by Earnan de Blaghd.

128. Puirséil, Niamh, *The Labour Party, 1922–73*, p. 24.

129. DÉD, Vol 21, 11 October 1927.

130. DÉD, 28 March 1930, Vol. 34, Cols. 276/7; also NAI, S 9331.

131. O'Higgins, T.F., *A Double Life*, p. 137.

132. Ó Longaigh, p. 90.

133. 23 April 1929, statement of Robert Briscoe T.D., NAI, S 5862. It is interesting to note that this statement, by an Opposition TD, was circulated to all members of the Executive Council.

134. 17 May 1929, Garda memorandum, NAI, S 5864 A.

135. O'Halpin, Eunan, *Defending Ireland*, p. 78.

136. Ibid., p. 78.

137. McGarry, p. 183.

138. 15 July 1931, O'Hegarty to private secretary, Minister for Justice, NAI, S 5864 B.

139. August 1931, D/J report on the present position, NAI, S 5864 B.

140. 27 July 1931, O'Duffy to Secretary, D/J, NAI, S 5864 B.

141. 17 August 1936, note by Stephen Roche, NAI, S 9249.

142. 13 August 1931, Cosgrave to McRory, NAI, S 5864 B.

143. 10 September 1931, Cosgrave to McRory, NAI, S 5864 B.

144. 18 September 1931, McGilligan to Walshe, UCDA, P35/d/113.

145. Constitution (Amendment No. 17) Act, 1931, No. 37/1931.

146. 17 October 1931, statement by the President, NAI, S 2449.

147. Ó Longaigh, p. 122.

148. 19 October 1931, "Note for the information of the Minister for Justice", NAI, S 2449.

149. See note on procedure, 15 June 1936, NAI, S 8974.

150. 20 October 1931, O'Duffy to Minister for Justice, NAI, S 2449.

151. 22 October 1931, note of special meeting of Ministers, NAI, S 2449.

152. O'Halpin, p. 79.

153. DÉD, 19 April 1939, Vol 75, Col. 730.

154. Brady, Conor, *Guardians of the Peace*, p. 163.

155. McGarry, p. 188, and footnote 83.

156. Ibid., p. 189.

157. MacMahon, Deirdre, *Republicans and Imperialists*, p. 38.

158. 16 December 1926, Costello to Secretary, D/J, JACP, P190/52.

159. J.P. Casey describes this as the "most outstanding" example of an Attorney's advice being published. Casey, p. 88.

160. White Paper, JACP, P190/59.

161. Forward by Oscar Traynor to Fianna Fáil legal opinion, JACP, P190/59.

162. McMahon, p. 40.

163. 11 July 1925, O'Hegarty to Secretary, Boundary Commission, in UCDA, P24/160.

164. Patterson, Henry, *Ireland since 1939: the persistence of conflict*, p. 16.

165. 29 July 1926, Cabinet conclusions, PRONI CAB/4/173.

166. 29 July 1926, Cabinet conclusions, PRONI, CAB/4/173.

167. 29 June 1926, Cabinet conclusions, PRONI CAB/4/172.

168. 29 July 1926, Cabinet conclusions, PRONI CAB/4/173.

169. See Babington to Costello, 30 July 1926, JACP, P190/61 and 31 July 1926, JACP, P190/62.

170. 8 March 1927, Craigavon to Cosgrave, in UCDA, P24/160.

171. 14 March 1927, McDunphy to Costello, NAI, S 3302 A.

172. 15 March 1927, Cosgrave to Costello, NAI, S 3302 A.

173. 18 March 1927, Cosgrave to Craigavon, UCDA, P24/160.

174. 21 March 1927, Cosgrave to Baldwin, UCDA, P24/160.

175. 23 March 1927, Craigavon to Cosgrave, NAI, S 3302 A.

176. 25 March 1927, Cosgrave to Craigavon, UCDA, P24/160.

177. 7 April 1927, Craigavon to Cosgrave, and reply 8 April 1927, NAI, S 3302 A.

178. 29 June 1926, Cabinet conclusions, PRONI CAB/4/172.

179. 13 April 1927, Cabinet meeting, PRONI CAB/4/191.

180. 19 April 1927, Babington to Costello, JACP, P190/63.

181. 13 May 1927, Babington to Costello, JACP, P190/66.

182. 20 June 1927, Costello memorandum, NAI, S 3302 B.

183. See Babington to Costello, 21 July 1927, 15 December 1927, and 4 January 1928, JACP, P190/68 to 70.

184. Babington to Costello, 7 February 1928, JACP, P190/71. Score from www.irishrugby.ie.

185. 13 February 1928, Babington to Costello, JACP, P190/72.

186. 16 February 1928, McDunphy to relevant Ministers, NAI, S 3302 B.

187. 21 February 1928, minutes of Cabinet sub-committee, NAI, S 3302 B.

188. 14 March 1928, McDunphy to McGilligan, NAI, S 3302 B.

189. 16 March 1928, minutes of Cabinet sub-committee, NAI, S 3302 B.

190. 29 March 1928, Baldwin to Cosgrave, in UCDA, P24/160.

191. 19 April 1928, Babington to Costello, JACP, P190/75.

192. 22 May 1928, Costello memo of meeting, in UCDA, P24/160.

193. 8 June 1928, Batterbee (Home Office) to O'Hegarty, UCDA, P24/160.

194. 13 July 1928, meeting with Irish Society, NAI, S 3302 C.

195. 31 July 1928, Babington to Costello, JACP, P190/78.

196. 28 June 1929, Whiskard, Dominions Office, to Murphy, D/EA, UCDA, P24/160.

197. 1 August 1929, Cosgrave to MacDonald, JACP, P190/60.

198. 8 August 1929, Craigavon to Cosgrave, JACP, P190/60.

199. 29 November 1929, memorandum on meeting in Dominions Office, UCDA, P24/160.
200. 2 July 1930, D/Justice memorandum, UCDA, P24/160.
201. 10 July 1924, Craig to Ramsay MacDonald, PRONI CAB/9R/47/5.
202. 17 July 1924, Ronald Waterhouse (Downing Street) to Craig, PRON CAB/9R/47/5.
203. Smith, Murray, "No Honours Please, We're Republicans", *Irish Student Law Review*, 1999.
204. 31 March 1927, McDunphy to Costello, NAI, S 5708 A.
205. 18 May 1928, Costello memorandum, NAI, S 5708 A.
206. 18 May 1928, Costello memorandum, NAI, S 5708 A.
207. 21 May 1928, Cabinet decision, NAI, S 5708 A.
208. NAI, S 5708 A.
209. Smith, loc. cit.
210. 26 May 1948, Nolan note, NAI, S 5708 B.
211. 26 June 1948, Lynch note, NAI, S 5708 B.
212. 20 November 1948, note of conversation between Attlee and Brooke in Chequers, PRONI CAB/9R/47/5
213. Sexton, pp 127/8.

Chapter 4 A long game (pp 75–100)

1. 24 December 1932, draft article by Costello, JACP, P190/56.
2. SÉD, 2 June 1932, Vol 15, Col. 938.
3. 6 December 1946, II, article by Costello on developments since the Treaty.
4. Harkness, David, *The Restless Dominion*, p. 12.
5. RTÉ Thomas Davis lecture, 1967, in Mansergh, Diana (ed.), *Nationalism and Independence: Selected Irish papers by Nicholas Mansergh*, pp 109.
6. 8 December 1969, Garret FitzGerald speech to Presentation Evening for John A. Costello, cassette recording, JACP, P190/350.
7. 7 June 1926, Executive Council decision, NAI, S 4754/1. They were at the time President of the Executive Council, Vice-President and Minister for Justice, Minister for External Affairs and Minister for Industry and Commerce.
8. 12 October 1926, O'Hegarty to James MacNeill, NAI, S 4754/2 for travelling arrangements for Irish delegation.
9. 5 October 1926, O'Hegarty to James MacNeill, NAI, S 4754/2.
10. 13 October 1926, MacNeill to Cosgrave, NAI, S 4654/2.
11. Undated, but probably October 1926, O'Higgins to his wife, UCDA, P197/95.
12. 21 April 1926, Joe Walsh preliminary memorandum, NAI, S 4754/1.
13. Attorney General memorandum, JACP, P190/100.
14. 5 July 1926, Joe Walshe to Secretaries of Departments, NAI, S 4754/1.
15. 6 July 1926, MacNeill to Walshe, NAI, S 4754/1.
16. Notes on Governor General, JACP, P190/112.
17. 9 November 1926, minutes of Committee on Inter-Imperial Relations, NAI, S 4754/6.

18. 27 October 1926, O'Hegarty to Boland, NAI, S 4754/3.

19. Undated (but October 1926) letter from O'Higgins to his wife, UCDA, P197/95.

20. Undated, O'Higgins to his wife, in UCDA, P197/96.

21. 27 October 1926, O'Higgins to his wife, UCDA, P197/98.

22. McCoole, Sinéad, *Hazel: a life of Lady Lavery*, pp 125–8.

23. 6 January 1927, O'Hegarty to Cosgrave, NAI, S 4754/3.

24. D/External Affairs preliminary memorandum, JACP, P190/100.

25. Mackenzie King diaries, 18 October 1926, p. 3.

26. Undated from O'Higgins to his wife, UCDA, P197/99.

27. Undated from FitzGerald to his wife, UCDA, P80/1410 (2).

28. Undated from O'Higgins to his wife, UCDA, P197/99.

29. Nicholas Mansergh, in Diana Mansergh (ed.), p. 111.

30. 24 July 1956, Costello to Bodkin, JACP, P190/813.

31. 25 October 1926, Kiernan, Secretary of Irish delegation, to Howarth, Conference Secretariat, NAI, S 4754/1.

32. 28 October 1926, minutes of first meeting of Treaty Procedure sub-committee, JACP, P190/106.

33. Notes of first meeting, JACP, P190/107.

34. 17 November 1926, notes of fifth meeting, JACP, P 190/107.

35. Quoted in Harkness, pp 121/2.

36. Undated letter from O'Higgins to his wife, UCDA, P197/96.

37. November 1926, O'Higgins to his wife, UCDA, P197/99.

38. 17 November 1926, O'Higgins to his wife, UCDA, P197/100.

39. DÉD, 19 November 1936, Vol 64, Col. 768.

40. Summary of Proceedings of Imperial Confernece, JACP, P190/108.

41. Amery quoted in de Vere White, p. 249.

42. Extract from Summary of Proceedings of 1926 Conference, NAI, S 5092.

43. Summary of Proceedings, JACP, P190/108.

44. Harkness, p. 99.

45. Undated text of Costello speech, JACP, P190/55.

46. 24 December 1932, draft article by Costello, JACP, P190/56.

47. 28 March 1927, T.M. Healy to Leo Amery, NAI, AG, 54/27.

48. 5 April 1927, Amery to Healy, NAI, AG, 54/27.

49. 17 May 1927, Walshe to O'Hegarty, NAI, AG, 54/27.

50. 19 May 1927, FitzGerald to Amery, NAI, AG, 54/27.

51. 24 December 1932, draft article by Costello, JACP, P190/56.

52. 30 June 1927, Walshe to O'Hegarty, JACP, P190/97.

53. 30 June 1927, O'Higgins to his wife, UCDA, P197/101.

54. 30 June 1927, Walshe to O'Hegarty, JACP, P190/97.

55. 24 December 1932, draft article by Costello, JACP, P190/56.

56. 30 June 1927, O'Higgins to his wife, UCDA, P197/101.

57. 24 December 1932, draft article by Costello, JACP, P190/56.

58. 9 July 1927, Walshe to O'Higgins, JACP, P190/97.

59. Official record of proceedings, NAI, AG, 54/27.

60. 9 July 1927, Walshe to O'Higgins, JACP, P190/97.

61. McCoole, p. 130.

62. 8 September 1927, McDunphy to Walshe, NAI, S 5166.

63. 19 September 1926, FitzGerald to his wife, UCDA, P80/1407 (4).

64. 6 August 1927, Walshe to O'Hegarty, NAI, S 5166.

65. 8 September 1927, MacDunphy to Walshe, NAI, S 5166.

66. League of Nations official journal, 1927, JACP, P190/157.

67. Report of delegation, JACP, P190/237.

68. Minutes of First Committee, 1928, League of Nations Official Journal, JACP, P190/159.

69. Report of delegation, JACP, P190/237.

70. Undated letters from FitzGerald to his wife, UCDA, P80/1408 (6) and (7).

71. Undated letter from FitzGerald to his wife, 1926, UCDA, P80/1407.

72. 14 April 1929, MacWhite memorandum, JACP, P190/239.

73. See website of the International Court of Justice, http://www.icj-cij.org/pcij/index.php?p1=9

74. 6 September 1924, Dominions Office to Governor General, NAI, S 4363 A.

75. Extract from summary of proceedings of Imperial Conference, 1926, NAI, S 4363 A.

76. 22 June 1929, MacDonald to Dominion Prime Ministers, NAI, S 4363 A.

77. 1 August 1929, MacDonald to Dominion Prime Ministers, NAI, S 4363 A.

78. 28 June 1929, McGilligan to Passfield, NAI, S 4363 A.

79. D/EA memo, JACP, P190/155.

80. 7 September 1930, Costello memorandum, JACP, P190/155.

81. 16 March 1929, minutes of League of Nations Committee of Jurists, JACP, P190/155.

82. 7 September 1929, Costello memorandum, JACP P190/155.

83. 14 September 1929, Costello memorandum, JACP, P190/155.

84. 14 September 1929, Costello memorandum, JACP, P190/155.

85. Summary of Proceedings, JACP, P 190/108.

86. 6 September 1929, Walshe to Dominions Secretary, NAI, S 5340/1

87. Hearne preliminary memorandum, JACP, P190/122.

88. 20 September 1929, memo by E.J. Smyth, D/I&C, NAI, S 5340/10.

89. 7 October 1929, Costello to O'Sullivan, UCDA, P24/546.

90. 17 October 1929, McGilligan report of meeting, NAI, S 5340/13.

91. 18 October 1929, O'Hegarty to McDunphy, NAI, S 5340/13.

92. 31 October 1929, minutes of first meeting, JACP, P190/115.

93. 4 November 1929, Gwyer draft, JACP, P190/115.

94. 12 November 1929, O'Hegarty report, NAI, S 5340/13.

95. 12 November 1929, note of discussion at Gwyer Committee, JACP, P190/115.

96. 14 November 1929, notes of Gwyer Committee meeting, UCDA, P35/134.

97. Discussion at Gwyer Committtee, JACP, P190/116.

98. 18 November 1929, Gwyer Committee minutes, JACP, P190/116.

99. 18 November 1929, Gwyer Committee minutes, JACP, P190/116.

100. 18 November 1929, Gwyer Committee minutes, JACP, P190/116.

101. 18 November 1929, Gwyer Committee minutes, JACP, P190/116.

102. 20 November 1929, discussion at Gwyer Committee, NAI, S 5340/19.

103. 21 November 1929, draft Statute, JACP, P190/115.

104. 29 November 1929, final draft report, JACP, P190/115.

105. 4 December 1929, draft minutes of final meeting of Conference, JACP, P190/115.

106. Harkness, p. 172.

107. 21 March 1930, Walshe to O'Hegarty, NAI, S 6009/1.

108. 24 March 1930, Walshe to O'Hegarty, NAI, S 6009/1.

109. 15 April 1930, McDunphy to Walshe, NAI, S 6009/1.

110. 15 April 1930, McDunphy to Walshe, NAI, S 6009/1.

111. 11 October 1930, Cosgrave to McGilligan, and reply, NAI, S 6009/4.

112. 12 September 1930, McGilligan to Thomas, NAI, S 6009/1.

113. D/EA preliminary note, JACP, P190/141.

114. 7 October 1930, Irish memorandum on treaties, JACP, P190/138.

115. Walshe memorandum, UCDA, P35/134.

116. 1 October 1930, minutes of first meeting of Conference, JACP, P190/140.

117. Text of address to Imperial Conference, JACP, P190/96.

118. Undated Irish memorandum on Privy Council, JACP, P190/96.

119. 29 October 1929, Edwards v. Canada (Attorney General).

120. 24 October 1929, Kennedy to Costello, JACP, P190/115.

121. 6 October 1930, afternoon meeting of Prime Ministers and Heads of Delegation, JACP, P190/141. Costello and McGilligan would encounter Jowitt again in 1948 when he was Lord Chancellor. Another observer at the meeting was the Chancellor of the Duchy of Lancaster, Clement Attlee.

122. 2 October 1930, meeting of Prime Ministers and Heads of Delegations, JACP, P190/141.

123. FitzGerald to his wife, received 8 October 1930, UCDA, P80/1411 (7).

124. 2 October 1930, meeting of Prime Ministers and Heads of Delegations, JACP, P190/141.

125. 17 October 1930, 6th meeting of Sankey Committee, JACP, P190/142.

126. 21 October 1930, 8th meeting of Sankey Committee, JACP, P190/142.

127. FitzGerald to his wife, UCDA, P80/1411 (3).

128. FitzGerald to his wife, UCDA, P80/1411 (4).

129. McMahon, p. 31.

130. 5 October 1930, FitzGerald to his wife, UCDA, P80/1411 (5).

131. Boland Memoir, p. 20.

132. FitzGerald to his wife, UCDA, P80/1411 (4).

133. 5 October 1930, FitzGerald to his wife, UCDA, P80/1411 (5).

134. 27 October 1930, FitzGerald to his wife, UCDA, P80/1411 (22).

135. 28 October 1930, FitzGerald to his wife, UCDA, P80/1411 (23).

136. 30 October 1930, summary of draft report, NAI, S 6009/5.

137. DÉD, 15 November 1934, Vol. 54, Col. 354.

138. 31 October 1930, heads of delegation meeting, JACP P190/141.

139. 7 November 1930, O'Hegarty to McDunphy, JACP, P190/96.

140. 4 November 1930, minutes of meeting, JACP, P190/141.

141. 4 November 1930, McGilligan to MacDonald, JACP, P190/96.

142. Undated memorandum, NAI, AG 2005/77/286.

143. 5 November 1930, heads of delegation meeting, NAI, S 4295 B.

144. 6 November 1930, FitzGerald to his wife, UCDA, P80/1411 (26).

145. 7 November 1930, McDunphy to O'Hegarty, JACP, P190/96.

146. 7 November 1930, McDunphy memorandum, NAI, S 4285 B.

147. 6 November 1930, note by J.V. Fahy, JACP, P190/96.

148. 7 November 1930, O'Hegarty to McDunphy, NAI, S 4285 B.

149. 7 November 1930, McDunphy to O'Hegarty, JACP, P190/96.

150. 8 November 1930, Cosgrave to Granard, JACP, P190/96.

151. 24 December 1932, draft article by Costello, JACP, P190/56.

152. 6 December 1946, *II*, Costello article on developments since the Treaty.

153. 13 November 1930, heads of delegation meeting, JACP, P190/141.

154. 14 November 1930, 3rd meeting of Conference, JACP, P190/140.

155. 3 November 1930, heads of delegation meeting, JACP, P190/141.

156. 20 November 1931, Hansard, Vol 259, No 12, col. 1196.

157. 21 November 1931, Cosgrave to MacDonald, UCDA, P35/146.

158. 21 November 1931, McGilligan to Thomas, UCDA, P35/146.

159. 23 November 1931, Dulanty to Walshe, UCDA, P35/146.

160. 23 November 1931, Dulanty to Walshe, UCDA, P35/146.

161. 24 November 1931, MacDonald to Cosgrave, NAI, S 5340/19.

162. 11 December 1931, Dominions Secretary telegram, NAI, S 5340/19.

163. Text of Statute of Westminster, NAI, S 5340/19.

164. 6 December 1946, *II*, Costello article on developments since the Treaty.

165. 2 June 1932, SÉD, Vol 15, Col. 938.

166. See McMahon, p. 47.

167. Quoted in Fanning, Ronan, *Independent Ireland*, p. 111.

168. Mansergh (ed.), p. 113.

169. Mansergh (ed.), pp 204/5.

170. Related by McGilligan to David Harkness. See Harkness, p. 225.

Chapter 5 The Blueshirts will be victorious (pp 101–126)

1. DÉD, 28 February 1934, Vol 50, Col. 2235.

2. "Seven Days".

3. DÉD, 28 February 1934, Vol 50, Col. 2235.

4. "Seven Days".

5. *II*, 28 February 1934.

6. "Seven Days".

7. DÉD, 28 February 1934, Vol 50, Col 2234.

8. DÉD, 28 February 1934, Vol 50, Col 2261.

9. DÉD, 28 February 1934, Vol 50, Col 2295.

10. 8 December 1969, Costello speech to retirement function, JACP, P190/350.

11. *II*, 13 February 1932.

12. *The Anglo-Celt*, 20 February 1932.

13. *II*, 15 February 1932.

14. 8 December 1969, Costello speech to retirement function, JACP, P190/350.

15. *The Anglo-Celt*, 20 February 1932.

16. FitzGerald, Garret, *Ireland in the World: Further Reflections*, p. 101.

17. Details of payment for burial by JAC, JACP, P190/957.

18. *IT*, 15 September 1930.

19. *II*, 27 August 1932.

20. Correspondence with John Costello.

21. *IT*, 8 June 1933.

22. *IT*, 20 July 1933.

23. Costello interview, *The Citizen*, May 1967.

24. *II*, 30 June 1936.

25. McGarry, Fearghal, *Eoin O'Duffy*, p. 191.

26. Costello interview, *IT*, 6 September 1967.

27. *II*, 16 January 1933.

28. Fanning, Ronan, *Independent Ireland*, p. 114.

29. All election figures from http://electionsireland.org.

30. 26 November 1932, *The Anglo-Celt*.

31. Interview with Tom Finlay.

32. 8 December 1969, Costello speech to retirement function, JACP, P190/350.

33. *IT*, 14 January 1933, report of speech in Town Hall, Dun Laoghaire.

34. 8 December 1969, Costello speech to retirement function, JACP, P190/350.

35. Quoted in Regan, John M., *The Irish Counter-Revolution*, p. 322.

36. 8 June 1933, parliamentary party minutes, UCDA, P39/MIN/3.

37. 2 March 1933 and 18 May 1933, Parliamentary Party minutes, UCDA, P39/MIN/3.

38. McGarry, p. 196.

39. 14 March 1933, notes on O'Duffy's dismissal, NAI, S 6485A.

40. 22 February 1933, Seán Moynihan to O'Duffy, NAI, S 6485 A.

41. DÉD, 1 March 1933, Vol 46, Cols 33–35.

42. 2 March 1933, Parliamentary Party minutes, UCDA, P39/MIN/3.

43. DÉD, 14 March 1933, Vol 46, Col 759, 794 and 807.

44. 20 November 1978, note in NAI, 2008/148/28.

45. Quoted in Regan, p. 296.

46. Fanning, Ronan, *The Irish Department of Finance*, p. 237.

47. DÉD, 31 March 1933, Vol 46, cols 1943 to 1947.

48. DÉD, 26 May 1933, Vol 47, Col 1819.

49. DÉD, 14 June 1933, Vol 48, Col 659.

50. DÉD, 3 August 1933, Vol 49, Cols 1208–9.

51. See file of Journals heavily annotated by Costello, JACP, P190/325.

52. *IT*, 12 August 1932.

53. Undated Mulcahy speech, JACP, P190/268.

54. 28 April 1983, Seán O'Rourke report on RTÉ Radio 1 News at 1.30.

55. Regan, p. 332.

56. DÉD, 27 February 1936, Costello speech, Vol 60, Col. 1427/8.

57. *IT*, 4 April 1935.

58. DÉD, 9 July 1936, Vol. 63, Cols. 1230/1.

59. 30 May 1933, Seán Moynihan to private secretaries of Ministers for Justice and Defence, NAI, S 6433.

60. 21 July 1933, Cronin to Secretary, Executive Council, NAI, S 6433.

61. 26 July 1933, McDunphy to Private Secretary, Minister for Finance, NAI, S 6433.

62. Manning, Maurice, *James Dillon*, p. 74.

63. DÉD, 1 August 1933, Vol 49, Cols 1041–3.

64. McGarry, p. 218.

65. *II*, 11 September 1933.

66. "Seven Days".

67. "Seven Days".

68. *IT*, 2 November 1974, Costello interview.

69. Regan, p. 343.

70. McGarry, p. 221.

71. 9 October 1934, Commandant Cronin speech, JACP, P190/316.

72. *II*, 29 September 1933.

73. 27 September 1933, parliamentary party minutes, in UCDA, P39/MIN/4.

74. Ó Longaigh, Seosamh, *Emergency Law in Independent Ireland*, p. 147.

75. DÉD, 28 September 1933, Vol 49, cols 1817–1827.

76. *II*, 29 September 1933.

77. Mulcahy, Risteard, *Richard Mulcahy: A family memoir*, p. 236.

78. DÉD, 4 October 1933, cols 2047/8.

79. 9 November 1933, FG Standing Committee minutes, UCDA, P39/MIN/2.

80. 11 November 1933, FG heads of policy, JACP, P190/268.

81. "Seven Days".

82. Regan, p. 347.

83. Quoted in McGarry, p. 229.

84. *IT*, 19 December 1933.

85. Ó Longaigh, p. 152.

86. McGarry, p. 229.

87. Quoted in McGarry, p. 230.

88. Summons in JACP, P190/16.

89. JACP, P190/16.

90. Judgment of Sullivan P, JACP, P190/16.

91. Costello's brief for Supreme Court Appeal, JACP, P190/16.

92. *IT*, 21 July 1934.

93. 24 July 1934, Cabinet Minutes, NAI, S 6647.

94. Ó Longaigh, p. 281.

95. DÉD, 19 April 1939, Vol. 75, Col. 729.

96. McGarry, p. 232.

97. DÉD, 18 April 1934, vol 51, cols 1885–1898.

98. DÉD, 8 May 1934, Vol 52, Col 527.

99. IT, 29 November 1934.

100. Cronin, Mike, *The Blueshirts in Irish Politics*, p. 24.

101. Undated memo, "The Opposition in the Dáil and Article 2A of the Constitution", NAI, JUS 8/444.

102. "Seven Days".

103. Tierney quoted in Manning, Maurice, *James Dillon*, p. 96.

104. Tierney quoted in Regan, p. 365.

105. 11 September 1934, O'Duffy to MacEoin, UCDA, P151/780.

106. Manning, pp 99/100.

107. 14 September 1934, Cosgrave to Costello, JACP, P190/330.

108. 20 September 1934, FG Standing Committee minutes, UCDA, P39/MIN/2.

109. 10 September 1936, Standing Committee minutes, UCDA, P39/MIN/2.

110. Cronin, pp 25/6.

111. 31 October 1934, parliamentary party minutes, UCDA, P39/MIN/4.

112. DÉD, 1 April 1937, Vol. 66, Cols. 193/5

113. DÉD, 4 April 1935, Vol. 55, cols. 1977/8.

114. DÉD, 4 April 1935, Vol. 55, cols. 2024/5.

115. DÉD, 22 May 1934, Vol. 52, Cols. 1478/9.

116. DÉD, 11 April 1935, Vol 55, Col. 2365.

117. 15 January 1936, Fine Gael party minutes, UCDA, P39/MIN/4.

118. DÉD, 29 May 1935, Vol. 56, Col 2136.

119. DÉD, 13 June 1934, Vol. 53, Cols 262/3.

120. DÉD, 28 November 1934, Vol 54, Col 396.

121. IT, 12 November 1934.

122. DÉD, 14 February 1935, Vol. 54, Col. 2031.

123. DÉD, 19 May 1937, Vol. 67, Col. 754.

124. IT, 6 June 1935, report of by-election rally in Blackrock.

125. DÉD, 19 November 1936, Vol 64. cols. 767/8.

126. DÉD, 20 February 1934, Vol. 54, Col. 2152.

127. DÉD, 18 November 1936, Vol 64, Cols 520–23.

128. 13 February 1935, Fine Gael party minutes, UCDA, P39/MIN/4.

129. DÉD, 20 February 1935, Vol. 54, Cols, 2140–2156.

130. DÉD, 13 November 1935, Vol. 59, Cols. 768 and 838.

131. 1 February 1936, D/Justice memorandum for Executive Council, NAI, S 8613.

132. DÉD, 12 February 1936, Vol. 60, Cols. 547/8.

133. DÉD, 26 June 1942, Vol. 87, Cols. 1912/13.

134. IT, 25 November 1935.

135. DÉD, 23 July 1935, Vol. 58, Cols. 1079–82.

136. DÉD, 25 July 1935, Vol 58, Col. 1418.

137. *IT*, 16 November 1935.

138. DÉD, 16 June 1936, Vol 62, Col. 2368.

139. DÉD, 3 June 1936, Vol. 62, Cols. 1656/7.

140. DÉD, 30 June 1936, Vol. 63, Col. 2510.

141. 19 February 1948, P. Nugent to Costello, JACP, P190/373.

142. DÉD, 9 July 1936, Vol. 63, cols. 1218–23.

143. DÉD, 20 May 1937, Vol. 67, Col. 859.

144. *IT*, 3 June 1935, report of election meeting in Rathmines.

145. DÉD, 25 June 1935, Vol. 57, Cols. 776/785.

146. DÉD, 27 June 1935, Vol. 57, Cols. 1193/4.

147. *IT*, 24 July 1935.

148. DÉD, 3 February 1937, Vol. 65, cols. 54/5 and 78.

149. DÉD, 3 February 1937, Vol. 65, col. 93.

150. 17 January 1935, Standing Committee minutes, UCDA, P39/MIN/2.

151. See meetings of 28 March 1935, 8 May 1935, and 19 September 1935, Standing Committee minutes, UCDA, P39/MIN/2.

152. 6 November 1935, parliamentary party minutes, UCDA, P39/MIN/4.

153. DÉD, 18 November 1936, Vol 64, Col. 554.

154. David Neligan, quoted in Ferriter, Diarmaid, *What If?*, p. 265.

155. *SI*, 3 November 1974.

156. 24 July 1936, Costello to MacEntee, UCDA, P67/113.

157. *II*, 19 June 1971, interview by Dermot Walsh on the eve of Costello's eightieth birthday.

158. 12 September 1935, Mulcahy to Cosgrave, JACP, P190/333.

159. 8 December 1969, Costello speech at retirement function, JACP, P190/350.

160. Quoted in McMahon, Deirdre, *Republicans and Imperialists*, pp 170/1.

161. DÉD, 11 December 1936, Vol 64, Cols. 1293–1306.

162. 15 December 1936, Mackenzie King diary, page 1.

163. DÉD, 12 December 1936, Vol. 64, Cols 1432–7.

164. DÉD, 12 December 1936, Vol. 64, Cols 1484–92.

165. DÉD, 24 February 1937, Vol. 65, Cols 955 and 984. As it happens, the chaplain concerned was something of a menace to discipline, and O'Duffy would have been better off without him. See Stradling, Robert, *The Irish and the Spanish Civil War*, p. 117.

166. DÉD, 19 May 1937, Vol. 67, Cols. 755/7 and 790/1.

Chapter 6 No hope whatever (pp 127–156)

1. DÉD, 11 December 1936, Vol. 64, Col. 1293.

2. "Seven Days".

3. DÉD, 17 May 1934, Vol. 52, Col. 1193.

4. Keogh, Dermot and McCarthy, Andrew J., *The Making of the Irish Constitution*, p. 65.

5. Costello's annotated copies of drafts of Bunreacht na hÉireann, JACP, P190/32.

6. Hogan, Gerard, foreword to Keogh and McCarthy, p. 27.

7. *II*, 6 May 1937, quoted in Keogh and McCarthy, pp 183/4.

8. *IT*, 10 May 1937, quoted in Keogh and McCarthy, p. 185.

9. DÉD, 11 May 1937, Vol. 67, Cols. 65 and 67.

10. DÉD, 13 May 1937, Vol. 67, Cols. 463–5.

11. DÉD, 28 May 1937, Vol. 67, Col. 1307.

12. DÉD, 2 June 1937, Vol. 67, Cols. 1580/1 and 1612.

13. DÉD, 4 June 1937, Vol. 67, Cols 1856 and 1858.

14. *IT*, 6 January 1976.

15. DÉD, 4 June 1937, Vol. 67, Col. 1882.

16. DÉD, 4 June 1937, Vol. 67, Cols 1883/4.

17. DÉD, 9 June 1937, Vol. 67, Col. 225/6.

18. Keogh and McCarthy, p. 181.

19. DÉD, 12 May 1937, Vol. 67. Cols. 301, 303 and 304.

20. DÉD, 13 May 1937, Vol 67, Col. 458.

21. DÉD, 26 May 1937, Vol. 67, Col. 1113.

22. DÉD, 11 May 1937, Vol. 67, Col. 67.

23. DÉD, 12 May 1937, Vol. 67, Col.s 305/6.

24. DÉD, 2 June 1937, Vol. 67, Col. 1520.

25. 8 June 1937, MacEntee to de Valera, with Revenue Commissioners memorandum, UCDA, P150/2441.

26. Mary Robinson advanced just such a view during her successful campaign for the presidency in 1990, although she backtracked after a controversial suggestion that she could look then Taoiseach Charles Haughey in the eye and tell him to "back off".

27. DÉD, 25 May 1937, Vol. 67, Cols. 1031, 1033, 1035 and 1071/2.

28. DÉD, 26 May 1937, Vol. 67, Cols. 1106, 1116 and 1128.

29. DÉD, 2 June 1937, Vol. 67, Cols. 1631, 1528 and 1613.

30. Notes for speech on new Constitution, JACP, P190/262.

31. DÉD, 25 May 1937, Vol. 67, Cols. 970/1.

32. DÉD, 26 May 1937, Vol. 67, Cols. 1178 and 1195/6.

33. DÉD, 1 June 1937, Vol. 67, Cols. 1341–5.

34. DÉD, 10 June 1937, Vol. 68, Cols. 264–6, 276, and 282–3.

35. DÉD, 12 May 1937, Vol. 67, Col. 297.

36. Quoted in Quinn, Ruairí, and Higgins, Ross, *A history of Dublin South-east constituency*, p. 36.

37. DÉD, 29 November 1939, Vol. 78, Col. 522.

38. DÉD, 28 November 1945, Vol. 98, Col. 1384.

39. DÉD, 6 November 1946, Vol. 103, Col. 466.

40. 12 August 1937, *II*.

41. 22 September 1937, MacEntee to Boland, UCDA, P67/358.

42. Figures calculated from Department of the Environment publication, Referenda Results 1937–2008, available through www.environ.ie/en/LocalGovernment/Voting/Referenda.

43. DÉD, 7 October 1937, Vol. 69, Cols. 335 and 336.

44. DÉD, 9 December 1937, Vol. 69, Cols. 2041 and 2043.

45. Elaine Byrne, *Political Corruption in Ireland*, (forthcoming), Chapter Four.

46. *IT*, 13 December 1937.

47. DÉD, 30 March 1938, Vol. 70, Cols. 1196 and 1199.

48. DÉD, 25 May 1938, Vol. 71, Col. 1864.

49. *IT*, 26 May 1938.

50. *IT*, 28 May 1938.

51. 10 June 1938, MacEntee letter to voters, UCDA, P67/359.

52. DÉD, 30 March 1938, Vol. 70, Col. 1196.

53. DÉD, 23 February 1965, Vol. 214, Col. 921.

54. DÉD, 9 May 1940, Vol. 80, Col. 345.

55. *IT*, 18 August 1938.

56. DÉD, 2 November 1938, Vol. 73, Col. 292.

57. *IT*, 19 August 1938.

58. *IT*, 28 October 1938.

59. DÉD, 2 November 1938, Vol. 73, Col. 290.

60. Ó Broin, Leon, *Just Like Yesterday*, p. 176.

61. DÉD, 14 July 1938, Vol. 72, Cols. 833–5.

62. In Mansergh, Diana (ed.), *Nationalism and Independence*, p. 157.

63. DÉD, 2 March 1939, Vol. 74, Cols. 1408–10.

64. DÉD, 19 April 1939, Vol. 75, Cols. 649, 667 and 728.

65. DÉD, 2 September 1939, Vol. 77, Cols. 50, 51, 54 and 57.

66. DÉD, 29 November 1939, Vol. 78, Cols. 524/5.

67. DÉD, 3 January 1940, Vol. 78, Cols 1339/40.

68. *IT*, 18 October 1940.

69. *IT*, 9 December 1941.

70. DÉD, 8 May 1940, Vol. 80, Col. 68.

71. DÉD, 9 May 1940, Vol. 80, Cols. 332/5.

72. DÉD, 16 January 1941, Vol. 81, Cols. 1448–52.

73. DÉD, 20 May 1942, Vol. 86, Cols 2452–67.

74. Interview with Declan Costello.

75. DÉD, 20 May 1942, Vol. 86, Cols 2452-67.

76. DÉD, 5 May 1942, Vol. 86, Col. 1541.

77. 28 February 1938, George Gavan Duffy, President of the High Court, to Costello, NAI, S 9879 B.

78. *IT*, 4 June 1941.

79. DÉD, 11 June 1941, Vol. 83, Cols. 1936/7 and 1964.

80. DÉD, 19 November 1941, Vol. 85, Col. 837.

81. DÉD, 3 December 1941, Vol. 85, Col. 1149.

82. DÉD, 3 December 1941, Vol. 85, Col. 1152.

83. DÉD, 25 February 1947, Vol. 104, Col. 1207.

84. DÉD, 26 March 1947, Vol. 105, Col. 245.

85. See NAI, S 9879 B.

86. DÉD, 8 July 1941, Vol. 84, Cols. 1196/1200.

87. DÉD, 28 January 1942, Vol. 85, Cols. 1469–1480; direct quotes from 1478 and 1480.

88. DÉD, 29 January 1942, Vol. 85, Cols 1707/8.

89. 15 February 1943, letter to Hyde, and undated opinion on Bill by Costello, JACP, P190/329.

90. IT, 26 March 1943.

91. IT, 16 April 1943.

92. IT, 29 May 1943.

93. IT, 22 June 1943.

94. 19 April 1943, Burke to MacEntee, UCDA, P67/363.

95. 10 June 1943, Lemass to MacEntee, and reply of same date, UCDA, P67/363.

96. Interview with Richie Ryan.

97. 28 June 1943, MacEntee to de Valera, UCDA, P67/366.

98. 31 May 1949, MacEntee to de Valera, UCDA, P150/2980.

99. 30 June 1943, FG parliamentary party minutes, UCDA, P39/MIN/4.

100. 24 December 1943, Dillon to McGilligan, UCDA, P35/176.

101. 18 January 1944, FG parliamentary party minutes, UCDA, P39/MIN/4.

102. Manning, p. 190.

103. 10 February 1944, Kearney to Ottawa, LAC, RG 25, Vol. 4480, File 50021-40, Part 1.

104. Interview with Risteárd Mulcahy.

105. Correspondence with John Costello.

106. Correspondence with Georgina Sutton.

107. 4 November 1970, Costello to M.G. Oddy, JACP, P190/924.

108. Interview with Declan Costello, 1 October 2007.

109. 24 February 1956, Hearne to Costello, NAI, S 16021 A.

110. 4 November 1970, Costello to M.G. Oddy, JACP, P190/924.

111. Interview with Declan Costello.

112. IT, 12 January 1946.

113. Ferriter, Diarmaid, *The Transformation of Ireland*, p. 496.

114. Interview with Jacqueline Armstrong.

115. IT, 13 December 1943.

116. McCague, Eugene, *Arthur Cox*, pp 56/7.

117. Interview with Tom Finlay.

118. Undated speech, JACP, P190/281—this speech is wrongly filed with material from the 1932 and 1933 elections, but from the content is clearly from 1944.

119. IT, 24 May 1944.

120. IT, 20 May 1944.

121. IT, 20 May 1944.

122. 19 June 1944 and 27 September 1944, Fine Gael parliamentary party minutes, UCDA, P39/MIN/4.

123. DÉD, 21 June 1944, Vol. 94, Cols. 870/1; 11 April 1945, Vol. 96, Cols 1833/4; 12 April 1945, Vol. 96, Col. 1973.

124. DÉD, 4 July 1945, Vol. 97, Cols. 1887, 1890 and 1891.

125. DÉD, 11 July 1945, Vol. 97, Col. 2147/8.

126. 14 June 1949, Taoiseach memorandum for the Government, NAI, S 12644 B.

127. DÉD, 13 December 1945, Vol. 98, Cols. 1945, 1946, 1954 and 1955.

128. DÉD, 27 March 1946, Vol. 100, Col. 686.

129. DÉD, 28 March 1946, Vol. 100, Col. 793.

130. DÉD, 3 April 1946, Vol. 100, Cols 1115/6.

131. DÉD, 3 April 1946, Vol. 100, Col 1134.

132. DÉD, 5 April 1946, Vol. 100, Cols. 1384–6.

133. DÉD, 11 April 1946, Vol. 100, Cols. 1816–8.

134. DÉD, 11 July 1946, Vol. 102, Cols. 655–68.

135. DÉD, 25 February 1947, Vol. 104, Col. 1252.

136. Manning, p. 219.

137. DÉD, 6 February 1946, Vol. 99, Col. 508.

138. DÉD, 14 February 1946, Vol. 99, Col. 1094.

139. DÉD, 27 February 1946, Vol. 99, Cols. 1656 and 1665.

140. DÉD, 11 April 1946, Vol. 100, Col. 1766.

141. DÉD, 21 May 1946, Vol. 101, Cols. 469–73.

142. DÉD, 27 June 1946, Col. 2605.

143. 4 July 1946, Stephen Roche to Gerry Boland, NAI, JUS 8/938.

144. General note on Deputy Costello's criticism of Emergency Powers Orders, NAI, JUS 8/938.

145. DÉD, 19 June 1946, Vol. 101, Cols 2183 and 2186; 2205; 2208; 2212; and 2213.

146. DÉD, 20 June 1947, Vol. 106, Col. 2322.

147. DÉD, 24 July 1946, Vol. 102, Cols. 1377/8, 1374 and 1376.

148. Feeney, Brian, *Sinn Féin*, pp 178–81.

149. DÉD, 24 April 1947, Vol. 105, Cols. 1456–8, and 1452.

150. *IP*, 24 February 1948.

151. 10 March 1948, P.P. O'Donoghue to Moynihan; 11 March 1948, Moynihan note on discussion with Lavery, and 12 March 1948, note of Government decision, NAI, S 12110 D/1.

152. Feeney, p. 180.

153. 21 June 1950, Casey to Moynihan, NAI, S 12110 D/1.

154. 23 January 1945, FG Parliamentary Party minutes, and 30 January 1945, note by P.S. Doyle, UCDA, P39/MIN/4.

155. 15 February 1945, parliamentary party minutes, and 13 March 1945, Chief Whip's report, UCDA, P39/Min/4.

156. 26 April 1945, parliamentary party minutes, UCDA, P39/MIN/4.

157. Stationery Office, Prl. 8624.

158. "Seven Days".

159. 14 May 1947, Cosgrave to Mulcahy, UCDA, P7/D/123.

160. DÉD, 30 October 1947, Vol. 108, Col. 1309.

161. See Manning, pp 209 and 220.

162. DÉD, 30 April 1947, Vol. 105, Col. 1767.

163. 3 January 1948, Costello speech at Fine Gael meeting in Donnybrook, JACP, P190/285.

164. Election leaflet in NAI, S 14224.

Chapter 7 Playing with fire (pp 157–196)

1. 8 December 1969, speech to retirement function, JACP, P190/350.

2. JAC to Declan Costello, 29 February 1948, in possession of Declan Costello.

3. Letter to Declan.

4. Healy, T.M. *Portmarnock Golf Club, 1894–1994: A Centenary History*, p. i.

5. Interview with Declan Costello.

6. Irishman's Diary, *IT*, 21 February 1948.

7. Letter to Declan.

8. Letter to Declan.

9. Based on MacEoin memorandum on the formation of the Government, UCDA, P151/1919.

10. 17 July 1967, Mulcahy to Costello, UCDA, P7/D/116.

11. MacEoin memorandum on the formation of the Government, UCDA, P151/1919.

12. 17 July 1967, Mulcahy to Costello, UCDA, P7/D/116.

13. 17 July 1967, Mulcahy to Costello, UCDA, P7/D/116.

14. "Seven Days".

15. 29 April 1967, Mulcahy to Costello, UCDA, P7/D/116.

16. May 1967, *The Citizen*, Vincent Browne interview with Costello.

17. 6 January 1976, RTÉ Radio, 1330 News.

18. Letter to Declan.

19. MacEoin memo on formation of Government, UCDA, P151/919.

20. 8 December 1969, speech to retirement function, JACP, P190/350.

21. Lynch, 'Pages from a Memoir', in Lynch and Meenan (eds), pp 37/8.

22. MacBride, Séan, *That Day's Struggle*, p. 144.

23. Ibid., p. 145.

24. 16 July 1996, letter to the author from Patrick Lynch.

25. Letter to Declan.

26. 2 August 1967, Seán MacEoin memo on formation of the government, JACP, P190/973.

27. 14 April 1949, *News Review* interview with Costello, JACP, P190/547.

28. MacDermott, Eithne, *Clann na Poblachta*, note 58, p. 192.

29. MacBride, pp 149/150.

30. 17 February 1948, Mulcahy statement, NAI, S 14165.

31. Undated memo signed by Costello, JACP, P190/973.

32. *IP*, 27 January 1969.

33. *EH*, 16 February 1973.

34. DÉD, 18 February 1948, Vol 110, Cols 22, 24, 25/6 and 27/8.

35. DÉD, 18 February 1948, Vol. 110, Col 48; also letter to Declan.

36. DÉD, 18 February 1948, Vol. 110, Col. 48.

37. O'Higgins, Tom, *A Double Life*, p. 134. For the strikingly similar impressions of Noël Browne, see EH, 16 February 1973.

38. 31 March 1948, Department of the Taoiseach note on appointment of Government, NAI, S 10719 A.

39. Letter to Declan. According to Alexis FitzGerald, McElligott told the new Taoiseach that the country had been a dictatorship under Fianna Fáil, and that it had been Lemass, not de Valera, who was the dictator. Horgan, John, *Seán Lemass*, p. 134.

40. 31 March 1948, Department of the Taoiseach note on appointment of Government, NAI, S 10719 A.

41. 8 March 1948, George Garrett to Norman Armour, USNA, RG 88, Dublin Legation, Security Segregated Reports, 1936–49, Box 16, 800—Ireland.

42. "Seven Days".

43. Interview with Patrick Lynch.

44. 25 October 1952, *The Leader*, profile of Norton.

45. McGilligan notes on formation of Inter-Party Government, UCDA, P35/177.

46. Mulcahy, p. 244.

47. Interview with Patrick Lynch.

48. *The Leader*, 28 February 1953, profile of McGilligan.

49. Browne, Noël, *Against The Tide*, p. 107.

50. Quoted in Fanning, Ronan, *Independent Ireland*, p. 168.

51. MacBride, pp 146/7.

52. Horgan, *Noël Browne*, p. 56.

53. Ibid., p. 149.

54. 25 November 1998, Liam Cosgrave speech at book launch.

55. 8 December 1969, Cosgrave speech at Costello retirement dinner, JACP, P190/350.

56. Ó Broin, Leon, *Just Like Yesterday*, p. 176.

57. Letter from Liam Cosgrave, 7 November 2008.

58. "This Week", RTÉ Radio, 11 February 1973.

59. IP, 20 February 1948.

60. 31 March 1948, Dept. of the Taoiseach note on appointment of Government, NAI, S 10719 A.

61. 25 November 1964, W.J. Hyland to Costello, JACP, P190/919.

62. Letter to Declan.

63. This phrase was a direct quote from an election flyer for Costello and his running mate, J. Harold Douglas, in the 1948 election, which also suggested that "even if a party has a parliamentary majority it should consult with and consider suggestions from other parties or groups". JACP, P190/284.

64. 24 February 1948, text of broadcast, JACP, P190/430.

65. II, 25 February 1948.

66. II, 19 February 1948.

67. IP, 19 February 1948.

68. Andrews, C.S., *Man of No Property*, p. 195.
69. 19 February 1948, Blythe to Costello, JACP, P190/363.
70. 19 February 1948, Kevin Liston to Costello, JACP, P190/371.
71. P.J. Smythe to Costello, JACP, P190/379.
72. Lindsay, Patrick, *Memories*, pp 151/2.
73. 10 March 1948, Costello to MacWhite, UCDA, P194/564.
74. 18 February 1948, Rugby to de Valera, and reply, 27 February 1948, UCDA, P150/2940.
75. 16 February 1948, Chapin to Secretary of State; 8 March 1948, Garrett to Norman Armour, Asst Sec of State; 29 July 1948, Robert M. Beaudry to Joseph Sweeny, Dept of State; all in USNA, RG 84, Dublin Legation, Security Segregated Records, 1936–49, Box 16, 800—Ireland.
76. Manning, p. 233; Dillon quotes from his memoir, p. 70, quoted in ibid.
77. Interview with Patrick Lynch.
78. Interview with Dr T.K. Whitaker.
79. Lynch, Patrick, "More Pages from a Memoir", in English and Skelly (eds), *Ideas Matter*, p. 129.
80. 5 March 1949, Costello to Bodkin, and 15 March 1949, Bodkin to Costello, in TCD, Bodkin Papers, MSS 7003/ 135 and 136.
81. 1 June 1950, Laithwaite report of conversation with Lord Glenavy, TNA, DO 130/110.
82. MacBride, p. 191.
83. Dillon memoir quoted in Manning, p. 233.
84. 17 December 1948, weekly report, in USNA, RG 84, Dublin Legation, Security Segregated Records, 1936–49, Box 12.
85. 18 January 1949, Parliamentary Party minutes, UCDA, P39/MIN/5.
86. 17 February 1948, Sheldon to Costello, JACP, P190/404.
87. 15 January 1949, Sheldon to Costello, JACP, P190/404.
88. 16 May 1950, Cogan to Costello, JACP, P190/387.
89. Browne, p. 125.
90. "Seven Days".
91. 5 May 1948, Parliamentary Party minutes, UCDA, P39/MIN/5.
92. 7 July 1948, Parliamentary Party minutes, UCDA, P39/MIN/5.
93. 10 March 1949, Parliamentary Party minutes, UCDA, P39/MIN/5.
94. 30 March 1949, P.F. Dineen, Director of Organisation, Quarterly Bulletin, NAI, Taoiseach's Private Office, 97/9/117.
95. 16 January 1949, notes on conference, UCDA, P35/c/184.
96. See NAI, Taoiseach's Private Office, 97/9/1083.
97. 7 June 1949, McElligott to Secretary, D/SW, JACP, P190/554; Costello's copy of the White Paper is in the same file.
98. 23 June 1949, Lynch notes on White Paper, JACP, P190/554.
99. 1 October 1949, memo, JACP, P190/554.
100. *IT*, 15 February 1950.
101. Browne, p. 126.

102. 28 November 1949, MacEoin to Costello, UCDA, P151/462.

103. 9 March 1949, minutes of Advisory Committee, UCDA, P35/c/184.

104. Lynch, p. 42.

105. 27 January 1948, Minister for Defence memorandum for Government, NAI, S 13315 A/61.

106. *11*, 10 March 1948.

107. Interview with Kyran FitzGerald.

108. Browne, p. 104.

109. See 3 May 1955, Moynihan to Sec, D/D, NAI, S 13315 A/61.

110. 16 August 1956, FitzGerald to Costello, in possession of Fergus and Jacqueline Armstrong.

111. *News Review*, 14 April 1949, JACP, P190/547.

112. 12 June 1951, Government decision, NAI, S 11832 C.

113. Interview with Kyran FitzGerald.

114. 20 February 1948, *News Chronicle* cutting, JACP, P190/354.

115. MacBride, p. 151.

116. 8 March 1948, George Garrett to Norman Armour, USNA, RG 84, Dublin Legation, Security Segregated Records, 1936–49, Box 16, 800—Ireland.

117. 26 February 1948, Roche to Moynihan, NAI, S 13262.

118. See NAI S 11931 B for MacCurtain and S 13975 for White.

119. See NAI, S 14380.

120. DÉD, 15 April 1948, Vol. 110, Cols 931/2.

121. O'Halpin, Eunan, *Defending Ireland*, p. 303.

122. Bell, J. Bowyer, *The Secret Army*, p. 249.

123. Ó Longaigh, Seosamh, *Emergency Law in Independent Ireland*, p. 277.

124. 19 August 1950, diary entry, UCDA, P122/83.

125. 27 February 1948, Government decision, NAI, S 14252. See S 10496 A for list of committees in different governments.

126. 26 August 1922, Provisional Government minutes, NAI, S 7870 A.

127. NAI, S 7871.

128. 28 April 1924, Cosgrave to J.C. Meredith, NAI, S 7869 A.

129. DÉD, 24 November 1948, Vol 113, Col 312.

130. DÉD, 23 March 1950, Vol. 119, Col. 2521.

131. 8 March 1950, Laithwaite report on developments in the Republic of Ireland, TNA, FO 371/84831.

132. Interview with Patrick Lynch.

133. Fanning, Ronan, *Independent Ireland*, p. 167, based on interview with MacBride.

134. 14 February 1933, note on Secretary, NAI, S 6378 A.

135. See for instance, 12 January 1949, Cosgrave to Costello, JACP, P190/414 setting out the decisions taken at the previous day's meeting, "as they may be useful to refresh your memory in view of the fact that we took no formal decision and consequently they will not be recorded in the Minutes".

136. 6 January 1949, Moynihan memo for Taoiseach, NAI, S 3635.

137. 10 January 1949, Moynihan note, NAI, S 3635, and 22 January 1949, Moynihan to Nolan, NAI, S 1646/4A.

138. 3 March 1948, Taoiseach to each Minister, NAI, S 14261.

139. 7 April 1948, speech to Federation of Irish Manufacturers, Cork, JACP, P190/436.

140. 1 November 1948, Chapin to Secretary of State, USNA, RG 58, Decimal File 1945–49, Box 3289, 711.41D2/10-2848.

141. McCague, Eugene, *Arthur Cox*, p. 63.

142. 17 December 1948, Garrett to Washington, USNA, RG 59, Decimal File 1945–49, Box 3289, 711.41D2/12-1748.

143. *IT*, 13 January 1949.

144. 20 January 1949, Garrett to Washington, USNA, RG 59, Decimal File 1945–49, Box 3289, 711.41D2/1-2049.

145. *IT*, 21 January 1949 and 22 January 1949.

146. 26 May 1948, address to Dublin Chamber of Commerce, JACP, P190/439.

147. Fanning, *Finance*, p. 427; the foregoing paragraph is based on Fanning, pp 424–7.

148. Dillon memoir quoted in Manning, *Dillon*, p. 240.

149. 8 December 1969, Costello speech at Presentation Evening, JACP, P190/350.

150. Manning, p. 249.

151. 11 December 1948, M/F memo for the Government, UCDA, P35/a/61.

152. 24 February 1949, McElligott to McGilligan, UCDA, P35/a/77.

153. 9 September 1949, McElligott to McGilligan, UCDA, P35/a/86.

154. 1 May 1949, McElligott to McGilligan, UCDA, P35/a/82.

155. 21 January 1949, Dillon to Costello, UCDA, P35/a/42.

156. 5 March 1949, Costello to Bodkin, TCD, Bodkin Papers, Mss 7003/103a-317, correspondence with John A. Costello.

157. 23 December 1949, Costello to McGilligan, UCDA, P35/c/48.

158. MacBride, p. 189.

159. 23 June 1949, M/EA memo for Govt, NAI, S 14617A.

160. 25 June 1949, O'Dowd note, NAI, S 14617 A.

161. Pink slips, NAI, S 14617A.

162. MacBride, p. 190.

163. 17 September 1949, Maurice Moynihan diary entry, UCDA, P122/84.

164. Fanning, *Finance*, p. 449.

165. Ibid., p. 449.

166. 27 September 1949, M/EA memo for Government, NAI, S 14617 A.

167. 11 February 1950, Moynihan note, NAI, S 14617 A.

168. Lynch, Patrick, "More pages from an Irish Memoir" in English and Skelly (eds) *Ideas Matter*, p. 129.

169. Discussion with Governor, UDCA, P35/c/60.

170. Moynihan, Maurice, *Currency and Central Banking in Ireland, 1922–60*, p. 352 and p. 341.

171. *IT*, 18 October 1949.

172. 19 October 1949 and 20 October 1949, McElligott to McGilligan, UCDA, P35/c/60.

173. Ó Broin, Leon, *No Man's Man*, pp 157/8.

174. Fanning, *Finance*, p. 455.

175. Brennan diary, quoted in Ó Broin, *No Man's Man*, p. 159.

176. *II*, 6 February 1950.

177. Fanning in Lynch and Meenan (eds), p. 7.

178. See NAI, S 6378 A.

179. Fanning, *Finance*, p. 457.

180. Interview with Patrick Lynch.

181. DÉD, 20 July 1949, Vol 117, Col 1373.

182. DÉD, 21 July 1949, Vol 117 Col. 1601.

183. Mulcahy, p. 245.

184. Patrick Lynch interview.

185. Lynch, "Pages from a Memoir", pp 36/7.

186. 19 November 1949, address to annual dinner of Institute of Bankers in Ireland, JACP, P190/488.

187. Girvin, Brian, *Between Two Worlds*, p. 170.

188. T.K. Whitaker interview.

189. Lynch, "Pages from a memoir", p. 36; also interview with Patrick Lynch.

190. Fanning, *Independent Ireland*, p. 171.

191. 18 November 1949, minutes of meeting, NAI, S 13749 C.

192. 28 November 1949, minutes of second meeting, NAI, S 13749 C.

193. Ó Gráda, Cormac, *A Rocky Road*, p. 25.

194. Whelan, Bernadette, *Ireland and the Marshall Plan*, p. 228.

195. Patterson, Henry, *Ireland since 1939*, p. 89.

196. Whelan, p. 399.

197. *IT*, 15 November 1949.

198. *IT*, 18 November 1949.

199. McCullagh, David, *A Makeshift Majority*, pp 237–9.

200. 14 April 1949, *News Review* interview with Costello, JACP, P190/547.

201. JACP, P190/406.

202. See for example entry for 24 January 1949, NAI, Taoiseach's Private Office, 97/9/928.

203. Correspondence with John Costello.

204. Interview with Jacqueline Armstrong.

205. Conversation with Joan Gleeson.

206. 29 August 1950, Bodkin to Costello, JACP, P190/408.

207. O'Byrne, Robert, *Hugh Lane*, p. 187.

208. O'Byrne, pp 231 and 232.

209. Kennedy, Brian P., *Dreams and Responsibilities*, p. 7.

210. Kennedy, pp 22 and 24.

211. Stanford, William Bedell, *Memoirs*, p. 77.

212. Verbatim report of speech, January 1931, and copy of The Catholic Bulletin, February 1931, NAI, S 2573.

213. Bodkin Papers, TCD, Ms. 7003/114, 19 May 1948.

214. 27 February 1947, Rugby to Machtig, TNA, DO 35/3993.

215. 11 March 1948, Cabinet conclusions, TNA, DO 35/3993.

216. 1 April 1948, Bodkin to Costello, JACP, P190/408.

217. *IT*, 7 September 1967.

218. 26 July 1948, Costello to Attlee, TNA, DO 35/3994.

219. 12 August 1948, Rugby to Machtig, TNA, DO 35/3994.

220. 12 November 1948, Attlee to Noel-Baker, TNA, DO 35/3994.

221. 8 January 1951, Rugby to Liesching, TNA, DO 35/3994.

222. O'Byrne, p. 239.

223. 14 April 1956, Hogan to Costello, JACP, P190/822.

224. 25 April 1958, Robbins to Pakenham, JACP, P190/408.

225. 13 May 1958, Costello to de Valera, JACP, P190/408.

226. 25 March 1959, Costello to de Valera, JACP, P190/408.

227. 10 August 1959, Lemass to Costello, JACP, P190/408.

228. Lemass and Costello Dáil statements, JACP, P190/408.

229. Kennedy, p. 55.

230. See Kennedy, pp 78–80.

231. 22 August 1950, Bodkin to Costello, Bodkin Papers, TCD, Ms 7003/167.

232. See 30 November 1950, Bodkin to Costello, JACP, P190/411.

233. 16 December 1950, Bodkin to Costello, Bodkin Papers, TCD, Ms 7003/180.

234. 1 January 1951, Costello to Bodkin, Bodkin Papers, TCD, Ms 7003/185.

235. 29 January 1951, Bodkin to Costello, Bodkin Papers, TCD, Ms 7003/186.

236. 16 February 1951, Costello to Bodkin, Bodkin Papers, TCD.

237. Bodkin to Paddy Lynch, 25 April 1951, Bodkin Papers, TCD, Ms 7003/199b.

238. Kennedy, pp 96/7.

239. Bruce Arnold, 'Politics and the Arts in Ireland' in Litton, Frank (ed.), *Unequal Achievement*, p. 287 and 285.

240. Kennedy, p. 94.

241. 26 January 1952, *IT* and *IP*.

Chapter 8 Mr Costello was rarin' to go (pp 197–231)

1. Boland manuscript, p. 25.

2. 1 June 1950, Chapedlaine to Norman Robertson, Ottawa, LAC, RG 25, Vol 4401, File 50021-40, Part 3.

3. A statue of her consort, Prince Albert, remains in the Leinster House grounds, on the Merrion Square side.

4. O'Higgins, T.F., *A Double Life*, pp 132/3.

5. 10 July 1948, Rugby to Machtig, TNA, DO 35/3957.

6. DÉD, 30 June 1948, Vol 111, Col 1785. The car park plan had originally been proposed the previous December by the then Fianna Fáil government.

7. 10 July 1948, Rugby to Machtig, TNA, DO 35/3957.

8. 21 July 1948, Machtig to Sir Alan Lascelles, Private Secretary to the King, and 27 July 1948, Lascelles to Machtig, TNA, DO 35/3957.

9. NAI, S 6412 A.

10. I paid a visit when I was in Australia in 1999. O'Higgins and Rugby were right!

11. Fanning, *Independent Ireland*.

12. 16 October 1947, note of meeting with de Valera, TNA, DO 35/3926.

13. 21 October 1947, Presidential (International Powers and Functions) Bill, 1947, UCDA, P150/2970.

14. 27 January 1948, Rugby to Machtig, TNA, DO/130/93.

15. 28 January 1948, Rugby to Machtig, TNA, DO/130/93.

16. FitzGerald, Garret, *All in a life*, p. 45.

17. Summary of Costello election address, UCDA, P104/1468.

18. 21 February 1948, Rugby to Secretary of State, TNA, DO/130/93.

19. *II*, 23 February 1948.

20. MacBride, Seán, *That Day's Struggle*, p. 156.

21. 24 July 1948, M/EA memorandum for Government, NAI, S 14210 B/1.

22. DÉD, 23 July 1948, Vol 112, Col. 1520.

23. Undated FitzGerald memorandum to Costello, JACP, P190/390.

24. 31 March 1948, Gallman, London, to Department of State, USNA, RG 84, Dublin Legation, Security Segregated Records, 1936–49, Box 15, 710 Political Relations, Treaties.

25. 8 July 1948, Costello to MacWhite, UCDA, P194/564.

26. 13 October 1996, interview with Risteárd Mulcahy.

27. *IT*, 7 February 1951.

28. Mansergh, Nicholas, *Survey of British Commonwealth Affairs*, p. 279.

29. 5 July 1948, Jowitt to Costello, NAI, Taoiseach's Private Office, 97/9/862. Jowitt was looking for the loan of a car while he was on holiday, so he may have been attempting to butter up the Taoiseach.

30. Cole, John, *As It Seemed To Me*, p. 11.

31. 16 August 1948, Garrett to Department of State, USNA, RG 84, Dublin Legation, Security Segregated Records, 1936–49, Box 15, 710 Political Relations, Treaties.

32. 22 June 1948, Nolan to Moynihan, and 23 June 1948, Moynihan note, NAI, S 13760 A.

33. Interview with Patrick Lynch.

34. He had been expelled after opposing the agreement with the United States on Marshall Aid.

35. DÉD, 28 July 1948, Vol. 112, Col. 1555.

36. DÉD, 5 August 1948, Vol. 112, Cols. 2105–7.

37. 29 July 1948, Turgeon to Ottawa, LAC, RG 25, Vol. 4480, file 50021-40 Part 1.

38. DÉD, 6 August 1948, Vol. 112, Col. 2382.

39. Costello memorandum on repeal of External Relations Act, JACP, P190/546.

40. 11 August 1948, Rugby to Machtig, TNA, PREM 8/1010.

41. 7 December 1948, Turgeon dispatch, LAC, RG 25, Vol. 4480, File 50021-40 Part 2.

42. 17 August 1948, CRO memo, TNA, PREM 8/1010.

43. 22 August 1948, Attlee note, and 23 August 1948, CRO telegram to UK High Commissioner in Canada, TNA, PREM 8/1010.

44. 9 September 1948, M/EA memo for Government, NAI, S 14333A.

45. 23 September 1948, Dulanty to Boland, UCDA, P104/4447.

46. 18 August 1948, M/EA memorandum for Government, NAI, S 14333A.

47. 19 August 1948, Cabinet Minutes, NAI, S 14333A.

48. Lynch, Patrick, "Pages from a Memoir" in Lynch and Meenan (eds), p. 46.

49. MacBride, p. 174.

50. 9 September 1948, M/EA memo for Govt, NAI, S 14333A.

51. 7 September 1948, Rugby to Machtig, TNA, DO/130/93.

52. 9 September 1948, Cabinet Minutes, NAI, S 14333A.

53. 23 September 1948, Dulanty to Boland, UCDA, P104/4447.

54. "Seven Days".

55. DÉD, 6 August 1948, Vol. 112, Cols 2440/1.

56. Costello memorandum on repeal of External Relations Act, JACP, P190/546.

57. 7 August 1948, Ó Dálaigh to de Valera, with draft of "The Presidential (International Powers and Fuctions) Bill, 1948", UCDA, P150/2970.

58. Costello memorandum, JACP, P190/546.

59. McDermott, Eithne, *Clann na Poblachta*, p. 114.

60. DÉD, 21 July 1959, Vol. 176, Col. 1602.

61. Notes on conversations, Frederick Boland, 1952, in Mansergh, Diana (ed.), *Nationalism and Independence*, p. 189.

62. RTÉ Archive Tape A 4184: The Republic of Ireland Act, 1948. Tx 26 March 1989.

63. Manning, Maurice, *James Dillon*, p. 244.

64. 7 September 1948, Rugby to Machtig, TNA, DO/130/93.

65. 30 September 1948, Rugby to Machtig, TNA, DO/130/93.

66. 9 September 1948, M/EA memo for government, NAI, S 14387.

67. 9 August 1948, Rugby to Machtig, recording a meeting involving them, Noel-Baker and Cabinet Secretary Sir Norman Brook on 5 August, i.e. the day *before* the Adjournment Debate. TNA, DO/130/93.

68. 18 May 1957, Rugby to de Valera, in UCDA, P150/2940. The irony of a British official complaining to de Valera about unilateral action appears not to have occurred to Rugby.

69. 27 March 1948, Costello to MacWhite, UCDA, P194/564, and 3 March 1948, Mulcahy to MacWhite, loc. cit, P194/567.

70. 2 September 1948, W. H. Measures to F.M. Maclennan, LAC, RG 25, Vol. 3981, File 9908-T-1-40.

71. 30 August 1948, King Diaries.

72. 16 August 1948, Turgeon to Pearson, and 25 August 1948, Pearson to Turgeon, LAC, RG 25, Vol. 4480, File 50021-40 Part 1.

73. 21 August 1948, Boland to Hearne, UCDA, P104/4442.

74. 14 August 1948, Turgeon to Ottawa and reply, LAC, RG 25, Vol. 4480; File 50021-40 Part 1

75. Unless otherwise stated, all details related to the trip come from Lynch's diary of the visit, JACP, P190/526.

76. See memo on cost of trip, NAI, S 14331.

77. MacBride, p. 172.

78. Boland manuscript, p. 24

79. Text of speech, JACP, P190/532.

80. 24 September 1948, High Commissioner to Noel Baker, TNA, DO 35/2749.

81. Memorandum in JACP, P190/546.

82. 14 December 1949, David Johnson memorandum of conversation with President O'Kelly, LAC, RG 25, Vol 4401, File 50021-40 Part 3.

83. Undated and unsigned memorandum, which from internal evidence was written by Joseph Chapdelaine, *chargé d'affaires,* around March 1950. LAC, RG 25, Vol 4480, File 50021-40 Part 2.

84. 4 September 1948, King Diaries.

85. 5 October 1948, Priestman to Ottawa, LAC, RG 25, Vol. 4480, File 50021-40 Part 1.

86. Table plan for dinner, JACP, P190/535.

87. 23 January 1949, Hearne to Costello, JACP, P190/414.

88. 28 February 1949, Memorandum for Pearson on Costello visit, LAC, RG 25, Vol. 4480, File 50021-40 Part 2.

89. Ibid.

90. 4 September 1948, King Diaries.

91. 7 December 1948, Turgeon despatch, LAC, RG 25, Vol 4480, File 50021-40 Part 2.

92. 28 February 1949, Memorandum for Pearson on Costello visit, LAC, RG 25, Vol 4480, File 50021-40 Part 2.

93. 21 December 1948, Rugby to Machtig, TNA, DO/130/94.

94. 14 December 1949, Johnson Memorandum on conversation with President O'Kelly, LAC, RG 25, Vol. 4401, File 50021-40, Part 3.

95. 1 June 1950, Chapedlaine to Norman Robertson, Ottawa, LAC, RG 25, Vol 4401, File 50021-40, Part 3.

96. Stanford, William Bedell, *Memoirs,* p. 128.

97. Lynch, Patrick, "More pages from an Irish memoir", in English and Skelly (eds), *Ideas Matter,* pp 126/7

98. Text of broadcast, JACP, P190/528.

99. 14 October 1948, Escott Reid, Ottawa, to Turgeon, LAC, RG 25, Vol 4480, File 50021-40.

100. *II,* 7 September 1948.

101. *IT,* 3 January 1979, reprint of letter to Norton from Costello, dated 11 September 1948.

102. 9 September 1948, Garrett to Secretary of State, USNA, RG 84 Dublin Legation Security Segregated Records, 1936–49, Box 16, 800 Ireland.

103. *IT,* 3 January 1979. He would of course have been better off if he had said this to MacDermott, O'Kelly, Stanford and others as well.

104. *SI,* 5 September 1948.

105. *IT,* 8 September 1967.

106. Notes on conversations, in Mansergh (ed.), p. 186.

107. Patrick Lynch, "Pages from a Memoir", p. 54.

108. Keane, Elizabeth, *Seán MacBride*, p. 106.

109. Interview with Louie O'Brien, 24 July 1996.

110. Patrick Lynch, "Pages from a Memoir", p. 54.

111. 7 September 1948, Rugby to Machtig, TNA, DO/130/93.

112. 26 August 1948, memorandum, in LAC, RG 25, Vol. 3981, File 9908-T-1-40.

113. Costello memorandum, JACP, P190/546.

114. Interview with Patrick Lynch.

115. RTÉ television documentary "The Republic: Leaving the Commonwealth", tx. 15 April 1999.

116. Boland manuscript, p. 24.

117. *IT*, 4 July 1962, Lord Rugby Remembers.

118. *IT*, 10 July 1962.

119. 9 September 1948, Rugby telegram to Secretary of State, TNA, DO/130/93.

120. Boland manuscript, p. 26.

121. 7 September 1948, King Diaries.

122. 9 September 1948, Hearne memorandum, UCDA, P104/4473.

123. 9 September 1948, King Diaries.

124. 11 September 1948, Costello to Norton, reprinted in *IT*, 3/1/79.

125. 9 September 1948, King Diaries.

126. Costello memorandum, JACP, P190/546.

127. 9 September 1948, King Diaries.

128. 10 September 1948, King Diaries.

129. 5 January 1949, Costello to MacWhite, UCDA, P194/564.

130. Lynch diary of visit, JACP, P190/526.

131. Interview with Patrick Lynch.

132. *SI*, 3 October 1948.

133. 6 October 1948, Priestman to Ottawa, LAC, RG 25, Vol 4480, File 50021-40 Part 1.

134. Interview with Patrick Lynch.

135. Browne, Noël, *Against the Tide*, p. 130.

136. 7 October 1948, note from Nolan, NAI, S 14470 A.

137. Entry for 7 October 1948, NAI, Taoiseach's Private Office, 97/9/928.

138. Note by Nolan on draft Cabinet minute, 11 October 1948, in NAI, S 14331. In the official records the minute is dated 11 October 1948.

139. RTÉ radio documentary, "The Republic of Ireland Act, 1948". Tx 26 March 1989.

140. In the National Archives, the note is stamped 8 October, presumably the date Costello gave it to his officials; it is clear from Rugby's records that it was handed over on the seventh. See NAI, S 14387, and Rugby telegram, 7 October 1948 in TNA, DO/130/93.

141. 11 October 1948, Cabinet minutes.

142. 26 October 1948, Rugby to Machtig, TNA, DO/130/93.

143. 24 November 1948, Turgeon to Ottawa, LAC, RG 25, Vol. 4480, File 50021-40 Part 1.

144. 15 October 1948, Rugby to Secretary of State, and 21 October 1948, Rugby to Machtig, TNA, DO130/93.

145. 28 October 1948, Chapin to Washington, USNA, FG 84, Dublin Legation Security Segregated Records, 1936–49, Box 16, 800—Ireland.

146. 12 October 1948, Rugby to CRO, TNA, DO/35/3962.

147. 13 October 1948, unsigned memo for Attlee, TNA, DO/35/3962.

148. 19 November 1948, Machtig to Rugby, TNA, DO/130/93.

149. 30 October 1948, draft bill, NAI, S 14387 A.

150. Costello's copy of the Bill is in NAI, S 14387 B.

151. Fanning, *Independent Ireland*, p. 175.

152. 15 November 1948, note by Nolan, NAI, S 14387 B.

153. Undated Alexis FitzGerald memorandum, JACP, P190/390.

154. *IT*, 20 April 1949.

155. *IT*, 22 May 1951, and letter from Alexis FitzGerald, 23 May 1951.

156. Interview with Ronan Keane.

157. Undated Alexis FitzGerald memorandum, JACP, P190/390.

158. DÉD, 24 February 1949, Vol 114, Cols 493/4.

159. UCDA, P104/1802.

160. DÉD, 7 April 1949, Vol 114, Col 2519.

161. DÉD, 24 November 1948, Vol 113, Cols 347, 348, 363, 374, 376, 378, 379 and 380.

162. 25 November 1948, Rugby to Machtig, TNA, DO/130/93.

163. 9 January 1949, Eavan Costello to Bodkin, TCD, Bodkin Papers, Ms 7003/130.

164. 25 November 1948, Cabinet conclusions, Prime Minister report on talks with Attlee on 20 November 1948, PRONI, CAB 4/769.

165. 30 December 1948, Cabinet meeting, PRONI, CAB 4/773.

166. 16 December 1948, Standing Committee minutes, UUP Papers, PRONI, D/1327/7/33.

167. 20 January 1949, Standing Committee minutes, UUP Papers, PRONI, D/1327/7/34.

168. *IT*, 26 January 1949.

169. M/EA memo, NAI, S 9361.

170. 28 January 1949, Chapin to Washington, USNA, RG 84, Dublin Security Segregated Records, Box 18, 350, Partition 1949.

171. 21 March 1949, Attlee to Brooke, PRONI, CAB 9B/2676.

172. 6 April 1949, Costello to de Valera, and reply 7/4/49, UCDA, P150/2990.

173. 18 April 1949, text of broadcast, JACP, P190/467.

174. Diary entries, 28 April 1949 and 3 May 1949, quoted in Barton, Brian, *Brookeborough*, p. 232.

175. 5 May 1949, de Valera to Costello, and reply, same date, UCDA, P150/2990.

176. 5 May 1949, Garrett to Sec of State, USNA, RG 84, Dublin Legation Security Segregated Records, 1936–49, Box 17, 320.1.

177. 7 May 1949, Cabinet conclusion, NAI, S 14528.

178. 8 May 1949, Laithwaite to CRO, TNA, DO 35/3971.

179. 10 May 1949, Johnson to Ottawa and 20/5/49, Johnson to Pearson, LAC, RG 25, Vol 4480, File 50021-40, Part 2.

180. DÉD, 10 May 1949, Vol 115, Cols 787/8, 791/2, 801/2, 807.

181. 19 May 1949, Laithwaite to Sec of State, TNA, DO/130/99.

182. Interview with Richie Ryan.

183. 4 May 1949, Garrett to Sec of State, USNA, RG 84, Dublin Legation Security Segregated records, 1936–49, Box 17, 320.1

184. 20 May 1949, Johnson to Pearson, LAC, RG 25, Vol. 4480, File 50021-40, Part 2.

185. Ibid.

186. Feeney, Brian, *Sinn Féin*, p. 193.

187. 25 October 1949, Laithwaite to Sir Percivale Liesching, TNA, CAB 21/407.

188. 15 April 1948, Hearne to Sec, D/EA, NAI, S 14291 A/1.

189. 4 May 1948, Hickerson to Garrett, USNA, RG 84, Dublin Legation Security Segregated Records, 1936–49, Box 15, 710.

190. CIA report on Ireland, 1 April 1949, Truman Library, HST Papers, PSF, Box 256, SR-48.

191. 24 January 1950, G.W. Perkins to Secretary of State, USNA, RG 59, Decimal File, Box 3289, 611.41/1-2450.

192. 27 December 1948, Hickerson to Garrett, USNA, RG 84, Dublin Legation Security Segregated Records, 1936–49, Box 15, 711.

193. 10 January 1949, Hickerson to Miller, British Embassy, Washington, TNA, DO/35/2749.

194. 14 January 1949, Rugby to Liesching, with memorandum of Pritchard discussion with Boland, TNA, DO/35/2749.

195. 8 February 1949, MacBride aide-memoire to United States, NAI, S 14291 A/1.

196. 14 April 1949, Hickerson to Garrett, USNA, RG 84, Dublin Legation Security Segregated Records, 1936–49, Box 17, 320.1.

197. 13 April 1949, MacWhite to Costello, UCDA, P194/564.

198. Boland memoir, pp 21–3.

199. 3 November 1948, Chapin to Secretary of State, USNA, RG 84, Dublin Security Segregated Records, Box 18, 821: Army Manoeuvres: Survey.

200. 9 May 1950, Laithwaite record of conversation with MacBride, and 30 May 1950, Laithwaite record of conversation with Boland, TNA, DO 130/110.

201. 2 May 1951, record of discussion at McKee Barracks, UCDA, P151/503.

202. 15 August 1950, State Department policy statement on Ireland, USNA, RG 59, Department of State Decimal File, 1950–54, Box 2768, 611.40A/8-1550.

203. 15 January 1951, Dillon to Costello, JACP, P190/562.

204. 23 March 1951, Acheson memorandum of conversation with MacBride and Truman, USNA, RG 59, Department of State Decimal File, 1950–54, Box 2768, 611.40A/3-2351.

205. 3 November 1950, Laithwaite review of affairs, TNA, FO 371/84832.

206. 3 April 1951, Troy to Laithwaite, TNA, DO 130/112.

207. 20 March 1951, IP, and 22 March 1951, Moynihan minute, NAI, S 9361 C.

208. Cosgrave quoted in Collins, Stephen, *The Cosgrave Legacy*, pp 69/70.

209. Memorandum, JACP, P190/546.

Chapter 9 A very happy success for the Church (pp 232–258)

1. DÉD, 12 April 1951, Vol 125, Col 767.
2. 15 April 1951, McQuaid to Felici, McQuaid Papers, DDA, AB8/B/XVIII/Box 5—Health, Mother and Child Scheme, Folder: Mother and Child Scheme, 1951.
3. 23 February 1948, Costello to Pope; 29 February 1948, reply NAI, S 9469 A.
4. 10 March 1948, Costello to MacWhite, UCDA, P194/564.
5. 10 April 1951, D'Alton to McQuaid, DDA, McQuaid Papers, AB8/B/XVIII/Box 5—Health, Mother and Child Scheme, Folder: Mother and Child Scheme, 1951.
6. SI, 12 April 1998.
7. "Seven Days".
8. Bolster, Evelyn, *The Knights of Saint Columbanus*, pp 14 and 95.
9. 28 February 1948, Costello to McQuaid; 2 March 1949, Costello to McQuaid; 9 May 1950, Griffin to Costello; 22 May 1950, Costello to McQuaid; DDA, McQuaid Papers, AB8/b/XVIII, Mr John A. Costello (first coalition period) 1948–51.
10. 21 November 1949, M/EA memo; 20 December 1949, Moynihan to Sec, D/EA; NAI, S 14597.
11. Cooney, John, *John Charles McQuaid*, p. 248.
12. Costello expressed this view privately to Patrick McCartan, according to his son. See Horgan, John, *Noël Browne*, p. 75 and Note 53, p. 303.
13. Quoted in Dunleavy and Dunleavy, *Douglas Hyde*, p. 434.
14. 2 December 1948, Browne to Walsh, NAI, S 15008.
15. 30 June 1949, Secretaries to the Hierarchy to Costello, NAI, S 15008.
16. 16 September 1949, Costello to Secretaries to the Hierarchy, NAI, S 15008.
17. Quoted in Keating, Anthony, "The legalisation of adoption in Ireland", *Studies*, 2003.
18. 15 November 1950, note on Parliamentary Party meeting, UCDA, P151/469.
19. Dillon memoir quoted in Manning, Maurice, *James Dillon*, p. 270.
20. Interview with Patrick Lynch.
21. Record of meeting with Franco, UCDA, P151/1913.
22. 17 October 1949, M/J memo for Government, and 28 October 1949, Cabinet conclusions, NAI, S 14620.
23. NAI, S 15131.
24. Manning, p. 269.
25. Interview with Patrick Lynch.
26. 13 October 1947, Staunton to de Valera, NAI, S 14227.
27. NAI, S 14227.
28. IT, 15 January 1948.
29. 10 December 1948, Mulcahy to Fine Gael Ministers, and 17 November 1948, D.J. Sheehan to Deputy Palmer, JACP, P190/412.
30. Health Bill 1950, Explanatory Memorandum, NAI, S 14227.
31. 9 June 1948, M/H memo for Government, NAI, S 13444 G.
32. Browne, Noël, *Against the Tide*, p. 153.
33. Horgan, John, *Noël Browne*, p. 101.

34. 13 February 1950, Nolan memo, and 27 March 1951, Moynihan to Costello, NAI, S 13444 G. It is not clear why he sought this information in early 1950, before the crisis had developed.

35. 2 April 1951, D/Taoiseach memo, NAI, S 13444 G.

36. Horgan, *Browne*, p. 105.

37. Marr, Andrew, *A History of Modern Britain*, p. 66.

38. *Irish News*, 18 April 1951, quoted in Staunton, Enda, *The Nationalists of Northern Ireland*, p. 363.

39. Horgan, *Browne*, p. 111.

40. *IT*, 21 February 1951.

41. *The Leader*, 3 March 1951.

42. *SP*, 7 December 1986, MacBride interview.

43. Interview with Patrick Lynch.

44. Interview with Alexis FitzGerald.

45. Interview with Patrick Lynch.

46. 19 November 1950, Brennan to Costello, NAI, S 14997 A.

47. 25 October 1950, minutes of meeting, McQuaid Papers, DDA, AB8/B/XVIII, Box 5—Health, Mother and Child Scheme, Folder: Mother and Child Scheme, 1950.

48. Undated speech to IMA, JACP, P190/424.

49. Undated notes for speech to RCPI, JACP, P190/427.

50. 25 November 1950, Delaney to Costello, NAI, S 14997 A.

51. 25 November 1950, Costello to Delaney, and notes, NAI, S 14227.

52. DÉD, 12 April 1951, Vol 125, cols 748–51.

53. 8 December 1950, Browne to Costello, NAI, S 14997 A.

54. 16 December 1950, Browne to Costello, NAI, S 14997 A.

55. 5 December 1950, Delaney to Costello, NAI, S 14997 A.

56. 5 March 1951, Browne to Costello, NAI, S 14997 A.

57. 10 October 1950, Staunton to Costello, NAI, S 14997 A.

58. DÉD, 12 April 1951, Vol 125, Col 742.

59. 21 March 1951, Browne to Costello, NAI, S 14997 A.

60. 19 March 1951, Browne to Costello, and 21 March 1951, Costello to Browne, NAI, S 14997 A.

61. Undated draft by Browne, NAI, S 14997 A.

62. 21 March 1951, Costello to Browne, NAI, S 14997 A.

63. 9 December 1950, McQuaid to Bishop Browne, McQuaid Papers, DDA, AB8/B/XVIII/Box 5—Health, Mother and Child Scheme, Folder: Mother and Child Scheme, 1950.

64. 16 January 1951, McQuaid report to Standing Committee of Hierarchy. Ibid. Emphasis in original.

65. Horgan, *Browne*, p. 111.

66. 8 March 1951, McQuaid to Costello, NAI, S 14997A.

67. DÉD, 12 April 1951, Vol 125, Cols 757–8.

68. 15 March 1951, Costello to Browne, NAI, S 14997 A.

69. 19 March 1951, Browne to Costello, NAI, S 14997 A.

70. Notes on events in March 1951, McQuaid Papers, DDA, AB8/B/XVIII/Box 5—Health, Mother and Child Scheme; folder: Mother and Child Scheme, 1951.

71. 21 March 1951, note by Moynihan, NAI, S 14997 A.

72. 21 March 1951, Costello to Browne, NAI, S 14997 A.

73. 21 March 1951, Browne to Costello, NAI, S 14997 A.

74. 22 March 1951, Moynihan note, NAI, S 14997 A.

75. 22 March 1951, Costello to Browne, NAI, S 14997 A.

76. 22 March 1951, handwritten note by Costello, NAI, S 14997A.

77. 3 April 1951, Report to Standing Committee, McQuaid Papers, DDA, AB8/B/XVIII/Box 5—Health, Mother and Child Scheme, Folder: Mother and Child Scheme, 1951.

78. Puirséil, Niamh, *The Irish Labour Party*, p. 155.

79. Notes on events in March 1951, McQuaid Papers, DDA, AB8/B/XVIII/Box 5—Health, Mother and Child Scheme; folder: Mother and Child Scheme, 1951.

80. Interview with Patrick Lynch.

81. O'Brien, Conor Cruise, *Memoir: My life and themes*, p. 153.

82. Lee, J.J., *Ireland 1912–1985*, p. 317.

83. 3 April 1951, Report to Standing Committee, McQuaid Papers, DDA, AB8/B/XVIII/Box 5—Health, Mother and Child Scheme, Folder: Mother and Child Scheme, 1951.

84. 5 April 1951, McQuaid to Costello enclosing Hierarchy documment, NAI, S 14227.

85. Notes on events since Hierarchy's meeting, McQuaid Papers, DDA, AB8/B/XVIII/Box 5—Health, Mother and Child Scheme, Folder: Mother and Child Scheme, 1951.

86. Ibid.

87. Ibid.

88. Browne, pp 176/7.

89. 7 April 1951, note, NAI, S 14997 D.

90. Fanning, *Independent Ireland*, pp 185/6.

91. 7 April 1951, Sec to Govt to Private Secretary, M/H, JACP, P190/557.

92. Notes on events since Hierarchy's meeting, McQuaid Papers, DDA, AB8/B/XVIII/Box 5—Health, Mother and Child Scheme, Folder: Mother and Child Scheme, 1951.

93. Draft letter to Minister for Health, NAI, S 14997 D.

94. "Seven Days".

95. MacBride, pp 222/3.

96. 11 April 1951, Browne to Costello, and reply, NAI, S 14165.

97. 20 April 1951, memo on resignation, NAI, S 10719 B.

98. DÉD, 12 April 1951, Vol 125, Cols 667, 668, 669, 672/3.

99. DÉD, 12 April 1951, Vol 125, Cols 732, 732, 737, 739/40, 740, 777–8, 783–4.

100. Horgan, *Browne*, p. 151.

101. Ibid., p. 150.

102. Interview with Ronan Keane; the reference was to Masefield's poem "Sea Fever", and to a favourite *Irish Times* pub.
103. 15 April 1951, McQuaid to Felici, McQuaid Papers, DDA, AB8/B/XVIII/Box 5—Health, Mother and Child Scheme, Folder: Mother and Child Scheme, 1951.
104. O'Brien, Conor Cruise, *States of Ireland*, p. 120.
105. Yeats, Michael B., *Cast a cold eye*, p. 50.
106. DÉD, 11 April 1951, Vol 125, Col 640.
107. Deeny, James, *To cure and to care*, p. 196.
108. Horgan, *Browne*, pp 156–8.
109. DÉD, 10 July 1951, Vol 126, Col 1231.
110. Horgan, pp 156–8.
111. DÉD, 10 July 1951, Vol 126, Cols 1223–6.
112. 4 January 1951, Norman Robertson memo, LAC, RG 25, vol 4401, File 50021-40 pt 3.
113. *The Leader*, 6 January 1951.
114. *EH*, 27 January 1951.
115. 16 February 1951, Costello to Bodkin, TCD, Bodkin Papers, MSS 7003/103a-317.
116. 3 January 1951, Dillon to Costello, JACP, P190/607.
117. *The Leader*, 28 April 1951.
118. Manning, pp 272/3.
119. 5 March 1951, Costello to Bodkin, TCD, Bodkin Papers, Ms 7003/197.
120. NAI, S 15017.
121. 5 May 1951, Laithwaite to CRO, and 8 May 1951, note by G.W. Sich, TNA, FO 371/91167.
122. 4 May 1951, Statement by Taoiseach, JACP, P190/294.
123. 7 May 1951, address to constituents, JACP, P190/294.
124. Horgan, p. 158.
125. *IT*, 22 May 1951.
126. 8 December 1969, retirement speech, JACP, P190/350.
127. Election itinerary, JACP, P190/294.
128. *IT*, 29 May 1951.
129. Appointment diary, NAI, Taoiseach's Private Office, 97/9/928.
130. Text with Costello's annotations, JACP, P190/294; recording of speech, loc. cit, P190/288.
131. Dublin South East election leaflet, JACP, P190/293.
132. 19 May 1951, speech in Cork, JACP, P190/294.
133. 28 May 1951, speech in Dublin, JACP, P190/294.
134. 15 May 1951, speech in Rathmines, JACP, P190/294.
135. 16 May 1951, Mullingar speech, JACP, P190/294.
136. 12 May 1951, Drogheda speech, JACP, P190/294.
137. 27 May 1951, Ennis speech, JACP, P190/294. Montagu Norman, the former Governor of the Bank of England, was noted for his conservatism.
138. 20 May 1951, Limerick speech, JACP, P190/294. 51 years later Fianna Fáil would employ a similar, if snappier, election slogan: "A lot done, more to do".

139. 19 May 1951, Cork speech, JACP, P190/294.
140. 29 May 1951, Bray speech, JACP, P190/294.
141. *The Leader*, 26 May 1951.
142. McCullagh, David, *A Makeshift Majority*, pp 246–8.
143. 2 June 1951, Laithwaite to CRO, TNA, FO 371/91167.
144. 4 June 1951, Lemass to Henry Harrison, quoted in O'Sullivan, Michael, *Seán Lemass*, p. 124.
145. Horgan, p. 163.
146. 7 June 1951, MacBride to Taoiseach, UCDA, P7/C/106.
147. *IT*, 5 June 1951.
148. Manning, pp 278/9.
149. 13 June 1951, Laithwaite to CRO, TNA, FO 371/91167.
150. Manning, p. 279.
151. DÉD, 13 June 1951, Vol 126, Col 16.
152. DÉD, 13 June 1951, Vol 126, Col 82.

Chapter 10 Trumpet-tongued denunciation (pp 259–287)

1. 9 July 1951, Costello to Monsignor M. Moloney, Limerick, JACP, P190/614.
2. 9 January 1955, Seamus McCall to Costello, JACP, P190/826.
3. DÉD, 30 June 1953, Vol 140, Col 39.
4. Interview with Ronan Keane.
5. 9 July 1951, Costello to Joseph Ronayne, JACP, P190/618.
6. Lindsay, Patrick, *Memories*, p. 156.
7. O'Leary, Cornelius, *Irish Elections*, p. 43.
8. Manning, p. 285.
9. 19 October 1951, Costello to Dillon, JACP, P190/607.
10. 27 August 1951, speech to Dublin SE constituency executive, JACP, P190/296.
11. *The Leader*, 16 August 1952.
12. 7 August 1951, Douglas to Costello, JACP, P190/607.
13. 27 August 1951, speech to Dublin SE constituency executive, JACP, P190/296.
14. *The Leader*, 24 November 1951.
15. Fanning, Ronan, "Alexis FitzGerald", in Lynch and Meenan (eds), *Essays in Memory of Alexis FitzGerald*, p. 9.
16. 21 July 1951, John Costello [junior] to Bodkin, TCD, Bodkin Papers, Ms 7003/204.
17. 16 October 1951, Costello to Bodkin, TCD, Bodkin Papers, Ms 7003/209.
18. 19 October 1951, Costello to Dillon, JACP, P190/607.
19. 19 October 1951, Rathmines speech, JACP, P190/576.
20. *IT*, 24 October 1951.
21. Central Bank Report for the year ending 31 March 1951.
22. 27 October 1951, Dillon memorandum, JACP, P190/558.
23. 14 November 1951, Bodkin to Costello, JACP, P190/813.
24. *IT*, 30 October 1951.
25. 3 November 1951, Cork speech, JACP, P190/577.

26. Feeney, *MacEntee*, p. 171.

27. DÉD, 20 November 1952, Vol. 134, Col. 2039.

28. The series appeared in *The Leader* on 2 August 1952, 16 August 1952 and 27 September 1952—Costello's annotated copy of the final part is in JACP, P190/570.

29. DÉD, 7 November 1951, Vol 127, Col 353.

30. *IT*, 8 November 1951.

31. 16 December 1951, Kilkenny speech, JACP, P190/578.

32. 18 May 1952, Athlone speech, JACP, P190/588.

33. DÉD, 12 March 1952, Vol 129, Col 1954/5.

34. 6 February 1952, Ard Fheis speech, JACP, P190/585.

35. Feeney, p. 186.

36. Lee, p. 325.

37. DÉD, 3 April 1952, Vol 130, cols 1268 and 1296.

38. DÉD, 13 May 1952, Vol 131, Col 1443.

39. Interview with Declan Costello.

40. 17 June 1954 and 26 April 1955, Moynihan notes, NAI, 96/6/106.

41. 31 March 1952, Costello to Commissioner M.J. Kinnane, JACP, P190/609.

42. Interview with Mick Kilkenny.

43. Feeney, pp 185–9.

44. DÉD, 13 May 1952, Vol. 131, Col. 1446.

45. Whitaker, T.K., *Interests*, p. 164.

46. Interview with Ken Whitaker.

47. 13 January 1952, Killarney speech, JACP, P190/583.

48. 22 January 1952, Shelbourne speech, JACP, P190/584.

49. 20 April 1952, Tralee speech, JACP, P190/587.

50. Yeats, p. 55.

51. DÉD, 24 July 1952, Vol 133, Cols 1759/60, 1761, 1764.

52. DÉD, 24 July 1952, Vol 133, Col 1880.

53. DÉD, 24 July 1952, Vol 133, Col 1893.

54. DÉD, 22 October 1952, Vol 134, Cols 56/7.

55. 11 October 1952, Grosvenor Hotel speech, JACP, P190/575.

56. *The Leader*, 28 February 1953.

57. 18 February 1953, Ard Fheis speech, JACP, P190/315.

58. 4 March 1953, Whitaker note for Minister, in UCDA, P67/220, and D/F memo, P67/223.

59. M/I&C memo, 28 July 1953; M/F memo, 31 July 1953; D/T memo, 13 August 1953; M/F memo, 25 August 1953; documents in the possession of Fergus and Jacqueline Armstrong.

60. 17 February 1954, Ard Fheis speech, JACP, P190/298.

61. DÉD, 7 May 1953, Vol. 138, Col. 1349.

62. DÉD, 12 March 1953, Vol. 137, Cols. 261–3.

63. 16 December 1951, Kilkenny speech, JACP, P190/578.

64. *The Leader*, 16 August 1952.

65. Horgan, pp 168/9.

66. 4 May 1953, Sweetman to Editor, Manchester Guardian, JACP, P190/608.

67. DÉD, 15 April 1953, Vol 138, Cols 47, 60 and 64.

68. DÉD, 15 April 1953, Vol 138, Cols 98 and 66.

69. DÉD, 9 June 1953, Vol 139, Col 798.

70. O'Higgins, T.F., *A Double Life*, pp 153–5.

71. 25 May 1952, Limerick speech, JACP, P190/589.

72. 7 June 1952, Waterford speech, JACP, P190/590.

73. 14 June 1952, Ballina speech, JACP, P190/591.

74. 3 July 1952, Costello to Bodkin, TCD, Bodkin Papers, Ms 7003/217.

75. 14 October 1952, Four Courts Hotel speech, JACP, P190/595.

76. Undated Lombard Street speech, JACP, P190/573.

77. 11 November 1952, final by-election rally, JACP, P190/596.

78. 27 November 1952, fortnightly summary of events, TNA, DO 35/5290.

79. 16 November 1952, Mullingar speech, JACP, P190/597.

80. 30 May 1953, Cobh speech, JACP, P190/598.

81. 7 June 1953, Arklow speech, JACP, P190/599.

82. 15 July 1953, Costello to Monsignor John Power, JACP, P190/617.

83. 22 June 1953, Government decision, and 30 June 1953, notes on speeches, NAI, S 15525.

84. DÉD, 30 June 1953, Vol. 140, Cols. 29–30, 41 and 33.

85. Glynn to Costello, undated, JACP, P190/609.

86. 30 November 1953, Dun Laoghaire speech, JACP, P190/603.

87. *IP*, 29 October 1953.

88. 16 January 1954, *The Leader*.

89. Cox was suggested to Churchill's lawyer, Sir Hartley Shawcross, by Freddie Boland. In lieu of a fee, Cox asked for autographed copies of the two volumes of Churchill's biography of his ancestor, the Duke of Marlborough. Boland memoir (unpaginated).

90. Entry on Costello, by Charles Lysaght, in Maguire, James and Quinn, James, *Dictionary of Irish Biography, Vol. 2*.

91. McCague, Eugene, *Arthur Cox*, p. 101.

92. *The Leader*, 11 October 1952.

93. Quinn, Antoinette, *Patrick Kavanagh*, pp 314–16.

94. 23 February 1954, Costello to Bodkin, TCD, Bodkin Papers, Ms 7003/225.

95. Interview with Ronan Keane.

96. Quinn, p. 326.

97. Quinn, p. 327.

98. Interview with Ronan Keane.

99. *The Leader*, 11 October 1952.

100. 10 February 1954, Seamus Behan to Costello, JACP, P190/605.

101. Quinn, p. 327.

102. Quinn, pp 328–9.

103. Interview with Ronan Keane.

104. Quinn, pp 328/9.

105. 9 January 1955, Seamus MacCall to Costello, JACP, P190/826.

106. Interview with Declan Costello.

107. Quinn, p. 345.

108. Quinn, p. 339.

109. 16 February 1955, Kavanagh to Costello, JACP, P190/823.

110. 4 June 1955, Costello to Little, NAI, S 15896.

111. Interview with Mick Kilkenny.

112. 23 May 1955, Costello to Kavanagh, JACP, P190/823.

113. 27 May 1955, Kavanagh to Costello, NAI, S 15896.

114. 2 July 1955, Kavanagh to Costello, NAI, S 15896.

115. 4 July 1955, Costello to Little, NAI, S 15896.

116. 18 July 1955, Dowd note, NAI, S 15896.

117. 26 July 1955 and 2 August 1955, NAI, S 15896.

118. Kennedy, *Dreams and Responsibilities,* p. 115.

119. 4 June 1956, Costello to Kavanagh, JACP, P190/835.

120. 4 July 1956, Moynihan note, NAI, S 15896.

121. Interview with Mick Kilkenny.

122. 26 November 1956, Costello to T.K. O'Toole, JACP, P190/821.

123. 17 September 1952, Ita McCoy to Deputy Paddy Cawley, JACP, P190/609.

124. 6 April 1953, R.L. McDowell to Costello, and reply, 8 May 1953, JACP, P190/615.

125. Interview with Jacqueline Armstrong. Her daughter, Katie, called her great-grandfather "Little Pam-pam", because he was smaller than her grandfather, Alexis FitzGerald.

126. Correspondence with Georgina Sutton.

127. 23 March 1953, Costello to Michael Tierney, UCDA, OA 30/452.

128. 20 February 1952, O'Dea to Costello, and reply, 28 February 1952, JACP, P190/616.

129. Interview with Declan Costello.

130. DÉD, 28 July 1953, Vol 141, Cols 807 and 805.

131. 28 January 1954, de Valera memo, UCDA, P150/2990.

132. *SI*, 3 November 1974.

133. Correspondence with Michael V. O'Mahony.

134. Interview with Declan Costello.

135. 21 January 1954, M/J memo, NAI, S 11602 B.

136. 29 June 1954, Taft to Secretary of State, USNA, RG 86, Dublin Legation Security Segregated Records, Box 21, 350: Ireland, Political, 1953–55.

137. 4 March 1954, Gallagher memo, NAI, S 15652.

138. *II*, 5 March 1954.

139. Lindsay, p. 155.

140. *The Leader,* 24 April 1954.

141. 9 March 1954 PQ submitted by Sweetman in Costello's name; 9 March 1954, Nolan note. NAI, S 15652.

142. 9 March 1954, Moynihan to Costello, JACP, P190/607.

143. 14 March 1954, Kilkenny speech, JACP, P190/298.

144. DÉD, 11 March 1954, Vol. 144, Col. 1628.

145. DÉD, 22 April 1954, Vol. 145, Col. 679.

146. 6 May 1954, Hankinson to Secretary of State, TNA, DO 35/5193.

147. *11*, 15 March 1954.

148. 14 March 1954, Kilkenny speech, JACP, P190/298.

149. 16 May 1954, Ballina speech, JACP, P190/298.

150. 8 May 1954, Ennis speech, JACP, P190/298.

151. 15 May 1954, Longford speech, JACP, P190/298.

152. 9 April 1954, Mills' Hall speech, JACP, P190/298.

153. 7 May 1954, Limerick speech, JACP, P190/298.

154. DÉD, 12 May 1955, Vol. 150, Col. 1391.

155. 9 April 1954, Mills' Hall speech, JACP, P190/298.

156. 24 April 1954, Sligo speech, JACP, P190/298.

157. 3 May 1954, Rathmines speech, JACP, P190/298.

158. 17 May 1954, O'Connell Street speech, JACP, P190/298.

159. 6 May 1954, Hankinson to Secretary of Sate, TNA, DO 35/5193.

160. 25 April 1954, Letterkenny speech, JACP, P190/298.

161. 26 April 1954, Fairview speech, JACP, P190/298.

162. 9 May 1954, Athlone speech, JACP, P190/298.

163. O'Brien, Mark, *De Valera, Fianna Fáil and the Irish Press*, p. 90.

164. 10 May 1954, Donnybrook speech, JACP, P190/298.

165. DÉD, 12 November 1952, Vol 134, Col. 1389.

166. 10 November 1951, John Mullin to Costello, JACP, P190/614.

167. 7 January 1954, Costello to Mullin, JACP, P190/614.

168. 14 June 1954, Senator James Douglas to Costello, JACP, P190/819.

169. Horgan, pp 178/9.

170. Browne, pp 221/2.

171. 8 December 1969, retirement dinner, JACP, P190/350.

172. 6 July 1954, Sandymount Branch annual report, UCDA, P39/C/D/90.

173. Mulcahy, Risteárd, *Richard Mulcahy*, p. 258.

174. Interview with Jacqueline Armstrong.

175. 26 May 1954, fortnightly summary, TNA, DO 35/5290.

176. Puirséil, Niamh, *The Irish Labour Party*, pp 175/6.

177. Drafts of Government programme, JACP, P190/551.

178. 29 June 1954, Taft to Secretary of State, USNA,RG 84, Dublin Legation Security Segregated Records, Box 21, 350—Ireland, Political, 1953–5.

179. DÉD, 6 July 1954, Vol. 146, Col. 1266.

180. DÉD, 12 May 1955, Vol. 150, Col. 1407.

181. Drafts of Government programme, JACP, P190/551.

182. DÉD, 1 April 1952, Vol. 130, Col. 993.

183. Drafts of Government programme, JACP, P190/551.

184. See drafts of Government programme, JACP, P190/551.

185. Copy of Statement in NAI, S 15713.

186. 15 June 1954, Hankinson to Lord Swinton, TNA, DO 35/5193.

187. DÉD, 2 June 1954, Vol. 146, Col. 26.

188. *IP*, 3 June 1954.

189. DÉD, 2 June 1954, Vol. 146, Col. 36.

190. *II*, 5 May 1969.

191. *The Leader*, 28 March 1953.

192. 15 June 1954, Hankinson to Swinton, TNA, DO 35/5193.

193. Quoted in Puirséil, p. 180.

194. O'Higgins, p. 186.

195. DÉD, 9 March 1955, Vol. 149, Col. 233.

196. 19 June 1954, memo on conversation with Boland, TNA, DO 35/5159.

197. MacDermott, p. 219, note 208.

198. *IT*, 2 June 1954.

199. 23 June 1954, Costello to Catalina MacBride, NAI, S 15719 B.

200. DÉD, 2 June 1954, Vol. 146, Col. 61.

201. Memo in NAI, S 15655.

202. Letter from Liam Cosgrave, 7 November 2008.

203. O'Higgins, p. 156.

204. Details in NAI S 15655 and 15656.

205. 23 February 1955, answer to parliamentary question, NAI, S 15656.

206. DÉD, 2 June 1954, Vol. 146, Col. 62.

207. 25 May 1954, Cox to Costello, NAI, S 15719 A.

Chapter 11 Giving the people quiet (pp 288–322)

1. DÉD, 9 March 1955, Vol. 149, Col. 230.

2. 26 November 1955, Rathkeale speech, JACP, P190/640.

3. 8 July 1954, Costello to Bodkin, TCD, Bodkin Papers, Ms 7003/227.

4. 19 June 1954, *The Leader*.

5. 7 November 2008, letter from Liam Cosgrave.

6. 29 June 1954, Taft to Secretary of State, USNA, RG 84, Dublin Legation Security Segregated Reports, Box 21, 350—Ireland—Political, 1953–55

7. Interview with Mick Kilkenny.

8. 24 June 1954, Nolan note, NAI, 96/6/106.

9. O'Higgins, *A Double Life*, pp 161/2.

10. Ibid., pp 163/4.

11. 22 July 1954, Nolan note, NAI, S 15655.

12. DÉD, 12 May 1955, Vol. 150, Col. 1418.

13. 16 August 1956, FitzGerald to Costello, letter in possession of Jacqueline and Fergus Armstrong.

14. O'Higgins, p. 172.

15. Keogh, Dermot, *Twentieth Century Ireland*, p. 227.

16. 17 June 1954, Minister for Finance memorandum for Government, and 28 June 1954, Nolan to Secretary of Department of Finance, NAI, S 15720.

17. DÉD, 9 March 1955, Vol. 149, Col. 219.

18. *The Leader*, 9 October 1954.

19. 24 December 1954, Sweetman to Costello, JACP, P190/831.

20. *The Leader*, 9 October 1954.

21. 7 January 1955 and 11 January 1955, notes in NAI, S 14470 D.

22. *The Leader*, 29 January 1955.

23. Annual review of 1954, TNA, DO 35/5379.

24. 2 February 1955, Ard Fheis speech, JACP, P190/758.

25. 11 February 1955, fortnightly report, TNA, DO 35/5291.

26. 4 May 1954, D/T memorandum, NAI, S 15725 A.

27. 24 June 1954, Moynihan to External Affairs, and 19 July 19, Boland to External Affairs, NAI, S 15725 A.

28. 13 October 1954, M/F memorandum for Government, NAI, S 15725 A.

29. 11 September 1956, D/T memorandum, NAI, S 15725 A.

30. 30 January 1956, General Survey of the State Capital Programme, JACP, P190/710.

31. 5 July 1956, M/F memorandum for the Government, NAI, S 15725 A.

32. 21 June 1956, minutes of meeting with Provisional United Trade Union Movement, NAI, S 15725 A.

33. 1 November 1948, Chapin to Secretary of State, USNA, RG 58, Decimal File 1945–9, Box 3289, 711.41D2/10-2848.

34. 25 June 1954, Moynihan to Industry and Commerce, NAI, S 15735 A.

35. 31 July 1954, Moynihan to Finance, and ICC report, January 1955, both in NAI, S 15735 A.

36. 30 June 1955, Redmond to Moynihan, NAI, S 15735 A.

37. Reservation to report by Alexis FitzGerald, and Minority Report by James Meenan, in NAI, S 2850 B.

38. 6 September 1954, Norton to Costello, NAI, S 2850 B.

39. 14 March 1955, Charles Murray note, NAI, S 2850 B.

40. He later made a similar observation in the Dáil in relation to forestry. "When a Department has a strong view, even the head of the Government is not always able to change it, no matter how much he wants to change it." DED, 7 November 1962, Vol. 197, Col. 734.

41. See NAI, S 2850 B.

42. Patterson, Henry, *Ireland since 1939*, pp 108/9.

43. 7 February 1956, FIM speech, NAI, S 2850 C.

44. DÉD, 14 July 1955, Vol. 152, Col. 1101.

45. Patterson, p. 108.

46. 25 January 1956, Cork Chamber of Commerce speech, JACP, P190/646.

47. Honohan and Ó Gráda, "The Irish macroeconomic crisis of 1955–56", *Irish Economic and Social History*, 1998, p. 65.

48. Puirséil, p. 186; Patterson, p. 108.

49. 25 January 1956, Cork Chamber of Commerce speech, JACP, P190/646.

50. 8 February 1956, Ard Fheis speech, JACP, P190/736.

51. Lindsay, pp 167/8.

52. Memoir, p. 79, quoted in Manning, *Dillon*, p. 294.

53. 23 March 1955, memorandum of conversation between O'Donovan and Louis M. Smith, Agricultural Attaché, USNA, RG 84, Dublin Legation Security Segregated Records, Box 21, 350: Ireland—political, 1953–5.

54. Lindsay, pp 168/9.

55. *The Leader*, 14 May 1955.

56. 23 May 1955, Department of the Taoiseach memorandum, NAI, S 13965 E. Between the end of 1951 and the end of 1954, earnings had increased from 228.5 to 256.8, while the Consumer Price Index went from 208 to 232. The Index of Real Earnings (earnings controlled for inflation) went up by just under 1%, from 109.9 to 110.7.

57. 29 September 1955, notice of motion, NAI, S 13965 E.

58. 20 October 1955, Government amendment, NAI, S 13965 F.

59. DÉD, 27 October 1955, Vol. 153, Cols. 219, 224, 233 and 243.

60. 26 November 1955, Rathkeale speech, JACP, P190/640.

61. 3 May 1956, minutes of meeting, NAI, S 13965 G.

62. *IT*, 13 October 1956.

63. *IT*, 30 May 1957.

64. Lindsay, pp 160–62.

65. See row over ESB funding in JACP, P190/779, or 2 September 1955, Sweetman to Norton, JACP, P190/831 for an argument over shipping.

66. 12 June 1956, CIÉ memo; 23 August 1956, Finance memo; 31 August 1956, Norton to Beddy; 4 September 1956, Norton to Sweetman; 5 September 1956, Norton to Costello; 3 September 1956, Sweetman to Norton; 6 September 1956, MacBride to Costello; 7 September 1956, Costello to MacBride; JACP, P190/717.

67. 22 April 1955, MacBride to Costello, JACP, P 190/826.

68. *IP*, 2 February 1957.

69. 1 November 1955, MacBride to Costello, and Department of the Taoiseach note, 20 December 1955, NAI, S 15965.

70. Puirséil, Niamh, "Political and party competition in post-war Ireland" in Girvin and Murphy (eds), *The Lemass Era*, p. 21.

71. 26 November 1955, Rathkeale speech, JACP, P190/640.

72. 28 October 1956, MacBride to Costello, JACP, P190/694.

73. 19 November 1956, MacBride to Cosgrave, copied to Costello, JACP, P190/694.

74. 24 November 1956, Cosgrave to Costello, JACP, P190/746.

75. 12 October 1955, Cabinet conclusions, PRONI CAB/4/982.

76. *IT*, 6 September 2003.

77. 12 July 1954, Vincent MacDowell to Costello, JACP, P190/562.

78. *IT*, 14 June 1954.

79. *IT*, 16 July 1954.

80. July 1954, Healy to Costello, PRONI, Healy Papers, D2991/B/51/1.

81. 6 August 1954, Costello to Labhras Ó Lochrainn, NAI, S 9361 D.

82. Currie, Austin, *All Hell Will Break Loose*, p. 29.

83. *II*, 20 August 1954.

84. *II*, 18 October 1954.

85. 18 October 1954, weekly report, NAI, JUS 8/1022.

86. 25 October 1954, note, in NAI, S 11564 B.

87. DÉD, 28 October 1954, Vol. 147, Cols. 194/5, 182 and 184.

88. *IT*, 29 October 1954, editorial.

89. November 1954, Army Council statement, JACP, P190/562.

90. 19 November 1954, Hankinson to Swinton, TNA, DO 35/5379.

91. 8 November 1954, record of meeting, TNA, DO 35/5207.

92. 15 December 1954, record of meeting, TNA, DO 35/5208.

93. 20 January 1955, Cabinet conclusions, and record of conversation with Boland, 24 January 1955, TNA, PREM 11/923.

94. Quoted in Kennedy, Michael, *Division and consensus*, p. 155.

95. 17 February 1955, Maginess statement, NAI, S 9561 E.

96. 18 February 1955, Taoiseach's statement, JACP, P190/631.

97. *The Leader*, 26 February 1955.

98. Quoted in Patterson, p. 154.

99. 18 April 1955, diary entry, UCDA, P122/85. Moynihan said this money was coming from "SS", presumably a reference to the Secret Service vote.

100. 19 April 1955 and 22 April 1955, diary entries, UCDA, P122/85.

101. 22 April 1955, Government decision, NAI, S 9361 E.

102. 9 November 1955, Embassy report on Clann na Poblachta convention, USNA, RG 84, Dublin Security Segregated Report, Box 21, 350: IRA—Partition.

103. See exchange in TNA, CAB 21/4407.

104. *II*, 28 and 29 November 1955.

105. 2 December 1955, T.J. Coyne to Costello, NAI, S 9361 F.

106. 4 December 1955, Abbeyfeale speech, JACP, P190/641.

107. 28 November 1955, Irish Times editorial.

108. 29 November 1955, Cabinet minutes, NAI, S 11564 C.

109. 30 November 1955, statement to Dáil, JACP, P190/639.

110. 1 December 1955, McQuaid to Costello, NAI, S 9361 E.

111. 1 December 1955, Taft to Secretary of State, and 30 December 1955, La Freniere to Department of State, USNA, RG 84, Dublin Security Segregated Reports, Box 21, 350: IRA—Partition.

112. 2 December 1955, fortnightly summary, TNA, DO 35/5291.

113. 19 January 1956, Cabinet conclusions, PRONI, CAB/4/1028.

114. Edmonds, Sean, *The gun, the law and the Irish people*, p. 189.

115. *The Leader*, Christmas 1955.

116. DÉD, 19 April 1939, Vol 75, Col. 730.

117. 6 December 1955, note of meeting with editors, NAI, S 9361 F.

118. 28 March 1951, Moynihan note, referring to an earlier (unsuccessful) attempt to stop publication of material tending to glorify the IRA, NAI, S 11564 B.

119. 23 January 1958, speech in Jury's Hotel, JACP, P190/935.

120. Bell, J. Bowyer, *The Secret Army*, p. 276.

121. 27 July 1956, Rodgers to Costello; 4 August 1956, Moynihan note; 14 August 1956, Costello to McQuaid; 16 August 1956, McQuaid to Costello; NAI, S 16073 A.

122. 9 November 1956, McQuaid to Costello, JACP, P190/704.

123. 17 October 1956, MacEoin to Costello, JACP, P190/826.

124. 12 December 1956, McQuaid to Costello, JACP, P190/816.

125. 28 September 1955, IP.

126. 4 October 1955, Cremin to Costello, JACP, P 190/694.

127. Keogh, *Twentieth Century Ireland*, p. 227.

128. Cooney, John, *John Charles McQuaid*, p. 311.

129. Coyne to Costello, undated, JACP, P190/704.

130. Undated note, NAI, S 2321B.

131. 16 August 1956, FitzGerald to Costello, in possession of Jacqueline and Fergus Armstrong.

132. 20 February 1958, Minister for Justice memorandum for Government, NAI, S 2321B.

133. 4 February 1958, Traynor to de Valera, NAI, S 2321 B.

134. 13 February 1958, note on file, NAI, S 2321 B.

135. Girvin, Brian, "Church, state and the moral community", in Girvin and Murphy (eds), p. 138.

136. See NAI, S 14815 A/1 to C for the background to the scheme.

137. 19 January 1955, note of discussion, NAI, S 14815 C.

138. Manning, p. 299.

139. 30 July 1955, D/T, JACP, P190/706.

140. 28 April 1955, Costello to Tierney, NAI, S 14815 C.

141. 25 July 1955, Costello to Walsh, NAI, S 14815 D.

142. 27 July 1955, Costello to D'Alton, NAI, S 14815 D.

143. 2 August 1955, Walsh to Costello, NAI, S 14815 E.

144. 30 July 1955, Browne to Costello, JACP, P 190/706.

145. 2 August 1955, Costello to de Valera, NAI, S 14815 E.

146. 4 August 1955, Moynihan to Nagle, NAI, S 14815 E.

147. 14 August 1955, Muintir na Tíre speech, JACP, P190/636.

148. 16 August 1955, note on meeting in Taoiseach's office with delegation from UCG, JACP, P190/706.

149. IT, 17 September 1955.

150. 18 September 1955, Sutton to Costello, JACP, P190/695.

151. 24 September 1955, Dillon to Costello, JACP, P190/695.

152. 18 October 1955, Fergus to Costello, NAI, S 14815F.

153. 21 October 1955, notes by Taoiseach, JACP, P190/706.

154. 2 November 1955, Nolan note, NAI, S 14815G.

155. 4 November 1955, Costello to Fergus, NAI, S 14815G.

156. 5 November 1955, McQuaid to Costello, NAI, S 14815G.

157. 19 January 1956, Fergus to Costello, NAI, S 14815G.

158. 25 January 1956, Moynihan note, NAI, S 14815G.

159. 18 May 1956, JACP, P190/814.

160. Undated memorandum on policy, JACP, P190/713.

161. 26 October 1956, draft heads of Agricultural Institute Bill, JACP, P190/706.

162. 2 November 1956, Costello to de Valera, JACP, P190/837.

163. 11 November 1956, McQuaid to Costello, JACP, P190/816.

164. 26 November 1956, William Taft to Dillon, JACP, P190/706; 7 November 1957, Minister for Agriculture memorandum for Government, NAI, S 14815I.

165. 8 February 1957, Nolan note, NAI, S 14815H.

166. 1 October 1957, MacNeely and Fergus to de Valera, NAI, S 14815H.

167. 16 October 1957, Moynihan note, NAI, S 14815 H.

168. 28 March 1957, Dillon confidential memorandum, JACP, P190/706.

169. See S 14470 D.

170. Interview with Richie Ryan.

171. 9 December 1954, M/J memorandum for Government, NAI, S 15782.

172. See DÉD, Vol. 147, 1 December 1954 and 24 November 1954.

173. 13 April 1956, Costello to Boris Kostelanetz, JACP, P190/788.

174. 18 November 1954, Little to Costello, Arts Council, 2609/1951/1.

175. Kennedy, *Dreams and Responsibilities*, p. 114.

176. 10 January 1951, Little to Bodkin, JACP, P190/408.

177. 15 January 1955, Costello to Bodkin, JACP, P190/408.

178. 19 April 1955, Costello to Bodkin, JACP, P190/408.

179. 4 June 1955, Costello to Bodkin, JACP, P190/813.

180. 17 December 1956, Costello to Sweetman, JACP, P190/837.

181. DÉD, 10 May 1960, Vol. 181, Col. 953.

182. DÉD, 22 June 1960, Vol. 183, Col. 210.

183. 12 May 1967, Lynch to Costello, JACP, P190/973.

184. 15 December 1958, O Faolain to Costello, JACP, P190/731.

185. 20 December 1956, Bodkin to McQuaid, Bodkin Papers, TCDA, Ms 7003/273a.

186. Kennedy, p. 117.

187. 20 December 1956, Costello to McQuaid, and 23 December 1956, McQuaid note, in DDA, AB8/b/XVIII—Government; Mr John A. Costello (second coalition period) 1954–7.

188. Horgan, p. 260.

189. See *IT*, 2 November 1956 and 27 December 1956.

190. 1 January 1957, M/J memorandum for Government, NAI, S 16116.

191. Interview with Richie Ryan.

192. 4 January 1957, Government decision, NAI, S 16116.

193. *II*, 10 March 1948.

194. 20 March 1948, Det Garda Thomas Boyle report, with note by Berry, NAI, 97/9/825.

195. 23 March 1948, Moynihan note, NAI, 97/9/825.

196. 13 July 1956, Cork speech, JACP, P190/659.

197. 26 November 1955, Rathkeale speech, JACP, P190/640.

198. 11 December 1955, Askeaton speech, JACP, P190/642.

199. Newcastle West speech, *II*, 28 November 1955.

200.Rafter, Kevin, *The Clann*, pp 170/1.

201. 1 March 1956, statement on by-election result, JACP, P190/650.

202. *The Leader*, 10 March 1956.

Chapter 12 We must have friends (pp 323–342)

1. April 1956, draft memorandum for Government, JACP, P190/900.

2. Undated letter from Jackie Kennedy to Costello, JACP, P190/960.

3. See addendum to draft resolution proposed by P.J. Little, JACP, P190/571.

4. Correspondence with John Costello.

5. 27 March 1956, John J. Hall to Costello, NAI, S 16021 C.

6. Declan Costello interview.

7. 23 April 1966, Lewis to Costello, JACP, P190/960.

8. Mick Kilkenny interview.

9. Appreciation of Father Leonard for 1966 *All Hallows Annual*, JACP, P190/960.

10. Cooney, *McQuaid*, p. 341.

11. Interview with Delcan Costello.

12. Family source.

13. 23 April 1966, Lewis to Costello, JACP, P190/960.

14. 11 November 1955, Lewis to Costello, NAI, S 16021 A.

15. The postgraduate students who benefited from the scholarships in his name used the nickname, but not to his face! Information from Patrick Russell.

16. Lewis, W.S., *One Man's Education*, p. 107.

17. Ibid., p. 320.

18. Ibid., p. 235.

19. Bradford, Sarah, *America's Queen*, pp 39/40.

20. Bradford, p. 62. The Taoiseach is misnamed "Patrick Costello" in this book.

21. Appreciation of Father Leonard for 1966 *All Hallows Annual,* JACP, P190/960.

22. Lewis, p. 235.

23. Dallek, Robert, *John F. Kennedy*, pp 192 and 194.

24. *IT*, 1 October 1955.

25. Declan Costello interview.

26. 29 April 1966, Jackie Kennedy to Costello, JACP, P190/960.

27. Appreciation of Father Leonard for 1966 All Hallows Annual, JACP, P190/960.

28. Undated letter from Jackie Kennedy to Costello, JACP, P190/960.

29. 9 November 1955, Griswold to Costello, NAI, S 16021 A.

30. 11 November 1955, Lewis to Costello, NAI, S 16021 A.

31. 3 December 1955, Costello to Griswold, NAI, S 16021 A.

32. 3 December 1955, Costello to Lewis, NAI, S 16021 A.

33. 13 January 1956, Jim Farley to Costello, NAI, S 16021 A.

34. 5 January 1956, Costello to Hearne, NAI, S 16021 A.

35. 18 January 1956, Hearne cable to D/EA, NAI, S 16021 A.

36. 23 January 1956, Murphy record of phone call to Hearne, NAI, S 16021 A.

37. 2 February 1956, Norton to Costello, NAI, S 16021 A.

38. 5 January 1956, Costello to Hearne, NAI, S 16021 A.

39. 16 January 1956, Taft to Costello, NAI, S 16021 A.

40. 6 February 1956, Costello to Hearne, JACP, P190/834.

41. 6 February 1956, Costello to Lewis, JACP, P190/834.

42. 13 February 1956, Lewis to Costello, NAI, S 16021 A.

43. 15 March 1956, Nolan to Aer Lingus, NAI, S 15987.

44. State Department programme for visit, JACP, P190/852.

45. 24 February 1956, Hearne to Costello, JACP, P190/859.

46. *II*, 29 March 1956. This must have included some shopping—his granddaughter Jacqueline Armstrong recalls him bringing her home two dresses from this trip.

47. *New York Times*, 15 March 1956. Unless otherwise stated, details of the visit are based on a State Department programme for the visit, giving times and dates of events, JACP, P190/852.

48. Black, Conrad, *Richard Milhous Nixon*, p. 303.

49. New York Times, 15 March 1956.

50. 14 March 1956, Eisenhower appointment books, Jan–June 1956, Eisenhower Presidential Library.

51. Menu in White House Social Office records, Box 54, Eisenhower Presidential Library.

52. Memorandum for Government on trip, JACP, P190/865.

53. 14 March 1956, Eisenhower appointment books, Jan–June 1956, Eisenhower Presidential Library.

54. *SI*, 25 March 1956.

55. 14 March 1956, Bowen to Costello, NAI, S 16021 B.

56. *Washington Star*, 11 March 1956.

57. *NYT*, 15 March 1956.

58. 18 March 1956, "Some West Point Cadets" to Costello, NAI, S 16021 C.

59. Undated newspaper cutting, by George Dixon, JACP, P190/852.

60. 3 May 1956, Frank Holman, President of the National Press Club, to Costello, JACP, P190/816.

61. *IT*, 16 March 1956.

62. 30 April 1956, Memorandum for Government, JACP, P190/865.

63. *NYT*, 16 March 1956.

64. 6 February 1956, Costello to Hearne, JACP, P190/834.

65. *NYT*, 16 March 1956.

66. 30 April 1956, Memorandum for Government, JACP, P190/865.

67. April 1956, draft memorandum, JACP, P190/900.

68. 21 March 1954, Walshe to Nunan, NAI, S 15291.

69. *II* and *IT*, 18 March 1952.

70. 1 May 1953, Nunan to Secretary, Department of the Taoiseach, NAI, S 15291.

71. 17 March 1953, Eisenhower to O'Kelly, NAI, S 15291—Eisenhower wrongly assumed the gift had been sent by the President of Ireland, rather than the Government.

72. 24 March 1969, William P. Fay to D/EA, NAI, S 15291.

73. *IP*, 17 March 1956.

74. 16 March 1956, Eisenhower appointment books, Jan–June 1956, Eisenhower Presidential Library.

75. 30 April 1956, Memorandum on trip, JACP, P190/865.

76. 16 March 1956, Eisenhower to Costello, JACP, P190/852.

77. April 1956, draft memorandum for government, JACP, P190/900.

78. 30 April 1956, Memorandum on trip, JACP, P190/865.

79. April 1956, draft memorandum on trip, JACP, P190/900.

80. Quoted in Keogh, Dermot, *Twentieth-Century Ireland*, pp 231/2.

81. 14 February 1956, Hoover to Eisenhower, Records as President (White House Central Files), Official File, Box 870, OF 183-5 Ireland (2), Eisenhower Library.

82. 7 March 1956, Garrett to Eisenhower, loc. cit.

83. 18 March 1956, *NYT*.

84. April 1956, draft memorandum on trip, JACP, P190/900.

85. Skelly, Joseph Morrison, *Irish Diplomacy at the United Nations*, pp 35/6.

86. 16 October 1956, Griswold to Costello, NAI, S 16021 D.

87. 30 April 1956, Memorandum on trip, JACP, P190/865.

88. *IP*, 19 March 1956.

89. April 1956, draft memorandum on trip, JACP, P190/900.

90. *Yale Alumni Magazine*, May 1956.

91. *Yale Alumni Magazine* online, http://www.yalealumnimagazine.com/issues/99_03/speakers.html

92. 7 March 1956, Hearne to Secretary, D/EA, NAI, S 16021B.

93. April 1956, draft memorandum on trip, JACP, P190/900.

94. May 1956, *Yale Alumni Magazine*.

95. *EP*, 21 March 1956.

96. 30 April 1956, Memorandum for Government, JACP, P190/865.

97. See correspondence in NAI, S 16022 A, and note of 17 May 1965 in the continuation of the file, 96/6/765.

98. 15 February 1956, record of conversation between J. Alfred LaFreniere, US Embassy Dublin, and Wilfred Lennon, D/EA, USNA, RG 59, State Department records, 1955–59, Central Decimal File, Box No. 2977, 611.40A97/2-1756; 13 April 1956, address to inaugural meeting of Atomic Energy Committee, JACP, P190/652.

99. 23 February 1956, Hearne to Costello, JACP, P190/858.

100. 30 April 1956, Memorandum for Government on trip, JACP, P190/865.

101. 28 March 1956, *Cork Examiner* and *Irish Times*.

102. DÉD, 17 April 1956, Vol. 156, Cols. 409–10.

103. April 1956, draft memorandum for Government, JACP, P190/900.

104. 13 March 1956, Fisher Howe, State, to Colonel Goodpaster, White House, Eisenhower Papers as President, 53–61, International Series, Box 32, Ireland (2).

105. Geiger, Till, "A belated discovery of internationalism", in Kennedy and McMahon (eds), *Obligations and Responsibilities*, p. 31.

106. O'Halpin, Eunin, *Defending Ireland*, p. 185.

107. 27 January 1945, Churchill to Roosevelt, USNA, RG 59 Department of State, Decimal File 1945–9, Vox 3289, 711.41D27/1-2945.

108. Girvin, Brian, *The Emergency*, p. 317.

109. 24 March 1948, Moreland to Washington, USNA, RG 59, Decimal File 1945–9, Box 3289, 711.41D/3-2448.

110. 29 September 1949, Garrett to Department of State, USNA, RG 59, Department of State Decimal File 1945–9, Box 3289, 711.41D27/10/1949.

111. 14 October 1949, Garrett to Secretary of State, USNA, RG 84, Dublin Legation Security Segregated Reports, 1936–49, Box 18, 320.12.

112. Dublin Legation to Department of State, USNA, RG 59, Department of State Decimal File 1945–9, Box 3289, 711.41D27/10-1149.

113. 15 April 1956, Hearne to Costello, "Secret. For the Taoiseach Only", JACP, P190/822.

114. 8 September 1956, Costello to Taft, JACP, P190/836.

115. 31 March 1956, Costello telegram to Eisenhower, Eisenhower Presidential Library, Records as President (White House Central Files), Official File, Box 870, OF 183–5 Ireland (2).

116. 11 April 1956, Eisenhower to Costello, Eisenhower Presidential Library, Papers as President, 53–61, International Series, Box 32, Ireland (2).

117. Sweetman comments on memorandum, JACP, P190/901.

118. 18 May 1956, Nolan to Secretary of each Department, NAI, S 2850 C.

119. April 1956, draft memorandum for Government, JACP, P190/900.

120. 6 August 1956, FitzGerald to Costello, letter in possession of Fergus and Jacqueline Armstrong.

121. Quoted in Collins, Stephen, *The Cosgrave Legacy*, p. 74.

122. Skelly, Joseph Morrison, *Irish Diplomacy at the United Nations*, pp 39 and 31.

123. 19 July 1956, Costello to McQuaid, DDA, AB8/b/XVIII—Government.

124. 25 September 1956, Costello to Síle Ní Lionnáin, JACP, P190/836.

125. Cosgrave quoted in Collins, p. 75.

126. 21 November 1956, Taft to Secretary of State, USNA, RG 84, Dublin Legation Security Segregated Records, Box 23, 313: United Nations, 1956.

127. 13 November 1956, Cosgrave to Costello, JACP, P190/746.

128. 3 December 1956, Boland to Murphy, JACP, P190/694.

129. DÉD, 28 November 1957, Vol. 164, Col. 1224.

Chapter 13 Something is wrong with the country (pp 343–371)

1. 27 April 1956, Costello to McQuaid, DDA, McQuaid Papers, AB8/B/XVIII—Government, John A. Costello (second coalition period).

2. Undated Costello memorandum, JACP, P190/713.

3. 9 April 1956, Costello to McQuaid, DDA, McQuaid Papers, AB8/B/XVIII—Government, John A. Costello (second coalition period).

4. 11 April 1956, McQuaid to Costello, JACP, P190/816.

5. 16 July 1956, Costello to Everett, JACP, P190/820.

6. Interview with Declan Costello; interview with Richie Ryan.

7. 19 April 1956, Costello to Eisenhower, JACP, P190/835.

8. Medical information from death certificate in the General Registry Office.

9. 27 April 1956, Costello to McQuaid, DDA, McQuaid Papers, AB8/B/XVIII—Government, John A. Costello (second coalition period).

10. 21 April 1956, Eisenhower telegram to Costello, and reply, 12 May 1956, Eisenhower Presidential Library, Papers as President, 53–61, International Series, Box 32, Ireland (2). The list of sympathisers in Costello's papers ran to 102 pages. JACP, P190/961.

11. Interview with Richie Ryan.

12. Interview with Mick Kilkenny.

13. Correspondence with John Costello.

14. 18 June 1956, O'Brien to Costello, JACP, P190/828.

15. 4 June 1956, Costello to Bill Taft, JACP, P190/835, and 22 August 1956, Costello to Cremin, JACP, P190/818.

16. 5 February 1957, Costello to B. O'Reilly, JACP, P190/838.

17. 24 January 1957, Costello to Mrs M. Doyle, JACP, P190/838.

18. 21 January 1957, Costello to Mrs Claire Kennedy, JACP, P190/838.

19. Costello to Tommy Robinson, JACP, P190/838.

20. Interview with Kyran FitzGerald.

21. Interview with Jacqueline Armstrong.

22. Dillon memoir, p. 82, quoted in Manning, p. 310.

23. Interview with Declan Costello.

24. Interview with Richie Ryan.

25. Puirséil, p. 350.

26. 12 March 1956, M/F memo for Government, NAI, S 16046 A.

27. P. Honohan and C. Ó Gráda, "The Irish macroeconomic crisis of 1955–56", in *Irish Economic and Social History*, 1998, p. 55.

28. 20 January 1956, McElligott to Sweetman, JACP, P190/708.

29. 21 March 1956, Nolan note, NAI, S 16046 A.

30. 26 April 1956, Costello to Hugh W. Kennedy, JACP, P190/835.

31. 23 February 1956, Clutterbuck to Laithwaite, CRO, TNA, DO 35/5194.

32. DÉD, 17 May 1956, Vol. 157, Col 638.

33. Puirséil, p. 188.

34. *IT*, 2 June 1956.

35. 21 June 1956, PUTU memorandum for Government, NAI, S 13965 G.

36. 13 July 1956, speech opening Cork by-election campaign, JACP, P190/659.

37. *NYT*, 29 July 1956.

38. Estimates speech, JACP, P190/657.

39. 20 July 1956, D/F circular, NAI, S 16046 A.

40. 24 July 1956, Government decision, NAI, S 1646 A.

41. *The Leader*, 4 August 1956.

42. 1 August 1956, eve of by-election speech, JACP, P190/662.

43. *II*, 4 August 1956.

44. 28 November 1956, Clutterbuck to Murphy, JACP, P190/729.

45. Interview with Declan Costello.

46. Interview with T.K. Whitaker.

47. *IP*, 27 September 1956.

48. See NAI, S 16046 B for decision on further levies, and text of Sweetman speech, 16 October 1956.

49. 19 September 1956, Minister for Finance memo for Government, NAI, S 16075 A.

50. DÉD, 26 April 1961, Vol. 188, Col. 1167, and 20 February 1963, Vol. 200, Col. 154.

51. Lindsay, p. 167.

52. O'Higgins, T.F., *A Double Life*, p. 185.

53. Undated memorandum, "Policy: items for discussion and decision", JACP, P190/713.

54. 16 August 1956, FitzGerald to Costello, letter in possession of Jacqueline and Fergus Armstrong.

55. Ibid.

56. 8 December 1969, Costello speech to retirement function, JACP, P 190/350.

57. FitzGerald, Garret, *All in a life*, pp 363/4.

58. Undated and unsigned memo (the contents indicate it was by Costello), JACP, P190/713.

59. Policy memorandum, JACP, P190/713.

60. M/EA memorandum, JACP, P190/713. The first quoted sentence was written in capital letters in Cosgrave's memorandum.

61. AG memorandum, JACP, P190/713.

62. 4 October 1956, Government decision, NAI, S 16095A.

63. Text of speech, JACP, P190/668.

64. *IT*, 6 October 1956.

65. 11 October 1956, fortnightly summary, TNA, DO 35/5291.

66. *II*, *IP* and *IT*, 6 October 1956.

67. Garvin, Tom, *Preventing the future*, p. 247.

68. 24 September 1956, Moynihan note, NAI, S 16095A.

69. 2 February 1957, D/F memo, NAI, S 16095B.

70. 12 May 1967, Lynch to Costello, JACP, P190/973.

71. 15 January 1957, Norton to Costello, NAI, S 2950 D.

72. 28 May 1957, Lemass speech to Dublin Chamber of Commerce, NAI, S 2850 D.

73. 19 October 1956, Government decision, NAI, S 15725 A.

74. 22 January 1957, first report of Capital Investment Advisory Committee, NAI, S 15725 B.

75. DÉD, 3 May 1962, Vol. 195, Col. 179.

76. Quoted in McCarthy, 'Ireland's turnaround' in McCarthy, John F. (ed.), *Planning Ireland's Future*, pp 68/9.

77. Telephone conversation with Liam Cosgrave, 28 November 2009.

78. Feeney, *MacEntee*, p. 201.

79. Fanning, *Finance*, pp 403/4.

80. Horgan, *Lemass*, p. 176.

81. 14 September 1956, Whitaker to Sweetman, quoted in Garvin, *Preventing the Future*, p. 233.

82. Garvin, *Preventing the Future*, p. 233.

83. Murphy, Gary, "From Economic Nationalism to European Union", in Girvin and Murphy (eds), p. 29.

84. Interview with T.K. Whitaker.

85. Whitaker, T.K., *Protection or Free Trade*, p. 8.

86. Horgan, *Lemass*, p. 167.

87. *The Leader*, 26 January 1957.

88. 16 August 1956, FitzGerald to Costello, letter in possession of Jacqueline and Fergus Armstrong.

89. 8 October 1956, Costello to Mulcahy, JACP, P190/700.

90. 20 September 1956, Everett to Costello, JACP, P190/704.

91. Sheehy Skeffington, *Skeff*, pp 172/3.

92. 9 October 1956, Mulcahy to Costello, JACP, P190/700.

93. *IT*, 1 October 1956.

94. *IT*, 4 October 1956.

95. 8 October 1956, Costello to Mulcahy, JACP, P190/700.

96. Undated memorandum, JACP, P190/700.

97. 4 November 1956, Mooncoin speech, JACP, P190/670.

98. 4 November 1956, Glenmore speech, JACP, P190/671.

99. 9 November 1956, Kilkenny speech, JACP, P190/673.

100. 6 November 1956, Dublin SW speech, JACP, P190/672.

101. 20 November 1956, Rathmines speech, JACP, P190/677.

102. 3 December 1956, Costello to Bodkin, JACP, P190/813.

103. Memoranda dates 17 November 1956 and 27 November 1956, in UCDA, P35/b/58.

104. 12 January 1957, MacBride to Costello, UCDA, P35/c/193.

105. 19 March 1957, Carroll to Sec, D/J, JACP, P190/708.

106. *IT* and *II*, 12 November 1956.

107. See Kennedy, Michael, *Division and Consensus*, pp 162/3.

108. 14 December 1956, Government statement, NAI, S 11564 C.

109. *IT*, 15 December 1956.

110. *SI*, 16 December 1956.

111. Bell, J. Bowyer, *The Secret Army*, p. 300.

112. 17 December 1956, Taft to Secretary of State, USNA, RG 84, Dublin Legation Security Segregated Records, Box 23, 350: IRA, Partition.

113. 21 December 1956, LaFreniere to Secretary of State, USNA, RG 84, Dublin Legation Security Segregated Records, Box 23, 350: IRA, Partition.

114. 19 December 1956, extract from Hansard, in NAI, S 11564 D.

115. 21 December 1956, La Freniere to Secretary of State, reporting Taft's conversation with Costello, USNA, RG 84, Dublin Embassy Security Segregated Records, Box 23, 350: IRA, Partition.

116. 24 December 1956, Aide-memoire to British Government, JACP, P190/763.

117. 29 January 1957, Minister for External Affairs memorandum for the Government, UCDA, P151/531. The memorandum is wrongly dated January 1956, but refers to newspaper reports from December 1956, so obviously was written in January 1957.

118. Staunton, Enda, *The Nationalists of Northern Ireland*, p. 216.

119. 13 February 1957, H.J.B. Lintott, CRO, to Clutterbuck, TNA, DO 35/5195.

120. 2 February 1957, Cabinet minutes, NAI, S 9361 F.

121. 3 June 1957, David Cole, CRO, to Philip de Zuletta, Downing Street, TNA, PREM 1/1901.

122. 16 April 1957, Taoiseach memo for government, NAI, S 16220.

123. 17 July 1957, handwritten note by Macmillan, TNA, PREM 11/1901.

124. 18 December 1956, Costello to McQuillan, JACP, P190/837.

125. *II*, 31 December 1956.

126. *II*, 2 January 1957

127. Kennedy, *Division and Consensus*, p. 163.

128. Currie, Austin, *All Hell Will Break Loose*, p. 32.

129. 3 January 1957, McQuillan and Finnucane telegram to Costello, NAI, S 11564 D.

130. *II*, 3 January 1957.

131. 4 January 1957, Costello to McQuillan and Finucane, NAI, S 11564D.

132. 21 January 1957, Costello to Pearse Morris, JACP, P190/825.

133. 6 January 1957, text of broadcast, JACP, P190/683.

134. 7 January 1957, Ambassador to Secretary, NAI, S 11564 D.

135. 8 February 1957, Costello to Michael Heffernan, JACP, P190/838.

136. Interview with Richie Ryan.

137. See Bell, p. 300; Kennedy, *Division and Consensus*, pp 163/4, and Feeney, Brian, *Sinn Féin*, p. 205.

138. 3 March 1957, Athlone speech, JACP, P190/310.

139. 19 March 1957, Carroll to Secretary, D/J, JACP, P190/708.

140. Edmonds, introduction and p. 196.

141. NAI, 2001/6/244.

142. Feeney, *Sinn Féin*, p. 208.

143. 14 January 1957, interview with Canadian Broadcasting Corporation, JACP, P190/687.

144. Horgan, *Lemass*, p. 173.

145. 16 January 1957, Costello to Breen, JACP, P190/838.

146. Bell, p. 303; Rafter, p. 172.

147. 28 January 1957, notice of motion, NAI, S 16170.

148. 30 January 1957, MacBride statement, UCDA, P104/1528.

149. 26 January 1957 (the document may be incorrectly dated), Ard Comhairle statement, NAI, S 16170

150. Stanford, William Bedell, *Memoirs,* p. 145.

151. 8 February 1957, Costello to MacBride, JACP, P190/838.

152. 31 January 1957, Clutterbuck to CRO, TNA, DO 35/5195.

153. Dillon memoir, p. 82, quoted in Manning, p. 311.

154. 2 July 1956, Finucane to Costello, JACP, P190/724.

155. Notes on Dáil numbers, NAI, S 16170.

156. 29 January 1957, notice of motion by de Valera, NAI, S 16170.

157. 18 February 1957, Clutterbuck to Lord Home, TNA, DO 35/5195.

158. 4 February 1957, GIB statement, NAI, S 16170.

159. 6 February 1957, Ard Fheis speech, JACP, P190/758.

160. 13 February 1957, H.J.B. Lintott, CRO, to Clutterbuck, TNA, DO 35/5195.

161. 9 November 1956, Government decision; 4 January 1957, M/F memo for Government; 24 January 1957, Government decision, NAI, S 16075 A.

162. 15 February 1957, Cork speech, JACP, P190/310.

163. *IP,* 25 February 1957.

164. 14 March 1957, Costello to Courtney, JACP, P190/838.

165. 15 February 1957, Cork speech, JACP, P190/310.

166. 13 February 1957, Mills Hall speech, JACP, P190/310.

167. 22 February 1957, Ballyshannon speech, JACP, P190/310.

168. *IP,* 19 February 1957.

169. *IP,* 26 February 1957.

170. *IP,* 16 February 1957.

171. 20 February 1957, Mallow speech, reproduced in Ferriter, Diarmaid, *Judging Dev,* p. 119.

172. 22 February 1957, Ballyshannon speech, JACP, P190/310.

173. *IP,* 26 February 1957.

174. 27 February 1957, Tralee speech, JACP, P190/310.

175. 2 March 1957, Galway speech, JACP, P190/310.

176. *IP,* 14 February 1957.

177. 15 February 1957, Cork speech, JACP, P190/310.

178. 19 February 1957, Ringsend speech, JACP, P190/310.

179. 22 February 1957, Costello to Michael MacWhite, JACP, P190/838.

180. 1 March 1957, radio broadcast, JACP, P190/310.

181. Horgan, *Browne,* p. 187.

182. 23 March 1957, Clutterbuck to Home, TNA, DO 35/5195.

183. *The Leader,* 16 March 1957.

184. Lindsay, pp 171/2.

185. 11 March 1957, Costello to McQuaid, DDA, McQuaid Papers, AB8/b/XVIII— Government; Mr John A. Costello (second coalition period), 1954–7.

186. 14 March 1957, Costello to Professor Desmond Williams, JACP, P190/838.
187. 15 March 1957, Costello to McQuaid, DDA, McQuaid Papers, AB8/b/XVIII—Government; Mr John A. Costello (second coalition period), 1954–7.
188. DÉD, 20 March 1957, Vol 161, Cols. 17/8 and 26.
189. DÉD, 20 March 1957, Vol. 161, Cols. 30 and 32.
190. 14 March 1957, Costello to Professor Desmond Williams, JACP, P190/838.
191. Puirséil, p. 203.

Chapter 14 A perfectly happy man (pp 372–408)

1. 14 December 1959, Costello to Father Patrick O'Carroll, California, JACP, P190/924.
2. 8 December 1969, Costello speech to retirement function, JACP, P 190/350.
3. *IT*, 2 November 1974, "Saturday Interview".
4. 25 March 1957, Costello to Miss E. Dodd, JACP, P190/838.
5. Interview with Tom Finlay.
6. 30 August 1957, Costello to Bodkin, TCD, Bodkin Papers, Ms 7003/290.
7. 24 September 1957, Ita McCoy to Con Cremin, JACP, P190/908.
8. 4 September 1957, Costello to P. Kehoe, Office of the Revenue Commissioners, JACP, P190/913.
9. 10 May 1957, Budget broadcast text, JACP, P190/796.
10. DÉD, 14 May 1957, Vol. 161, Col 1136.
11. 5 February 1958, Ard Fheis speech, JACP, P190/315.
12. DÉD, 3 July 1957, Vol. 163, Cols. 632 and 636.
13. DÉD, 4 July 1957, Vol. 163, Col. 792.
14. DÉD, 13 March 1958, Vol. 166, Cols. 229 to 230.
15. McCarthy, 'Ireland's turnaround' in McCarthy (ed.), *Planning Ireland's Future*, p. 29.
16. Interview with T.K. Whitaker.
17. DÉD, 28 April 1959, Vol. 174, Col. 1148.
18. DÉD, 23 June 1959, Vol. 176, Col. 96.
19. DÉD, 21 July 1959, Vol. 176, Cols 1592/3.
20. John Bradley, "The Legacy of Economic Development", in McCarthy (ed.), p. 132.
21. Ronan Fanning, "The Genesis of Economic Development", in McCarthy (ed.), p. 104.
22. Quoted in Ronan Fanning, "Alexis FitzGerald", in Lynch, Patrick and Meenan, James (eds), *Essays in Memory of Alexis FitzGerald*, p. 10.
23. 24 November 1959, Hayes to O'Higgins, UCDA, P53/270.
24. 25 April 1959, Bishop Browne to Costello; 29 April 1959, FitzGerald to Costello; 2 May 1959, Costello to Browne. Correspondence in possession of Kyran FitzGerald.
25. "One to One" interview with Declan Costello, RTÉ 1 television, 14 September 2009.
26. *The Leader*, 8 February 1958.

27. 1 February 1958, Costello to FitzGerald; 10 February 1958, FitzGerald to Mrs McCoy; 20 April 1958, Sunday Review article; JACP, P190/920.

28. FitzGerald, Garret, *All in a life*, p. 127.

29. 11 March 1958, Costello to Mrs McCoy, JACP, P190/811. He wasn't joking, either. There are many examples in his private papers of notes which are utterly unintelligible.

30. 8 December 1969, Costello speech to retirement function, JACP, P 190/350.

31. DÉD, 4 July 1957, Vol 163, Col 805.

32. Harte, Paddy, *Young Tigers and Mongrel Foxes*, pp 95/6.

33. Manning, p. 314.

34. Ibid, p. 318.

35. 29 September 1957, Dillon speech, Ballybay, JACP, P190/321.

36. 17 October 1957, Dublin North Central by-election speech, JACP, P190/933.

37. *IT*, 16 November 1957.

38. *The Leader*, 12 July 1958.

39. DÉD, 1 June 1937, Vol. 67, Cols. 1341–5.

40. DÉD, 12 November 1958, Vol. 171, Cols 613 to 618.

41. DÉD, 26 November 1958, Vol. 171, Cols 1007, 1017 and 1023.

42. DÉD, 28 January 1959, Vol. 172, Col. 1270.

43. DÉD, 25 February 1959, Vol. 173, Col. 156.

44. 23 November 1958, Carlow speech, JACP, P190/947.

45. 7 December 1958, Navan speech, JACP, P190/948.

46. 11 February 1959, Ard Fheis speech, JACP, P190/315.

47. 25 April 1959, Cork speech, JACP, P190/949.

48. 12 June 1959, text of broadcast, JACP, P190/952.

49. DÉD, 23 June 1959, Vol. 176, Cols. 2 and 4.

50. Interview with Declan Costello.

51. Conversation with Harvey Kenny.

52. Interview with Ronan Keane.

53. 13 November 1958, Costello to Bodkin, TCD, Bodkin Papers, Ms 7003/283.

54. For his travel arrangements, see 9 March 1959, Ita McCoy to J.R. Miley, JACP, P190/918 and 12 March 1959, Ita McCoy to Terence de Vere White, JACP, P190/929; for Dáil business, see DÉD, Vol 173, 10 and 11 March 1959.

55. Note on conversation, September 1959, UCDA, P7/C/150.

56. Manning, pp 323/4.

57. Note on conversation, September 1959, UCDA, P7/C/150.

58. 6 October 1959. Lynch to Costello, JACP, P190/953.

59. Manning, p. 325.

60. Collins, Stephen, *The Cosgrave Legacy*, p. 78.

61. Interview with Declan Costello.

62. Interview with Mick Kilkenny.

63. 20 October 1959, Costello to Mulcahy, JACP, P190/953.

64. Manning, pp 326 and 327.

65. 8 March 1960, Kimber to Chadwick, and 22 March 1960, Clutterbuck note, TNA, DO 35/7941.

66. *IP*, 21 October 1959; O'Higgins, T.F., *A Double Life*, p. 188.

67. Puirséil, Niamh, *The Irish Labour Party*, p. 211.

68. 14 December 1959, Costello to Father Patrick O'Carroll, Riverside, California, JACP, P190/924.

69. 13 January 1960, Costello to Dillon, UCDA, Costello Papers, P190/340. In 1968, Whitaker managed to convince the Devlin Review of Public Service Organisation that the economic planning function should remain attached to the Department of Finance. It was, according to Ronan Fanning, an example of Whitaker's success as "an administrative conservative who not merely preserved the power of the Department of Finance but who established it on a firmer footing than before". Fanning, Ronan, "The Genesis of Economic Development" in McCarthy (ed.), p. 102.

70. *IT*, 2 May 1961.

71. 28 March 1960, Costello to Ryan, JACP, P190/340.

72. DÉD, 7 November 1967, Vol. 230, Cols. 2021/2.

73. DÉD, 13 November 1968, Vol. 237, Col. 231.

74. 24 February 1961, Costello to Deputy Mary Reynolds, JACP, P190/340.

75. 29 March 1960, Costello to Bernard Brady, JACP, P190/340.

76. DÉD, 29 May 1962, Vol. 195, Cols. 1687, 1684 and 1690; 18 May 1965, Vol. 215, Col. 1562.

77. Interview with Ronan Keane.

78. *IT*, 30 March 1960.

79. *IT*, 31 March 1960.

80. *IT*, 12 May 1960.

81. *IT*, 15 December 1961.

82. *IT*, 16 December 1961.

83. Correspondence with Michael V. O'Mahony.

84. Interview with Tom Finlay.

85. Interview with Mick Kilkenny.

86. Correspondence with Michael V. O'Mahony.

87. Interviews with Tom Finlay and Ronan Keane.

88. Conversation with Harvey Kenny.

89. Correspondence with Michael V. O'Mahony; interview with Ronan Keane—Mr Keane was also on the plaintiff's legal team.

90. Interview with Mick Kilkenny.

91. Correspondence with Georgina Sutton.

92. Correspondence with Isabelle Sutton.

93. *IT*, 2 March 1968.

94. Correspondence with Georgina Sutton.

95. Conversation with Harvey Kenny.

96. All references to the visit are from Costello's 15-page report, which he delivered to Dillon on 15 October 1960. JACP, P190/341.

97. Although their exchanges appear to have been entirely formal, Costello and Adenauer had quite a lot in common—both sons of civil servants who went to university on scholarships, they were devout Catholics who were widowed in office, in Adenauer's case twice. See Williams, Francis, *Adenauer, the Father of New Germany.*

98. See Horgan, *Noël Browne*, p. 210, for the suggestion about vote splitting with O'Donovan. With just over 11 per cent of the first-preference vote, the latter had his best ever vote in the constituency, which supports Horgan's belief. O'Donovan later joined Labour and was elected for Dublin South Central in 1969.

99. DÉD, 11 November 1961, Vol. 192, Cols. 62, 64 and 69.

100. DÉD, 3 May 1961, Vol. 188, Cols. 1605 and 1652.

101. DÉD, 3 December 1964, Vol. 213, Col. 485.

102. DÉD, 29 June 1965, Vol. 217 Col. 123.

103. *IT*, 6 January 1976.

104. 8 November 1966, Colm Condon to Costello, and reply 18 November 1966, JACP, P190/916.

105. Draft report, August 1968, NAI, 2002/16/227.

106. 18 August 1964, McQuillan to Costello, JACP, P190/923.

107. Puirséil, pp 234/5; MacDermott, note 60, p. 211.

108. DÉD, 30 January 1963, Vol. 199, Cols. 731 to 739.

109. DÉD, 16 July 1963, Vol. 204, Col. 969.

110. DÉD, 23 February 1965, Vol. 214, Col. 913.

111. Calculation from the Central Statistics Office.

112. DÉD, 18 May 1965, Vol. 215, Col. 1554.

113. DÉD, 23 February 1965, Vol. 214, Cols. 920 and 919.

114. "One to One" interview with Declan Costello.

115. 27 April 1964, Declan Costello to each member of the Fine Gael parliamentary party, UCDA, P151/812.

116. Interview with Mick Kilkenny.

117. Mair, Peter, *The changing Irish party system,* pp 184/5.

118. *The Citizen,* May 1967.

119. 8 December 1969, Costello speech to retirement function, JACP, P 190/350.

120. See correspondence with Alexis FitzGerald, JACP, P190/918.

121. O'Higgins, T.F., *A Double Life,* pp 194/5.

122. FitzGerald, Garret, *All in a life,* p. 74.

123. Interview with Alexis FitzGerald.

124. 16 September 1963, Costello to Matthew Byrne, JACP, P190/915.

125. DÉD, 23 February 1965, Vol. 214, Col. 914.

126. DÉD, 18 May 1965, Vol. 215, Col. 1552.

127. Harte, p. 101.

128. 17 September 1968, Four Courts Hotel speech, UCDA, P39/PR/128.

129. DÉD, 20 March 1968, Vol. 233, Col. 760.

130. See, for example, the copy sent to Archbishop McQuaid in February 1968, DDA, McQuaid Papers, AB8/b/XVIII—Government; Mr John A. Costello.

131. The correspondence is in JACP, P190/963.

132. See correspondence with David Harkness, JACP, P190/920; with A.S. Cohan, ibid., P190/916; with Brian Farrell, ibid., P190/918.

133. Brady, Conor, *Up With the Times*, p. 156.

134. Interview with Muiris Mac Conghail.

135. "Seven Days".

136. Interview with Muiris Mac Conghail.

137. 4 March 1969, Tony Keane to Costello, and reply, 5 March 1969, JACP, P190/921.

138. DÉD, 22 April 1969, Vol. 239, Col. 1875; 29 April 1969, Vol. 240, Col. 85.

139. *IT*, 26 April 1969.

140. *IT*, 26 April 1969.

141. 29 May 1969, Lynch speech in Mallow, NAI, 2001/6/12. I am grateful to Dr Elaine Byrne for this reference.

142. Interview with Alexis FitzGerald.

143. 11 June 1969, Sandymount Green speech, UCDA, P39/GE/162, document 43.

144. 4 July 1969, Alexis FitzGerald to Costello, JACP, P190/918.

145. 8 December 1969, Costello speech to retirement function, JACP, P190/350.

146. 1 August 1961, Costello to MacBride, JACP, P190/340.

147. 2 August 1961, Nolan to Costello, and 24 August 1961, MacBride to Costello, JACP, P190/799.

148. 17 July 1964, AG memo, NAI, 2003/16/605; 1 January 1965, Nolan to Committee members, and 13 January 1965, Costello to Nolan, JACP, P190/799.

149. 6 November 1969, Costello to Nolan, JACP, P190/799.

150. 26 October 1971, minutes of Committee meeting, NAI, 2003/16/605.

151. 8 November 1974, note on file, NAI, 2005/7/671.

152. 12 April 1972, MacEoin memorandum; 14 April 1972, Cosgrave to Costello; undated Costello memorandum; JACP, P190/812.

153. *IT*, 21 August 1972.

154. 20 August 1972, Béal na mBláth speech, JACP, P190/280.

155. Letters of congratulation, including Walsh to Costello, 19 June 1961, JACP, P190/915.

156. 31 October 1964, Stephen Barrett to Dermot Kinlen, JACP, P190/915.

157. Interview with Ronan Keane.

158. 18 April 1962, Costello to Cardinal Amleto Cicognani, JACP, P190/916.

159. The only living Irish politician to hold the honour is Liam Cosgrave. Information from Peter Durnin, Secretary, Papal Knights Association of Ireland.

160. 15 November 1961, Costello to Lemass; 7 December 1961, Costello to D'Alton; 7 December 1961, Costello to Barrett. JACP, P190/345.

161. See JACP, P190/346.

162. Interview with Declan Costello, 8 October 2007.

163. Interview with Kyran FitzGerald.

164. Reports of ceremony in *IT* and *IP* 8 March 1975.

165. 30 September 1970, Costello to Mike Burns, JACP, P190/915.

166. Quoted in *IT*, 5 September 1975. He had been equally critical of Lemass when he died, saying he was "ruthless in his efforts to achieve what he desired ... impatient of criticism and immune to logical argument", although he added that Lemass was also "a great debater, a forceful personality and a great leader of his party". 11 May 1971, RTÉ 1330 News.

167. 25 September 1975, Hickman to Harding, TNA, PREM 16/324.

168. De Valera, Terry, *A Memoir*, p. 205.

169. Interview with Tom Finlay.

170. De Valera, pp 205/6.

171. *IT*, 2 November 1974.

172. Interview with Jacqueline Armstrong.

173. Interview with Mick Kilkenny.

174. Correspondence with Georgina and Isabelle Sutton.

175. Interview with Tom Finlay.

176. Interview with Kyran FitzGerald.

177. Correspondence with Isabelle Sutton.

178. Interview with Kyran FitzGerald.

179. Interview with Jack Christal.

180. Interview with Jack Christal.

181. Interview with Kyran FitzGerald.

182. Interview with Jacqueline Armstrong.

183. Death certificate, General Register Office.

184. Interview with Kyran FitzGerald.

185. Interview with Jack Christal.

186. Conversation with Harvey Kenny.

187. Interview with Kyran FitzGerald.

188. Correspondence with Michael V. O'Mahony; Costello spoke on this topic at Mr O'Mahony's inaugural address as Auditor of the Solicitors Apprentices Debating Society on 28 November 1963.

189. *SI*, 3 November 1974.

190. Interview with Tom Finlay.

191. Correspondence with Michael V. O'Mahony. In fact, one of the judges, Frederick Budd, was born in 1904, 10 years before Costello's call. The other judges were Chief Justice Tom O'Higgins, born in 1916, Brian Walsh (1918), Seamus Henchy (1917) and Frank Griffin (1919).

192. 12 December 1969, motion establishing Tribunal, in NAI, 200/6/518.

193. *Hibernia*, 19 December 1969.

194. Interview with Muiris Mac Conghail.

195. 23 January 1970, *This Week in Ireland*.

196. Interview with Muiris Mac Conghail.

197. 6 August 1970, D/T summary of findings, NAI, 2001/6/440.

198. 16 February 1972, Condon to Jack Lynch, NAI, 2003/16/417.

199. 11 February 1973, "This Week", RTÉ Radio.

200. 5 March 1973, "1330 News", RTÉ Radio.

201. Collins, Stephen, *The Cosgrave Legacy*, p. 140.

202. Interview with Alexis FitzGerald.

203. Interview with Muiris Mac Conghail.

204. Interview with Jacqueline Armstrong.

205. 6 September 1966, Lefty Lewis to Costello, JACP, P190/960.

206. Interview with Kyran FitzGerald.

207. Death certificate, General Register Office.

208. Interview with Mick Kilkenny.

209. Interview with Jack Christal.

210. Interview with Kyran FitzGerald.

211. Calculation by Central Statistics Office. The exact equivalent is €688,996.46.

212. Will, NAI.

213. *IT*, 19 December 1975. Mr Justice Budd did not long survive Costello, dying in February; *IT*, 10 February 1976.

214. 7 January 1976, Bishop Carroll homily, in possession of Costello family.

215. *IP*, 6 January 1976.

216. 7 January 1976, Wilson to Cosgrave, and 7 January 1976, Ford to Cosgrave, both in NAI, 2006/133/405.

217. *II*, 7 January 1976.

218. 7 January 1976, note by Dermot Nally on funeral arrangements, NAI 2006/133/405.

219. Carroll was titular Bishop of Quaestoriana.

220. 7 January 1976, Bishop Carroll homily, in possession of Costello family.

221. *IT*, 13 January 1976.

Chapter 15 Measuring up (pp 409–414)

1. 8 December 1969, speech to retirement function, JACP, P190/350.

2. *The Leader*, 17 February 1951.

3. 8 December 1969, speech to retirement function, JACP, P190/350.

4. Manning, *Dillon*; Keane, *MacBride*; Horgan, *Browne*.

5. The 28-pence stamp featured a charcoal drawing of Costello by Sean O'Sullivan; the other stamps in the series were a 32-pence commemoration of the death of Charles Stewart Parnell and a 52-pence stamp commemorating the bicentenary of the first meeting of the United Irishmen.

6. Hartnett profile of Costello, *Development* magazine, JACP, P190/969.

7. CIA report on Ireland, HST, PSF Box 256, SR-48, p. 38

8. *The Leader*, 17 February 1951.

9. Interview with T.K. Whitaker.

10. 13 May 1944, Costello to Burke, NLI, John L. Burke Papers, Ms. 36,101 (7).

11. Garvin, Tom, *Preventing the future*, p. 254.

12. Puirséil, Niamh, *The Irish Labour Party*, p. 311.

13. Letter from Liam Cosgrave, 7 November 2008.

14. Horgan, John, *Seán Lemass*, p. 120.

15. Horgan, *Lemass*, p. 138. The advice was given to Seán Flanagan.

16. Entry on Costello, by Charles Lysaght, in McGuire, James and Quinn, James, *Dictionary of Irish Biography*, p. 894.

17. Interview with Jacqueline Armstrong.

18. Conversation with Ronan Fanning.

19. Interview with Declan Costello.

20. Hartnett profile of Costello, *Development* magazine, JACP, P190/969.

BIBLIOGRAPHY

PRIMARY SOURCES:
Archives:
The various archives consulted are referred to in the Notes as follows:
— DDA—Dublin Diocesan Archives
   McQuaid Papers
— DDE—Dwight D. Eisenhower Presidential Library
   Eisenhower Appointment Books
   Eisenhower Papers as President, International Series
   White House Social Office records
   White House Central Files
— HST—Harry S Truman Presidential Library
   HST Papers
— JACP—John A. Costello Papers, Archives Department, UCD.
— LAC—Libraries and Archives of Canada
   Department of External Affairs, RG 25
   Diaries of William Lyon Mackenzie King. Available online: http://king. collections
   canada.gc.ca/EN/default.asp
— NAI—National Archives of Ireland
   Attorney General's Office (AG files)
   Department of Justice (JUS files)
   Department of the Taoiseach (S files)
   Department of Foreign Affairs (DFA files)
   Taoiseach's Private Office
   John A. Costello's Will
— NLI—National Library of Ireland Manuscripts Department
   Joseph Bigger Papers
   John L. Burke Papers
   W.G. Fallon Papers
   Frank Gallagher Papers
   Seán T. O'Kelly Papers
— PRONI—Public Records Office of Northern Ireland
   CAB files
   Cabinet conclusions
   Prime Minister's files
   Personal Papers: Ulster Unionist Council; papers of Cahir Healy, Sir Douglas
   Savoury

— TCD—Manuscripts Department, Trinity College Dublin
 F.H. Boland Papers
 Thomas Bodkin Papers
— TNA—The National Archives, Kew
 Dominions Office
 Foreign Office
 Prime Minister's office (PREM)
 Cabinet Office (CAB)
— UCDA—Archives Department, University College Dublin
 P 4: Hugh Kennedy papers
 P 6: T.M. Healy papers
 P 7: Richard Mulcahy papers
 P 24: Ernest Blythe papers
 P 35: Patrick McGilligan papers
 P 39: Fine Gael papers
 P 53: Michael Hayes papers
 P 67: Seán MacEntee papers
 P 80: Desmond FitzGerald papers
 P 104: Frank Aiken papers
 P 122: Maurice Moynihan papers
 P 150: Eamon de Valera papers
 P 151: Seán MacEoin papers
 P 194: Michael MacWhite papers
 P 197: Kevin O'Higgins papers
 SOC 2: Literary and Historical Society (L&H) papers
 LA 30: Michael Tierney papers
— USNA—United States National Archives, College Park, Maryland
 RG 59, Department of State Decimal File
 RG 84, Dublin Legation, General Records
 RG 84, Dublin Legation, Security Segregated Records

Other Archives:
— Allen Library—records of the O'Connell School
— Bar Council—records of King's Inns
— Census 1911—available online: http://www.census.nationalarchives.ie/search/
— GRO—General Register Office for certificates of birth, marriage and death
— Irish Jesuit Archives—Arthur Cox Papers
— Arts Council Archive

Papers in private possession:
— F.H. Boland memoir—in the possession of his daughter, Mrs Mella Crowley
— Papers of Alexis FitzGerald—in possession of Kyran FitzGerald, and of Jacqueline
  and Fergus Armstrong

Interviews and Correspondence:
— Jacqueline Armstrong (granddaughter)
— Jack Christal (driver)
— Liam Cosgrave (fellow Fine Gael TD; Chief Whip 1948–51, Minister for External Affairs 1954–57, Party Leader 1966–77)
— Declan Costello (son)
— John Costello (son)
— Tom Finlay (fellow barrister, Fine Gael TD 1954–57, Chief Justice 1985–94)
— Alexis FitzGerald (constituency organiser, Fine Gael TD and senator)
— Kyran FitzGerald (grandson)
— Ronan Keane (fellow barrister, Chief Justice 2000–04)
— Harvey Kenny (fellow barrister, later Circuit Court Judge)
— Mick Kilkenny (driver)
— Patrick Lynch (1996) (Private Secretary 1948–51; later Professor of Economics, UCD)
— Muiris Mac Conghail (Editor, "Seven Days", RTÉ)
— Risteard Mulcahy (1996) (son of Richard Mulcahy)
— Louie O'Brien (1996) (personal secretary to Seán MacBride)
— Michael V. O'Mahony (solicitor, legal colleague)
— Richie Ryan (Fine Gael activist, solicitor, TD, later Minister for Finance)
— Georgina Sutton (granddaughter)
— Isabelle Sutton (granddaughter)
— T.K. Whitaker (1998 and 2010) (Secretary, Department of Finance, 1956–69)

Online resources:
— Oireachtas Debates: Available online at http://historical-debates.oireachtas.ie/index.html
  DÉD—Dáil Éireann Debates
  SÉD—Seanad Éireann Debates
— Election results—http://electionsireland.org/
— Irish Statute Book—http://acts.oireachtas.ie/en.toc.decade.html

Broadcast:
Apart from news programmes referenced in the notes, the following were used:
— "Seven Days"—Interview with John A. Costello by David Thornley, broadcast 24 June 1969
— "The Mother and Child Scheme"—radio documentary, broadcast 7 October 1980
— "The Republic of Ireland Act"—radio documentary, broadcast 26 March 1989
— "The Republic: Leaving the Commonwealth"—television documentary, broadcast 15 April 1999
— "One to One: Declan Costello"—television interview, broadcast 14 September 2009

Newspapers and Journals:
- EH—*Evening Herald*
- EP—*Evening Press*
- FJ—*Freeman's Journal*
- II—*Irish Independent*
- ILT&SJ—*Irish Law Times and Solicitors Journal*
- ILTR—*Irish Law Times Reports*
- IT—*Irish Times*
- IP—*Irish Press*
- SI—*Sunday Independent*
- SP—*Sunday Press*
- NS—*National Student* (UCD student newspaper)
- *Studies*
- *Thom's Directory*
- *The Leader*
- *This Week in Ireland*

SECONDARY SOURCES:

Books:

- Andrews, C.S., *Man of No Property*, The Lilliput Press, Dublin, 2001.
- Attlee, Clement, *As It Happened*, William Heinemann Ltd, London, 1954.
- Barrington, Ruth, *Health, Medicine and Politics in Ireland, 1900–1970*, IPA, Dublin, 1987.
- Barton, Brian, *Brookeborough: the making of a Prime Minister*, The Institute of Irish Studies, Queen's University, Belfast, 1988.
- Bell, J. Bowyer, *The Secret Army: The IRA 1916–1979*, Poolbeg, Dublin, 1989 edition.
- Bewley, Charles, *Memoirs of a Wild Goose*, The Lilliput Press, Dublin, 1989.
- Black, Conrad, *Richard Milhous Nixon: The Invincible Quest*, Quercus, London, 2007.
- Bolster, Evelyn, *The Knights of Saint Columbanus*, Gill & Macmillan, Dublin, 1979.
- Bowman, John, *De Valera and the Ulster Question, 1917–1973*, Oxford University Press, 1989.
- Bradford, Sarah, *America's Queen: The life of Jacqueline Kennedy Onassis*, Viking, London, 2000.
- Brady, Conor, *Guardians of the Peace*, Gill & Macmillan, Dublin, 1974.
- Brady, Conor, *Up With The Times*, Gill & Macmillan, Dublin, 2005.
- Browne, Noël, *Against the Tide*, Gill & Macmillan, Dublin, 1986.
- Browne, Vincent (ed.), *The Magill Book of Irish Politics*, Magill, Dublin, 1981.
- Burridge, Trevor, *Clement Attlee: a political biography*, Jonathan Cape, London, 1985.
- Byrne, Elaine, *Political Corruption in Ireland*, Manchester University Press (forthcoming).
- Callanan, Frank, *T.M. Healy*, Cork University Press, 1996.
- Callanan, Frank (ed.), *The Literary and Historical Society, 1955–2005*, A & A Farmar, Dublin, 2005.

— Casey, J.P., *The Office of the Attorney-General in Ireland*, IPA, Dublin, 1980.

— Chubb, Basil, *Cabinet Government in Ireland*, IPA, Dublin, 1974.

— Chubb, Basil, *The Government and Politics of Ireland*, Longman, London and New York, second edition, 1982.

— Cole, John, *As It Seemed To Me*, revised edition, Phoenix, London, 1996.

— Collins, Stephen, *The Cosgrave Legacy*, Blackwater Press, Dublin, 1996.

— Cooney, John, *The Crozier and the Dáil: Church and State 1922–1986*, Mercier Press, Cork and Dublin, 1986.

— Cooney, John, *John Charles McQuaid: Ruler of Catholic Ireland*, O'Brien Press, Dublin, 1999.

— Cronin, Mike, *The Blueshirts and Irish Politics*, Four Courts Press, Dublin, 1997.

— Cronin, Mike, and John M. Regan (eds), *Ireland: The Politics of Independence, 1922–1949*, Macmillan Press, London, 2000.

— Cronin, Patrick, *Boss Croker of New York City and Glencairn*, Foxrock Local History Club, 1983.

— Cronin, Seán, *Washington's Irish Policy, 1916–86*, Anvil, Dublin, 1987.

— Currie, Austin, *All Hell Will Break Loose*, O'Brien, Dublin, 2004.

— Dallek, Robert, *John F. Kennedy: An Unfinished Life*, Allen Lane, London, 2003.

— Daly, Paul, *Creating Ireland: the words and events that shaped us*, Hachette Books Ireland, Dublin, 2008.

— Davis, Troy D., *Dublin's American Policy: Irish-American Diplomatic Relations, 1945–52*, The Catholic University of America Press, Washington, D.C., 1998.

— Deeny, James, *To cure and to care: memories of a Chief Medical Officer*, Glendale Press, Dun Laoghaire, 1989.

— Desmond, Barry, *Finally and In Conclusion*, New Island, Dublin, 2000.

— De Valera, Terry, *A Memoir*, Currach Press, Dublin, 2004.

— De Vere White, Terence, *A Fretful Midge*, Routledge and Kegan Paul, London, 1957.

— De Vere White, Terence, *Kevin O'Higgins*, Anvil Books, Dublin, 1986.

— Dunleavy, Janet Egleson and Gareth W., *Douglas Hyde: A maker of modern Ireland*, University of California Press, Berkeley, 1991.

— Dwyer, T. Ryle, *Nice Fellow: A biography of Jack Lynch*, Mercier Press, Cork, 2001.

— Edmonds, Seán, *The gun, the law and the Irish people*, Anvil Books, Tralee, 1971.

— English, Richard, and Joseph Morrison Skelley (eds), *Ideas Matter: Essays in Honour of Conor Cruise O'Brien*, University Press of America, Lanham, MA, 2000.

— English, Richard, *Irish Freedom: The History of Nationalism in Ireland*, Macmillan, London, 2006.

— Fanning, Ronan, *The Irish Department of Finance, 1922–58*, Institute of Public Administration, Dublin, 1978.

— Fanning, Ronan, *Independent Ireland*, Helicon, Dublin, 1983.

— Farrell, Brian, *Chairman or Chief? The role of Taoiseach in Irish Government*, Gill & Macmillan, Dublin, 1971.

— Faulkner, Pádraig, *As I saw it: reviewing over 30 years of Fianna Fáil and Irish politics*, Wolfhound, Dublin, 2005.

— Feeney, Brian, *Sinn Féin: A hundred turbulent years*, O'Brien Press, Dublin, 2002.

— Feeney, Tom, *Seán MacEntee*, Irish Academic Press, Dublin, 2009.

— Ferguson, Kenneth (ed.), *King's Inns Barristers, 1868–2004*, The Honorable Society of King's Inns, Dublin, 2005.

— Ferriter, Diarmaid, *The Transformation of Ireland, 1900–2000*, Profile Books, London, 2004.

— Ferriter, Diarmaid, *What If?*, Gill & Macmillan, Dublin, 2006.

— Ferriter, Diarmaid, *Judging Dev*, Royal Irish Academy, Dublin, 2007.

— FitzGerald, Garret, *All in a life*, Papermac edition, London, 1992.

— FitzGerald, Garret, *Reflections on the Irish State*, Irish Academic Press, Dublin, 2003.

— FitzGerald, Garret, *Ireland in the world: Further Reflections*, Liberties, Dublin, 2005.

— Fitzpatrick, David, *The Two Irelands, 1912–1939*, OPUS, Oxford, 1998.

— Foxton, David, *Revolutionary lawyers: Sinn Féin and Crown Courts in Ireland and Britain, 1916–1923*, Four Courts Press, Dublin, 2008.

— Garvin, Tom, *Preventing the future: Why was Ireland so poor for so long?*, Gill & Macmillan, Dublin, 2004.

— Garvin, Tom, *Judging Lemass*, Royal Irish Academy, Dublin, 2009.

— Girvin, Brian, *Between Two Worlds: Politics and Economy in Independent Ireland*, Gill & Macmillan, Dublin, 1989.

— Girvin, Brian, *The Emergency: Neutral Ireland 1939–45*, Pan Books, London, 2007.

— Girvin, Brian, and Gary Murphy (eds), *The Lemass Era: Politics and Society in the Ireland of Seán Lemass*, UCD Press, Dublin, 2005.

— Gray, Tony, *Mr Smyllie, Sir*, Gill & Macmillan, Dublin, 1994.

— Harkness, David, *The Restless Dominion: the Irish Free State and the British Commonwealth of Nations, 1921–31*, Gill & Macmillan, Dublin, 1969.

— Harte, Paddy, *Young Tigers and Mongrel Foxes*, O'Brien Press, Dublin, 2005.

— Healy, Maurice, *The Old Munster Circuit*, Mercier, Dublin and Cork, 1979.

— Healy, T.M., *Portmarnock Golf Club, 1894–1994: A Centenary History*, Portmarnock Golf Club, Dublin, 1993.

— Henderson, Nicholas, *The Private Office Revisited*, Profile Books, London, 2001.

— Hennessy, Peter, *The Prime Minister: The office and its holders since 1945*, Allen Lane, London, 2000.

— Hogan, Daire, *The Legal Profession in Ireland 1789–1922*, Incorporated Law Society of Ireland, Dublin, 1986.

— Hogan, Daire, *The Honorable Society of King's Inns*, The Council of King's Inns, Dublin, 1987.

— Hopkinson, Michael (ed.), *The Last Days of Dublin Castle: The Mark Sturgis Diaries*, Irish Academic Press, Dublin, 1999.

— Hopkinson, Michael, *The Irish War of Independence*, Gill & Macmillan, Dublin, 2002.

— Horgan, John, *Seán Lemass: The Enigmatic Patriot*, Gill & Macmillan, Dublin, 1997.

— Horgan, John, *Noël Browne: Passionate Outsider*, Gill & Macmillan, Dublin, 2000.

— Jordan, Anthony J., *Seán MacBride: A biography*, Blackwater Press, Dublin, 1993.

— Jordan, Anthony J., *W.T. Cosgrave: Founder of Modern Ireland*, Westport Books, Dublin, 2006.

— Jordan, Anthony J., *John A. Costello: Compromise Taoiseach*, Westport Books, Dublin, 2007.

— Judge, Patrick (ed.), *O'Connell School: 150 Years, 1828–1978*, O'Connell School Union, Dublin, 1978.

— Keane, Elizabeth, *Seán MacBride: A Life*, Gill & Macmillan, Dublin, 2007.

— Kennedy, Brian P, *Dreams and Responsibilities: The State and the Arts in Independent Ireland*, The Arts Council, Dublin, 1990.

— Kennedy, Michael, *Ireland and the League of Nations, 1919–1946: International Relations, Diplomacy and Politics*, Irish Academic Press, Dublin, 1996.

— Kennedy, Michael, *Division and Consensus: The politics of cross-Border relations in Ireland, 1925–1969*, IPA, Dublin, 2000.

— Kennedy, Michael, and Deirdre McMahon (eds), *Obligations and Responsibilities: Ireland and the United Nations, 1955–2005*, IPA, Dublin, 2005.

— Keogh, Dermot, *Twentieth-Century Ireland, Nation and State*, Gill & Macmillan, Dublin, 1994.

— Keogh, Dermot, *Jack Lynch: A biography*, Gill & Macmillan, Dublin, 2008.

— Keogh, Dermot, Finbarr O'Shea and Carmel Quinlan (eds), *Ireland in the 1950s— the lost Decade*, Mercier Press, Cork, 2004.

— Keogh, Dermot, and McCarthy, Andrew J, *The Making of the Irish Constitution, 1937*, Mercier Press, Cork, 2007.

— Kershaw, Ian, *Fateful Choices: Ten decisions that changed the world, 1940–41*, paperback edition, Penguin Books, London, 2008.

— Kissane, Bill, *Explaining Irish Democracy*, UCD Press, Dublin, 2002.

— Kotsonouris, Mary, *Retreat from Revolution: The Dáil Courts, 1920–24*, Irish Academic Press, Dublin, 1994.

— Laffan, Michael, *The Resurrection of Ireland: The Sinn Féin Party, 1916–1923*, Cambridge University Press, 1999.

— Lee, J.J., *Ireland, 1912–1985: Politics and Society*, Cambridge University Press, 1989.

— Lewis, Wilmarth Sheldon, *One Man's Education: The autobiography of a distinguished American scholar, author, editor and collector*, Knopf, New York, 1967.

— Lindsay, Patrick, *Memories*, Blackwater Press, Dublin, 1992.

— Lynch, Patrick, and James Meenan (eds), *Essays in Memory of Alexis FitzGerald*, Incorporated Law Society of Ireland, Dublin, 1987.

— Lyons, F.S.L., *Ireland since the Famine*, Fontana, London, 1973.

— MacBride, Seán, *That Day's Struggle: A memoir 1904–1951*, edited by Caitriona Lawlor, Currach Press, Dublin, 2005.

— McCague, Eugene, *Arthur Cox, 1891–1965*, Gill & Macmillan, Dublin, 1994.

— McCarthy, John F. (ed.), *Planning Ireland's Future: the legacy of T.K. Whitaker*, Glendale, Dublin, 1990.

— McCoole, Sinéad, *Hazel: A life of Lady Lavery, 1880–1935*, Lilliput Press, Dublin, 1996.

— McCullagh, David, *A Makeshift Majority: The first Inter-party Government, 1948–51*, IPA, Dublin, 1998.

— MacDermott, Eithne, *Clann na Poblachta*, Cork University Press, 1998.

— Macready, Sir Nevil, *Annals of an active life*, Hutchinson, London, 1924, Volume 2.

— McGarry, Fearghal, *Eoin O'Duffy: A self-made hero*, Oxford University Press, 2005.

— McGuire, James, and James Quinn, *Dictionary of Irish Biography*, Royal Irish Academy and Cambridge University Press, 2009.

— McMahon, Deirdre, *Republicans and Imperialists: Anglo-Irish relations in the 1930s*, Yale University Press, New Haven and London, 1984.

— Mackey, Rex, *Windward of the Law*, 2nd edition, Round Hall Press, Dublin, 1991.

— Maguire, Martin, *The Civil Service and the revolution in Ireland*, Manchester University Press, 2008.

— Mair, Peter, *The changing Irish party system*, Pinter Publishers, London, 1987.

— Manning, Maurice, *James Dillon: A Biography*, Wolfhound Press, Dublin, 1999.

— Mansergh, Diana (ed.), *Nationalism and Independence: Selected Irish Papers by Nicholas Mansergh*, Cork University Press, Cork, 1997.

— Mansergh, Nicholas, *Survey of British Commonwealth Affairs: Problems of Wartime Co-operation and post-war change, 1939–52*, Oxford University Press, 1958.

— Mansergh, Nicholas, *The Commonwealth Experience, Volume II: From British to Multiracial Commonwealth*, Macmillan, London, 1982.

— Marr, Andrew, *A History of Modern Britain*, paperback edition, Pan Books, London, 2008.

— Meenan, James, *George O'Brien: A biographical memoir*, Gill & Macmillan, Dublin, 1980.

— Meenan, James (ed.), *Centenary History of the Literary and Historical Society of University College Dublin, 1855–1955*, A & A Farmar, Dublin, 2005 (reprint of 1955 edition).

— Moynihan, Maurice, *Currency and Central Banking in Ireland, 1922–60*, Central Bank of Ireland and Gill & Macmillan, Dublin, 1975.

— Mulcahy, Risteárd, *Richard Mulcahy: A family memoir*, Aurelian Press, Dublin, 1999.

— Munger, Frank, *The Legitimacy of Opposition: The Change of Government in Ireland in 1932*, SAGE Publications, Beverley Hills, 1975.

— Nolan, Aengus, *Joseph Walshe: Irish Foreign Policy, 1922–46*, Mercier Press, Cork, 2008.

— O'Brien, Conor Cruise, *States of Ireland*, Panther Books, St Albans, 1974.

— O'Brien, Conor Cruise, *Memoir: My life and themes*, Poolbeg Dublin, 1999.

— O'Brien, Mark, *De Valera, Fianna Fáil and the Irish Press: The truth in the news?* Irish Academic Press, Dublin, 2001.

— Ó Broin, Leon, *No Man's Man: A biographical memoir of Joseph Brennan*, IPA, Dublin, 1982.

— Ó Broin, Leon, *Just Like Yesterday*, Gill & Macmillan, Dublin, 1985.

— O'Byrne, Robert, *Hugh Lane*, Lilliput Press, Dublin, 2000.

— *O'Connell School Centenary Record*, Dublin, June 1928.
— Ó Gráda, Cormac, *A Rocky Road: The Irish Economy since the 1920s*, Manchester University Press, 1997.
— O'Halpin, Eunan, *Defending Ireland: The Irish State and its enemies since 1922*, Oxford University Press, 1999.
— O'Higgins, T.F., *A Double Life*, Town House, Dublin, 1996.
— O'Leary, Cornelius, *Irish Elections, 1918–77*, Gill & Macmillan, Dublin, 1977.
— Ó Longaigh, Seosamh, *Emergency Law in Independent Ireland, 1922–1948*, Four Courts Press, Dublin, 2006.
— O'Neill, Tom, *The Battle of Clonmult: The IRA's Worst Defeat*, Nonsuch Publishing, Dublin, 2006.
— O'Sullivan, Michael, *Seán Lemass: A biography*, Blackwater Press, Dublin, 1994.
— Patterson, Henry, *Ireland since 1939: The persistence of conflict*, Penguin Books, 2007.
— Puirséil, Niamh, *The Irish Labour Party, 1922–73*, UCD Press, Dublin, 2007.
— Quinn, Antoinette, *Patrick Kavanagh: A Biography*, Gill & Macmillan, Dublin, 2001.
— Quinn, Ruairí, and Ross Higgins, *A history of Dublin South-East constituency*, Labour Party, 2006.
— Rafter, Kevin, *The Clann: The Story of Clann na Poblachta*, Mercier Press, Cork, 1996.
— Regan, John M., *The Irish Counter-Revolution, 1921–1936*, Gill & Macmillan, Dublin, 2001.
— Sexton, Brendan, *Ireland and the Crown, 1922–36: The Governor-Generalship of the Irish Free State*, Irish Academic Press, Dublin, 1989.
— Sheehy Skeffington, Andrée, *Skeff: The life of Owen Sheehy Skeffington*, The Lilliput Press, Dublin, 1991.
— Skelly, Joseph Morrison, *Irish Diplomacy at the United Nations, 1945–1965: National Interests and the International Order*, Irish Academic Press, Dublin, 1997.
— Stanford, William Bedell, *Memoirs*, Hinds Publishing, Dublin, 2001.
— Staunton, Enda, *The Nationalists of Northern Ireland 1918–73*, Columba Press, Dublin, 2001.
— Stradling, Robert A., *The Irish and the Spanish Civil War, 1936–39*, Mandolin, Manchester, 1999.
— Whelan, Bernadette, *Ireland and the Marshall Plan, 1947–57*, Four Courts Press, Dublin, 2000.
— Whitaker, T.K., *Interests*, IPA, Dublin, 1983.
— Whitaker, T.K., *Protection or Free Trade: The Final Battle*, IPA, Dublin, 2006
— White, Robert M., *Ruairí Ó Brádaigh: The life and politics of an Irish revolutionary*, Indiana University Press, 2006.
— Whyte, J.H., *Church and State in Modern Ireland*, second edition, Gill & Macmillan, Dublin, 1980.
— Williams, Francis, *Adenauer, the Father of New Germany*, Abacus, London, 2003.

— Yeats, Michael B., *Cast a cold eye: Memories of a poet's son and politician*, Blackwater Press, Dublin, 1998.

Articles:

— Arnold, Bruce, "Politics and the Arts in Ireland: the Dáil debates", in Litton, Frank (ed.), *Unequal Achievement: The Irish Experience, 1957–82*, IPA, Dublin, 1982.
— Costello, John A., "The leading principles of the Brehon Law", *Studies*, 1913.
— Farrell, Michael, "The Extraordinary Life and Times of Seán MacBride", part 2, *Magill*, January 1983.
— Honohan, Patrick, and Ó Gráda, Cormac, "The Irish macroeconomic crisis of 1955–56: how much was due to monetary policy?" *Irish Economic and Social History*, 1998.
— Keating, Anthony, "The legalisation of adoption in Ireland", *Studies*, 2003.
— McInerney, Michael, "John A. Costello Remembers", *IT*, 4 to 8 September 1967.
— Smith, Murray, "No Honours Please, We're Republicans", *Irish Student Law Review*, 1999.

INDEX